T0135049

# Communications in Computer and Information Science     1600

More information about this series at https://link.springer.com/bookseries/7899

Lazaros Iliadis · Chrisina Jayne ·
Anastasios Tefas · Elias Pimenidis (Eds.)

# Engineering Applications of Neural Networks

23rd International Conference, EAAAI/EANN 2022
Chersonissos, Crete, Greece, June 17–20, 2022
Proceedings

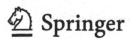

*Editors*
Lazaros Iliadis
Democritus University of Thrace
Xanthi, Greece

Chrisina Jayne
Teesside University
Middlesbrough, UK

Anastasios Tefas
Aristotle University of Thessaloniki
Thessaloniki, Greece

Elias Pimenidis
University of the West of England
Bristol, UK

ISSN 1865-0929    ISSN 1865-0937 (electronic)
Communications in Computer and Information Science
ISBN 978-3-031-08222-1    ISBN 978-3-031-08223-8 (eBook)
https://doi.org/10.1007/978-3-031-08223-8

This Springer imprint is published by the registered company Springer Nature Switzerland AG
The registered company address is: Gewerbestrasse 11, 6330 Cham, Switzerland

# Preface

The first International Conference on Engineering Applications of Neural Networks (EANN) was held in Otaniemi, Finland, in August 1995. Since then, it has been continuously held with great success, as an annual event from 1995–2001, as a biannual event from 2001–2012, and finally as an annual event from 2013 till today. So far, EANN has been organized in 10 different European countries, namely, Finland, the UK, Greece, Bulgaria, Sweden, Gibraltar, Italy, France, Poland, and Spain.

After 27 years, it is time for change. EANN is adapting to the demands of the times and expanding its horizons by changing its name to Engineering Applications and Advances of Artificial Intelligence (EAAAI). The conference topics are opening to a broader spectrum of algorithmic approaches, applications, and advances of artificial intelligence (AI).

The event will continue to be technically supported by the International Neural Networks Society (INNS) and more specifically by the EANN Special Interest Group. In addition, the name EANN will continue to accompany the conference for historical reasons but also for substantive ones. More specifically, EANN will be a parallel satellite event of EAAAI, for the members of our scientific family, who would like to continue submitting to EANN.

Since the first conference in 1995, EANN has provided a great discussion forum on engineering applications of all artificial intelligence technologies, focusing on artificial neural networks. It has managed to promote the use of modeling techniques from all subdomains of AI in diverse application areas, where significant benefits can be derived. The conference also covers advances in theoretical AI aspects. Thus, both innovative applications and methods are particularly appreciated.

The 23rd International Conference on Engineering Applications of Neural Networks (EAAAI/EANN 2022) was collocated with the 18th International Conference on Artificial Intelligence Applications and Innovations (AIAI 2022) and held at the Aldemar Knossos Royal in Chersonisos, Crete, Greece. EAAAI/EANN 2022 brought together scientists from all AI domains and offered them the chance to exchange ideas and to announce their achievements.

This proceedings volume in the INNS (International Neural Networks) series published by Springer contains the papers that were accepted to be presented orally at EAAAI/EANN 2022. The diverse nature of papers presented demonstrates the vitality of artificial intelligence algorithms and approaches. The conference not only covered neural networks but also provided a forum for a diverse range of AI applications reflecting the scope of EAAAI.

The event was held in a hybrid mode from June 17 to June 20, 2022. The vast majority of the authors attended the conference on site. Moreover, it was also broadcast live over the internet to offer all conference delegates who could not travel the chance to present and attend in real time.

The response of the international scientific community to the EAAAI/EANN 2022 call for papers was more than satisfactory, with 83 papers initially submitted by authors from 11 different countries worldwide: Brazil, Bulgaria, the Czech Republic, Germany, Greece, Italy, Japan, Norway, Romania, Spain, and the UK. All papers were peer reviewed by at least two independent academic referees. Where needed a third referee was consulted to resolve any potential conflicts.

A total of 49% of the submitted manuscripts (41 papers) were accepted to be published as full papers (12 pages long) in the proceedings. Due to the high quality of the submissions, the Program Committee also decided to accept one short paper (10 pages long) for publication. The accepted papers are related to the following thematic topics:

- Classification in Machine Learning
- Machine Learning for Medical Images
- Genome Classification
- Robotics
- Autonomous Vehicles
- Photonic Neural Networks
- Bio inspired Modeling
- Novel Neural Architectures
- Data Mining
- Autoencoders
- Convolutional Neural Networks
- Deep Learning
- Reinforcement Learning
- Generative Adversarial Neural Networks
- Echo State Neural Networks
- Classification
- Clustering
- Machine Learning
- Blockchain
- Text Classification
- Natural Language
- Knowledge Graphs
- Evolutionary Computing
- Ensemble Learning
- Security Modeling
- Spiking Neural Networks

In addition to the paper presentations, five invited speakers gave keynotes on timely aspects or state-of-the-art applications of artificial intelligence. Hojjat Adeli from Ohio State University, USA, gave a speech on "Machine Learning: A Key Ubiquitous Technology in the 21st Century". Riitta Salmelin from Aalto University, Finland, addressed "What neuroimaging can tell about human brain function". Elisabeth André from the University of Augsburg, Germany, discussed "Socially Interactive Artificial Intelligence: Perception, Synthesis and Learning of Human-like Behaviors". Verena Rieser from Heriot-Watt University, UK, gave a speech on the subject of "Responsible Conversational AI: Trusted, Safe and Bias-free" and John Macintyre from the University of Sunderland,

UK, addressed the wider AI and ethics area in his talk "Is Big Tech Becoming the Big Tobacco of AI?".

On behalf of the organizers, we would like to thank everyone involved in EAAAI/EANN 2022, and we hope that you find the proceedings interesting and insightful.

June 2022

Lazaros Iliadis
Chrisina Jayne
Anastasios Tefas
Elias Pimenidis

# Organization

## General Co-chairs

Ilias Maglogiannis      University of Piraeus, Greece
John Macintyre      University of Sunderland, UK
George Magoulas      Birkbeck College, University of London, UK

## Program Co-chairs

Lazaros Iliadis      Democritus University of Thrace, Greece
Anastasios Tefas      Aristotle University of Thessaloniki, Greece
Chrisina Jayne      Teesside University, UK
Elias Pimenidis      University of the West of England, UK

## Steering Committee

Giacomo Boracchi      Politecnico di Milano, Italy
Lazaros Iliadis      Democritus University of Thrace, Greece
Elias Pimenidis      University of the West of England, UK

## Doctoral Consortium Co-chairs

Antonios Papaleonidas      Democritus University of Thrace, Greece
Peter Hajek      University of Parduvice, Czech Republic
Harris Papadopoulos      Frederick University, Cyprus

## Liaison Chair

Panagiotis Kikiras      European Défense Systems, Belgium

## Publication and Publicity Co-chairs

Antonios Papaleonidas      Democritus University of Thrace, Greece
Anastasios Panagiotis Psathas      Democritus University of Thrace, Greece

## Advisory Chair

Chrisina Jayne      Teesside University, UK

## Honorary Chairs

Nikola Kasabov          Auckland University of Technology, New Zealand
Vera Kurkova            Czech Academy of Sciences, Czech Republic

## Workshops Co-chairs

Phivos Mylonas          Ionian University, Greece
Christos Makris         University of Patras, Greece

## Special Sessions and Tutorials Co-chairs

Ilias Sakellariou       University of Makedonia, Thessaloniki, Greece
Katia Kermanidis        Ionian University, Greece

## Program Committee

| | |
|---|---|
| Aiello Salvatore | Politecnico di Torino, Italy |
| Aldanondo Michel | IMT Mines Albi, France |
| Alexandridis Georgios | University of the Aegean, Greece |
| Alexiou Athanasios | Novel Global Community Educational Foundation, Australia |
| Aloisio Angelo | University of L'Aquila, Italy |
| Alonso Serafin | University of Leon, Spain |
| Amato Domenico | University of Palermo, Italy |
| Anagnostopoulos Christos-Nikolaos | University of the Aegean, Greece |
| Badica Costin | University of Craiova, Romania |
| Bezas Napoleon | Centre for Research and Technology Hellas, Greece |
| Bobrowski Leon | Bialystok University of Technology, Poland |
| Bozanis Panayiotis | International Hellenic University, Greece |
| C. Sousa Joana | NOS Inovação SA, Portugal |
| Campos Souza Paulo Vitor | Federal Center for Technological Education of Minas Gerais, Brazil |
| Caridakis George | National Technical University of Athens, Greece |
| Cavique Luis | University of Aberta, Portugal |
| Chamodrakas Ioannis | National and Kapodistrian University of Athens, Greece |
| Chochliouros Ioannis | Hellenic Telecommunications Organization S.A. (OTE), Greece |
| Delibasis Konstantinos | University of Thessaly, Greece |
| Demertzis Konstantinos | Democritus University of Thrace, Greece |

| | |
|---|---|
| Dimara Asimina | Centre for Research and Technology Hellas, Greece |
| Diou Christos | Harokopio University of Athens, Greece |
| Dominguez Manuel | University of Leon, Spain |
| Drakopoulos Georgios | Ionian University, Greece |
| Drousiotis Efthyvoulos | University of Liverpool, UK |
| Ferreira Luis | Polytechnic of Porto, Portugal |
| Fiannaca Antonino | National Research Council, Italy |
| Frittoli Luca | Politecnico di Milano, Italy |
| Fuertes Juan J. | University of León, Spain |
| Gaggero Mauro | National Research Council, Italy |
| Georgopoulos Efstratios | University of Peloponnese, Greece |
| Giancarlo Raffaele | University of Palermo, Italy |
| Giarelis Nikolaos | University of Patras, Greece |
| Giunchiglia Eleonora | University of Oxford, UK |
| Gonzalez-Deleito Nicolas | Sirris, Belgium |
| Grivokostopoulou Foteini | University of Patras, Greece |
| Hága Péter | Ericsson Research, Hungary |
| Hajek Petr | University of Pardubice, Czech Republic |
| Haralabopoulos Giannis | University of Nottingham, UK |
| Hatzilygeroudis Ioannis | University of Patras, Greece |
| Hichri Bassem | GCL International, Luxembourg |
| Hristoskova Anna | Sirris, Belgium |
| Humm Bernhard | Darmstadt University of Applied Sciences, Germany |
| Iakovidis Dimitris | University of Thessaly, Greece |
| Iliadis Lazaros | Democritus University of Thrace, Greece |
| Ishii Naohiro | Aichi Institute of Technology, Japan |
| Islam Shareeful | University of East London, UK |
| Ivanovic Mirjana | University of Novi Sad, Serbia |
| Jeannin-Girardon | Anne University of Strasbourg, France |
| Kalamaras Ilias | Centre for Research and Technology Hellas/Information Technologies Institute, Greece |
| Kallipolitis Athanasios | University of Piraeus, Greece |
| Kanakaris Nikos | University of Patras, Greece |
| Kanavos Andreas | University of Patras, Greece |
| Kapetanakis Stelios | University of Brighton, UK |
| Karacapilidis Nikos | University of Patras, Greece |
| Karatzas Kostas | Aristotle University of Thessaloniki, Greece |
| Karpouzis Kostas | National and Kapodistrian University of Athens, Greece |

Kassandros Theodosios        Aristotle University of Thessaloniki, Greece
Kazemian Hassan              London Metropolitan University, UK
Kefalas Petros               CITY College, Greece
Kermanidis Katia Lida        Ionian University, Greece
Kokkinos Yiannis             University of Macedonia, Greece
Kollia Ilianna               IBM/National Technical University of Athens,
                               Greece
Kontos Yiannis               Aristotle University of Thessaloniki, Greece
Koprinkova-Hristova Petia    Bulgarian Academy of Sciences, Bulgaria
Korkas Christos              Democritus University of Thrace/Centre for
                               Research and Technology Hellas, Greece
Kosmopoulos Dimitrios        University of Patras, Greece
Kotis Konstantinos           University of the Aegean, Greece
Kotsiantis Sotiris           University of Patras, Greece
Koukaras Paraskevas          Centre for Research and Technology Hellas,
                               Greece
Koussouris Sotiris           Suite5 Data Intelligence Solutions Ltd., Cyprus
Koutras Athanasios           University of Peloponnese, Greece
Krejcar Ondrej               University of Hradec Kralove, Czech Republic
Krinidis Stelios             Centre for Research and Technology Hellas,
                               Greece
Kyriakides George            University of Macedonia, Greece
La Rosa Massimo              National Research Council, Italy
Lalas Antonios               Centre for Research and Technology
                               Hellas/Information Technologies Institute,
                               Greece
Lazaridis Georgios           Centre for Research and Technology
                               Hellas/Information Technologies Institute,
                               Greece
Lazic Ljubomir               UNION University, Serbia
Lederman Dror                Holon Institute of Technology, Israel
Leon Florin                  Technical University of Iasi, Romania
Likas Aristidis              University of Ioannina, Greece
Likothanassis Spiros         University of Patras, Greece
Livieris Ioannis             University of Patras, Greece
Lo Bosco Giosuè              University of Palermo, Italy
Logofatu Doina               Frankfurt University of Applied Sciences,
                               Germany
Longo Luca                   Technological University of Dublin, Ireland
Maghool Samira               University of Milan, Italy
Maglogiannis Ilias           University of Piraeus, Greece
Magoulas George              Birbeck University of London, UK
Magri Luca                   Politecnico di Milano, Italy

| Makris Christos | University of Patras, Greece |
| Malialis Kleanthis | University of Cyprus, Cyprus |
| Maragoudakis Manolis | Ionian University, Greece |
| Marano Giuseppe Carlo | Politecnico di Torino, Italy |
| Margaritis Konstantinos | University of Macedonia, Greece |
| Martins Nuno | NOS Inovação SA, Portugal |
| Melnik Andrew | Bielefeld University, Germany |
| Menychtas Andreas | University of Piraeus, Greece |
| Mezaris Vasileios | Centre for Research and Technology Hellas, Greece |
| Michailidis Iakovos | Centre for Research and Technology Hellas, Greece |
| Mitianoudis Nikolaos | Democritus University of Thrace, Greece |
| Morán Antonio | University of León, Spain |
| Moutselos Konstantinos | University of Piraeus, Greece |
| Muhr David | Johannes Kepler University Linz, Austria |
| Müller Wilmuth | Fraunhofer IOSB, Germany |
| Munk Michal | Constantine the Philosopher University in Nitra, Slovakia |
| Mylonas Phivos | National Technical University of Athens, Greece |
| Nikiforos Stefanos | Ionian University, Greece |
| Ntalampiras Stavros | University of Milan, Italy |
| Oprea Mihaela | Petroleum-Gas University of Ploiesti, Romania |
| Papadopoulos Symeon | Centre for Research and Technology Hellas/Information Technologies Institute, Greece |
| Papadourakis Giorgos | Hellenic Mediterranean University, Greece |
| Papaioannou Vaios | University of Patras, Greece |
| Papaleonidas Antonios | Democritus University of Thrace, Greece |
| Papastergiopoulos Christoforos | Centre for Research and Technology Hellas/Information Technologies Institute, Greece |
| Papatheodoulou Dimitris | KIOS Research and Innovation Center of Excellence, Cyprus |
| Passalis Nikolaos | Aristotle University of Thessaloniki, Greece |
| Paulus Jan | Nuremberg Institute of Technology, Germany |
| Pérez Daniel | University of León, Spain |
| Perikos Isidoros | University of Patras, Greece |
| Pimenidis Elias | University of the West of England, UK |
| Pintelas Panagiotis | University of Patras, Greece |
| Prada Miguel | Ángel Universidad de León, Spain |
| Pradat-Peyre Jean-François | Paris Nanterre University and LIP6, France |
| Psathas Anastasios Panagiotis | Democritus University of Thrace, Greece |

| | |
|---|---|
| Racz Andras | Ericsson Research, Hungary |
| Rankovic Dragica | UNION University, Serbia |
| Reitmann Stefan | TU Bergakademie Freiberg, Germany |
| Rosso Marco Martino | Politecnico di Torino, Italy |
| Ryjov Alexander | Lomonosov Moscow State University, Russia |
| Sarafidis Michail | National Technical University of Athens, Greece |
| Scheele Stephan | Fraunhofer IIS/University of Bamberg, Germany |
| Scherrer Alexander | Fraunhofer ITWM, Germany |
| Seferis Manos | National Technical University of Athens, Greece |
| Serrano Will | University College London, UK |
| Shi Lei | Durham University, UK |
| Siccardi Stefano | University of Milan, Italy |
| Spyrou Evaggelos | Technological Educational Institute of Sterea Ellada, Greece |
| Staiano Antonino | University of Naples Parthenope, Italy |
| Stamate Daniel | Goldsmiths University of London, UK |
| Stefanopoulou Aliki | Centre for Research and Technology Hellas, Greece |
| Stucchi Diego | Politecnico di Milano, Italy |
| Stylianou Nikolaos | Aristotle University of Thessaloniki, Greece |
| Theocharides Theo | University of Cyprus, Cyprus |
| Theodoridis Georgios | Aristotle University of Thessaloniki, Greece |
| Timplalexis Christos | Centre for Research and Technology Hellas/Information Technologies Institute, Greece |
| Trakadas Panagiotis | National and Kapodistrian University of Athens, Greece |
| Treur Jan | VU Amsterdam, The Netherlands |
| Trovò Francesco | Politecnico di Milano, Italy |
| Tsadiras Athanasios | Aristotle University of Thessaloniki, Greece |
| Tsaknakis Christos | Democritus University of Thrace, Greece |
| Van-Horenbeke Franz | Alexander Free University of Bozen-Bolzano, Italy |
| Versaci Mario | University of Reggio Calabria, Italy |
| Vidnerová Petra | Czech Academy of Sciences, Czech Republic |
| Vilone Giulia | Technological University Dublin, Ireland |
| Vonitsanos Gerasimos | Ionian University, Greece |
| Votis Kostas | Centre for Research and Technology Hellas, Greece |
| Vougiatzis Georgios | Information Technologies Institute/Centre for Research and Technology Hellas, Greece |
| Wan Cen | Birkbeck University of London, UK |
| Yang Xin-She | Middlesex University London, UK |

| | |
|---|---|
| Zender Alexander | Darmstadt University of Applied Sciences, Germany |
| Zervas Panagiotis | University of Peloponnese, Greece |
| Zimmermann Tobias | Fraunhofer ITWM, Germany |

# Abstracts of Invited Talks

# Machine Learning: A Key Ubiquitous Technology in the 21st Century

Hojjat Adeli

Ohio State University, Columbus, USA, Fellow of the Institute of Electrical and Electronics Engineers (IEEE) (IEEE), Honorary Professor, Southeast University, Nanjing, China, Member, Polish and Lithuanian Academy of Sciences, Elected corresponding member of the Spanish Royal Academy of Engineering
adeli.1@osu.edu

**Abstract.** Machine learning (ML) is a key and increasingly pervasive technology in the 21st century. It is going to impact the way people live and work in a significant way. In general, machine learning algorithms simulate the way brain learns and solves an estimation/recognition problem. They usually require a learning phase to discover the patterns among the available data, similar to the humans. An expanded definition of ML is advanced as algorithms that can learn from examples and data and solve seemingly interactable learning and unteachable problems, referred to as ingenious artificial intelligence (AI). Recent and innovative applications of ML in various fields and projects currently being pursued by leading high-tech and industrial companies such as Boeing, Google, IBM, Uber, Baidu, Facebook, and Tesla are reviewed. Then, machine learning algorithms developed by the author and his associates are briefly described. Finally, examples are presented in different areas from health monitoring of smart highrise building structures to automated EEG-based diagnosis of various neurological and psychiatric disorders such as epilepsy, the Alzheimer's disease, Parkinson's disease, and autism spectrum disorder.

# What Neuroimaging Can Tell About Human Brain Function

Riitta Salmelin

Department of Neuroscience and Biomedical Engineering Aalto University, Finland
riitta.salmelin@aalto.fi

**Abstract.** Over the past few decades, real-time tracking of cortical current flow (magneto/electroencephalography, MEG/EEG) and accurate localization of blood oxygenation changes (functional magnetic resonance imaging, fMRI) have offered windows to the functional architecture of the human brain. The neuroimaging domain has reached its first level of maturity: we now know how to measure and quantify different types of signals and, phenomenologically, we know what type of group-level functional effects to expect in a large variety of experimental conditions. Specific brain areas, networks and electrophysiological dynamics have been proposed to be linked with various perceptual, motor and cognitive functions and their disorders. To reach the next phase in human neuroscience, we need to advance from group-level descriptions to quantitative model-based individual-level predictions. These developments will be illustrated with focus on language function for which descriptive models, largely based on observations of patients with language disorders, are being supplemented by computationally explicit models of mechanisms and representations. Machine learning approaches are essential tools in this endeavor.

# Socially Interactive Artificial Intelligence: Perception, Synthesis and Learning of Human-Like Behaviors

Elisabeth Andre

Human-Centered Artificial Intelligence, Institute for Informatics, University of Augsburg, Germany
andre@informatik.uni-augsburg.de

**Abstract.** The automatic analysis and synthesis of social signals conveyed by voice, gestures, mimics, etc., will play a vital role for next-generation interfaces as it paves the way towards a more intuitive and natural human-computer interaction with robots and virtual agents. In my talk, I will present computational methods to implement socially interactive behaviors in artificial agents, focusing on three essential properties of socially interactive interfaces: Social Perception, Socially Aware Behavior Synthesis, and Learning Socially Aware Behaviors. I will highlight opportunities and challenges that arise from deep learning approaches that promise to achieve the next level of human-likeness in virtual agents and social robots. I will illustrate my talk with examples from various applications with socially interactive characters or robots, including art and entertainment, cultural training and social coaching, and personal well-being and health.

# Responsible Conversational AI: Trusted, Safe and Bias-free

Verena Rieser

School of Mathematical and Computer Sciences (MACS) at Heriot Watt University, Edinburgh
V.T.Rieser@hw.ac.uk

**Abstract.** With recent progress in deep learning, there has been an increased interest in learning dialogue systems from data, also known as "Conversational AI". In this talk, I will focus on the task of response generation, for which I will highlight lessons learnt and ongoing challenges, such as reducing 'hallucinations for task-based systems, safety critical issues for open-domain chatbots, and the often-overlooked problem of 'good' persona design. I will argue that we will need to solve these challenges to create trusted, safe and bias-free systems for end-user applications.

# Is Big Tech Becoming the Big Tobacco of AI?

John Macintyre

Dean of the Faculty of Applied Sciences and Pro Vice Chancellor at University of Sunderland
John.Macintyre@sunderland.ac.uk

**Abstract.** The future of AI is being shaped by many forces – politics, economics, and technology all play their part. Whilst science and academia continue to push forward the boundaries of knowledge, private sector investment in AI is growing exponentially, with commercial revenues from AI expected to exceed $500 billion in the near future. At the forefront of this commercial boom in AI is so-called "Big Tech" – the biggest technology companies driving the commercialization of AI products and systems for profit. These companies have vast R&D budgets, and employ an increasingly large fraction of the AI R&D workforce globally. The question is: are they living up to their responsibilities to develop AI for the good of society, or are they just pursuing profit? Will Big Tech follow the very negative pattern of huge companies prepared to inflict harms on society to boost their profits and shareholder dividends? Professor John MacIntyre's talk will look at the emerging issues in AI and examine what impact the behaviour of Big Tech is having on the whole field of AI.

# Is Big Tech Becoming the Big Tobacco of AI?

John MacIntyre

Dean of the Faculty of Applied Sciences and Pro Vice Chancellor at University of
Sunderland
john.MacIntyre@sunderland.ac.uk

Abstract. The future of AI is being shaped by many forces – politics, economics, and technology all play their part. Whilst science and academia continue to push forward the boundaries of knowledge, private sector investment in AI is growing exponentially with commercial revenues from AI expected to exceed $500 billion in the near future. At the forefront of this commercial boom in AI is so-called "Big Tech" – the biggest technology companies driving the commercialization of AI products and systems for profit. These companies have vast R&D budgets, and employ an increasingly large fraction of the AI R&D workforce globally. The question is: are they living up to their responsibilities to develop AI for the good of society, or are they just pursuing profit? Will Big Tech follow the very negative pattern of huge companies prepared to inflict harms on society to boost their profits and shareholder dividends? Professor John MacIntyre's talk will look at the emerging issues in AI and examine what impact the behaviour of Big Tech is having on the whole field of AI.

# Contents

## Convolutional/Deep Learning

## Datamining/Learning/Autoencoders

**Deep Learning/Blockchain**

**Machine Learning for Medical Images/Genome Classification**

## Text Classification/Natural Language

# Bio Inspired Modeling/Novel Neural Architectures

# Evaluating Acceleration Techniques for Genetic Neural Architecture Search

Foteini Dervisi[✉][iD], George Kyriakides[iD], and Konstantinos Margaritis[iD]

Department of Applied Informatics, University of Macedonia, 156 Egnatia Street,
54636 Thessaloniki, Greece
{aid21006,ge.kyriakides,kmarg}@uom.edu.gr

**Abstract.** The increase in the available data and computational power
has led to the rapid evolution of the field of deep learning over the last
few years. However, the success of deep learning methods relies on making appropriate neural architecture choices, which is not a straightforward task and usually requires a time-consuming trial-and-error procedure. Neural architecture search is the process of automating the design
of neural network architectures capable of performing well on specific
tasks. It is a field that has emerged in order to address the problem of
designing efficient neural architectures and is gaining popularity due to
the rapid evolution of deep learning, which has led to an increasing need
for the discovery of high-performing neural architectures. This paper
focuses on evolutionary neural architecture search, which is an efficient
but also time-consuming and computationally expensive neural architecture search approach, and aims to pave the way for speeding up such
algorithms by assessing the effect of acceleration methods on the overall
performance of the neural architecture search procedure as well as on
the produced architectures.

**Keywords:** Neural architecture search · Evolutionary algorithms ·
Candidate evaluation · NAS-Bench-101

## 1 Introduction

Deep learning is a subfield of machine learning inspired by the function of the
human brain that uses multi-layer artificial neural networks to understand the
world as a hierarchy of concepts and learn complicated concepts by using simpler
ones as a basis, thus succeeding in automating feature engineering [3]. The use
of deep learning techniques has led to significant advancements in various fields,
such as information retrieval, computer vision and natural language processing.
The successful application of deep learning techniques largely relies on selecting
an appropriate neural network architecture for the task at hand, which is a
time-consuming process that requires prior knowledge of the field and is also
likely to lead to errors if performed manually by a human. The field of neural
architecture search, which has emerged in recent years as part of the shift towards

L. Iliadis et al. (Eds.): EANN 2022, CCIS 1600, pp. 3–14, 2022.
https://doi.org/10.1007/978-3-031-08223-8_1

automated machine learning, allows for the automatic design of optimal neural network architectures by using optimisation algorithms.

Neural architecture search is a subfield of automated machine learning that emerged in recent years due to the desire for automating the neural architecture design process and has succeeded in producing state-of-the-art neural network architectures that outperform manually designed ones without exhausting the available resources [7,10,11,14]. A neural architecture search procedure can be divided into the following components: search space, optimisation method and candidate evaluation method [5]. The search space defines which neural network architectures are eligible to be selected by the neural architecture search algorithm and may be influenced by prior experience in solving problems similar to the one the produced neural network architecture is intended to tackle. However, this may introduce bias, meaning that it may exclude architectures that have not previously been used for similar problems but would have been capable of achieving high performance [2]. The exploration of the search space is performed by using various optimisation methods, such as evolutionary algorithms, reinforcement learning and Bayesian optimisation [12]. Finally, candidate evaluation methods are used to assess the quality of candidate neural network architectures and thus guide the optimisation methods towards selecting the best candidates. The most straightforward approach for candidate evaluation is to perform a standard training and validation procedure of each neural architecture on a specific dataset. However, this approach is computationally expensive, which is why alternative approaches have been proposed, such as the reduction of the number of training epochs, the reduction of the number of cells or filters used and the use of predictive models to guide the search.

This paper focuses on the assessment of the quality of candidate evaluation acceleration techniques in evolutionary neural architecture search algorithms. The options that are explored for speeding up the process of evaluating candidate architectures are the use of fitness approximation and the use of a method for the partial prediction of the candidates' trained accuracy from their initial state. The rest of the paper is organised as follows: first, we briefly present the considered methods, as well as the NAS-Bench-101 dataset, which is the dataset that has been used to perform our experiments. We then describe the experiments that were conducted to determine the effect of the acceleration techniques on the overall performance of the search procedure. Finally, we present and interpret the results of our experiments and draw our final conclusions.

## 2   Related Work

As mentioned above, this paper examines the effect of techniques for accelerating the process of evaluating neural architectures on the performance of evolutionary neural architecture search algorithms. This section introduces the acceleration methods that are considered and also presents the NAS-Bench-101 dataset, which has been used to perform experiments for the comparison of the aforementioned techniques.

## 2.1 Evolutionary Neural Architecture Search with Fitness Approximation

Evolutionary algorithms are population-based metaheuristics inspired by Darwin's theory of evolution. They use mechanisms such as mutation, crossover, selection and reproduction to find acceptable solutions to optimisation problems. These algorithms treat candidate solutions to an optimisation problem as individuals in a population and use a fitness function to assess the quality of each candidate solution. An approximate solution is typically reached through an iterative procedure that simulates the natural selection process. Evolutionary algorithms are commonly used as an optimisation method in neural architecture search algorithms, as they succeed in producing high-performing neural architectures. However, they usually require immense computational resources due to the fact that they evaluate candidate architectures by performing a standard training and validation procedure. In order to overcome this difficulty and improve the time efficiency of such algorithms, the use of fitness approximation has been proposed.

NAS-EA-FA V2 [9] is an evolutionary algorithm that uses an XGBoost [1] model to estimate the fitness of candidate architectures, thus reducing the algorithm running time. The algorithm uses an iterative procedure, where only a small number of architectures are trained and evaluated in each iteration in order to provide training data for the XGBoost model. The XGBoost model is then trained and used to estimate the fitness of the remaining architectures. The $K$ architectures with the highest fitness and the $H$ architectures with the largest distance from the previously evaluated architectures are selected for training in each iteration, thus increasing the diversity of the trained architectures and improving the stability of the algorithm. Furthermore, the algorithm uses data augmentation, as it identifies the isomorphisms of each of the trained architectures and includes them in the training set, thus attempting to improve the performance of the predictive model by providing it with a larger training dataset.

## 2.2 Neural Architecture Search Without Training

An alternative solution that has been proposed for the acceleration of the neural architecture search process is to evaluate architectures based solely on their initial state. For this purpose, Mellor et al. introduced the NAS without training score [8], henceforth called NASWT score, which is able to perform a partial prediction of a neural network's accuracy without requiring any training. This score can be calculated for neural networks with rectified linear unit (ReLU) activations, as it evaluates untrained networks by looking at the overlap of these activations between data points. There seems to be a positive correlation between the aforementioned score and the accuracy of a network after training, meaning that this score can quickly give a rough estimate of a network's performance and serve as a means of guiding neural architecture search algorithms towards discovering efficient neural architectures. The calculation of this score requires minimal computational power as it can be performed within a few seconds on a single GPU, thus offering promising prospects in the sense that it has the potential of enabling a considerable reduction of the running time of neural architecture search algorithms.

## 2.3 NAS-Bench-101

As mentioned above, neural architecture search algorithms require immense computational power, as they typically evaluate candidate neural network architectures by performing a standard training and validation procedure for each architecture. This leads to difficulties regarding the reproducibility of experiments and excludes researchers without access to adequate computational resources from developing and testing novel ideas in the field. In order to overcome this issue, various benchmark datasets have been introduced. Each of these datasets contains a large number of trained and evaluated architectures, allowing for the assessment of neural architecture search techniques in minimal time. NAS-Bench-101 [13] is the first neural architecture dataset that was publicly released. It contains a search space of 423,624 unique convolutional architectures that are suitable for the task of image classification. These architectures have been trained and evaluated multiple times with three different initialisations on CIFAR-10 for four different numbers of epochs, thus resulting in a dataset of over 5 million trained architectures. The NAS-Bench-101 search space consists of neural architectures that are constructed as follows: the neural architecture search algorithm defines the architecture of a specific cell, which is represented in the form of a directed acyclic graph and has a maximum of 7 nodes, which represent layers, and a maximum of 9 edges, which represent connections between layers. Each generated cell has an input layer, an output layer and a maximum of 5 intermediate layers that are chosen from the following available operations: $3 \times 3$ convolution, $1 \times 1$ convolution and $3 \times 3$ max pool. An example of a NAS-Bench-101 cell is displayed in Fig. 1a. The overall architecture is then constructed with the use of a pre-defined skeleton (Fig. 1b) that is based on stacking multiple cells. The best architecture in NAS-Bench-101 achieves a mean test accuracy of 94.32% on the CIFAR-10 dataset.

## 3   Experiments

We conduct four experiments to determine the effect of acceleration techniques on the performance of evolutionary neural architecture search. In the first two experiments, we use a simple genetic algorithm. Two options are examined regarding candidate evaluation; in the first experiment, the validation accuracy is used to determine the fitness of individuals, whereas in the second experiment the NASWT score is used as a measure of individuals' fitness. The remaining experiments concern NAS-EA-FA V2, the aforementioned evolutionary algorithm that uses fitness approximation to speed up the search procedure. In the third experiment, the validation accuracy is used as the fitness score, whereas in the fourth experiment the fitness of individuals is determined by using the NASWT score.

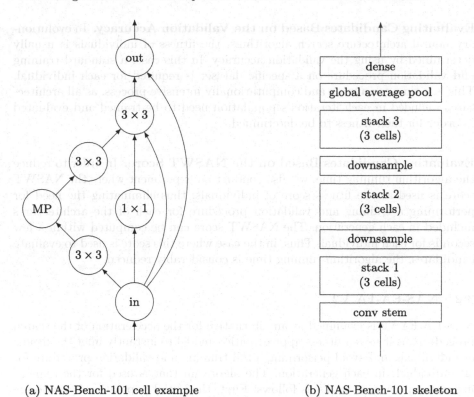

(a) NAS-Bench-101 cell example      (b) NAS-Bench-101 skeleton

**Fig. 1.** NAS-Bench-101 cell and skeleton

## 3.1   Genetic Algorithm

Genetic algorithms are evolutionary algorithms that are based on the biological process of natural selection and are used as a means of discovering high-quality solutions to optimisation problems by performing a natural selection process on an initial population. In our case, the genetic algorithm is used for the discovery of high-performing neural architectures, thus each individual in the population is a neural network architecture. The genetic algorithm that is used for our experiments works as follows: First, the initial population is randomly sampled and assigned an initial fitness equal to zero, as there is no available information regarding the behaviour of the produced architectures yet. We then perform an iterative procedure for a fixed number of iterations, where in each iteration the parents are defined by using tournament selection and the offsprings are generated from the parents by using bitwise mutation. The initial population of each iteration is the population derived by mutation from the previous iteration's population.

**Evaluating Candidates Based on the Validation Accuracy.** In evolutionary neural architecture search algorithms, the fitness of individuals is usually determined by using the validation accuracy. In this case, a standard training and validation procedure on a specific dataset is required for each individual. This is a time-consuming and computationally intensive process, as all architectures included in each iteration's population need to be trained and evaluated in order for their fitness to be determined.

**Evaluating Candidates Based on the NASWT Score.** In order to reduce the algorithm running time, we also conduct an experiment where the NASWT score is used as the fitness score of individuals, thus eliminating the need for performing a training and validation procedure for each of the architectures included in each generation. The NASWT score can be computed within a few seconds for each individual. Thus, in the case where this score is used to evaluate candidates, the algorithm running time is considerably reduced.

### 3.2    NAS-EA-FA V2

NAS-EA-FA V2 is examined as an alternative for the acceleration of the search procedure, as it uses a fitness approximation model to instantly infer the fitness of individuals and avoid performing a full training and validation procedure for all individuals in each generation. The algorithm that is used for the remaining two experiments works as follows: First, the initial population is randomly sampled and assigned a fitness score equal to zero. Then, an iterative procedure is performed for a fixed number of iterations $(T)$, where in each iteration the first step is to sort the current population in descending order based on the fitness of its individuals. The $K$ architectures with the highest fitness and the $H$ architectures with the largest distance from the previously evaluated architectures are then selected to be trained and evaluated in order to provide training data for the fitness approximation model. The training set is enhanced by using data augmentation, as the isomorphisms of the $K + H$ evaluated architectures are also appended to the training set. An XGBoost model is then trained based on the provided training data (which consist of all the architectures that have been trained and evaluated in all iterations up until that point) in order to be able to estimate the fitness of the remaining architectures. Once the XGBoost model training has been performed, a genetic algorithm with a fixed number of generations $(G)$ is used to evolve the population and generate architectures with higher performance. The algorithm chooses the parents by using tournament selection and produces the offsprings by performing bitwise mutation. The main difference between this approach and the simple genetic algorithm used in the first two experiments is the fact that the fitness of offsprings is now instantly estimated by using the trained XGBoost model.

**Evaluating Candidates Based on the Validation Accuracy.** In the third experiment, we use the validation accuracy as the fitness score, meaning that a training and validation process is still required for $K + H$ architectures in each iteration. However, a considerable amount of time is saved compared to the simple genetic algorithm, where all individuals need to be trained and evaluated.

**Evaluating Candidates Based on the NASWT Score.** In the last experiment, we use the NASWT score as the fitness score, thus completely eliminating the need for training and evaluating networks. In this case, only the NASWT score is calculated for each architecture, a calculation that can be performed relatively quickly and requires minimal computational resources. The algorithm running time is therefore drastically reduced. However, some extra noise is introduced, as the NASWT score is not a definitive measure of the architectures' performance after training. This may lead to a considerable reduction of the performance of the algorithm, as the use of fitness approximation to infer the fitness of offsprings already induces some noise in the process. Based on the results, the validity of this method will be assessed and conclusions as to whether the reduction in the algorithm running time can compensate for the algorithm's performance drop will be reached.

## 3.3 Experimental Setup

**The NORD Framework.** Neural Operations Research and Development [6] (NORD) is a Python framework that simplifies the design of neural architecture search procedures by decoupling the design and implementation of networks and enables the fair comparison of neural architecture search approaches by facilitating their application on benchmarks and custom datasets. The NORD framework contains a neural descriptor class, which enables building neural networks simply by describing their topology, i.e. its layers and the connections between them. It also contains a neural evaluator class, which automates the process of either training and evaluating networks on real datasets or using benchmarks to retrieve the pre-computed performance statistics of candidate architectures. The NORD framework is used in all the experiments presented in this paper to perform the calculations required for the performance evaluation of individuals.

**Handling Nodes Without Input or Output Connections.** The initial population of the examined evolutionary algorithms is created by building random cells whose layer types and connections are randomly decided by taking into account the NAS-Bench-101 requirements. However, this means that some invalid cells are created along the way, as it is possible to generate cells that contain layers without any input or output connections. In order to overcome this issue, the layers without input or output connections are removed from each randomly generated cell before the start of the iterative procedure.

**Experimental Parameter Settings.** Table 1 displays the values of the parameters that are used in our experiments, which have been selected in accordance with [9].

**Table 1.** Parameter values

| Algorithm | Parameter | Value |
|---|---|---|
| Genetic algorithm | Population size | 100 |
| | Tournament size | 20% |
| | Layer mutation rate | $1/5$ |
| | Connection mutation rate | $1/21$ |
| | Number of generations | 100 |
| NAS-EA-FA V2 | Population size | 100 |
| | Tournament size | 20% |
| | Layer mutation rate | $1/5$ |
| | Connection mutation rate | $1/21$ |
| | Number of iterations ($T$) | 10 |
| | Number of generations ($G$) in each iteration | 10 |
| | $K$ | 30 |
| | $H$ | 20 |
| | XGBoost learning rate | 0.1 |
| NASWT score | Batch size | 32 |

## 4   Results

In order to produce representative results and draw accurate conclusions regarding the efficiency of the considered evolutionary neural architecture search acceleration techniques, each experiment was repeated ten times, resulting in ten independent sets of results. The results were then post-processed and analysed in order to draw conclusions regarding the effect of the examined acceleration techniques on the efficiency of the neural architecture search process.

The conclusion that can be drawn from Figs. 2a and 2b is that NAS-EA-FA introduces some noise to the process due to the use of a predictive model to estimate the individuals' fitness. It is apparent that the simple genetic algorithm that performs a direct calculation of each individual's fitness succeeds in producing better architectures than NAS-EA-FA, thus leading to the conclusion that NAS-EA-FA somehow narrows down the search space, as the best architectures it produces perform slightly worse than the best architecture in NAS-Bench-101 , which is more frequently found by the simple genetic algorithm. This may be caused due to the introduction of bias by the process that is used for the selection of the training data for the fitness approximation model and the fact that this bias is then reflected in the fitness approximation model's predictions.

Figures 2c and 2d show the best accuracies as selected based on the algorithm's fitness measure, i.e. the validation accuracy or the NASWT score. The results show that although NAS-EA-FA introduces some limitations, the version of NAS-EA-FA that evaluates individuals based on the validation accuracy is the best choice for the acceleration of the neural architecture search procedure. This conclusion is based on the fact that the NASWT score seems to be unable to recognise better-performing architectures, probably due to the fact that its correlation with the validation accuracy is not strong enough to enable it to accurately distinguish the best-performing architectures. Therefore, although the search procedures that are guided by the NASWT score succeed in producing high-performing architectures in just a few epochs, it is unfortunately impossible for them to identify the best-performing architectures, as the fitness score that they use is not an accurate enough measure of an architecture's performance.

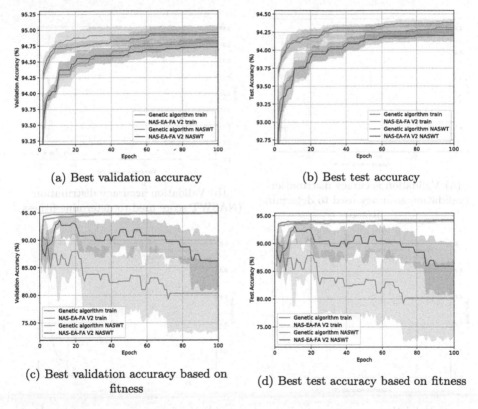

(a) Best validation accuracy

(b) Best test accuracy

(c) Best validation accuracy based on fitness

(d) Best test accuracy based on fitness

**Fig. 2.** Best accuracy of 10 runs on NAS-Bench-101 (mean and 95% confidence interval displayed)

Figure 3 displays the distributions of the validation accuracies of the architectures produced by all the considered algorithms. In all experiments, the majority of the generated architectures have a validation accuracy ranging between 90% and 95%, whereas there are also a few architectures with a validation accuracy of around 85%, which are probably generated at the start of the search procedure. The main conclusion that can be drawn is that the simple genetic algorithm and NAS-EA-FA produce different architectures regardless of the chosen fitness score. This has also been confirmed by a two-sample Kolmogorov-Smirnov test [4], which has been used to compare the distributions of the validation accuracies of the produced architectures. We conducted two tests, one for the case where we use the validation accuracy to determine the fitness of individuals and one for the case where the fitness is determined by the NASWT score. The tests resulted in p-values of $1.84 \cdot 10^{-121}$ and $1.89 \cdot 10^{-160}$ respectively, thus leading to the conclusion that the validation accuracies of the architectures generated by the simple genetic algorithm belong to a different distribution than the validation accuracies of the architectures generated by NAS-EA-FA.

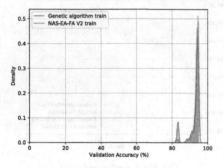

(a) Validation accuracy distribution (validation accuracy used to determine fitness)

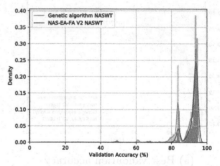

(b) Validation accuracy distribution (NASWT score used to determine fitness)

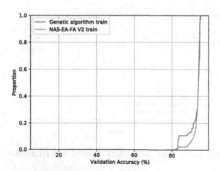

(c) Validation accuracy empirical cumulative distribution (validation accuracy used to determine fitness)

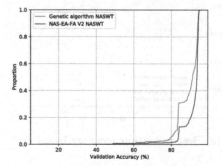

(d) Validation accuracy empirical cumulative distribution (NASWT score used to determine fitness)

**Fig. 3.** Distributions of the validation accuracies of the produced architectures

# 5   Conclusions and Future Work

Due to the increasing popularity of deep learning techniques, there is also an increasing need for automating the design of neural network architectures that are capable of performing well and solving specific problems. Neural architecture search, a subfield of automated machine learning that uses optimisation algorithms in order to automatically design optimal neural architectures, has succeeded in producing state-of-the-art architectures for various problems.

This paper examines the use of techniques for accelerating evolutionary neural architecture search and their effect on the search procedure and its ability to identify high-performing neural architectures. We considered the use of a fitness approximation model to estimate the individuals' fitness instead of evaluating them based on their accuracy, which would require a time-consuming training and validation procedure, as well as guiding the search with the use of the NASWT score, which estimates a network's performance based on its initial state. A thorough computational study was conducted to determine the effect of the aforementioned techniques on the search procedure and the quality of the produced architectures. The results lead to the conclusion that the fitness approximation model for the estimation of the individuals' fitness introduces some noise to the process and also restricts the produced architectures to a subset of the search space, thus failing to discover the optimal architectures. However, it is apparent that the use of a fitness approximation model to estimate the validation accuracy is preferred over the use of the NASWT score as a fitness measure, as although the NASWT score does not impose any restrictions on the search space, it is not capable of accurately identifying the best-performing architectures even though it succeeds in guiding the algorithm to discover some of them.

Future work in this direction includes experimenting with the NASWT score by using different batch sizes in order to determine whether the batch size influences the score's correlation with the networks' performance. Another possible task is to examine the behaviour of other fitness approximation models, such as graph convolutional networks, as well as the use of other metaheuristic optimisation methods, such as particle swarm optimisation and ant colony optimisation.

**Acknowledgements.** This paper is a result of research conducted within the "MSc in Artificial Intelligence and Data Analytics" of the Department of Applied Informatics of the University of Macedonia. The presentation of the paper is funded by the University of Macedonia Research Committee.

# References

1. Chen, T., Guestrin, C.: XGBoost: a scalable tree boosting system. In: Proceedings of the 22nd ACM SIGKDD International Conference on Knowledge Discovery and Data Mining, pp. 785–794. KDD 2016. Association for Computing Machinery, New York, NY (2016). https://doi.org/10.1145/2939672.2939785

2. Elsken, T., Metzen, J.H., Hutter, F.: Neural architecture search: a survey. J. Mach. Learn. Res. **20**(55), 1–21 (2019). http://jmlr.org/papers/v20/18-598.html
3. Goodfellow, I., Bengio, Y., Courville, A.: Deep Learning. MIT Press (2016). http://www.deeplearningbook.org
4. Hodges, J.L.: The significance probability of the Smirnov two-sample test. Arkiv för Matematik **3**(5), 469–486 (1958). https://doi.org/10.1007/BF02589501
5. Kyriakides, G., Margaritis, K.: An introduction to neural architecture search for convolutional networks. arXiv preprint arXiv:2005.11074 (2020)
6. Kyriakides, G., Margaritis, K.: NORD: a python framework for neural architecture search. Softw. Impacts **6**, 100042 (2020). https://doi.org/10.1016/j.simpa.2020.100042
7. Liu, H., Simonyan, K., Yang, Y.: DARTS: differentiable architecture search. In: International Conference on Learning Representations (2019). https://openreview.net/forum?id=S1eYHoC5FX
8. Mellor, J., Turner, J., Storkey, A., Crowley, E.J.: Neural architecture search without training. In: Meila, M., Zhang, T. (eds.) Proceedings of the 38th International Conference on Machine Learning. Proceedings of Machine Learning Research, vol. 139, pp. 7588–7598. PMLR, 18–24 July 2021. https://proceedings.mlr.press/v139/mellor21a.html
9. Pan, C., Yao, X.: Neural architecture search based on evolutionary algorithms with fitness approximation. In: 2021 International Joint Conference on Neural Networks (IJCNN), pp. 1–8 (2021). https://doi.org/10.1109/IJCNN52387.2021.9533986
10. Pham, H., Guan, M., Zoph, B., Le, Q., Dean, J.: Efficient neural architecture search via parameters sharing. In: Dy, J., Krause, A. (eds.) Proceedings of the 35th International Conference on Machine Learning. Proceedings of Machine Learning Research, vol. 80, pp. 4095–4104. PMLR, 10–15 July 2018. https://proceedings.mlr.press/v80/pham18a.html
11. Real, E., Aggarwal, A., Huang, Y., Le, Q.V.: Regularized evolution for image classifier architecture search. In: Proceedings of the Thirty-Third AAAI Conference on Artificial Intelligence and Thirty-First Innovative Applications of Artificial Intelligence Conference and Ninth AAAI Symposium on Educational Advances in Artificial Intelligence. AAAI Press (2019). https://doi.org/10.1609/aaai.v33i01.33014780
12. Wistuba, M., Rawat, A., Pedapati, T.: A survey on neural architecture search. arXiv preprint arXiv:1905.01392 (2019)
13. Ying, C., Klein, A., Christiansen, E., Real, E., Murphy, K., Hutter, F.: NAS-Bench-101: towards reproducible neural architecture search. In: Chaudhuri, K., Salakhutdinov, R. (eds.) Proceedings of the 36th International Conference on Machine Learning. Proceedings of Machine Learning Research, vol. 97, pp. 7105–7114. PMLR, Long Beach, California, USA, 09–15 June 2019. http://proceedings.mlr.press/v97/ying19a.html
14. Zoph, B., Le, Q.V.: Neural architecture search with reinforcement learning. In: 5th International Conference on Learning Representations, ICLR 2017, Toulon, France, 24–26 April 2017, Conference Track Proceedings. OpenReview.net (2017). https://openreview.net/forum?id=r1Ue8Hcxg

# Generation of Orthogonality for Feature Spaces in the Bio-inspired Neural Networks

Naohiro Ishii[1]($\boxtimes$), Toshinori Deguchi[2], Masashi Kawaguchi[3], Hiroshi Sasaki[4], and Tokuro Matsuo[1]

[1] Advanced Institute of Industrial Technology, Tokyo, Japan
nishii@acm.org, matsuo@aiit.ac.jp
[2] Gifu National College of Technology, Gifu, Japan
deguchi@gifu-nct.ac.jp
[3] Suzuka National College of Technology, Mie, Japan
masashi@elec.suzuka-ct.ac.jp
[4] Fukui University of Technology, Fukui, Japan
h-sasaki@fukui-ut.ac.jp

**Abstract.** Neural networks are extensively developed for the deep learning and intelligent processing. To improve the performance of neural networks, the biological inspired neural networks are often studied for artificial neural networks. Models for motion processing in the biological systems have been used, which consist of the symmetric networks with quadrature functions of Gabor filters. This paper proposes a model of the bio-inspired asymmetric neural networks with nonlinear characteristics, which are the squaring and rectification functions. These functions are observed in the retinal and visual cortex networks. In this paper, the proposed asymmetric network with Gabor filters and the conventional energy model are compared from the orthogonality characteristics. To show the role of the orthogonality in the feature space, tracking characteristics to input stimulus are experimented. Then, the orthogonality basis functions create better tracking results. Thus, asymmetric structure of the network and its nonlinear characteristics are shown to be effective factors for generating orthogonality.

**Keywords:** Asymmetric neural network · Gabor filter · Correlation and orthogonality analysis · Energy model · Nonlinear characteristics

## 1 Introduction

Neural networks currently play an important role in the processing complex tasks for the visual perception and the deep learning. To estimate the visual motion, sensory biological information models have been studied [1]. For the deep learning efficiently, an independent projection [2] from the inputs are studied in the convolutional neural networks. Further, in the deep learning, the orthogonalization in the weight matrix of neural networks are studied using optimization methods [3]. In the network learning, the feature vectors from different classes are expected to be as orthogonal as possible [4]. It is important to make clear the network structures and functions how to generate

© Springer Nature Switzerland AG 2022
L. Iliadis et al. (Eds.): EANN 2022, CCIS 1600, pp. 15–26, 2022.
https://doi.org/10.1007/978-3-031-08223-8_2

orthogonality relations, which will make it possible to respond correctly and effectively in the feature spaces. By using Gabor filters, a symmetric network model was developed for the motion detection, which is called energy model [1]. The energy model is applied to maximizing independence for neural networks [5, 6]. Further, in the sparse coding, the non-orthogonal basis functions cause deviation of input-output linearity [7]. This paper develops asymmetrical networks, which are based on the catfish retina. This is an extended version of an earlier article [12] developed for feature spaces. Then, the orthogonality characteristics between the asymmetric networks and the conventional energy model are compared. In the biological visual systems, the nonlinear characteristics are observed as the squaring function and rectification function [10]. It is shown that asymmetric structure networks and nonlinear functions generate orthogonal characteristics. To verify the orthogonal properties in the feature spaces, the tracking problems are experimented. It is shown that the asymmetric networks with nonlinear function work effectively for tracking characteristics in the feature spaces, in which the orthogonal wavelet basis functions play an effective role for following to the input stimulus.

## 2   Bio-inspired Neural Networks

### 2.1   Background of Bio-inspired Neural Networks

In the biological neural networks, the structure of the network, is closely related to the functions of the network. Naka et al. [10] presented a simplified, but essential networks of catfish inner retina as shown in Fig. 1. Visual perception is carried out firstly in the retinal neural network as the special processing between neurons.

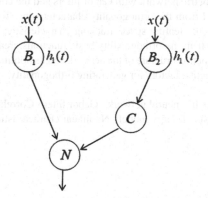

**Fig. 1.** Asymmetric network with linear and squaring nonlinear pathways

Visual perception is carried out firstly in the retinal neural network as the special processing between neurons. The following asymmetric neural network is extracted from the catfish retinal network [10]. The asymmetric structure network with a quadratic nonlinearity is shown in Fig. 1, which composes of the pathway from the bipolar cell B to the amacrine cell N and that from the bipolar cell B, via the amacrine cell C to the N [9, 10]. Figure 1 shows a network which plays an important role in the movement perception as the fundamental network. It is shown that N cell response is realized by a linear filter, which is composed of a differentiation filter followed by a low-pass filter. Thus, the asymmetric network in Fig. 1 is composed of a linear pathway and a nonlinear pathway with the cell C, which works as a squaring function.

## 3 Orthogonal Characteristics of Asymmetric Networks

### 3.1 Orthogonality of Asymmetric Network Under the Stimulus Condition

The inner orthogonality under the moving stimulus conditions is computed in the asymmetric networks as shown in Fig. 2, which are derived from the systematic functions in Fig. 1. The impuse functions of the cells are shown in $h_1(t)$ and $h_1'(t)$.

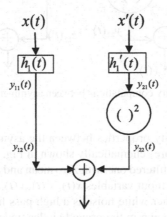

**Fig. 2.** Asymmetric network unit with Gabor filters

In the biological visual systems, Gabor filters are often used as the impulse functions.

The variable $t$ in the Gabor filters is changed to $t'$, where by setting $\xi \triangleq 2\pi\omega$ in the Eq. (1), $t' = 2\pi\omega t = \xi t$ and $dt = dt/\xi$ hold. Then, Gabor filters become to the following equation.

$$G_s(t') = \frac{1}{\sqrt{2\pi}\sigma}e^{-\frac{t'^2}{2\sigma^2\xi^2}}sin(t') \text{ and } G_c(t') = \frac{1}{\sqrt{2\pi}\sigma}e^{-\frac{t'^2}{2\sigma^2\xi^2}}cos(t') \quad (1)$$

The impulse response functions $h_1(t)$ and $h_1'(t)$ are often replaced by $G_s(t')$ and $G_c(t')$ or vice versa. The outputs of these linear filters are given as follows,

$$y_{11}(t) = \int_0^\infty h_1(t')x(t-t')dt' \quad (2)$$

$$y_{21}(t) = \int_0^\infty h_1'(t')x(t-t')dt' \quad (3)$$

## 3.2 Orthogonality Between the Asymmetric Networks Units

We compute orthogonality properties between the asymmetric networks units in Fig. 3. Orthogonal or non-orthogonal properties of the networks depend on the input stimulus to the networks.

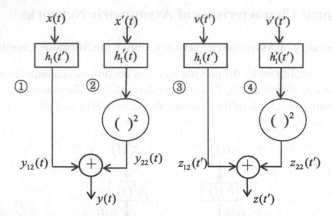

**Fig. 3.** Orthogonality computations between asymmetric networks units

To check the orthogonality properties between the asymmetric networks units, the white noise moving stimuli are schematically shown in Fig. 4. In the first row in Fig. 4, one white noise is a low pass filtered one with zero mean and its power $p$, which is shown in the circles only under the input variables $x(t)$, $x'(t)$, $v(t)$ and $v'(t')$. Similarly, in the second row in Fig. 4, the other white noise is a high pass filtered one with zero mean and its power $p'$, which is shown in the grayed circles under input variable $v'(t')$. The impulse response functions $h_1(t)$ and $h'_1(t)$ are replaced by the Gabor filters, $G_s(t')$ and $G_c(t')$ as shown in the Eq. (1). The stimulus with the high pass filtered noise is moved from the right to the left according to $(a)$, $(b)$, $(c)$, $(d)$ and $(e)$ in front of the visual space.

Under the stimulus condition $(a)$ in Fig. 4, the correlation between outputs $y(t)$ and $z(t)$ between the asymmetrical networks with Gabor filters in Fig. 3, is computed as follows,

$$
\int_{-\infty}^{\infty} y(t)z(t)dt = \int_{-\infty}^{\infty} dt\{ \int_{0}^{\infty} h_1(\tau)x(t-\tau)d\tau
$$

$$
+ \int_{0}^{\infty} \int_{0}^{\infty} h'_1(\tau_1)h'_1(\tau_2)x'(t-\tau_1)x'(t-\tau_2)d\tau_1 d\tau_2 \}
$$

$$
\{ \int_{0}^{\infty} h'_1(\sigma)v(t-\sigma)d\sigma + \int_{0}^{\infty} \int_{0}^{\infty} h_1(\sigma_1)h_1(\sigma_2)v'(t-\sigma_1)v'(t-\sigma_2)d\sigma_1 d\sigma_2 \} \quad (4)
$$

$$
= \int_{0}^{\infty} \int_{0}^{\infty} h_1(\tau)h'_1(\sigma)d\tau d\sigma E[x(t-\tau)v(t-\sigma)]
$$

$$
+ \int_{0}^{\infty} \int_{0}^{\infty} \int_{0}^{\infty} h_1(\tau)h_1(\sigma_1)h_1(\sigma_2)E[x(t-\tau)v'(t-\sigma_1)v'(t-\sigma_2)]d\tau d\sigma_1 d\sigma_2
$$

$$+ \int_0^\infty \int_0^\infty \int_0^\infty h_1'(\sigma)h_1'(\tau_1)h_1'(\tau_2)E[v(t-\sigma)x'(t-\tau_1)x'(t-\tau_2)]d\sigma d\tau_1 d\tau_2$$

$$+ \int_0^\infty \int_0^\infty \int_0^\infty \int_0^\infty h_1'(\tau_1)h_1'(\tau_2)h_1(\sigma_1)h_1(\sigma_2)$$

$$E[x'(t-\tau_1)x'(t-\tau_2)v'(t-\sigma_1)v'(t-\sigma_2)]d\tau_1 d\tau_2 d\sigma_1 d\sigma_2$$

$$= \{\int_0^\infty h_1(\tau)d\tau \int_0^\infty h_1'(\sigma)d\sigma\} \cdot p + 0 + 0 + 3p^2 \{\int_0^\infty h_1'(\tau)d\tau\}^2 \{\int_0^\infty h_1(\tau)d\tau\}^2 \qquad (5)$$

$$①③ \qquad\qquad ①④ \quad ②③ \qquad ②④$$

where the first term of Eq. (5) shows a path way of ① and ③ and the second and third terms are to be 0 in ①④ and ② ③, respectively. The fourth term is in ②④.

The terms ①③ and ②④ are not zero, because the following equations hold,

$$\int_0^\infty h_1(\tau)d\tau = \frac{1}{\sqrt{2\pi}\sigma} \int_0^\infty e^{-\frac{\tau^2}{2\sigma^2\xi^2}} \sin(\tau)d\tau = \frac{\xi}{\sqrt{\pi}} e^{-\frac{1}{2}\sigma^2\xi^2} \int_0^{\frac{1}{\sqrt{2}}\sigma\xi} e^{\tau^2} d\tau > 0$$

$$(6)$$

and

$$\int_0^\infty h_1'(\tau)d\tau = \frac{1}{\sqrt{2\pi}\sigma} \int_0^\infty e^{-\frac{\tau^2}{2\sigma^2\xi^2}} \cos(\tau)d\tau = \frac{\xi}{2} e^{-\frac{1}{2}\sigma^2\xi^2} > 0 \qquad (7)$$

where $\xi$ is the center frequency of the Gabor filter. Thus, since two pathways are zero in the correlation, while other two pathways (25% and 25%) are non-zero, the orthogonality becomes 50% for the stimuli (a) in Fig. 4. Similarly, under the stimulus conditions, (b), (c), (d) and (e) in Fig. 4, the correlations are computed [16].

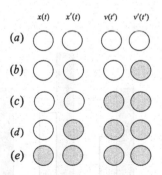

**Fig. 4.** White noise stimuli for checking orthogonality and non-orthogonality

## 4 Orthogonal Properties of Conventional Energy Model

A symmetric network with Gabor filter were proposed by Adelson and Bergen [1] as the energy model of the perception of the visual motion.

### 4.1  Orthogonality Under the Stimulus Condition

Symmetric network is shown in Fig. 5, which is derived from the systematic functions.

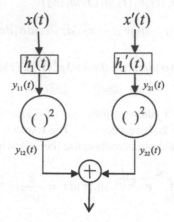

**Fig. 5.** Symmetric network unit, which is called energy model

### 4.2  Comparison Between the Asymmetric Network and the Energy Model

In Fig. 6, the filled bar shows the orthogonality ratio value in the asymmetric neural networks under the moving stimulus conditions, while the dotted bar shows by two units of the symmetric network in Fig. 5. Figure 6 shows that the asymmetric network shows higher orthogonality ratio, compared with the symmetric network.

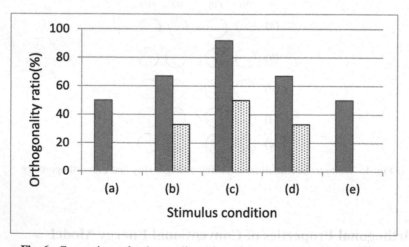

**Fig. 6.** Comparison of orthogonality ratio under moving stimulus conditions

# 5   Generation of Orthogonality in the 1st Layer Network

The two types of the units are shown in Fig. 7, which are constructed with two asymmetric networks in Fig. 1. Two amacrine cells $Na$ and $Nb$ are experimentally clarified [9] and the outputs of them are inputted to the Ganglion cell, $G$

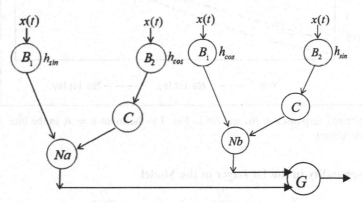

**Fig. 7.** First layer for the generation of orthogonality components

We assume here the impulse response functions of the bipolar cells $B_1$ are different, which are described in $h_{sin}$ and $h_{cos}$, respectively. Output responses of the $Na$ cell and $Nb$ cell are shown in $\widehat{Na}$ and $\widehat{Nb}$. Their responses are given in the Eq. (8),

$$\widehat{Na} = \int_0^T (\int_0^T e^{-\frac{\tau^2}{2\sigma^2\xi^2}} sin(\tau)x(t-\tau)d\tau)dt + \int_0^T (\int_0^T e^{-\frac{\tau^2}{2\sigma^2\xi^2}} cos(\tau)x(t-\tau)d\tau)^2 dt$$

$$\widehat{Nb} = \int_0^T (\int_0^T e^{-\frac{\tau^2}{2\sigma^2\xi^2}} cos(\tau)x(t-\tau)d\tau)dt + \int_0^T (\int_0^T e^{-\frac{\tau^2}{2\sigma^2\xi^2}} sin(\tau)x(t-\tau)d\tau)^2 dt$$

$$(8)$$

We assume here the static feature is represented in the linear equation $y = x(t)$. Then, the least square optimization $\widetilde{Na}$ of the $Na$ is realized by setting coefficients $\{a, b\}$ for respective pathways as follows,

$$\widetilde{Na} = a\int_0^T (\int_0^T e^{-\frac{\tau^2}{2\sigma^2\xi^2}} sin(\tau)x(t-\tau)d\tau)dt + b\int_0^T (\int_0^T e^{-\frac{\tau^2}{2\sigma^2\xi^2}} cos(\tau)x(t-\tau)d\tau)^2 dt \qquad (9)$$

Then, the optimization is realized by the equation

$$Minimize \int_0^T (x(t)-\widehat{Na})^2 dt \qquad (10)$$

The minimization of Eq. (10) is solved by the differentiations $(d\widetilde{Na}/da)$ and $(d\widetilde{Na}/db)$. Thus, the optimized coefficients $\{a, b\}$ are obtained.

By setting $T = \pi$, we can obtain the optimized coefficients, $a = 0.489$, $b = 0.0215$. Using these values, the comparison between the feature $y = x$ and the optimized value $\widetilde{Na}$ in the Eq. (9) is shown in dashed line in Fig. 8. Similarly, the optimized responses $\widetilde{Nb}$ is computed in dotted line in Fig. 8.

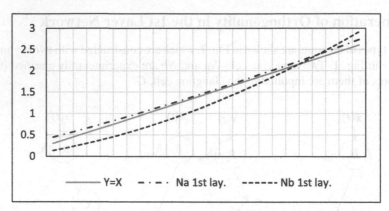

**Fig. 8.** Optimized responses of *Na* and *Nb* in Fig. 7 to the input $y = x$( in the blue solid line) (Color figure online)

## 5.1 Orthogonality in the 1st Layer in the Model

The orthogonality between $Ae^{-\frac{t'^2}{2\sigma^2\xi^2}}\sin(t')$ and $Ae^{-\frac{t'^2}{2\sigma^2\xi^2}}\cos(t')$ is shown in the following procedure. The orthogonality is computed in the correlation

$$\int_{-\pi}^{\pi} e^{-\frac{\tau^2}{2\sigma^2\xi^2}}\sin(t)\cdot e^{-\frac{\tau^2}{2\sigma^2\xi^2}}\cos(t)dt = \int_{-\pi}^{\pi} e^{-\frac{\tau^2}{\sigma^2\xi^2}}\sin(t)\cdot\cos(t)dt \qquad (11)$$

In Fig. 9, the Gaussian function is included between the approximated by triangle functions (a) and (b) in Fig. 9, which are shown in Eq. (12) with $a > 0$ and $b > 0$.

$$at + b\,, t < 0 \text{ and } -at + b,\ t \geq 0 \qquad (12)$$

Similarly, the triangle function (b) in Fig. 9 is represented using the coefficients $a'$ and $b'$ in Eq. (12).

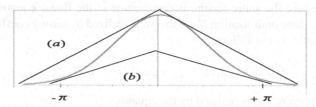

**Fig. 9.** Gaussian function is included between two triangle functions (a) and (b)

Since the cross product of the trigonometric functions, $\sin t$ and $\cos t$ of the Gabor filters in Eq. (1) on the $[-\pi, +\pi]$, becomes an odd function shown in $f(-t) = -f(t)$ using function $f(t)$, the following equations are derived.

$$\int_{-\pi}^{\pi} |a't + b'| \cdot f(t)dt \leq \frac{1}{\sqrt{2\pi}\sigma}\int_{-\pi}^{\pi} (e^{-\frac{\tau^2}{2\sigma^2\xi^2}})^2\sin(t)\cdot\cos(t)dt \leq \int_{-\pi}^{\pi} |at + b| \cdot f(t)dt = 0$$

$$(13)$$

These orthogonal relations are generated in the cell $G$, which are based on the two asymmetric networks $Na$ and $Nb$. The optimized responses of the G is shown in dotted line in Fig. 10, which we call the optimized responses in the asymmetric 1-st layer of the model.

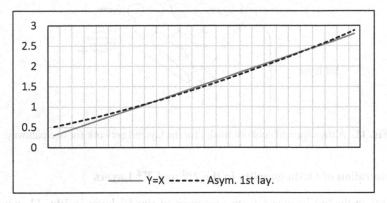

**Fig. 10.** Optimized responses of the asymmetric 1-st layer of the model to the input $y = x$

## 6   Extension of Asymmetric Networks Based on Bio-inspired Neural Networks

Here, we present an example of layered neural network in Fig. 11, which is developed from the neural networks in the brain cortex model V1 followed by MT [8].

### 6.1   Extension of the Asymmetric Networks to the 2-nd and 3-rd Layers

An extended asymmetric network is developed by the approximated network with Tailor expansion in Fig. 11, in which the basic asymmetric networks in Fig. 2 are included. The half-wave rectification is approximated in the following equation.

$$f(x) = \frac{1}{1 + e^{-\eta(x-\theta)}}$$

By Taylor expansion of Eq. (14) at $x = \theta$, the Eq. (15) is derived as follows,

$$f(x)_{x=\theta} = f(\theta) \mid f'(\theta)(x - \theta) + \frac{1}{2!}f''(0)(x - 0)^2 + \dots$$

$$= \frac{1}{2} + \frac{\eta}{4}(x - \theta) + \frac{1}{2!}(-\frac{\eta^2}{4} + \frac{\eta^2 e^{-\eta\theta}}{2})(x - \theta)^2 + \dots \qquad (15)$$

In Fig. 11, the nonlinear terms, $x^2, x^3, x^4, \dots$ are generated in Eq. (15). Thus, the combination of Gabor function pairs are generated in Fig. 11, in which the transformed network consists of two layers of the extended asymmetrical network in Fig. 2.

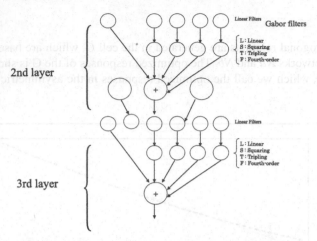

**Fig. 11.** A transformed network model for the layered network for one pathway

## 6.2 Generation of Orthogonality in the 2$^{nd}$ and 3$^{rd}$ Layers

The inputs in the2nd layer are from responses of the 1$^{st}$ layer in Fig. 11, which are wavelets of the product of Gaussian and trigonometric functions in the following.

$$Ae^{-\frac{t^2}{2\sigma^2\xi^2}}\sin(t),\ A^2(e^{-\frac{t^2}{2\sigma^2\xi^2}})^2\sin^2(t), A^3(e^{-\frac{t^2}{2\sigma^2\xi^2}})^3\sin^3(t)... \tag{16}$$

$$Ae^{-\frac{t^2}{2\sigma^2\xi^2}}\cos(t),\ A^2(e^{-\frac{t^2}{2\sigma^2\xi^2}})^2\cos^2(t), A^3(e^{-\frac{t^2}{2\sigma^2\xi^2}})^3\cos^3(t)... \tag{17}$$

By applying the power reducing formula in the trigonometric functions, the following functions hold for the integer n to be odd,

$$\sin^n t = C_{1n}\sum_{k=0}^{(n-1)/2}\binom{n}{k}\cos((n-2k)t),\quad \cos^n t = C_{1n}\sum_{k=0}^{(n-1)/2}(-1)^{(\frac{n-1}{2}-k)}\binom{n}{k}\sin((n-2k)t) \tag{18}$$

The correlation of the right term in Eq. (18) becomes

$$\int_{-\pi}^{\pi}\sin((n-2k)t)\cdot\cos((m-2k')t)dt$$

$$=\frac{1}{2}\int_{-\pi}^{\pi}\{\sin((n-m)-2(k-k'))t+\sin((n-m)+2(k-k'))t\}dt=0 \tag{19}$$

Thus, the pair $\{(\sin^n t),(\cos^m t)\}$ becomes to be orthogonal. Similarly, the pair $\{(\sin^n t), (\cos^m t)\}$becomes orthogonal in case of n to be odd and m to be even, and in case of n to be even and m to be odd. Only the pair $\{(\sin^n t), (\cos^m t)\}$is not orthogonal in case of n to be even and m to be even. The tracking results in the 2$^{nd}$ layer are shown in Fig. 12.

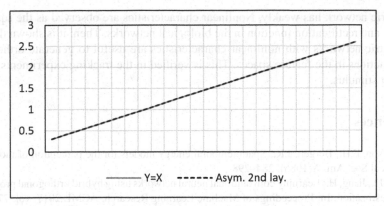

**Fig.12.** Optimized tracking results in the 2$^{nd}$ layer network

## 6.3 Tracking Characteristics in the Conventional Symmetric Network

Tracking characteristics in the conventional symmetric network are shown in Fig. 13. The 1$^{st}$ layer consists of the network in Fig. 5, while the 2$^{nd}$ layer has squaring terms of the 1$^{st}$ layer. In Fig. 13, the difference between y = x and the tracking results in the 1st and 2$^{nd}$ layers shows insufficient tracking ability in the symmetric networks.

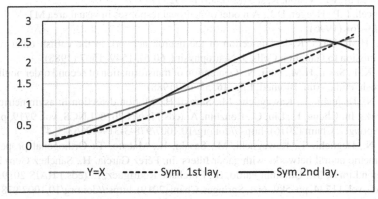

**Fig.13.** Tracking characteristics in the 1$^{st}$ and 2$^{nd}$ layers of the symmetric networks

## 7 Conclusion

It is important to make clear the structures functions how to generate the orthogonality relations in the neural networks, which will create exact features in the spaces, effectively. In this paper, the bio-inspired neural networks are proposed to generate the orthogonal functions in their networks. It is shown that the asymmetric network with Gabor filters has orthogonal properties strongly under stimulus conditions, while the conventional energy symmetric network has weakly. Nonlinear characteristics are observed as the squaring function and rectification function in the biological networks. Then, it is shown that the asymmetric networks with nonlinear characteristics are useful to generate orthogonal basis functions in the feature spaces. This is verified in the tracking experiments under the input stimulus.

# References

1. Adelson, E.H., Bergen, J.R.: Spatiotemporal energy models for the perception of motion. J. Optical Soc. Am. A(1985), 284–298
2. Pan, H., Jiang, H.: Learning convolutional neural networks using hybrid orthogonal projection and estimation. In: Proceedings of Machine Learning Research, ACML 2017, vol. 77, 1–16 (2017)
3. Huang, l., Liu, X., Lang, B., Yu, A.W., Wang, Y., Li, B.: Orthogonal weight normalization: solution to optimization over multiple dependent stiefel manifolds in deep neural networks. In: 32nd AAAI Conference on AI, AAAI-18, pp. 3271–3278 (2018)
4. Shi, W., Gong, Y., Cheng, D., Tao, X., Zheng, N.: Entropy orthogonality based deep discriminative feature learning for object recognition. Pattern Recogn. 81, 71–80 (2018)
5. Hashimoto, W.: Quadratic forms in natural images 14, 765–788 (2003)
6. Hyvarinen, A., Hoyer, P.: Emergence of phase-and shiftinvariant features by decomposition of natural images into independent feature subspaces. Neural Comput. 12, 1705–1720 (2000)
7. Olshausen, B.A., Field, D.J.: Sparse coding with an overcomplete basis set: a strategy employed by V1? Vision. Res. 37(23), 3311–3325 (1997)
8. Simonceli, E.P., Heeger, D.J.: A model of neuronal responses in visual area MT. Vision. Res. 38, 743–761 (1996)
9. Sakai, H.M., Naka, K.-I.: Dissection of the neuron network in the catfish inner retina. I. Transmission to Ganglion Cells. J. Neurophysiol. 60(5), 1549–1567 (1988)
10. Naka, K.-I., Sakai, H.M., Ishii, N.: Generation of transformation of second order nonlinearity in catfish retina. Ann. Biomed. Eng. 16, 53–64 (1988)
11. Ishii, N., Deguchi, T., Kawaguchi, M., Sasaki, H.: Motion detection in asymmetric neural networks. In: Cheng, L., Liu, Q., Ronzhin, A. (eds.) ISNN 2016. LNCS, vol. 9719, pp. 409–417. Springer, Cham (2016). https://doi.org/10.1007/978-3-319-40663-3_47
12. Ishii, N., Deguchi, T., Kawaguchi, M., Sasaki, H., Matsuo, T.: Orthogonal properties of asymmetric neural networks with gabor filters. In: Pérez García, H., Sánchez González, L., Castejón Limas, M., Quintián Pardo, H., Corchado Rodríguez, E. (eds.) HAIS 2019. LNCS (LNAI), vol. 11734, pp. 589–601. Springer, Cham (2019). https://doi.org/10.1007/978-3-030-29859-3_50

# Route Scheduling System for Multiple Self-driving Cars Using K-means and Bio-inspired Algorithms

Clênio E. Silva[1]($\boxtimes$), Tiago S. César[2], Iago P. Gomes[2], Júnior A. R. Silva[2], Denis F. Wolf[2], Raulcézar Alves[1], and Jefferson R. Souza[1]($\boxtimes$)

[1] Faculty of Computing, Federal University of Uberlandia, Uberlandia, Brazil
clenioeduardo@yahoo.com.br, jrsouza@ufu.br
[2] Institute of Mathematical and Computer Sciences, University of São Paulo, São Paulo, Brazil

**Abstract.** This paper presents the development of a hybrid approach as a solution to the multiple Traveling Salesman Problem (mTSP) applied to the route scheduling for self-drive cars. First, we use k-means to generate routes that equality distribute delivery locations among the cars. Then, these routes are set as the initial population for bio-inspired algorithms, such as Genetic Algorithm (GA) and Ant Colony System (ACS), that perform an evolutionary process in order to find a route which minimizes the overall distance while keeping the balance of individual tours of each car. The experiments were conducted with our route scheduling system in real and virtual environments. We compared our hybrid approaches using k-means in conjunction with GA and ACS against GA, ACS and Particle Swarm Optimization (PSO) initialized with random population. The results showed that, as the number of cars and target locations increase, the hybrid approaches outperform GA, ACS and PSO without any pre-processing.

**Keywords:** multiple Traveling Salesman Problem (mTSP) · Route scheduling system · Bio-inspired algorithms

## 1 Introduction

Self-driving vehicles is an essential issue for the field of Intelligent Transportation Systems (ITS) and its application on Smart Cities such as the improvement of traffic flow, automated intersection management, finding parking spots, reduction of accidents.

Although the purpose of self-driving cars is to transport people, other tasks can be automated like delivering goods. For instance, companies can provide their products autonomously to customers at several locations 24/7. To optimize

Supported by the University of São Paulo, Federal University of Uberlândia, and by the CNPq under Grant 400699/2016-8.

L. Iliadis et al. (Eds.): EANN 2022, CCIS 1600, pp. 27–39, 2022.
https://doi.org/10.1007/978-3-031-08223-8_3

the efficiency of the deliveries, car routing strategies can be applied to schedule delivery locations.

The scheduling for a single vehicle can be seen as an instance of the TSP, which is a combinatorial optimization problem. Combinatorial optimization problems are problems that attempt to find an optimal solution from a finite set of solutions. In TSP, given a set of $n$ cities and the cost of traveling (or distance) between each possible pair, the goal is to find the best possible way of visiting all cities that minimizes the final traveling cost [5].

While the TSP is restricted to a single salesman, the multiple Traveling Salesman Problem (mTSP) generalizes the problem for multiple salesmen, which is more common in real-world applications, such as school bus routing [2,11] and management of pickup and delivery [3,14]. Thus, the mTSP consists of finding routes for $m$ salesmen, who start and finish their routes at a single spot, known as a depot. Also, each city must be visited exactly once by any salesman, and the total distance of visiting all cities should be minimized.

However, when applying mTSP in the multiple self-driving car scenario the balance of distance traveled by each car must be taken into account in addition to the total distance minimization [1,15]. Depending on the distribution of delivery locations along the map, some cars may travel more than others to keep the lowest total distance, but eventually they may run out of fuel and not complete the entire route.

Our work aims at describing the development of a centralized system to schedule routes for a fleet of the cars using mTSP model. In this case, cities are delivery locations to be visited, and salesmen are cars. The system uses bio-inspired algorithms to generate solutions that minimize the total distance traveled by the fleet and also balance the routes of the vehicles. In addition, we use k-means as a pre-processing for generating the initial population with good individuals for bio-inspired algorithms. Experiments were carried out using 3D models of our self-driving cars in a virtual city and a real experiment at university campus with two cars, being one autonomous and another driven manually. The main contributions of this work are as follows: K-means as a population generator; Comparison between well-known algorithms - GA, ACS, and PSO - and our hybrid approaches k-means-GA and k-means-ACS; Proposing a centralized system to schedule routes for delivery; Conduct a study using virtual and real self-driving cars.

The remainder of the paper is organized as follows. Section 2 presents related work. The methodology describing strategies and algorithms are shown in Sect. 3. Finally, the results and conclusion are discussed in Sects. 4 and 5 respectively.

## 2    Related Work

Many studies have been conducted with the application of evolutionary algorithms to mTSP, and with that the use of this modeling has also been applied to the vehicle routing problem (VRP). Below are some works that aim to solve the mTSP and works that apply evolutionary algorithms to the VRP.

In [13], the development of a GA and ACO applied to the Shortest Path (SP) problem is presented. The problem was modeled as mTSP, and the authors use Two Phase Hybrid AI-heuristics as method. In the first, k-means is used to group cities according to their adjacency. In the second, the clustered cities are presented as inputs for GA and ACO to optimize the routes for each cluster. Another similar work is presented in [15], the work introduces k-means for clustering cities. The authors propose a workload balance method, which minimizes and balances the distances of salesmen.

With the idea of division to conquer, [16] considered mTSP as a multi-agent system. The authors separate cities into $N$ groups using k-means. Thus mTSP is decomposed into a set of $N$ TSP, with each group having the maximum number of cities based on the constraint, which is the division of the number of cities by the number of salesmen. For each group, a GA is performed with the 2-opt local search operator to search for an optimal route.

With the emergence of the Covid-19 pandemic, mTSP approaches can also be used to support the distribution of medical supplies, such as respirators and test kits. In [10] a GA combined with the 2-Opt algorithm was implemented to solve the problem of distribution of pharmaceutical products. The mTSP approach was used to optimize the distribution points of pharmaceutical products for each vehicle.

Another work that approaches the optimization of routes is presented in [12], where the problem of optimization of school bus routes is treated with the application of a genetic algorithm. In this problem, it was necessary to optimize the path of multiple buses by modeling a genetic algorithm to choose the shortest path. The experimental results showed that the genetic algorithm can generate good solutions for school bus routing problems.

The proposed approaches addressed in this papers aim at applying k-means as a pre-processing for generating the initial population for bio-inspired algorithms, such as GA and ACS. These algorithms optimize solutions considering the trade-off between reducing the total distance and balancing individual tours. Our approach differs from the related works, as they apply a clustering method and run for each cluster a bio-inspired algorithm, decomposing mTSP into k TSP. Unlike our work that applies the clustering technique for generating initial solutions and combines the fitness function to ensure the balance of routes to mTSP.

## 3   Methodology

The route optimization task for vehicles can be seen as an instance of the mTSP, where each car is a salesman and delivery locations are cities. Our approach uses bio-inspired algorithms to o obtain approximation solutions in a reasonable time and minimize the total distance of the fleet and balancing the distances traveled by each car.

## 3.1    Bio-inspired Algorithms

Bio-inspired algorithms have a generic architecture. To solve a problem using this architecture, some of its components must be designed considering the constraints of the problem. As components of the architecture, we have the structure of the individual and evaluation function in algorithms like GA, PSO and ACS. Other components are more specific, such: crossover and mutation for GA, transposition and particle velocity for PSO, and state transition rules for ACS. This section describes how these components were designed for the algorithms and how k-means was applied to develop hybrid approaches with GA and ACS.

**Individual Structure.** mTSP is a TSP extension for a multi-agent model, where multiple salesmen can be used to visit $n$ cities on a map. Thus each city should be visited only once by one of the salesmen. Each city on the map has its coordinates. The coordinates are used to estimate the distance between a pair of cities. In this way, an individual can be modeled as depicted by Fig 1.

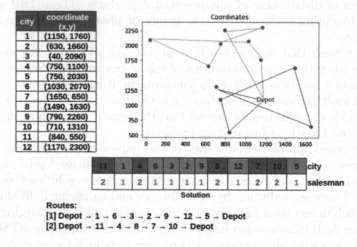

**Fig. 1.** Example of the individual. The individual is a solution to the problem. This scenario shows an instance in which two salesmen must visit twelve cities and return to the depot.

The length of the individual is equal to the number of cities, as all of them must be visited only once. Each column assigns a salesman to a city. The sort of the cities is also essential as it shows the sequence in which the salesmen will perform their visits, i.e., their routes.

**Road Map and Complete Graph.** Different from the example of Fig. 1, where paths between locations are represented by straight lines on a plan, route scheduling for cars on road maps requires the computation of feasible paths.

Therefore, before scheduling the routes, our approach creates a path matrix $P$ using A* algorithm for all pairs of locations, including the depot location, as illustrated by Fig. 2.

Thus, the dimension of $P$ is $|L|+1 X |L|+1$ where $L$ is the list of locations to be visited. To optimize the computation, elements of the main diagonal in $P$ are set as being empty, which correspond to paths where the source and destination are the same locations. Also, when the element $P_{ij}$ is computed, which corresponds to the path from $i$ to $j$, the inverse path is automatically stored at $P_{ji}$. This matrix represents a complete graph connecting all desired locations with real paths, which are used later by the scheduling process.

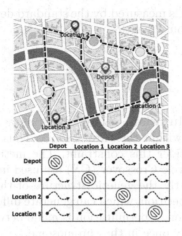

**Fig. 2.** Path Matrix stores paths computed by A* based on road maps. Paths are calculated for all pairs of locations to be visited, including the depot.

**Objectives.** The goal of mTSP is to minimize the total distance traveled by all salesmen. However, it may cause an imbalance in the distance traveled by them. This may occur when a salesman travels far away to visit a city. Since mTSP aims to reduce the total distance, this salesman tends to cover all the cities around, as sending another salesman there, for visiting just a few cities, can increase the total distance. As a result, some salesmen might travel much more than others.

For some real domains, this behavior is not suitable. For example, in a delivery company, there might be some overloaded vehicles making many deliveries and driving long distances, while others remain nearby the company. Therefore, some customers have to wait more time than others to receive their deliveries, which is a problem for some services like food delivery. Hence, we proposed the use of two objectives. The first is responsible for minimizing total distance traveled by the set of salesmen, while the second aims to reduce the difference of distance traveled individually.

Given the path matrix $P$, the route distance traveled by a salesman $i$ is calculated by the sum of path lengths within its route $R_i$:

$$R_i = \sum_{j=1}^{n} |P_{j,j+1}|, \forall j \in Cities_i \tag{1}$$

The total distance traveled by all salesmen in a given solution is:

$$\Delta = \sum_{i=1}^{m} R_i \tag{2}$$

The balance of the routes is measured by the standard deviation of route lengths, where $\bar{R}$ is the average route length.

$$\sigma = \sqrt{\frac{\sum_{i=1}^{m}(R_i - \bar{R})^2}{m-1}} \tag{3}$$

**GA - Crossover and Mutation.** mTSP is a permutation problem as the cities should not be repeated within the chromosome. Thus, methods for crossover and mutation must consider this constraint. The methods Partially Matched Crossover (PMX) and Cycle Crossover (CX) are used in such cases.

While CX keeps exactly the genetic structure of the parents, PMX makes some changes to avoid repetition, which can generate different genetic structures.

Regarding the mutation, a permutation is made between two random genes. Each city will appear only once in the chromosome.

The our implementation of GA algorithm was inspired by the traditional GA [8]. A population is randomly generated with $T_p$ individuals and subjected to the evaluation process. Each individual represents a route scheduling for $m$ salesmen traveling through $n$ cities without repetition.

The fitness function $F$ used in this GA combines both objectives by summing the total distance $\Delta$ and the standard deviation $\sigma$, as shown in the following formula:

$$F = \Delta + \sigma \tag{4}$$

For the next step, $P_{rec}$ individuals must be selected from the current population. For this work, PMX was used for crossover and Stochastic Tournament for selection. Other crossover methods such as CX and other selection methods such as Roulette Wheel and Tournament were analyzed but preliminary experiments showed that PMX with Stochastic Tournament yield better results as they are more random and escape easily from local optima.

**PSO - Velocity and Position.** In discrete PSO velocity is a list of swaps. For mTSP swaps should be made for the routes and the salesmen, and the routes should not be repeated. The list of swaps is obtained by the subtraction of the positions, and the movement is performed with addition. Assuming $P$ as a position, and $V$ as the velocity, then $P'$ is a new position where $P' = P + V$, where all swaps belonging to $V$ must be applied. In Fig. 3 the velocity $V$ is obtained subtracting one position from the other, $V = A - B$. Through this difference, the list of swaps is result of the equation $A = B + V$.

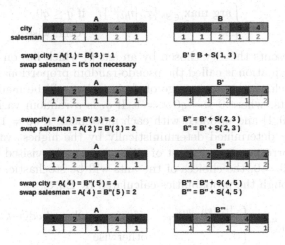

**Fig. 3.** Example of swaps in the position of an individual used in PSO. The blocks in green represent the routes for salesman 1 and blocks in are routes of salesman 2. End of process $V = [(1,3),(2,3),(4,5)]$.

The our implementation of PSO algorithm was inspired by the Discrete Particle Swarm Optimization [4]. First, a population with a number of particles (individuals) is generated with random positions. The position of each particle is represented by the structure of an individual shown in Fig. 1 and the velocity is initially an empty list of swaps. The evaluation is performed by the fitness function presented in Eq. 4. After the evaluation, an update is done on the best local particle $p_{Best}$ and the best global particle $g_{Best}$. The particles $p_{Best}$ and $g_{Best}$ influence the calculation of the velocity of each particle, being updated directly. The update for particle velocity is calculated by $w$ (inertia weight), $c1$ and $c2$ (accelerator constants), and $r1$ and $r2$ (matrices of random variables between 0 and 1). Equations 5 and 6 present the calculation to update the velocity and position of the particles.

$$v_i(t + 1) = v_i(t) \cdot w + c1 \cdot r1 \cdot (p_{Best} - x_i(t)) + c2 \cdot r2 \cdot (g_{Best} - x_i(t)) \quad (5)$$

$$x_i(t + 1) = x_i(t) + v_i(t + 1) \quad (6)$$

**ACS - Solution Building.** In the phase of constructing routes, the ACS algorithm uses a deterministic State Transition Rule (STR) while the AS (Ant System) uses an stochastic STR. STR is a rule that determines the probability that a vertex will be chosen by an ant, $i$ represents the vertex in which the ant $k$ is found and $j$ one of the possible vertices to which it can move. The ant $k$ should only visit the vertices not yet visited in the current phase of the construction. Each ant has in memory the vertices already visited. The ACS STR is presented in Eq. 7.

$$
j = \begin{cases} \arg \max_{\iota \in S_i^k} \{\tau_{i\iota}[\eta_{i\iota}]^{\beta}\}, & \text{if } q \leq q0 \\ J, & \text{otherwise} \end{cases} \tag{7}
$$

In Eq. 7 $j$ represents the city chosen by an ant $k$, which lies on the vertex $i$ as it moves. This equation is called the pseudo-random proportional rule, since the parameter $q0$ defines the percentage of choices that will be made deterministically by the ants, where $0 <= q0 <= 1$. If $q$, is a random variable uniformly distributed in $[0, 1]$ and updated with each movement, if $q0 = 1$, the choices of the ants will be determined deterministically by the highest value of $\tau_{i\iota}[\eta_{i\iota}]^{\beta}$, where $\iota \in S_i^k$ corresponds to the set of cities that can be visited by ant $k$ in the movement. If $q0 = 0$, the choices of the ants will be stochastic, with $J$ being a city chosen through the probabilities calculated by Eq. 8.

$$
p_{ij}^k = \begin{cases} \frac{[\tau_{ij}(t)]^{\alpha}[\eta_{ij}]^{\beta}}{\sum[\tau_{ij}(t)]^{\alpha}[\eta_{ij}]^{\beta}} & \text{if } j \text{ is an allowed edge } k \\ 0 & \text{otherwise} \end{cases} \tag{8}
$$

In Eq. 8 $i$ represents the vertex in which the ant $k$ is found, $j$ one of the possible vertices for displacement $\eta_{ij}$ corresponds to the visibility of the edge, $\alpha$ and $\beta$ are parameters that define the weight of the pheromone trail and the visibility, respectively.

The our algorithm was inspired by the Ant Colony System [6]. Initially, a population with $T_p$ ants (individuals) is generated, and the pheromone trail table is initialized. The Eq. 7 is applied to each ant $k$. In each vertex visited by the ant, the evaporation is carried out for the trail of pheromone in the edge of that vertex. After the construction of the ant route $k$, the salesmen are randomly added to the route forming the structure shown in Fig 1. The fitness function presented in Eq. 4 performs the evaluation of the route of the ant $k$. After the construction of the routes for all the ants, the algorithm performs a global update for pheromone trails.

## 3.2   Hybrid Algorithms k-means-GA and k-means-ACS

In addition to GA, PSO and ACS algorithms, hybrid approaches using k-means with GA and ACS were implemented. The k-means is one of the most popular clustering algorithms, [9]. The algorithm has the task of partitioning a dataset into $k$ clusters according to the similarity of the data. In this work, k-means generates the initial population for a GA and the neighbor list in the construction of the ACS solution. Thus, two algorithms were developed, k-means-GA and k-means-ACS.

For generating the initial population, k-means is executed based on the map coordinates. First, k-means is executed once, where the number of clusters $k$ is equal to the number of salesmen. After that, the construction of the individuals in the $k$ clusters begins. For a population with $Tp$ individuals, in each generation, the sequence of the coordinates are shuffled in the clusters. Thus, it is not necessary to run k-means $Tp$ times for each generated individual. Shuffling the coordinate sequence within each cluster allows the population diversity while maintaining the quality obtained by k-means.

For k-means-GA, the first step is the generation of a population with $T_p$ individuals based in the result of the k-means, and subjected to step of evaluation of GA algorithm. Likewise, in k-means-ACS, for each ant $k$ is constructed a route based on the k-means result, which builds the list of neighbors that are passed to the calculation of the STR, presented in Eq. 7. The ACS is a constructive algorithm, where for each individual of the population, a stepwise route is constructed according to the neighbors list and STR (Eq. 7). Thus, the combination of k-means with ACS is done in the construction process of individuals and not only for the initial population as it is done in GA.

In previous experiments it was proved that GA and ACS surpass discrete PSO, as a way to validate pre-processing with k-means we chose GA and ACS for a meaningful comparison with their versions without pre-processing.

### 3.3    Route Scheduling System

The route scheduling system was developed in *Java*, along with the algorithms presented. The process of route scheduling works as follows (Fig. 4).

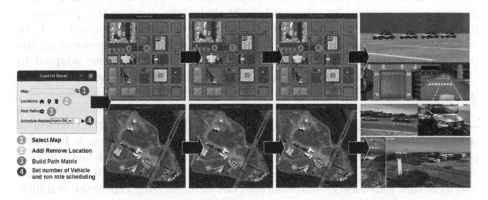

**Fig. 4.** Route Scheduling. This process shows the flow of our route scheduling system: 1) Select a road map; 2) Set depot and desired locations on the map; 3) Build complete graph and path matrix; 4) Schedule routes for each vehicle using a system algorithm; 5) Send routes to cars.

To schedule the routes using our k-means-GA and k-means-ACS, or other algorithms such as GA, PSO, and ACS, the user must select one of them on the combobox, fill the number of salesmen (cars) to be used, and click on run. The user can follow the progress from the execution panel as the system plots the best solution found after each iteration. Different colors are used to represent the route of each salesman. A message appears to the user when the route scheduling is done.

## 4   Experimental Results

The experiments were conducted in the route scheduling system with a virtual city and a real road on university campus using two cars, one completely autonomous and another manually driven. The autonomous car used in the experiment was CaRINA-2 [7].

For the experiments in simulation, 13 scenarios were defined with different amounts of cars and delivery locations. Each scenario was generated by selecting visit locations in a virtual map of the route scheduling system, where each instance is computed through the path matrix. As real experiments are more difficult to deploy, we set only one scenario with 2 cars and 9 locations.

Several parameter combinations were tested, but the algorithms performed better with the following configurations: iteration and population size were defined equally for the five algorithms, with population size = 160 and iterations = 200. For k-means-GA and GA, crossover rate = 60%, mutation rate = 30% and tour = 3. Both k-means-GA and GA were developed using PMX and Stochastic Tournaments. For the PSO, inertia weight = 0.5, cognitive and social parameters = 2.0. In k-means-ACS the parameters also follow the same parameters defined in ACS, influence of pheromone = 1, heuristic information = 2, pheromone evaporation rate = 0.1, STR choice parameter = 0.9, pheromone initiation rate = $10^{-4}$ and amount of pheromone excreted by an ant = 1. In order to validate the improvement of the algorithms with pre-processing, the parameters adopted for hybrid approaches are the same as those adopted in their versions without pre-processing. We run 50 trials for each algorithm on the maps of both scenarios. Results for simulation are presented in Table 1.

The results presented in the Table 1 show that with the increase of cars and locations, the application of k-means as pre-processing for the creation of individuals obtained a better minimization of the fitness function 4. It is also possible to observe that the standard deviation of the 50 executions had a smaller variation comparing GA and k-means-GA. Thus, when applied to several cars and locations, k-means-GA outperformed GA in minimizing fitness and stability. Another important factor is the reduction of the average execution time, where k-means-GA had a faster execution time for all scenarios and k-means-ACS was dominated only in the first scenario. The traditional ACS algorithm also presents competitive results with hybrid approaches.

To validate and demonstrate an application of the route scheduling system, we conducted an experiment on a real road.

The video for this experiment is available online at: https://youtu.be/mmuW17mbJXQ.

**Table 1.** Comparison between algorithms in 50 runs.

| Scenario | Algorithm | Best | Worst | Mean | Deviation | Time (s) |
|---|---|---|---|---|---|---|
| 2 cars 10 locations | GA | **2925,83** | 3111,59 | 2929,55 | 26,27 | 20,37 |
| | PSO | **2925,83** | 3592,61 | 3192,66 | 162,16 | 20,63 |
| | ACS | **2925,83** | **2925,83** | **2925,83** | **0,00** | 21,35 |
| | k-means-GA | **2925,83** | 3111,59 | 3044,72 | 90,07 | **20,32** |
| | k-means-ACS | **2925,83** | 3111,59 | 3041,00 | 91,08 | 21,47 |
| 3 cars 15 locations | GA | **3953,32** | 4196,01 | 3963,95 | 36,64 | 20,49 |
| | PSO | 3988,48 | 5707,88 | 4785,62 | 304,20 | 21,11 |
| | ACS | **3953,32** | **4009,45** | **3961,76** | **9,96** | 22,24 |
| | k-means-GA | 3973,14 | 4698,04 | 4275,84 | 235,61 | **20,44** |
| | k-means-ACS | 3973,14 | 4617,12 | 4316,25 | 204,85 | 22,43 |
| 4 cars 20 locations | GA | **6026,60** | 6688,24 | **6229,37** | 175,77 | 20,69 |
| | PSO | 7294,01 | 8883,62 | 8355,64 | 374,71 | 21,26 |
| | ACS | 6060,96 | **6416,10** | 6279,99 | **69,51** | 24,02 |
| | k-means-GA | 6173,94 | 7553,31 | 6716,81 | 423,21 | **20,58** |
| | k-means-ACS | 6183,23 | 7966,73 | 6657,75 | 441,65 | 23,77 |
| 5 cars 25 locations | GA | **7429,69** | 9169,72 | 8202,52 | 369,86 | 20,83 |
| | PSO | 11015,94 | 12972,52 | 11930,34 | 458,84 | 22,02 |
| | ACS | 7686,07 | **8329,09** | **8080,90** | **150,62** | 25,76 |
| | k-means-GA | 8080,11 | 10075,86 | 8904,84 | 432,27 | **20,74** |
| | k-means-ACS | 7868,69 | 10100,67 | 8996,26 | 468,98 | 25,85 |
| 6 cars 30 locations | GA | **9240,22** | 11996,49 | 10331,17 | 698,06 | 21,00 |
| | PSO | 13405,41 | 16910,23 | 15892,88 | 608,51 | 22,67 |
| | ACS | 9429,44 | **10478,92** | **9998,96** | **197,50** | 27,60 |
| | k-means-GA | 999,74 | 12075,83 | 10785,83 | 477,90 | **20,83** |
| | k-means-ACS | 9781,14 | 12165,11 | 10897,04 | 574,64 | 27,29 |
| 7 cars 35 locations | GA | 11055,28 | 14809,37 | 12495,03 | 786,49 | 21,17 |
| | PSO | 17796,26 | 21131,67 | 19514,50 | 744,73 | 23,28 |
| | ACS | **10963,57** | **11894,61** | **11517,36** | **206,97** | 28,88 |
| | k-means-GA | 11192,60 | 13451,09 | 12141,79 | 564,55 | **21,00** |
| | k-means-ACS | 11230,23 | 13840,17 | 12166,42 | 595,73 | 28,72 |
| 8 cars 40 locations | GA | **12785,44** | 18154,30 | 15367,24 | 1072,89 | 21,26 |
| | PSO | 21570,04 | 25383,06 | 23807,85 | 896,76 | 23,87 |
| | ACS | 13306,51 | **14443,05** | **13875,16** | **224,71** | 30,19 |
| | k-means-GA | 12986,58 | 15600,32 | 14352,58 | 579,36 | **21,17** |
| | k-means-ACS | 12947,84 | 16273,53 | 14511,97 | 732,04 | 29,96 |
| 9 cars 45 locations | GA | 15813,65 | 20286,78 | 17448,53 | 1049,42 | 21,57 |
| | PSO | 25262,51 | 29072,77 | 27936,12 | 767,99 | 24,55 |
| | ACS | 14889,47 | **16087,27** | **15637,93** | **287,32** | 31,84 |
| | k-means-GA | 14988,96 | 17603,22 | 16187,69 | 562,10 | **21,23** |
| | k-means-ACS | **14254,77** | 17894,15 | 16065,20 | 738,21 | 31,67 |
| 10 cars 50 locations | GA | 17936,78 | 25424,75 | 20742,51 | 1503,45 | 21,73 |
| | PSO | 29927,16 | 33807,63 | 32231,72 | 857,00 | 25,23 |
| | ACS | 16604,97 | **17720,00** | **17253,56** | **275,44** | 33,21 |
| | k-means-GA | **16152,93** | 20685,47 | 18624,81 | 1121,24 | **21,48** |
| | k-means-ACS | 16452,19 | 21524,24 | 19126,22 | 1226,43 | 32,09 |
| 11 cars 55 locations | GA | 20290,11 | 28252,24 | 23203,83 | 1474,05 | 21,81 |
| | PSO | 34233,02 | 38070,09 | 36503,01 | 894,03 | 23,88 |
| | ACS | 18873,22 | **20466,42** | 20006,13 | **302,22** | 35,39 |
| | k-means-GA | 18276,86 | 21534,84 | **19756,62** | 769,92 | **21,43** |
| | k-means-ACS | **17933,28** | 21927,44 | 19793,24 | 862,78 | 34,31 |
| 12 cars 60 locations | GA | 22838,16 | 31307,42 | 26986,15 | 2019,37 | 21,98 |
| | PSO | 39593,40 | 43236,54 | 41626,36 | 900,06 | 25,16 |
| | ACS | 21583,88 | **22998,77** | 22220,57 | **285,68** | 37,90 |
| | k-means-GA | **20472,43** | 24199,00 | **21945,19** | 811,96 | **21,57** |
| | k-means-ACS | 20917,43 | 24134,55 | 22333,77 | 837,99 | 36,54 |
| 13 cars 80 locations | GA | 31761,18 | 42083,95 | 36765,01 | 2181,92 | 22,57 |
| | PSO | 54283,33 | 59134,66 | 56922,85 | 1050,89 | 26,88 |
| | ACS | 24937,75 | **27115,26** | 26391,50 | **408,79** | 51,84 |
| | k-means-GA | 23877,73 | 27618,35 | 25829,58 | 879,96 | **22,10** |
| | k-means-ACS | **23576,45** | 28803,86 | **25827,42** | 1087,65 | 50,54 |
| 14 cars 100 locations | GA | 41294,79 | 54287,20 | 45962,00 | 2869,84 | 23,09 |
| | PSO | 65912,16 | 73511,49 | 69968,29 | 1672,09 | 27,01 |
| | ACS | 27879,07 | **30011,62** | 29459,72 | **428,44** | 80,21 |
| | k-means-GA | **26805,59** | 30409,54 | 28484,69 | 871,44 | **22,50** |
| | k-means-ACS | 26962,16 | 30272,42 | **28403,41** | 838,27 | 73,43 |

## 5    Conclusions

This work presents the problem of scheduling routes for multiples cars and locations. This problem can be seen as an instance of the mTSP, in which cars are salesmen and cities are locations to be visited. As mTSP is considered NP-hard, approximation and heuristic methods are more suitable to be used. This paper discusses the use of the k-means as pre-processing for the generation good individuals for the initial population assign to bio-inspired algorithms, in this case GA and ACS.

Experiments were performed in our centralized route scheduling system for self-driving cars. We compared our approaches to traditional implementations of GA, PSO, and ACS. We noticed that for many vehicles and locations, the application of the k-means as pre-processing can provide better results, leading to a faster minimization of the proposed fitness function for GA and ACS.

For future work, we are interested in developing a centralized system for online route rescheduling, focusing on autonomous vehicles.

**Acknowledgements.** This work was supported by the University of São Paulo, Federal University of Uberlândia, and by the CNPq under Grant 400699/2016-8.

## References

1. Alves, R.M.F., Lopes, C.R.: Using genetic algorithms to minimize the distance and balance the routes for the multiple traveling salesman problem. In: Congress on Evolutionary Computation (CEC). IEEE (2015)
2. Angel, R.D., Caudle, W.L., Noonan, R., Whinston, A.: Computer-assisted school bus scheduling. Manag. Sci. **18**(6), 279–288 (1972)
3. Christofides, N., Eilon, S.: An algorithm for the vehicle-dispatching problem. J. Oper. Res. Soc. **20**(3), 309–318 (1969)
4. Clerc, M.: Discrete particle swarm optimization, illustrated by the traveling salesman problem. In: New Optimization Techniques in Engineering. Studies in Fuzziness and Soft Computing, vol. 141. Springer, Heidelberg (2004). https://doi.org/10.1007/978-3-540-39930-8_8
5. Davendra, D.: Traveling Salesman Problem. Theory and Applications (2010). https://doi.org/10.5772/547
6. Dorigo, M., Gambardella, L.M.: Ant colony system: a cooperative learning approach to the traveling salesman problem. IEEE Trans. Evol. Comput. **1**, 53–66 (1997)
7. Fernandes, L.C., et al.: Carina intelligent robotic car: architectural design and applications. J. Syst. Archit. - Embedded Syst. Des. **60**, 372–392 (2014)
8. Goldberg, D.E.: Genetic Algorithms in Search, Optimization, and Machine Learning. Addison-Wesley, Boston (1989)
9. Jain, A.K.: Data clustering: 50 years beyond k-means. Pattern Recogn. Lett. **31**(8), 651–666 (2010). https://doi.org/10.1016/j.patrec.2009.09.011
10. Kocyigit, E., Sahingoz, O.K., Diri, B.: An evolutionary approach to multiple traveling salesman problem for efficient distribution of pharmaceutical products. In: 2020 International Conference on Electrical Engineering (ICEE), pp. 1–7. IEEE (2020)

11. Orloff, C.S.: Routing a fleet of m vehicles to/from a central facility. Networks **4**(2), 147–162 (1974)
12. Ozmen, M., Sahin, H.: Real-time optimization of school bus routing problem in smart cities using genetic algorithm. In: 2021 6th International Conference on Inventive Computation Technologies (ICICT), pp. 1152–1158. IEEE (2021)
13. Sathya, N., Muthukumaravel, A.: Two phase hybrid AI-heuristics for multiple travelling salesman problem. Int. J. Appl. Eng. Res. **12**, 12659–12664 (2017)
14. Savelsbergh, M.W.P., Sol, M.: The general pickup and delivery problem. Transp. Sci. **29**, 17–29 (1995)
15. Xu, X., Yuan, H., Liptrott, M., Trovati, M.: Two phase heuristic algorithm for the multiple-travelling salesman problem. Soft Comput. **22**, 6567–6581 (2018)
16. Yang, C., Szeto, K.Y.: Solving the traveling salesman problem with a multi-agent system. In: Congress on Evolutionary Computation (CEC). IEEE (2019)

# SNNs Model Analyzing and Visualizing Experimentation Using RAVSim

Sanaullah[1]([✉]), Shamini Koravuna[2], Ulrich Rückert[2], and Thorsten Jungeblut[1]

[1] Bielefeld University of Applied Science, Bielefeld, Germany
{sanaullah,thorsten.jungeblut}@fh-bielefeld.de
[2] Bielefeld University, Bielefeld, Germany

**Abstract.** Spiking Neural Networks (SNNs) reduce the computational complexity compared to traditional artificial neural networks (ANN) by introducing the spike coding method and the nonlinear activated neuron model and transmitting only the binary spike events. However, these complex model simulations and behavioral analysis are a standard approach of parametric values verification prior to their physical implementation on the hardware. Recently some popular tools have been presented, but we believe that none of the tools allow users to interact with the model simulation in run-time. The run-time interaction with the simulation creates a full understanding of these complex SNNs model mechanisms which is a quite challenging process, especially for early-stage researchers and students. In this paper, we present the first version of our novel spiking neural network user-friendly software tool named RAVSim (Real-time Analysis and Visualization Simulator), which provides a runtime environment to analyze and simulate the SNNs model. It is an interactive and intuitive tool designed to help in knowing considerable parameters involved in the working of the neurons, their dependency on each other, determining the essential parametric values, and the communication between the neurons for replicating the way the human brain works. Moreover, the proposed SNNs model analysis and simulation algorithm used in RAVSim takes significantly less time in order to estimate and visualize the behavior of the parametric values during a runtime environment.

**Keywords:** Spiking Neural Network · WTA networks · Neural model · Runtime simulator · Machine learning

## 1 Introduction

The human brain is a fascinating mystery. It controls our body which is a very complicated non-linear dynamic system and the brain can control it at an extremely fast speed. Neuromorphic intelligence is showing promising results

This research was supported by the research training group "Dataninja" (Trustworthy AI for Seamless Problem Solving: Next Generation Intelligence Joins Robust Data Analysis) funded by the German federal state of North Rhine-Westphalia.

L. Iliadis et al. (Eds.): EANN 2022, CCIS 1600, pp. 40–51, 2022.
https://doi.org/10.1007/978-3-031-08223-8_4

for achieving this brain-like functionality and efficiency by building artificial neural systems that implement "neurons" and "synapses" to transfer electrical signals using analog circuitry. This enables them to modulate the amount of electricity flowing between those nodes to mimic the varying degrees of strength that naturally occurring brain signals have. The growth of the experimental findings and evidence that spike timing is essential to explain neural computations has motivated the use of Spiking Neural Networks (SNNs). SNNs can efficiently process data in the form of spikes [1–3]. Numerous SNN-based systems have demonstrated superior energy efficiency [4–7]. However, a significant amount of dedicated simulators have been developed to analyze and visualize the SNNs behavior. Such simulators are providing the users to acquire precise simulations in a relatively short period of time. Nevertheless, there are many challenges and computational issues related to SNN. In some cases, it requires the use of accurate biological representations of the neurons. Although some of the existing state-of-the-art SNN simulators Brian2 [8] and NEST [9] have been primarily built for exploring brain functionalities and neuronal dynamics, they are not user-friendly. Adding new functionalities to some simulators requires specifying them in a low-level programming language for example C++ and integrating them with the simulator code [9]. Also, some of the simulators need domain-specific languages, for instance, NESTML for NEST simulator, NMODL for NEURON [10]. With all these constraints, for early-stage researchers and students, a lot of time is consumed for understanding the behavior of SNNs and exploiting the significant features of SNNs for adapting them for run-time scenarios. There is a requirement of an interactive simulator with low or no-code as the existing simulators require a lot of time and huge lines of code for designing the neural network architectures, analyzing, and visualizing their behavior. On the other hand, the run-time environment-based simulator also helps to decrease the learning period of the early-stage researchers, students, and those who don't have or limited programming backgrounds for understanding the mechanism of the SNN models.

To perform analysis, in order to gain accurate parametric values and observe the complete behavior of an SNN model, a different set of input conditions, i.e., what values are required, which component values are dependent on each other, must be defined in each event. Even the group of neurons is moderate-sized, the combinations of these component inputs into the model may require very precious values to be defined and simulated. Alternately, a run-time capability provides a more appropriate way to understand the model and allows users to make direct changes at any instant of time into a simulation to observe the model behavior. This kind of simulator not only helps the SNN community to analyze and visualize the model easily by increasing or decreasing the input at any level and any instant of time but also gives the user to fully understand the complex structural model. Additionally, a fast, run-time visualization and user-friendly simulator not only speeds up existing simulations. It accelerates the process of designing, prototyping, parameter tuning, and so on. Also, research into other algorithms, including training, advancing the field as a whole. To this effect and with this motivation behind and the existing challenges in understanding and leveraging the promising features of SNNs, we are proposing a novel run-time simulator "RAVSim", a state of the art SNN simulator, implemented using Lab-VIEW (Laboratory Virtual Instrument Engineering Workbench) [11] and also, RAVSim v1.0 was successfully accepted and published on LabVIEW's official website [12] after being reviewed by their developer team. It is an interactive simulation environment tool that allows the user to interact with the model, observe its behavior, and make direct changes in the parameters of input models at run-time. This is the first version of our simulator and it is mainly designed for early-stage researchers and students who are interested in this area of research. RAVSim provides a substitute for the time-consuming code-based experiments for analyzing and designing models with correct values and helps users to fully understand the SNN mechanism. It is capable of spike detection by using the continuous noisy input, spike detection by using input current, and generating a winner takes all network (WTA), which establishes communication between the neurons. Our proposed approach allows the SNN architecture to be defined completely in software, which negates the need to re-synthesize the hardware implementation when any parameter in the SNN architecture is changed. Also, our design is user-friendly and provides a run-time user interaction, which makes it is suitable for visualizing and analyzing the model in a more precious way where users can understand the complex model in a short period of time.

## 2  Related Work

A significant amount of effort has been devoted to developing simulators of SNNs. Some of the popular software including, the Brian simulator [8] and the NEST simulator [9] among others [13–17]. Brian simulator is an open-source python library that enables the users to simply and efficiently simulate SNN models. These SNN models can characterize novel dynamical equations, their experimental protocols, and their interactions with the environment. NEST simulator is ideal for SNNs of any size, for example, models of information processing, network activity dynamics, learning, and plasticity. Some recent approaches like SPIKE [18], Brian2GeNN [19], CARLsim [20], GeNN [21], Kasap et al. [22], Fujita et al. [23] are designed and accelerated using GPUs. In comparison to all these simulators, SPIKE and GeNN are acknowledged to be the fastest with comparative pros and cons. SPIKE simulator is mainly designed for boosting up the simulation speed because of which it loses some generality and compromises on the efficiency of the memory. heavily optimized for simulation speed, and in doing so, sacrifices some generality and memory efficiency. On the contrary, GeNN exhibits a flexible programming interface to the users enabling them to design custom models, at the expense of some speed. Some of the simulators like SpykeTorch [24] and BindsNet [25] are leveraging the popularity of Deep Learning frameworks like PyTorch in simulating SNNs. But practically these kinds of approaches are not completely supporting the general SNN simulation, which is restricting their applicability.

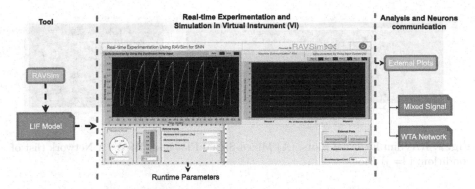

**Fig. 1.** Analyses and Simulation flow of RAVSim VI. [Left Plot]: Spikes Generated by using continuous Noisy Input, [Right Plot]: Neurons Communication Plot and Plot which shows the detection of spikes using the Input Current, [Bottom left]: External Neural Model Parameters, and [Bottom Right]: Selection of the External Plots and the Simulation Speed control option.

## 3   RAVSim Tool

Real-time Analyzing and Visualization Simulator or RAVSim is an interactive virtual experiment environment for the simulation and analysis of spike neural network models. RAVSim tool used Leaky Integration and Fire model by using the continuous noisy input [26], Spike detection by using input current [27], and generating a winner takes all network (WTA) [28], which establishes communication between the neurons. It is solely designed with the aim of helping early-stage researchers and students to fully understand the mechanism of SNNs where users can interact with the simulator in run-time by providing the essential parameters. There are a lot of parameters involved in the designing of SNNs and it is extremely important to understand the significance of these parameters for designing optimal neural networks. The run-time simulation environment is important in that the input-output value is critical for extracting the correct logic behavior of an SNN model. Thus, it is necessary to visualize the value of this parameter before applying it directly to the hardware. One should be aware of which parameters are essential, how the parameters interact and are dependent on each other, the optimal values of these parameters for achieving accurate and efficient SNNs to be as realistic as biological neurons.

The run-time environment is also very important in the following sense: Let us assume that a user has concluded an analysis with some random parametric value settings (such as threshold value, reset potential, membrane capacitance, and so on). If the user conducts another analysis with different parametric value settings and the computation time in the current analysis exceeds abnormally compared to the previous analysis, the user can deduce that he/she might have selected some invalid parametric value settings for the current analysis. Below we provide some results to support the above thesis. But, we must first recall the definition of the LIF model: In order to perform correct analysis, it is therefore

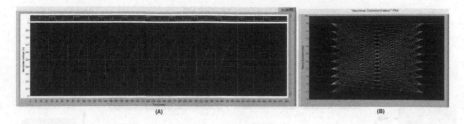

**Fig. 2.** RAVSim External Plots: (A) Mixed-Signal Plot and (B) WTA Network (list of condition: i != j) Plot.

required to initialize all of the model parameters to a stable value. If the values are not initialized or entered wrong, the run-time simulator visualization feature helps the user, and that is the reason we set some default parametric values at the start of the simulation and also using menu bad user can see the default values at any time during the simulation. The default parameter VI helps the user to specify a correct value during which the SNN model output is expected to become stable.

RAVSim is fastest simulator (in terms of execution time, parametric values setup time) and easy to use. As shown in Fig. 1, the basic flow of the RAVSim run-time virtual simulation environment, our design is also user-friendly and a run-time user interaction environment, which makes it is suitable for visualizing and analyzing the model in a more precious way where users are able to understand the complex model in a short period of time and also able to estimate a stable parametric value faster as compared to other simulators (witness our evolution and implementations all the way to outperform the state of art is discussed in section Discussion and Results). The left plot(shown in Fig. 1), shows the spikes generated with the values which the user has inserted. And they can change the values of the parameters like the threshold, reset potential, etc. during the run-time. In the right plot, the users can see how the neurons are communicating with each other and how many times one neuron is interacting with the other, and also visualize the plot that shows the detection of spikes using the input current. In the bottom right, we have provided the selection of the external plots, mixed-signal plots, and WTA network for the ease of the user and unlike any biologically computational experiment [29,30], users can increase or decrease the speed of the simulation with the help of the speed control function displayed on the right-bottom side in Fig. 1. With the mixed-signal plot, one can visualize the spike detection using input currents and the spike detection using continuous signals values which are depicted in Fig. 2(A). And for navigating to the WTA mechanism the user can visualize the neuron communication which is shown in Fig. 2(B). The overall RAVSim demonstration using default parametric values are shown in [31] (section User Manual).

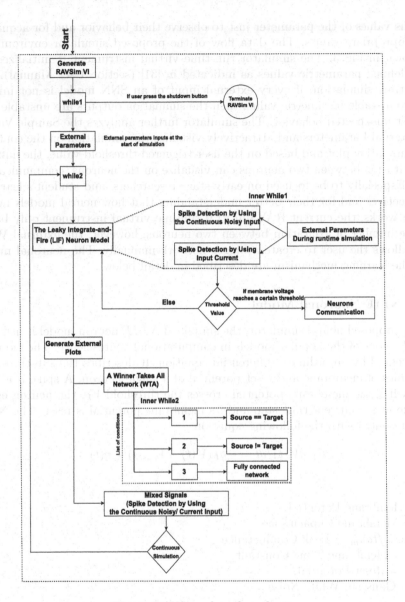

**Fig. 3.** RAVSim: data flow chart.

## 4   Discussion and Results

RAVSim allows the users to observe the SNN parameter reactions graphically and interact with the model in run-time. This process is analogous to setting up parameters for experimentation and testing of a model in any other programming language like Python. But, for doing so we require huge lines of code to wholly understand these parameters and the model needs to be fine-tuned with various values of the parameter just to observe their behavior and for acquiring the appropriate values. The data flow of the proposed simulator environment is shown in Fig. 3. The simulator run-time virtual instrument is initialized by user-defined parametric values as indicated in [31] (section User Manual). For a runtime simulation, if every external input of an SNN model is not initialized to a stable parametric value, then the simulation outputs are unstable and exhibit unexpected behavior. The simulator further analyzes the Sample Values of External Parameters and attractively visualize the simulation on the continuous simulation plot and based on the user-triggered threshold value, the number of excitation between two neurons can visualize on the neurons' communication plot. Especially to be focused on early-stage researchers' and student's learning perspectives and for their better understanding that how neural models mechanism works, the current RAVSim v1.0 runtime virtual instrument only based on the number of excitation between two neurons, however, the external WTA plot allows the user to create a bigger network manually. The neuronal model and the learning mechanism are described in detail below.

### 4.1   NLIF Neuronal Model

In the proposed neural simulator, the simplified $NLIF$ neuron model is utilized. $NLIF$ is one of the popular models in computational neuroscience. The model is represented by an ordinary differential equation. It describes the sub-threshold dynamics of membrane and reset potential of a single neuron. A spike is generated when the membrane potential crosses the threshold $V_T$, the neuron emits a spike at the current time step and its membrane potential is reset. The NLIF is represented with the following equation:

$$C_m dV(t)/dt = -g_L(V(t) - V_{reset}) + \eta(t)$$

Where:

$V_t$ = Membrane Potential
$C_m$ = Membrane Capacitance
$g_L = C_m/tau_m$ = Leak Conductance
$tau_m$ = Membrane Time Constant
$V_{reset}$ = Reset Potential
$\eta(t)$ = Gaussian White Noise

### 4.2   Learning Mechanism Using WTA Network

The winner takes it all network or WTA network [28] generally serves as a fundamental building block for many tasks involving neural networks, for example, learning, clustering, pattern recognition, etc. We have two important parameters for WTA networks:

- Weight between noisy input and neurons ($weight$)
- Weight for self-excitation ($weight_{exc}$)

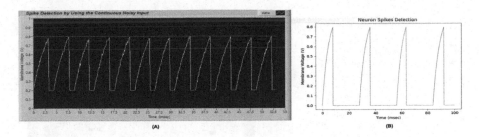

**Fig. 4.** RAVSim (A) and Brian2 (B) simulator output by using the same input of parametric values

The logic for tuning this kind of network can be summarized as follows.

- Initializing the two weights parameters mentioned above to 0, then start increasing the (input) 'weight' until neurons start spiking randomly.
- Increase '$weight_{exc}$' for self excitation until the neurons fire continuously.

We have implemented this in our interactive simulator RAVSim v1.0 in three types:

- WTA with $i = j$ where '$i$' is the source neuron index, and '$j$' is the target neuron index.
- WTA with fully connected network
- WTA with $i \mathrel{!=} j$

### 4.3 Simulator Comparison

The current simulators to designing SNNs model is time-consuming in both prospectives studying and understanding, as many of times model may need to run with different parametric values, out of which only a few would function for the following reasons:

- The SNNs model requires a precise balancing of parametric values.
- Different components are combined to build a model and their function can vary depending on a threshold value, membrane capacitance, and membrane time constant.
- These models are defined by more than one state (their output to different inputs or how they change with different input).

We have mentioned some of the key design features that make RAVSim a standalone simulator and to the best of our knowledge, there is no tool that exists that allows the user to interact with the model during runtime. These features represent that RAVSim simulator is a particular balance between the conflicting demands of flexibility, friendly user interface, and faster performance and compare the results of these available simulators. The RAVSim is also very helpful

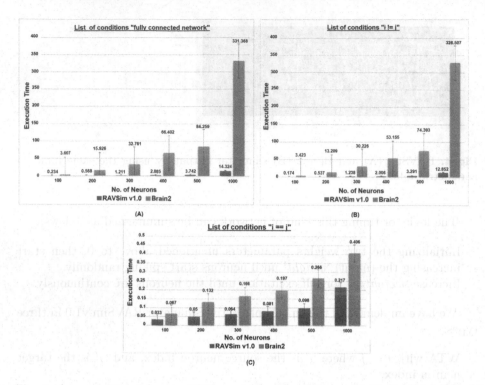

**Fig. 5.** Average time taken in WTA analysis using LIF model by the Brain2 and proposed RAVSim simulator for six test cases using different number of neurons, along with standard deviation error bars. (A) Average time taken in fully connected network analysis, (B) Average time taken in $'i \mathrel{!=} j'$ analysis, and (C) Average time taken in $'i == j'$ analysis,

in the following sense: let's assume that a user has implemented 10,000 neurons based network with some random parametric value settings on the hardware and results of accuracy or whatever users are looking for output, comes after several hours of analysis and in case the user didn't satisfy the output then run analysis again after changing the values of the parameters and so on. Additionally, this is also a time-consuming and costly procedure, and most important to perform a correct experiment user needs to verify each parametric value with different combinations every time, which is also a very lengthy and complex procedure. However, RAVSim run-time environment offers the user to visualize the experiment before starting a practical implementation to verify the stability of each parameter.

As you can see in Fig. 4, the output of our RAVSim (Fig. 4[A]) and Brian2 (Fig. 4[B]) simulator by using the same input of parametric values (shown in [31]). The simulated plot results on both simulators are almost similar. As shown in Fig. 4, neuron spike detection simulation for Brain2 used 100 msec time period and RAVSim simulation stopped after approximate 55 msec due to run-time environment, users are able to stop the simulation at any time, however, the output simulation of RAVSim based on the default parametric values never falls below the triggered threshold value at any point of time during the overall simulation time unit. In Fig. 5, the Average time taken in WTA analysis using LIF model by the Brain2 and proposed RAVSim simulator for six test cases using a different number of neurons (minimum 100 and maximum 1000 neurons), along with standard deviation error bars. (A) The average time taken in fully connected network analysis, (B) Average time taken in $'i \,!= j'$ analysis, and (C) Average time taken in $'i == j'$ analysis, the experimental results clearly showed that the Brian2 simulator uses quite a long time for execution as it needs to execute a couple of libraries before the simulation, on the other hand, RAVSim was fully developed in the LabVIEW platform and no external library required for model simulation. We have tested RAVSim v1.0 using up to 1000 neurons, as you can be seen in Fig. 5, in the most complex model'i != j's case the maximum amount of time consumed by the simulator is an average of approximately 12 s to analyzed and visualize the WTA network, however, brain2 simulator in the same case consumed approximate 328 s. The details of each experimental result are presented in [31] (section Experimental Results).

## 5 Conclusion

To summarize, a simple yet effective run-time simulator, "RAVSim" has been developed, which is very interactive, faster, and easy to use for understanding the mechanism of SNNs. This tool is ideal for early-stage researchers and students. Which helps them to interact with the simulator in run-time and understand the working of SNNs for designing optimal neural networks. It saves a lot of time for the users as it is an interactive tool. It does not require any programming skills and helps them learn things quickly. For future work, we are continuously working on improving RAVSim and will implement other SNN neuron and synapse models, and various learning techniques which avoid huge lines of code for simulating the models. On the other hand, deploying the computer-vision-based application directly into the hardware and visualizing, analyzing, and exploring with the different parametric values and allowing direct change at any time during designing a neural network with a run-time simulator based environment is also under consideration. We believe that this work (RAVSim Simulator), run-time analysis, and visualization of the SNNs model will be an interesting area for further research.

**Availability.** All of the experiments have been performed using run-time simulations on RAVSim v1.0. The RAVSim (v1.0) is an open-source simulator and it is published on LabVIEW official website and available publicly at [12]. The user manual [32] and video demonstration of RAVSim can be accessed at,

– https://www.youtube.com/watch?v=Ozv0MXXj89Y

**Supporting Information.** The Supporting Information including the detailed result of each test is available at [31]. The data for each test results is enclosed in its respective "Experimental Results" section.

**Acknowledgements.** The authors would like to thank Christopher Ostrau from the Center for Cognitive Interaction Technology (CITEC) at Bielefeld University, for his contribution to the development of earlier versions of RAVSim.

This research was supported by the research training group "Dataninja" (Trustworthy AI for Seamless Problem Solving: Next Generation Intelligence Joins Robust Data Analysis) funded by the German federal state of North Rhine-Westphalia.

# References

1. Tavanaei, A., Ghodrati, M., Kheradpisheh, S.R., Masquelier, T., Maida, A.: Deep learning in spiking neural networks. Neural Networks **111**, 47–63 (2019)
2. Pfeiffer, M., Pfeil, T.: Deep learning with spiking neurons: opportunities and challenges. Frontiers in neuroscience **12**, 774 (2018)
3. Roy, K., Jaiswal, A., Panda, P.: Towards spike-based machine intelligence with neuromorphic computing. Nature **575**(7784), 607–617 (2019)
4. Schuman, C.D., Potok, T.E., Patton, R.M., Birdwell, J.D., Dean, M.E., Rose, G.S., Plank, J.S.: A survey of neuromorphic computing and neural networks in hardware. arXiv preprint arXiv:1705.06963 (2017)
5. Bouvier, M., Valentian, A., Mesquida, T., Rummens, F., Reyboz, M., Vianello, E., Beigne, E.: Spiking neural networks hardware implementations and challenges: A survey. ACM Journal on Emerging Technologies in Computing Systems (JETC) **15**(2), 1–35 (2019)
6. Merolla, P.A., Arthur, J.V., Alvarez-Icaza, R., Cassidy, A.S., Sawada, J., Akopyan, F., Jackson, B.L., Imam, N., Guo, C., Nakamura, Y., et al.: A million spiking-neuron integrated circuit with a scalable communication network and interface. Science **345**(6197), 668–673 (2014)
7. Davies, M., Srinivasa, N., Lin, T.H., Chinya, G., Cao, Y., Choday, S.H., Dimou, G., Joshi, P., Imam, N., Jain, S., et al.: Loihi: A neuromorphic manycore processor with on-chip learning. Ieee Micro **38**(1), 82–99 (2018)
8. Stimberg, M., Brette, R., Goodman, D.F.: Brian 2, an intuitive and efficient neural simulator. Elife **8**, e47314 (2019)
9. Eppler, J.M., Helias, M., Muller, E., Diesmann, M., Gewaltig, M.O.: Pynest: a convenient interface to the nest simulator. Frontiers in neuroinformatics **2**, 12 (2009)
10. Hines, M.: ExpandingNEURON's RepertoireofMechanisms withNMODL
11. LabVIEW: laboratory virtual instrument engineering workbench. https://www.ni.com/de-de/shop/labview.html, accessed: January 2022
12. RAVSim v1.0: https://www.ni.com/de-de/support/downloads/tools-network/download.run-time-analysis-and-visualization-simulator-ravsim-.html#443936, accessed: March 2022
13. Pecevski, D., Kappel, D., Jonke, Z.: Nevesim: event-driven neural simulation framework with a python interface. Frontiers in neuroinformatics **8**, 70 (2014)

14. Morrison, A., Straube, S., Plesser, H.E., Diesmann, M.: Exact subthreshold integration with continuous spike times in discrete-time neural network simulations. Neural computation **19**(1), 47–79 (2007)
15. Brette, R., Rudolph, M., Carnevale, T., Hines, M., Beeman, D., Bower, J.M., Diesmann, M., Morrison, A., Goodman, P.H., Harris, F.C., et al.: Simulation of networks of spiking neurons: a review of tools and strategies. Journal of computational neuroscience **23**(3), 349–398 (2007)
16. Ros, E., Carrillo, R., Ortigosa, E.M., Barbour, B., Agís, R.: Event-driven simulation scheme for spiking neural networks using lookup tables to characterize neuronal dynamics. Neural computation **18**(12), 2959–2993 (2006)
17. Ahmad, N., Isbister, J.B., Smithe, T.S.C., Stringer, S.M.: Spike: A gpu optimised spiking neural network simulator. bioRxiv p. 461160 (2018)
18. Rudolph, M., Destexhe, A.: Analytical integrate-and-fire neuron models with conductance-based dynamics for event-driven simulation strategies. Neural computation **18**(9), 2146–2210 (2006)
19. Stimberg, M., Goodman, D.F., Nowotny, T.: Brian2genn: a system for accelerating a large variety of spiking neural networks with graphics hardware. bioRxiv p. 448050 (2018)
20. Chou, T.S., et al.: Carlsim 4: an open source library for large scale, biologically detailed spiking neural network simulation using heterogeneous clusters. In: 2018 International Joint Conference on Neural Networks (IJCNN), pp. 1–8. IEEE (2018)
21. Yavuz, E., Turner, J., Nowotny, T.: Genn: a code generation framework for accelerated brain simulations. Scientific reports **6**(1), 1–14 (2016)
22. Kasap, B., van Opstal, A.J.: Dynamic parallelism for synaptic updating in GPU-accelerated spiking neural network simulations. Neurocomputing **302**, 55–65 (2018)
23. Fujita, K., Okuno, S., Kashimori, Y.: Evaluation of the computational efficacy in GPU-accelerated simulations of spiking neurons. Computing **100**(9), 907–926 (2018)
24. Mozafari, M., Ganjtabesh, M., Nowzari-Dalini, A., Masquelier, T.: Spyketorch: efficient simulation of convolutional spiking neural networks with at most one spike per neuron. Front. Neurosci. **13**, 625 (2019)
25. Hazan, H., et al.: Bindsnet: a machine learning-oriented spiking neural networks library in python. Front. Neuroinform. **12**, 89 (2018)
26. Dumont, G., Henry, J., Tarniceriu, C.O.: Noisy threshold in neuronal models: connections with the noisy leaky integrate-and-fire model. J. Math. Biol. **73**(6), 1413–1436 (2016)
27. Fourcaud-Trocmé, N., Hansel, D., Van Vreeswijk, C., Brunel, N.: How spike generation mechanisms determine the neuronal response to fluctuating inputs. J. Neurosci. **23**(37), 11628–11640 (2003)
28. Chen, Y.: Mechanisms of winner-take-all and group selection in neuronal spiking networks. Front. Comput. Neurosci. **11**, 20 (2017)
29. Sanaullah, Baig, H., Madsen, J., Lee, J.A.: A parallel approach to perform threshold value and propagation delay analyses of genetic logic circuit models. ACS Synthetic Biol. **9**(12), 3422–3428 (2020)
30. Baig, H., Madsen, J.: D-vasim: an interactive virtual laboratory environment for the simulation and analysis of genetic circuits. Bioinformatics **33**(2), 297–299 (2017)
31. Supporting information: Detailed results. https://github.com/Rao-Sanaullah/RAVSim/tree/main/Results. Accessed Mar 2022
32. RAVSim: User manual guide. https://github.com/Rao-Sanaullah/RAVSim/tree/main/User-Manual. Accessed Mar 2022

# The Effectiveness of Synchronous Data-parallel Differentiable Architecture Search

George Kyriakides[(✉)] [ID] and Konstantinos Margaritis[ID]

University of Macedonia, 55236 Thessaloniki, Greece
{ge.kyriakides,kmarg}@uom.edu.gr

**Abstract.** DARTS is a popular gradient-based method for Neural Architecture Search (NAS). Many extensions have been introduced in the literature, resulting in various state-of-the-art models for many datasets. As such, DARTS can now be regarded as a family of methods. Most proposed extensions focus on improving DARTS' computational and memory demands and its effectiveness in generating competent architectures. Nonetheless, as with most NAS methods, DARTS is quite computationally expensive. Furthermore, despite the method's popularity, there is little research concerning its parallelization feasibility and the behavior of parallel DARTS methods. This paper studies the speedup, efficiency, and quality of a synchronous data-parallel DARTS scheme on the Fashion-MNIST dataset. We argue that although data-parallel methods can introduce noise to the search phase, this should not significantly affect the final results due to the pruning before extracting the final network. As a result, we achieve a speedup of 1.82 for two GPU workers and a 3.18 speedup for four GPU workers while retaining the same qualitative results as serially executing DARTS.

**Keywords:** Neural architecture search · DARTS · Synchronous data-parallel

## 1 Introduction

In recent years, neural architecture search (NAS) has enabled the automatic design of state-of-the-art neural architectures for various problems [11,15,16,18]. NAS emerged from the need to systematically design neural architectures, as a network's topology and layer design greatly affect its data-modeling efficiency. NAS capabilities greatly complement deep learning by allowing the problem of learning from data to be solved from a higher level. Reinforcement learning [25], metaheuristics [11], and differentiable methods [8] have been utilized in NAS, with the aim to find competent architectures for various tasks. A problem that arises with traditional reinforcement learning and metaheuristic approaches is re-training from scratch each candidate architecture. To solve this problem, weight-sharing through a supernet has been proposed [20]. As such, differentiable

© Springer Nature Switzerland AG 2022
L. Iliadis et al. (Eds.): EANN 2022, CCIS 1600, pp. 52–63, 2022.
https://doi.org/10.1007/978-3-031-08223-8_5

methods can be seen as the most natural approach to supernets due to the simultaneous utilization of the whole supernet.

One of the most popular and successful differentiable NAS methodologies is DARTS [8], which enables the employment of back-propagation in order to find optimal network architectures. An extension of the method has led to the discovery of the current state-of-the-art architecture for the Fashion-MNIST data set [19]. Due to its popularity, there have been many improvements since its initial inception [21–23]. However, when compared to reinforcement learning and metaheuristics, one of the main disadvantages is that differentiable methods have a larger memory footprint, as the whole supernet must constantly be in GPU memory. This requirement also indirectly limits the maximum batch size utilized during the search due to memory limitations. Furthermore, the parallelization of such methods is usually not straightforward.

There are many asynchronous approaches to parallelizing mini-batch gradient descent (SGD) [4,9,14], but most of them require special handling of the optimization process while introducing noise. The most straightforward synchronous method is to average the weights of all parallel copies of the network after each epoch [2]. Although it is possible to converge to local optima for non-convex models, neural networks show an increasingly convex loss surface landscape as they increase in size [3].

In this paper, we explore the behavior of first-order DARTS under synchronous data-parallel SGD, for one, two, and four parallel workers, by generating architectures for the Fashion-MNIST dataset [19]. Although parallel training is expected to introduce noise to the model, it will only affect the search phase. As such, we aim to study the behavior of the method and the quality of the generated models under a data-parallel scheme. To the best of our knowledge, this is the first paper studying the behavior of data-parallel DARTS. We aim to compare the serial and parallelized methods' ability to generate competent architectures, as well as the potential speedup. We first briefly present the DARTS algorithm, as well as the dataset. Following, we explain our methodology and our experimental results. Finally, we present the limitations and findings of our research.

## 2    Background

In this section, we provide a brief overview of DARTS and the Fashion-MNIST dataset.

### 2.1    DARTS

Differentiable architecture search(DARTS) is a NAS method that relaxes the discrete problem of selecting layers and connections between layers into a continuous one. The search space of DARTS is a cell search space. It generates architectures for two types of small, repeating cells (reduction and normal cells).

These cells are repeated in a pre-determined pattern to generate the actual network. Each cell has four aggregation nodes, and each node is connected to all following nodes through a neural layer (such as pooling or convolutional layers).

In order to treat the problem as continuous, all possible layer types exist simultaneously in the supernet, and a weight is assigned to each layer output, referred to as architecture weight $a$. Cells of the same type share architecture weights. Normal cells have a stride of 1 for their layers, while reduction cells have a stride of 2. To simplify the notion of having all possible layers and connections, the authors define a mixed operation layer type (MixOp), which contains all available layer types and their respective connection weights (see Fig. 1). As such, each cell has 6 MixOp layers. By including the "zeroize" layer type, which always outputs zero, the cell has the option to deactivate a connection between two nodes, while "identity" layers enable the implementation of skip-connects. As the optimizer has to train two sets of weights, the traditional layer weights and the architecture weights, the optimization becomes bi-level. At each training step, the weights of each individual layer are first optimized utilizing the training set ($L_{train}$), while the architecture weights are then optimized utilizing the validation set ($L_{val}$). Thus, the optimization problem is to minimize the loss on the validation set w.r.t. $a$ (1a), given the layer weights $w^*$, as they were optimized on the training set (1b).

$$\min_{a} \quad L_{val}(w^*(a), a) \tag{1a}$$

$$\text{s.t.} \quad w^*(a) = \arg\min_{w} L_{train}(w, a) \tag{1b}$$

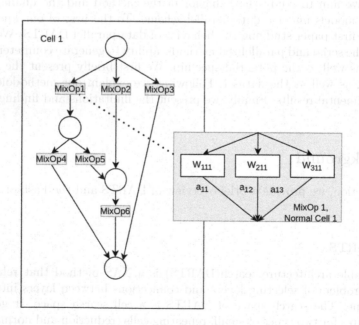

**Fig. 1.** Example cell architecture.

## 2.2   Fashion-MNIST in NAS

Fashion-MNIST [19] is a $28 \times 28$ grayscale image classification dataset with 60,000 training and 10,000 testing examples. It is intended as a direct replacement for the traditional hand-written digits MNIST dataset, although it is considerably harder to model. It contains ten different classes, which refer to distinct clothing items. There are several NAS papers concerned with generating architectures for this dataset. Employing the experts' advice framework, XNAS [12] was able to achieve a 96.36% accuracy, while a modified version of DARTS with attention modules in the macro architecture and an extended input head block was able to achieve the current state-of-the-art, 96.91%. Other cell-search methods are presented in Asap [13], which can also produce competent architectures.

## 3   Methodology and Experimental Setup

This study employs the original DARTS framework with a synchronous data-parallel optimization approach. Aiming to study its behavior under data-parallel training, we employ a synchronous approach, as we hope to curtail the impact on solving the bi-level optimization problem. In order to minimize the communication between nodes, we perform a single collective communications operation at the end of each epoch, a reduction (averaging) of all network parameters (Algorithm 1). Compared to a more common synchronous approach, such as gradient aggregation (Algorithm 2), where the gradients for each parameter are aggregated after each mini-batch step, we considerably reduce the communication instances. The reduction factor is $N/B$, where $N$ is the number of training examples and $B$ is the batch size. For Fashion-MNIST with a batch size of 64, the reduction factor is 937.5, as all 60,000 training samples are utilized for the update of the layer and architecture weights. Furthermore, we reduce the possible occurrences of stragglers [2], where many processes are waiting for another to finish by the same factor.

Our experiments are implemented in the Neural Architecture Search framework "NORD" [7], which relies on PyTorch. NVIDIA's NCCL was utilized as the communications back-end, allowing fast collective communication operations between GPU nodes. For the search phase, we utilize 16 initial channels and 8 cells. The layers' weights are trained with mini-batch SGD with an annealing learning rate schedule (starting at 0.025 and gradually reducing to 0.001), while the architecture weights are optimized with Adam [5]. There are 8 different layer types for each MixOp layer: zeroize, identity, max and average pooling with kernels of size $3 \times 3$, separable convolutions with kernel sizes $3 \times 3$ and $5 \times 5$, and dilated convolutions with kernel sizes $3 \times 3$ and $5x$. Random horizontal flips and random erasing are utilized as data augmentation. Half of the training set is utilized as a validation set. The architecture parameters are also optimized on the validation set. Experiments are conducted on 1, 2, and 4 NVIDIA Tesla A100 GPUs. We run the experiment 4 times with a different initial seed for each setup to mitigate the fact that initial architecture and layer weights can both favor and disfavor a particular run.

---

**Algorithm 1:** Weight-based data-parallel DARTS, worker k

---

**Data:** $L_{train}, L_{valid}, n_{batches}, n_{epochs}$
**Result:** $a$
$w \leftarrow$ broadcast$(w)$ from worker 0;
$a \leftarrow$ broadcast$(a)$ from worker 0;
**for** $e = 0, 1, ..., n_{epochs}$ **do**
    **for** $i = 0, 1, ..., n_{batches}$ **do**
        $train \leftarrow L_{train}[i]; \; valid \leftarrow L_{valid}[i];$
        $G_w \leftarrow \frac{\partial Error(train;w,a)}{\partial w};$
        $w \leftarrow w - lr * (G_w);$
        $G_a \leftarrow \frac{\partial Error(valid;w,a)}{\partial a};$
        $a \leftarrow a - lr * (G_a);$
    **end**
    $w \leftarrow$ allreduce$(w)$;
    $a \leftarrow$ allreduce$(a)$;
    /* Wait for allreduce to complete                    */
**end**

---

Following the search phase, we select the best architecture of each GPU setup. Then, using the architecture weights, we generate the final networks. For these models, only the operation with the strongest $a$ is retained for each MixOp layer. As such, each node is connected to the next through a single layer. These networks are the final result of the search phase. The resulting architectures are fully trained for 100 epochs to compare their performances. In this fine-tuning phase, we utilize 36 channels and 20 cells in order to increase the final network's number of parameters, as in [8]. During fine-tuning, the validation set is only 10% of the training set, while the optimizer is Stochastic Gradient Descent with momentum. The parameters for both the search as well as the fine-tuning training phase are depicted in Table 1.

## 4 Results

In this section, we present the results of the two approaches. First, we analyze their behavior during the search phase and the resulting networks. Following, we construct extended networks from the best architectures found for each group. Finally, by fully training these architectures, we extract information regarding the equivalence of the data-parallel and serial approaches.

### 4.1 Search Phase

During the search phase, single GPU runs seem to out-perform multi-GPU runs. In both training and validation accuracy, single-GPU runs achieve higher scores early in the training phase while also having higher final train and validation accuracy. Nonetheless, the discrepancy is more profound in the training accuracy

---

**Algorithm 2:** Gradient-based data-parallel DARTS, worker k

---

**Data:** $L_{train}, L_{valid}, n_{batches}, n_{epochs}$
**Result:** $a$
$w \leftarrow$ broadcast($w$) from worker 0;
$a \leftarrow$ broadcast($a$) from worker 0;
**for** $e = 0, 1, ..., n_{epochs}$ **do**
    **for** $i = 0, 1, ..., n_{batches}$ **do**
        $train \leftarrow L_{train}[i]$; $valid \leftarrow L_{valid}[i]$;
        $G_w \leftarrow \frac{\partial Error(train;w,a)}{\partial w}$;
        $w \leftarrow w - lr*$allreduce($G_w$);
        /* Wait for allreduce to complete        */
        $G_a \leftarrow \frac{\partial Error(valid;w^*,a)}{\partial a}$;
        $a \leftarrow a - lr*$allreduce($G_a$);
        /* Wait for allreduce to complete        */
    **end**
**end**

---

**Table 1.** Search and training parameters

| Search phase | | Training phase | |
|---|---|---|---|
| Layer optimizer | SGD | Layer optimizer | SGD |
| Learning rate | 0.025–0.001 | Learning rate | 0.025 |
| Momentum | 0.9 | Momentum | 0.9 |
| Architecture optimizer | Adam | – | |
| Channels | 16 | Channels | 36 |
| Cells | 8 | Cells | 20 |
| Layer types | 8 | – | |
| Batch size | 64 | Batch size | 96 |
| Validation percentage | 50% | Validation percentage | 10% |
| Epochs | 50 | Epochs | 100 |

than validation accuracy (Figs. 2 and 3, respectively). In terms of validation accuracy, all experiments could produce results within a 1% validation accuracy in the range of [92.2%, 93.2%]. Nonetheless, these results concern only the search phase. Although indicative of the final network's fully trained performance, they serve more as a guide to the search rather than an absolute measure that can be directly compared.

The method seems to speed up almost linearly, with speedup values of 1.82 for the two-GPU setup and 3.2 for the four-GPU setup (Table 2. As such, efficiency is at 90% for the two-GPU setup and 80% for the four-GPU setup. This reduction in efficiency is probably due to stragglers, as there is minimal communication overhead. Adding a backup worker [2], and assuming that a speedup of 4 is achieved with 4+1 workers, the efficiency would remain at 80%. Backup workers would be a viable option for any number of GPUs greater than 4, as a 10% efficiency loss is observed for each doubling of the GPU workers, implying that at 8 nodes, the efficiency would drop at least to 70%. With $8+1$ workers and a speedup of 8, the efficiency would be at 88%.

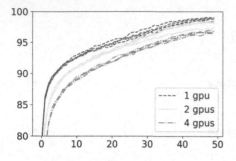

**Fig. 2.** Training accuracy curves for the search phase.

**Fig. 3.** Validation accuracy curves for the search phase.

**Table 2.** Key performance metrics

| GPUs | Best test accuracy | Best validation accuracy | Average time (secs) | Speedup |
|------|--------------------|--------------------------|---------------------|---------|
| 1    | 99.06%             | 93.19%                   | 26708               | –       |
| 2    | 98.52%             | 92.99%                   | 14659               | 1.82    |
| 4    | 96.92%             | 92.63%                   | 8393                | 3.18    |

To study the discrepancy between the generated architectures, we calculate the graph edit distance (GED) for intra-group and inter-group results for both normal and reduction cells (Figs. 4 and 5). Graph edit distance is calculated based on topology and layer operations. The same topology with a single different layer operation would give a GED of 2. This value results from the two operations required to edit one of the graphs to match the other; first, delete the existing operation and add the missing one. Intra-group GED values (1, 2, and 4 GPUs) have a smaller deviation than inter-group GED values (1 vs. 4, 1 vs. 2, and 2 vs. 4 GPUs). Nonetheless, applying a Kruskal-Wallis H test [6] on the normal cell GED values yields a p-value of 0.4, while the same test on the reduction cell GED values yields a p-value of 0.29. As such, we cannot confidently say that any group significantly differs from the rest for a specific cell type. We can see that the differences between cell architectures gave a mean GED value of 8. As each node has exactly one connection with all previous nodes, it implies that, on average, the layer selections differ in four connections, while the cells are computationally similar, as seen in Fig. 3. The data-parallel approach seems to produce, on average, the same deviation within its final generated architectures as the deviation produced between the final architectures of all approaches.

Looking at Fig. 5 we even see a tendency for the serial approach to producing slightly higher intra-group GED, compared to the data-parallel approaches.

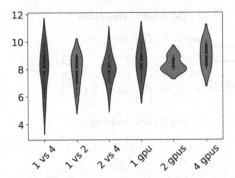

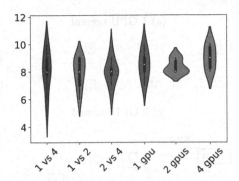

**Fig. 4.** Graph edit distance values for the normal cells.

**Fig. 5.** Graph edit distance values for the reduction cells.

## 4.2   Best Model Analysis

The best architecture of each setup (1, 2, and 4 GPU runs) was selected and trained for 100 epochs with an increased number of layers and channels to compare each approach's results. The cell architectures of each model are depicted in Fig. 6. We can see that for all normal cells, the inputs are followed mainly by dilated and separable convolutions, with a minimal amount of pooling operations. It is interesting to note that although all groups produced final cells with predominately pooling operations in their reduction cells, they were not the best-performing ones on our specific dataset.

Although the single-GPU setup had the best performance in the search phase, the generated architecture under-performed in training set accuracy, while the other two networks followed a similar trajectory (Fig. 7). More importantly, all three networks seemed to have comparable performance on the validation set. Nonetheless, we would like to examine more systematically their similarity. Assuming that the first 10 training epochs are greatly dependent on weight initialization, we apply a Kolmogorov-Smirnov test [10] for equality of distributions between the validation accuracies of the three networks for epochs 10 to 100. Following, we correct for false discovery rate, utilizing the Benjamini/Hochberg correction [1]. The results are depicted in Table 3, prohibiting us from rejecting the null hypothesis that the distributions of the accuracies are the same. This further validates the visual information in Fig. 8, which shows a remarkably similar trend with noise for all networks.

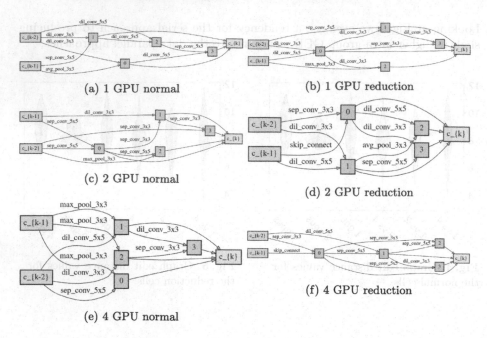

(a) 1 GPU normal

(b) 1 GPU reduction

(c) 2 GPU normal

(d) 2 GPU reduction

(e) 4 GPU normal

(f) 4 GPU reduction

**Fig. 6.** Best models cell architectures.

**Table 3.** Kolmogorov-Smirnov and Benjamini/Hochberg-corrected p-values

| Model | Kolmogorov-Smirnov | Benjamini/Hochberg-corrected |
|-------|--------------------|------------------------------|
| 1 vs 2-GPUs | 0.51 | 0.71 |
| 1 vs 4-GPUs | 0.08 | 0.15 |
| 2 vs 4-GPUs | 0.87 | 0.88 |

## 5   Limitations

Although this study tries to analyze the behavior of a data-parallel DARTS as
thoroughly as possible, its main limitation is the small number of executions for
each setup (number of parallel GPUs). The results seem consistent, although a
more significant number of executions for each setup would provide more insights
into the properties of a data-parallel DARTS approach. Furthermore, a more
significant number of GPU nodes would allow for a comprehensive assessment
of the speedup and efficiency of this approach.

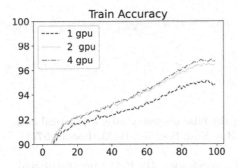

**Fig. 7.** Best model training fine-tune accuracy.

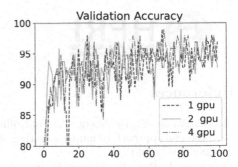

**Fig. 8.** Best model validation fine-tune accuracy.

# 6   Discussion and Future Work

In this paper, we study the behavior of Differentiable Architecture Search [8] under a data-parallel synchronous training approach, utilizing groups of 1, 2, and 4 GPU workers. We observe an almost linear speedup, with a 10% drop in efficiency for each doubling of GPU workers. As such, we argue that a backup-worker approach [2] would benefit the method for more than four GPU setups. Furthermore, the generated architectures' quality seems to be stable, and also their diversity does not change between the serial and data-parallel approaches. This consistency is confirmed by analyzing the graph edit distance values for cells of the same group and cells between different groups.

We observe similar behavior for all three groups by generating enlarged networks from the best architecture cells for each group and training them for an extended number of epochs. Moreover, their validation accuracy performance follows the same trajectory, while their distributions do not differ at the 0.05 and 0.1 significance levels. This observation indicates that the generated architectures are computationally equivalent. In contrast, their difference in performance and architecture can be attributed to different initial conditions, states of random number generators (although having the same initial seed at each run for all groups, different number of workers translates to different number of steps performed, and as such different internal states for the generators at each step), and inherent stochasticity in the execution of some GPU operations.

Concluding, in this paper, we show that synchronous data-parallel optimization is viable for DARTS, resulting in similarly performing architectures to the serial approach. As our future work, we aim to study larger and more diverse datasets, investigate asynchronous approaches [17,24] to evaluate their feasibility, as well as extensions of DARTS [22], in order to assess the merit of parallelizing such methods.

**Acknowledgments.** The research work was supported by the Hellenic Foundation for Research and Innovation (HFRI) under the HFRI PhD Fellowship grant (Fellowship Number: 646).

# References

1. Benjamini, Y., Hochberg, Y.: Controlling the false discovery rate: a practical and powerful approach to multiple testing. J. Roy. Stat. Soc. Ser. B (Methodol.) **57**(1), 289–300 (1995)
2. Chen, J., Pan, X., Monga, R., Bengio, S., Jozefowicz, R.: Revisiting distributed synchronous sgd. arXiv preprint arXiv:1604.00981 (2016)
3. Choromanska, A., Henaff, M., Mathieu, M., Arous, G.B., LeCun, Y.: The loss surfaces of multilayer networks. In: Artificial intelligence and statistics, pp. 192–204. PMLR (2015)
4. Dean, J., et al.: Large scale distributed deep networks. Advances in Neural Information Processing Systems, vol. 25 (2012)
5. Kingma, D.P., Ba, J.: Adam: a method for stochastic optimization. arXiv preprint arXiv:1412.6980 (2014)
6. Kruskal, W.H., Wallis, W.A.: Use of ranks in one-criterion variance analysis. J. Am. Stat. Assoc. **47**(260), 583–621 (1952)
7. Kyriakides, G., Margaritis, K.: Nord: a python framework for neural architecture search. Softw. Impacts **6**, 100042 (2020)
8. Liu, H., Simonyan, K., Yang, Y.: Darts: differentiable architecture search. In: 7th International Conference on Learning Representations, ICLR 2019,June 2018. http://arxiv.org/abs/1806.09055
9. Maleki, S., Musuvathi, M., Mytkowicz, T.: Parallel stochastic gradient descent with sound combiners. arXiv preprint arXiv:1705.08030 (2017)
10. Massey, F.J., Jr.: The Kolmogorov-Smirnov test for goodness of fit. J. Am. Stat. Assoc. **46**(253), 68–78 (1951)
11. Miikkulainen, R., et al.: Evolving deep neural networks. In: Artificial Intelligence in the Age of Neural Networks and Brain Computing, pp. 293–312. Elsevier (2019)
12. Nayman, N., Noy, A., Ridnik, T., Friedman, I., Jin, R., Zelnik, L.: XNAS: neural architecture search with expert advice. In: Advances in Neural Information Processing Systems, pp. 1975–1985 (2019)
13. Noy, A., et al.: Asap: architecture search, anneal and prune. arXiv preprint arXiv:1904.04123 (2019)
14. Pan, X., et al.: Cyclades: conflict-free asynchronous machine learning. Advances in Neural Information Processing Systems, vol. 29 (2016)
15. Pham, H., Guan, M.Y., Zoph, B., Le, Q.V., Dean, J.: Efficient neural architecture search via parameter sharing. In: 35th International Conference on Machine Learning, ICML 2018,vol. 9, pp. 6522–6531,February 2018. http://arxiv.org/abs/1802.03268
16. Real, E., Aggarwal, A., Huang, Y., Le, Q.V.: Regularized evolution for image classifier architecture search. In: Proceedings of the AAAI Conference on Artificial Intelligence, vol. 33, pp. 4780–4789, July 2019. https://doi.org/10.1609/aaai.v33i01.33014780
17. Recht, B., Re, C., Wright, S., Niu, F.: Hogwild!: A lock-free approach to parallelizing stochastic gradient descent. Advances in neural information processing systems 24 (2011)

18. Tanveer, M.S., Khan, M.U.K., Kyung, C.M.: Fine-tuning darts for image classi-fication. In: 2020 25th International Conference on Pattern Recognition (ICPR), pp. 4789–4796. IEEE (2021)
19. Xiao, H., Rasul, K., Vollgraf, R.: Fashion-MNIST: a novel image dataset for bench-marking machine learning algorithms (2017)
20. Xie, L., et al.: Weight-sharing neural architecture search: a battle to shrink the optimization gap (2021)
21. Xie, S., Zheng, H., Liu, C., Lin, L.: SNAS: stochastic neural architecture search. arXiv preprint arXiv:1812.09926 (2018)
22. Xu, Y., et al.: PC-DARTS: partial channel connections for memory-efficient archi-tecture search (2019)
23. Yao, Q., Xu, J., Tu, W.W., Zhu, Z.: Efficient neural architecture search via proximal iterations (2020)
24. Zheng, S., et al.: Asynchronous stochastic gradient descent with delay compen-sation. In: International Conference on Machine Learning, pp. 4120–4129. PMLR (2017)
25. Zoph, B., Le, Q.V.: Neural architecture search with reinforcement learning, Novem-ber 2016. http://arxiv.org/abs/1611.01578

18. Tauvou, M.S., Khan, M.U.K., Ayoub, C.M.: Fine-tuning darts for image classification. In: 2020 25th International Conference on Pattern Recognition (ICPR), pp. 4789–4796. IEEE (2021)

19. Xiao, H., Rasul, K., Vollgraf, R.: Fashion-MNIST: a novel image dataset for benchmarking machine learning algorithms (2017)

20. Xie, L., et al.: Weight sharing neural architecture search: a battle to shrink the optimization gap (2021)

21. Xie, S., Zheng, H., Liu, C., Lin, L.: SNAS: stochastic neural architecture search. arXiv preprint arXiv:1812.09926 (2018)

22. Xu, Y., et al.: PC-DARTS: partial channel connections for memory-efficient architecture search (2019)

23. Yao, Q., Xu, J., Tu, W.W., Zhu, Z.: Efficient neural architecture search via proximal iterations (2020)

24. Zhang, S., et al.: Asynchronous stochastic gradient descent with delay compensation. In: International Conference on Machine Learning, pp. 4120–4129. PMLR (2017)

25. Zoph, B., Le, Q.V.: Neural architecture search with reinforcement learning. November 2016. http://arxiv.org/abs/1611.01578

# Classification/Clustering - Machine Learning

# Automatic Accent and Gender Recognition of Regional UK Speakers

Chrisina Jayne[1](✉) (iD), Victor Chang[2](iD), Jozeene Bailey[1],
and Qianwen Ariel Xu[1]

[1] Teesside University, Middlesbrough TS1 3BX, UK
c.jayne@tees.ac.uk
[2] Aston University, Aston St, Birmingham B4 7ET, UK
http://tees.ac.uk

**Abstract.** With the ubiquity of voice assistants across the UK and the
world, speech recognition of the regional accents across the British Isles
has proven challenging due to varying pronunciations. This paper proposes an automated recognition of the geographical origin and gender of
a voice sample based on the six regional dialects of the United Kingdom.
Twenty six features are extracted from 17,877 voice samples and then
used to design, implement and evaluate machine learning classifiers based
on Artificial Neural Networks (ANNs), Support Vector Machine (SVM),
Random Forest (RF) and $k$-nearest neighbors ($k$-NN) algorithms. The
results suggest that the proposed approach could be applicable for areas
such as e-commerce and the service industry, and it provides a contribution to NLP audio research.

**Keywords:** Deep learning · Artificial neural networks · Speech
recognition · Accent classification

## 1 Introduction

Across the United Kingdom, approximately 20% of homes are estimated to be
using a voice assistant according to a report by [7]. These voice-based artificial
intelligence systems respond to vocal commands from their users with a synthesized voice. According to a report by [31], 74% of consumers prefer to use voice
assistants in the comfort of their homes, rather than out in public while doing
domestic tasks. While voice assistants are used for daily tasks such as home
automation, controlling other devices and purchasing, commercial interests are
pushing the limits of their capabilities. Through voice assistant, customers are
able to communicate with customer service more directly and efficiently, especially in some complicated transaction processes. 61% of consumers surveyed
in the report by [31] expected, as a bare minimum, that their voice assistants
understand their accent/diction every time they speak. For a vast majority of
UK residents, this is far from their reality. In a survey done by Newcastle Life Sciences Centre through their 'Robots - then and now' exhibit, 79% of respondents

L. Iliadis et al. (Eds.): EANN 2022, CCIS 1600, pp. 67–80, 2022.
https://doi.org/10.1007/978-3-031-08223-8_6

who identified as speaking with a regional accent or dialect stated that they had to alter the way they spoke to voice assistants at least "a little bit", [29]. It was of such concern for 48% of respondents, who were of the opinion that increased use of voice recognition systems could lead to an "eradication" of regional accents [29]. According to a Spike Digital survey in 2018, [33], 67.3% of UK residents "feel that voice recognition devices should be adapted to recognize, or distinguish between, regional accents". Oral communications between members of different cultures have increasingly become important in various fields, including organizations with multinational employers, education (teacher-student interaction), health (better providing consulting services), as well as personal relationships [30]. In the e-commerce sector, the dialect effect also plays a role in the pre-sale and post-sale stages. For example, the initial contacts with the company's service representatives portray the first impressions, which may result in whether buyers view the company as a potential supplier. At the after-sale stage, a local dialect can also affect the relationship between buyers and sellers: the same dialects can raise the seller's credibility in the service restoration, which can help influence the purchaser's evaluation of how the seller deals with the complaints [26]. The quality of communication in the e-commerce sector has direct correlations to customer satisfaction as well as purchase decisions and customer retention. At a time when the general population demographic is constantly changing, decreasing communication quality (related to accents and dialect) is a growing issue in customer service delivery.

This paper investigates machine learning models capable of classifying regional accents of the United Kingdom for use in speech recognition systems applicable to the e-commerce and service industry. In an era where online shopping is becoming more and more popular, most voice assistants and customer service staff are familiar with Standard English and Received Pronunciation but not with regional dialects. Persons who live remotely from metropolitan areas are less likely to speak Standard English and can be at a disadvantage. Using audio-based tools that cater to regional accents can improve the quality of customer services. A high-quality dataset from Google Research is utilized, with 17,877 transcribed audio recordings of persons, male and female, speaking/reading sentences from various regions in the United Kingdom [11] available at [15]. Several models are designed, implemented and evaluated for detecting regional accents. The main contributions are:

- Experiments with different classification models to recognize multiple accents and gender of the speaker
- Novel approach to speech recognition for accents rather than standard language
- Evaluation of the proposed classification models for English-based accents

The rest of this paper is organized as follows: Sect. 2 presents related work on the accent classification methodologies and their significance for e-commerce and society. Section 3 introduces the dataset and methodology used in this research. Models based on Artificial Neural Networks (ANNs), Random Forest, Support Vector Machine (SVM) and k-nearest neighbors (kNN) algorithms are employed to perform accent classification. Section 4 compares and discusses the results of the models in terms of accuracy, precision, recall, and F1-score. Section 5 gives the conclusions and future work direction.

## 2 Related Work

### 2.1 Importance of Accent/Dialect Classification

With the rapid development of the Internet, in the current e-commerce field, communication between customers and customer service personnel can be carried out in various forms, which are no longer limited to text messages, but also include voice messages and voice calls. At present, more and more customers tend to use voice messages or voice calls because, in some complicated transaction processes, text messages cannot effectively express the content they want to ask. Compared with text messages, communicating with customer service through voice is more direct and efficient. Languages that are similar (such as dialects based on English) are often maintained in such societal groups, but this comes with some extent of miscommunication and misunderstanding in communal interactions. Therefore, while accents or dialects are natural entities of human speech, they can present a barrier to effective communication in the e-commerce or service sectors [1]. These challenges have the potential of negatively affecting the industries that require more effective communication and developing intelligent customer service [28,36]. In the e-commerce sector and service industry, the recognition of different accents or dialects is beneficial in matching voice recordings to the customer's place of origin or assigning a customer to a customer service representative who may speak in similar ways. This can help companies to understand customers' behavior, deal with their requests better, and improve customer satisfaction.

It is well known that customer satisfaction is a key element in service marketing since it can foster purchase intention and re-intention, loyalty, public praise, profitability and market share. Satisfaction is mainly an emotional state and response to service, not limited to quality. Therefore, satisfaction tends to be the relevant outcome variable of regional dialect affecting service experience. The customer service personnel are the key to influence the customer's evaluation of the company. Compatibility between customer service staff and buyers' accents or dialects can increase their satisfaction with the company and their intention to buy because regional dialects and accents may promote the fluidity of social interaction [26,35].

Different accents may indicate cultural differences. Research work in [4] suggests that based on service provider verbal interaction, customers with diverse cultures perceive they may receive inequitable service and consequently experience low levels of satisfaction. Therefore, accent recognition may enable assigning relevant customer service staff to improve services. With the rapid development of communications, such as the recent emergence of 5G, more applications rely on automatic voice recognition, e.g., voice assistants [32], education [22], and customer service [36]. However most of the research focuses on identifying customer emotions [6,24,30], and only rarely considers the issue of accent or dialect [12]. This paper addresses the problem of automatic recognition of the geographical origin and gender of a voice sample based on the six regional dialects of the United Kingdom, which can be utilized in practical applications of e-commerce or the service industry.

## 2.2   Automatic Methods for Accent/Dialect Classification

Typically, conversational Artificial Intelligence (AI) technology refers to artificial intelligence, which detects, processes, and responds using natural human language, whether spoken or written. This would include Natural Language Processing (NLP) and Natural Language Generation (NLG), as well as Automatic Dialect Classification (ADC). NLP tries to interpret the meaning of the language inputs it receives, including vocabulary, context and intent. ADC tends to be part of this NLP process. It is a technique that can automatically recognize a regional dialect of a particular language from voice samples, which is difficult as dialects often have smaller discernible variations than languages [12]. Inclusive AI systems that combat cultural biases are built from the ground up. Numerous datasets currently used to train AI systems are rife with biases (Google Translate commonly assigns gender stereotypes to occupations when a phrase is being translated from a language with gender-neutral pronouns). Machine learning algorithms thrive on data patterns, but this means they can form inaccurate conclusions from biased data. We also see these biases in commercial facial recognition applications when dealing with minorities. Daugherty et al. [10] suggest that this can be corrected by curating new datasets with a 'better representation of minorities' or adjusting the weights in classification algorithms.

A dialect is a variation of a standard language, like English, specific to geographical regions or cultural and social groups [23]. They can be influenced or stem from a single language or a mixture of multiple. Some dialects only exist in their spoken form, but for many, it is the only language they know or are familiar with, and it is important that technology is accessible in a way that allows such people to communicate in their familiar language. Yoo et al. [34] propose that a direct way to build a single acoustic model (AM) for multiple dialects is to train the AM on assorted samples from multiple dialects. This is similar to what Li et al. [23] propose, that is, to explore the possibility of training a single model serving multiple dialects, thereby simplifying the process of training multi-dialect models without the need for multiple Acoustic Models (AM), Pronunciation Models (PM) and Language Models (LM) for each dialect. Yoo et al.'s [34] approach to the problem was to dynamically adapt an acoustic model based on dialect information with a single AM. Their approach results in a highly adaptive AM for handling multiple dialects simultaneously. Ali's [2] propose generative and discriminative classifiers, in addition to deep learning approaches for Arabic dialects recognition.

# 3  Methodology

## 3.1  Data and Features Extraction

We utilize the UK dialect dataset, which can be found at Google Research [15]. It consists of 17,877 transcribed high-quality audio recordings (approximately 31 h) collected from native English speakers from a few areas in the UK and Ireland, including native speakers of Southern England, Midlands, Northern England, Welsh, Scottish and Irish variants of English. Recordings were performed by volunteers who self-reported their dialect. There are  2,400 unique speech specimens (quotes) of varying lengths. The audio is high quality (48 kHz, 16-bit, mono, Wave audio), recorded in a quiet environment [11]. The corpus was created with the intent of linguistic analysis as well as for use in speech technologies. Special characteristics of this dataset that make it a valuable choice for analysis over audio datasets like LibriSpeech Corpus and the Speech Accent Archive include high sampling rate for intelligibility, high phoneme coverage, and the curation of scripts that enhanced accent and idiolect elicitation [11]. Another important feature is the inclusion of words and names (for example, Gaelic names) that were specific to the region of the speaker (native pronunciations). The average length of recordings is 6.3 s, with the longest being 20.1 s long and the shortest being 1.62 s long. Table 1 shows the numbers of samples per regional dialect recorded and transcribed.

**Table 1.** Number of samples per regional dialect recorded and transcribed

| Region | Male | Female |
|---|---|---|
| Irish English | 450 | 0 |
| Midland English | 450 | 246 |
| Northern English | 2097 | 750 |
| Scotish English | 1649 | 894 |
| Southern English | 4331 | 4161 |
| Welsh English | 1650 | 1199 |

Audio features that capture the speech-relevant information need to be extracted from the audio wave files. For feature extraction of the audio file, we used the Python 'librosa' package[1]. Table 2 shows the various spectral features that were utilized.

The features in Table 2 are described as follows:

– **Chroma stft** Chroma Feature analysis [13] and synthesis is a representation of music audio, in which the entire spectrum is divided into 12 bins which represent12 distinct chromas (semitones) of the musical octave. We use the

---

[1] https://librosa.org/doc/latest/index.html.

**Table 2.** Features extracted

| No. | Feature |
|-----|---------|
| 1 | Chroma stft |
| 2 | MFCC (Mel-frequency cepstral coefficients) |
| 3 | RMS (Root Mean Square) |
| 4 | Zero-crossing rate |
| 5 | Spectral roll-off |
| 6 | Spectral centroid |
| 7 | Spectral bandwidth |

librosa.sftf function to create a spectrogram. This is a Short-time Fourier transform (STFT) representing a signal in the time-frequency domain by computing discrete Fourier transforms (DFT) over short overlapping windows. The DFT can be efficiently computed using the fast Fourier transform (FFT). The FFT window size $n\_fft$ parameter is set to 2048 samples, which corresponds to a physical duration of 93 ms at a sample rate 22050 Hz (the default sample rate in librosa). The number of audio samples between adjacent STFT columns $hop\_length$ parameter is set to 512. Figure 1 is a visualization of the spectrogram for the phrase "When the sunlight strikes raindrops in the air they act as a prism and form a rainbow", as spoken by a female from the North of England.

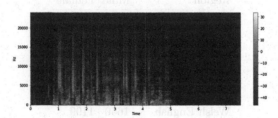

**Fig. 1.** Spectrogram of a Northern English female saying: "When the sunlight strikes raindrops in the air they act as a prism and form a rainbow"

- **MFCC (Mel-frequency cepstral coefficients).** Mel-frequency cepstral coefficients (MFCCs) [25] of a signal are a set of features used to estimate the important features that the human auditory system detects in audio signals. They are obtained by taking the Fourier transform of the audio signal, mapping the spectrum powers to the mel scale, and then taking the discrete cosine transform of the logarithms of the powers. For use in audio classification problems, between 12 to 20 coefficients are typically used. In this work, 20 coefficients are utilized in the lower order (at the bottom of the graph Fig. 2), which provides information about the overall extent of the audio spectrum. The mel-frequency cepstral coefficients indicate various rates of change in the cepstral domain. They also contain information about the shape of the vocal cords.

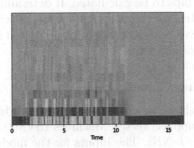

**Fig. 2.** MFCCs of a Northern English female saying: "When the sunlight strikes raindrops in the air they act as a prism and form a rainbow"

- **RMS (Root Mean Square).** The Root Mean Square (RMS) [8] is used to compute the root mean-square (RMS) energy for each frame, either from the audio samples or from a spectrogram. A Short-time Fourier Transform window of continuous ones with no frame centering is used to get consistent results from the RMS that would be computed from audio samples.

- **Zero-crossing rate.** The zero-crossing rate (ZCR) [16] is a fundamental spectral measurement technique that is used to estimate central frequency, also known as the lowest possible frequency of an intermittent waveform. It measures the number of times in each time interval/frame that the amplitude of the speech signals passes through the zero mark. As a pertinent feature used to categorize percussive sounds, the ZCR is widely used in other audio application domains, such as musical genre classification, speech analysis, and singing voice detection in music. It is the simplest method to perceive voice, unvoiced, or silent speech frames. Unvoiced segments of audio are anticipated to produce higher ZCRs than for voice segments.

- **Spectral roll-off.** The spectral roll-off frequency is defined for each frame as the center frequency for a spectrogram bin such that at least roll_percent (0.85 by default) of the energy of the spectrum in this frame is contained in this bin and the bins below [17].

- **Spectral centroid.** The spectral centroid [27] indicates the weighted average of the frequencies present in a given signal with the magnitudes of frequency as the weights. It characterizes the "center of mass" of a given spectrum. If the frequencies in a specific sample are the same throughout, then spectral centroid would be clustered and if there are high frequencies at the end of the sample, then the centroid would be towards the end. Perceptually, it has a strong relationship with the perception of sound "brightness", which has been formalized to indicate the amount of high-frequency content in a sound.

- **Spectral bandwidth.** The spectral bandwidth [27] draws on the centroid and the spectrogram bins to be calculated. It determines the quality of sound and indicates the extent of the spectrum of sound within a frame. It is the interval along the wavelength axis whereby a radiated spectral measure is not less than half its maximum value.

## 3.2   Machine Learning Classification Models

We design, train and evaluate machine learning models based on Artificial Neural Networks (ANN), Support Vector Machines (SVMs), Random Forest (RF) and $k$-Nearest Neighbor ($k$-NN). The inputs for the models are the 26 features, namely: 20 Mel-frequency cepstral coefficients (MFCCs) and 6 spectral features: RMS (Root Mean Square Error), Zero-crossing rate, Spectral roll-off, Spectral centroid, Spectral bandwidth and Chroma_stft. The individual frame features have been averaged to obtain these 26 features.

ANN models resemble the concept of the human brain's neural network and its neurons. ANN model typically consists of artificial neurons organized in layers known as the input, hidden and output layers. The model essentially processes data through a series of functions to optimize an error function and determine the parameters (weights associated with the neurons) within the network to solve a classification/prediction problem. Figure 3 illustrates the architecture of the ANN model utilized in this paper with an input layer of 26 inputs, 2 hidden layers with 100 and 50 neurons, respectively and an output layer with 11 neurons corresponding to the 11 classes. The number of neurons and hidden layers have been selected by experimentation. We utilize for the experiments the Keras[2] framework, which is the most used deep learning framework among top-5 winning teams on Kaggle[3]. The activation function utilised in in the hidden layers is the ReLU (rectified linear unit) activation function $f(x) = max(0, x)$. SoftMax activation function is applied to the output layer $\sigma(z) = \frac{\exp^{z_i}}{\sum_{j=1}^{11} e^{z_j}}$. We utilize Dropout and Batch Normalisation to reduce overfitting [14]. The Adam optimiser proposed in [21] is used as optimization algorithm.

SVMs [9] are supervised machine learning models that provide robust classification accuracy by projecting the data points to a higher dimensional feature space aiming at finding an optimal hyperplane that separates positive and negative classes. The mapping into high-dimensional feature spaces is achieved by the so-called kernel trick. In this work we use scikit-learn[4] library to implement SVM and a Radial Basis Function (RBF) kernel.

---

[2] https://keras.io/.
[3] https://www.kaggle.com/.
[4] https://scikit-learn.org/stable/.

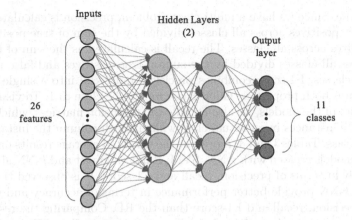

**Fig. 3.** ANN model architecture illustration

RF is an ensemble classification and regression technique [5,18,19] that has proved to be highly accurate. The ensemble is designed to train more than one classifier and then aggregate the predictions of all models and perform predictions by majority voting, i.e., the class selected by most trees. RF reduces the overfitting of the individual trees and outperforms decision trees. A good ensemble needs models to be diverse enough and independent from each other to ensure good performance. RF generates a diversified ensemble using Bootstrap aggregating (Bagging). Bagging is a sampling method that samples data from the training set with replacement. With such an approach, an instance in the dataset can be sampled more than once for the same model. At the same time, other instances may not appear at all during the training process. We use scikit-learn[5] library for the implementation of RF and set the maximum depth of the tree to 20.

K-nearest neighbors algorithm (k-NN) [3] is a non-parametric classification method where the input consists of the $k$ closest training examples in a data set and the output in the case of classification is a class membership. A sample is assigned to the class most common among its $k$ nearest neighbors. The number $k$ is typically chosen by heuristics. After experimentation we selected $k = 3$ and used scikit-learn (see Footnote 5) library for the implementation.

## 4    Results and Discussion

We split the data into training and testing subsets at ratios 0.7 and 0.3 accordingly. 10% from the training data is used as a validation dataset, which reduces the training data to 63%. The ANNs model was trained for 150 epochs, while for the SVM model, the maximum iterations parameter was set to 500. The performance of the models is evaluated in terms of accuracy, precision, recall

---

[5] https://scikit-learn.org/stable/.

and F1-score. Since we have a multi-class problem, precision is calculated as the sum of true positives across all classes divided by the sum of true positives and false positives across all classes. The recall is calculated as the sum of true positives across all classes divided by the sum of true positives and false negatives across all classes. F1-score combines precision and recall into a single measure that captures both properties. Good F1-score will be close to 1. To visualize the performance of the models, we also include the confusion matrices, which display in a row the instances in an actual class while in each column the instances in a predicted class. Tables 3 and 4, represent the weighted average results on the test set of the models created with ANN, SVM, Random Forest and $k$-NN algorithms respectively in terms of precision, recall and F1-score. It is observed that ANN, SVM and $k$-NN provide better performance in terms of accuracy and weighted average precision, recall and F1-score than the RF. Comparing the results in 3 and 4 with respect ti the weighted average precision, recall and F1-score for the four methods we find that the best result is achieved with $k$-NN accuracy 0.988. This accuracy is slightly better than previously reported accuracy Hossain et al. [20] but it should be noted that in the paper [20] the gender classification was not considered and the results are not directly comparable. Figure 4 presents the confusion matrix for test results obtained with the $k$-NN. It can be noted that Scottish male can be confused with Northern male or Southern male, Southern male with Northern male, Scottish female with Southern female in a small number of cases. However, confusing the gender seems very rare. Confusing Scottish speakers with Northern speakers may be due to some extent to the proximity of the geographical regions. The results suggest that utilizing machine learning methods is feasible for detecting dialects as well as the gender of a speaker based on features extracted from the voice sample.

**Table 3. ANN(left) and SVM(right) results**

| | Precision | Recall | F1-score | Precision | Recall | F1-score | Support |
|---|---|---|---|---|---|---|---|
| irm | 0.993 | 1.000 | 0.996 | 1.00 | 0.985 | 0.993 | 135 |
| mif | 0.974 | 1.00 | 0.987 | 1.00 | 1.00 | 1.00 | 74 |
| mim | 0.985 | 0.970 | 0.978 | 1.00 | 0.926 | 0.962 | 135 |
| nof | 0.969 | 0.982 | 0.976 | 0.996 | 0.996 | 0.996 | 225 |
| nom | 0.970 | 0.983 | 0.976 | 0.952 | 0.979 | 0.966 | 629 |
| scf | 0.981 | 0.963 | 0.972 | 0.989 | 0.963 | 0.975 | 268 |
| scm | 0.986 | 0.974 | 0.980 | 0.989 | 0.939 | 0.964 | 495 |
| sof | 0.991 | 0.993 | 0.992 | 0.992 | 0.995 | 0.994 | 1248 |
| som | 0.978 | 0.980 | 0.979 | 0.967 | 0.988 | 0.978 | 1300 |
| wef | 0.994 | 0.989 | 0.992 | 0.989 | 0.994 | 0.992 | 360 |
| wem | 0.990 | 0.982 | 0.986 | 1.000 | 0.982 | 0.991 | 495 |
| accuracy | 0.983 | 0.983 | 0.983 | 0.982 | 0.982 | 0.982 | |
| macro avg | 0.983 | 0.983 | 0.983 | 0.988 | 0.977 | 0.983 | 5364 |
| weight. avg | 0.983 | 0.983 | 0.983 | 0.982 | 0.982 | 0.982 | 5364 |

Table 4. RF(left) and KNN(right) results

| | Precision | Recall | F1-score | | Precision | Recall | F1-score | Support |
|---|---|---|---|---|---|---|---|---|
| irm | 0.985 | 0.970 | 0.978 | | 1.00 | 0.993 | 0.996 | 135 |
| mif | 1.00 | 0.932 | 0.965 | | 0.974 | 1.000 | 0.987 | 74 |
| mim | 1.00 | 0.807 | 0.893 | | 0.963 | 0.963 | 0.963 | 135 |
| nof | 0.990 | 0.907 | 0.947 | | 0.978 | 0.991 | 0.985 | 225 |
| nom | 0.930 | 0.946 | 0.938 | | 0.965 | 0.994 | 0.979 | 629 |
| scf | 0.987 | 0.877 | 0.929 | | 0.974 | 0.970 | 0.972 | 268 |
| scm | 0.991 | 0.867 | 0.925 | | 0.994 | 0.974 | 0.984 | 495 |
| sof | 0.950 | 0.997 | 0.973 | | 0.997 | 0.995 | 0.996 | 1248 |
| som | 0.913 | 0.985 | 0.947 | | 0.991 | 0.991 | 0.991 | 1300 |
| wef | 0.989 | 0.967 | 0.978 | | 0.989 | 0.992 | 0.990 | 360 |
| wem | 0.979 | 0.933 | 0.956 | | 0.998 | 0.976 | 0.987 | 495 |
| accuracy | 0.952 | 0.952 | 0.952 | | 0.988 | 0.988 | 0.988 | |
| macro avg | 0.974 | 0.926 | 0.948 | | 0.984 | 0.985 | 0.984 | 5364 |
| weight. avg | 0.954 | 0.952 | 0.952 | | 0.988 | 0.988 | 0.988 | 5364 |

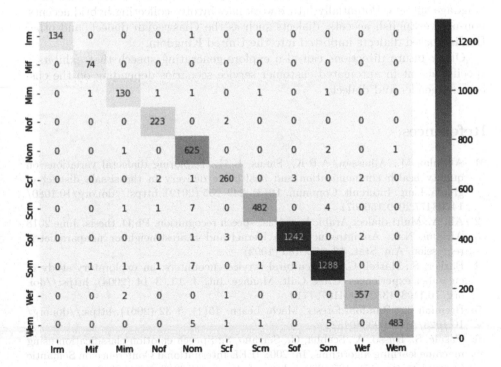

Fig. 4. k-NN confusion matrix

# 5   Conclusions

In this paper, we have reviewed the importance of recognition of dialects and gender in relation to automated customer services, e-commerce, or the service industry. We have addressed the problem of automatic recognition of the geographical origin and gender based on six regional dialects of the United Kingdom. We presented several classification algorithms for recognizing dialects and gender of an English speaker. We have used 26 features, namely: 20 Mel-frequency cepstral coefficients (MFCCs) and 6 spectral features to train models based on ANN, SVMs, RF and $k$-NN and subsequently evaluated the performance of models. The ANN, SVM and $k$-NN performed better than the RF, but it was observed that all models provide reasonable performance. The results show the potential of the proposed approach for speech recognition of dialects and the gender of the speaker.

While the quality of recorded speech datasets is continuously improving, there are still numerous gaps in terms of human mistakes and natural-sounding recordings. Furthermore, while machine learning is growing in its capacity to handle low-resource categories of speech, such as indigenous languages and informal dialects, there is a need to collect data and more intensive studies into these language subsets. Potentially future work may involve collecting hybrid accents, non-native English accents, dialects such as the Glaswegian dialect, and other English-based dialects imported into the United Kingdom.

Other future directions can also explore generating speech that exhibits a specific accent in automated customer service scenarios depending on the customers' gender and dialect.

# References

1. Abdulai, M., Alhassan, A.R.K., Sanus, K.M.: Exploring dialectal variations on quality health communication and healthcare delivery in the sissala district of ghana. Lang. Intercult. Commun. **19**(3), 242–255 (2019). https://doi.org/10.1080/14708477.2019.1569671
2. Ali, A.: Multi-dialect Arabic broadcast speech recognition. Ph.D. thesis, June 2018
3. Altman, N.S.: An introduction to Kernel and nearest-neighbor nonparametric regression. Am. Stat. **46**, 175–185 (1992)
4. Barker, S., Hartel, C.: Intercultural service encounters: an exploratory study of customer experiences. Cross Cult. Manage. Int. J. **11**, 3–14 (2004). https://doi.org/10.1108/13527600410797710
5. Breiman, L.: Random forests. Mach. Learn. **45**(1), 5–32 (2001). https://doi.org/10.1023/A:1010933404324
6. Casale, S., Russo, A., Scebba, G., Serrano, S.: Speech emotion classification using machine learning algorithms. In: 2008 IEEE International Conference on Semantic Computing, pp. 158–165 (2008). https://doi.org/10.1109/ICSC.2008.43
7. CDEI: Smart speakers and voice assistants. CDEI Report at https://www.gov.uk/government/publications/cdei-publishes-its-first-series-of-three-snapshot-papers-ethical-issues-in-ai/snapshot-paper-smart-speakers-and-voice-assistants (2019)

8. Chai, T., Draxler, R.R.: Root mean square error (RMSE) or mean absolute error (MAE)?-arguments against avoiding RMSE in the literature. Geosci. Model Dev. **7**(3), 1247–1250 (2014)
9. Cortes, C., Vapnik, V.: Support-vector networks. Mach. Learn. **20**(3), 273–297 (1995). https://doi.org/10.1023/A:1022627411411
10. Daugherty, P.R., Wilson, H.J., Chowdhury, R.: Using artificial intelligence to promote diversity. MIT Sloan Manage. Rev. **60**(2), 1 (2019)
11. Demirsahin, I., Kjartansson, O., Gutkin, A., Rivera, C.: Open-source multi-speaker corpora of the English accents in the British Isles. In: Proceedings of The 12th Language Resources and Evaluation Conference (LREC), pp. 6532–6541. European Language Resources Association (ELRA), Marseille, France, May 2020. https://www.aclweb.org/anthology/2020.lrec-1.804
12. Dobbriner, J., Jokisch, O.: Towards a dialect classification in German speech samples. In: Salah, A.A., Karpov, A., Potapova, R. (eds.) SPECOM 2019. LNCS (LNAI), vol. 11658, pp. 64–74. Springer, Cham (2019). https://doi.org/10.1007/978-3-030-26061-3_7
13. Ellis, D.: Chroma feature analysis and synthesis. Resources of Laboratory for the Recognition and Organization of Speech and Audio- LabROSA (2007)
14. Goodfellow, I.J., Bengio, Y., Courville, A.: Deep Learning. MIT Press, Cambridge (2016). http://www.deeplearningbook.org
15. Google.: Crowdsourced high quality UK and Ireland English dialect speech data set by google. SLR83. http://www.openslr.org/83 (2019)
16. Fabien, F.P.G., Delerue, O.: On the use of zero-crossing rate for an application of classification of percussive sounds. In: Proceedings of the COST G-6 Conference on Digital Audio Effects (DAFX-00) (2000)
17. Harako, K., et al.: Roll-off factor dependence of Nyquist pulse transmission. Opt. Express **24**(19), 21986–21994 (2016)
18. Ho, T.K.: Random decision forests. In: Proceedings of 3rd International Conference on Document Analysis and Recognition, vol. 1, pp. 278–282 (1995). https://doi.org/10.1109/ICDAR.1995.598994
19. Ho, T.K.: The random subspace method for constructing decision forests. IEEE Trans. Patt. Anal. Mach. Intell. **20**(8), 832–844 (1998). https://doi.org/10.1109/34.709601
20. Hossain, M.F., Hasan, M.M., Ali, H., Sarker, M.R.K.R., Hassan, M.T.: A machine learning approach to recognize speakers region of the united kingdom from continuous speech based on accent classification. In: 2020 11th International Conference on Electrical and Computer Engineering (ICECE), pp. 210–213 (2020). https://doi.org/10.1109/ICECE51571.2020.9393038
21. Kingma, D.P., Ba, J.: Adam: a method for stochastic optimization. In: Bengio, Y., LeCun, Y. (eds.) 3rd International Conference on Learning Representations, ICLR 2015, San Diego, CA, USA, 7–9 May 2015, Conference Track Proceedings (2015). http://arxiv.org/abs/1412.6980
22. Konda, A.K.R., Jimada, S., Cherukuri, P.A.A., Sarma, M.J.: Chatbot implementation for enhancement of student understanding—a natural language processing approach. In: Singh Mer, K.K., Semwal, V.B., Bijalwan, V., Crespo, R.G. (eds.) Proceedings of Integrated Intelligence Enable Networks and Computing. AIS, pp. 171–180. Springer, Singapore (2021). https://doi.org/10.1007/978-981-33-6307-6_18
23. Li, B., et al.: Multi-dialect speech recognition with a single sequence-to-sequence model, pp. 4749–4753 (2018). https://doi.org/10.1109/ICASSP.2018.8461886

24. Li, B., Dimitriadis, D., Stolcke, A.: Acoustic and lexical sentiment analysis for customer service calls. In: ICASSP 2019–2019 IEEE International Conference on Acoustics, Speech and Signal Processing (ICASSP), pp. 5876–5880 (2019). https://doi.org/10.1109/ICASSP.2019.8683679
25. Logan, B.: Mel frequency cepstral coefficients for music modeling. ISMIR 270 (2000)
26. Mai, R., Hoffmann, S.: Four positive effects of a salesperson's regional dialect in services selling. J. Serv. Res. **14**(4), 460–474 (2011). https://doi.org/10.1177/1094670511414551
27. McKinney, M., Breebaart, J.: Features for audio and music classification, November 2003
28. Nie, J., Wang, Q., Xiong, J.: Research on intelligent service of customer service system. Cogn. Comput. Syst. **3**(3), 197–205 (2021). https://doi.org/10.1049/ccs2.12012, https://ietresearch.onlinelibrary.wiley.com/doi/abs/10.1049/ccs2.12012
29. NLS: Prepare for the voice revolution, newcastle life sciences centre. https://www.pwc.com/us/en/services/consulting/library/consumer-intelligence-series/voice-assistants.html (2018)
30. Paulmann, S., Uskul, A.K.: Cross-cultural emotional prosody recognition: evidence from Chinese and British listeners. Cogn. Emotion **28**(2), 230–244 (2014). https://doi.org/10.1080/02699931.2013.812033, pMID: 23862740
31. PwC: Research fears technology could eradicate regional accents. https://www.life.org.uk/news/technology-could-eradicate-regional-accents (2018)
32. Sahu, M.P.: Automatic speech recognition in mobile customer care service. Int. J. New Pract. Manage. Eng. **4**(01), 07–11 (2015). https://doi.org/10.17762/ijnpme.v4i01.34, http://ijnpme.org/index.php/IJNPME/article/view/34
33. Spike: The dialect of tech. https://spike.digital/2018/08/28/the-dialect-of-tech/ (2018)
34. Yoo, S., Song, I., Bengio, Y.: A highly adaptive acoustic model for accurate multi-dialect speech recognition. In: ICASSP 2019–2019 IEEE International Conference on Acoustics, Speech and Signal Processing (ICASSP), pp. 5716–5720 (2019). https://doi.org/10.1109/ICASSP.2019.8683705
35. Zhong, J., Zhang, P., Li, X.: Adaptive recognition of different accents conversations based on convolutional neural network. Multimed. Tools Appl. **78**(21), 30749–30767 (2019). https://doi.org/10.1007/s11042-018-6590-4
36. Zhu, J., Wu, D.: Application of new artificial intelligence technology in the voice recognition and analysis system of electric power information customer service. In: Proceedings of the 2020 International Conference on Computers, Information Processing and Advanced Education, pp. 187–193. CIPAE 2020, Association for Computing Machinery, New York, NY, USA (2020). https://doi.org/10.1145/3419635.3419686

# Complex Layers of Formal Neurons

Leon Bobrowski[1,2]([✉]) [ID]

[1] Faculty of Computer Science, Bialystok University
of Technology, Wiejska 45A, Bialystok, Poland
l.bobrowski@pb.edu.pl
[2] Institute of Biocybernetics and Biomedical Engineering, PAS, Warsaw, Poland

**Abstract.** Data sets consisting of a relatively small number of high-dimensional feature vectors often appear, e.g. in bioinformatics preoblems. This data structure complicates the design of classification or regression models.

Complex layers of formal neurons (linear classifiers) can be designed on the basis of data sets composed of high-dimensional feature vectors. Linear classifiers of a given complex layer are designed on disjoint subsets of features obtained as a result of well-conditioned clustering. This feature clustering technique is related to matrix regularization.

**Keywords:** Formal neurons · Data mining · Complex layers of linear classifiers · Feature clustering

## 1 Introduction

Data sets consisting of a small number of high-dimensional feature vectors appear frequently in practice [1]. For example, genetic data sets have this structure. High-dimensional feature vectors representing the measurement results of a large number of different types of features can create difficulties in developing appropriate classification or regression models [2]. A large number of features results in many parameters in the model [3]. Overfiiting models can result from a large number of parameters [4]. Numerical difficulties appear in high-dimensional parameter spaces when inverting matrices or solving large scale eigenvalue problems [5]. Formal neuron netprks can also be designed (learned) from large data sets [6].

A dataset consisting of a small number of multivariate feature vectors enables the design of complex layers of formal neurons [7]. In this approach, a number of low-dimensional feature subspaces related to particular neurons in the layer are extracted from the multidimensional feature space [8]. The extracted feature subspaces are disjoint and have a dimension no greater than the number of feature vetors (objects) in a given dataset [9]. The presented work broadens the theoretical basis for designing complex layers of formal neurons. In particular, the problem of extracting linearly dependent feature vectors from a given data set is considered.

L. Iliadis et al. (Eds.): EANN 2022, CCIS 1600, pp. 81–89, 2022.
https://doi.org/10.1007/978-3-031-08223-8_7

## 2 Linear Separability With Margin

Consider the data set $C$ consisting $m$ feature vectors $\mathbf{x}_j = \left[x_{j,1}, ..., x_{j,n}\right]^T$ from the $n$-dimensional feature space $F[n]$ ($\mathbf{x}_j \in F[n]$):

$$C = \left\{\mathbf{x}_j\right\}, \text{ where } j = 1, ..., m \tag{1}$$

The feature vectors $\mathbf{x}_j$ in data set $C$ (1) represent individual patients (objects) $P_j$. The components $x_{j,i}(x_{j,i} \in R^1$ or $x_{j,i} \in \{0, 1\})$ of the feature vector $\mathbf{x}_j$ are numerical values of ndividual features (genes, measurements) $X_i(i = 1, ...., n)$ of the $j$-th patient $P_j$. We consider a situation in which the number $m$ of feature vectors $\mathbf{x}_j$ in the data set $C$ (1) is much smaller than the dimension $n$ of these vectors ($m << n$).

The selected feature vectors $\mathbf{x}_j$ from the data set $C$ (1) form the positive learning set $G_k^+$ and the negative learning set $G_k^-$ ($k = 1, ..., K$):

$$\mathbf{G}_k^+ = \{\mathbf{x}_j : j \in J_k^+\}, \text{ and } \mathbf{G}_k^- = \{\mathbf{x}_j : j \in J_k^-\} \tag{2}$$

where $J_k^+$ and $J_k^-$ are non-empty and disjoint sets ($J_k^+ \cap J_k^- = \varnothing$) of indices $j$ of selected feature vectors $\mathbf{x}_j$ from the data set $C$ (1).

The *positive* learning set $G_k^+$ consists of $m_k^+$ feature vectors $\mathbf{x}_j$ ($j \in J_k^+$) representing the category (class) $\omega_k^+$. Similarly, the *negative* learning set $G_k^-$ consists of $m_k^-$ feature vectors $\mathbf{x}_j(j \in J_k^-)$ representing the category $\omega_k^-$, where $m_k^+ + m_k^- \leq m$. The possibility of separating the learning sets $G_k^+$ and $G_k^-$ (2) by a certain hyperplane $H(\mathbf{w}_k, \theta_k)$ is investigated in neural networks or pattern recognition methods [10]. The hyperplane $H(\mathbf{w}_k, \theta_k)$ in the feature space $F[n]$ is defined as follows:

$$H(\mathbf{w}_k, \theta_k) = \{\mathbf{x} : \mathbf{w}_k^T\mathbf{x} = \theta_k\} \tag{3}$$

where $\mathbf{w}_k = \left[w_{k,1}, ..., w_{k,n}\right]^T \in R^n$ is the weight vector, $\theta_k \in R^1$ is the threshold, and $\mathbf{w}_k^T\mathbf{x} = \Sigma_i w_{k,i}x_i$ is the inner product.

*Definition 1:* The learning sets $G_k^+$ and $G_k^-$ (2) are *linearly separable with margin* in the feature space $F[n]$, if and only if there exists such a weight vector $\mathbf{w}_k(\mathbf{w}_k \in R^n)$, and a threshold $\theta_k(\theta_k \in R^1)$ that the hyperplane $H(\mathbf{w}_k, \theta_k)$ (3) separates these sets:

$$\begin{aligned}(\exists \mathbf{w}_k, \theta_k)(\forall \mathbf{x}_j \in G_k^+) \ \mathbf{w}_k^T\mathbf{x}_j \geq \theta_k + 1 \text{ and} \\ (\forall \mathbf{x}_j \in G_k^-) \ \mathbf{w}_k^T\mathbf{x}_j \leq \theta_k - 1\end{aligned} \tag{4}$$

According to the above inequalities, all feature vectors $\mathbf{x}_j$ from the learning set $G_k^+$ (2) lie on the positive side of the hyperplane $H(\mathbf{w}_k, \theta_k)$ (3), and all vectors $\mathbf{x}_j$ from the set $G_k^-$ are on the negative side of this hyperplane. The linear inequalities (4) can be represented as follows:

$$\begin{aligned}(\forall \mathbf{x}_j \in G_k^+) \ (\mathbf{w}_k/\|\mathbf{w}_k\|)^T\mathbf{x}_j \geq \theta_k/\|\mathbf{w}_k\|+1/\|\mathbf{w}_k\|, \text{ and} \\ (\forall \mathbf{x}_j \in G_k^-) \ (\mathbf{w}_k/\|\mathbf{w}_k\|)^T\mathbf{x}_j \leq \theta_k/\|\mathbf{w}_k\|-1/\|\mathbf{w}_k\|\end{aligned} \tag{5}$$

where $\|\mathbf{w}_k\|$ is the length of the vector $\mathbf{w}_k = \left[w_{k,1}, ..., w_{k,n}\right]^T$.

Inequalities (5) describe the linear separation of the learning sets $G_k^+$ and $G_k^-$ (2) with the margin $\delta(\mathbf{w_k})$ determined as follows in the case of the Euclidean ($L_2$) norm [10]:

$$\delta(\mathbf{w_k})_{L2} = 2/\left(\mathbf{w_k^T w_k}\right)^{1/2} = 2/(\Sigma_i w_{k,i}^2)^{1/2} \tag{6}$$

The margin $\delta(\mathbf{w_k})_{L1}$ based on the $L_1$ norm is determined below [9]:

$$\delta(\mathbf{w_k})_{L1} = 2/(\Sigma_i |w_{k,i}|) \tag{7}$$

Parameters $\mathbf{w_k} = \left[w_{k,1}, ..., w_{k,n}\right]^T$ and $\theta_k$ which allow the separation (5) of the learning sets $G_k^+$ and $G_k^-$ (2) can be used in the below classification rule in the feature space $F[n]$ ($\mathbf{x} \in F[n]$):

$$(\forall \mathbf{x_j} \in F[n])$$
$$\text{if } \mathbf{w_k^T x_j} > \theta_k, \text{ then } \mathbf{x_j} \in \omega_k^+, \text{ and if } \mathbf{w_k^T x} < \theta_k, \text{ then } \mathbf{x_j} \in \omega_k^- \tag{8}$$

where $\omega_k^+$ is the positive category represented by $m_k^+$ feature vectors $\mathbf{x_j}$ ($j \in J_k^+$) creating the learning set $G_k^+$ (1) and $\omega_k^-$ is the negative category represented by $m_k^-$ vectors $\mathbf{x_j}$ forming the set $G_k^-$.

It can be seen that the rule (8) correctly classifies all feature vectors $\mathbf{x_j}$ from the linearly separable learning sets $G_k^+$ and $G_k^-$ (2). Such feature vectors $\mathbf{x_{j'}}$ which are not included in the learning sets may, however, be incorrectly identified. The generalization power of the classification rule (8) is characterized by the frequency of misclassified feature vectors $\mathbf{x_{j'}}$ not belonging to the learning sets $G_k^+$ or $G_k^-$ (2). The power of generalization is high when a large number of new vectors $\mathbf{x_{j'}}$ ($\mathbf{x_{j'}} \notin G_k^+ \cup G_k^-$) are correctly classified. Increasing the margins $\delta(\mathbf{w_k})_{L2}$ (6) or $\delta(\mathbf{w_k})_{L1}$ (7) is aimed at increase the generalization power of the classification rule (8).

## 3 Complex Layers of Formal Neurons

The formal neuron is a simplified mathematical model of neuronal activity in the brain. The formal neuron was used in the *Perceptron*, one of the first model of neural networks plasticity proposed by F. Rosenblatt around 1950 [6]. Formal neurons can work as linear classifiers in pattern recognition tasks [2].

Formal neurons are usually defined on the feature vectors $\mathbf{x_j} = \left[x_{j,1}, ..., x_{j,n}\right]^T$ belonging to the $n$-dimensional feature space $F[n]$ ($\mathbf{x_j} \in F[n]$). The feature space $F[n]$ is represented by the set $F(n)$ of n features $X_i (i = 1, ...., n)$:

$$F(n) = \{X_1, ..., X_n\}. \tag{9}$$

The $i$-th component $x_{j,i}$ of the vector $\mathbf{x_j}$ is a numerical result of the feature $X_i$ measurement.

The *vertexial feature subspace* $R_k[n_k]$ of the dimension $n_k$ is represented by the subset $R_k(n_k)(R_k(n_k) \subset F(n))$ of $n_k$ selected features $X_{i(l)}$ [8]:

$$R_k(n_k) = \{X_{i(1)}, ..., X_{i(nk)}\} = \{X_i : i \in I_k\}. \tag{10}$$

where $I_k$ is a subset of the indices of $n_k$ selected features $X_i (X_i \in R_k(n_k))$.

The decision rule $r(\mathbf{w}_k[n_k], \theta_k; \mathbf{x}[n_k])$ of the $k$-th formal neuron $FN(\mathbf{w}_k[n_k], \theta_k)$ operating in the vertexial feature subspace $R_k[n_k]$ $(\mathbf{x}[n_k] \in R_k[n_k])$ is defined as [9]:

$$(\forall \mathbf{x}[n_k] \in R_k[n_k])$$

$$r_k = r(\mathbf{w}_k[n_k], \theta_k; \mathbf{x}) = \begin{array}{l} 1 \; if \; \mathbf{w}_k[n_k]^T \mathbf{x}[n_k] \geq \theta_k \\ \\ 0 \; if \; \mathbf{w}_k[n_k]^T \mathbf{x}[n_k] < \theta_k \end{array} \tag{11}$$

where $\mathbf{w}_k[n_k] = [w_1, \ldots, w_{nk}]^T$ is a weight vector of dimenstion $n_k (\mathbf{w}_k[n_k] \in R^{nk})$ and $\theta_k$ is the threshold $(\theta_k \in R^1)$.

In accordance with the decision rule (11), the formal neuron $FN(\mathbf{w}_k[n_k], \theta_k)$ is activated $(r_k = 1)$ by the input vector $\mathbf{x}[n_k] (\mathbf{x}[n_k] \in F_k[n_k])$ of the dimension $n_k$ if the weighted sum of the input signals (features) $X_i (i \in I_k$ (10)) is greater or equal to the threshold $\theta_k$.

Let us assume that the complex layer consists of $L$ formal neurons $FN(\mathbf{w}_{k(l)}[n_{k(l)}], \theta_{k(l)})$ (11), where $l = 1, \ldots, L$. Each of the neurons $FN(\mathbf{w}_{k(l)}[n_{k(l)}], \theta_{k(l)})$ (11) of the complex layer works in its own feature subspace $R_{k(l)}[n_{k(l)}]$ of the dimension $n_{k(l)}$. This means that the neuron $FN(\mathbf{w}_{k(l)}[n_{k(l)}], \theta_{k(l)})$ (11) receives only input vectors $\mathbf{x}[n_{k(l)}]$ belonging to the vertexial feature subspace $R_{k(l)}[n_{k(l)}]$ $(\mathbf{x}[n_{k(l)}] \in R_k[n_{k(l)}])$.

An additional assumption is made when designing complex layer of formal neurons $FN(\mathbf{w}_{k(l)}[n_{k(l)}], \theta_{k(l)})$ (11). Namely, it is assumed that the subsequent feature subsets $R_{k(l)}(n_{k(l)})$ (10) are disjoint:

$$(\forall l \in \{1, \ldots, L-1\}) \; R_{k(l)}(n_{k(l)}) \cap R_{k(l+1)}(n_{k(l+1)}) = \emptyset \tag{12}$$

## 4 Perceptron Penalty Functions with Zero Threshold

Consider the linear separability inequalities (4) in the following form:

$$(\exists \mathbf{w}_k) \; (\forall \mathbf{x}_j \in G_k^+) \; \mathbf{w}_k^T \mathbf{x}_j \geq 1 \; and$$
$$(\forall \mathbf{x}_j \in G_k^-) \; \mathbf{w}_k^T \mathbf{x}_j \leq -1 \tag{13}$$

The above inequalities result from (4) by setting the threshold $\theta_k$ equal zero $(\theta_k = 0)$. Iinequalities (13) can be represented in a simplified form:

$$(\forall \mathbf{w}_k) \; (\forall \mathbf{x}_j') \; \mathbf{w}_k^T \mathbf{x}_j \geq 1 \tag{14}$$

where $\mathbf{x}_j'$ is the veature vector $\mathbf{x}_j$ (2) signed with " $+$ " or "–":

$$(\forall \mathbf{x}_j \in G_k^+) \; \mathbf{x}_j' = \mathbf{x}_j \; and \; (\forall \mathbf{x}_j \in G_k^-) \; \mathbf{x}_j' = -\mathbf{x}_j \tag{15}$$

*Lemma 1:* The learning sets $G_k^+$ and $G_k^-$ (2) composed of linearly independent feature vectors $\mathbf{x}_j (\mathbf{x}_j \in F[n])$ are linearly separable with zero threshold (14) [8].

Perceptron penalty functions $\varphi_j(\mathbf{w})$ related to inequalities (14) are defined for each element $\mathbf{x}_j$ of the learning sets $G_k^+$ and $G_k^-$ (2) as:

$$(\forall \mathbf{x}_j \in G_k^+ \cup G_k^-) \; \varphi_j(\mathbf{w}) = \begin{cases} 1 - (\mathbf{x}_j')^T \mathbf{w} & \text{if } (\mathbf{x}_j')^T \mathbf{w} < 1 \\ \\ 0 & \text{if } (\mathbf{x}_j')^T \mathbf{w} \geq 1 \end{cases} \qquad (16)$$

The *perceptron* criterion function $\Phi_k(\mathbf{w})$ is defined as the sum of the penalty functions $\varphi_j(\mathbf{w})$ (16) [10]:

$$\Phi_k(\mathbf{w}) = \Sigma_j \varphi_j(\mathbf{w}) \qquad (17)$$

where the summation (17) follows the indices $j$ from the subset $J_k$:

$$J_k = \{j : \mathbf{x}_j \in G_k^+ \cup G_k^- (2)\} \qquad (18)$$

The criterion function $\Phi_k(\mathbf{w})$ (17) is related to the *error correction* algorithm, the basic algorithm in the *Perceptron* model [6].

The perceptron criterion function $\Phi_k(\mathbf{w})$ (17) is *convex and piecewise-linear (CPL)* with the global minimum in the optimal vertex $\mathbf{w}_k^*$:

$$(\exists \mathbf{w}_k^*) \; (\forall \mathbf{w} \in R^n) \; \Phi_k(\mathbf{w}) \geq \Phi_k(\mathbf{w}_k^*) = \Phi_k^* \geq 0 \qquad (19)$$

The below theorem can be proved [10]:

*Theorem 1:* The minimum value $\Phi_k^* = \Phi_k(\mathbf{w}_k^*)$ (19) of the perceptron criterion function $\Phi_k(\mathbf{w})$ (17) is equal to zero ($\Phi_k^* = 0$) if and only if the learning sets $G_k^+$ and $G_k^-$ (2) are linearly separable (14) with the threshold $\theta_k$ equal zero ($\theta_k = 0$).

The proof of Lemma 1 and Theorem 1 can be based on the vertexical linear equation defined in the work [9], and also described later in this text. In this approach, the optimal vertex $\mathbf{w}_{k(l)}^*$ is calculated as a solution of a well-defined system of $m$ linear equations, where $m$ is the number of feature vectors $\mathbf{x}_j$ with dimension $n$ in the learning sets $G_k^+$ and $G_k^-$ (2) ($m << n$).

The regularized criterion function $\Psi_{k,\lambda}(\mathbf{w})$ is defined as the weighted sum of the perceptron criterion function $\Phi_k(\mathbf{w})$ (17) and the absolute values $|w_i|$ of weighs $w_i$ [9]:

$$\Psi_{k,\lambda}(\mathbf{w}) = \Phi_k(\mathbf{w}) + \lambda \Sigma_{i\in\{1,...,n\}} |w_i| \qquad (20)$$

where $\mathbf{w} = [w_1, ..., w_n]^T$ and $\lambda \geq 0$ is the *cost level*.

The optimal vector $\mathbf{w}_{k,\lambda}^*$ constitutes the global minimum $\Psi_{k,\lambda}(\mathbf{w}_{k,\lambda}^*)$ of the *CPL* criterion function $\Psi_{k,\lambda}(\mathbf{w})$ (20) defined on elements $\mathbf{x}_j$ of the learning sets $G_k^+$ and $G_k^-$ (2):

$$(\exists \mathbf{w}_{k,\lambda}^*) \; (\forall \mathbf{w} \in R^n) \; \Psi_{k,\lambda}(\mathbf{w}) \geq \Psi_k(\mathbf{w}_{k,\lambda}^*) = \Psi_{k,\lambda}^* > 0 \qquad (21)$$

The minimum value $\Psi_{k,\lambda}^*$ of the criterion function $\Psi_k(\mathbf{v})$ (20) is used, among others, in the *relaxed linear separability (RLS)* method of selecting optimal subsets of genes [11]. It has been shown that the minimization of the regularized criterion function $\Psi_{k,\lambda}(\mathbf{w})$ (20) allows for the maximization of the margin $\delta(\mathbf{w}_k)_{L1}$ (7) in the decision rule (8) [9].

## 5   Dual Hyperplanes and Vertices in the Parameter Space

The dual hyperplanes $h_j^1$ are defined in the parameter space $R^n$ by signed feature vectors $x_j{'}$ (15):

$$(\forall x_j \in G_k^+ \cup G_k^- (2))\ h_j^1 = \{w \in R^n : (x_j{'})^T w = 1\} \tag{22}$$

The dual hyperplanes $h_j^0$ are defined by unit vectors $e_i$ [10]:

$$\left(\forall i \in (1, \ldots, n) h_i^0 = \left\{w \in R^n : e_i^T w = 0\right\} = \left\{w \in R^n : w_i = 0\right\}\right. \tag{23}$$

*Definition 2:* The vertex $w_k$ of the rank $r$ in the parameter space $R^n$ ($r \leq n$) is located at the intersection of $r$ hyperplanes $h_j^1$ (22) and $n$ - $r$ hyperplanes $h_i^0$ (23), where $i \in I_k(r)$.

The vertex $w_k$ of the rank $r = m_k^+ + m_k^-$ (2) is defined by the below system of $n$ linear equations:

$$(\forall x_j \in G_k^+ \cup G_k^- (2)) \left(x_j'\right)^T w_k = 1$$
$$(\forall i(l) \in I_k(r)) \quad e_{i(l)}^T w_k = 0 \tag{24}$$

where $I_k(r) = \{i(1), \ldots, i(n - r)\}$ is the $k$-th subset of indices $i(l)$ defining $n - r$ unit vectors $e_i$ with the hyperplanes $h_i^0$ (23) passing through the vertex $w_k$.

The linear Eqs. (24) can be given in the matrix form [8]:

$$B_k(r) w_k(r) = 1_k(r) \tag{25}$$

where $1_k(r) = [1, \ldots, 1, 0, \ldots, 0]^T$ is a vector in which the first $r$ components are equal to one and the remaining $n - r$ components are zero.

The square matrix $B_k(r)$ in Eq. (25) contains $r$ signed vectors $x_j'$ (15) ($j = 1, \ldots, r$) and has the following structure [8]:

$$B_k(r) = \left[x_1', \ldots, x_r', e_{i(r+1)}, \ldots, e_{i(n)}\right]^T \tag{26}$$

where the symbol $e_{i(l)}$ denotes such unit vector, which forms the $l$-th row ($l = r + 1, \ldots, n$) of the matrix $B_k(r)$.

The non-singular matrix $B_k(r)$ (26) formed by $r$ linearly independent feature vectors $x_j'$ (17) ($j \in J_k$) from the learning sets (2) and $n - r$ unit vectors $e_i(i \in I_k(r)$ (24)) is the *basis* of the feature space $F[n]$ related to the vertex $w_k(r)$ [8]:

$$w_k(r) = B_k(r)^{-1} 1_k(r) = r_1 + \ldots + r_r \tag{27}$$

where $B_k(r)^{-1} = \left[r_1(r), \ldots, r_r(r), r_{r+1}(r), \ldots, r_n(r)\right]$ is the inverse matrix.

*Lemma 2:* The last $n$ - $r$ components $w_{k,i}$ of the parameter vector (vertex) $w_k(r) = \left[W_{k,1}, \ldots, W_{k,n}\right]^T$ (27) are equal to zero

$$(\forall l \in \{r + 1, \ldots, n\})\ w_{k,l} = 0 \tag{29}$$

The thesis of this lemma results directly from the equations $w_k(r)^T e_i = 0$ (24).

# 6  Minimization of the Perceptron Criterion Function

The global minimum value $\Phi_k^* = \Phi_k(w_k^*)$ (19) of the perceptron criterion function $\Phi_k(w)$ (17) can be found in one of vertices using the basis exchange algorithm [10]. In this approach, the optimal vertex $w_k^*$, which is the minimum $\Phi_k(W_k^*)$ (19), is reached after a finite number $L$ of steps $l$ between vertices $w_k(l)$ (27) [9]:

$$w_k(0) \rightarrow w_k(1) \rightarrow \ldots . \rightarrow w_k(L) = w_k^* \tag{30}$$

The sequence of vertices $w_k(l)$ (30) is related by the Eq. (27) to the following sequence of the inverse matrices $B_k(l)^{-1}$:

$$B_k(0)^{-1} \rightarrow B_k(1)^{-1} \rightarrow \ldots . \rightarrow B_k(L)^{-1} \tag{31}$$

The sequence of vertices $w_k(l)$ (30) usually starts with the vertex $w_k(0) = [0,\ldots, 0]^T$ related to the identity matrix $B_k(0) = I_n = [e_1, \ldots, e_n]^T$ of the dimension $n \times n$ [10]. The final vertex $w_k(l)$ (30) provides the minimal value $\Phi_k(w_k^*)$ (19) of the perceptron criterion function $\Phi_k(w)$ (17).

During the $l$-th step one of the unit vectors $e_i$ contained in the matrix (basis) $B_k(l - 1) = [x_1', \ldots, x_{l-1}', e_{i(l)}, \ldots, e_{i(n)}]^T$ (26) is replaced by the signed vector $x_l'$ (17) and the matrix $B_k(l) = [x_1', \ldots, x_l', e_{i(l+1)}, \ldots, e_{i(n)}]^T$ related to the vertex $w_k(l)$ (30) appears:

$$(\forall l \in \{1, \ldots, L\})\ \ B_k(l - 1) \rightarrow B_k(l) \tag{32}$$

According to the vector Gauss-Jordan transformation, replacing the unit vector $e_{i(l)}$ with the feature vector $x_l'$ (15) during the $l$ - th step results in the following modifications of the columns $r_i(l - 1)$ of the inverse matrix $B_k(l - 1)^{-1} = [r_1(l - 1), \ldots, r_l(l - 1), r_{l+1}(l - 1), \ldots, r_n(l - 1)]$ [10]:

$$r_{i(l)}(l) = \left(1/r_{i(l)}(l - 1)^T x_l'\right) r_{i(l)}(l - 1)$$

and $(\forall i \neq i(l))\ \ r_i(l) = r_i(l - 1) - \left(r_i(l - 1)^T x_l'\right) r_{i(l)}(l) \tag{33}$

$$= r_i(l - 1) - \left(r_i(l - 1)^T x_l'/r_{i(l)}(l - 1)^T x_l'\right) r_{i(l)}(l - 1)$$

where $i(l)$ is the index of the unit vector $e_{i(l)}$ leaving the basis $B_k(l - 1)$ (26) during the $l$-th step.

The design procedure can ensure that the perceptron criterion function $\Phi_k(W)$ (17) decreases in successive vertices $w_k(l)$ (30) [10]:

$$\Phi_k(w_k(0)) > \Phi_k(w_k(1)) > \ldots > \Phi_k(w_k(L)) \tag{34}$$

The *exit criterion* allows to choose such a unit vector $e_{i(l)}$ leaving the basis $B_k(l)$ (28), that the condition (34) is satisfied at the vertex $w_k(l)$.

88    L. Bobrowski

## 7  Selected Properties of Optimal Vertices

The optimal vertex $\mathbf{w}_k^*$ constituting the minimum $\Phi_k\left(\mathbf{w}_k^*\right)$ (19) of the perceptron criterion function $\Phi_k(\mathbf{w})$ (17) can be obtained as end vertex $\mathbf{w}_k(L)$ in the sequence (30) associated with the sequence (31) of the inverse matrices $\mathbf{B}_k(l)^{-1}$. The vector Gauss-Jordan transformation (33) allows to compute efficiently the colums $\mathbf{r}_i(l)$ of the inverse matrix $\mathbf{B}_k(l)^{-1}$ on the basis of the colums $\mathbf{r}_i(l-1)$ of the inverse matrix $\mathbf{B}_k(l-1)^{-1}$.

During the $l$-th step (33) the $i(l)$-th unit vector $\mathbf{e}_{i(l)}$ is removed from the basis $\mathbf{B}_k(l-1) = \left[\mathbf{x}_1', \ldots, \mathbf{x}_{l-1}', \mathbf{e}_{i(l)},\ldots \mathbf{e}_{i(n)}\right]^T$ and the signed feature vector $\mathbf{x}_l'$ (15) is introduced into this basis. The transformation (33) related to the introduction of the vector $\mathbf{x}_l'$ (15) to the basis $\mathbf{B}_k(l-1)$ cannot be realized due to division by zero if the following *condition of collinearity* is met [10]:

$$\mathbf{r}_{i(l)}(l-1)^T\mathbf{x}_l' = 0 \tag{35}$$

The new feature vector $\mathbf{x}_l'$ (15) is a linear combination of vectors $\mathbf{x}_j'$ already contained in the basis $\mathbf{B}_k(l-1) = \left[\mathbf{x}_1', \ldots, \mathbf{x}_{l-1}', \mathbf{e}_{i(l)}, \ldots, \mathbf{e}_{i(n)}\right]^T$ (28) if the following equation holds:

$$\mathbf{x}_l' = \alpha_1\mathbf{x}_1' + \ldots + \alpha_{l-1}\mathbf{x}_{l-1}' \tag{36}$$

where $(\forall i \in \{1, \ldots, l-1\})\alpha_i \in R^1$.

*Lemma 3:* Such a feature vector $\mathbf{x}_l'$ (15) which satisfies the condition of collinearity (35), is a linear combination (36) of the vectors $\mathbf{x}_j'$ already contained in the basis $\mathbf{B}_k(l-1) = \left[\mathbf{x}_1', \ldots, \mathbf{x}_{l-1}', \mathbf{e}_{i(l)}, \ldots, \mathbf{e}_{i(n)}\right]^T$.

The proof of this lemma can be based on the inversion equation $\mathbf{B}_k(l-1) \mathbf{B}_k(l-1)^{-1} = \mathbf{I}_n$ of the matrix $\mathbf{B}_k(l-1)$. The Eq. (35) holds because:

$$(\forall i \in \{1, \ldots, l-1\}) \quad \mathbf{r_i}(l-1)^T\mathbf{x}_l' = 0 \tag{37}$$

It can also be shown that the condition of collinearity (35) means a linear dependendce (36) of the feature vector $\mathbf{x}_l'$ (15) on the vectors $\mathbf{x}_j'$ contained in the basis $\mathbf{B}_k(l-1) = \left[\mathbf{x}_1', \ldots, \mathbf{x}_{l-1}', \mathbf{e}_{i(l)}, \ldots, \mathbf{e}_{i(n)}\right]^T$ (28).

*Lemma 4:* The vector $\mathbf{r}_l(l-1)$ forming the $l$-th column of the inverse matrix $\mathbf{B}_k(l-1)^{-1} = \left[\mathbf{r}_1(l-1), \ldots, \mathbf{r}_{l-1}(l-1), \mathbf{r}_l(l-1), \ldots, \mathbf{r}_n(l-1)\right]$ during the $(l-1)$ - th step has the following structure:

$$\mathbf{r}_l(l-1) = \left[\mathbf{r}_{l,1}(l-1), \ldots, \mathbf{r}_{l,l-1}(l-1), 0, \ldots, 0, 1, 0, \ldots, 0\right]^T \tag{38}$$

The last $n-1+1$ components $\mathbf{r}_{l,i}(l-1)$ of the vector $\mathbf{r}_{l,i}(l-1)$ (38) are equal to zero or one. The $l$-th component $\mathbf{r}_{l,l}(l)$ is equal to one $\left(\mathbf{r}_{l,l}(l) = 1\right)$.

The proof of this lemma can also be based on the inversion equation.

The condition of collinearity (35) can be *relaxed* on the basis of the vector $\mathbf{r}_l(l-1)$ (38) omitting components $\mathbf{r}_{l,i}(l-1)$ equal to zero [11]. The related components $\mathbf{x}_{l,i'}'$ of the vector $\mathbf{x}_l'$ (15) are also omitted.

## 8 Concluding Remarks

The relaxed collinearity condition (35) can be used to design complex layers of formal neurons $FN(\mathbf{w}_k[n_k], \theta_k)$ (11), for example to find and exclude such features $X_i$ which are linearly dependent [10].

Complex layers can be designed on the basis of the data set $C$ (1) consisting of a small number $m$ of high-dimensional ($m << n$) feature vectors $\mathbf{x}_j$ (1) by minimizing the perceptron criterion function $\Phi_k(\mathbf{w})$ (17) or the criterion function $\Psi_{k,\lambda}(\mathbf{w})$ (20) with regularization [10].

An important property of complex layers is that each neuron $FN(\mathbf{w}_k[n_k], \theta_k)$ (11) in the layer receives input vectors $\mathbf{x}_j[n_k]$ from its own channel. In other words, each neuron operates in a separate feature subspace $R_k[n_k]$ (10).

The described methodology of designing complex layers enables the exploration of large, multi-dimensional data sets with a heterogeneous structure (big data). Such a property is based on the decomposition of feature space $F[n]$ into separate feature subspaces $R_k[n_k]$ (signal channels) (11) linked to individual neurons of the layer. The described method of decomposition and reduction of high-dimensional feature spaces $F[n]$ may also be useful in developing new, more effective deep learning procedures.

**Acknowledgments.** The presented study was supported by the grant WZ/WI-IIT/3/2020 from the Bialystok University of Technology and funded from the resources for research by the Polish Ministry of Science and Higher Education.

## References

1. Duda, O.R., Hart, P.E., Stork, D.G.: Pattern Classification. Wiley, New York (2001)
2. Bishop C.M.: Pattern Recognition and Machine Learning. Springer, Cham (2006)
3. Kuncheva, L.: Combining Pattern Classifiers: Methods and Algorithms, 2nd edn. J. Wiley, New Jersey (2014)
4. Johnson, R.A., Wichern, D.W.: Applied Multivariate Statistical Analysis. Prentice- Hall Inc., Englewood Cliffs (2002)
5. Jolliffe, I.T.: Principal Component Analysis. Springer, NY (2002)
6. Rosenblatt, F.: Principles of neurodynamics. Spartan Books, Washington (1962)
7. Bobrowski, L.: Complexes of low dimensional linear classifiers with $L_1$ margins. In: Nguyen, N.-T., et al. (eds.) Intelligent Information and Database Systems. Springer, pp. 29–40 (2021)
8. Bobrowski, L., Łukaszuk, T.: Repeatable functionalities in complex layers of formal neurons. In: Iliadis, L., Macintyre, J., Jayne, C., Pimenidis, E. (eds.) EANN 2021. PINNS, vol. 3, pp. 436–447. Springer, Cham (2021). https://doi.org/10.1007/978-3-030-80568-5_36
9. Bobrowski, L.: Computing on vertices in data mining, pp. 1–19, Data mining, Intech Open (2021)
10. Bobrowski, L.: Data Exploration and Linear Separability, pp. 1–172, Lambert Academic Publishing (2019)
11. Bobrowski, L., Łukaszuk, T.: Relaxed Linear Separability (RLS) approach to feature (gene) subset selection. In: Selected Works in Bioinformatics X Xia, INTECH, pp. 103–118 (2011)

# Novel Decision Forest Building Techniques by Utilising Correlation Coefficient Methods

Efthyvoulos Drousiotis[1]([✉]), Lei Shi[2]([✉]), Paul G. Spirakis[3,4], and Simon Maskell[1]

[1] Department of Electrical Engineering and Electronics, University of Liverpool, Liverpool L69 3GJ, UK
{E.Drousiotis,S.Maskell}@liverpool.ac.uk
[2] Department of Computer Science, Durham University, Durham DH1 3DE, UK
lei.shi@durham.ac.uk
[3] Department of Computer Science, University of Liverpool, Liverpool L69 3BX, UK
spirakis@liverpool.ac.uk
[4] Department of Computer Engineering and Informatics, University of Patras, 26504 Patras, Greece

**Abstract.** Decision Forests have attracted the academic community's interest mainly due to their simplicity and transparency. This paper proposes two novel decision forest building techniques, called Maximal Information Coefficient Forest (MICF) and Pearson's Correlation Coefficient Forest (PCCF). The proposed new algorithms use Pearson's Correlation Coefficient (PCC) and Maximal Information Coefficient (MIC) as extra measures of the classification capacity score of each feature. Using those approaches, we improve the picking of the most convenient feature at each splitting node, the feature with the greatest Gain Ratio. We conduct experiments on 12 datasets that are available in the publicly accessible UCI machine learning repository. Our experimental results indicate that the proposed methods have the best average ensemble accuracy rank of 1.3 (for MICF) and 3.0 (for PCCF), compared to their closest competitor, Random Forest (RF), which has an average rank of 4.3. Additionally, the results from Friedman and Bonferroni-Dunn tests indicate statistically significant improvement.

**Keywords:** Decision forests · Tree-based learning · Ensemble learning · Classification · Machine learning

## 1 Introduction

Technological development has altered our approach to data management throughout the years. Data mining is currently being used for diverse datasets, aiming to discover hidden patterns and generate suitable predictions and/or descriptions. Data mining is set of techniques that extract hidden information such as patterns, correlations, or rules from massive data. Classification is highly

© Springer Nature Switzerland AG 2022
L. Iliadis et al. (Eds.): EANN 2022, CCIS 1600, pp. 90–102, 2022.
https://doi.org/10.1007/978-3-031-08223-8_8

essential in the field of data mining for both predicting the 'class' of an unknown instance and identifying trends in data. Furthermore, machines are increasingly being held accountable for societal decisions and various domains such as injustice [24], medicine [20], policing [19], and education [8,9], while the algorithmic transparency is an undeniable characteristic, they must have. Algorithms functioning as black boxes produce results and decisions that humans are eager to follow since they are proven to be helpful. Errors do exist and will continue to occur regardless of how much the underlying systems grow as more data becomes accessible to them, and more sophisticated algorithms learn from it. This awareness has given rise to either focusing more on more transparent algorithms such as decision trees and decision forests or trying to transparentise classical blackbox algorithms such as Neural Networks.

Decision forests are a popular classification method, as they can learn the patterns in a dataset in an easy way that closely matches human thinking. Importantly, unlike other classifiers (e.g., neural networks, k-nearest neighbours, and support vector machines), decision forests can train on both categorical and numerical data [18], and generate human-interpretable knowledge [22], which enable them to increase their application domains further. Decision forests are considered among the fastest machine learning algorithms in terms of training, testing, and predicting. It comes as no surprise that improving classification accuracy on unknown data within the restrictions given by the training data is a desirable goal.

In this paper, we propose two novel decision forest building methods, i.e., the Maximal Information Coefficient Forest (MICF) and the Pearson's Correlation Coefficient Forest (PCCF). We aim to achieve a higher classification accuracy, than other famous variants of the decision forest algorithms, including Bagging, Random Subspace, Random Forest and Random Features Weights.

The rest of the present paper is organised as follows: Sect. 2 describes the related work. Our novel approach and the new algorithm are denoted in Sect. 3. Experimental results are drawn in Sect. 4 with a conclusion in Sect. 5.

## 2    Related Work

Many forest building methods have been proposed to produce more accurate and diversified trees by distinguishing the training dataset in various ways. As follows, we will examine several well-known algorithms.

*Bagging:* In Bagging [3], the dataset is randomly divided into a test set $T$ and a learning set $L$. A new learning set $L'$ is created randomly from the original learning set $L$, containing the same number of samples. Consequently, some samples in $L$ may be selected several times and others may not be selected at all. This method of generating a new learning set is called bootstrap sampling. In bagging, bootstrap sampling is used to generate number ($|T|$) of bootstrap samples $L_1, L_2, L_3, ...., L_r$. Afterwards, a decision tree algorithm uses each bootstrap sample $L_i (i = 1, 2, 3..., |T|)$ to build ($|T|$) number of trees for the forest.

*Random Subspace:* The Random Subspace method [14] is also called attribute bagging and feature bagging. It attempts to reduce the correlation between individual weak learners in an ensemble by training them on random selection of a subset $D'$ of features from the entire attribute space $D$. Features in $D'$ can be drawn at both node level and tree level. When drawn at the tree level, features in $D'$ continue to be the same for the tree, whereas when drawn at the node level, features $D'$ vary from one node to another in a tree. Through any known decision tree algorithms such as CART [5], the best attribute in $D'$ is calculated and determined to be the best splitting feature for the corresponding node.

*Random Feature Weights:* Random Feature Weights [17] is a tree ensemble construction method, where diversity is introduced into each individual tree using a random weight from a uniform distribution associated with each attribute. A weight stays the same for every node of a tree, while each tree acquires a different weight. In order to determine the best splitting feature at each node, merit values are calculated for each feature by multiplying their classification capacities such as Gini Index [5] by their respective random weights. Finally, the attribute with the highest excellence value is chosen as the splitting feature.

*Random Forest* [4] *(RF):* RF is considered to be among the state-of-the-art decision forest building algorithms, as it simply combines Random Subspace and Bagging algorithms where, in its simplest form, features $D'$ are randomly selected at the node level. Despite all the variants of decision forests algorithms, RF is the most popular among the research community mainly because of its publicly availability through the sci-kit learn Python library[1]. Moreover, [6] compared 179 classification algorithms emerging from 17 learning families over 121 datasets where it concluded that forests, and specifically random forests, tend to outperform the rest of the classification algorithms. Those results indicate that any enhancement beyond Random Forest will have a substantial impact on its broad application scope.

*Parallel Random Forest (PRF):* PRF [16] is a modification of RF to be more suitable for 'big data'. A PRF algorithm is optimised using the MIC optimisation technique as a single splitting criterion. Firstly, each feature correlation capacity score is calculated through MIC, and then, according to the level of score, the features are divided into three groups: 'low', 'medium', and 'high'. Features fell in the 'low' group are discarded, and thus a new feature subset ($D'$) with all the features from the 'medium' and 'high' groups is created. For each node, the splitting feature is chosen randomly from $D'$. A similar approach but for regression problems utilises MIC with information gain [13] as well, and it discards the low correlation features similarly to the PRF algorithm. Interestingly, they employ the roulette method so as to keep only the features with a high correlation capacity score.

   Therefore, intending to provide an enhanced generic decision forest building technique, this study considers satisfying two splitting criteria (MIC and Gain Ratio, PCC and Gain Ratio) focusing on classification tasks as well as taking

---

[1] https://scikit-learn.org.

into consideration low correlation features as hidden patterns that may still exist. Moreover, in contrast to the latest trend of improving decision forest algorithms in a problem specific manner, we present two generic methods, which improves the overall predictive accuracy.

In general, our experimental result shows that MICF and PCCF are more balanced and accurate decision forest algorithms. In brief, we itemise the novel contributions of both algorithms as follows:

- Proposing a weight assignment strategy that works in favour of the features with the highest classification capacity, but it does not discard features with lower classification capacity.
- Proposing a double metric strategy (Gain Ratio and MIC, Gain Ratio and PCC), which determines the best feature and threshold on each node on classification problems.
- Proposing a weight assignment strategy that helps maintain the diversity among the individual decision trees.

## 3    Proposed Methods

We propose two methods that create subsets from the feature space of the whole original dataset using correlation capacity scores(MIC and PCC), resulting in a higher predictive accuracy. In this paper, to the best of our knowledge, it is the first time the MIC and Gain Ratio (for MICF) and the PCC and Gain Ratio (for PCCF) are combined as splitting criteria (impurity measure) to improve the overall accuracy of a decision forest classifier algorithm. Next, we present the splitting criteria and learning algorithms, including the two main functions for MICF and PCCF methods. The other steps of the algorithms are identical to existing decision tree building algorithms such as CART.

### 3.1    Splitting Criteria

**Gain Ratio.** The normalisation of the Information gain of an attribute against how much entropy that attribute has. Entropy (see Eq. 1, $p_i$ is the probability of a data point in the subset of $D_i$ of a dataset $D$) can be described as the degree of uncertainty or a measure of purity, and it is bounded between 0 and 1. The higher entropy the higher diversion in data, while our aim is to determine a split to create a purer distribution (close to 0) of class values in the succeeding partitions than the original dataset $D$.

Entropy plays an important role in estimating the Information Gain, which is used in ID3(the preliminary Decision Tree algorithm) [21] to determine the best features that provide as much information about a class as possible. The aim is to decrease the level of entropy, as it begins with the root node and progresses to the leaf nodes by computing the difference in entropy before and after the split (see Eq. 2, where $Entropy_{t-1}$ is the entropy before splitting and $Entropy_t$ is the entropy after splitting).

Gain Ratio normalises Information Gain of a feature based on the amount of entropy it has (see Eq. 3). As shown in Eq. 3, when entropy is low, the Gain Ratio will be high, and vice versa.

$$Entropy(P) = -\sum_{i=1}^{n} p_i \log_2(p_i) \tag{1}$$

$$InformationGain = Entropy_{t-1} - Entropy_t \tag{2}$$

$$GainRatio = Information\ Gain\ /Entropy \tag{3}$$

**Pearson's Correlation Coefficient.** In statistics, Pearson's correlation coefficient is used to measure the statistical relationship or correlation among variables. It is based on the covariance matrix of the data to determine the strength of the connection between two vectors. Pearson's correlation coefficient between two vectors $a_i$ and $a_j$ is:

$$P(a_i, a_j) = \frac{cov(a_i, a_j)}{\sqrt{var(a_i) \times var(a_j)}} \tag{4}$$

where $cov(a_i, a_j)$ is the covariance, $var(a_i)$ is the variance of $a_i$ and $var(a_j)$ is the variance of $a_j$.

**Maximal Information Coefficient.** Maximal Information Coefficient (MIC) is a powerful approach to measuring the correlation between two features. MIC can deal with the correlation analysis of linear, nonlinear, and potential nonfunctional relationships in large datasets. The fundamental idea of MIC is that if a specific relationship exists between two features, a grid can be drawn on the scatter-plot to partition them. Then, it will be able to encapsulate the mutual information of the two features according to the approximate probability density distribution in the grid. MIC is calculated based on mutual information and the grid partition method. Given two independent features with $n$ samples, $x = \{x_i | i = 1..., n\}$ and the target variable $y = \{y_i | 1, .., n\}$, a finite set $D = (x_i, y_i | i = 1, .., n)$ of ordered pairs can be obtained. Given a grid $G$, we can partition the $x_i$ values of $D$ into $x$ bins and the $y_i$ values of $D$ into $y$ bins. MIC is obtained according to the following equations:

$$MI(D, x, y) = \max MI(D|G) \tag{5}$$

where $MI(D, x, y)$ denotes the maximum mutual information of $D$ over grids $G$. $D|G$ represents the distribution induced by the data points in $D$ on the cells of grid $G$. The characteristic matrix of $D$ is defined by the following equation:

$$M(D)_{xy} = \frac{MI(D, x, y)}{\log \min\{x, y\}} \tag{6}$$

The MIC of $D$ with grid size less than $B(n)$ is defined as:

$$MIC(D)_{xy} = \max_{xy < B(n)} \{M(D)_{xy}\} \tag{7}$$

where $B(n)$ is the upper limit of the mesh division $xy$. In general, $B(n) = n^{0.6}$. MIC is normalised into a range $[0, 1]$. A higher MIC value indicates a stronger correlation between the variables/features.

First, we use the training dataset to calculate the MIC (in the case of MICF) and PCC (in the case of PCCF) (see Table 1) between $x$ and $y$. We then normalise those values between 0 and 1, to create an interval for the features space $[0, 1]$. Features with stronger correlation (Linear correlation for PCCF; both linear and nonlinear for MICF) given the target variable having more possibilities to be selected uniformly.

When the tree grows, at each split node, we draw random uniform numbers between $[0, 1]$ equivalent to the number of features. Then, we remove the duplicated values, and we end up with a sub-sample of the training dataset. Thereafter, we calculate the Gain Ratio of the new feature space to determine the best split for the current node. In this step, we apply any existing decision tree algorithm such as CART. In our study, we examine the effectiveness of this particular method, specifically on classification problems. To better explain the algorithms and the functions, we explain the key functions below.

## 3.2   Function $Features Importance$

Let $D$ be the training dataset with $d$ original features. Thus, the original feature space $A_o = A_1, A_2, ..A_d$. In this function, we use the training dataset $D$ to calculate whether a feature $d$ has a positive, neutral, or negative correlation, given the target feature either with PCC or MIC depending on the algorithm we test (see Table 4). At this point, in the case of PCC, we also calculate its absolute values, which range in $[-1, 1]$. Then, we normalise them (see Eq. 5) to be 0 to 1, so as to create an interval for the features space in the range of $[0, 1]$ (see Table 1). Features $d$ with stronger correlation (linear correlation for the PCC; linear and nonlinear for MIC) given the target variable have more possibilities to be selected uniformly. Features Importance function returns an array with the features intervals (see Table 1).

## 3.3   Function $growTree$

The following steps happen every time we grow the tree until the stopping criteria are met. Providing the algorithm with the stopping criteria is crucial on individual decision trees and consequently on decision forests. On the one hand, the data are generally over-fitted if we continue to expand the tree until each leaf node equates to the highest Gain Ratio; and on the other hand, if splitting is halted too soon, the error on the training data is insufficiently large, and thus the performance suffers as a result of bias. As such, avoiding over-fitting and under-fitting is crucial. In our case, we deployed the *maximum depth stopping criterion* and the *numbers of labels criterion*, where we check if the current node is homogeneous. We draw random uniform numbers equal to the number of features between 0 and 1, and we store the indexes of the $d'$ features intervals they fall within (see Table 4), so we end up with an array containing less of the original feature space with $D' \subseteq D$. It is noteworthy that, at this point, we do not allow duplicate feature indexes as it does not make any difference in the final result. Then, we calculate the *Gain Ratio* of the new dataset feature space $D'$ to determine the best split for the current node. This step, may apply any existing decision tree algorithm such as CART on the reduced space dataset $D'$. This particular decision tree can be used for classification based on the training dataset and prediction based on the testing dataset, which contains unlabelled samples. Using two splitting criteria (PCC and Gain Ratio or MIC and Gain Ratio), we promote the features with the best predictive ability without heavily biasing the algorithm (see Algorithm 1).

**Table 1.** Pearson's correlation coefficient example

| Feature ID | Scores | Absolute values | Normalised scores | Thresholds |
|---|---|---|---|---|
| 0 | −0.255 | 0.255 | 0.322 | 0.322 |
| 1 | 0.075 | 0.075 | 0.094 | 0.417 |
| 2 | 0.143 | 0.143 | 0.180 | 0.597 |
| 3 | −0.282 | 0.282 | 0.356 | 0.954 |
| 4 | −0.035 | 0.035 | 0.045 | 1.000 |

## 4　Experimental Setup and Results

This section presents the proposed methods' experimental results in predictive accuracy and running time. The following results were obtained on an Intel(R) Core(TM) i7-10875H CPU @ 2.30 GHz (16 CPUs) processor, with 64 GB RAM and 16 MB CACHE memory.

In order to demonstrate the accuracy improvement of MICF and PCCF, we experiment on 12 widely known datasets that are publicly available through UCI Machine Learning Repository listed in Table 2. In particular, the median average number of records used is 354, with the lowest having 27 records and the largest 4,177. The median average number of features used is 9, with the lowest having 4 features and the largest 279.

For testing purposes, we generate 100 trees for each contending decision forest algorithm since the number is considered to be large enough to ensure convergence of the ensemble effect [2]. We apply majority voting to aggregate results for the forests. Moreover, we test the model with 10-Fold Cross-Validation to ensure that every observation from the original dataset has the possibility of appearing in the training and test sets. We perform hyperparameter optimization for each dataset using Grid Search and Random Search techniques to ensure the best possible accuracies for each case. All the prediction accuracies reported in this paper are in percentage, and the best results are presented in bold-face. As MICF and PCCF are designed for parallel forest algorithms, for a fair evaluation, we compare them with other parallel forest algorithms, including Bagging (BG), Random Subspace (RS), Random Forest (RF), and two variants of Random Features Weights (RFW) with $p = 1$ and $p = 2$. Moreover, for consistency with RF, CART is utilised as the tree induction algorithm, and Gini Index is employed as the measure of classification capacity for every forest algorithm mentioned above. Finally, both versions of RFW ($P = 2$ and $p = 1$) are applied on bootstrap samples, as a better performance can be observed using this particular technique [17].

Generally, an essential aim for forest algorithms is to improve the Ensemble Accuracy (EA) [1]. As such, every single contending forest algorithm described in this paper aims to increase EA as their principal performance metric. Metrics such as Precision and Recall [23] are mainly and primarily used on imbalanced datasets, therefore evaluating PCCF and MICF as general purpose forest algorithms, we have not involved any imbalance dataset in our experimental evaluation. Table 3 presents the results on EA for all the contending algorithms while all datasets are taken into consideration. Results are presented in the shape of EA Rank, where EA is the Ensemble Accuracy in percentage for the algorithm in

---

**Algorithm 1:** Features Importance and Grow tree functions in algorithmic notation

---

**Input:** Training Dataset D with original attribute space Ao = {A1,A2,...,Ad}, number of features of the new Dataset D' where D'features < D features(NumFeat)

**Output:** A Decision Tree(T)

**Function** Features_Importance(*D*):

> FeaturesImportance = Calculate the features importance(MIC or PCC) of Training Dataset D
>
> FeaturesImportanceInterval = Create a features importance interval from 0 to 1 such as
> ($F_1 = 0.1, F_2 = 0.3, F_3 = 0.55, ..., F_n = 1$)
>
> return FeaturesImportanceInterval

**Function** Grow_Tree(*FeaturesImportanceInterval,NumFeat*):

> for *i until stopping criteria met* **do**
>
> UniformDraw = draw uniform numbers between 0 and 1
>
> FeaturesIndex = get the features index using the uniform numbers using UniformDraw
>
> D' = generate the dataset using the column index using FeaturesIndex
>
> T = growTree using the D'
>
> **End for**
>
> return T

comparison, and EA Rank is the Ensemble Accuracy Rank for the corresponding algorithm to other contending algorithms according to the rank-ordering used in Friedman Test [12]. Amongst the 7 contending algorithms, the one with the highest EA is assigned an EA Rank of 1, the second highest as EA Rank of 2, and so on. Hence, the lower the EA Rank, the better the EA. In the case of a tie, we average the two or three or the number of algorithms having equal EA. Thus, for example, if two algorithms become the worst in EA, their EA Rank is calculated by $\frac{6+7}{2} = 6.5$. The last row of Table 3 shows the average EA and the average EA Rank in parentheses.

In Table 3, we present the EA percentage of the contenting algorithms for all 12 datasets considered. From Table 3 we observe that $PCCF$ provides the best EA on 1 dataset with an EA Rank of 3.0, and $MICF$ obtains the best EA on 11 datasets out of 12 with an EA Rank of 1.3. $BG$ does not get any first place in an EA, resulting in an EA Rank of 5.4. $RS$ obtains the best EA on 1 dataset with an EA Rank of 4.2. $RF$ does not manage to get any first place in an EA resulting in an EA Rank of 4.3. $RFWp = 1$ obtains higher EA on 1 dataset with EA Rank of 4.3. Finally, $RFWp = 2$ does not manage to get any first place in an EA, resulting in an EA Rank of 5.5. The last row of Table 3 shows that $MICF$ achieves the best overall average performance based in an EA and EA Rank compared to all other contending algorithms.

**Table 2.** Datasets specifications

| Dataset name | Number of records | Number of features |
|---|---|---|
| Abalone (AB) | 4177 | 8 |
| Arrythma (AR) | 452 | 279 |
| Balance scale (BS) | 625 | 4 |
| Dermatology (DER) | 358 | 34 |
| Glass identification (GI) | 214 | 9 |
| Ionosphere (ION) | 351 | 34 |
| Liver disorders (LD) | 345 | 6 |
| Lung cancer (LC) | 27 | 56 |
| Pima indians diabetes (PID) | 768 | 8 |
| SCADI (SCD) | 206 | 70 |
| Teaching assistant evaluation (TAE) | 1515 | 5 |
| Yeast (YST) | 1484 | 9 |

**Table 3.** Ensemble Accuracy (EA) in percentage with Ensemble Accuracy Rank (EA Rank).

| Dataset | PCCF | MICF | BG | RS | RF | RFW p = 1 | RFW p = 2 |
|---|---|---|---|---|---|---|---|
| AB | 21.3 (7.0) | 27.5 (1.0) | 25.1 (2.5) | 25.0 (4.5) | 25.0 (4.5) | 25.1 (2.5) | 23.7 (6.0) |
| AR | 81.2 (7.0) | 82.8 (4.0) | 81.6 (6.0) | 83.7 (1.0) | 83.0 (2.5) | 82.6 (5.0) | 83.0 (2.5) |
| BS | 84.2 (1.5) | 84.2 (1.5) | 77.5 (6.0) | 72.2 (7.0) | 80.5 (5.0) | 81.1 (4.0) | 82.5 (3.0) |
| DER | 96.0 (2.0) | 96.7 (1.0) | 88.5 (4.0) | 89.0 (3.0) | 87.0 (7.0) | 87.5 (5.0) | 87.3 (6.0) |
| GI | 76.7 (2.0) | 77.2 (1.0) | 74.1 (3.5) | 73.2 (5.5) | 74.1(3.5) | 73.2 (5.5) | 72.2 (7.0) |
| ION | 93.7 (3.0) | 94.5 (1.0) | 92.6 (7.0) | 93.4 (5.0) | 93.7 (3.0) | 93.7 (3.0) | 92.9 (6.0) |
| LD | 72.1 (2.0) | 73.6 (1.0) | 68.7 (6.0) | 69.8 (5.0) | 71.5 (3.0) | 71.0 (4.0) | 67.3 (7.0) |
| LC | 76.6 (2.0) | 84.4 (1.0) | 63.9 (7.0) | 68.9 (4.5) | 68.9 (4.5) | 68.9 (4.5) | 68.9 (4.5) |
| PID | 76.2 (2.5) | 77.9 (1.0) | 75.6 (6.0) | 76.2 (2.5) | 75.9 (4.0) | 75.6 (6.0) | 75.6 (6.0) |
| SCD | 83.7 (3.0) | 84.3 (1.5) | 80.0 (6.5) | 82.9 (4.5) | 80.0 (6.5) | 84.3 (1.5) | 82.9 (4.5) |
| TAE | 60.6 (2.0) | 62.4 (1.0) | 53.6 (7.0) | 59.5 (3.0) | 56.3 (4.0) | 54.3 (5.0) | 54.2 (6.0) |
| YST | 60.3 (2.0) | 60.9 (1.0) | 60.5 (3.0) | 58.6 (5.0) | 59.5 (4.0) | 57.9 (6.0) | 48.9 (7.0) |
| **Average** | 73.9 (3.0) | **75.7 (1.3)** | 70.1 (5.4) | 71.0 (4.2) | 71.4 (4.3) | 71.3 (4.3) | 69.9 (5.5) |

In the following, we further examine the enhancement we achieved by performing statistical significance tests as recommended in [7]. First, we perform the Friedman test [11], which is a popular non-parametric test for examining various classifiers on multiple datasets. Friedman statistic is distributed according to Eq. 8, where $k$ is the number of algorithms, and $N$ is the number of datasets. As a generic rule, $k > 5$ and $N > 10$ must be hold. In Eq. 9, let $r_i^j$ be the rank of the $j_{th}$ of $k$ algorithms on the $i_{th}$ of $N$ datasets. [15] suggests that Eq. 8 is undesirably conservative, and it derives a better statistical measure, as shown in Eq. 10:

$$x_F^2 = \frac{N}{nk(k+1)} \sum_{j=1}^{k} R_j^2 - 3n(k+1) \tag{8}$$

$$R_j = \frac{1}{N} \sum_i r_i^j \tag{9}$$

$$F_f = \frac{(N-1)x_F^2}{N(k-1) - x_F^2} \tag{10}$$

With 7 algorithms and 14 datasets, $F_f$ is distributed according to the F distribution with 66 degrees of freedom, which is calculated using Eq. 11. The critical value of $F(6, 66)$ for $\alpha = 0.05$ is 2.24 and our value of $F_f$ is calculated to be 8.7. As the critical value is lower than our $F_f$ value, the *null hypothesis* is rejected, and so we can proceed with a post-hoc test, i.e., the Bonferroni-Dunn test [10] for detecting pairwise differences of EA Ranks between the controlled classifiers (MICF and PCCF) and the rest of the contending classifiers.

$$FD = (k-1)(N-1) \tag{11}$$

For the Bonferonni-Dunn test, we calculate the critical difference using Eq. 12 to compare our first novel algorithm (MICF) with the rest of the contending algorithms. In Eq. 12, $q_a$ represents the bold number in the last row of Table 3 in brackets (EA Rank). The Critical Difference(CD) is calculated to be 1.14. At this point we observe that CD remains lower than the pairwise difference of EA Ranks between the classifier MICF and the other contending classifiers ( $MICF \ vs \ BG$ : 4.1, $MICF \ vs \ RS$ : 2.9, $MICF \ vs \ RF$ : 3.0, $MICF \ vs \ RFWp = 1$ : 3.0, $MICF \ vs \ RFWp = 3 : 4.2$). This indicates that MICF outperforms the rest classifiers in terms or EA, in a statistically significant manner.

Now, we repeat the same test for our second novel algorithm (PCCF) with the rest of the contending classifiers. The critical difference is calculated to be 1 and as before we observe that CD remains lower than the pairwise difference of EA Ranks between classifier PCCF and the other contending algorithms ( $PCCF \ vs \ BG$ : 2.4, $PCCF \ vs \ RS$ : 1.2, $PCCF \ vs \ RF$ : 1.3, $PCCF \ vs \ RFWp = 1$ : 1.3, $PCCF \ vs \ RFWp = 3 : 2.5$). This indicates that the performance improvement in PCCF in terms of EA is statistically significant.

$$CD = q_a\sqrt{\frac{k(k+1)}{6N}} \tag{12}$$

Table 4 contains correlation scores, which indicate the main differences between our two novel algorithms - MICF and PCCF. The results suggest that MIC can identify more accurately the correlation between the features and the target, as well as take into consideration the uncertainty, which results in a more accurate algorithm. Both MICF and PCCF algorithms outperform their competitors by achieving 4.4 and 2.6% more accurate results, respectively, compared with the third highest accurate algorithm, RF.

**Table 4.** Comparison between MIC and PCC scores.(left-PCC, right-MIC)

| Feature space | AB | | TAE | | YST | | GI | | LD | | BS | |
|---|---|---|---|---|---|---|---|---|---|---|---|---|
| 1 | 0.009 | 0.071 | 0.323 | 0.079 | 0.071 | 0.208 | 0.056 | 0.132 | 0.166 | 0.081 | 0.242 | 0.242 |
| 2 | 0.155 | 0.204 | 0.417 | 0.275 | 0.191 | 0.389 | 0.227 | 0.252 | 0.344 | 0.330 | 0.485 | 0.485 |
| 3 | 0.306 | 0.341 | 0.598 | 0.559 | 0.221 | 0.515 | 0.481 | 0.428 | 0.408 | 0.505 | 0.742 | 0.742 |
| 4 | 0.452 | 0.471 | 0.955 | 0.647 | 0.357 | 0.764 | 0.685 | 0.552 | 0.694 | 0.642 | 1.000 | 1.000 |
| 5 | 0.593 | 0.604 | 1.000 | 1.000 | 0.499 | 0.857 | 0.736 | 0.626 | 0.960 | 0.887 | | |
| 6 | 0.704 | 0.723 | | | 0.570 | 0.871 | 0.740 | 0.741 | 1.000 | 1.000 | | |
| 7 | 0.836 | 0.855 | | | 0.174 | 0.903 | 0.740 | 0.825 | | | | |
| 8 | 1.000 | 1.000 | | | 0.724 | 0.928 | 0.936 | 0.961 | | | | |
| 9 | | | | | 1.000 | 1.000 | 1.000 | 1.000 | | | | |

# 5   Conclusion

In this paper, we have proposed two novel decision forest building algorithms - Maximal Information Coefficient Forest ($MICF$) and Pearson's Correlation Coefficient Forest ($PCCF$). They combine Gain Ratio with PCC and MIC, which are used to determine the best feature on each splitting node. The larger the correlation score (either MIC or PCC), the greater the possibility of ending up on the newly created dataset $D'$ at each splitting node. To the best of our knowledge, our work of combining Gain Ratio with MIC or PCC in classification problems is the first of its kind and can help improve the accuracy in classification problems significantly. The experimental results have shown that $MICF$ performs significantly better in Ensemble Accuracy than some highly esteemed existing algorithms, including Bagging, Random Subspace, Random Forest, Random Feature Weight, and the newly proposed $PCCF$ algorithm. Moreover, the generation of individual decision trees in both $MICF$ and $PCCF$ is in no way dependent on any previous tree(s) and, therefore, can be generated in parallel. Moreover, considering the consistent performance of both $MICF$ and $PCCF$, makes them a great fit within the big data context and thus enabling it to be used by non-technical individuals.

For future work, we aim to test our algorithms against imbalanced datasets and compare them with probabilistic trees, which are known to capture the uncertainty in the data effectively.

# References

1. Adnan, N.: Decision tree and decision forest algorithms: on improving accuracy, efficiency and knowledge discovery (2017)
2. Bernard, S., Heutte, L., Adam, S.: Forest-rk: a new random forest induction method. In: ICIC (2008)
3. Breiman, L.: Bagging predictors. Mach. Learn. **24**, 123–140 (2004)
4. Breiman, L.: Random forests. Mach. Learn. **45**, 5–32 (2004)
5. Breiman, L., Friedman, J.H., Olshen, R.A., Stone, C.J.: Classification and regression trees (1983)
6. Delgado, M.F., Cernadas, E., Barro, S., Amorim, D.G.: Do we need hundreds of classifiers to solve real world classification problems? J. Mach. Learn. Res. **15**, 3133–3181 (2014)
7. Demsar, J.: Statistical comparisons of classifiers over multiple data sets. J. Mach. Learn. Res. **7**, 1–30 (2006)
8. Drousiotis, E., Pentaliotis, P., Shi, L., Cristea, A.I.: Capturing fairness and uncertainty in student dropout prediction – a comparison study. In: Roll, I., McNamara, D., Sosnovsky, S., Luckin, R., Dimitrova, V. (eds.) AIED 2021. LNCS (LNAI), vol. 12749, pp. 139–144. Springer, Cham (2021). https://doi.org/10.1007/978-3-030-78270-2_25
9. Drousiotis, E., Shi, L., Maskell, S.: Early predictor for student success based on behavioural and demographic indicators. In: Cristea, A.I., Troussas, C. (eds.) ITS 2021. LNCS, vol. 12677, pp. 161–172. Springer, Cham (2021). https://doi.org/10.1007/978-3-030-80421-3_19

102    E. Drousiotis et al.

10. Dunn, O.J.: Multiple comparisons among means. J. Am. Stat. Assoc. **56**(293), 52–64 (1961)
11. Friedman, M.: The use of ranks to avoid the assumption of normality implicit in the analysis of variance. J. Am. Stat. Assoc. **32**(200), 675–701 (1937)
12. Friedman, M.: A comparison of alternative tests of significance for the problem of $m$ rankings. Ann. Math. Stat. **11**, 86–92 (1940)
13. Guo, Z., Yu, B., Hao, M., Wang, W., Jiang, Y., Zong, F.: A novel hybrid method for flight departure delay prediction using random forest regression and maximal information coefficient (2021)
14. Ho, T.K.: The random subspace method for constructing decision forests. IEEE Trans. Pattern Anal. Mach. Intell. **20**, 832–844 (1998)
15. Iman, R.L., Davenport, J.M.: Approximations of the critical region of the Fbietkan statistic. Commun. Stat.-Theory Methods **9**, 571–595 (1980)
16. Liu, S., Hu, T.: Parallel random forest algorithm optimization based on maximal information coefficient. In: 2018 IEEE 9th International Conference on Software Engineering and Service Science, pp. 1083–1087 (2018)
17. Maudes, J., Rodríguez, J.J., García-Osorio, C., García-Pedrajas, N.: Random feature weights for decision tree ensemble construction. Inf. Fusion **13**(1), 20–30 (2012)
18. Murthy, S.K.: Automatic construction of decision trees from data: a multidisciplinary survey. Data Mining Knowl. Disc. **2**, 345–389 (2004)
19. Nasridinov, A., Ihm, S., Park, Y.H.: A decision tree-based classification model for crime prediction. In: ITCS (2013)
20. Podgorelec, V., Kokol, P., Stiglic, B., Rozman, I.: Decision trees: an overview and their use in medicine. J. Med. Syst. **26**, 445–463 (2004)
21. Quinlan, J.R.: Induction of decision trees. Mach. Learn. **1**, 81–106 (1986)
22. Salzberg, S., Murthy, K.: On growing better decision trees from data (1996)
23. Tan, P.N., Steinbach, M., Kumar, V.: Introduction to Data Mining. Pearson Education India (2016)
24. Zeleznikow, J.: Using web-based legal decision support systems to improve access to justice. Inf. Commun. Technol. Law **11**, 15–33 (2002)

# On Forecasting Project Activity Durations with Neural Networks

Peter Zachares, Vahan Hovhannisyan(✉), Carlos Ledezma, Joao Gante,
and Alan Mosca

nPlan, London, UK
{peter,vahan,carlos,alan}@nplan.io

**Abstract.** Accurately forecasting project end dates is an incredibly valuable and equally challenging task. In recent years it has gained added attention from the machine learning community. However, state of the art methods both in academia and in industry still rely on expert opinions and Monte-Carlo simulations. In this paper, we formulate the problem of activity duration forecasting as a classification task using a domain specific binning strategy. Our experiments on a data set of real construction projects suggest that our proposed method offers several orders of magnitude improvement over more traditional approaches where activity duration forecasting is treated as a regression task. Our results suggest that posing the forecasting problem as a classification task with carefully designed classes is crucial for high quality forecasts both at an activity and a project levels.

**Keywords:** Forecasting · Project management · Neural network applications

## 1 Introduction

Many economic endeavours require undertaking complex projects which can only be completed over long time spans [10]. In the planning phase, projects are allocated budgets which rely on the completion of the project in a similar manner to which it was planned. If a project's completion is delayed, this can lead to ballooning costs, which can have a major negative impact on the project stakeholders including failure to complete the project [9]. To mitigate the risk of delay, stakeholders of the project require an accurate time estimate of project duration. With this knowledge, stakeholders can assess the risk of delay and even execute mitigation actions to reduce this risk.

While it is impossible to estimate the duration of a complex project exactly [6], it is possible to determine which durations are more likely than others, i.e. in almost all cases a project will not take one hundred times longer to complete than planned. Consequently, it is more useful to stakeholders to forecast the duration of a project rather than to predict it.

Supported by nPlan.

J. Gante—For contributions made while employed at nPlan.

L. Iliadis et al. (Eds.): EANN 2022, CCIS 1600, pp. 103–114, 2022.
https://doi.org/10.1007/978-3-031-08223-8_9

Each complex project is unique, but can share many similarities with past projects. Using a data-driven modelling approach and details from past projects, it is possible to accurately forecast a project's duration providing stakeholders with useful information for mitigating the risk of delay.

Complex projects involve the completion of numerous tasks. Each task in the project has a state with respect to the current time which could be *not started*, *in progress* or *completed*. In a project, the state of a task can depend not only on the current time, but also on the state of many other tasks within the project i.e. the facade structure must be completed before facade window installation can begin. It is possible to model these state dependencies using a directed acyclic graph (DAG) [5], where nodes represent activities and links represent dependency constraints.

If provided with a duration forecast for each task in the project and an estimated start date for the project, it is possible to estimate the end date, and thus duration, of the entire project using an uncertainty propagation method such as Monte Carlo sampling [32]. This simplifies the problem of forecasting a project's duration to forecasting the durations of tasks in the project. In addition, past projects are more likely to contain similar tasks to a future project than they are to mimic the future project exactly. Consequently, past project data can provide more useful information for forecasting at a task level than a project level.

Taking the approach described above to project duration forecasting, the quality of the forecasts at a task-level will determine the quality of the forecast of project duration. Neural networks have achieved state-of-the-art performance in a number of forecasting tasks (also known as uncertainty estimation) both by combining results from ensembles of models [11,23,28] and applying post-hoc calibration [15].

In this paper we perform experiments to determine which training objectives and inductive biases applied to neural networks yield the most accurate task-level forecasts on project data. We perform experiments using a data set of construction projects. Our results suggest that a neural network that outputs a histogram distribution over task duration trained with a classification objective and using a domain specific binning strategy to define the classes leads to the most accurate forecasts.

The contributions of our work are threefold;

- To the best of our knowledge this is the first machine learning model used to forecast project activity durations.
- A novel problem formulation which poses task duration forecasting as a classification problem.
- A novel binning strategy incorporating domain knowledge about how humans complete tasks which leads to higher quality forecasts when used as an inductive bias to train models on project data.

**Notation.** We follow standard notation practices using bold lower case letters for vectors and bold upper case letters for matrices. For scalars we use both lower and upper case non-bold letters. Subscripts on vectors and matrices refer to its elements. We use superscripts to indicate indices for vectors and matrices.

## 2   Related Work

Forecasting is an age old problem. Early on, humans used empirical observations to forecast the weather, but now we apply complex mathematical models to forecast whether multi-billion dollar mega projects will finish on time and on budget [33]. Currently, forecasting is a very broad field of research with applications in environment sciences [21], economics, supply chain management, project controls and many other industries [13,31]. For a comprehensive review of forecasting theory and practice we refer the reader to [29]. In this paper our focus is on forecasting time durations of activities in project schedules.

While there has been some recent work on using machine learning algorithms to forecast project durations using handcrafted features [7,24,25] (also see reference therein), traditionally task duration forecasting has been implemented using a blanket distribution for all tasks [8] or with added expert opinion [16,26,27] for individual activities. The latter, more specialised solution is, of course, more accurate, however, it is based on human inputs and inherently suffers from various biases [2].

In a recent work [17] proposes a machine learning algorithm to learn activity types in construction projects using a manually labelled database of activities. This work is closest to ours in the literature, however, it does not address the much more challenging problem of forecasting activity durations.

Our proposed method is based on the observation that task duration forecasts are inherently heavy-tailed [16] and that Gaussian distributions are not suitable to represent such distributions [35]. Hence, we pose task duration forecasting as a multi-class classification problem to train neural networks to output a histogram distribution describing the uncertainty in tasks' durations [3].

Since the majority of all activities in a project complete on time, even if the project suffers from large delays[1], splitting the activity duration range into uniform intervals for a histogram distribution creates a large class imbalance. We mitigate this well-known problem [15,19] by proposing equibins - a novel binning strategy which calculates a more balanced class distribution than using uniform intervals. We also use domain knowledge about how humans accomplish tasks to further improve our models.

## 3   Problem Formulation

Each task in a project has an associated feature vector $\mathbf{x}$ and duration label $y$. We address the problem of learning the parameters $\theta$ of a neural network

---

[1] 2.977 million of 5.693 million (or 52.3%) activities in our database have completed exactly on time.

$f_\theta : \mathbf{x} \to P(\mathcal{Y})$ that maps a task's feature vector to a probability distribution over its duration with the objective;

$$\theta^* = \arg\max_\theta f_\theta(\mathbf{x})\Big|_{\mathcal{Y}=y} \tag{1}$$

The objective is to maximise the likelihood of the neural network's output distribution evaluated at $y$. We assume that each task also has a planned duration $y_{plan}$ and define a new quantity, completion ratio as:

$$c = \frac{y}{y_{plan}} \tag{2}$$

When actualised, each task will have a completion ratio whose magnitude will indicate the accuracy of the planner in estimating the duration of a task. We assume that all tasks will be completed within some completion ratio range $c \in [c_{min}, c_{max}]$, $c_{min} > 0$, $c_{max} > c_{min}$ and separate the interval $[c_{min}, c_{max})$ into $n$ intervals of $([c_{min}, c_1), [c_1, c_2), ..., [c_{n-2}, c_{n-1}), [c_{n-1}, c_{max}), i > j \to c_i > c_j)$.

We assume the associated distribution of the random variable $\mathcal{Y}$ is a histogram distribution composed of the following intervals:

$$y_{plan} \times \{[c_{min}, c_1), [c_1, c_2), ..., [c_{n-2}, c_{n-1}), [c_{n-1}, c_{max})\} \tag{3}$$

We assume that within each bin the distribution's probability density is uniform. Hence, each task's duration $y$ will fall within one of the histogram's bins scaled by $y_{plan}$:

$$y \in [c_{n-1}y_{plan}, c_{max}y_{plan}) \tag{4}$$

Using this formulation, it is possible to generate a one-hot vector $\mathbf{y}$ of size $n$ with zeros in all dimensions except the dimension corresponding to the index of the interval the duration falls in, where the vector has value 1. With these assumptions we can optimise our original objective by reposing forecasting task duration as a classification problem where $f_\theta$ maps to a multinomial distribution (a vector of non-negative numbers which sum to one with $n$ dimensions) over completion ratio ($f_\theta : \mathbf{x} \to P(\mathcal{C})$) and we optimise the equivalent objective;

$$\theta^* = \arg\max_\theta f_\theta(\mathbf{x})^T \mathbf{y} \tag{5}$$

## 4    Method

We assume access to a data set of related tasks from past projects which is split into a training set and a validation set. Each split contains two matrices; a feature matrix $\mathbf{X} \in \mathbb{R}^{k \times m}$ and a label matrix $\mathbf{Y} \in \mathbb{R}^{m \times n}$, where $k$ is the number of data points, $m$ is the number of features and $n$ is the number of classes.

We assume the mapping from task features to the task's distribution over completion ratio can be expressed by a multi-layer perceptron [30] with a softmax operation as its final layer. For completeness, we define the softmax operation below:

$$\sigma(\mathbf{z})_i = \frac{e^{z_i}}{\sum_{l=1}^{m} e^{z_l}}, \tag{6}$$

where $\mathbf{z}$ is a vector of size $n$. We train our model using a variant of stochastic gradient descent [22] to minimise the negative loglikelihood (also known as cross-entropy loss) of the true class of each task in our training set i.e. if $\mathbf{X}_{batch}$ is a batch of feature vectors of $k'$ tasks from our training set and $\mathbf{Y}_{batch}$ are the tasks' corresponding label vectors. Then we minimise the loss:

$$Loss = \sum_{i=1}^{k'} -log(f_\theta(\mathbf{x}_i)^T \mathbf{y}_i) \tag{7}$$

The majority of all tasks in a project complete on time, even if the project suffers from large delays. In addition, there are certain values of completion ratio that are very common i.e. 1.0, 1.5, 2.0 in our data set (see Fig. 1 for the data distribution). This indicates that when stakeholders work on a project, if a task cannot be finished on time, then they set a new deadline which is some multiple of original task's planned duration. Consequently, tasks tend to be delivered late and early in a predictable manner. This means, splitting a task's completion ratio support $[c_{min}, c_{max})$ into uniform intervals can create a large class imbalance in the data set. If intervals are all of uniform size, then an interval can contain many commonly appearing completion ratio values in the data set and consequently contain a much larger proportion of the data set than other intervals.

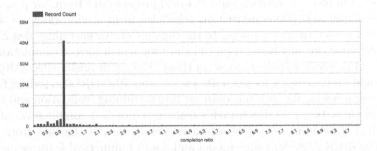

**Fig. 1.** Completion ratios (training labels) of all construction schedule activities in our database: over half of them have completion ratio 1, aka completed on time. There are also noticeable spikes at 0.5, 2, 3, etc. points.

To mitigate this issue, we propose binning strategy called **equibins**, which helps create a more balanced class distribution. **equibins** is an iterative algorithm. Before starting, the algorithm stores a count of all completion ratio values in the training and validation set which occur more than once. A hyperparameter of the algorithm is how many bins $n_{bins}$ the algorithm should split the support into. The algorithm starts out with all labels in training and validation sets union $c \in \mathcal{C}_{train+val}$. At each iteration the algorithm calculates how many data points would be within intervals of uniform size i.e. $n_{uniform} = \lfloor \frac{|\mathcal{C}_{train+val}|}{n} \rfloor$. If it finds a completion ratio value $c$ which occurs more than $n_{uniform}$ times, then the algorithm creates a bin centred at $c$ with bounds $[c - \epsilon, c + \epsilon)$ where $\epsilon$ is another hyperparameter of this binning strategy. Then the algorithm removes the points within the defined interval from the set of completion values considered, sets $n_{bin} = n_{bin} - 1$ and repeats the steps described above until there are no completion ratio values which occur more than $n_{uniform}$ times. Then the algorithm splits the remaining intervals in the support into bins by finding the boundaries which separate the remaining data into $n_{bin}$ equally sized quantiles. Note that $n_{bin}$ could be less than the originally specified value depending on the number of iterations of the algorithm required to remove common completion ratio values from the set of considered values.

## 5 Experiments

Our experiments are designed to answer two questions:

1. Does posing task duration forecasting as a classification problem yield higher quality forecasts?

2. Does our proposed binning strategy equibins improve the quality of forecasts outputted by a task duration model trained as a classifier in comparison to a naive binning strategy?

We perform our experiments on real world project data from our proprietary database of over $400,000$ construction schedules from a wide range of sectors. The labels for each task correspond to the one-hot vector encodings described in Sect. 3. We filter out any tasks from our data set which have a completion ratio less than 0.1 or greater than 10, viewing them as noisy or mislabelled. After data cleaning and preprocessing we get a data set of over $70,000,000$ activities to train and test our models. We split our data set into a training, validation and test set using split ratio $16 : 4 : 5$. Each task's feature vector is a combination of a 128 dimensional embedding vector of a textual description of the task from a pretrained tiny-BERT [20] language model and a set of numerical features including the tasks planned duration $y_{plan}$ and numerical features which describe the date at which the task is planned to start.

For our proposed model, we used a 5-layer fully-connected network. Each layer, except the last layer is composed of a linear layer, a batch normalisation layer [18], a Relu layer [1] and a dropout layer [34]. Figure 2 presents the model architecture. The last layer uses a softmax operation as its activation function and is not followed by a drop-out layer. For our experiments we used a dropout rate of 0.3 and the internal layers of the model had 3968 hidden units. The model was trained using ADAM [22] with a learning rate of 2.0e–4. The hyperparameters of the model architecture and training were determined using a Bayesian hyperparameter search[2]. We trained our model for 64 epochs with an early stopping condition: model training terminated if the model's performance on the validation set did not improve for five consecutive epochs. For evaluation, we used the parameters for each model which resulted in the lowest validation loss. For our `equibins` binning strategy, we separated the support of the histogram into 53 bins and used an $\epsilon$ value of 1e–3.

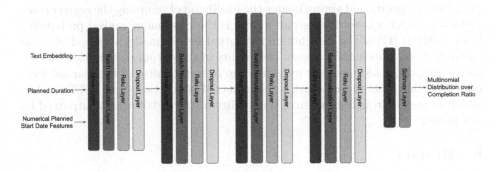

**Fig. 2.** Representative multi-layer perceptron used in our experiments.

We compare our proposed model to three baselines. All baselines share the same model architecture up to their last layer and were trained using the training procedure described above. The first baseline poses task duration forecasting as a regression task where the model outputs a Gaussian distribution. The model output is two parameters; a mean and log standard deviation. We further process the log standard deviation by performing a softplus operation on it [37] to ensure stability during training. This baseline outputs a uni-modal distribution.

If our data is inherently multi-modal, the baseline could perform poorly due to its inability to describe a multi-modal distribution. Consequently, our second baseline also poses task duration forecasting as a regression task where the model outputs a Gaussian mixture model with 3 modes. The model also outputs a log standard deviation for each mode (as opposed to standard deviation) which is processed by applying softplus operation to it. The model outputs 3 terms for the weighting terms of the Gaussian mixture model which are processed by performing a softmax operation on them to ensure they sum to one. Both regression baselines are trained by minimising the negative log-likelihood of each task's actualised completion ratio with respect to the distribution they output. The third baseline poses task duration forecasting as a classification task, but uses uniformly sized bin intervals as opposed to the `equibins` strategy we propose.

---

[2] https://cloud.google.com/blog/products/ai-machine-learning/hyperparameter-tuning-cloud-machine-learning-engine-using-bayesian-optimization.

For our purposes, classification metrics such as F1-score are not very informative, since we do not intend to use the predicted class in any downstream task. Instead, the entire distribution outputted by the classifier is used as a forecast for the duration of a task. Consequently, we report metrics commonly used to measure forecast quality.

The first metric is the probability mass within 1e–2 of a task's actualised completion ratio averaged over the entire test set. This metric measures local distribution quality and approximates the likelihood of sampling the correct completion ratio for a task. The second metric is the continuous ranked probability score (CRPS) [12] of the distribution outputted by our model averaged over the entire test set. This metric assesses the quality of the output distribution over its entire support, which roughly measures the overall quality of the learned forecast. The third metric we report is the expected calibration error (ECE) [4,14], which is another rough measure of the quality of the distributions outputted by our model.

## 6   Results

Table 1 records the performance of our proposed model and the three baselines described above. The results show clearly that in terms of likelihood there is an order of magnitude increase in performance ($\sim$0.001$\rightarrow\sim$0.01) when using models trained using a classification objective versus a model trained using a regression objective to forecast task duration.

A possible reason for the improved performance of models trained using classification objectives as opposed to regression objectives is that continuous distributions like Gaussian and Gaussian mixture models use distance metrics to calculate likelihood. These density functions contain an implicit locality assumption where points close to each other have similar likelihoods. In addition, Gaussian likelihoods decay exponentially as they move away from the mean of the distribution. If the underlying distribution a model is trying to learn does not meet this locality assumption or exponential decay assumption, then a Gaussian density functions will struggle to approximate it. Using a classification objective, the model learns a histogram distribution which makes fewer assumptions about the underlying distribution. Specifically, it makes a strong locality assumption within bins, but no locality assumption across bins. In our experiments, histogram distributions trained using a classification objective (which makes no locality assumption across bins) yield better uncertainty estimates from the trained model.

In addition, there is another order of magnitude increase ($\sim$0.01$\rightarrow\sim$0.1) in performance in terms of likelihood when using the equibins binning strategy as an inductive bias in the model as opposed to uniformly sized bins. As explained in Sect. 4, equibins leads to a more balanced class distribution. A more balanced class distribution encourages sensitivity in our models as they see more variation in their targets during training and consequently are more likely to identify statistical relationships in their training set than models trained on a highly unbalanced class distribution.

In terms of CPRS on the test set, the combination of training the model using a classification objective and using an equibins strategy yielded the same improvement in CRPS over the three baselines ($\sim$0.060→$\sim$0.044). Finally in terms of ECE, there was not much of a difference between the models trained using classification objectives ($\sim$1.7 versus $\sim$1.9), but there was a large jump in performance when comparing models trained using regression objectives as opposed to classification objectives ($\sim$7.0 versus $\sim$1.8). To calculate the ECE for the two regression baselines, we first approximated them as histogram distributions within the completion ratio support $[0.1, 10)$.

In our experiments, the performance of the models in terms of likelihood and CRPS suggest that training models using a classification objective and incorporating an **equibins** binning strategy improves the performance of neural networks on task duration forecasting. On the other hand, the performance of models in terms of ECE suggest that only training models using a classification objective is important.

**Table 1.** Performance metrics on the test set of models trained to perform task duration forecasting. Higher likelihood and higher CRPS mean better forecasting power; lower ECE means better forecasting power.

| Model | Likelihood | CRPS | ECE |
|---|---|---|---|
| Unimodal Gaussian regressor | 0.0058 | 0.0600 | 7.1043 |
| Gaussian mixture model with 3 modes regressor | 0.0062 | 0.0582 | 7.0310 |
| Uniform bin size classifier | 0.0368 | 0.0602 | 1.7416 |
| Equibins classifier | 0.3680 | 0.0443 | 1.8973 |

Better activity level forecasts should result in better project end date forecasts. To demonstrate this, we ran Monte-Carlo simulations on various projects for which we have both initially planned and fully actualised schedules. We report the difference in performance between the two best performing models: our proposed **equibins** classifier and the uniform bin size classifier baseline on the project end-date forecasting task. We report the probability density function calculated by performing a Monte Carlo simulation on a project using the distributions outputted by these models.

We found a very consistent behaviour across all tested project, and we report visual representative results of project end date forecasting in Fig. 3. Visually the results suggest that using the **equibins** classifier results in probability density functions for project end-date forecasts which place a much higher likelihood on the project's actual end-date with more mass around this date than when using a uniform bin size classifier.

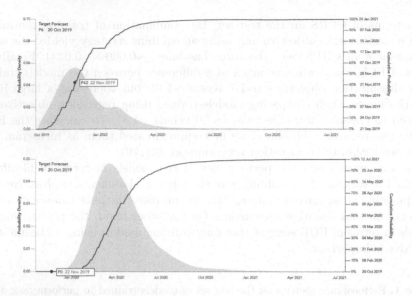

**Fig. 3.** Comparison of project level forecasts after running Monte-Carlo simulations using samples from a classification model with `equibin` classes (above) versus a regression Gaussian mixture model (below). The same true end date for the project is marked on each graph.

## 7   Discussion and Conclusions

Accurately forecasting project end dates is a valuable, yet challenging task, traditionally solved by relying on heuristics provided by experts to forecast activity durations and Monte-Carlo simulations. In recent years, the problem of forecasting task durations has gained a growing amount of attention from the machine learning community. However, there is still no consensus on what is best practice when it comes to forecasting activity durations using neural networks. In this paper, we experiment with different problem formulations and inductive biases to determine which are important when training neural networks to forecast activity durations.

Experiments on our data set of real world construction projects suggest the performance benefits of our proposed method for forecasting activity duration, as well as forecasting project end dates. We show that posing the forecasting problem as a classification task with carefully designed classes is crucial for high quality results.

The next natural step in our research is to replace the simple feed forward neural networks used here with ones that can take advantage of the underlying graph structure in project schedules. In recent years graph neural networks have been deployed in a wide range of applications from molecular biology to social sciences [36], however graph neural networks have not yet been effectively applied to project duration forecasting problems. Another interesting direction is searching for methods to train models end-to-end, meaning directly to forecast project end dates, possibly removing the need to perform Monte-Carlo sampling as part of the model when forecasting project end dates.

# References

1. Agarap, A.F.: Deep learning using rectified linear units (relu). arXiv preprint arXiv:1803.08375 (2018)
2. Bhandari, S., Molenaar, K.R.: Using debiasing strategies to manage cognitive biases in construction risk management: recommendations for practice and future research. Pract. Period. Struct. Design Constr. **25**(4), 04020033 (2020)
3. Bishop, C.M.: Pattern Recognition and Machine Learning. Springer, Heidelberg (2006)
4. Culakova, N., et al.: How to calibrate your neural network classifier: getting true probabilities from a classification model. In: Proceedings of the 26th ACM SIGKDD International Conference on Knowledge Discovery & Data Mining (2020)
5. Malcolm, D.G., Roseboom, J.H., Clark, C.E., Fazar, W.: Application of a technique for research and development program evaluation. Oper. Res. **7**(5), 646–669 (1959)
6. Dubois, D., Fargier, H., Fortemps, P.: Fuzzy scheduling: modelling flexible constraints vs. coping with incomplete knowledge. Eur. J. Oper. Res. **147**(2), 231–252 (2003)
7. Egwim, C.N., et al.: Applied artificial intelligence for predicting construction projects delay. Mach. Learn. Appl. **6**, 100166 (2021)
8. Fazar, W.: Program evaluation and review technique. Am. Stat. **13**(2), 10 (1959)
9. Fiori, C., Kovaka, M.: Defining megaprojects: learning from construction at the edge of experience. In: Construction Research Congress 2005: Broadening Perspectives (2005)
10. Flyvbjerg, B., Bruzelius, N., Rothengatter, W.: An Anatomy of Ambition: Megaprojects and Risk. Cambridge University Press, Cambridge (2003)
11. Gal, Y., Ghahramani, Z.: Dropout as a bayesian approximation: representing model uncertainty in deep learning. In: International Conference on Machine Learning. PMLR (2016)
12. Gneiting, T., Raftery, A.E.: Strictly proper scoring rules, prediction, and estimation. J. Am. Stat. Assoc. **102**(477), 359–378 (2007)
13. Gneiting, T., Katzfuss, M.: Probabilistic forecasting. Ann. Rev. Stat. Appl. **1**, 125–151 (2014)
14. Guo, C., et al.: On calibration of modern neural networks. In: International Conference on Machine Learning. PMLR (2017)
15. Guo, X., et al.: On the class imbalance problem. In: 2008 Fourth International Conference on Natural Computation, vol. 4. IEEE (2008)
16. Hahn, E.D.: Mixture densities for project management activity times: a robust approach to PERT. Eur. J. Oper. Res. **188**(2), 450–459 (2008)
17. Hong, Y., et al.: Determining construction method patterns to automate and optimise scheduling-a graph-based approach. In: European Conference on Computing in Construction (2021). https://doi.org/10.17863/CAM.Vol.68385
18. Ioffe, S., Szegedy, C.: Batch normalization: accelerating deep network training by reducing internal covariate shift. In: International Conference on Machine Learning. PMLR (2015)
19. Japkowicz, N., Stephen, S.: The class imbalance problem: a systematic study. Intell. Data Anal. **6**, 429–449 (2002)

20. Jiao, X., et al.: Tinybert: distilling bert for natural language understanding. arXiv preprint arXiv:1909.10351 (2019)
21. Jolliffe, I.T., Stephenson, D.B. (eds.): Forecast Verification: A Practitioner's Guide in Atmospheric Science. John Wiley & Sons, Hoboken (2012)
22. Kingma, D.P., Ba, J.: Adam: a method for stochastic optimization. arXiv preprint arXiv:1412.6980 (2014)
23. Lakshminarayanan, B., Pritzel, A., Blundell, C.: Simple and scalable predictive uncertainty estimation using deep ensembles. In: Advances in Neural Information Processing Systems, vol. 30 (2017)
24. Mahdi, M.N., et al.: Software project management using machine learning technique-a review. Appl. Sci. **11**(11), 5183 (2021)
25. Mahmoodzadeh, A., Mohammadi, M., Daraei, A., Farid Hama Ali, H., Ismail Abdullah, A., Kameran Al-Salihi, N.: Forecasting tunnel geology, construction time and costs using machine learning methods. Neural Comput. Appl. **33**(1), 321–348 (2020). https://doi.org/10.1007/s00521-020-05006-2
26. Mahmoodzadeh, A., et al.: Predicting construction time and cost of tunnels using Markov chain model considering opinions of experts. Tunnel. Undergr. Space Technol. **116**, 104109 (2021)
27. Maravas, A., Pantouvakis, J.-P.: Project cash flow analysis in the presence of uncertainty in activity duration and cost. Int. J. Proj. Manag. **30**(3), 374–384 (2012)
28. Mosca, A., Magoulas, G.D.: Boosted residual networks. In: Boracchi, G., Iliadis, L., Jayne, C., Likas, A. (eds.) EANN 2017. CCIS, vol. 744, pp. 137–148. Springer, Cham (2017). https://doi.org/10.1007/978-3-319-65172-9_12
29. Petropoulos, F., et al.: Forecasting: theory and practice. Int. J. Forecast. (2022)
30. Popescu, M.-C., et al.: Multilayer perceptron and neural networks. WSEAS Trans. Circ. Syst. **8**(7), 579–588 (2009)
31. Raftery, A.E.: Use and communication of probabilistic forecasts. Stat. Anal. Data Mining ASA Data Sci. J. **9**(6), 397–410 (2016)
32. Van Slyke, R.M.: Letter to the editor-monte carlo methods and the PERT problem. Oper. Res. **11**(5), 839–860 (1963)
33. Sanderson, J.: Risk, uncertainty and governance in megaprojects: a critical discussion of alternative explanations. Int. J. Proj. Manag. **30**(4), 432–443 (2012)
34. Srivastava, N., et al.: Dropout: a simple way to prevent neural networks from overfitting. J. Mach. Learn. Res. **15**(1), 1929–1958 (2014)
35. Taleb, N.N.: The Black Swan: The Impact of the Highly Improbable, vol. 2. Random house (2)007
36. Wu, Z., et al.: A comprehensive survey on graph neural networks. IEEE Trans. Neural Netw. Learn. Syst. **32**(1), 4–24 (2020)
37. Zheng, H., et al.: Improving deep neural networks using softplus units. In: 2015 International Joint Conference on Neural Networks (IJCNN). IEEE (2015)

# On the Suitability of Neural Networks as Building Blocks for the Design of Efficient Learned Indexes

Domenico Amato, Giosué Lo Bosco[✉], and Raffaele Giancarlo

Dipartimento di Matematica e Informatica, Universitá degli Studi di Palermo,
Palermo, Italy
giosue.lobosco@unipa.it

**Abstract.** With the aim of obtaining time/space improvements in classic Data Structures, an emerging trend is to combine Machine Learning techniques with the ones proper of Data Structures. This new area goes under the name of *Learned Data Structures*. The motivation for its study is a perceived change of paradigm in Computer Architectures that would favour the use of Graphics Processing Units and Tensor Processing Units over conventional Central Processing Units. In turn, that would favour the use of Neural Networks as building blocks of Classic Data Structures. Indeed, Learned Bloom Filters, which are one of the main pillars of Learned Data Structures, make extensive use of Neural Networks to improve the performance of classic Filters. However, no use of Neural Networks is reported in the realm of Learned Indexes, which is another main pillar of that new area. In this contribution, we provide the first, and much needed, comparative experimental analysis regarding the use of Neural Networks as building blocks of Learned Indexes. The results reported here highlight the need for the design of very specialized Neural Networks tailored to Learned Indexes and it establishes solid ground for those developments. Our findings, methodologically important, are of interest to both Scientists and Engineers working in Neural Networks Design and Implementation, in view also of the importance of the application areas involved, e.g., Computer Networks and Databases.

## 1 Introduction

Learned Data Structures is a new research area based on the combination of Machine Learning (ML) techniques with the ones proper of Data Structures, with the aim of obtaining time/space improvements in classic Data Structures. It was initiated by [18], it has grown very rapidly [11] and now it has been extended to include also Learned Algorithms [22].

This research is funded in part by MIUR Project of National Relevance 2017WR7SHH "Multicriteria Data Structures and Algorithms: from compressed to learned indexes, and beyond". We also acknowledge an NVIDIA Higher Education and Research Grant (donation of a Titan V GPU).

© Springer Nature Switzerland AG 2022
L. Iliadis et al. (Eds.): EANN 2022, CCIS 1600, pp. 115–127, 2022.
https://doi.org/10.1007/978-3-031-08223-8_10

## 1.1   Computer Architectures as a Motivation for Learned Data Structures

The ML models with the most potential in this area are undoubtedly Neural Networks (NNs), because of their learning power, e.g., [24]. Unfortunately, they require prohibitive computational power. In recent years, the introduction of Graphics Processing Unit (GPU) and Tensor Processing Unit (TPU) architectures in commercial computers [25,27], and the deployment of highly engineered development platforms such as Tensorflow [2], has *de facto* removed the computational bottleneck referred to earlier. In fact, ML Models, and in particular NNs, have been increasingly used in many application domains [19].

The major strength of these new architectures is that they can parallelise math operations made by NNs very well, compared to a general-purpose set of instructions. In particular, recent studies even argue that the power of the GPU can be improved by 1000x in terms of time in the next few years, while, due to Moore's Law constraints [23], those improvements are not seen for classic CPUs. Furthermore, a programming paradigm based on branches of the if-then-else type seems to have been overcome in favour of a paradigm that promotes straight-line mathematical operations, which can be pipelined efficiently on those modern architectures. For these reasons, using ML models such as NNs, on such advanced architectures instead of the classic Data Structures, which make extensive use of branch instructions in their code, may lead to the deployment of substantially better Data Structures, with benefits in many areas such as Computer Networks and Data Bases.

Unfortunately, although the above motivation for the design of Learned Data Structures based on NNs is indeed a strong one, the potential gain that can be achieved is either at an initial stage of assessment or it has not been assessed at all, as we outline next.

## 1.2   From Motivation to Design and Implementation of Learned Data Structures: The Role of NNs

- **Learned Bloom Filters.** NNs have been extensively used within the design and implementation of Learned Bloom Filters, since the very start of the area of Learned Data Structure [18]. We recall that, given a universe $U$ of elements, a Bloom Filter [6] is a Data Structure to solve the *Approximate Membership Problem* for a given set $A \subset U$. That is, given a query element $x \in U$, establish whether $x \in A$, with a specific False Positive Rate (FPR) $\epsilon$ and zero False Negatives. Essential parameters for the evaluation of the performance of Bloom Filters are FPR, Query Time and Space Occupancy. Those parameters are very intimately connected, as well explained in [8]. The current versions of Learned Bloom Filters that have been proposed in the literature [9,18,21,26] use convolutional and recurrent neural networks. The interested reader can find details in [14], together with an experimental comparative performance analysis.

- **Learned Indexes.** Learned Indexes [18] have been introduced to solve the so-called *Predecessor Search Problem*. Given a sorted table $A$ of $n$ keys taken from a universe $U$, and a query element $x$ in $A$, the Predecessor Search Problem consists in finding the $A[j]$ such that $A[j] \leq x < A[j + 1]$. A synopsis of the Learned Indexes Methodology is presented in Sect. 2. Although several versions of Learned Indexes have been proposed, e.g., [3,4,11,12,18,20], surprisingly, none of them use NNs. Even more surprisingly, no comparative performance analysis regarding the use of NNs in Learned Indexing has been carried out.
- **Additional Learned Data Structures.** Learned Hash Functions [18] as well as Learned Rank and Select Data Structures [7] do not use NNs. Again, no performance analysis regarding those models has been carried out.

### 1.3    Our Results: The Role of Neural Networks in the Design of Learned Indexes - The Atomic Case

In view of the State of the Art reported in Sect. 1.2, our novel contribution to the advancement of the area of Learned Data Structures is the first assessment of the suitability of NNs as building blocks of Learned Indexes. Indeed, in order to provide a clear comparative assessment of the potential usefulness of NNs in the mentioned domain, we consider Atomic Models for Learned Indexes, defined in Sect. 3. Intuitively, they are the simplest models one can think of. The rationale for their choice is that, if NNs do not provide any significant advance with respect to very simple Learned Indexes, in view of the results in [3,4], they have very little to offer to Learned Indexing in their current generic, if not "textbook", form even with the advantage of GPU processing. Technically, we offer the following contributions:

- The first design of a Learned Index based on NNs Models only. We choose Feed Forward NNs because they offer a good compromise between time efficiency, space occupancy and ability to learn [5]. Since this Learned Index has no other ML subcomponent, we refer to it as an Atomic Learned Index.
- An extensive experimental study about the effectiveness of this Atomic Learned Index, both in the case of CPU and GPU processing.
- An extensive comparison of this Atomic Learned Index with respect to analogous Atomic Indexes that use only Linear Regression [13] as the learned part. Those models have been formalized and studied in [3,4] and they are valid building blocks of more complex models used for Learned Indexes, e.g., the **RMI** family [20].

As opposed to Learned Bloom Filters, our results clearly indicate the need to design NNs specifically focused on their use in the Learned Indexing paradigm. A study analogous to ours, that paves the way to development of NNs more specific for Learned Indexing, is not available in the Literature and it is of methodological importance.

The software we have used for our experiments is available at [1].

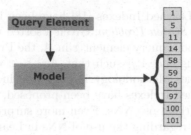

**Fig. 1. A general paradigm of Learned Searching in a Sorted Set** [20]. The model is trained on the data in the table. Then, given a query element, it is used to predict the interval in the table where to search (included in brackets in the figure).

### 1.4 Organization of the Paper

This paper is organized as follows. Section 2 provides a synoptic description on Learned Indexing. Section 3 presents the Atomic Models that we consider for this research. In Sect. 4, we illustrate the adopted experimental methodology. Section 5 reports experiments and findings. Finally, in Sect. 6, we provide conclusions and future direction of research.

## 2   Learned Indexes: A Synopsis

Consider a sorted table $A$ of $n$ keys, taken from a universe $U$. It is well known that Sorted Table Search can be phrased as the Predecessor Search Problem: for a given query element $x$, return the $A[j]$ such that $A[j] \leq x < A[j+1]$. Kraska et al. [18] have proposed an approach that transforms such a problem into a learning-prediction one. With reference to Fig. 1, the model learned from the data is used as a predictor of where a query element may be in the table. To fix ideas, Binary Search is then performed only on the interval returned by the model.

We now outline the basic technique that one can use to build a model for $A$. It relies on Linear Regression [13]. With reference to the example in Fig. 2 and assuming that one wants a linear model, i.e., $F(x) = ax + b$, Kraska et al. note that one can fit a straight line to the CDF and then use it to predict where a point $x$ may fall in terms of rank and accounting also for approximation errors. In terms of regression, the function $F$ is a *Model* for the CDF function.

More in general, in order to perform a query, the model is consulted and an interval in which to search for is returned. Then, to fix ideas, Binary Search on that interval is performed. Different models may use different schemes to determine the required range, as outlined in Sect. 3. The reader interested in a rigorous presentation of those ideas can consult Markus et al. [20].

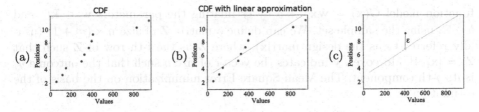

**Fig. 2. The Process of Learning a Simple Model via Linear Regression.** Let $A$ be $[47, 105, 140, 289, 316, 358, 386, 398, 819, 939]$. (a) The CDF of A. In the diagram, the $x$ coordinate indicates the value of an element in the table, while the $y$ is its rank. (b) Values $a$ and $b$ of the straight line $F(x) = ax + b$ are obtained solving Linear Regression. (c) The maximum error $\epsilon$ one can incur in using $F$ is $\epsilon = 3$, i.e., accounting for rounding, it is the maximum distance between the rank of a point in the table and its rank as predicted by $F$. In this case, the interval to search into, for a given query element $x$, is given by $I = [F(x) - \epsilon, F(x) + \epsilon]$.

## 3    Atomic Models for Learned Indexes

As outlined in Sect. 2, a simple linear function that provides a model for the CDF of the data is a model for Learned Indexes. With reference to Fig. 1, when the model consists of either a closed-form formula or a simple program that provides an estimation of the CDF on a given point, we refer to it as *Atomic*. That is, it has no sub-component that has been learned from the data. As stated in the Introduction, more complex models exist. However, as already outlined, for the aim of this research, it is best to consider Atomic Models only. In particular, we consider models that come from an analytical solution to regression problems (see Sect. 3.1), and models that use NNs (see Sect. 3.2).

### 3.1    CDF Function Models Based on Analytic Solutions to Regression Problems

Regression is a methodology for estimating a given function $G : \mathbb{R}^m \to \mathbb{R}$ via a specific function model $\tilde{G}$. The independent variables in $x \in \mathbb{R}^m$ and the dependent variable $y \in \mathbb{R}$ are usually referred to as predictors and outcomes, respectively. The parameters of $\tilde{G}$ are estimated by minimizing an error function, computed using a sample set of predictors-outcome measurements. The most commonly used Regression Loss Function is the Mean Square Error. Such a task can be accomplished in several ways. Here we follow the method outlined in [15]. In particular, we present linear (as a matter of fact, polynomial) closed-form formulae solving the posed minimization problem.

Linear regression (**LR** for short) is the case when a geometric linear form is assumed as a model. In the case, when $m = 1$, it is referred to as Simple Linear Regression (**SLR** for short) and as Multiple Linear Regression (**MLR** for short), otherwise.

For the general case of **LR**, given a training set of $n$ predictor-outcome couples $(\mathbf{x}_i, y_i)$, where $\mathbf{x}_i \in \mathbb{R}^m$ and $y_i \in \mathbb{R}$, the goal is to characterize the linear function model $\tilde{G}(\mathbf{x}) = \hat{\mathbf{w}}\mathbf{x}^T + \hat{b}$ by estimating the parameters $\hat{\mathbf{w}} \in \mathbb{R}^m$ and $\hat{b} \in \mathbb{R}$, using the sample set. We can define a matrix $\mathbf{Z}$ of size $n \times (m+1)$ (usually referred to as the design matrix), where $\mathbf{Z}_i$ is the $i$-th row of $\mathbf{Z}$ such that $\mathbf{Z}_i = [\mathbf{x}_i, 1]$. Moreover, $\mathbf{y}$ indicates the vector of size $n$ such that the outcome $y_j$ is its $j$-th component. The Mean Square Error minimization on the basis of the estimation is:

$$\mathbf{MSE}(\mathbf{w}, b) = \frac{1}{n} \left\| [\mathbf{w}, b]\mathbf{Z}^T - \mathbf{y} \right\|_2^2 \tag{1}$$

**MSE** is a convex quadratic function on $[\mathbf{w}, b]$, so that the unique values that minimize it can be obtained by setting its gradient $\nabla_{\mathbf{w}, b}$ equal to zero. The closed form solution for the parameters $\mathbf{w}, b$ is

$$[\hat{\mathbf{w}}, \hat{b}] = \mathbf{y}\mathbf{Z}(\mathbf{Z}^T\mathbf{Z})^{-1} \tag{2}$$

It is to be noted that the **SLR** case is characterized by the choice of a polynomial of degree $g = 1$. The general case of Polynomial Regression (**PR** for short), using polynomials with degree $g > 1$, are special cases of **MLR**. Indeed, we can consider the model:

$$\tilde{G}(\mathbf{z}) = \mathbf{w}\mathbf{z}^T + b$$

where $w$ is of size $g$, $\mathbf{z} = [x, .., x^{g-1}, x^g] \in \mathbb{R}^g$ is the predictor vector for **MLR**.

In this paper, we use linear, quadratic and cubic regression models to approximate the function $F$ given by the $CDF$ of the data. In particular, the corresponding models are prefixed by **L**, **Q**, or **C**.

### 3.2   CDF Function Models Based on Neural Networks

Another method to learn a function $G : \mathbb{R}^m \rightarrow \mathbb{R}$ is to use NNs. In particular, we focus on Feed-Forward NNs, where the general strategy consists of an iterative training phase during which an improvement of the $\tilde{G}$ approximation is made. Starting from an initial approximation $\tilde{G}_0$, at each step $i$, an attempt is made to minimize an error function $E$ so that $E(\tilde{G}_{i-1}) \geq E(\tilde{G}_i)$. The minimization is carried out on a training set $T$ of examples. The process can stop after a fixed number of steps or when, given a tolerance $\delta$, $| E(\tilde{G}_{i-1}) - E(\tilde{G}_i) | \leq \delta$. In the following, we report the basic elements that characterize the type of NN we use.

1. **ARCHITECTURE TOPOLOGY.**
   (a) As atomic element of our NN, we use a standard Perceptron [5] with *relu* activation function.
   (b) The number of Hidden Layers $H$.
   (c) For each hidden layer $h_i$, its number of Perceptrons $n_{h_i}$.
   (d) The connection between each layer. In our case, a Fully Connected NN is used, i.e. each Perceptron of layer $h_i$ is connected with each Perceptron of the next layer $h_{i+1}$.
2. **THE LEARNING ALGORITHM.**

(a) The error function $E$, that is used to measure how close is $\tilde{G}$ to $G$.
(b) The gradient descent iterative process that starts from a $\tilde{G}_0$ and, at each step, better approximates $G$ reducing $E$, changing layer by layer, by a backward and forward pass, the parameters of each layer. It can be characterized by a learning rate, i.e. the multiplicative constant of the gradient error.

3. **THE TRAINING SCHEME**.
  (a) The size of a batch $B$, i.e., the number of elements to extract from the training set $T$. At each extraction of the batch, the parameters are updated.
  (b) The number of epochs $ne$ that corresponds to the number of times the training set $T$ is presented to the NN for the minimization of $E$.

The learning algorithm of a NN uses a proper training set to perform the gradient descent iterative process. For the purpose of indexing, which is our goal, the training data are in the form of scalar integers. To perform a Regression using a NN, it is mandatory to represent the scalar integer $x$ with a vector representation $\overrightarrow{x}$. In this work, $\overrightarrow{x}$ is a string containing the 64-bit binary representation of $x$, as suggested also by Kraska et al. [18].

### 3.3   Prediction Accuracy of an Atomic Model

As well illustrated in Fig. 2, the approximation error is very important in reducing the size of the interval to be searched into. Smaller the error, the smaller the portion of the table in which the final search must be performed. In this paper, we characterize the accuracy in prediction of a model via the *reduction factor* (**RF**): the percentage of the table that is no longer considered for searching after a prediction. Because of the diversity across models to determine the search interval, and in order to place all models on a par, we estimate empirically the **RF** of a model. That is, with the use of the model and over a batch of queries, we determine the length of the interval to search into for each query (the interval $I$ in Fig. 2). Based on it, it is immediate to compute the reduction factor for that query. Then, we take the average of those reduction factors over the entire set of queries as the reduction factor of the model for the given table.

## 4   Experimental Methodology

### 4.1   Hardware and Datasets

Experiments have been performed using a workstation equipped with an Intel Core i7-8700 3.2 GHz CPU and an Nvidia Titan V GPU. The total amount of system memory is 32 Gbyte of DDR4. The GPU is also supplied with its own 12 Gbyte of DDR5 memory and adopts a CUDA parallel computing platform. CPU and GPU are connected with a PCIe 3 bus with a bandwidth of 32Gbyte/s. The operating system is Ubuntu LTS 20.04.

We have used both synthetic and real datasets, taken from previous studies on Learned Indexes [12,18]. The synthetic ones have been generated using random sampling in $[1, 2^{r-1}-1]$, with $r = 64$. Datasets are sorted and without duplicates. We anticipate that, as evident from the analysis in Sect. 5, the use of GPU training for the NNs severely limits the size of the datasets that we can use.

1. **Uni** that contains data sample from a Uniform distribution defined as

$$U(x, a, b) = \begin{cases} \frac{1}{b-a} & \text{if } x \in [a, b] \\ 0 & otherwise \end{cases} \tag{3}$$

   where $a = 1$ e $b = 2^{r-1} - 1$. Its size is 1.10e+04 Kb and it contains 1.05e+06 integers.
2. **Logn** that contains data sample from a Log-normal distribution defined as

$$L(x, \mu, \sigma) = \frac{e^{-\frac{(lnx-\mu)^2}{2\sigma^2}}}{x\sqrt{2\pi}\sigma} \tag{4}$$

   where $\mu = 0$ e $\sigma = 1$ are respectively mean and variance of the distribution. Its size is 1.05e+04 Kb and it contains 1.05e+06 integers.

1. **Real-wl** that contains timestamps of about 715M requests performed by a web server during 2016. Its size is 3.48e+05 Kb and it contains 3.16e+07 integers.
2. **Real-iot** that consists of timestamps of about 26M events recorded during 2017 by IoT sensors deployed in academic buildings. Its size is 1.67e+05 Kb and it contains 1.52e+07 integers.

As for the query dataset, for each of the above tables, it has a size equal to 50% of the reference table and contains, in equal parts, both elements present and not present in the table. For all the experiments, the query datasets are not sorted.

### 4.2    Binary Search and the Corresponding Atomic Learned Indexes

For the final search stage, in addition to a standard Binary Search method, we use also Uniform Binary Search [17] (see also [16]). Indeed, based on work by Khuong and Morin [16], it can be streamlined to avoid "branchy" instructions in its implementation. Such a streamlining results in a speed-up in regard to the standard procedure. The interested reader can find details in [16]. We refer to the standard procedure as Branchy Binary Search (**BBS**) and to the other version as a Branch-Free (**BFS**).

As for Atomic Models, we use **L, Q,** and **C**. Additional Atomic Models are obtained via NNs. Indeed, we consider three types of NNs with different hidden layers, as specified next. **NN0** for zero hidden layers, **NN1** for one hidden layer, **NN2** for two hidden layers, each layer consisting in 256 units.

Each of the above models provides two Atomic Learned Indexes, one for each Binary Search routine used for the final search stage.

# 5   Experiments and Findings

We use the datasets described in Sect. 4.1. Both training and query datasets are transformed, as outlined in Sect. 3.2, to use them as input of the NNs. For NN training, we use the highly-engineered Tensorflow platform, with GPU support. The results are reported in Sect. 5.1.

As for queries, we perform the following experiments.

- **TensorFlow.** We have carried out query experiments by uploading the platform to GPU, in order to perform query searches with the Learned Indexes based on NNs. Because of the overhead to upload Tensorflow in the GPU, results are very disappointing and therefore not reported. This is in agreement with considerations in [18].
- **NVIDIA CUDA Implementation.** We use our own implementation of the Learned Index corresponding to **NN0** and with **BBS** for the final search stage. The results are reported in Sect. 5.2. As discussed in that Section, this experiment indicates that the use of the GPU is not advantageous, even with respect to the baseline **BBS**, implemented in a parallel version. Therefore, no further experiment on the GPU has been performed.
- **CPU.** In this case, we have performed the entire set of experiments. For conciseness, we report the results only with the use of **BFS**, since the ones involving **BBS** would add very little to the discussion. They are reported and discussed in Sect. 5.3.

## 5.1   Training: GPU vs CPU

In Table 1, we report the training times per element for each method described in the preceding Section, and we also indicate the respective **RF**, computed as indicated in Sect. 3.3. For what concerns Atomic Models **L**, **Q** and **C**, the training time is the time needed to solve Eq. 2. Regarding the NN models, the used learning algorithm is stochastic gradient descent with momentum parameter equal to 0.9 and a learning rate equal to 0.1. The Batch size is 64, and the number of epochs is 2000.

As is evident from the results reported in Table 1, even with GPU support and the use of the highly-engineered Tensorflow platform, NNs are not competitive with respect to the **L**, **Q** and **C** Atomic Models, both in training time and **RF**. Indeed, for each dataset, the NNs training time per item is four orders of magnitude higher than the one obtained with the non-NN Atomic Models, with comparable **RF**.

## 5.2   Query: GPU only for NNs

We perform an experiment, only on **NN0** and **uni**, to see if there could be a real advantage from using the GPU for queries. In Table 2, we report the query time per element resulting from this experiment. As evident from that Table, on GPUs, the copy operations from CPU to GPU, and vice versa, cancel the

**Table 1. Atomic Indexes Training Time and Reduction Factor.** For each datasets and each model, it is shown: the training time per element expressed in seconds (column **TT (s)**) and the percentage of the table reduction (column **RF (%)**), as described in Sect. 3.3.

|  | uni | | logn | | real-wl | | real-iot | |
|---|---|---|---|---|---|---|---|---|
|  | TT (s) | RF (%) | TT (s) | RF (%) | TT (s) | RF (%) | TT (s) | RF (%) |
| NN0 | 2.55e−04 | 94.08% | 1.39e−04 | 54.40% | 2.50e−04 | 99.99% | 1.28e−04 | 89.90% |
| NN1 | 4.18e−04 | 99.89% | 3.79e−04 | 94.21% | 2.31e−04 | 99.88% | 4.20e−04 | 98.54% |
| NN2 | 4.49e−04 | 99.87% | 8.60e−04 | 97.14% | 2.33e−04 | 99.8% | 3.57e−04 | 97.31% |
| L | 8.20e−08 | 99.94% | 5.61e−08 | 77.10% | 5.82e−08 | 99.99% | 7.70e−08 | 96.48% |
| Q | 1.27e−07 | 99.98% | 1.02e−07 | 90.69% | 1.14e−07 | 99.99% | 1.25e−07 | 99.1% |
| C | 1.84e−07 | 99.97% | 1.74e−07 | 95.76% | 1.24e−07 | 99.45% | 1.63e−07 | 98.87% |

**Table 2. Query Time on GPUs. NN0-BBS** refers to Binary Search with **NN0** as the prediction step, while **BBS** is the parallel Binary Search executed on GPU without a previous prediction. For each of these methods executed on GPU, we report: the time for CPU-GPU, and vice versa, copy operations (column **Copy (s)**), the time for math operations (column **Op. (s)**), the time to search into the interval (column **Search (s)**) and the total time to complete the query process (column **Query (s)**). Every time in the Table is per element and is expressed in seconds.

| Methods | Copy (s) | Op. (s) | Search (s) | Query (s) |
|---|---|---|---|---|
| NN0-BBS | 3.27e−08 | 4.20e−09 | 1.84e−09 | 3.27e−08 |
| BBS | 2.55e−09 | – | 1.89e−09 | 4.44e−09 |

one order of magnitude speed-up of the math operations. In addition, a classic parallel Binary Search **BBS** on the GPU is by itself faster than its Learned counterparts, making the use of NNs on this architecture unnecessary.

### 5.3  Query: CPU only for All Atomic Models

The query experiments results are summarized in Tables 3 and 4. As we can see, NNs are also not competitive for the query phase.

The query time on **NN1** and **NN2** is even two orders of magnitude greater than the one obtained with the simple **L** Model. In addition, in some cases, the transformed dataset is too large to be stored entirely in the CPU memory, causing a space allocation error.

**Table 3. CPU Prediction Effectiveness-NN Atomic Models. NN0-BFS** refers to Binary Search with **NN0** as the prediction step, while the other two columns refer to the time taken by **NN1** and **NN2** to predict the search interval only. The time is reported as time per query in second. When the model and the queries are too big to fit in the main memory, a space error is reported.

| Dataset | BFS | NN0-BFS | NN1 | NN2 |
|---------|-----|---------|-----|-----|
| uni | 2.81e−07 | 1.31e−07 | 1.56e−06 | 5.16e−06 |
| logn | 2.08e−07 | 1.92e−07 | 1.69e−06 | 5.24e−06 |
| real-wl | 3.38e−07 | 4.59e−07 | Space error | Space error |
| real-iot | 3.07e−07 | 4.76e−07 | 1.90e−06 | 1.94e−05 |

**Table 4. CPU Prediction Effectiveness-Non NN Atomic Models.** The Table reports results with Linear, Quadratic and Cubic models. The Legend is as in Table 3.

| Dataset | BFS | L-BFS | Q-BFS | C-BFS |
|---------|-----|-------|-------|-------|
| uni | 2.81e−07 | 9.42e−08 | 8.11e−08 | 9.39e−08 |
| logn | 2.08e−07 | 1.60e−07 | 1.59e−07 | 1.54e−07 |
| real-wl | 3.38e−07 | 5e05e−08 | 2.12e−7 | 1.80e−7 |
| real-iot | 3.07e−07 | 8.32e−08 | 1.99e−7 | 2.57e−7 |

## 6   Conclusions

A perceived paradigm shift is one of the motivations for the introduction of the Learned Indexes. Despite that, the use of a GPU architecture for Learned Indexes based on NNs seems not to be appropriate when we use generic NNs as we have done here. It is to be pointed out that certainly, the use of a GPU accelerates the performance of math operations, but the data transfer between CPU and GPU is a bottleneck in the case of NNs: not only data but also the size of the model matters. When we consider CPU only, NN models are not competitive with very simple models based on Linear Regression. This research clearly points to the need to design NN architectures specialized for Learned Indexing, as opposed to what happens for Bloom Filters where generic NN models guarantee good performance to their Learned versions. In particular, those new NN models must be competitive with the Atomic Models based on Linear Regression, which are widely used as building blocks of more complex models [3,4,20]. It is to be remarked that we have considered the static case only, i.e., no insertions or deletions are allowed in the table. The dynamic case has also been considered in the literature, i.e., [10,12]. However, for that setting, no NN solution is available. In conclusion, this study provides solid grounds and valuable indications for the future development of Learned Data Structures, which would include a pervasive presence of NNs.

# References

1. https://github.com/globosco/A-Benchmarking-platform-for-atomic-learned-indexes
2. Abadi, M.: Tensorflow: Large-scale machine learning on heterogeneous distributed systems (2015). http://download.tensorflow.org/paper/whitepaper2015.pdf
3. Amato, D., Lo Bosco, G., Giancarlo, R.: Learned sorted table search and static indexes in small model space. CoRR, abs/2107.09480 (2021)
4. D. Amato, G. Lo Bosco, and R. Giancarlo. Learned sorted table search and static indexes in small model space (Extended Abstract). In Proc. of the 20-th Italian Conference in Artificial Intelligence (AIxIA), to appear in Lecture Notes in Computer Science, 2021
5. Bishop, C.M.: Neural Networks for Pattern Recognition. Oxford University Press, USA (1995)
6. Bloom, B.H.: Space/time trade-offs in hash coding with allowable errors. Commun. ACM **13**(7), 422–426 (1970)
7. Boffa, A., Ferragina, P., Vinciguerra, G.: A "learned" approach to quicken and compress rank/select dictionaries. In: Proceedings of the SIAM Symposium on Algorithm Engineering and Experiments (ALENEX) (2021)
8. Broder, A., Mitzenmacher, M.: Network applications of bloom filters: a survey. Internet Math. **1**(4), 485–509 (2003)
9. Dai, Z., Shrivastava, A.: Adaptive learned bloom filter (Ada-BF): efficient utilization of the classifier with application to real-time information filtering on the web. In: Larochelle, H., Ranzato, M., Hadsell, R., Balcan, M.F., Lin, H. (eds.) Advances in Neural Information Processing Systems, vol. 33, pp. 11700–11710. Curran Associates Inc. (2020)
10. Ding, J., et al.: Alex: an updatable adaptive learned index. In: Proceedings of the 2020 ACM SIGMOD International Conference on Management of Data, SIGMOD 2020, pp. 969–984. Association for Computing Machinery, New York (2020)
11. Ferragina, P., Vinciguerra, G.: Learned data structures. In: Oneto, L., Navarin, N., Sperduti, A., Anguita, D. (eds.) Recent Trends in Learning From Data. SCI, vol. 896, pp. 5–41. Springer, Cham (2020). https://doi.org/10.1007/978-3-030-43883-8_2
12. Ferragina, P., Vinciguerra, G.: The PGM-index: a fully-dynamic compressed learned index with provable worst-case bounds. PVLDB **13**(8), 1162–1175 (2020)
13. Freedman, D.: Statistical Models: Theory and Practice. Cambridge University Press, August 2005
14. Fumagalli, G., Raimondi, D., Giancarlo, R., Malchiodi, D., Frasca, M.: On the choice of general purpose classifiers in learned bloom filters: an initial analysis within basic filters. In: Proceedings of the 11th International Conference on Pattern Recognition Applications and Methods (ICPRAM), pp. 675–682 (2022)
15. Goodfellow, I., Bengio, Y., Courville, A.: Deep Learning. The MIT Press (2016)
16. Khuong, P.V., Morin, P.: Array layouts for comparison-based searching. J. Exp. Algorithmics **22**, 1.3:1–1.3:39 (2017)
17. Knuth, D.E.: The Art of Computer Programming, vol. 3 (Sorting and Searching) (1973)
18. Kraska, T., Beutel, A., Chi, E.H., Dean, J., Polyzotis, N.: The case for learned index structures. In: Proceedings of the 2018 International Conference on Management of Data, pp. 489–504. ACM (2018)
19. LeCun, Y., Bengio, Y., Hinton, G.: Deep learning. Nature **521**(7553), 436 (2015)

20. Marcus, R., Kipf, A., van Renen, A., Stoian, M., Misra, S., Kemper, A., Neumann, T., Kraska, T.: Benchmarking learned indexes. Proc. VLDB Endow. **14**(1), 1–13 (2020)
21. Mitzenmacher, M.: A model for learned bloom filters and optimizing by sandwiching. In: Bengio, S., Wallach, H., Larochelle, H., Grauman, K., Cesa-Bianchi, N., Garnett, R. (eds.) Advances in Neural Information Processing Systems, vol. 31. Curran Associates Inc. (2018)
22. Mitzenmacher, M., Vassilvitskii, S.: Algorithms with predictions. CoRR, abs/2006.09123 (2020)
23. Moore, G.E.: Cramming more components onto integrated circuits. Electronics, 38(8), April 1965
24. Ohn, I., Kim, Y.: Smooth function approximation by deep neural networks with general activation functions. Entropy **21**(7), 627 (2019)
25. Sato, K., Young, C., Patterson, D.: An in-depth look at Google's first tensor processing unit (2017). https://cloud.google.com/blog/products/ai-machine-learning/an-in-depth-look-at-googles-first-tensor-processing-unit-tpu
26. Vaidya, K., Knorr, E., Kraska, T., Mitzenmacher, M.: Partitioned learned bloom filter. ArXiv, abs/2006.03176 (2020)
27. Wang, B.: Moore's law is dead but GPU will get 1000x faster by 2025 (2017). https://www.nextbigfuture.com/2017/06/moore-law-is-dead-but-gpu-will-get-1000x-faster-by-2025.html

# Supporting Patient Nutrition in Critical Care Units

Kamran Soomro[1] , Elias Pimenidis[1(✉)] , and Chris McWilliams[2]

[1] University of the West of England, Britol BS16 1QY, UK
{kamran.soomro,elias.pimenidis}@uwe.ac.uk
[2] University of Bristol, Bristol BS8 1TW, UK
chris.mcwilliams@bristol.ac.uk

**Abstract.** Critical Care Unit (CCU) patients often benefit from being referred to dietitians for various reasons. This can help improve recovery time, resulting in more effective utilisation of valuable resources within the NHS (National Health Service) in the United Kingdom. However, said resources are often in high demand with scarce availability. Therefore, in this paper we propose an AI-based dashboard that can help clinicians automatically identify such patients, thereby reducing workload as well as cognitive load on clinical staff. We have trained various machine learning classifiers using various physiological measures of CCU patients and have identified a Support Vector Machine (SVC) classifier as the best performing model (AUC: 0.78). Our investigation shows promise results that significantly improve quality of patient care within the NHS. In future we intend to undertake more extensive evaluation of the dashboard developed as well as extend this work to paediatric patients.

**Keywords:** Critical care units · Patient referrals · Clinical decision support · Supervised classification · KNN

## 1 Introduction

Critical Care Units (CCUs) are the sections of hospitals where severely ill patients are treated. Their importance has been widely appreciated during the current Covid-19 pandemic where millions of ill people were treated in such units across the globe [1]. The condition of each patient at admission to the unit and their potential recovery route will dictate requirements for appropriate nutrition. This will require relevant assessment by a qualified dietitian. An early referral to such a healthcare professional can have a positive impact on the patient's outlook, rate and quality of recovery [2].

There are differences in the dietary/nutritional requirements of patients depending on their health condition at admission to the unit. There are also considerable differences between the nutritional needs of adult and children patients. Critical Care Units employ smart beds that collect a lot of data about a patient. The significance of a lot of these data is lost either due to the way it recorded and stored, or due to the inability of being able to interrelate it with other data relating to a patient's health and using it to support effective decision making.

© Springer Nature Switzerland AG 2022
L. Iliadis et al. (Eds.): EANN 2022, CCIS 1600, pp. 128–136, 2022.
https://doi.org/10.1007/978-3-031-08223-8_11

This work attempts to improve the situation by employing machine learning in analysing patient data and enhancing the speed and accuracy of prioritization of referring patients to dietitians in a Critical Care Unit, focusing on adult patients only. The authors present an early attempt in automating the referral process alleviating the burden on nursing staff who could be overwhelmed by the demand in patient care.

A number of supervised classification models were chosen for processing the patient data that was collected from different databases within the hospital and the NHS records systems and a comparative evaluation was performed. The challenge in collecting, collating and filtering the data is a major problem in the case of NHS (National Health System) in the United Kingdom as different hospitals may use different systems and the formatting of data storage is not always compatible across these [3]. Thus a lot of preparation work is required and this may raise challenges to the use of data supporting automated decision support for staff at the CCUs.

At the time of writing the Dashboard application presented here is being upgraded with further evaluation pending. The work is ongoing and further results are expected to be available over the next few months.

## 2   Problem Definition

Dietitians, as well as many other healthcare professionals, are in high demand among various other organizations and publicly funded hospitals often struggle to find such resources to staff their critical care units. At the same time they are important resources and their effective utilisation can support not just the quality of care of patients at hand, but the effective management of CCU beds which are at a premium [4].

With the advent of smart beds, a large number of physiological measurements are automatically collected for all patients under critical care in the CCU. This data is currently available to CCU staff, but due to cognitive overload, they often miss patients that require attention and there are no automated mechanisms in place to help them identify such patients.

Many patients are also sedated and need regular monitoring and external feeding. Furthermore, the data collected from patients is stored in many different places in the information system, and is often distributed across various information systems. An automated system that can automatically monitor and analyse patient data and flag patients that need referral and immediate attention by a dietitian, can significantly improve quality of patient care. Proper use of the data that is collected but not utilized to its full potential could prove a real catalyst in changing the quality of care that patients receive. Determining how routine clinical data collected in critical care units can be used to optimise patient outcomes, can lead to augmenting clinician decision-making and altering clinician behaviour to optimise patient clinical outcomes. Developing a system that can automatically screen CCU patients and prioritize the need to referral to a dietitian. Having alleviated the pressure of routine work on clinicians and dietitians could allow for further analysis of the collected data. With the aid of Machine Learning develop further interrelationships between health conditions, nutrition and its impact on health care and recovery.

## 3  Related Work

Critical Care Units (CCUs) are specific hospital wards where the sickest patients are admitted and where large amounts of detailed clinical data are collected (usually every hour) for the duration of the patient's stay. Many CCUs have moved from paper to clinical information systems to capture all this data from the patients' monitor, ventilator and other equipment such as drug infusions into a very extensive database. The data is captured using the facilities of smart beds that are utilized in CCUs gathering up to 200 different patient measurements. Gholami et al. [5] though, have established that CCUs are not using such systems and this data to their advantage, with much of the data being captured not being analysed or used for maximal benefit. In an era of limited NHS resources, these digital resources have the potential to both optimise patient outcomes and make systems more efficient and effective.

Data analysis and machine learning have been explored on several research cases and have been utilised widely in health care and Critical Care Units. They are usually used to automate processes where problems are well known and fully defined and there the deliverables to efficiency and accuracy achieved are well within the expected levels [6, 7].

The goal for CCUs is to optimise the patients' survival, clinical outcomes and to reduce harm caused by therapies (iatrogenic harm). All critical care units have a number of recognised targets to improve outcomes such as maintaining an optimal level of sedation (not too high or low), maintain lung volumes delivered by the ventilator within a specific range to minimise lung injury and trying to deliver a minimum amount of nutrition to patients whilst they are critically ill. Yet these seemingly simple targets, are often not achieved. Nutritional practices have been long proven to have a direct relationship to clinical outcomes in patients in CCUs and particularly so in patients in the paediatric sections of CCUs [8].

Accessing data in effective and efficient way can contribute towards better utilization and leading to reaping the benefits of exploring it with machine learning algorithms. Although this has been identified as a priority and the United Kingdom has over the past few years made considerable plans and advances towards such a target, the status of patient and hospital records is such that still pauses a challenge for intelligent solutions [9].

## 4  An Automation Prototype

A prototype data dashboard was developed to demonstrate how an automated system could assist staff in screening patients, shown in Fig. 1. The dashboard provides a quick overview to clinical staff about all patients in the CCU and at any time highlights those who need to see a dietitian. The dashboard shows the patient ID, and any relevant treatments that each patient is receiving, along with specialist feeding guidelines. Dietitian users of the system can filter patients accordingly, to prioritise seeing only those that are recommended for referral.

Patient prioritisation is based on an automated rule of thumb algorithm that staff nurses will have to apply manually and slowly over a range of data that could be confusing or could be interpreted inconsistently with fatigue building in during long shifts at intense working conditions. The data on the dashboard can be refreshed frequently during the day as new data can be captured from smart beds.

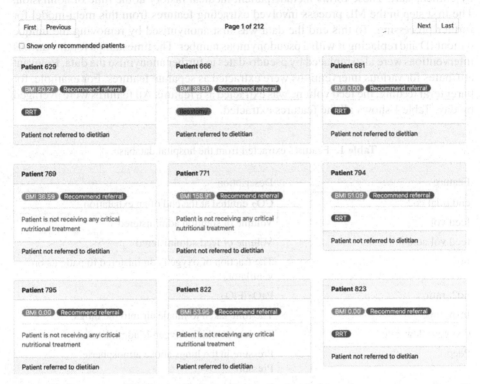

Fig. 1. Automated patient screening dashboard.

## 5 Applying Machine Learning

For Machine Learning purposes, the target variable was defined as a categorical variable indicating whether a patient should or should not be referred to a dietitian, thus formulating this as a classification problem.

### 5.1 Feature Extraction

The data in the hospital database is stored in a meta-model that is described elsewhere [2]. Treatments that patients receive as well as any interventions by clinical staff are recorded as *interventions*. Interventions in turn have *attributes*.

For example, when a patient receives parenteral feeding, a new intervention is created with attributes such as the volume of the feed, mix of solution being fed, time of feed etc. Interventions are linked to instances of patients being treated in the CCU by an *encounterID*. Every time a patient is admitted in the CCU, a new *encounterID* is assigned to the visit, which is linked to a unique *patientID*. Furthermore, each *encounterID* has an assessment form associated with it that contains free text data about the patient recorded by clinical staff. These forms include patient medical history at the time of admission. The first step in the ML process involved extracting features from this meta-model for further processing. To this end the data was first anonymised by removing the unique patient ID and replacing it with a pseudonymous number. The timestamps for the various interventions were also replaced by pseudo-dates to further anonymise the data. Relevant attributes for various interventions were extracted as separate features. For example, for parenteral feeding, the feed volume was extracted as a feature. All features were averaged by day. Table 1 shows all the features extracted.

**Table 1.** Features extracted from the hospital database.

| Feature | Description |
| --- | --- |
| end tidal co2 | $CO_2$ emitted at the end of an exhalation |
| feed vol | Volume of solution administered |
| feed vol adm | Volume of feed administered |
| fio2 | The fraction of oxygen administered to patients on ventilators |
| fio2_ratio | $PaO_2/FiO_2$ |
| Insp_time | The time taken to inhale air into the lungs |
| Oxygen_flow_rate | The rate at which oxygen is administered |
| Peep | Pressure in the lungs above atmospheric Pressure |
| Pip | Peak Inspiratory Pressure |
| resp rate | Spontaneous respiratory rate |
| Sip | Set Inspiratory Pressure |
| tidal vol Tidal Volume | Tidal Volume |
| tidal vol actual Actual Tidal Volume | Actual Tidal Volume |
| tidal vol kg Tidal Volume/KG | Tidal Volume/KG |
| tidal vol spon | Spontaneous Tidal Volume |
| Bmi | Body-Mass Index |

## 5.2  Feature Engineering

The BMI of the patients was calculated from their height and weight and outliers as well as missing values were filtered as part of the cleaning process. Furthermore, if a patient's record contained a note from a dietitian, indicating that the patient had been referred to a dietitian, the corresponding target variable was set to 1, otherwise it was set to 0. This allowed the problem to be formulated as supervised classification problem. Missing values for included features were replaced with 0.

### 5.3  Model Training

Various supervised classification models were chosen for this step. Since the target classes were unbalanced in this case (80% non-referrals vs 20% referrals), the AUC rather than the overall accuracy was chosen as the performance metric. Based on hyper-parameter tuning coupled with 10-fold cross validation, the best performing models for each algorithm were compared using the AUC. Training vs test sets were also compared (70/30 split) in order to check whether overfitting had occurred.

### 5.4  Evaluation

The models were evaluated using the Area Under the Curve (AUC). The performance of the models was evaluated using the test dataset and validated against the training dataset. Furthermore, sensitivity analysis was performed by imputing the missing values using a KNN Imputer and the results compared against the non-imputed datasets.

### 5.5  Results

Figure 2 shows the feature importance as determined by a Random Forest Classifier. Based on these results, four features were shortlisted; feed_vol, oxygen_flow_rate,

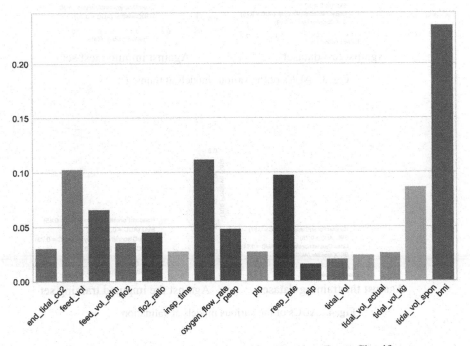

**Fig. 2.** Feature importance as returned by a Random Forest Classifier.

resp_rate and bmi. Figure 3 shows the AUCs of the models when applied to the four short listed features, while Fig. 4 shows the AUCs of the models when validated against the training data. The best performing model is a Random Forest Classifier with an AUC of 0.83. However, the results of the validation data show that it is likely overfit (AUC 0.87). Therefore, for practical purposes we consider the SVC to be the best performing model (AUCs 0.78).

## 6  Sensitivity Analysis

A sensitivity analysis was also performed by filling in the missing values using a K-Nearest Neighbor algorithm to impute the missing values. The results of the training and validation sets are shown in Figs. 3 and 4. The results clearly demonstrate the missing values do not demonstrably affect the resultant models, indicating that our models are robust. Table 2 shows the hyperparameters for the best performing classifiers.

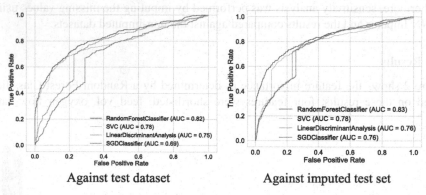

Against test dataset                    Against imputed test set

**Fig. 3.** AUCs of the various models at training

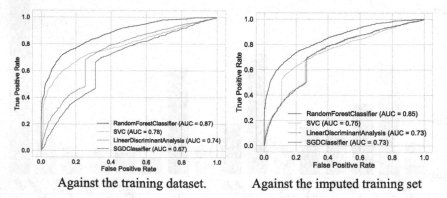

Against the training dataset.           Against the imputed training set

**Fig. 4.** AUCs of the various models at validation

**Table 2.** Parameters giving the best results for the various models.

| Classifier | Best parameters |
|---|---|
| Random forest | Max depth: 7 |
| svc | Kernel: rbf |
| Linear discriminant | Solver: svd |
| sgd | Alpha: 0.01, loss: modified_huber, penalty: l2 |

## 7  Discussion and Conclusions

Often patients admitted in CCUs would benefit from being attended by a dietitian. This can help improve recovery time as well as patient outcomes, resulting in more effective management of CCU beds which are often at a premium. Smart beds that monitor various patient physiological measurements allow automatic monitoring of patients, thus introducing the possibility of using AI-based solutions to automatically identify patients that would benefit from being referred to dietitians. This would also help reduce cognitive load on clinical staff as the various patient physiological measurements are often quite numerous and scattered across different elements of the system, making it difficult for the clinical staff to manually monitor the measurements.

To this end, we have developed a dashboard that allows clinicians to identify at a glance what patients should be referred to a dietitian. The dashboard uses an AI-based approach to identify the patients. We formulate the problem of referring patients to dietitians as a classification problem with the various patient physiological measurements as inputs to the classifiers. Our investigation shows that four measurements in particular; feed_vol, oxygen_flow_rate, resp_rate and bmi; are high predictors of the target variable. This finding is at odds with the established clinical guidelines issued by the NHS Trust and constitutes new information for clinicians. We also found that after experimenting with various classification algorithms, an SVC classifier performs the best (AUC: 0.78).

Future directions include transferring the learning from this project to paediatric patients as well as enhancing the dashboard and undertaking further evaluation of the models developed during this project.

## References

1. Bambi, S., Iozzo, P., Rasero, L., Lucchini, A.: COVID-19 in critical care units: rethinking the humanization of nursing care. Dimens Crit Care Nurs. **39**, 239–241 (2020). https://doi.org/10.1097/DCC.0000000000000438
2. Soomro, K., Pimenidis, E.: Automated screening of patients for dietician referral. In: Iliadis, L., Angelov, P.P., Jayne, C., Pimenidis, E. (eds.) EANN 2020. PINNS, vol. 2, pp. 319–325. Springer, Cham (2020). https://doi.org/10.1007/978-3-030-48791-1_24
3. NHS: Interoperability. https://www.england.nhs.uk/digitaltechnology/connecteddigitalsystems/interoperability/
4. Anandaciva, S.: Critical care services in the English NHS. https://www.kingsfund.org.uk/publications/critical-care-services-nhs

5. Gholami, B., Haddad, W.M., Bailey, J.M.: AI in the ICU: in the intensive care unit, artificial intelligence can keep watch. IEEE Spectr. **55**, 31–35 (2018). https://doi.org/10.1109/MSPEC.2018.8482421
6. Saeed, M., et al.: Multiparameter intelligent monitoring in intensive care II: a public-access intensive care unit database*: Critical Care Med. **39**, 952–960 (2011). https://doi.org/10.1097/CCM.0b013e31820a92c6
7. Salman, I., Vomlel, J.: A machine learning method for incomplete and imbalanced medical data. Presented at the 20th Czech-Japan Seminar on Data Analysis and Decision Making Pardubice. University of Ostrava, Czech, September 2017
8. Mehta, N.M., Bechard, L.J., Cahill, N., Wang, M., Day, A., Duggan, C.P., Heyland, D.K.: Nutritional practices and their relationship to clinical outcomes in critically ill children—An international multicenter cohort study*. Critical Care Med. **40**, 2204–2211 (2012). https://doi.org/10.1097/CCM.0b013e31824e18a8
9. Kelsey, T.: Digital health services by 2020: Delivering Interoperability at Point of Care to Support Safe, Effective, Efficient and High Quality Care. NHS England (2015)

# Convolutional/Deep Learning

# An Accurate Convolutional Neural Networks Approach to Wound Detection for Farmed Salmon

Aditya Gupta[1]([✉]) [ID], Even Bringsdal[2], Nicole Salbuvik[2],
Kristian Muri Knausgård[3] [ID], and Morten Goodwin[1] [ID]

[1] Centre for Artificial Intelligence Research, University of Agder, Grimstad, Norway
aditya.gupta@uia.no
[2] CreateView AS, Molde, Norway
[3] Top Research Centre Machatronics, University of Agder, Grimstad, Norway

**Abstract.** Fish is one of the most important food sources worldwide and for people in Nordic countries. For this reason, fish has been widely cultivated, but aquacultural fish are severely affected by lice, maturity, wounds, and other harmful factors typically part of agricultural fish, resulting in millions of fish deaths. Unfortunately, diagnosing injuries and wounds in live salmon fish is difficult. However, this study uses image-based machine learning approaches to present a wound detection technique for live farmed salmon fish. As part of this study, we present a new dataset of 3571 photos of injured and non-wounded fish from the Institute of Marine Research's genuine fish tank. We also propose a Convolutional Neural Network tailored for such wound detection with 20 convolutional and five subsequent dense layers. The model incorporates methods such as dropout, early halting, and Gaussian noise to avoid overfitting. Compared to the established VGG-16 and VGG-19 models, the proposed approaches have a validation accuracy of 96.22%. The model has low 0.0199 and 0.941 false positive and true positive rates, making it a good candidate for accurate live production.

**Keywords:** Fish wound detection · Convolutional neural network · Machine learning · Salmon fish

## 1 Introduction

Due to harsh environmental conditions, Nordic Country such as Norway has only 3% of agricultural lands [1]. Thus, they rely very much on Salmon fish to supply food for every citizen. Fishing agriculture remains one of the essential lifelines for the economic survival of its citizen. As a result, according to reports from the Food and Agriculture Organization of United Nations, Norway exports 7% of total world fish export making it second in the world after Chile [2]. It has annual fish consumption rate per person of 59 kg [3]. The Aquacultural fish effects by diseases such as bacterial infection causing wounds, the presence of water lice, and fish maturity causing fish wounds [4]. Fish containing wounds gives a signal about irregularities rising inside the aquaculture. These irregularities can

© Springer Nature Switzerland AG 2022
L. Iliadis et al. (Eds.): EANN 2022, CCIS 1600, pp. 139–149, 2022.
https://doi.org/10.1007/978-3-031-08223-8_12

lead to fish mortality. In 2019, Norway had a mortality of 52.8 million captive salmon [5]. Automatic detection of fish containing wounds in a real scenario can help in saving the ecosystem. The underwater scenario contains oxygen bubbles contamination of dust particles that can be misclassified as small wounds, low illumination, etc., making wound classification difficult in a live scenario. Also, sometimes wounds are very small, which can be misclassified as non-wound. The presence of dust particles captured in an image can be detected as wounds [6].

Machine learning techniques using underwater images have made underwater fish monitoring easier by analyzing fish behavior, identifying fish species, fish counting, etc. Some of the recent useful contributions are enlisted by Li, Daoliang [7] and Goodwin et al. [18]. The presence of labeled datasets has been concluded as one of the major reasons for this rapid development. Ahmed M. S. et al. [8] has recently proposed an image-based fish disease detection by performing wound detection utilizing K-Means clustering and Support Vector Machine (SVM). K-Means clustering is used for image segmentation and feature extraction. Based upon extracted features SVM classifiers are trained to detect fish diseases. The system gives an accuracy of 94% with a dataset of 210 fish images. A similar study was performed on fish images to identify Epizootic Ulcerative Syndrome (EUS) diseases in fish by identifying the wounds in fish [9]. The study performs edge detection and segmentation technique using canny edge detector and K-means cluster by segmenting wounds. After segmentation, a histogram of Gradient (HOG) is used for feature extraction and Nearest Neighbor (K-NN) technique is utilized for disease classification. The algorithm is applied on dead fish and achieved an accuracy of 86%.

Carrión uses image-based wound tracking, and assessment techniques on a mouse with the aim is to replace the laborious manual process of wound measurement. Wound images are captured at regular intervals. The wound is detected using the YOLO-3 technique, after wound detection its size is analyzed to track the healing process. YOLO-3 has been demonstrated to be an accurate model for fish detection [19] and fish species identification [19] but is still not established for wound detection. Earlier techniques also utilize chemical analysis tests for finding out the diseases in Fish. Sture et al. [10] utilize 3-D imaging for quality grading of salmon fish. Irregularities in fish such as deformation and wounds are detected by performing shape analysis and color analysis utilizing the red channel only. 45 dead fish are utilized for this, among which 16 have wounds. The proposed study has an accuracy of 90%. Balaban et al. [11] has utilized 2-D imaging in order to identify blood spots in fish. Adaptive thresholding techniques are utilized in order to find out the threshold value to identify the blood spots in fish. The study is successfully performed on 10 fish. Pate [12] uses AccuProbe Mycobacterium gordonae assay and Restriction enzyme analysis of PCR products (PCRRFLP) test in the identification of fish diseases. The study is performed on 35 fish.

## 1.1 Drawbacks

In past literature, researchers have used dead fish for wound or disease detection that too on a smaller dataset sometimes even less than 50 fish. Some of them use complex 3-D cameras on the dead fish. Some of the techniques are also focused on chemical analysis which is not possible to perform on each fish, especially in a live environment.

To make things simple and cost-effective 2-D techniques need to be utilized to make it practically implementable. Earlier techniques utilizing 2-D images have used small datasets. These techniques are applied on dead fish only, hence such techniques cannot be utilized for practical implementation. Not much of the work is done in the wound detection of Salmon fish. There are no dedicated datasets for salmon fish containing wounds. Hence there is a need to fill this space by creating the datasets which can be used by other researchers also later.

The objective of this study is to:

1) Prepare a robust dataset of images of live Salmon fish consisting of different kinds of wounds in an underwater scenario under various lighting conditions.
2) To develop 2-D image-based fish wound detection techniques.
3) The Convolutional Neural Network (CNN) should be strong enough to counter underwater scenarios and detect fish as a wound or absence of a wound (non-wounded).
4) Compare the developed CNN model with existing CNN models.

The arrangement of the paper is as follows: Sects. 2 and 3 give a detailed description of the prepared dataset and the methodology. The outcomes of the proposed models are discussed in Sect. 4 i.e., results and discussions. Based upon the results the conclusions are drawn in Sect. 5. The simulations are performed using Python 3 utilizing the TensorFlow library. The proposed model is trained on Tesla v100 GPU.

## 2   Dataset

The goal of this dataset generation is to include the salmon fish having a different kind of wounds. The images have been captured from the welfare 2-D camera from a Norwegian industry known as CreateView[1]. The cameras are installed in the Live fish tanks of the Norwegian Institute of Marine Research (IMR), Bergen, Norway as shown in Fig. 1. As cameras are installed in different fish tanks therefore it has a very limited number of wounded fish. The images are captured in day and night mode to get the images with illumination. A total of 125 non-wounded fish images have been captured compared to 101 wounded fish images. Non-wounded fish images are abundant but to avoid data imbalance only a limited number of non-wounded fish images are captured.

### 2.1   Datasets Creation

The datasets contain a total of total 3571 images among which wounded and non-wounded fish are in a ratio of 45:55. The data are split into 80:20 ratio for training and validation. A total of 2830 and 741 fish images are used for training and testing respectively. The images are captured in a fish tank under different illumination conditions day and night to match them up with the practical scenario. The images are captured in a live fish tank hence acquired images contains dust particles, water bubble, different kind of wounds from small to large as shown in Fig. 1.

---

[1] http://CreateView.ai.

142     A. Gupta et al.

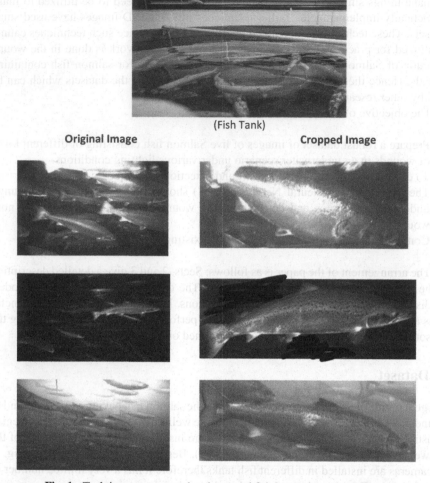

(Fish Tank)

Original Image                              Cropped Image

**Fig. 1.** Tank images, captured and cropped fish image from the fishtank

It is visible from the figure that a single image contains a lot of fish containing wounded and non-wounded fish. In order to train a model wounded fish are cropped from the images. The figure also shows the variation in image capturing under different light conditions. The figure shows different kinds of wounds in the image. It can be observed that some of the fish have very small wounds whereas are the other fish has a bigger wound. Various light illumination condition makes it harder to identify these smaller wounds.

Applying the CNN model on such a small dataset can't cook a good result. Thus, the data generator model has been utilized to generate larger datasets. For data generation strategies such as Zooming, Vertical and Horizontal flipping, rotation, image cropping, contrast variation, etc. are utilized. Thus, from one image a total of 15 images are generated. An example of data generation can be seen in Fig. 2.

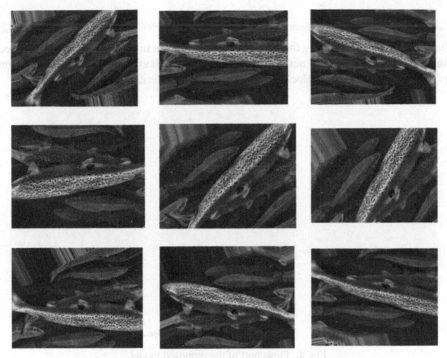

**Fig. 2.** Example of the data generation

The goal of the study is to cover different kinds of wounds such as wounds due to small skin rupture (Fig. 3 (b)), wounds due to lice attack (Fig. 3 (d)), regular wounds (Fig. 3 (a)) due to fights among themselves. Figure 3 shows some of the wounds undertaken in the dataset. Whereas Fig. 3(e) shows different lighting conditions.

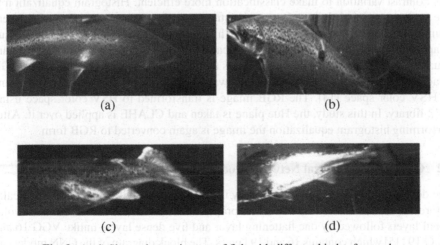

**Fig. 3.** (a–d) Shows dataset images of fish with different kinds of wounds

# 3 Methodology

After generating and splitting the datasets in test and train images. The model is trained using a convolutional neural network (CNN). The flow chart of the proposed algorithm can be seen in Fig. 4. Each block is further explained individually in subsections.

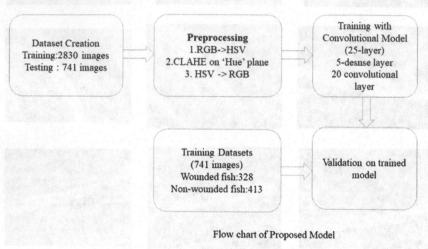

Flow chart of Proposed Model

**Fig. 4.** Flowchart of the proposed model

## 3.1  Preprocessing

Images are captured underwater day and night under different lighting conditions due to this the dataset has variations in terms of lightning. It is equally important to eliminate this contrast variation to make classification more efficient. Histogram equalization is one such promising technique for contrast stretching. To eliminate the effect of different illumination, the Contrast limited adaptive histogram equalization (CLAHE) technique is applied. CLAHE prevents over-amplification of noise unlike traditional histogram equalization [13]. Previous literature shows that applying CLAHE on underwater RGB images corrupts the color sense. A better way to perform it is by using the Hue plane of HSV color space [14]. The RGB image is transformed to HSV color space using CV2 library. In this study, the Hue plane is taken and CLAHE is applied over it. After performing histogram equalization the image is again converted to RGB form.

## 3.2  Convolutional Neural Network Model

The developed CNN model is inspired by the well-known VGG model but specifically tailored to wound detection in fish. The proposed CNN model consists of 20 convolutional layers followed by one flattening layer and five dense layers unlike VGG 16 and VGG 19 [15] which contains 16 and 19 layers. The block diagram of the CNN model can be understood from Fig. 5. 20 convolutional layers are divided into five convolutional blocks. Each block contains four convolutional layers connected back-to-back followed by the Max-Polling layer of size 2 × 2. Convolutional block 1,2,3,4 and 5 contains 64,128,256, 512 and 512 number of filters. Each filter is of size 3 × 3. (Refer Fig. 5) 'Leaky-Relu' is used here as an activation function. 'Relu' function is also used here but Leaky-Relu performs better and differences in the results are compared later in the section. 'Softmax' function is utilized as an activation function in the last dense layer i.e., dense layer 5.

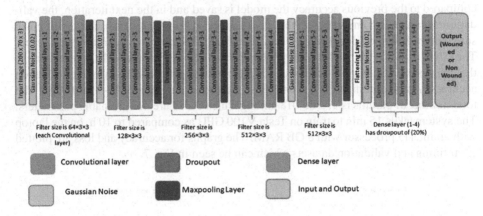

**Fig. 5.** Block diagram of convolutional neural network (CNN) model

To reduce the overfitting dropout of 20% is introduced in every dense layer. A dropout of 10% is also introduced between the second and third convolutional blocks. Adding a dense layer in convolutional blocks will have a negative effect on results hence dropout layer is avoided in a convolutional layer. Training CNN model with Gaussian noise also reduces overfitting and creates a regularizing effect [16]. For this study Gaussian noise with a mean of 0.0 and a standard deviation of 0.01 and 0.02 is utilized (refer to Fig. 5). L1 regularization is also added in the dense layer of CNN to avoid overfitting.

## 4 Result

The proposed CNN model is applied to the created dataset containing 3571 images of wounded and non-wounded salmon fish from a live fish tank. The dataset is splitted in a ratio of 80:20 for training and testing purposes. Fish are cropped from captured images for dataset creation. As a result, all images are of different sizes. In preprocessing every input image is resized to 200 × 70 × 3 (width × height × no. of channels). RGB color space is converted into HSV color space. CLAHE is applied on the Hue plane and again the image is transformed to RGB color space. It can be observed from Fig. 6 that after performing CLARE the wounds are distinguishable.

After performing preprocessing, the model is trained in the CNN model explained earlier. During training model checkpoint is used which continuously monitors the validation accuracy results every iteration. In the case of validation, accuracy is improved

**Fig. 6.** Comparative result after applying CLARE on image

compared to the previous accuracy the model is saved and in the next iteration, the validation accuracy is compared with this save a model. Utilizing this procedure will make sure that the best model will be stored and can be utilized later to produce the best result. The CNN model is trained for 125 epochs. Early stopping for 30 epochs is used here so that the system will stop automatically if CNN model is unable to improve the validation accuracy. Adam optimizer [20] is used here with a learning rate of 1e-4 or 0.0001. The total number of params is 27,366,018 among which 3,712 are non-trainable parameters. The system takes 15 min to train on Tesla V100 GPU as compared to 10 h. on the laptop with an intel i5 processor with 8 GB RAM. The graphs for accuracy and loss are plotted for training and validation datasets which can be seen in Fig. 7.

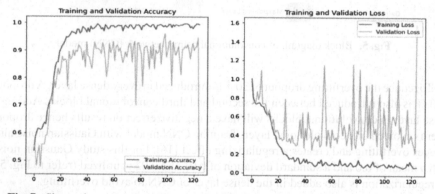

**Fig. 7.** Shows the accuracy and loss invalidation and training dataset against 125 epochs

The system has a training accuracy of 99.32 in the training dataset containing 2830 images. There are a total of 328 and 413 wounded and non-wounded images in the validation dataset. The proposed model has a validation accuracy of 96.22% Based upon the obtained results the confusion matrix is plotted which can be seen in Fig. 8. It can be observed that only 8 wounded fish are misclassified as non-wounded fish whereas 20 non-wounded fish are classified as wounded fish. False-positive rate (FPR) and true positive rate (TPR) is determined by using Eq. (1) and (2), respectively [17].

$$FPR = \frac{FP}{FP + TN} \qquad (1)$$

$$TPR = \frac{TP}{FN + TP} \qquad (2)$$

where FP and TN are false positives and true negatives, respectively, TP and FN are True positives and false negatives. The result shows that model has a False positive of 8 images and a true negative of 393 images. Similarly, the model has the true positive and false negative of 320 and 20 respectively. The False-positive and true positive rate comes out to be 0.0199 and 0.058 respectively.

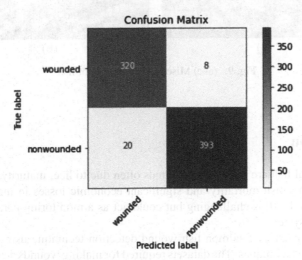

**Fig. 8.** Shows the confusion metrics of the result

**Table 1.** Comparison of proposed model with other models

| Model utilized | Validation accuracy | FPR | TPR |
|---|---|---|---|
| Proposed CNN model (with Leaky-Relu) | 96.22% | 0.0199 | 0.941 |
| Proposed CNN model (with Relu) | 93.69% | 0.073 | 0.926 |
| VGG-16 | 91.2% | 0.090 | 0.908 |
| VGG-19 | 92.81% | 0.078 | 0.917 |

Table 1 shows the comparison of the proposed model with different models. The proposed CNN model (With Leaky-Relu) gives the validation accuracy of **96.22%** compared to 91.2% and 92.81% for VGG-16 and VGG-19 models, respectively. The CNN model also gives better FPR and TPR of 0.019 and 0.941 when compared with the VGG-16 and VGG-19 models. The CNN model with 'relu' functions also gives an accuracy of 93.69%. Although accuracy is increased when 'Leaky-Relu' is used.

It is important to analyze the misclassification results also. It can be seen from Fig. 9(a) which is misclassified as non-wounded fish that the wound is almost healed and looks like skin deformation. Fig. 9 (b) and (c) are misclassified as wounded fish, affected by high illumination in small parts which can be misunderstood as wounds by the CNN model.

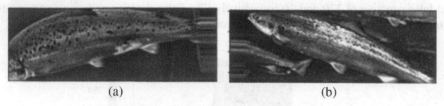

(a)                                                    (b)

**Fig. 9.** (a–c) Misclassified images of fish

## 5    Conclusion

The Aquacultural fish are affected by wounds often due to lice, maturity, fighting with other fish, causing fish mortality and significant economic losses in millions. Identifying such injured fish is challenging but could act as a monitoring parameter for the aquaculture ecosystem.

This study proposes a salmon fish wound detection technique using image-based machine learning techniques. The datasets required for making wounds detection models for salmon fish have previously not been present but is published as part of this study. The new dataset contains 3571 images of wounded and nonwounded fish in a ratio of 45:55, captured from a real fish tank from the Institute of Marine Research.

We present a CNN model, layers to detect the fish with wounds with 20 convolutional and five dense layers, leaky-relu activation, and dropout and gaussian noise layer in the CNN model to avoid overfitting. The model is trained on Tesla V100 GPU.

The proposed CNN model gives the validation accuracy of 96.22%, which is significantly higher than the to 91.2% and 92.81% for VGG-16 and VGG-19 models, respectively. The false-positive and true positive rates are 0.0199 and 0.941. The current model can only detect the wounded fish but cannot localize the wound in fish, but it is part of our future work.

Currently the proposed methodology can only classify the wound and non-wounded fish, but the system cannot locate the wound in fish. Hence locating wounds in fish using object detection techniques can be seen as future work.

**Fundings.** The authors are supported by the Norwegian Research Council HAVBRUK2 innovation project CreateView Project nr. 309784.

**Conflict of Interest.** Authors state no conflict of interest.

## References

1. Knutsen, H.: Norwegian agriculture status and trends 2019. NIBIO POP **6**(8) (2020)

2. FAO: The state of world fisheries and aquaculture 2020. In: Sustainability in Action, Rome (2022). https://doi.org/10.4060/ca9229en
3. Barange, M., Bahri, T., Beveridge, M.C., Cochrane, K.L., Funge-Smith, S., Poulain, F.: Impacts of climate change on fisheries and aquaculture: synthesis of current knowledge, adaptation and mitigation options. Fao (2020)
4. Kabir, S.R., Kousher, Kh., Abu, Al.: Fish disease detection system using machine learning. Daffodil International University, Bangladesh (2021)
5. Oliveira, V.H., Dean, K.R., Qviller, L., Kirkeby, C., Bang, J.B.: Factors associated with baseline mortality in Norwegian Atlantic salmon farming. Sci. Rep. **11**(1), 1–4 (2021)
6. Noga, E.J.: Fish Disease: Diagnosis and Treatment. Wiley, Hoboken (2010)
7. Li, D., Du, L.: Recent advances of deep learning algorithms for aquacultural machine vision systems with emphasis on fish. Artif. Intell. Rev. **55**, 1–40 (2021). https://doi.org/10.1007/s10462-021-10102-3
8. Ahmed, Md.S., Aurpa, T.T., Azad, Md.A.K.: Fish disease detection using image based machine learning technique in aquaculture. J. King Saud Univ. Comput. Inf. Sci. (2021)
9. Malik, S., Kumar, T., Sahoo, A.K.: Image processing techniques for identification of fish disease. In: 2017 IEEE 2nd International Conference on Signal and Image Processing (ICSIP), 55–59 (2017)
10. Sture, Ø., Øye, E.R., Skavhaug, A., Mathiassen, J.R.: A 3D machine vision system for quality grading of Atlantic salmon. Comput. Electron. Agric. **123**, 142–148 (2016)
11. Balaban, M.O., ÜnalŞengör, G.F., Soriano, M.G., Ruiz, E.G.: Quantification of gaping, bruising, and blood spots in salmon fillets using image analysis. J. Food Sci. **76**(3), 291–297 (2011)
12. Pate, M., Jencic, V., Zolnir-Dovc, M., Ocepek, M.: Detection of mycobacteria in aquarium fish in Slovenia by culture and molecular methods. Dis. Aquat. Org. **64**(1), 29–35 (2005)
13. Pizer, S.M., Johnston, R.E., Ericksen, J.P., Yankaskas, B.C., Muller, K.E.: Contrast-limited adaptive histogram equalization: speed and effectiveness. In: 1990 Proceedings of the First Conference on Visualization in Biomedical Computing, pp. 337–338. IEEE Computer Society (1990)
14. Yussof, W.N., Hitam, M.S., Awalludin, E.A., Bachok, Z.: Performing contrast limited adaptive histogram equalization technique on combined color models for underwater image enhancement. Int. J. Interact. Digit. Media **1**(1), 1–6 (2013)
15. Simonyan, K., Zisserman, A.: Very deep convolutional networks for large-scale image recognition. arXiv preprint arXiv:1409.1556 (2014)
16. Wang, K., Thrampoulidis, C.: Binary classification of Gaussian mixtures: abundance of support vectors, benign overfitting and regularization. arXiv preprint arXiv:2011.09148, 18 November 2020
17. Amin, M.A., Yan, H.: High speed detection of retinal blood vessels in fundus image using phase congruency. Soft Comput. **15**(6), 1217–1230 (2011)
18. Goodwin, M., et al.: Unlocking the potential of deep learning for marine ecology: overview, applications, and outlook. ICES J. Mar. Sci. **79**(2), 319–336 (2022)
19. Olsvik, E., et al.: Biometric fish classification of temperate species using convolutional neural network with squeeze-and-excitation. In: Wotawa, F., Friedrich, G., Pill, I., Koitz-Hristov, R., Ali, M. (eds.) IEA/AIE 2019. LNCS (LNAI), vol. 11606, pp. 89–101. Springer, Cham (2019). https://doi.org/10.1007/978-3-030-22999-3_9
20. Kingma, D.P., Ba, J.: Adam: a method for stochastic optimization. arXiv preprint arXiv:1412.6980 (2014)

# Autoregressive Deep Learning Models
# for Bridge Strain Prediction

Anastasios Panagiotis Psathas[1](✉) ⓘ, Lazaros Iliadis[1] ⓘ, Dimitra V. Achillopoulou[2,3],
Antonios Papaleonidas[1] ⓘ, Nikoleta K. Stamataki[2], Dimitris Bountas[1] ⓘ,
and Ioannis M. Dokas[4] ⓘ

[1] Department of Civil Engineering-Lab of Mathematics and Informatics (ISCE), Democritus
University of Thrace, 67100 Xanthi, Greece
{anpsatha,liliadis,papaleon,dibounta}@civil.duth.gr
[2] Department of Civil Engineering-Laboratory of Reinforced Concrete and Seismic Design of
Structures, Democritus University of Thrace, 67100 Xanthi, Greece
d.achillopoulou@surrey.ac.uk, nstamata@civil.duth.gr
[3] Department of Civil and Environmental Engineering, University of Surrey, Guildford, UK
[4] Department of Civil Engineering-Lab of Project Management, Democritus University of
Thrace, 67100 Xanthi, Greece
idokas@civil.duth.gr

**Abstract.** Infrastructures are often subjected to harsh loading scenarios and
severe environmental conditions, not anticipated during design, which result in
their long-term structural deterioration. Thus, monitoring and maintaining the
urban infrastructure is critical for the resilience. In this research, the authors present
a modeling approach, for the prediction of future strain values in a *Dutch Highway*
Bridge, based on eleven Deep Learning (DL) algorithms. Previous strain measurements were used as input. The performance of the developed Machine Learning
model was evaluated using the Root Mean Square Error (RMSE), Mean Absolute
Error (MAE) and R square ($R^2$) indices. The Fast Fourier Transform (FFT) was
employed for the pre-processing of the involved time series. The obtained results
are extremely promising for predicting the performance under design loads. All
algorithms have proven their capacity to successfully predict the fluctuations of
strain values. The authorities responsible for the function and management of the
bridge, can feel confident to rely on these models in order to schedule in time
proper maintenance works.

**Keywords:** Deep learning · Univariate · Autoregression · Strain · Prediction ·
Bridge · Infrastructure

## 1 Introduction

Urban Infrastructures (UIN) such as public buildings (e.g. hospitals, schools), transport
hubs, pipelines, transport assets (e.g. highways, bridges), are built to withstand not only
extreme weather and environmental conditions but also human induced stressors [19,
47]. In fact, their lifetime is limited yet desired to expand. In the long run, catastrophic

© Springer Nature Switzerland AG 2022
L. Iliadis et al. (Eds.): EANN 2022, CCIS 1600, pp. 150–164, 2022.
https://doi.org/10.1007/978-3-031-08223-8_13

events or cumulative phenomena aggravate and wear down the infrastructures over time, and often the safety or functionality level is decreased, therefor repair or strengthening is decided. Especially transport assets, such as bridges, need to be frequently monitored for the undisrupted traffic flow and for assessment of the risk level [18, 48, 49]. In cases that retrofitting measures are applied, the assets can be shut down during works, with great impact in the economic activities [9].

It is crucial to model the structural integrity of such infrastructure assets, over time. The recent development in Structural Health Monitoring (SHM) techniques, the rapidly decreasing cost for sensors and data collection-storage devices, have offered more sophisticated hardware, software, and data storage (local or cloud) solutions. [16, 50], SHM systems are employed to continuously monitor the actual operation status of critical infrastructure, in various domains, (e.g. in civil engineering and aviation). More and more, sensor networks, consisting of multiple sensor types are being employed, and large quantities of data are gathered [7, 51]. Most of the SHM tools, detect damages and the degradation of physical properties, such as geometry changes, stiffness or natural period [1, 52]. These fundamental changes can have serious effect on important attributes (e.g. response frequencies, mode shapes, and modal damping) [2]. However, in real-life, the transportation related features are also subject to a variety of stressors natural and human induced hazards and events, such as traffic level and temperature [3, 4]. In most studies, the laboratory tests are considering systems with simple structure, rather than cases similar to the actual operating environment [10]. In the vast majority of works, the environmental conditions are considered unchanged whereas natural hazards, such as catastrophic events e.g. earthquakes, floods, wildfire, or human induced hazards, e.g. terror, fire, collision, are studied independently or in sequence, whereas a study with the combination of such is missing.

In this research effort, the authors are using a public dataset, derived from a large Dutch monitoring project, known as the *InfraWatch* [9, 53]. The data was obtained from a sensor network installed on a highway bridge in August 2008, during its maintenance, after 40 years of service. The network is comprised of 145 sensors that measure different features, related to the condition of the bridge. These sensors include strain gauges (measuring horizontal strain on various locations) vibration sensors, and thermometers (to measure both the air and structure temperature) [5]. Moreover, it is equipped with a weather station and a video-camera [13]. The objective of this paper is the reliable prediction of future strain values under expected design traffic and operational loads. For this purpose, the deployment of autoregressive models using Deep Learning (DL) techniques was employed. The dataset consists of a timeseries acquired from the strain sensor. For the first time in the literature, the development of autoregressive models employing DL algorithms is attempted on this dataset.

The paper is organized in the following five Sections. Section 2 describes the area of research and pinpoints some notable research efforts. Section 3 describes the dataset, its features and the pre-processing of the input. Section 4 provides the architecture of the proposed models and the evaluation method. Section 5 presents the SHM results and the evaluation of the model. Finally, Sect. 6 summarizes the main conclusions.

## 2  Area of Research – Literature Review

This study uses the available public data from the *InfraWatch project* [53]. The *InfraWatch* project investigates a highway bridge in the Netherlands named Hollandse Brug [9, 11, 15]. The bridge is the oldest bridge to the Flevopolder, is located on A6 motorway and connects the east side of Gooimeer with the west side of IJmeer as Fig. 1 captures [9, 11, 15].

**Fig. 1.** The *Hollandse Brug* bridge [11]

The Hollandse Brug Bridge is in function since June of 1969 [9, 11, 15]. In 1993 and 1999 the bridge was widened to the south and north as the traffic increased and it was considered overloaded back in 1980 [11]. In April of 2007 the bridge's safety level was considered low and therefore bridge shutdown (27 April 2007) [9, 15]. Immediately the rehabilitation of the bridge began in August of 2007 and was completed in 2009 [9, 11, 15]. During this period a SHM system was installed [9, 11, 15].

The SHM system consists of 145 different sensors that are located in different parts of the bridge [9, 15, 53]. Specifically, there are **a)** *34 vibration sensors* that measure the vertical movement of the bottom of the road-deck as well as the supporting columns (geo-phones), **b)** *16 strain-gauges embedded in the concrete* that measure the horizontal longitudinal stress, and an additional *34 gauges attached to the outside*, **c)** *28 strain-gauges embedded in the concrete* that measure horizontal stress perpendicular to the first *16 strain-gauges*, and an additional *13 gauges attached to the outside* and **d)** *10 thermometers embedded in the concrete, and 10 attached on the outside* [9, 15, 53]. Also, there is a weather station that gathers respective data and a video camera that provides a continuous video stream of the actual traffic. Additionally, there were also plans to monitor the adjacent railway bridge. The data that are collected from the SHM system at a frequency of 100 Hz, are related to traffic loads and the environmental conditions of the bridge. [9, 15]. Overall, it was estimated that 56 kB of data/sec were stored. This amounts to about 5 GB per day, and over 1.7 TB on a yearly basis. The video camera produced a data stream in a similar range, with 46 kB/s of compressed video, for a typical daytime situation. The data available for analysis, consisted of short snapshots of strain and videos, which were manually transported from the site to the monitoring location (typically an office environment in Leiden University) [15].

There are several publications in the literature that exploited data from this maintenance project. In 2014, Miao et al. [5], present a baseline correction method to deal with the baseline of the strain signals, collected from a sensor network installed on *Hollandse Brug*. In 2012, Vespier et al. [8], proposed a combination of the *Minimum Description Length* (MDL) feature selection strategy, with *Convolutional* techniques, for the decomposition of a time series on artificial data related to the aforementioned Bridge. In 2010, Koopman et al. [17], introduced a pattern selection method, considering collections of patterns discovered in timeseries obtained from the *Hollandse Brug*. This is an optimization approach, which captures the dependencies between the different time-series, while minimizing potential redundancies. Important attempts to further analyze the *Hollandse Brug* time series, were published by Vespier et al. (2012), Miao et al. (2013), Miao et al. (2014) and Vespier et al. (2011) [6, 7, 13, 14].

## 3   Dataset

As it was already mentioned, the dataset used in this research effort, is related to measurements obtained by a strain sensor, attached on the *Hollandse Brug*, a Dutch Highway Bridge. This specific sensor collects data at a frequency of 10 Hz. The dataset deals with finite sequences of numerical measurements (samples), collected by observing some properties of the system and stored as timeseries [6]. A timeseries of length n is an ordered sequence of values $x = x[1],\ldots, x[n]$ of finite precision. A subsequence $x[a: b]$ of x is defined as follows:

$$x[a : b] = (x[a], \ x[a+1], \ldots, x[b]), \ 1 \leq a < b \leq n \qquad (1)$$

More specifically, the dataset comprises of 10,280,939 strain measurements over a period of 12 days, from Saturday 2008/11/15 to Wednesday 2008/11/26. The timeseries is presented in the following Fig. 2.

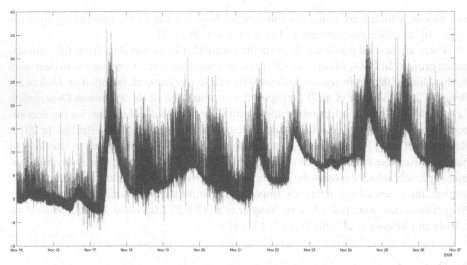

**Fig. 2.** The 10,280,939 strain values from 2008/11/15 to 2008/11/26

The dataset is publicly available and it can be found at the following website: https://infrawatch.liacs.nl/.

### 3.1 Dataset Preprocessing

As it has already been mentioned, the sensor collects data at frequency of 10 Hz. This means that there 10 values are obtained for every second. The measurements are very dense. In the cases of Infrastructures' modeling, it does not make much sense to predict a feature's value for every next second. The forecast, should be usually related to specific most interesting daily temporal moments, under the worst (most critical) conditions, such as traffic jams, or very high and very low temperature conditions. The variable data segmentation was performed by using *Fast Fourier Transformation* (FFT).

Fourier analysis converts a signal from its original domain (often time or space) to a representation in the frequency domain and vice versa. FFT is a specific implementation that computes the *Discrete Fourier Transformation* (DFT) of a sequence. It is an extremely powerful mathematical tool that allows to observe the obtained signals in a different domain, inside which several difficult problems become very simple to analyse [18].

The DFT is obtained by decomposing a sequence of values into components of different frequencies. Any periodic function g(x) integrable in the domain $D = [-\pi, \pi]$ can be written as an infinite sum of sine and cosine as follows:

$$g(x) = \sum_{k=-\infty}^{\infty} \tau_k e^{jkx} \tag{1}$$

$$\tau_k = \frac{1}{2\pi} \int_D g(x) e^{-jkx} dx \tag{2}$$

where $e^{\iota\theta} = \cos(\theta) + j\sin(\theta)$. The idea that a function can be broken down into its constituent frequencies is a powerful one and forms the backbone of the Fourier transformation [19].

An FFT rapidly computes such transformations by factorizing the DFT matrix into a product of sparse (mostly zero) factors. As a result, it manages to reduce the complexity of computing the DFT from $O(N^2)$, which arises if one simply applies the definition of DFT, to $O(N.logN)$, where $N$ is the size of data [20]. FFT was performed on the dataset as it is presented in Fig. 3 and the FFT timeseries is presented in Fig. 4.

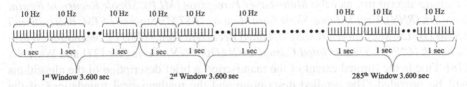

**Fig. 3.** Applying FFT for window length of 3,600 s (36,000 Hz)

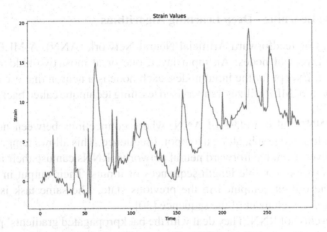

**Fig. 4.** Strain values after FFT is applied

As it can be seen from Fig. 4, the processed dataset still captures the flow of strain values, without much deviation. Usually in such time series there is almost always seasonality or trending, that makes the timeseries non-stationary [21]. In such cases one can use stationarity tests such as the *Augmented Dickey–Fuller* (ADF) Test [22] or the *Kwiatkowski-Phillips-Schmidt-Shin* (KPSS) Test [23]. If the timeseries proves to be non-stationary, then some steps must be taken to make it stationary, such as the First Difference method [24]. However, the biggest advantage of the *Deep Learning* algorithms versus the *Shallow Machine Learning* (SML) ones, or versus classical methodologies for timeseries such as the *Autoregressive Integrated Moving Average* (ARIMA) [25] is that DL can recognize the patterns and the seasonality of the timeseries without doing any additional processing in the data [26]. The preprocessing of the dataset was performed in Matlab with code written from scratch.

# 4 Algorithmic Approaches

After completion of the data processing, the obtained dataset consisted of a timeseries of 285 strain values. The goal of this research effort was to predict the future values of the strain, based on previous values. It is of major importance to predict the high strain values' trend, when the bridge has accepted high levels of stress and it has to be maintained, or the bridge responders have to schedule any other action to ensure its resilience overtime.

Thus, for the purpose of this research, the dataset was fed in 11 different Machine Learning algorithms, namely: *Multi-Layer Perceptron (MLP), Simple Recurrent Neural Network (RNN), Vanilla Long-Short Term Memory (LSTM), Stacked LSTM, Bidirectional LSTM (Bi-LSTM), Stacked Bi-LSTM, Gated Recurrent Unit, (GRU), Convolution Neural Network (CNN)-LSTM, Dilated Casual CNN (DC-CNN), SeriesNet* [27] and WaveNet [28]. Due to the limited extent of the manuscript, a brief description of the algorithms will be provided. The detailed description and the mathematical foundations of the algorithms, can be studied by a more detailed search in the literature.

## 4.1 Machine Learning - Deep Learning Algorithms

MLP is a class of feedforward Artificial Neural Network (ANN). A MLP consists of at least three layers of nodes: An input layer, one or at most two hidden layers and an output layer. Except for the input nodes, each node is a neuron that uses a nonlinear activation function. MLP utilizes a supervised learning technique called backpropagation for training [29].

Simple RNN is also a class of ANN, where connections between nodes form a directed or undirected graph, along a temporal sequence. This allows temporal dynamic behavior. Derived from feedforward neural networks, RNNs can use their internal state (memory) to process variable length sequences of inputs. Their output in each phase, depends on the output computed in the previous state. The same task is recurrently performed for every element of the sequence [30].

LSTM is a class of RNN. They deal with the backpropagated gradients' problem that Simple RNNs suffer. A typical LSTM unit is composed of three gates, an *input gate, an output gate, and a forget gate*, which regulate information into and out of the memory cell. The cell remembers values over arbitrary time intervals, and the three *gates* regulate the flow of information in and out of the cell. [31]. Vanilla LSTM is an LSTM model that has a single hidden layer of LSTM units, apart from the input and output layers [32]. Stacked LSTM comprises of multiple hidden layers stacked one on top of another [34]. Bi-LSTM is and LSTM that learns the input sequence both forward and backwards and concatenate both interpretations [33]. Stack Bi-LSTM Comprises of multiple hidden Bi-LSTM layers stacked one on top of another [35].

GRU is a Gating mechanism in RNN. GRU also deals with the vanishing gradient problem, just like the LSTM do. GRU has fewer parameters than LSTM and it has a simpler architecture. There are primarily two gates in a GRU as opposed to three gates in an LSTM cell. The first gate is the *Reset gate* and the other one is the *update gate* [36].

A CNN is defined as a neural network that extracts features at a higher resolution, and then converts them into more complex features at a coarser resolution. Therefore, CNN is based on three types of layers, namely: The *Convolutional*, the *Pooling* and the *Fully-Connected* ones. When these layers are stacked, a CNN architecture has been formed [37]. A CNN model can be used in a hybrid model with an LSTM backend where the CNN is used to interpret subsequences of input that together are provided as a sequence to an LSTM model to interpret (CNN-LSTM) [38]. Causal CNN (C-CNN) are a type of CNN used for temporal data. [39]. A DC-CNN is a C-CNN where the filter is applied over an area larger than its length, by skipping input values with a certain step. A DC-CNN effectively allows the network to have very large receptive fields with just a few layers [40].

SeriesNet was developed by Shen et al. in 2018 and it consists of two networks. The LSTM network aims to learn holistic features and to reduce dimensionality of multi-conditional data, and the dilated causal convolution network aims to learn different time intervals. This model can learn multi-range and multi-level features from time series data. It adopts residual learning and batch normalization to improve generalization [27].

WaveNet was developed by Oord et al. in 2016 and it is a deep generative model. It is autoregressive and combines causal filters with DC-CNN (without Maxpooling Layers) to allow their receptive fields to grow exponentially with depth, which is important to model the long-range temporal dependencies in audio signals [28].

## 4.2  Evaluation of Deep Learning Algorithms

The three typical evaluation indices presented in Table 1, were used for the evaluation of the aforementioned DL algorithms.

**Table 1.** Calculated indices for the evaluation of the binary classification approach

| Index | Abbreviation | Calculation |
|---|---|---|
| Root mean square error | RMSE | $\sqrt{\frac{\sum_{i=1}^{N}(y_i-\hat{y}_i)^2}{N}}$ |
| Mean absolute error | MAE | $\frac{1}{N}\sum_{i=1}^{N}\lvert y_i-\hat{y}_i\rvert$ |
| R square | $R^2$ | $1-\frac{\sum_i(y_i-\hat{y}_i)^2}{\sum_i(y_i-\overline{y})^2}$ |

It should be clarified that $y_i$ is the actual value, $\hat{y}_i$ is the predicted value, $\overline{y}$ is the mean value, and N is the total number of the instances. The Coefficient of determination $R^2$ is a statistical measure that represents the proportion of the variance for a dependent variable that is explained by an independent variable or variables, in a regression model. It takes values in the closed interval [0, 1] and a higher value indicates a better fit [41]. Root-mean-square error (RMSE) is a measure of the differences between the values of the sample or population that were predicted by a model and the actual observed ones. It is an absolute measure of the goodness for the fit. It offers a real number to compare against other model results [42]. The Mean Average Error (MAE) measures the average magnitude of the errors in a set of forecasts, without considering their direction. The RMSE gives larger penalization to higher prediction errors by square it while MAE treats all errors the same [42].

## 5   Evaluation and Experimental Results

An original, case specific Program, was developed in Python Language, in order to perform the training-testing processes of the employed algorithms and their respective evaluation. The *Keras* [43] and *Tensorflow* [44] libraries were employed to build the models' architectures. The dataset was split in **Training Data** (65%), **Validation** Data (15%) and **Testing Data** (20%). Training of all models was performed for 200 epochs. Based on the literature, the *RMSE was used as the Loss Function,* the *Adam Optimizer* was used to Optimize the models and the *Rectified Linear Unit (ReLU)* was employed as the *Activation Function*. The learning rate was set at a $= 0.001$. The algorithms were trained for 10 lags. The 10 previous measurements, were always considered for the prediction of the next measurement. Thus, the dimensions of the vectors were $1 \times 10$ (1 instance, 10 previous values). The values of all hyperparameters were chosen through a trial and error process. Table 2 describes the architecture of each model. Figure 5, presents a comparison between the true values vs the predicted ones for all algorithms.

**Table 2.** Architectures of the proposed algorithms

| Model | Layers |
|---|---|
| Vanilla LSTM | lstm (500 nodes) |
| Bi-LSTM | bidirectional lstm (200 nodes) |
| Stacked LSTM | lstm (500 nodes), lstm (250 nodes) |
| Stacked Bi-LSTM | bidirectional lstm (50 nodes), bidirectional lstm (50 nodes) |
| RNN | simple_rnn (400 nodes) |
| GRU | gru (400 nodes) |
| MLP | dense (500 nodes), dense (250 nodes), dense (50 nodes) |
| CNN-LSTM | $\left. \begin{array}{c} Convolution \ 1 - D \ (filters, \ kernel, \ stride = 32, 2, 1) \\ Maxpooling\,(Maxpool = 2) \end{array} \right\} x3$ <br> Flatten, lstm (50 nodes) |
| DC-CNN | Convolution 1-D (filters, kernel, stride = 32,2,1) x6, dense (64 nodes), dense (32 nodes) |
| SeriesNet | [27] |
| WaveNet | [28] |

*The dimensions of the input Vectors for all algorithms is $1 \times 10$
*The last layer (output) of each algorithm is a Dense Layer with one node.

Table 3 presents the performance indices RMSE, MAE and $R^2$ for each algorithm in the Testing phase.

The deviations of the predicted values from the actual ones, are presented in Fig. 5 below. They can be due to many things.

**Table 3.** Evaluation indices for HEDL-IDS and the machine learning algorithms

| Model | RMSE | MAE | $R^2$ |
|---|---|---|---|
| Vanilla LSTM | **1.369** | **0.917** | **0.880** |
| Bi-LSTM | 1.413 | 0.864 | 0.871 |
| Stacked LSTM | 4.350 | 3.770 | 0.549 |
| Stacked Bi-LSTM | 3.380 | 2.701 | 0.570 |
| RNN | 2.611 | 1.874 | 0.373 |
| GRU | 1.835 | 1.101 | 0.774 |
| MLP | 1.807 | 1.304 | 0.805 |
| CNN-LSTM | 1568 | 1.003 | 0.842 |
| DC-CNN | 1.496 | 0.983 | 0.856 |
| SeriesNet | 1.769 | 1.098 | 0.793 |
| WaveNet | 3.138 | 2.441 | 0.093 |

As Fig. 5 indicates, although no preprocessing has been done for the trend or seasonality of the time series, all models can successfully predict the fluctuations of the strain, which was the main objective of this research. The diagrams clearly reveal the temporal points corresponding to high or low strain, regardless the model employed by the maintenance responders. Table 3 proves that the models employing *Long-Short Term Memory* (LSTM) Layers, respond better to the nature of the problem, as it was expected from the literature [45, 46]. More specifically, the models comprising of a single LSTM layer (*Vanilla* and *Bi-LSTM*) can predict the values with greater accuracy. The more complex approaches have been proved to be less efficient (e.g. *Stacked* and *WaveNet* models). On the other hand, RNN have completely failed to adapt to the time series. SeriesNet, GRU and MLP struggle, but their prediction is decent enough. Last but not least, the hybrid models with CNN show promising results. The poor performance of Wavenet and Stacked LSTM is surprising. And so is the good performance of the MLP that does not include explicitly any memory/recurrent layer. Perhaps the most complex models would benefit from more data.

Overall, the models predict the trend of future strain values, with high accuracy. Especially, as it can be seen in Table 3, the values of the performance indices related to the cases of Vanilla LSTM and Bi-LSTM, are very high ($R^2 = 0.880$ and $R^2 = 0.871$ respectively).

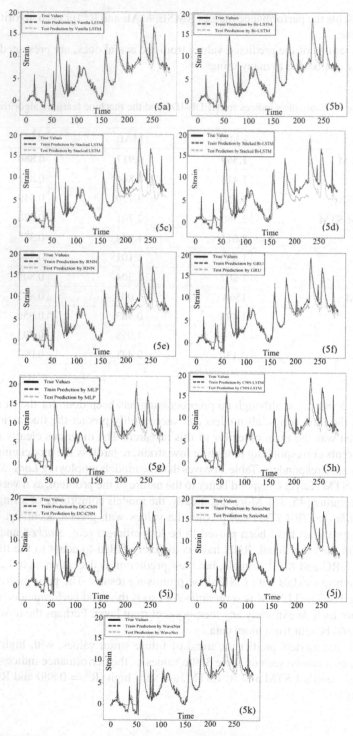

**Fig. 5.** True (black) Strain vs Predicted (blue for test and red for train) strain values for vanilla LSTM (5a), Bi-LSTM (5b), stacked LSTM (5c), stacked Bi-LSTM (5d), RNN (5e), GRU (5f), MLP (5g), CNN-LSTM (5h), DC-CNN (5i), SeriesNet (5j), WaveNet (5k). (Color figure online)

# 6 Conclusions and Future Work

This paper deals with a univariate autoregression problem. It aims to predict the future strain values of the *Hollandse Brug*, a Dutch Highway Bridge by considering the 10 previous strain measurements. Fast Fourier Transformation was used for the case of signal processing. Eleven Machine Learning and Deep Learning algorithms have been employed to cope with the autoregression problem. The results are promising, as all algorithms seem to be able to predict the fluctuation of strain values (to a different extend). RMSE, MAE and $R^2$ were used as the evaluation indices. The values of the aforementioned indices were high and adequate for the majority of the models. The Vanilla LSTM and the Bi-LSTM have proved to respond better for the specific dataset and problem. The predicted values of all models have a reasonable, small level of deviation from the actual ones, as it would be expected in all similar time series research efforts. This is due to the fact that according to the literature, strain values at any temporal moment, not only depend on previous values, but on other factors such as traffic loads, structural integrity of the asset and climatic conditions.

Despite the excellent agreement of a SHM data and predictions, a future extension of this research is orientated to find a better number of time lags that increases the performance of the model. Additionally, a more comprehensive study can be done on the window length of the FFT, followed by a better fine tuning of the hyperparameters' values. A significant improvement of the developed models would be enhanced by accounting for more extensive datasets or diverse input data, e.g. temperature, traffic loads, in order to make the model a practical and useful prediction tool for designers and operators and for the management of the asset.

**Acknowledgments.** We acknowledge support of this work by the project "Risk and Resilience Assessment Center – Prefecture of East Macedonia and Thrace - Greece." (MIS 5047293) which is implemented under the Action "Reinforcement of the Research and Innovation Infrastructure", funded by the Operational Programme "Competitiveness, Entrepreneurship and Innovation" (NSRF 2014-2020) and co-financed by Greece and the European Union (European Regional Development Fund).

# References

1. Fallahian, M., Khoshnoudian, F., Meruane, V.: Ensemble classification method for structural damage assessment under varying temperature. Struct. Health Monit. **17**(4), 747–762 (2018)
2. Cunha, A., Caetano, E., Magalhes, F., Moutinho, C.: Recent perspectives in dynamic testing and monitoring of bridges. Struct. Control Health Monit. **20**, 853877 (2013)
3. Li, H., Li, S., Ou, J., Li, H.: Modal identification of bridges under varying environmental conditions: temperature and wind effects. Struct.Control Health Monit. **17**, 495512 (2010)
4. Xia, Y., Chen, B., Zhou, X.Q., Xu, Y.L.: Field monitoring and numerical analysis of Tsing Ma suspension bridge temperature behavior. Struct. Control. Health Monit. **20**(4), 560–575 (2013). https://doi.org/10.1002/stc.515
5. Miao, S., Koenders, E.A.B., Knobbe, A.: Automatic baseline correction of strain gauge signals. Struct. Control Health Monit, **22**(1), 36–49 (2014). ISSN 1545-2263

6. Vespier, U., Nijssen, S., Knobbe, A.: Mining characteristic multi-scale motifs in sensor-based time series. In: International Conference on Information and Knowledge Management, Proceedings, pp. 2393–2398 (2013). https://doi.org/10.1145/2505515.2505620
7. Miao, S., Vespier, U., Vanschoren, J., Knobbe, A., Cachucho, R.: Modeling sensor dependencies between multiple sensor types (2013)
8. Vespier, U., Knobbe, A.J., Nijssen, S., Vanschoren, J.: MDL-based identification of relevant temporal scales in time series (2012)
9. Knobbe, A., et al.: InfraWatch: data management of large systems for monitoring infrastructural performance. In: Cohen, P.R., Adams, N.M., Berthold, M.R. (eds.) IDA 2010. LNCS, vol. 6065, pp. 91–102. Springer, Heidelberg (2010). https://doi.org/10.1007/978-3-642-13062-5_10
10. Farrar, C., Hemez, F., Shunk, D., Stinemates, D., Nadler, B.: A review of structural health monitoring literature: 1996–2001 (2004)
11. Wegenwiki: Hollandse Brug. https://www.wegenwiki.nl/index.php?title=Hollandse_Brug&mobileaction=toggle_view_mobile. Accessed 23 Feb 2022
12. Witkin, A.P.: Scale-space filtering. In: IJCAI (1983)
13. Miao, S., Knobbe, A., Vanschoren, J., Vespier, U., Chen, X.: A range of data mining techniques to correlate multiple sensor types (2011)
14. Vespier, U., et al.: Traffic events modeling for structural health monitoring. In: Gama, J., Bradley, E., Hollmén, J. (eds.) IDA 2011. LNCS, vol. 7014, pp. 376–387. Springer, Heidelberg (2011). https://doi.org/10.1007/978-3-642-24800-9_35
15. Knobbe, A.J., Koopman, A., Kok, J.N., Obladen, B., Bosma, C., Koenders, E.: Large data stream processing for bridge management systems (2010)
16. Li, X., Yu, W., Villegas, S.: Structural health monitoring of building structures with online data mining methods. IEEE Syst. J. **10**, 1–10 (2015). https://doi.org/10.1109/JSYST.2015.2481380
17. Seborg, D.: Pattern matching in multivariate time series databases using a moving-window approach. Ind. Eng. Chem. Res. **41**, 3822–3838 (2002). https://doi.org/10.1021/ie010517z
18. Brigham, E.O.: The FAST FOURIER TRANSFORM and Its Applications. Prentice-Hall, Inc., Hoboken (1988)
19. Zhang, Z.: Photoplethysmography-based heart rate monitoring in physical activities via joint sparse spectrum reconstruction. IEEE Trans. Biomed. Eng. **62**(8), 1902–1910 (2015)
20. Nussbaumer, H.J. The fast Fourier transform. In: Prince, E. (ed.) Fast Fourier Transform and Convolution Algorithms, pp. 80–111. Springer, Heidelberg (1981). https://doi.org/10.1007/978-3-642-97576-9_10
21. Rhif, M., Ben Abbes, A., Farah, I.R., Martínez, B., Sang, Y.: Wavelet transform application for/in non-stationary time-series analysis: a review. Appl. Sci. **9**(7), 1345 (2019)
22. Paparoditis, E., Politis, D.N.: The asymptotic size and power of the augmented Dickey-Fuller test for a unit root. Economet. Rev. **37**(9), 955–973 (2018)
23. Baum, C.: KPSS: stata module to compute Kwiatkowski-Phillips-Schmidt-Shin test for stationarity (2018)
24. Churchill, S.A., Inekwe, J., Ivanovski, K., Smyth, R.: Stationarity properties of per capita $CO_2$ emissions in the OECD in the very long-run: a replication and extension analysis. Energy Econ. **90**, 104868 (2020)
25. Peter, Ď., Silvia, P.: ARIMA vs. ARIMAX–which approach is better to analyze and forecast macroeconomic time series. In: Proceedings of 30th International Conference Mathematical Methods in Economics, vol. 2, pp. 136–140, September 2012
26. Reese, H.: Understanding the differences between AI, machine learning, and deep learning (2017). https://www.techrepublic.com/article/understandingthedifferencesbetweenaimachinelearninganddeeplearning

27. Papadopoulos, K.: SeriesNet: a dilated causal convolutional neural network for forecasting. In: Proceedings of the International Conference on Pattern Recognition and Machine Intelligence, Union, NJ, USA, pp. 1–4, August 2018
28. Oord, A.V.D., et al.: WaveNet: a generative model for raw audio. arXiv preprint arXiv:1609.03499 (2016)
29. Gardner, M.W., Dorling, S.R.: Artificial neural networks (the multilayer perceptron)—a review of applications in the atmospheric sciences. Atmos. Environ. **32**(14–15), 2627–2636 (1998)
30. Zaremba, W., Sutskever, I., Vinyals, O.: Recurrent neural network regularization. arXiv preprint arXiv:1409.2329 (2014)
31. Hochreiter, S., Schmidhuber, J.: Long short-term memory. Neural Comput. **9**(8), 1735–1780 (1997)
32. Sherstinsky, A.: Fundamentals of recurrent neural network (RNN) and long short-term memory (LSTM) network. Physica D **404**, 132306 (2020)
33. Huang, Z., Xu, W., Yu, K.: Bidirectional LSTM-CRF models for sequence tagging. arXiv preprint arXiv:1508.01991 (2015)
34. Dyer, C., Ballesteros, M., Ling, W., Matthews, A., Smith, N.A.: Transition-based dependency parsing with stack long short-term memory. arXiv preprint arXiv:1505.08075 (2015)
35. Cui, Z., Ke, R., Pu, Z., Wang, Y.: Stacked bidirectional and unidirectional LSTM recurrent neural network for forecasting network-wide traffic state with missing values. Transp. Res. Part C Emerg. Technol. **118**, 102674 (2020)
36. Gao, S., et al.: Short-term runoff prediction with GRU and LSTM networks without requiring time step optimization during sample generation. J. Hydrol. **589**, 125188 (2020)
37. O'Shea, K., Nash, R.: An introduction to convolutional neural networks. arXiv preprint arXiv:1511.08458 (2015)
38. Psathas, A.P., Iliadis, L., Papaleonidas, A., Bountas, D.: A hybrid deep learning ensemble for cyber intrusion detection. In: Iliadis, L., Macintyre, J., Jayne, C., Pimenidis, E. (eds.) EANN 2021. PINNS, vol. 3, pp. 27–41. Springer, Cham (2021). https://doi.org/10.1007/978-3-030-80568-5_3
39. Brazil, T.J.: Causal-convolution - a new method for the transient analysis of linear systems at microwave frequencies. IEEE Trans. Microw. Theory Tech. **43**(2), 315–323 (1995)
40. Robinson, J., Kuzdeba, S., Stankowicz, J., Carmack, J.M.: Dilated causal convolutional model for RF fingerprinting. In: 2020 10th Annual Computing and Communication Workshop and Conference (CCWC), pp. 0157–0162. IEEE, January 2020
41. Israeli, O.: A Shapley-based decomposition of the R-square of a linear regression. J. Econ. Inequal. **5**(2), 199–212 (2007)
42. Chai, T., Draxler, R.R.: Root mean square error (RMSE) or mean absolute error (MAE)?–Arguments against avoiding RMSE in the literature. Geosci. Model Dev **7**(3), 1247–1250 (2014)
43. Ketkar, N.: Introduction to keras. In: Deep learning with Python, pp. 97–111. Apress, Berkeley (2017)
44. Dillon, J.V., et al.: Tensorflow distributions. arXiv preprint arXiv:1711.10604 (2017)
45. Li, Y., Zhu, Z., Kong, D., Han, H., Zhao, Y.: EA-LSTM: evolutionary attention-based LSTM for time series prediction. Knowl.-Based Syst. **181**, 104785 (2019)
46. Siami-Namini, S., Tavakoli, N., Namin, A.S.: A comparison of ARIMA and LSTM in forecasting time series. In: 2018 17th IEEE International Conference on Machine Learning and Applications (ICMLA), pp. 1394–1401. IEEE, December 2018
47. Nations, U.: Transforming our world: the 2030 agenda for sustainable development. Department of Economic and Social Affairs, United Nations, New York (2015)
48. Kromanis, R.: Health monitoring of bridges. In: Start-Up Creation, pp. 369–389. Woodhead Publishing (2020)

49. Argyroudis, S.A., Achillopoulou, D.V., Livina, V., Mitoulis, S.A.: Data-driven resilience assessment for transport infrastructure exposed to multiple hazards. In: Proceedings of the 10th International Conference on Bridge Maintenance, Safety and Management (IABMAS2020). University of Surrey, April 2021
50. Argyroudis, S.A., et al.: Digital technologies can enhance climate resilience of critical infrastructure. Clim. Risk Manag. **35** (2022)
51. Achillopoulou, D.V., Mitoulis, S.A., Argyroudis, S.A., Wang, Y.: Monitoring of transport infrastructure exposed to multiple hazards: a roadmap for building resilience. Sci. Total Environ. **746**, 141001 (2020)
52. Tatsis, K., Dertimanis, V., Ou, Y., Chatzi, E.: GP-ARX-Based structural damage detection and localization under varying environmental conditions. J. Sens. Actuator Netw. **9**(3), 41 (2020)
53. InfraWatch progect. https://infrawatch.liacs.nl/. Accessed 23 Feb 2022

# Ground Penetrating Radar Fourier Pre-processing for Deep Learning Tunnel Defects' Automated Classification

Giulia Marasco[1], Marco M. Rosso[1](✉), Salvatore Aiello[1],
Angelo Aloisio[2], Giansalvo Cirrincione[3], Bernardino Chiaia[1],
and Giuseppe C. Marano[1]

[1] DISEG, Dipartimento di Ingegneria Strutturale, Edile e Geotecnica,
Politecnico di Torino, Corso Duca Degli Abruzzi, 24, Turin 10128, Italy
{giulia.marasco,marco.rosso,salvatore.aiello,bernardino.chiaia,
giuseppe.marano}@polito.it
[2] Università degli Studi dell'Aquila, via Giovanni Gronchi n.18, L'Aquila 67100, Italy
angelo.aloisio1@univaq.it
[3] University of Picardie Jules Verne, Lab. LTI, Amiens, France
exin@u-picardie.fr

**Abstract.** Nowadays, drawing up plans to control and manage infrastructural assets has become one of the most important challenges in most developed countries. The latter must cope with issues relating to the aging of their infrastructures, which are getting towards the end of their useful life. This study proposes an automatic approach for tunnel defects classification. Starting from non-destructive investigations using Ground Penetrating Radar (GPR), the deep convolutional neural networks (CNNs), with and without the application of bidimensional Fourier Transform (2D FT), have allowed the classification of several structural defects (e.g., crack, voids, anomaly, etc.) with high accuracy. The proposed methodology eliminates the need for human interpretation of Ground Penetrating Radar profiles and the use of integrative investigations (e.g., video-endoscopy, core drilling, jacking, and pull-out testing) for defects classification. As a result, it has significant speed and reliability that make it both time and cost-efficient.

**Keywords:** Road tunnels · Fourier transform · Convolutional neural network · Structural health monitoring · Ground penetrating radar

## 1 Introduction

The development of automated systems for current structural state of the infrastructural heritage is critical for the implementation of cost-effective maintenance plans that ensure a high level of safety [1–7]. In developed countries, the extent of the infrastructure asset in developed countries that need to be controlled is significant. As a result, developing robust, reliable, and timely structural

© Springer Nature Switzerland AG 2022
L. Iliadis et al. (Eds.): EANN 2022, CCIS 1600, pp. 165–176, 2022.
https://doi.org/10.1007/978-3-031-08223-8_14

health monitoring (SHM) programs are especially important for high-impact structures, like bridges [8] and underground structures [9–11]. Focusing on tunnels, the number of them in the proximity of their design life end, and so at high risk, is extremely high. Thus, degradation phenomena and structural damages may have irreversibly changed the original structural characteristics and severe consequences may occur [12]. Consequently, systems that rely exclusively on traditional routine inspections are not sufficient and effective [13]. Since they are based on human judgment and require specialist personnel, who is frequently exposed to dangerous environments, they are time-consuming and expensive [14]. Therefore, image recognition-based structural health monitoring (SHM) algorithms are frequently leveraged to detect the presence and nature of potential infrastructural deterioration [15]. The use of deep convolutional neural networks (CNNs) that exploit transfer learning processes has been proven effective in many applications [16]. It's really interesting how much support they can provide in identifying and classifying defects that can be extracted from the results of non-destructive structural testing (NDT) techniques. Among the most relevant non-destructive methods, for the quantity and quality of information that can be obtained, emerges the Ground Penetrating Radar (GPR). It overcomes the limitations of visual inspection techniques that are only adapted to detect surface defects [10]. Nevertheless, since GPR data is typically scaled and manually interpreted or stored and subsequently processed off-line, its analysis is generally computationally costly [17]. This paper presents the results of a proposed multi-level methodology for defect classification starting from GPR profiles, with and without the use of the 2D Fourier Transform as a pre-processing operation. The obtained outcomes are promising and encourage further developments.

## 2    Monitoring Road Tunnels with GPR

Among the several non-destructive testing (NDT) methods [18] for defect characterization in engineering materials, the Ground Penetrating Radar has been chosen [19]. Due to the ease of use and transportation [20] and to its penetration capacity, such an instrument turned out to be a valuable tool for damage detection, localization, and classification. GPR is a geophysical technique [21] that involves transmitting high-frequency electromagnetic wave impulses into the investigated material using an antenna with a frequency of 10 to 2600 MHz MHz. The propagation of such an impulse is influenced by the dielectric characteristics of the material. The GPR campaign has focalized on Italian tunnels most dated between 1960s s and 1980s.s. Two types of GPR have been used in such campaigns. The first uses a dual-frequency antenna, the second involves a high-frequency one. The technical characteristics are shown in the following Table 1 and 2. GPR profiles have a vertical axis that shows the depth of the examined thickness and a horizontal axis that indicates the progressive distance from the structure's beginning. In the investigation campaign, each GPR profile was interpreted by specialized personnel. An example of a GPR profile with defect interpretation is shown in the Fig. 1.

**Table 1.** Technical characteristics of GPR with dual frequency antenna.

| GPR with dual frequency antenna features | Value |
|---|---|
| Minimum number of channels | 4 |
| Pulse repetition frequency (kHz) | 400 |
| Range (ns) | 0–9999 |
| Min. number of scans (1/s) | 400 |
| Voltage (V) | 12 |
| Primary dual-frequency antenna (MHz) | 400–900 |
| Secondary dual-frequency antenna (MHz) | 200–600 |

**Table 2.** Technical characteristics of GPR with high-frequency antenna.

| GPR high-frequency antenna features | Value |
|---|---|
| Minimum number of channels | 4 |
| Pulse repetition frequency (kHz) | 400 |
| Range (ns) | 0–9999 |
| Min. number of scans (1/s) | 400 |
| Voltage (V) | 12 |
| High-frequency antenna (GHz) | ≥2 |

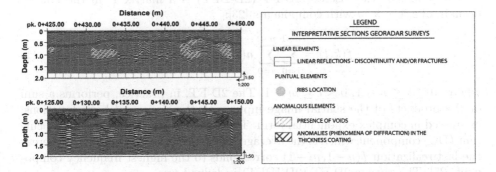

**Fig. 1.** Two examples of a GPR profile with defect patterns interpretation by human experts.

## 3   Two Dimensional Fourier Transform for Image Processing

The Fourier Transform (FT) is one of the most powerful tools for signal processing which provides a decomposition of a signal into its fundamental components. Moreover, it performs a domain mapping by changing the representation of the problem by passing from the input (spatial or time) domain to output (Fourier or frequency) domain. For continuous phenomena, the FT expresses a signal as an infinite sum of harmonics characterized by different frequencies and denoting the frequency content of each one. In real-world, even with the most sophisticated instrumentation, data are collected discretely through a sampling process. The sampling or Nyquist-Shannon theorem states that any continuous signal can be uniquely reconstructed in a reliable way starting from its samples when the sampling frequency is two times the Nyquist frequency, which represents the highest signal representable frequency [22]. Thus, for discrete signals, the Discrete version of the FT (DFT) has been developed to deal with real-world sampled signals.

In general, a digital image is represented by a matrix/tensor of pixels, where each pixel contains certain values. An 8-bit precision gray-scale images is a matrix in which each pixel can assume an integer value between 0 and 255. On the other hand, with a red-green-blue (RGB) image, the data are expressed by a tensor with a depth-size of three, in which each pixel is represented by three bytes since each color channel can assume integer values between 0 to 255 [23]. Without loss of generality, an image can be interpreted as two-dimensional signals of pixel values by looking to vertical and horizontal directions [24]. Therefore, the FT can be adopted to decompose a 2D discrete-space signal (digital image) into its main sinusoidal components. Due to the sampling frequency, only a certain number of harmonics is obtained. However, it must be sufficient to fully describe the information contained in the image [25]. Considering a digital image in the spatial domain $A$ of size $n \times m$ with components $a_{rs}$, with $0 \leq r \leq n - 1$, $0 \leq s \leq m - 1$, the discrete 2D-FT (2D-DFT) is a matrix $F$ in the Fourier domain of size $n \times m$ with components [23]:

$$f(k,l) = \sum_{r=0}^{n-1} \sum_{s=0}^{m-1} a(r,s) e^{-2\pi i \left( \frac{kr}{m} + \frac{ls}{n} \right)} \tag{1}$$

where: $0 \leq k \leq n - 1$, $0 \leq l \leq m - 1$. The 2D-FT, in practice, performs a sum of the products of the spatial image input with the sinusoidal basis functions, expressed in complex exponential form. The term $f(0,0)$ denotes the direct current (DC) component which is the average brightness of the input image, whereas the last realization $f(n-1, m-1)$ corresponds to the highest frequency component [25]. The inverse 2D-FT (2D-IDFT) is defined as:

$$a(r,s) = \frac{1}{n \cdot m} \sum_{k=0}^{n-1} \sum_{l=0}^{m-1} f(k,l) e^{2\pi i \left( \frac{kr}{m} + \frac{ls}{n} \right)} \tag{2}$$

To lower the computational effort, it is possible to demonstrate that the 2D-DFT can be computed as a series of $2n$ one-dimensional FT [25], which leads to a computational complexity of $O(n^2)$. Fast Fourier formulations (2D-FFT) have been developed in order to further reduce the complexity to $O(n \log_2(n))$ [25]. The FT operation delivers a complex matrix which can be displayed in terms of real and imaginary parts, or, usually, in terms of magnitude and phase. Since most of the information are contained into the magnitude, the phase is not considered in many applications. However, if it were necessary to reconstruct again the original image with the 2D-IDFT, the phase information would be strictly required in order to avoid corrupted image reconstruction [25]. Since the magnitude may present very scattered values comparing the largest DC component with respect to the other frequencies, a logarithmic transformation is usually applied to enhance the information contained in low-frequency components:

$$\tilde{f}(k,l) = c\log(1 + |M_{k,l}|) \tag{3}$$

where c is a scaling factor set to unity in the present study, and

$$M_{k,l} = \sqrt{\mathrm{Re}(f(k,l))^2 + \mathrm{Im}(f(k,l))^2} \tag{4}$$

is the magnitude for each pixel in the frequency domain. Among the many useful properties of the FT, the most important in the present case is related to the convolution property: the convolution operation in the input domain becomes a simple multiplication in the Fourier domain. In image processing, digital filters can be used to smooth the image, by suppressing high frequencies in the image, or to detect edges by removing the low frequencies [25]. These operations are accomplished by a filter kernel function $h(r,s)$ which slides on the image and computes a correlation between the kernel receptive field and the input image: $g(r,s) = h(r,s) * a(r,s)$. Specifically, the convolution is a correlation operation acting with a flipped kernel $h(-r,-s)$. Throughout the convolution property, the above-mentioned computation, which is the core of the convolutional neural networks (CNN), can be performed more efficiently in the frequency domain.

In the present work, the 2D-FFT has been adopted to perform a pre-processing of the road tunnel GPR linings profiles. This may help to compress data, maintaining the geometric structure of the starting digital image. The 2D-FFT identifies the vertical and horizontal patterns in the input image, preserving information of such alignments in the most dominant frequency components in the Fourier domain. Furthermore, as evidenced in Fig. 2, the 2D-FFT allows removing horizontal periodic components, typical of the GPR profiles in the depth direction. In Fig. 2, two illustrative examples have been depicted to highlight the effects of the 2D-FFT pre-processing on the road tunnels GPR profiles.

## 4  Methodology

The dataset considered in the current study comes from tunnel lining defects classification concerned structures dating from most 1960s s to 1980s.s. Specifically, after the human defect recognition, the entire GPR profiles were cut with a constant step of 5.00 m long along the horizontal axis. In this way, sample images were obtained for classification task. These samples have been labeled according to the human experts defect-recognition phase. To avoid that some defects were placed across two different images, the cutting step was occasionally manually altered to provide samples which allowed for a more clear classification.

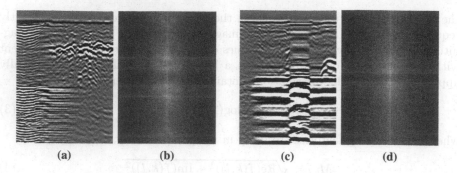

**Fig. 2.** Two examples of 2D-FFT pre-processing of road tunnels GPR profiles. (a) and (c): samples extracted from the entire GPR profile; (b) and (d): 2D-FFT magnitude pre-processed images.

## 4.1  Multi-level Defect Classification

The classification has been performed in a hierarchical multi-level procedure. As depicted in Fig. 3, this procedure allowed to perform a more detailed classification of the defect. Based on the structure of the hierarchical classification tree, 7 models were trained. Each of them performs a binary classification task. Following in depth the tree depicted in Fig. 3, the total number of available samples for each level gradually decreases. Moreover, since each class presents an unbalanced number of images, in order to train a good classification model, a balanced approach was forced by the class with the minimum number of samples. To accomplish the classification tasks, a deep learning model has been trained based on convolutional neural networks, discussed in the following section.

## 4.2  Convolutional Neural Network: ResNet50

Convolutional neural networks (CNN) algorithms are one of the most used deep learning techniques capable of solving categorization problems based on image recognition. To solve this kind of task, ResNet-50 was trained to detect structural states of tunnels lining through the transfer learning approach. Indeed, such networks are pre-trained on the ImageNet Large Scale Visual Recognition Challenge (ILSVRC) dataset based on 1,281,167 training, 50,000 validation, and 100,000 test images [26,27]. The chosen CNN was used within the MATLAB2021a programming environment [28]. Its architecture is composed of 177 layers of which 49 are convolutional and 1 is fully connected and it is designed in 2015 by He et al. [29]. It is defined as a "feed-forward" neural network with "residual/skip connections" that leverages Rectified Linear Units (ReLu) and softmax as activation functions exploiting 25 million parameters. Among the different layers of the network, it is possible to acknowledge the four types of layers that distinguish the neural networks as the activation and the pooling layer in addition to convolutional and fully connected ones, previously cited [30]. The convolutional layer contains neurons that interact with the other one in the next layer

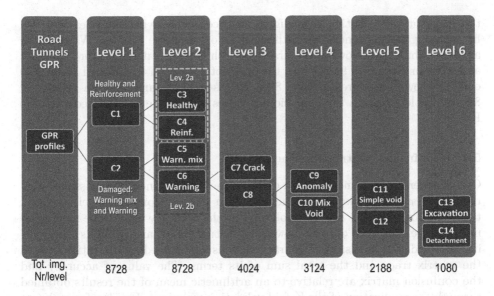

**Fig. 3.** Hierarchical tree multi-level classification representation.

through convolutional kernels while the nonlinear features are extracted using the activation layer. The pooling one improve the performance of the algorithm and reduces the cost by compressing the convolutional features. The last one is the layer that interprets the extracted features and creates a vector containing the probability of the analysed image to belong to each class [31]. In the literature, deeper neural networks are expected to perform better than shallower ones especially in the training phase, as shown in several studies [32,33]. However, it is recognized that the improvement in accuracy is not always related to an increase in network depth, which could generate degradation problems. The innovative element that makes ResNet superior compared to other CNNs is the presence of skip connections (residual units). This particular unit allows the learning of the differences between the input and output layers, mitigating, in this way, the problems deriving from excessive depth. The choice of network architecture has fallen on ResNet for the depth of the network and for the relatively reduced computational level. In particular, ResNet-50 has been adopted as a pre-trained network to perform a binary classification of GPR profile image and their FFT transform, previously described, using these hyperparameters: learning rate equal to 0.001, mini-batch size equal to 32, and maximum number of epochs equal to 12.

## 5   Results and Discussion

The classification of tunnel lining defects concerned structures dating from most 1960s s to 1980s s following the procedure described in the previous sections. The results obtained by training the network with the GPR profiles, extracted during the different investigation campaigns, were compared with the ones achieved by training the same network with the FTs of the same profiles. Whereas the accuracy obtained following the first approach showed values greater than 90% and with an average of 94.5% [31], the ones obtained with the trained ResNet-50 on FTs show values greater than 80%, unless level 2b, and with an average of 86.8%. Table 3 reports the confusion matrices for each level obtained with the FT.

## 5.1  Confusion Matrix for Each Level

Out of several useful methods for defining the performance of a classifier algorithm, the most well-known is the confusion matrix. For each level of detail, the confusion matrix is reported followed by the accuracy value. The mentioned matrices are composed of rows showing the actual classes and columns representing the predicted labels. The accuracy value is determined by the ratio between the matrix trace and the total sum of its terms. The value of accuracy and the confusion matrix are relative to an arithmetic mean of the results obtained through the application of the K-fold validation technique. Besides, for each test fold, an error estimation through the RMSE (Root Mean Square Error) index was performed and then their average was calculated and used as a final indicator. The data for each classification were casually divided into k groups (folds) in which a "fold" is used for testing, one for validation, and (k−2) for network training [34,35]. The used value of k is equal to 10. Such choice is based on empirical demonstrations that highlight the ability of it to produce test error rate estimates that have neither excessive bias nor much variance [36].

## 5.2  Comparison with the Authors' Previous Work

The authors in [31] have already performed a study on the multilevel tunnel linings defects classification working with raw GPR data profiles. On the other hand, the strategy proposed in this work is related to the possibility of using as input data of a CNN, not only GPR profile images, but also the FTs of the same ones. The outcomes obtained with this last one showed a decrease in accuracy for all levels with respect to the results obtained by training ResNet-50 with GPR profiles, keeping an accuracy higher than 90% for the levels 3,5, and 6. [31]. Comparing the results of the two different training and test valuation of the ResNet-50 proposed, level 1 (healthy and reinforced/damaged) shows an accuracy of 88% compared to 92.6% previously obtained, level 2a (healthy/reinforced) shows an accuracy of 83.1% compared to 97.3%. The accuracy for level 2b (warning mix/warning) shows a value of 76.3% compared to the respective value of 90.4%. Regarding the accuracy in level 3 (crack/C8) the value obtained by training on the FTs of the GPR profiles equal to 94.4% is very similar to the previous one equal to 95.9%. Level 4 (Anomaly/mix void) shows an accuracy of 85.1%compared to 91.8%. In the last two levels, the CNN with FTs showed the highest accuracy values of 90% and 91% for levels 5 and

**Table 3.** Confusion Matrix for Levels 1, 2a, 2b, 3, 4, 5 and 6.

| Confusion Matrix - Level 1 | | | |
|---|---|---|---|
| Real Class | C1: predicted | C2: predicted | Performance Metrics |
| C1 | 87.9% | 12.1% | Accuracy: 88% |
| C2 | 11.4% | 88.6% | RMSE: 31.5% |
| Confusion Matrix - Level 2a | | | |
| Real Class | C3: predicted | C4: predicted | Performance Metrics |
| C3 | 79.3% | 20.7% | Accuracy: 83.1% |
| C4 | 13.0% | 87.0% | RMSE: 37.2% |
| Confusion Matrix - Level 2b | | | |
| Real Class | C5: predicted | C6: predicted | Performance Metrics |
| C5 | 73.5% | 26.5% | Accuracy: 76.3% |
| C6 | 20.9% | 79.1% | RMSE: 44.3% |
| Confusion Matrix - Level 3 | | | |
| Real Class | C7: predicted | C8: predicted | Performance Metrics |
| C7 | 97.8% | 0.22% | Accuracy: 94.4% |
| C8 | 9.0% | 91.0% | RMSE: 20.6% |
| Confusion Matrix - Level 4 | | | |
| Real Class | C9: predicted | C10: predicted | Performance Metrics |
| C9 | 83.9% | 16.1% | Accuracy: 85.1% |
| C10 | 13.6% | 86.4% | RMSE: 38.3% |
| Confusion Matrix - Level 5 | | | |
| Real Class | C11: predicted | C12: predicted | Performance Metrics |
| C11 | 85.7% | 14.3% | Accuracy: 90% |
| C12 | 5.9% | 94.1% | RMSE: 28.6% |
| Confusion Matrix - Level 6 | | | |
| Real Class | C13: predicted | C14: predicted | Performance Metrics |
| C13 | 92.4% | 7.6% | Accuracy: 91% |
| C14 | 11.3% | 88.7% | RMSE: 25.8% |

6 respectively, compared to the values of 98.2% and 95.3% of the same CNN trained with simple GPR profiles.

# 6   Conclusions

In the present work, a hierarchical multi-level classification approach is discussed related to road tunnels linings GPR assessment for automated defects classification. The GPR profiles are sampled and pre-processed with 2D-FFT technique performing data compression and making convolution more efficient.

Seven different CNN models have been trained with the transfer learning approach starting from pre-trained ResNet-50 model. A final comparison with respect to the model trained without image pre-processing pointed out the reliability of the proposed approach for automated road tunnel defects classification. However, the pre-processing phase probably produces an excessive compression of the data, providing lower accuracy levels with respect to the model trained on raw GPR images samples. Future developments of the present work may virtually involve some further comparisons not only from the pre-processing side, but even on the neural architecture which could lead to further improvements and a more reliable system for automated road tunnels linings defect classification.

**Acknowledgments.** This research was supported by project MSCA-RISE-2020 Marie Skłodowska-Curie Research and Innovation Staff Exchange (RISE) - ADDOPTML (ntua.gr) The authors would like to thank G.C. Marano and the project ADDOPTML for funding supporting this research.

# References

1. Chiaia, B., Marasco, G., Ventura, G., Zannini Quirini, C.: Customised active monitoring system for structural control and maintenance optimisation. J. Civil Struct. Health Monit. **10**(2), 267–282 (2020). https://doi.org/10.1007/s13349-020-00382-8
2. Aloisio, A., et al.: Indirect assessment of concrete resistance from FE model updating and young's modulus estimation of a multi-span PSC viaduct: experimental tests and validation. Elsevier Struct. **37**, 686–697 (2022)
3. Rosso, M.M., Cucuzza, R., Aloisio, A., Marano, G.C.: Enhanced multi-strategy particle swarm optimization for constrained problems with an evolutionary-strategies-based unfeasible local search operator. Appl. Sci. **12**(5), 2285 (2022)
4. Asso, R., Cucuzza, R., Rosso, M.M., Masera, D., Marano, G.C.: Bridges monitoring: an application of AI with gaussian processes. In: 14th International Conference on Evolutionary and Deterministic Methods for Design, Optimization and Control. Institute of Structural Analysis and Antiseismic Research National Technical University of Athens (2021)
5. Rosso, M.M., Cucuzza, R., Di Trapani, F., Marano, G.C.: Nonpenalty machine learning constraint handling using PSO-svm for structural optimization. Adv. Civil Eng. **2021** (2021)
6. Cucuzza, R., Costi, C., Rosso, M.M., Domaneschi, M., Marano, G., Masera, D.: Optimal strengthening by steel truss arches in prestressed girder bridges. In: Proceedings of the Institution of Civil Engineers - Bridge Engineering, pp. 1–51 (2022)
7. Marasco, G., Chiaia, B., Ventura, G.: AI based bridge health assessment. In: 9th International Workshop on Reliable Engineering Computing (REC 2021) is "Risk and Uncertainty in Engineering Computations" (2021)
8. Chiaia, B., Ventura, G., Quirini, C.Z., Marasco, G.: Bridge active monitoring for maintenance and structural safety. In: Arêde, A., Costa, C. (eds.) ARCH 2019. SI, vol. 11, pp. 866–873. Springer, Cham (2020). https://doi.org/10.1007/978-3-030-29227-0_96
9. Davis, A.G., Lim, M.K., Petersen, C.G.: Rapid and economical evaluation of concrete tunnel linings with impulse response and impulse radar non-destructive methods. NDT & E Int. **38**(3), 181–186 (2005)

10. Dawood, T., Zhu, Z., Zayed, T.: Deterioration mapping in subway infrastructure using sensory data of GPR. Tunnel. Undergr. Space Technol. **103**, 103487 (2020)
11. Bhalla, S., Yang, Y., Zhao, J., Soh, C.: Structural health monitoring of underground facilities - technological issues and challenges. Tunnel. Undergr. Space Technol. **20**(5), 487–500 (2005)
12. Di Trapani, F., et al.: Dynamic response of infilled frames subject to accidental column losses. In: Pellegrino, C., Faleschini, F., Zanini, M.A., Matos, J.C., Casas, J.R., Strauss, A. (eds.) EUROSTRUCT 2021. LNCE, vol. 200, pp. 1100–1107. Springer, Cham (2022). https://doi.org/10.1007/978-3-030-91877-4_125
13. Jiang, Y., Zhang, X., Taniguchi, T.: Quantitative condition inspection and assessment of tunnel lining. Autom. Constr. **102**, 258–269 (2019)
14. Attard, L., Debono, C.J., Valentino, G., Di Castro, M.: Tunnel inspection using photogrammetric techniques and image processing: a review. ISPRS J. Photogram. Remote Sens. **144**, 180–188 (2018)
15. Lei, M., Liu, L., Shi, C., Tan, Y., Lin, Y., Wang, W.: A novel tunnel-lining crack recognition system based on digital image technology. Tunnel. Undergr. Space Technol. **108**, 103724 (2021)
16. Feng, C., Zhang, H., Wang, S., Li, Y., Wang, H., Yan, F.: Structural damage detection using deep convolutional neural network and transfer learning. KSCE J. Civil Eng. **23**(10), 4493–4502 (2019)
17. Al-Nuaimy, W., Huang, Y., Nakhkash, M., Fang, M., Nguyen, V., Eriksen, A.: Automatic detection of buried utilities and solid objects with GPR using neural networks and pattern recognition. J. Appl. Geophys. **43**(2), 157–165 (2000)
18. Dwivedi, S.K., Vishwakarma, M., Soni, P.: Advances and researches on non destructive testing: a review. Mater. Today Proc. **5**(2, Part 1), 3690–3698 (2018)
19. Tosti, F., Ferrante, C.: Using ground penetrating radar methods to investigate reinforced concrete structures. Surv. Geophys. **41**(3), 485–530 (2020)
20. Davis, A.G., Lim, M.K., Petersen, C.G.: Rapid and economical evaluation of concrete tunnel linings with impulse response and impulse radar non-destructive methods. NDT & E Int. **38**(3), 181–186 (2005)
21. Cardarelli, E., Marrone, C., Orlando, L.: Evaluation of tunnel stability using integrated geophysical methods. J. Appl. Geophys. **52**(2), 93–102 (2003)
22. Farrar, C.R., Worden, K.: Structural Health Monitoring: A Machine Learning Perspective. John Wiley & Sons, Hoboken (2012)
23. Broughton, S.A., Bryan, K.: Discrete Fourier Analysis and Wavelets: Applications to Signal and Image processing. John Wiley & Sons, Hoboken (2018)
24. Lim, J.S.: Two-dimensional signal and image processing. Englewood Cliffs (1990)
25. Fisher, R., Perkins, S., Walker, A., Wolfart, E.: Hypermedia Image Processing Reference, pp. 118–130. John Wiley & Sons Ltd., Hoboken (1996)
26. Russakovsky, O., et al.: Imagenet large scale visual recognition challenge. Int. J. Comput. Vision **115**(3), 211–252 (2015)
27. Markoff, J.: For web images, creating new technology to seek and find. New York Times (2012)
28. MATLAB version 9.10.0.1649659 (R2021a) Update 1. Natick, Massachusetts (2021)
29. He, K., Zhang, X., Ren, S., Sun, J.: Deep residual learning for image recognition. In: 2016 IEEE Conference on Computer Vision and Pattern Recognition (CVPR), pp. 770–778 (2016)
30. Rawat, W., Wang, Z.: Deep convolutional neural networks for image classification: a comprehensive review. Neural Comput. **29**(9), 2352–2449 (2017)

31. Chiaia, B., Marasco, G., Aiello, S.: Deep convolutional neural network for multi-level non-invasive tunnel lining assessment. Front. Struct. Civil Eng. **16**, 214–223 (2022)
32. Anitescu, C., Atroshchenko, E., Alajlan, N., Rabczuk, T.: Artificial neural network methods for the solution of second order boundary value problems. Comput. Mater. Continua **59**(1), 345–359 (2019)
33. Guo, H., Zhuang, X., Rabczuk, T.: A deep collocation method for the bending analysis of Kirchhoff plate. Comput. Mater. Continua **59**(2), 433–456 (2019)
34. Rodriguez, J.D., Perez, A., Lozano, J.A.: Sensitivity analysis of k-fold cross validation in prediction error estimation. IEEE Trans. Pattern Anal. Mach. Intell. **32**(3), 569–575 (2010)
35. Refaeilzadeh, P., Tang, L., Liu, H.: Cross-Validation, pp. 1–7. Springer, New York (2016). https://doi.org/10.1007/978-1-4899-7993-3_565-2
36. James, G., Witten, D., Hastie, T., Tibshirani, R.: An Introduction to Statistical Learning. STS, vol. 103. Springer, New York (2013). https://doi.org/10.1007/978-1-4614-7138-7

# ITSC Fault Diagnosis in Permanent Magnet Synchronous Motor Drives Using Shallow CNNs

Vera Szabo[1,2]([✉]), Saeed Hasan Ebrahimi[1], Martin Choux[1],
and Morten Goodwin[1]

[1] University of Agder, Jon Lilletuns Vei 9, 4879 Grimstad, Norway
{vera.szabo,saeed.ebrahimi,martin.choux,morten.goodwin}@uia.no
[2] MHWirth AS, Butangen 20, 4639 Kristiansand, Norway

**Abstract.** Due to its features, permanent magnet synchronous motor (PMSM) has gained popularity and is used in various industrial applications, including those with high downtime costs like offshore equipment. Inter-turn short-circuit (ITSC) fault is one of the most typical PMSM faults and therefore is its early diagnostics in real-time highly valuable. Solving the problem using conventional signal, model-based, or data-driven approaches faces challenges such as computational complexity, time demand, or need for detailed domain expertise. This paper presents a computationally simple, robust, and accurate method based on the 2D convolutional neural network (CNN). The proposed data-driven model has first been validated with the help of experimental data obtained from an inverter fed PMSM subject to ITSC faults in different time intervals, and secondly its performances have been compared to a model-based structural analysis approach using Dulmage-Mendelsohn decomposition tool. The comparison is based on the same data. Results show that the accuracy of the CNN model for diagnosing early faults is more than 98% without doing additional comprehensive fine-tuning. In addition, the paper presents a robust method that can be successfully used as a metric for fast fault detection benchmark.

**Keywords:** Fault diagnosis · Permanent magnet synchronous motor · Intern-turn short-circuit fault · Convolutional neural network

## 1 Introduction

Permanent magnet synchronous motors (PMSMs) are deployed in various industrial systems, such as offshore equipment, wind generators, robotics or electric vehicles. While having conventional three phase windings in the stator, PMSMs produce their rotor magnetic flux by the mean of permanent magnets, either embedded tangentially around the rim of the rotor as seen in Fig. 1, or buried radially for higher performances. Their efficiency (92%–97%) is significantly higher compared to traditional asynchronous motors (75%–92%) [3], while low

© Springer Nature Switzerland AG 2022
L. Iliadis et al. (Eds.): EANN 2022, CCIS 1600, pp. 177–189, 2022.
https://doi.org/10.1007/978-3-031-08223-8_15

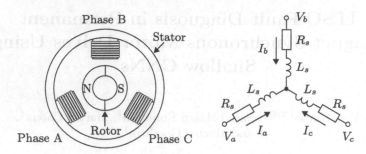

**Fig. 1.** Basic structure of a PMSM

reactive power consumption, improved dynamic performance, light weight, and small dimensions are further reasons for their increased popularity. More than 40% of all faults in synchronous motors start as stator related [16]. Among those, the inter-turn short-circuit (ITSC) faults are the most common, however difficult to detect automatically [15], which is partially caused by ITSC faults having little effect to the motor performance in early stages. However, if not discovered and mended in time, the ITSC fault can quickly grow into severe motor damage and consequently lead to total failure of the system [1]. The drive to cut operating and maintenance costs and increase operational safety is pushing the agenda in the industry towards the adoption of predictive maintenance strategies. In this process, fault diagnosis, i.e. fault detection and isolation, represents an important part. A proven method for diagnosis of ITSC faults in their early phase, that is easy to implement in practice, is therefore in great demand.

This paper focuses on a simple detection and diagnosis method for ITSC faults. While deep CNNs have several layers, often of various types, shallow CNNs have only one besides the input and the output layer. One objective of this study is to explore whether the simplest CNNs can be successfully used as ITSC fault classifiers, i.e. with high enough accuracy, as they do not overfit on small datasets and require less computational time and energy consumption than deep CNNs. Indeed, awareness about $CO_2$ emission in machine learning research started to arise lately [5]. According to the EU Annual Report on SMEs (2019), in the EU just 6% of the SMEs use AI, although they represent 99.8% of all enterprises in the EU-27, with lack of skill to be one of the main obstacles. Therefore, any model that is easy to use, does not require high computational power and shows robustness is of huge demand by the industry.

Following a short literature overview in Sect. 2, the proposed method is described in Sect. 3 while Sect. 4 details the results and compares the performances with a model-based method using the same experimental setup and dataset. Finally, conclusions are drawn in Sect. 5.

## 2   Literature Review

Fault diagnosis can be divided from data processing into model-based, signal-based and data-driven methods. The literature on PMSMs show that faults, as for example inter-turn short circuit or demagnetisation faults, can be early detected using either of the methods. Comprehensive reviews of methods for detection and diagnosis of ITSC faults in PMSMs are presented in [15] and [2].

The model-based methods establish a mathematical model based on principles of physics that describes the actual machine. The most accurate results have been achieved with finite element analysis (FEA) models which compared to other models also have the highest computational cost as well [2]. Other types of models, such as equivalent circuit, field reconstruction and linear PMSM models, are beneficial in understanding how the fault behaves assuming that they are detailed enough [15]. The signal-based and data driven methods use statistical tools and mathematical transformations to identify and extract fault patterns from signals such as current, voltage, vibrations and so on. Motor current signal analysis (MCSA) is the most common model and is extensively studied [2].

Artificial intelligence (AI) and machine learning (ML)-based approaches show increased performance compared to conventional signal-based models providing a solution for the complexity introduced by increased data quantity. However, it is often not easy to apply traditional ML techniques in practice, due to lack of efficient methods to obtain training data, and specific knowledge needed to train the models [8,14]. The traditional ML with tailor made and handcrafted features—typically used by applying feature extraction and learning algorithms such as support vector machine (SVM), random forest (RF), principal component analysis (PCA) or linear decrement analysis (LDA) [19]—has been used for many years while deep learning (DL) methods emerged in 2006.

DL represents a breakthrough in the field of AI and shows state-of-the-art performance when compared to traditional machine learning in many fields. Constructing a ML system needs careful engineering and high domain expertise to design a feature extractor that transforms the raw data into a suitable representation from which the learning model can detect or classify patterns [11].

In contrast, when it comes to DL, the features are learned automatically from raw data. DL models used in motor fault detection and diagnosis include for instance deep belief networks [20], generative adversarial networks (GAN) [12,17], long short-term memory models (LSTM) [6]. Among DL methods for fault diagnosis, extensively used are CNNs [9]. 1D CNNs are, among others, used with direct input of time-domain signals collected in motors [7,10], while 2D CNNs are, among others, used by converting the time-domain raw signals into 2D grey images without further feature extraction [18].

## 3   The Proposed Method

This section presents the proposed data-driven method based on a shallow 2D CNN. The input to the model is obtained from an experimental setup where a PMSM is run through a healthy and three faulty sequences. Switching the faults on and off is done by controllable relays placed between the winding taps. The three faulty sequences represent the three ITSC faults. Each fault is applied on a designated phase by short-circuiting different numbers of turns, resulting in different fault percentage, enabling establishing a fault of less than 1% in terms of number of short-circuited turns per total number of turns in one phase. Altogether, ten different features (four voltages, four currents, position of the rotor and speed) in their raw form, without any prepossessing, have been used as input to the model.

CNNs, primarily used for pattern recognition tasks, especially within images, usually consist of three types of layers: convolutional, pooling, and fully-connected layers. As the name indicates, the convolutional layers play the most important role, where the learnable parameters origin from kernels. The structure of the proposed classification model is outlined in Fig. 2. It has only one convolutional layer. The output of the model is one of the 4 classes: no-fault and ITSC faults at phases A, B and C.

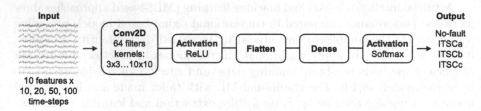

Fig. 2. The proposed shallow 2D CNN architecture

We use SHAP (Shapley Additive exPlanations), a method introduced in 2017 [13] to explain individual predictions of models on global and local level. On the global level it can show which features contribute to the model output and how significant their contribution is. On the local level it can examine each data point and investigate why the model made a certain decision.

## 4   Experiment and Results

The proposed method has been validated on the experimental setup used in [4], i.e. with a 4-pole PMSM whose parameters are given in Table 1. Each of the motor phase windings consists in two coils of 51 turns in series, with hence 102 turns per phase. As shown in Fig. 3, ITSC faults have been applied on each phase by short-circuiting different number of turns resulting in a different fault percentage at each phase as shown in Table 2.

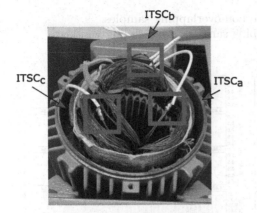

**Fig. 3.** Applied ITSC faults [4]

**Table 1.** Motor parameters

| Parameter | Value |
|---|---|
| Rated DC bus voltage | 280 V |
| Rated rms phase current | 5 A |
| Rated output torque | 7 Nm |
| Rated speed | 1500 rpm |
| Stator resistance | 0.8 $\Omega$ |
| Stator inductance | 8.5 mH |
| Rotor inertia | 0.0026 kgm$^2$ |
| Pole pairs | 2 |

**Table 2.** Applied ITSC faults per phase

| Fault type | Phase | Nr. of short-circuited turns | Applied ITSC fault in % | Nr. of records |
|---|---|---|---|---|
| ITSCa | A | 1 | 0.98 | 55300 |
| ITSCb | B | 3 | 2.94 | 62800 |
| ITSCc | C | 5 | 4.90 | 56000 |
| No-fault | — | 0 | 0.00 | 185600 |

The experiment lasted for 20 s with sampling time for data acquisition of 50 $\mu$s. ITSC faults in phase A, B and, C were applied in the time intervals $t = 4.471 - 7.238$ s, $t = 9.613 - 12.760$ s and, $t = 15.600 - 18.410$ s respectively, see Fig. 4.

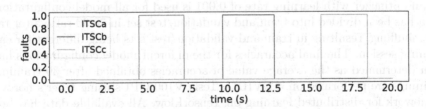

**Fig. 4.** Timeline of applied ITSC faults

The 10 inputs of the model are shown in Fig. 5 around the transition between the no fault region (green) and the ITSC fault in phase A (red) at t = 4.471 s. Samples of different lengths have been stacked one under the other making a 2D input of size 10 times sample length. The proposed method is evaluated using two approaches:

- Approach 1 - input data as separate non-overlapping samples.
- Approach 2 - input data as overlapping samples using sliding windows.

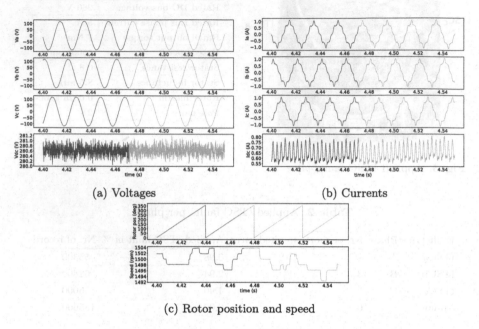

(a) Voltages                                    (b) Currents

(c) Rotor position and speed

**Fig. 5.** 10 features - input to 2D CNN (Color figure online)

Sample sizes range over 10, 20, 50 and 100 time-steps corresponding to 0.5, 1, 2.5 and 5 ms. Each model is trained on 500 epochs using kernel sizes from $3 \times 3$ to $10 \times 10$ in order to achieve optimal results in terms of accuracy, simplicity, computational and energy efficiency. The number of filters has been set to 64. Adam optimizer with learning rate of 0.001 is used for all model configurations. Data has been divided into train and validation/test set in 70:30 ratio after random shuffling, resulting in train and validation/test sets being different for each training session. The final accuracies for the different model configurations have been determined as the average value of accuracies obtained after 30 trainings. Trainings are performed on 4 NVIDIA Tesla V100 GPUs using Uber's horovod framework for distributed learning on TensorFlow. All available data has been used for training and testing, which results in slightly imbalanced classification due to data size in ratios of 52% (no fault), 15% (ITSCa), 17% (ITSCb), 16% (ITSCc).

## 4.1 Approach 1 - Non-overlapping Samples

This subsection investigates what is the optimal length of the input samples. We start with the simplest approach, slicing the sequences into non-overlapping segments of 10, 20, 50 and 100 time-steps. By using 2D inputs into the convolutional network we expect from the model to find pattern between the different features sampled at the same time. In case of clear patterns, we expect that shorter lengths can deliver as good results as longer ones, potentially even better. The attributes of the model variations, together with the average time needed for training are given in Table 3 while Table 4 shows the corresponding validation accuracies. The max accuracies achieved for the best performing models are given in Fig. 6 and Fig. 7.

**Table 3.** Model attributes - approach 1

| Sample length [time-steps] | No. of training samples | Batch size | Learning rate | Average training time [min] |
|---|---|---|---|---|
| 10 | 25 177 | 32 | 0.001 | 6.14 |
| 20 | 12 588 | 32 | 0.001 | 3.48 |
| 50 | 5 035 | 32 | 0.001 | 2.08 |
| 100 | 2 517 | 32 | 0.001 | 1.37 |

**Discussion.** The proposed method results in high accuracies. The accuracy of the models shows general increase with the length of timesteps for all kernels, except for kernels $9 \times 9$ and $10 \times 10$ that show slight deviation. The best performing model is the one based on 100 time-steps and kernel size $4 \times 4$. It achieves an average accuracy of 98.42%. Figure 8 shows SHAP values corresponding to four different outcomes: no-fault, and three ITSC faults. As seen, the voltages in phases A, B and C play an important role together with the currents. However, the last two features (rotor position and speed) have a minimum or no impact on the results. Figure 8 shows the best performing model for time-steps length of 10, however the conclusions are valid for all models.

## 4.2  Approach 2 - Sliding Windows

In this subsection we investigate whether we can get better results by using overlapping segments of 10, 20, 50 and 100 time-steps. We approximately double the number of train input samples and test whether introducing additional sequences of data gives more information. The model attributes and the validation accuracies are given in Table 5 and Table 6. The max accuracies achieved for the best performing models (kernel size $4 \times 4$) are given in Fig. 9 and Fig. 10.

**Table 4.** Validation acc. [%] - approach 1

| Kernel size | Sample length [time-steps] | | | | | | | |
|---|---|---|---|---|---|---|---|---|
| | 10 | | 20 | | 50 | | 100 | |
| | $\mu$ | $\sigma$ | $\mu$ | $\sigma$ | $\mu$ | $\sigma$ | $\mu$ | $\sigma$ |
| $3 \times 3$ | 91.00 | 1.81 | 94.92 | 1.76 | 94.95 | 2.46 | 97.91 | 0.90 |
| $4 \times 4$ | 92.46 | 1.23 | 96.33 | 0.95 | 96.74 | 0.61 | 98.42 | 0.72 |
| $5 \times 5$ | 88.16 | 2.68 | 94.49 | 2.53 | 93.73 | 4.64 | 97.32 | 1.54 |
| $6 \times 6$ | 88.26 | 2.45 | 94.18 | 2.82 | 94.49 | 2.45 | 97.04 | 1.85 |
| $7 \times 7$ | 87.81 | 2.27 | 94.25 | 3.74 | 95.41 | 0.93 | 96.36 | 3.57 |
| $8 \times 8$ | 88.00 | 1.56 | 94.60 | 1.12 | 94.82 | 2.57 | 96.60 | 2.80 |
| $9 \times 9$ | 86.68 | 1.44 | 92.79 | 2.15 | 93.84 | 2.23 | 86.11 | 11.59 |
| $10 \times 10$ | 67.20 | 12.42 | 61.13 | 14.73 | 66.29 | 15.11 | 58.96 | 10.41 |

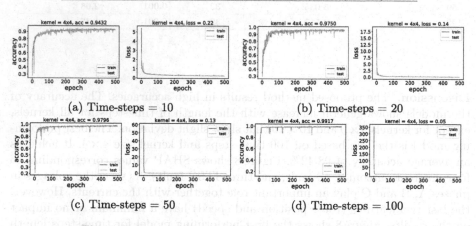

(a) Time-steps = 10          (b) Time-steps = 20

(c) Time-steps = 50          (d) Time-steps = 100

**Fig. 6.** Best performing models - max accuracies - appr. 1

**Discussion.** This approach shows similar results as approach 1, however it generally achieves slightly lower accuracies for the same number of epochs (97.47% compared to 98.42%). The best performing model is again the one based on 100 time-steps and kernel size $4 \times 4$. Figure 11 shows SHAP values for four different outcomes with the same conclusions as earlier. The voltages and currents in phases A, B and C play an important role while the last two features contribute less.

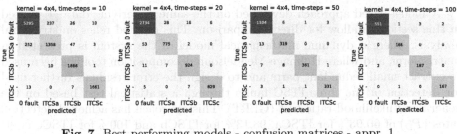

**Fig. 7.** Best performing models - confusion matrices - appr. 1

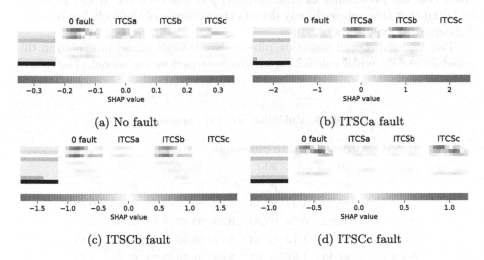

(a) No fault

(b) ITSCa fault

(c) ITSCb fault

(d) ITSCc fault

**Fig. 8.** SHAP values: kernel $= 4 \times 4$, time-steps $= 10$, appr.1

**Table 5.** Model attributes - approach 2

| Sample length [time-steps] | No. of training samples | Batch size | Learning rate | Average training time [min] |
|---|---|---|---|---|
| 10 | 50350 | 32 | 0.001 | 12.93 |
| 20 | 25171 | 32 | 0.001 | 7.03 |
| 50 | 10065 | 32 | 0.001 | 3.45 |
| 100 | 5028 | 32 | 0.001 | 2.31 |

## 4.3 Comparison with Model-based Approach

The main difference between data-driven (NNs) approach and signal- or model-based approach is the need of a priori understanding of the system. While both signal- and model-based approaches require a deep domain knowledge of the underlying system, data-driven approach discovers dependencies automatically. However, large amount of historical data for training the models, both healthy and faulty, is needed which is usually not available in such scale. Moreover, producing such data comes with high cost.

A model-based approach developed on the same underlying data [4] is used in this section to allow for direct comparison. This method relies on structural analysis, where a dynamic mathematical model of the system is presented in matrix form, and where Dulmage-Mendelsohn decomposition tool has been used to extract small redundant parts and to design the error residuals further used for detection of the three ITSC faults through a statistical test based on the generalized likelihood ratio test (GLRT). This approach has achieved detection rates ($P_D$) of 60.93% for ITSCa, 98.13% for ITSCb and 100% for ITSCc fault, given that the probability of false alarm ($P_{FA}$) has been set to 2%. It should be noted that this approach only detects the presence of the fault but does not distinguish among types of faults.

The achieved overall detection rate of the 2D CNN model presented in this paper is 98.83% when calculating on the best performing model. The overall

**Table 6.** Validation acc. [%] - approach 2

| Kernel size | Sample length [time-steps] | | | | | | | |
|---|---|---|---|---|---|---|---|---|
| | 10 | | 20 | | 50 | | 100 | |
| | $\mu$ | $\sigma$ | $\mu$ | $\sigma$ | $\mu$ | $\sigma$ | $\mu$ | $\sigma$ |
| $3 \times 3$ | 89.89 | 1.42 | 92.43 | 1.02 | 89.52 | 2.12 | 95.75 | 0.89 |
| $4 \times 4$ | 90.92 | 0.90 | 93.80 | 0.86 | 93.83 | 1.54 | 97.47 | 0.51 |
| $5 \times 5$ | 86.78 | 1.72 | 88.93 | 2.77 | 86.96 | 2.48 | 92.64 | 5.87 |
| $6 \times 6$ | 87.40 | 1.67 | 88.67 | 2.68 | 87.76 | 2.23 | 95.07 | 1.74 |
| $7 \times 7$ | 87.52 | 2.13 | 90.42 | 0.87 | 89.64 | 1.65 | 94.44 | 3.10 |
| $8 \times 8$ | 87.34 | 1.79 | 90.20 | 1.67 | 90.32 | 1.58 | 95.28 | 1.24 |
| $9 \times 9$ | 87.17 | 1.74 | 87.98 | 1.06 | 87.77 | 2.63 | 88.99 | 7.20 |
| $10 \times 10$ | 67.15 | 12.33 | 56.60 | 10.14 | 51.61 | 0.00 | 58.90 | 11.16 |

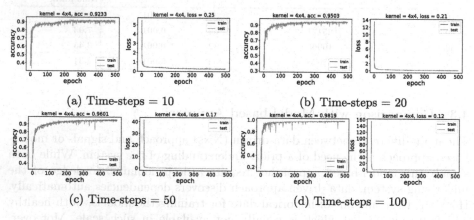

(a) Time-steps = 10        (b) Time-steps = 20

(c) Time-steps = 50        (d) Time-steps = 100

**Fig. 9.** Best performing models - max accuracies - appr. 2

and the detection rates for ITSCa, ITSCb and ITSCc faults, together with other performance metrics are shown in Table 7. The main limitation of the model is the need for sufficient amount of training data, especially faulty data that can be challenging to obtain outside of experimental setup.

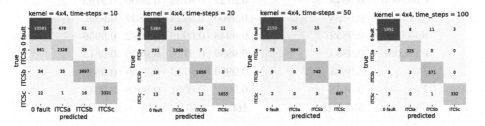

**Fig. 10.** Best performing models - confusion matrices - appr. 2

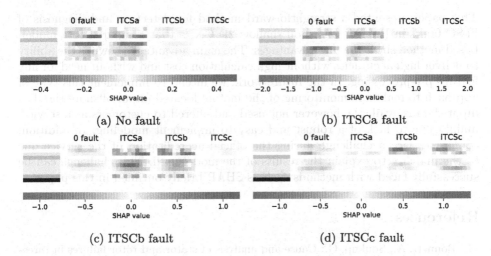

(a) No fault

(b) ITSCa fault

(c) ITSCb fault

(d) ITSCc fault

**Fig. 11.** SHAP values: kernel = $4 \times 4$, time-steps = 10, appr.2

**Table 7.** Best performing model - appr. 1 - performance metrics

| Metrics | Binary classification | Multiclass classification | | | |
|---|---|---|---|---|---|
| | No-fault/fault | ITSCa | ITCSb | ITSCc | W. average |
| Precision | 0.9843 | 0.9722 | 0.9759 | 0.9900 | 0.9793 |
| Sensitivity | 0.9883 | 0.9960 | 0.9713 | 0.9839 | 0.9832 |
| Specificity | 0.9852 | 0.9948 | 0.9949 | 0.9982 | 0.9959 |
| F1 score | 0.9863 | 0.9839 | 0.9736 | 0.9870 | 0.9812 |
| $P_D$ | 0.9883 | 0.9960 | 0.9713 | 0.9839 | 0.9832 |
| $P_{FA}$ | 0.0148 | 0.0052 | 0.0051 | 0.0018 | 0.0041 |
| Support | 557/523 | 166 | 189 | 168 | – |

## 5  Conclusions

This paper presented a straightforward method for detection and diagnosis of ITSC faults in PMSMs based on shallow 2D CNNs that compared to a model-based method showed a few advantages. The main advantage shown is the ability to deliver high accuracies without high calculation cost and without need for any feature pre-processing. In the future work, we intend to implement this type of approach to real-time monitoring of the motors located on an offshore rig. The input data is available, however not used and offered to customers as a service, mainly due to lack of a robust and easy to implement modeling. In addition, companies face a challenge during the official accreditation of the service due to the inability to explain the results of the model used. This challenge can be successfully faced with methods such as SHAP briefly outlined in this paper.

## References

1. Bonnett, A., Soukup, G.: Cause and analysis of stator and rotor failures in three-phase squirrel-cage induction motors. IEEE Trans. Ind. Appl. **28**, 921–937 (1992)
2. Chen, Y., Liang, S., Li, W., Liang, H., Wang, C.: Faults and diagnosis methods of permanent magnet synchronous motors: a review. Appl. Sci. **9**, 2116 (2019)
3. Dambrauskas, K., Vanagas, J., Zimnickas, T., Kalvaitis, A., Ažubalis, M.: A method for efficiency determination of permanent magnet synchronous motor. Energies **13**, 1004 (2020)
4. Ebrahimi, S.H., Choux, M., Huynh, V.K.: Real-time detection of incipient inter-turn short circuit and sensor faults in permanent magnet synchronous motor drives based on generalized likelihood ratio test and structural analysis (2022). https://doi.org/10.3390/s22093407
5. García-Martín, E., Rodrigues, C.F., Riley, G., Grahn, H.: Estimation of energy consumption in machine learning. J. Para. Distrib. Comput. **134**, 75–88 (2019)
6. Husari, F., Seshadrinath, J.: Sensitive inter-turn fault identification in induction motors using deep learning based methods. In: 2020 IEEE International Conference on Power Electronics, Smart Grid and Renewable Energy (PESGRE2020) (2020)

7. Ince, T., Kiranyaz, S., Eren, L., Askar, M., Gabbouj, M.: Real-time motor fault detection by 1-d convolutional neural networks. IEEE Trans. Ind. Electron. **63**, 7067–7075 (2016)

8. Jardine, A.K., Lin, D., Banjevic, D.: A review on machinery diagnostics and prognostics implementing condition-based maintenance. Mech. Syst. Signal Process. **20**, 1483–1510 (2006)

9. Jiao, J., Zhao, M., Lin, J., Liang, K.: A comprehensive review on convolutional neural network in machine fault diagnosis. Neurocomputing **417**, 36–63 (2020)

10. Kao, I.H., Wang, W.J., Lai, Y.H., Perng, J.W.: Analysis of permanent magnet synchronous motor fault diagnosis based on learning. IEEE Trans. Instrument. Meas. **68**(2), 310–324 (2019)

11. LeCun, Y., Bengio, Y., Hinton, G.: Deep learning. Nature **521**, 436–444 (2015)

12. Li, Y., Wang, Y., Zhang, Y., Zhang, J.: Diagnosis of inter-turn short circuit of permanent magnet synchronous motor based on deep learning and small fault samples. Neurocomputing **442**, 348–358 (2021)

13. Lundberg, S.M., Lee, S.I.: A unified approach to interpreting model predictions. In: Guyon, I., Luxburg, U.V., Bengio, S., Wallach, H., Fergus, R., Vishwanathan, S., Garnett, R. (eds.) Advances in Neural Information Processing Systems, vol. 30. Curran Associates, Inc. (2017)

14. Opalic, S.M.: Ann modelling of co2 refrigerant cooling system cop in a smart warehouse. J. Cleaner Prod. **260**, 120887 (2020)

15. Qi, Y., Bostanci, E., Zafarani, M., Akin, B.: Severity estimation of interturn short circuit fault for PMSM. IEEE Trans. Ind. Electron. **66**, 7260–7269 (2019)

16. Donnel, P.O.: Report of large motor reliability survey of industrial and commercial installations, part ii. IEEE Trans. Ind. Appl. **IA–21**(4), 865–872 (1985)

17. Wang, S., Yan, H.: Research on interturn short circuit fault identification method of PMSM based on deep learning. In: 22nd International Conference on Electrical Machines and Systems (ICEMS) (2019)

18. Wen, L., Li, X., Gao, L., Zhang, Y.: A new convolutional neural network-based data-driven fault diagnosis method. IEEE Trans. Ind. Electron. **65**, 5990–5998 (2018)

19. Zhao, R., Yan, R., Chen, Z., Mao, K., Wang, P., Gao, R.X.: Deep learning and its applications to machine health monitoring. Mech. Syst. Signal Process. **115**, 213–237 (2019)

20. Zhao, X., Jia, M., Liu, Z.: Semisupervised graph convolution deep belief network for fault diagnosis of electormechanical system with limited labeled data. IEEE Trans. Ind. Inf. **17**, 5450–5460 (2021)

# Synopsis of Video Files Using Neural Networks

Georgi Kostadinov(✉) ⓘ

New Bulgarian University, 21 Montevideo street, 1618 Sofia, Bulgaria
grgkostadinov@gmail.com

**Abstract.** The following paper examines the development of a framework that allows the generation of video synopsis. That is a video file obtained by overlaying the main moving objects in a single scene. This allows for file length reduction thus optimization of the analysis and storage of video surveillance footage. The proposed framework is based on modern methods in the field of machine learning for the automatic recognition and localization of objects in the video frames, their segmentation, tracking, and merging on the extracted background. Machine learning models based on convolutional neural networks were used for this purpose.

**Keywords:** Video synopsis · Convolutional neural networks · Machine learning · Object localization · Multiple object tracking · Feature extraction · Background segmentation · Person re-identification

## 1 Introduction

### 1.1 Current Challenges and Opportunities

Over the last few decades, video surveillance systems have grown steadily in popularity and accessibility. The need for constant video monitoring is strongly felt world-wide by governments and privately owned companies with the aim of increasing public safety and service efficiency. While round-the-clock video surveillance allows for the permanent and complete recording of all possible events, the challenges related to the efficient storage and analysis of these videos are becoming increasingly prevalent.

In the present work, an end-to-end framework is proposed, that can generate a synopsis of CCTV video materials. A "synopsis" of a video file refers to an output file obtained by extracting the main moving objects from the input video file and placing them on the same output scene. The output file generated during the process is both smaller in terms of file size than the input file, making it more cost-effective to store, and shorter in duration due to the removal of unnecessary static scenes, which eases the manual video analysis.

### 1.2 Proposed Work

The widespread methodology for creating a video synopsis consists of two processes. *Analysis* process where the static background is extracted, the objects are localized and segmented, and the individual sequences for each object – created. These sequences

© Springer Nature Switzerland AG 2022
L. Iliadis et al. (Eds.): EANN 2022, CCIS 1600, pp. 190–202, 2022.
https://doi.org/10.1007/978-3-031-08223-8_16

are also called *tubes*. The second process is the *generation* process, where each tube is shifted along temporally and placed together on the extracted background for their joint visualisation.

The proposed video synopsis framework can be divided into several main components that implement different synopsis tasks - extracting the main background from the video, localizing the main moving objects in a scene, extracting their discriminatory visual features, tracking them, and creating the tubes, and generating the synopsis file. Figure 1 graphically presents the framework and its components.

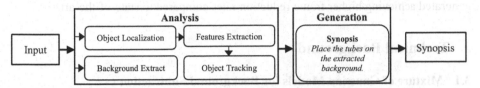

**Fig. 1.** The main components of the system and their connections.

The *analysis* step is applied on each frame of the input video file. During the analysis, each object detected on the scene is presented in a structure with additional data such as the order and time in which it appeared in the input video, as well as a mathematical vector corresponding to the visual features generated using convolutional neural network (CNN). Using this metadata, objects are registered linearly over time and during the *generation* step are placed in the extracted from the original video background. The whole process of the framework provides the ability to automatically create a synopsis of video files, which in turn greatly optimizes and upgrades the traditional methods of manually analysing video footage from security cameras. The current research is focused primarily on the synopsis of CCTV footage with pedestrians, but the proposed methodology can be applied for other types of objects. For simplicity in the following pages, *a tube* or sequence of occurrences of the same person will be called *an identity*.

The rest of the paper is organized as follows. Section 2 discusses some previous work related to generating synopsis of video files. Sections 3 and 4 present the theoretical fundamentals, the methodologies used in the framework, as well as its implementation details. In Sect. 5, metrics for evaluating the synopsis efficiency, as well as results achieved by the proposed framework and compared with state-of-the-art, are presented. Finally, in Sect. 6, the conclusion is drawn, and future work is presented.

## 2 Related Work

Numerous methods have been proposed related to video condensation and summarization. Most of them are based on the principle of deleting duplicate frames from the video and extracting the key ones, without making any additional analysis via the objects in the frames [1]. Other works use geometric primitives and minimize a cost function within each frame [2]. State-of-the-art methods use higher level approaches by extracting tubes of objects, which are temporarily shifted and placed together on the extracted background. For example, both [3] and [4] are using estimation algorithms where object's positions are chronologically rearranged without the need of knowing their trajectories. Whereas [5] is based on clustering of trajectories via event-based trajectory kinematics descriptors of the objects.

The contributions of this paper are two-folds. First, a novel framework for video synopsis for CCTV footage of pedestrians has been presented coupling machine learning methodologies for localizing and tracking people. For this, a popular online tracking method is implemented and combined with a state-of-the-art object detection methodology and state-of-the-art person re-identification convolutional neural network. Second, metrics for determining the efficiency of the video synopsis are defined and results are generated achieving higher frame reduction rates compared to state-of-the-art.

## 3  Technical Background

### 3.1  Mixture of Gaussian Models for Background Subtraction

The aim of the background subtraction task is to obtain the static background of the video scene, on which the extracted video objects will be placed to create the synopsis video. The algorithm used as part of the proposed framework is based on the adaptive Gaussian mixture models, presented by Stauffer and Grimson [6]. It is representative of an adaptive method that uses a mixture of normal distributions to model a multimodal background image sequence. For each pixel, its history is modelled by a mixture of Gaussian models consisting of $K$ normal distributions. In each consecutive video frame, each pixel is compared with the mixture model corresponding to that pixel. If the new pixel value is within 2.5 standard deviation of any of the $K$ normal distributions, it is considered a background candidate. The algorithm relies on assumptions that the background is visible more often than any foreground and that there are modes with relatively small variance.

Each background candidate is then checked if it belongs to a background distribution. The mixture of Gaussian models for each pixel is updated for each frame. This online adaptation allows the algorithm to adaptively deal with noise and illumination changes that may occur in video surveillance footage.

The framework uses mixture of Gaussian pixel models to iteratively accumulate background surfaces during the span of the input video. The output of the method is the static background of the video which is used as the base for overlaying the extracted identities and generating the synopsis file.

### 3.2  Convolutional Neural Network for Visual Feature Extraction

Artificial neural networks (ANN) are weighted graphs that consist of an ordered set of layers, where each layer is a set of nodes called neurons or perceptrons. The first layer of the neural network is called the input layer, and the last is called the output layer. The connections between the layers are weighted edges and are referred to as weights. At a given input data, each neural network node has numeric outputs. By sequentially calculating the outputs of the layers, we also calculate that of the final layer. Therefore, the structure of the neural network is determined by the number of layers and the functions that determine the outputs of those layers.

$$o^{(k)} = \begin{cases} \psi_{(k)}\left(o^{(k-1)}\right), & \text{if } k \geq 1 \\ x_n, & \text{if } k = 0 \end{cases} \tag{1}$$

where $o^{(k)}$ is the output of layer $k$, and $\psi_{(k)}$ is a function inferring $o^{(k)}$ with an input $o^{(k-1)}$.

One such function $\psi_{(k)}$ represents the fully connected layers in an ANN. As the name suggests, in order for two consecutive layers to be fully connected, all nodes in the previous layer must be connected to all the nodes in the next layer. The output of a fully connected layer is calculated using the function $\psi^{(FC)}$:

$$\psi_{(k)}^{(FC)}\left(o^{(k-1)}\right) = \phi\left(\left(o^{(k-1)}\right)^{T} w^{(k)} + b^{(k)}\right) \tag{2}$$

where, if $m^{(k)}$ is the number of nodes in layer $k$, $w^{(k)} \in \mathbb{R}^{m^{(k-1)} \times m^{(k)}}$ is the weight matrix connecting both layers, $b^{(k)} \in \mathbb{R}^{m^{(k)}}$ is the bias which controls the constants in the neural network, and $\phi$ is the activation function.

By arranging fully connected layers one after the other, the depth of the neural network can be increased, and by applying an activation function $\phi$ non-linearity is achieved, which increases the approximation accuracy of a neural network. There are many different types of activation functions (such as hyperbolic tangent or sigmoid), but the Rectified Linear Unit (ReLU) [7] is the most common nowadays. ReLU leads to reduced nodes, which in turn leads to a much faster training process.

For a neural network to be used with images or video frames as input data, convolutional layers can be defined using convolutional operations. Artificial neural networks with convolutional layers are called convolutional neural networks (CNN). CNNs are named after the linear mathematical operation called convolution. In image processing, convolution is a two-matrix operation that also results in a matrix $o^{(k)} \in \mathbb{R}^{\mathcal{H}_k \times \mathcal{W}_k \times m^{(k)}}$, where $\mathcal{H}_k$ is the height, and $\mathcal{W}_k$ is the width of the given level $k$. For each pair of indices $(I, J)$, where $0 < I \leq \mathcal{W}_k$ and $0 < J \leq \mathcal{H}_k$, there is a sliding window $p_{(I,J)}^{(k-1)}$ centred in $(I, J)$, defined by the outputs of the previous layers. It is then multiplied by the weight matrix. The bias values of layer $k$ are also added and the result is used as an input of the activation function $\phi$, to obtain the output of $\psi_{(k)}^{(Conv)}$:

$$\psi_{(k)}^{(Conv)}\left(o^{(k-1)}\right) = \left\{o_{(I,J)}^{(k)} | \forall (I,J)\left(\exists p_{(I,J)}^{(k-1)}\right)\left[o_{(I,J)}^{(k)} = \phi\left(p_{(I,J)}^{(k-1)} w^{(k)} + b^{(k)}\right)\right]\right\} \tag{3}$$

The feature matrices representing the outputs of a given convolutional or fully connected layer can be then used as inputs to a variety of other algorithms. Moreover, the feature matrices extracted from images can be used in conjunction with a similarity or distance metrics for calculating the visual similarity of two images. In the proposed framework, a specifically designed CNN for person re-identification called *Omni-Scale Feature Learning for Person Re-Identification* (OSNet) [8] is used.

The structure of the OSNet model is visualized on Fig. 2 and is based on residual blocks composed of multiple convolutional streams that detect features from different

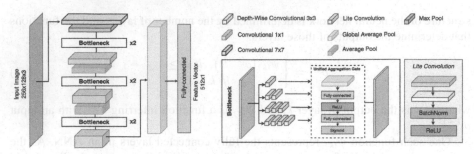

**Fig. 2.** Architecture of OSNet [8]. The model produces a 512-D feature vector.

spatial dimensions. Features corresponding to small, local regions (shoes, glasses) and global regions of the whole body (size and age of the person, rough combinations of clothes such as a white T-shirt and gray shorts) are extracted. Moreover, it uses a novel unified aggregation gate [8] that dynamically fuses these multi-scale features with the input-dependent weights to efficiently learn spatial-channel correlations. The output of the model is a fully connected layer that generates 512-D feature vector with features from different-sized convolutional streams. By using these visual features, the identity problem where the tracking algorithm could confuse one person with another is mitigated.

### 3.3 You Only Look Once v3 for Object Localization

Object localization is a process that involves both classification of objects and the extraction of their position. The spatial orientation of the detected object is marked by a rectangular box, which determines its width and height. The proposed framework uses the localization algorithm *You Only Look Once v3* (YOLOv3) [9]. YOLOv3 is a one-stage object detection method that considers object detection as a regression problem. It uses the feature matrices from the last convolutional levels of a single feed-forward 53-layer convolutional neural network Darknet-53 [9] to make predictions for both the locations of potential objects and their class affiliation at the same time. Its architecture detail is visualized on Fig. 3.

YOLOv3 divides the input image into three grids of feature maps with dimensions $S \times S$, $S \in \{13, 26, 52\}$ and each cell of each grid is responsible for giving an approximation of what object is in its center. The feature maps scales correspond to different object sizes and are fused together to make spatial correlations. Each grid cell makes a total of $B = 3$ proposals for regions, composed of 5 different components - $(x, y, w, h, o)$, where $x \in [0..1]$ and $y \in [0..1]$ indicate the coordinates of the centre of the region, and $w \in [0..1]$ and $h \in [0..1]$ - the width and height dimensions of the object. The fifth component $o \in [0..1]$ is the probability corresponding to how much a given proposal is related to an object. These probabilities are formally represented as $P(Object)IOU_{pred}^{truth}$, which simultaneously infer the probability of having an object in the region ($P(Object) \geq 0$) and the correctness of the detected object ($IOU_{pred}^{truth}$). At the same time, regardless of the number of regions, approximations are given for $C \in \mathbb{Z}^+$ class probabilities $P(Class_c|Object)$, $\forall c \in [1, \ldots, C]$ determining the probability that an object belongs to class $c$. In the proposed framework, the YOLOv3 model is trained on only one class and $C = 1$. Therefore, the size of each feature map scale is $S \times S \times [B * (5 + C)] = S \times S \times 18$, $S \in \{13, 26, 52\}$.

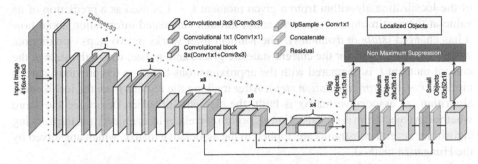

**Fig. 3.** Architecture of YOLOv3 [9] with Darknet-53 as the backbone CNN.

Finally, as seen in Fig. 3, the three scaled feature maps are fused together and using a confidence threshold to filter out low scoring predictions, and a Non-maximum Suppression [10] algorithm for post-processing, the final bounding boxes output is created.

The YOLOv3 model can process images at nearly 300 frames per second. This makes it an extremely good choice for real-time video processing applications.

### 3.4 Deep Simple Online and Realtime Tracking for Object Tracking

To retrieve all moving objects from a scene in a video data stream, the localization technologies are not sufficient. Since the object localization works on each frame individually, when there are sudden changes in brightness or in the environment, the algorithm may not fully recognize all objects on the scene. To fill these gaps, additional video context-aware information about the direction and trajectory of each object must be considered. This class of algorithms is called real-time object tracking algorithms. They store the history of the positions of the objects over time so that based on the past state of an object from previous frames its future state can be approximated in subsequent frames. The state data include both the position of the object and its size.

The algorithm used to track multiple objects and create the final identities in the proposed framework is *Deep Simple Online and Realtime Tracking* (DeepSORT) [11]. DeepSORT is a tracking-by-detection algorithm that considers both the positions of the detected objects and their visual appearance, to compare them with the positions and the appearance of the tracked objects from previous frames in order to associate them in the new frame. It is based on Simple Online and Realtime Tracking (SORT) [12], which is a pragmatic method using simple but effective algorithms such as the Kalman filter and the Hungarian method for object association. The main problem of SORT comes from the fact that in order to preserve the identity of a tracked object, a metric is used, which only evaluates the overlap of the region of the object with that from the previous scene – i.e., it does not consider any visual characteristics of the objects. DeepSORT improves

SORT by employing a convolutional neural network for more accurate estimation by comparing the visual features of the objects.

The tracking algorithm used in the DeepSORT system is the Kalman filter. Kalman filtering is a recursive estimation method in which the value of each estimated region of the localization algorithm from a given moment $k - 1$ is used as a prediction of its value at the next moment $k$ (*current state*) through calculated information about how it has changed (*state of dynamics*). The Kalman filter works in two steps - prediction, where approximations for the current state are given, and update, where the state at the current moment $k$ is compared with the approximations based on the previous state at moment $k - 1$ (*error calculation step*). After tracking the regions from the localization algorithm, an associative matrix is built, the elements of which determine the score whether an object from the localization algorithm correlates to an object from the tracking algorithm. Several constraints are applied to the associative matrix, which are solved by the Hungarian method.

In the proposed framework the associative matrix of the DeepSORT algorithm is composed of the linear combination of two distance metrics - (1) the Mahalanobis distance between the states of the Kalman filter on two objects of the localization algorithm and (2) the minimum Euclidean distance between the OSNet-generated visual features of a given localized object and the those of the last 100 tracked identities.

## 4    Implementation of the Synopsis Framework

### 4.1    Datasets and Training Details

Two convolutional neural networks were trained - (1) YOLOv3 for localizing the pedestrians on a given video scene and (2) OSNet for retrieving their visual features and creating the identities when tracking via DeepSORT.

Two datasets were selected for training the YOLOv3 model: *Common Objects in Context (COCO)* [13] and *Pascal Visual Objects Classes (VOC)* [14]. Since the focus of the paper is videos with pedestrians, the categories related to the object *person* were extracted from both datasets. The final dataset for pedestrian localization consisted of *66,109* images for training and *4,786* images for validation. The SGD algorithm was chosen for the training process with *15,000* total iterations and a learning step of *0.001*. The accuracy achieved on the dataset for validation during training was *93%*.

The following training datasets were used for training the OSNet model: *Market1501* [15], *DukeMTMC* [16] and *CUHK03* [17]. The final dataset obtained after merging them consisted of *36,823* training images and *6,996* validation images, structured in *2,152* categories corresponding to different pedestrian identities. The SGD algorithm with *150,000* iterations and a training step of *0.065* was used to train the model.

### 4.2    Video Synopsis Algorithm

Two things are needed in order to create the video synopsis: the extracted background, and the list of the identities (tubes). Before the algorithm starts, the identities are preprocessed by sorting them by the number of frames in which each identity is found in the original video, as well as removing those whose occurrence count is less than 10. This way all insignificant identities are removed and those that are more frequent in the original video are shown first.

It is also possible to set a small delay ($k$ frames) before adding a new identity to the scene to avoid overlapping in the opening frames. The number of simultaneous identities can also be controlled so that the scene is not overloaded using an additional parameter $m$. Thus, when this constraint is reached, the algorithm waits for an identity from the scene to disappear before adding a new one. Finally, when the last identity is added to the scene, the synopsis is considered complete and saved as an output file. The video synopsis algorithm is presented as Algorithm 1 below.

---

**Algorithm 1.** The video synopsis algorithm.

**Data:** The extracted background, list of identities, $k$ for the number of frames to wait before adding a new identity to the rendering queue, $m$ for the number of identities to render simultaneously.
**Result:** A list of frames for the generated synopsis.

---

```
begin
   while there are identities in the identities list do
      while the number of identities to process is < m and
the frames counter >= k do
         pop the next identity from the identities list
         add the identity to the processing list
         reset the frames counter
      end while
      for each identity from the processing list do
         get the identity video occurrences
         pop the first identity occurrence
         add it to the rendering queue
         if there are no more occurrences then
            delete the identity from the processing list
         end if
      end for
      create a new synopsis frame
      while there are items in the rendering queue do
         pop and overlay each item on the new synopsis frame
      end while
      add the new frame to the output and increase the
frames counter
   end while
   return the output synopsis frames
end
```

The output file generated by Algorithm 1 has the following characteristics:

- *Compressed file size* – the size of the output file is smaller than the input file, making its storage more cost-effective.
- *Shorter duration* – the output file consists of only the main person identities from the input file, eliminating any unnecessary static scenes that can last for hours.
- *Quality* – the use of the machine learning models makes for a smooth overlay on the extracted background, thus preventing any visual interruptions and loss of frames, which increases the realistic look of the synopsis.

## 5  Experimental Results and Discussions

### 5.1  Control Datasets

To generate experimental results for the proposed framework the *Oxford Town Centre* [18] dataset has been selected. It represents a video from a video surveillance camera shot in the centre of Oxford and consists of *4,500* frames with a duration of *3* min as well as annotations of a total of *230* different pedestrians (identities), or an average of *16* pedestrians per frame. Figure 4 visualizes sample frames from the dataset.

**Fig. 4.**  Samples from the dataset *Oxford Town Centre* [18] with rectangular annotations.

Additionally, comparison results with prior works are presented. Due to lack of standardized datasets, however, evaluation of such is a challenging task. Fortunately, the authors of [4] have published their synopsis dataset that consists of four videos, shot in different locations. Three of the videos are shot outdoors and capture different situations involving both pedestrians and vehicles, whereas one of them with a length of one hour is shot indoors and captures a hall scene with pedestrians coming from several entrances. As the proposed synopsis framework is primarily focused on pedestrian CCTV footage, the hall video has been chosen as the primary comparison set. Original frames from this video are presented on Fig. 5.

**Fig. 5.**  Example frames from the synopsis dataset video *hall* [4], consisting of *66,771* frames.

## 5.2  Metrics

As part of the framework for video synopsis, the following metrics for generating quantitative results of the quality of the synopsis process are proposed:

- **SynopsisO:** Optimization or the frame reduction that the synopsis algorithm does to the input file. Equals to the ratio between the length of the output and input files:

$$SynopsisO = 1 - F_O/F_I \qquad (4)$$

where $F_I \in \mathbb{N}^0$ and $F_O \in \mathbb{N}^0$ are the number of frames of the input and output files.

- **ObjAVG:** Average identities (pedestrians) per frame in the output file:

$$ObjAVG = \frac{\sum_{t=0}^{F_O} Obj_t}{F_O} \qquad (5)$$

where $Obj_t \in \mathbb{N}^0$ is the number of identities in synopsis frame $t \in \{0, \ldots, F_O\}$.

- **SynopsisT:** The total time to generate the output video file (in seconds):

$$SynopsisT = T_{final} - T_O \qquad (6)$$

where $T_O$ and $T_{final}$ are the start and end timestamp of the synopsis generation process.

## 5.3  Results

To evaluate and analyze the performance of the proposed synopsis framework multiple results were generated for the Oxford Town Centre [18] dataset and presented in Table 1. Several values of the control parameters of the algorithm were used: the maximum number of objects $m \in \{100, 50, 30\}$ to be displayed in one scene and the number of frames $k \in \{10, 3\}$ to wait before adding a new object to the scene.

The results reveal that high values of SynopsisO and ObjAVG are achieved at lower values of $k$ and higher values of $m$. Moreover, both parameters affect the duration $F_O$ of the output file. On the other hand, the generation speed SynopsisT directly depends on the number of output frames, therefore it also implicitly depends on the values of the algorithm parameters $k$ and $m$. Figure 6 visualizes the highest achieved SynopsisO for $m = 100$ and $k = 3$.

Furthermore, to compare the proposed framework with state-of-the-art the SynopsisO metric has been calculated on the hall video [4] (Fig. 5) and the results are presented

**Table 1.** Results of the video synopsis framework on the *Oxford Town Centre* [18] dataset. Arrows are an indicator of low or high optimal values.

| m | k | $F_O \downarrow$ | SynopsisO ↑ | ObjAVG ↑ | SynopsisT ↓ |
|---|---|---|---|---|---|
| 100 | 10 | 2767 | 0.385 | 21.123 | 9.166 |
| 100 | 3 | **925** | **0.794** | **63.187** | 7.970 |
| 50 | 10 | 1451 | 0.678 | 40.281 | 7.965 |
| 50 | 3 | 1266 | 0.719 | 46.167 | **7.855** |
| 30 | 10 | 2122 | 0.528 | 27.544 | 8.043 |
| 30 | 3 | 2020 | 0.551 | 28.935 | 7.972 |

**Fig. 6.** Visualization of the Oxford Town Centre [18] synopsis for $m = 100$ and $k = 3$.

**Table 2.** Comparison with prior art on the hall video dataset [4].

| Metric | Huang et al. [3] | Huang et al. [4] | Wang et al. [5] | Proposed |
|---|---|---|---|---|
| $F_O$ | 14379 | 11271 | 8814 | **1566** |
| SynopsisO | 0.785 | 0.831 | 0.868 | **0.977** |

in Table 2. The synopsis parameters used in this evaluation are the best performing on the Oxford Town Centre [18] dataset, that is, $m = 100$ and $k = 3$.

The resulting synopsis file for the hall dataset has a length $F_O$ of 1566 frames, five of which taken with 10s difference are visualized on Fig. 7. The achieved frame reduction is 97.7% which is 10.9% improvement over prior methodologies. Further tests with other synopsis parameter values used in Table 1 achieved the same frame reduction. This is due to two pedestrians being in the scene for a minute in the original video (ten times longer than the average) that can be also seen in the last frame on Fig. 7.

**Fig. 7.** Visualization of the hall dataset [4] synopsis for $m = 100$ and $k = 3$.

# 6   Conclusions

This paper presents a framework for creating a synopsis of a CCTV footage. This allows for cutting long security camera videos into significantly shorter files while giving much more viable information on each frame. The amount of information to be displayed in each frame can be controlled via parameters used during the synopsis process. Combining the latest developments in multi-object tracking as well as convolutional neural networks, the proposed framework achieves state-of-the-art frame reduction rate. In the future, a quantitative analysis of the quality of each framework component will be introduced to understand the impact that each algorithm has on the final synopsis result. Furthermore, creating a systematic approach to evaluating each component will allow them to be improved individually.

# References

1. Fu, W., Wang, J., Gui, L., Lu, H., Ma, S.: Online video synopsis of structured motion. Neurocomputing **135**, 155–162 (2014)
2. Salehin, M.M., Paul, M., Kabir, M.A.: Video summarization using line segments, angles, and conic parts. PloS ONE **12**(11) (2017)
3. Huang, C.R., Chen, H.C., Chung, P.C.: Online surveillance video synopsis. In: IEEE International Symposium on Circuits and Systems (ISCAS), pp. 1843–1846. IEEE (2012)
4. Huang, C.R., Chung, P.C.J., Yang, D.K., Chen, H.C., Huang, G.J.: Maximum a posteriori probability estimation for online surveillance video synopsis. IEEE Trans. Circuits Syst. Video Technol. **24**(8), 1417–1429 (2014)
5. Wang, W.C., Chung, P.C., Huang, C.R., Huang, W.Y.: Event based surveillance video synopsis using trajectory kinematics descriptors. In: Fifteenth IAPR International Conference on Machine Vision Applications, pp. 250–253 (2017)
6. Stauffer, C., Grimson, W.E.L.: Adaptive background mixture models for real-time tracking. In: CVPR (1999)
7. Nair, V., Hinton, G.E.: Rectified linear units improve restricted Boltzmann machines. In: ICML (2010)
8. Zhou, K., Yang, Y., Cavallaro, A., Xiang, T.: Omni-scale feature learning for person re-identification. In: ICCV, pp. 3702–3712 (2019)
9. Redmon, J., Farhadi, A.: Yolov3: an incremental improvement. arXiv preprint arXiv arXiv: 1804.02767 (2018)
10. Neubeck, A., Van Gool, L.: Efficient non-maximum suppression. In: ICPR (2006)
11. Wojke, N., Bewley, A., Paulus, D.: Simple online and realtime tracking with a deep association metric. In: ICIP, pp. 3645–3649 (2017)
12. Bewley, A., Ge, Z., Ott, L., Ramos, F., Upcroft, B.: Simple online and realtime tracking. In: ICIP, pp. 3464–3468 (2016)
13. Lin, T.-Y., et al.: Microsoft COCO: common objects in context. In: Fleet, D., Pajdla, T., Schiele, B., Tuytelaars, T. (eds.) ECCV 2014. LNCS, vol. 8693, pp. 740–755. Springer, Cham (2014). https://doi.org/10.1007/978-3-319-10602-1_48
14. Hoiem, D., Divvala, S.K., Hays, J.H.: Pascal VOC 2008 challenge. World Lit. Today **24** (2009)
15. Zheng, L., Shen, L., Tian, L., Wang, S., Wang, J., Tian, Q.: Scalable person re-identification: a benchmark. In: ICCV, pp. 1116–1124 (2015)

16. Ristani, E., Solera, F., Zou, R., Cucchiara, R., Tomasi, C.: Performance measures and a data set for multi-target, multi-camera tracking. In: Hua, G., Jégou, H. (eds.) ECCV 2016. LNCS, vol. 9914, pp. 17–35. Springer, Cham (2016). https://doi.org/10.1007/978-3-319-48881-3_2
17. Li, W., Zhao, R., Xiao, T., Wang, X. DeepReid: deep filter pairing neural network for person re-identification. In: CVPR, pp. 152–159 (2014)
18. Benfold, B., Reid, I.: Stable multi-target tracking in real-time surveillance video. In: CVPR 2011, pp. 3457–3464 (2011)

# TrojanDroid: Android Malware Detection for Trojan Discovery Using Convolutional Neural Networks

Saeed Seraj, Michalis Pavlidis, and Nikolaos Polatidis(✉)

School of Architecture, Technology, and Engineering, University of Brighton,
BN2 4GJ Brighton, U.K.
{S.Seraj,M.Pavlidis,N.Polatidis}@Brighton.ac.uk

**Abstract.** Android platforms are widely used nowadays in different forms such as mobile phones and tablets, and this has made the Android platform an attractive target for hackers. While there are many solutions available for detecting malware on Android devices there aren't that many that are concentrated on specific malware types. To this extent, this paper delivers a new dataset for Trojan detection for Android apps based on the permissions of the apps, while the second contribution is a neural network architecture that can classify with very high accuracy if an Android app is a genuine app or a Trojan pretending to be a normal app. We have run extensive evaluation tests to validate the performance of the proposed method and we have compared it to other well-known classifiers using well-known evaluation metrics to show its effectiveness.

**Keywords:** Android · Malware detection · Trojan · Convolutional Neural Networks

## 1 Introduction

Nowadays, in the world people can get all types of Android devices such as mobile phones and tablets and numerous applications (apps) can be easily downloaded from available websites in cyberspace. However, many apps are being produced daily, with some of which being infected and being malware instead of a genuine app. Many exploiters infect applications using malicious approaches for their profit to steal information from mobile devices. Malware can come in various forms, such as viruses, trojans, worms, botnets, and many others and among that malware, trojans are a type of malware that is often disguised as legitimate software; however, they will perform malicious activities on the operating system that most of the users will not even notice or understand [1, 6, 18].

Therefore, in this article, we study how to detect Android Trojans using the permissions of the applications. To do this we have collected and processed data and created a new dataset that is described in detail in Sect. 3. The Trojan dataset is a classification dataset that contains only Trojan and genuine Android applications and to this extent, we have developed a Convolutional Neural Network (CNN) architecture that detects

© Springer Nature Switzerland AG 2022
L. Iliadis et al. (Eds.): EANN 2022, CCIS 1600, pp. 203–212, 2022.
https://doi.org/10.1007/978-3-031-08223-8_17

Trojans with very high accuracy. To achieve this, we first had a theory that a Trojan can be identified based on the requested permissions during app installations.

The contributions of the paper are as follows:

• We introduce a novel dataset for Android Trojan detection based on the permissions of the applications.
• We deliver a CNN neural network architecture for Trojan detection.

The rest of the paper is organized as follows: Sect. 2 is the related work, Sect. 3 describes the dataset, Sect. 4 explains the proposed method, Sect. 5 delivers the experimental evaluation and Sect. 6 contains the conclusions.

## 2    Related Work

In the Android platform, there are several works available in the literature due to its popularity and numerous malware, that exist. We have identified recent relevant works and discussed them here but the related works that are about Trojan detection are non-existent in the literature. To the best of our knowledge, there is only one related work about Trojan detection that is based on dynamic analysis and not on permissions which are discussed later in [2].

We start with MCDM which is 'a multi-criteria decision-making based' mobile malware detection system that uses a risk-based fuzzy analytical hierarchy process (AHP) approach to evaluate the Android mobile applications. This research concentrated on static analysis by using permission-based features to assess the Android mobile malware detection system approach [1]. In another research dynamic analysis was used to detect their features. Therefore, a parameter such as a system call was investigated in this study. The purpose of this research is to detect android Trojan based on dynamic analysis [2]. Another research paper proposes a novel detection technique called PermPair that builds and compares the graphs for malware and normal samples by extracting the permission pairs from the manifest file inside the application [3]. Yet another research presents a platform named DroidCat which is a novel dynamic application classification model to complement those methods that are existing. DroidCat uses various sets of dynamic features based on method calls and inter-component communication (ICC) Intents without involving any permission, application resources, or system calls [4]. One other study proposes an innovative Android malware detection framework based on feature weighting with the joint optimization of weight-mapping and the parameters of the classifier named JOWMDroid [5].

In [6] the study introduces a new scheme for Android malware detection and familial classification based on the Graph Convolutional Network (GCN). The general idea is to map Android applications and APIs into a large heterogeneous graph and convert the original problems into a node classification task. The study in [7] was a novel hybrid-featured Android dataset that provides timestamps for each data sample which covers all years of Android history from the years 2008 to 2020 and considers the distinct dynamic data sources. Researchers presented a new malware detection framework for Android applications that are evolutionary'HAWK'. Their model can pinpoint rapidly the proximity between a new application and existing applications and assemble their numerical embeddings under different semantics as described in [8]. MAPAS is a malware detection platform that achieved high accuracy and adaptable usage of computing resources. Moreover, MAPAS analyzed malicious apps behaviors based on API call graphs of them by using convolution neural networks (CNN) [9]. NSDroid is 'a time-efficient malware multi-classification approach based on neighborhood signatures in local function call graphs (FCGs). This method uses a scheme based on neighborhood signature to calculate the similarity of the different applications which is significantly faster than traditional approaches according to subgraph isomorphism [10]. A work that presents a web-based framework that helped to detect malware from Android devices is named 'MLDroid'. The proposed framework detects Android malware applications by performing its dynamic analysis measures can be found in [11].

In their work 'NATICUSdroid' a new Android malware detection system that investigates and classifies benign and malware using statistically selected native and custom Android application permissions as features for various machine learning classifiers [12]. One more work is an innovative android malware detection framework that uses a deep CNN neural network. In this system, Malware classification is performed based on static analysis of the raw opcode sequence from a disassembled program [13]. A machine learning-based malware detection platform is proposed to distinguish Android malware from benign applications. It is aimed to remove unnecessary features by using a linear regression-based feature selection approach at the feature selection stage of the proposed malware detection framework. [14]. Another research proposes a novel approach based on behavior for Android malware classification. In the proposed method, the Android malware dataset is decompiled to identify the suspicious API classes and generate an encoded list. In addition, this framework classifies unknown applications as benign or malicious applications based on the log-likelihood score generated [15]. In their paper researchers have delivered a completely novel and innovative dataset of malicious or benign Android anti-malware detection, including, and a customized multilayer perceptron neural network (MLP) that is being used to detect fake anti-malware that pretend to be genuine ones based on the permissions of the applications [16].

In their article researchers introduced a novel TAN (Tree Augmented naive Bayes)-based—a hybrid Android malware detection mechanism that involves the conditional dependencies which are required for the functionality of an application among relevant static and dynamic features [17]. The next work is a survey aimed to provide an overview of the way machine learning (ML) has been employed in the context of malware analyses. They also conducted survey papers based on their objectives, what kind of information about malware they used specifically, and what type of machine learning techniques they employed [18]. DAE is a hybrid model based on a deep autoencoder and a CNN. This mechanism is proposed to improve the Android malware detection accuracy. To achieve this, they reconstructed the high-dimensional features of Android applications and employed multiple CNN to detect Android malware [19]. In the next research article, a new detection approach is introduced based on deep learning techniques to detect Android malware from trusted applications. To achieve that, they treat one system call sequence as a sentence in the language and build a classifier according to the Long Short-Term Memory (LSTM) language model [20].

An EfficientNet-B4 CNN-based model is presented for Android malware detection by employing image-based malware representations of the Android DEX file. This model extracts relevant features from the Android malware images [21]. In the following paper, a new classifier fusion scheme based on a multilevel architecture is introduced that enables an effective combination of machine learning algorithms for improved accuracy which is called DroidFusion. The induced multilevel model can be utilized as an improved accuracy predictor for Android malware detection [22]. A Machine Learning-based method that utilizes more than 200 features extracted from both static analysis and dynamic analysis of Android applications for malware detection was proposed in [23]. A platform that is capable to detect android malware applications is introduced to support the organized Android Market. The proposed framework intended to develop a machine learning-based malware detection framework on Android to detect malware applications and to increase the security and privacy of smartphone users [24]. CoDroid is a hybrid Android malware detection approach based on the sequence which utilizes the sequences of static opcode and dynamic system call [25]. Finally, researchers have combined the high accuracy of the traditional graph-based method with the high scalability of the social network analysis-based approach for Android malware detection [26].

Although all these works are interesting there is only one work that is about Trojan detection that is based on dynamic analysis. Therefore, in this work, we developed a new dataset about Trojan detection using permissions to fill this gap and we have developed a CNN architecture to detect trojans with high accuracy.

## 3  Dataset

With regards to trojan detection in Android platforms, we introduce a new dataset based on Android app permissions. To this extent, we developed an Android Trojan dataset that contains 2593 entries. To do this we downloaded 1058 Android Trojan malware and 1535 general benign apps from various categories from Google Play. We analyzed all apk files using VirusTotal.com to extract all their features including internet access and other required app permissions. Moreover, we have used over 70 reputed anti-malware detection engines to classify the apk files. The android Trojan dataset consists of the following families: BankBot, Binv, Citmo, FakeBank, LegitimateBankApps, Sandroid, SmsSpy, Spitmo, Wroba, ZertSecurity and Zitmo. For the dataset to be in a usable form, we added all the information in a file.csv file format which can be easily opened and processed. There is a total number of 450 columns in the dataset that includes 449 specific permissions plus the label which is the last column. The first row in the dataset describes column titles, and the rest are features from 2593 android Trojans and benign applications apk files. All values are in binary format i.e., 0 or 1. When an app requires permission, then the value in the respective entry of the dataset is 1, and unnecessary permissions of an app are set to zero. An Android app that is recognized as malware by most antivirus companies based on VirusTotal report, is considered risky and the value in the label column is set as 1, being Trojan. However, the other Android genuine apps have zero value. The complete dataset is accessible at: https://www.kaggle.com/saeeds eraj/trojandroidpermissionbased-android-trojan-dataset/.

| | A | B | C | D | E | F | G | H | I | J | K | L | M |
|---|---|---|---|---|---|---|---|---|---|---|---|---|---|
| 1 | internet | access | access | get | change | write | read | system | c2d | camera | call | bluetooth | bluetooth |
| 2 | 1 | 1 | 1 | 0 | 0 | 1 | 0 | 0 | 1 | 0 | 0 | 0 | 0 |
| 3 | 1 | 1 | 1 | 0 | 1 | 1 | 1 | 0 | 0 | 0 | 0 | 1 | 1 |
| 4 | 1 | 0 | 1 | 0 | 0 | 0 | 0 | 1 | 0 | 0 | 0 | 0 | 0 |
| 5 | 1 | 1 | 1 | 0 | 0 | 0 | 0 | 0 | 1 | 0 | 0 | 0 | 0 |
| 6 | 1 | 1 | 1 | 0 | 0 | 1 | 0 | 0 | 1 | 0 | 0 | 0 | 0 |
| 7 | 1 | 0 | 1 | 0 | 0 | 0 | 0 | 0 | 0 | 1 | 0 | 0 | 0 |
| 8 | 1 | 0 | 1 | 0 | 0 | 0 | 0 | 0 | 1 | 0 | 0 | 0 | 0 |

**Fig. 1.** An illustration of a small part of the proposed dataset

## 4 Proposed Method

A 1-dimensional CNN sequential architecture has been developed to classify trojans using the above dataset and the Python programming language with the Keras library. The architecture includes one 1D-CNN layer, followed by a 1D MaxPooling layer, followed by a Flatten layer, followed by 2 dense layers. The architecture is presented in detail in Fig. 2. The Specific settings are as follows:

- A learning rate of 0.01 has been used and the optimizer is Adam
- The number of epochs is 6
- The batch size is 16
- The activation functions used are the Relu for the 1D CNN layer and the first dense layer and the Sigmoid for the final dense layer
- Bias has been set to true in the 1D CNN layer

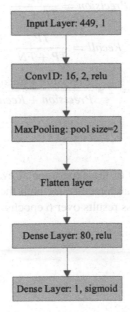

**Fig. 2.** Proposed method architecture

## 5 Experimental Evaluation

For the experimental evaluation, we have proposed the CNN architecture described in Sect. 4 developed using the Python programming language and the Keras library. For all experiments, 5-fold cross-validation has been used.

### 5.1 Evaluation Metrics

For the experimental evaluation, we have used the Python programming language and the Keras machine learning library. With regards to evaluation metrics, we have used the Accuracy, Precision, Recall, and F1 which are described in Eqs. 1, 2, 3, and 4 respectively. TP stands for true positive, TN for true negative, FP for false positive, and FN for false negative. Accuracy, which is Eq. 1, shows the overall performance. Another significant metric is Precision which describes the portion of predicted Trojans and is calculated by Eq. 2. Equation 3 explains the Recall metric which is the portion of Trojan that is correctly classified. The F1-score is a number between 0 and 1 and is the harmonic mean of precision and recall which is computed according to Eq. 4. These are well-known metrics that have been used in recent studies for similar problems in Android malware detection [5, 6, 21]. Overall, our proposed method outperforms alternative classifiers in all metrics.

$$Accuracy = \frac{TP + TN}{TP + TN + FP + FN} \tag{1}$$

$$Precision = \frac{TP}{TP + FP} \tag{2}$$

$$Recall = \frac{TP}{TP + FN} \tag{3}$$

$$F1 = 2 * \frac{Precision * Recall}{Precision + Recall} \tag{4}$$

### 5.2 Results

This section delivers the results of the experimental evaluation. Figure 3 presents the results of the proposed method architecture for both the train and test accuracy over 6 epochs. Figure 4 presents the loss results over 6 epochs.

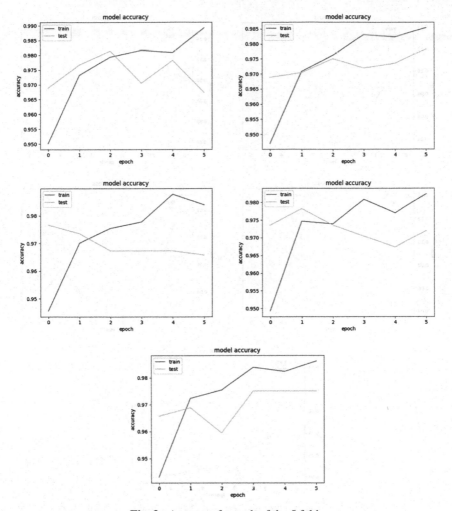

**Fig. 3.** Accuracy for each of the 5 folds

## 5.3 Comparisons with Other Classifiers

The algorithms used in the comparisons are the following with the default settings used from the sci-kit learn library: Decision Tree, Random Forest, Multi-Layer Perceptron. The results are presented in Table 1 which provides a comparison between the proposed method and the other well-known classifiers using accuracy, precision, recall, and F1. 5-fold cross-validation has been used throughout.

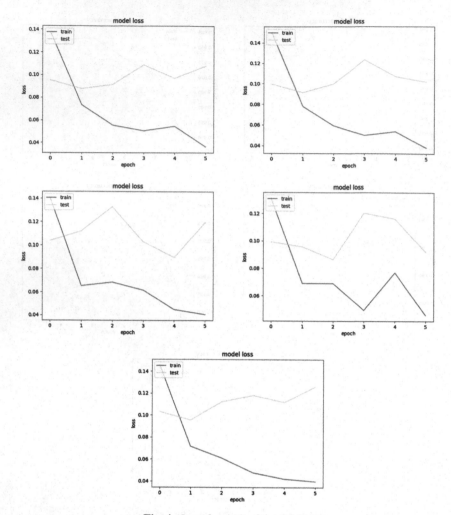

**Fig. 4.** Loss for each of the 5 folds

**Table 1.** Comparison results

| Algorithm | Accuracy | Precision | Recall | F1 |
|---|---|---|---|---|
| Decision Tree | 96.1% | 95.8% | 95.7% | 95.9% |
| Random Forest | 97.9% | 97.7% | 97.3% | 97.5% |
| Multi-Layer Perceptron | 97.8% | 97.8% | 96.7% | 97.7% |
| **TrojanDroid** | **98.06%** | **99%** | **97.71%** | **98%** |

## 6  Conclusions

In this paper, we have concentrated on Trojan detection on android platforms. We have collected a new dataset which we have made available, and we delivered a novel neural network architecture that can detect trojans with very high accuracy. The results indicate that by using the permissions of Trojan and genuine Android apps, trojans can be detected in a straightforward way which can be useful to the research community and beyond.

In the future, we plan to extend our proposed method to include the specific trojan family that a trojan belongs to and adjust it accordingly to detect the family with high accuracy as well. Moreover, we plan to investigate how to use permissions to detect other types of malware such as botnets.

## References

1. Arif, J.M., Ab Razak, M.F., Mat, S.R.T., Awang, S., Ismail, N.S.N., Firdaus, A.: Android mobile malware detection using fuzzy AHP. J. Inf. Secur. Appl. **61**, 102929 (2021)
2. Aminuddin, N.I., Abdullah, Z.: Android trojan detection based on dynamic analysis. Adv. Comput. Intell. Syst. **1**(1), 1–7 (2019)
3. Arora, A., Peddoju, S.K., Conti, M.: Permpair: Android malware detection using permission pairs. IEEE Trans. Inf. Forensics Secur. **15**, 1968–1982 (2019)
4. Cai, H., Meng, N., Ryder, B., Yao, D.: DroidCat: effective android malware detection and categorization via app-level profiling. IEEE Trans. Inf. Forensics Secur. **14**(6), 1455–1470 (2018)
5. Cai, L., Li, Y., Xiong, Z.: JOWMDroid: Android malware detection based on feature weighting with joint optimization of weight-mapping and classifier parameters. Comput. Secur. **100**, 102086 (2021)
6. Gao, H., Cheng, S., Zhang, W.: GDroid: Android malware detection and classification with graph convolutional network. Comput. Secur. **106**, 102264 (2021)
7. Guerra-Manzanares, A., Bahsi, H., Nõmm, S.: KronoDroid: time-based hybrid-featured dataset for effective android malware detection and characterization. Comput. Secur. **110**, 102399 (2021)
8. Hei, Y., et al.: Hawk: rapid android malware detection through heterogeneous graph attention networks. IEEE Trans. Neural Netw. Learn. Syst. (2021, in press). https://doi.org/10.1109/TNNLS.2021.3105617
9. Kim, J., Ban, Y., Ko, E., Cho, H., Yi, J.H.: MAPAS: a practical deep learning-based android malware detection system. Int. J. Inf. Secur. 1–14 (2022). https://doi.org/10.1007/s10207-022-00579-6
10. Liu, P., Wang, W., Luo, X., Wang, H., Liu, C.: NSDroid: efficient multi-classification of android malware using neighborhood signature in local function call graphs. Int. J. Inf. Secur. **20**(1), 59–71 (2020). https://doi.org/10.1007/s10207-020-00489-5
11. Mahindru, A., Sangal, A.L.: MLDroid—framework for Android malware detection using machine learning techniques. Neural Comput. Appl. **33**(10), 5183–5240 (2020). https://doi.org/10.1007/s00521-020-05309-4
12. Mathur, A., Podila, L.M., Kulkarni, K., Niyaz, Q., Javaid, A.Y.: NATICUSdroid: a malware detection framework for Android using native and custom permissions. J. Inf. Secur. Appl. **58**, 102696 (2021)
13. McLaughlin, N., et al.: Deep android malware detection. In: Proceedings of the Seventh ACM on Conference on Data and Application Security and Privacy, pp. 301–308, March 2017

14. Şahin, D.Ö., Kural, O.E., Akleylek, S., Kılıç, E.: A novel permission-based Android malware detection system using feature selection based on linear regression. Neural Comput. Appl. 1–16 (2021). https://doi.org/10.1007/s00521-021-05875-1
15. Sasidharan, S.K., Thomas, C.: ProDroid—an Android malware detection framework based on profile hidden Markov model. Pervasive Mob. Comput. 72, 101336 (2021)
16. Seraj, S., Khodambashi, S., Pavlidis, M., Polatidis, N.: HamDroid: permission-based harmful android anti-malware detection using neural networks. Neural Comput. Appl. 1 (2021). https://doi.org/10.1007/s00521-021-06755-4
17. Surendran, R., Thomas, T., Emmanuel, S.: A TAN based hybrid model for Android malware detection. J. Inf. Secur. Appl. 54, 102483 (2020)
18. Ucci, D., Aniello, L., Baldoni, R.: Survey of machine learning techniques for malware analysis. Comput. Secur. 81, 123–147 (2019)
19. Wang, W., Zhao, M., Wang, J.: Effective android malware detection with a hybrid model based on deep autoencoder and convolutional neural network. J. Ambient. Intell. Humaniz. Comput. 10(8), 3035–3043 (2018). https://doi.org/10.1007/s12652-018-0803-6
20. Xiao, X., Zhang, S., Mercaldo, F., Hu, G., Sangaiah, A.K.: Android malware detection based on system call sequences and LSTM. Multimedia Tools Appl. 78(4), 3979–3999 (2017). https://doi.org/10.1007/s11042-017-5104-0
21. Yadav, P., Menon, N., Ravi, V., Vishvanathan, S., Pham, T.D.: EfficientNet convolutional neural networks-based android malware detection. Comput. Secur. 115, 102622 (2022)
22. Yerima, S.Y., Sezer, S.: DroidFusion: a novel multilevel classifier fusion approach for android malware detection. IEEE Trans. Cybern. 49(2), 453–466 (2018)
23. Yuan, Z., Lu, Y., Wang, Z., Xue, Y.: Droid-Sec: deep learning in android malware detection. In: Proceedings of the 2014 ACM Conference on SIGCOMM, pp. 371–372, August 2014
24. Zarni Aung, W.Z.: Permission-based android malware detection. Int. J. Sci. Technol. Res. 2(3), 228–234 (2013)
25. Zhang, N., Xue, J., Ma, Y., Zhang, R., Liang, T., Tan, Y.A.: Hybrid sequence-based Android malware detection using natural language processing. Int. J. Intell. Syst. 36(10), 5770–5784 (2021)
26. Zou, D., et al.: IntDroid: Android malware detection based on API intimacy analysis. ACM Trans. Softw. Eng. Methodol. (TOSEM) 30(3), 1–32 (2021)

# Datamining/Learning/Autoencoders

# A Methodology to Manage Structured and Semi-structured Data in Knowledge Oriented Graph

Valerio Bellandi$^{(\boxtimes)}$ (iD), Paolo Ceravolo, Giacomo Alberto D'Andrea,
and Samira Maghool, and Stefano Siccardi

Computer Science Department, Università Degli Studi di Milano, Via Celoria 18,
Milano, Italy
{valerio.bellandi,paolo.ceravolo,giacomo.alberto,samira.maghool,
stefano.siccardi}@unimi.it

**Abstract.** Data has become fundamental to every business process and research area like never before. To date, one of the main open points of research activities is to manage the data acquired in the field by sensors, logs etc. by modeling the data structures according to the analyzes that will be carried out. In fact, with the advent of Big Data, the need to have a single reference data structure has been reduced, but with modern architectures there is a tendency to generate specific and optimized data structures for the analyzes that will be carried out. In this work we propose an agile data modeling methodology guided by analytics focused on the management of structured and semi-structured data sources.

**Keywords:** Events graphs · Graph rewriting · Data management

## 1  Introduction

We consider the problem of merging data coming from heterogeneous source in the best suited way to perform analyses in a specific domain and describe in depth each step of a method aiming to automate the whole procedure as much as possible. We deal with a rather particular set of cases, namely structured and semi-structured data like e.g. tagged unstructured data. We also suppose that data has both a graph structure and a measurable content, e.g. times, positions, physical quantities, amounts of money and so on.

We are looking for merging methods that: are well suited for graph databases; enhance the understandability of the data (as these databases are often manually queried using visual tools); improve the performance of analysis programs; can easily accommodate semi-structured data with variable information contents.

Inspired by [7], we model both the source and the target data as graphs and define graph rewriting rules to map the first model to the latter.

It is the type of the analyses, or the type of knowledge one wants to extract from the data, that should guide the data transformation. For this reason, we

L. Iliadis et al. (Eds.): EANN 2022, CCIS 1600, pp. 215–222, 2022.
https://doi.org/10.1007/978-3-031-08223-8_18

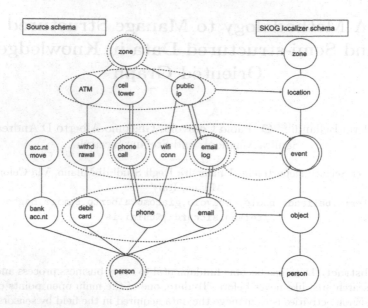

**Fig. 1.** A Source and a SKOG devoted to localization of people.

call the transformed graph a Specific Knowledge Oriented Graph (SKOG). We will define an automated procedure to find the transformations mapping the source graph to a SKOG.

## 2    Related Work

The **data fusion** task identifies the values of data records among multiple observed values acquired from different sources of varying reliability. Data fusion has been thoroughly studied in [10] and [14] considering deep learning methods; [13] compares the performances of early and late fusion, [17] proposes knowledge base representations, [9] surveys data driven methods; a taxonomy of methods intended for machine learning can be found in [1] and surveys in [16] and [8].

The basic principle of **graph rewriting** is the step-wise replacement of subgraphs inside a host graph [12] or the rule-based modification of graphs [5]. Two classical approaches have been proposed: the Double Pushout (DPO) and the Single Pushout (SPO). When a subgraph is replaced, its links with the rest of the graph that remain dangling must be addressed. The DPO approach forbids replacements leading to any dangling edges, while in SPO replacements are always allowed and dangling edges are simply removed. More general approaches, as the Sesqui-pushout rewriting and others have been recently proposed [2] and [6]. For our purposes, we need three basic operations on graphs: deleting, merging and splitting nodes.

## 3    Method

The method consists of several steps, described in the following paragraphs.

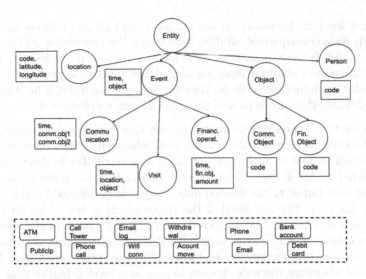

**Fig. 2.** A tree to describe the environment for the Source and SKOG of the example.

**The definition of the Source model**, that should be prepared by the user, is as follows: data sets are nodes; data sets attributes are nodes, linked to the data set nodes by edges with label *contained*; attributes categories are nodes, linked to data set attributes by edges with label *category*; external keys are edges, linking corresponding data set attributes. With data sets we mean individual data sets that hold the data.

Categories are used to recognise attributes holding the same type of information, for instance timestamps and amounts. An example can be found in Fig. 1, on the left. For the sake of simplicity, only data set nodes and external key edges have been drawn.

**The Environment Tree** describes the environment of the application and is prepared by the user to specify which source data must be included. The tree considers generic entities, specifying the minimum set of attributes that is required at each level (basic information pieces, like timestamps, codes etc. or pointers to other entities). The tree is built so that it is possible to replace iteratively the pointers to obtain attribute sets containing only basic information types.

An example is shown in Fig. 2. Circles represent entities and squares required attributes. Entities in the bottom dotted square represent source data sets; the rewriting is based on the presence of the required attributes in each source.

The same Environment Tree can be used to manage several instances of Source data and SKOG, automatically checking if a source data set can fit a node of the tree, that is if it has all the fields with required categories. We say that the Source model is mapped to the tree.

**The Choice of the Levels to Include.** The Environment Tree is traversed from top left to bottom right and the user is asked if he wants to keep each node.

218 V. Bellandi et al.

At the first level, if the answer is *no*, the node and all its children are marked to discard. As a consequence, all data sets fitting the tree nodes will be deleted from the model. If the answer is *yes*, the user will go down one level and choose which of the node's children must be kept. From level two onward, if the user discards all the children of a node, they are merged together; if he accepts one or more children they are kept and the other children are deleted.

**Computing the Transformations.** The first transformation set managed consists of deletions: a rewrite rule is computed, where the left hand part consists of the pattern to match, including data sets and attributes to delete and their links to other nodes, if any. The preserved and right hand parts consist of the nodes that were linked to the deleted ones. A split is performed for the data sets chosen by the user. The left hand of the rule consists of the nodes for the data sets and their attributes. The preserved and right hand parts of the rule consist of the new entities to be created, each with the source attributes used; moreover edges are created to link the source attributes to the entity attributes. A merge is performed whenever the user chooses to stop at a level $L$ higher than the leaf one: all the data sets in leaves under the $L$ level must be merged. The resulting entity keeps all the attributes common to the merged data sets. The category of the attributes is used to identify attributes with the same meaning in different data sets.

**The SKOG Model.** The structure of the SKOG model is as follows: entities in the SKOG database are nodes; entity attributes in the SKOG database are nodes, linked to the entity nodes by edges with label *property*; a special attribute for each entity records the type of the source data used for import; source data sets to be actually imported are nodes; source data attributes are nodes, linked to the data set nodes by edges with label *contained*; entity attributes are linked to source data set attributes by edges with label *source*; relations of type *external key* between source data set attributes are kept and result in relations between entity attributes.

A SKOG model is obtained applying the transformations computed in Sect. 3 to a source model. See Fig. 1 for an example.

**Loading the Data.** The data is loaded using Algorithm 31. Lists $L_i$ of entities with external keys must be such that entities in $L_k$ contain external keys to entities in $L_i$ only if $i < k$.

**Algorithm 31.** [Data import] To load source data to the SKOG database:

1: read the SKOG model, prepare list $L_1$ of entities without external keys, $L_2 \dots L_n$ of entities with external keys
2: $i = 1$
3: **while** $i \leq n$ **do**
4:    **while** Entity $E$ in $L_i$ **do**
5:       **while** Source data set $S$ for $E$ **do**
6:          create a node of type $E$ for each record in $S$ using SKOG model edges between entity attributes and source attributes

(a) A small source graph.        (b) The moneyflow SKOG derived from the
                                 graph in fig. 3a

**Fig. 3.** Graph models snapshots

7:        keep track of data needed                 as specified in the SKOG
          for external keys for entities            model
          in other $L_k$                   9:       **end while**
8:        add external key edges   10:     **end while**
          to already created nodes  11:    **end while**

## 4    Experiments

We applied the method to synthetic data sets including ATMs, Bank Accounts,
Cell Towers, Debit Cards, Email Addresses, Persons, Public IPs, Phones, Phone
Calls, Withdrawals of debit cards, Bank Account Moves, Wi-Fi connections,
Email Logs, Person State Changes.

Person state changes is a fictitious data set, that was generated to mimic any
changes in a person state or behaviour, that may be spontaneous or induced by
the encounter with another person; it might be for instance buying a product
after word of mouth advice or being infected with some diseases. All the tables
contain some descriptive information too.

We used three SKOG models: the "Localizer", with entities Location, Event,
Object and Person; the "MoneyFlow", with entities Financial Operation, Communication, Financial Object, Communication Object and Person; "Wordofmouth", with entities Location, Event, State Change and Person. Models and
rewriting rules were obtained and the data was loaded.

The goals of our experiments were: 1. show that we can obtain several different graphs from the same source data sets, 2. highlight the optimal expressiveness
of visual queries in each graph 3. show examples of analytic results both general and specific for each graph 4. show that new data set types can be easily
accommodated in the graphs in a meaningful way

**Visual Queries.** Figures 3a and 3b compare a small source graph, created from
data sets described above, and the corresponding Moneyflow SKOG. The source
contains 4115 nodes e 5278 edges, the Moneyflow 2731 nodes and 2261 edges. It
is obvious that the latter is much more readable than the first.

**Analytics.** We used the Wordofmouth SKOG to cluster locations where persons' states most likely spread. Data was generated assigning an "active" state

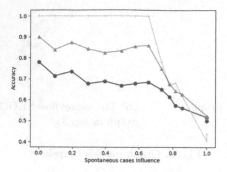

**Fig. 4.** Comparison of accuracy of analysis using the SKOG (red crosses), the source (blue circles) graph and source after LDA (green triangles). (Color figure online)

to a subset of the persons and a "type" (0, 1 or 2) to each location (ATMs, cell towers and IPs). As each event (withdrawal, phone call and email log) demonstrates presence of somebody in a location at a time, we considered a potential meeting of two persons when they were present at the same location within a time window. Then, depending on the location type, a person active state could activate the other person. The goal of the analysis was to cluster the locations according to their ability to favor the spreading of active states, and it was expected that the clusters correspond to the assigned location types. Several use cases might fit this scenario: for instance the active status might be interpreted as having bought a specific book, the interactions as talking of the book with people met at a location so that they become interested in the book and buy it in turn. Another interpretation of the status might be having got some disease and infect people met at locations. Some amount of spontaneous changes of state, that is not induced by encounters, are expected.

According to their nature and the type of encounters that happen therein, locations can favor the spreading, discovering the most conductive ones is the goal of the clustering.

Some simplifications were done: locations correspond one to one to an ATM, a cell tower or an IP; we did not try to find the optimal number of clusters from the data; we supposed that the active status of the "infecting" agent has always been detected before he gets in touch with the "infected" one.

As in a real application one would not know the location types in advance, we used an unsupervised algorithm, namely a K means clustering and a posteriori compared the results with the types. We transformed both the source and the SKOG graphs in event graphs in the sense of [11] and [15], see also [4]. In event graphs, nodes are events and edges link nodes sharing an entity and happening at other moments in some time windows.

Figure 4 compares results of clustering using the SKOG graph (red crosses) and the source graph (blue circles). Several runs have been done for each value of the "confusion" induced by spontaneous changes of state (the abscissa of the graph is the percentage of spontaneous cases with respect to number of encounters found in the patterns). To compare results to a classical method to reduce dimensions, we computed a 1-dimensional versions of the source data of emails and phone calls using Linear Discriminant Analysis (green triangles in the plot). Note that this would not be possible in a real case, as the method is supervised. Using the SKOG, greater accuracy can be achieved until confusion is less than $\approx 75\%$, then results are comparable to the expectation for random data, given the construction of the Source and SKOG graphs. The main reason for the good accuracy of the SKOG is that some collateral phenomena can be at work and create noise when clustering the source data; for instance there may be locations where some types of links are found more often (e.g. between caller and called). These may be due to fluctuations, so that they will disappear continuing the observations for a longer time, or to some specific cause that, however, is not important for the purpose of the analysis. Linear Discriminant Analysis enhances the accuracy, but is not able to completely filter out the collateral phenomena found in the data.

**Adding New Sources.** When a new source data set must be taken into consideration, the whole process can be repeated, starting from the source model definition. The case of semi structured data, however, must be managed in a slightly different way as each record may contain more or less fields to be matched to the environment tree. For the sake of clarity, we will discuss an example, generalization is straightforward. Consider as source a set of photographs, tagged with timestamp, IDs of persons that have been recognized and location. The source data set is e.g. a json file with an entry for each picture. Suppose that we want to add this info to the Localizer, generating events when a photograph contains a person at some locations. The environment tree in Fig. 2 is modified adding a second type of Visit events with a person instead of an object; each input record is mapped to a small source graph with nodes for attributes; then the tree is matched to the environment tree. If no locations or no persons are found in the source graph, the record is discarded, otherwise it is split into a Visit event for each person it contains.

## 5 Conclusion

As described in the initial sections, data modeling for generating data structures in analytics platforms is a crucial and critical step. In this work, an analytics-driven methodology for managing source data has been proposed. It was also applied and validated with different analytics to synthetic data derived from real cases.

## References

1. Baltrusaitis, T., Ahuja, C., Morency, L.-P.: Multimodal machine learning: a survey and taxonomy. IEEE Trans. Pattern Anal. Mach. Intell. **41**(2), 423–443 (2019). https://doi.org/10.1109/TPAMI.2018.2798607

2. Behr, N., Sobocinski, P.: Rule Algebras for Adhesive Categories, **1807**, 00785. arXiv (2018)
3. Bellandi, V., Ceravolo, P., Maghool, S., Siccardi, S.: Toward a General Framework for Multimodal Big Data Analysis, Big Data (2021)
4. Bellandi, V., Ceravolo, P., Maghool, S., Pindaro, M., Siccardi, S.: Correlation and pattern detection in event networks. In: 2021 IEEE International Conference on Big Data (Big Data) (2021). https://doi.org/10.1109/BigData52589.2021.9671512
5. Campbell, G. Efficient Graph Rewriting. arXiv 1906.05170v2 (2019)
6. Corradini, A., Duval, D., Echahed, R., Prost, F., Ribeiro, L.: Algebraic graph rewriting with controlled embedding. Theoret. Comput. Sci. **802**, 19–32 (2020). https://doi.org/10.1016/j.tcs.2019.06.004
7. Damiani, E., Oliboni, B., Quintarelli, E., Tanca, L.: A graph-based meta-model for heterogeneous data management. Knowl. Inf. Syst. **61**(1), 107–136 (2018). https://doi.org/10.1007/s10115-018-1305-8
8. Gao, J., Li, P., Chen, Z., Zhang, J.: A survey on deep learning for multimodal data fusion. Neural Comput. **32**(5), 829–864 (2020)
9. Lahat, D., Adali, T., Jutten, C.: Multimodal data fusion: an overview of methods, challenges, and prospects. In: Proceedings of the IEEE, vol. 103 (2015)
10. Liu, J., Li, T., Xie, P., Du, S., Teng, F., Yang, X.: Urban big data fusion based on deep learning: an overview. Inf. Fusion **53**, 123–133 (2020)
11. Mellor, A.: The temporal event graph. J. Complex Networks **6**(4), 639–659 (2017)
12. Overbeek, R., Endrullis, J.: Patch graph rewriting. In: Gadducci, F., Kehrer, T. (eds.) ICGT 2020. LNCS, vol. 12150, pp. 128–145. Springer, Cham (2020). https://doi.org/10.1007/978-3-030-51372-6_8
13. Snoek, C.G.M., Worring, M., Smeulders, A.W.M.: Early versus late fusion in semantic video analysis. In: Proceedings 13th Annual ACM International Conference on Multimedia (2005)
14. Tan, W., Tiwari, P., Pandey, H.M., Moreira, C., Jaiswal, A.K.: Multimodal medical image fusion algorithm in the era of big data. Neural Comput. Appl. **1**, 1–21 (2020). https://doi.org/10.1007/s00521-020-05173-2
15. Torricelli, M., Karsai, M., Gauvin, L.: weg2vec: event embedding for temporal networks. Sci. Rep. **10**, 7164 (2020). https://doi.org/10.1038/s41598-020-63221-2
16. Wang, Y.: Survey on deep multi-modal data analytics: collaboration, rivalry, and fusion. ACM Trans. Multimedia Comput. Commun. Appl. **17**(1s), 1–25 (2021). https://doi.org/10.1145/3408317
17. Zhu, Y., Zhang, C., Ré, C., Fei-Fei, L.: Building a large-scale multimodal knowledge base system for answering visual queries. arXiv 1507.05670 (2015)

# Discriminant Analysis on a Stream of Features

Jan Motl$^{(\boxtimes)}$ ⓘ and Pavel Kordík ⓘ

Czech Technical University in Prague, Prague, Czech Republic
jan.motl@fit.cvut.cz

**Abstract.** Online learning is a well-established problem in machine learning. But while online learning is commonly concerned with learning on a stream of samples, this article is concerned with learning on a stream on features. A modified quadratic discriminant analysis (QDA) is proposed because it is fast, capable of modeling feature interactions, and it can still return an exact solution. When a new feature is inserted into a training set, the proposed implementation of QDA showed a 1000-fold speed up to scikit-learn QDA. Fast learning on a stream of features provides a data scientist with timely feedback about the importance of new features during the feature engineering phase. In the production phase, it reduces the cost of updating a model when a new source of potentially useful features appears.

**Keywords:** Incremental learning · Online learning · Sequential learning · Stream learning

## 1 Introduction

A common issue in machine learning is the need to update machine learning models based on changing data. This issue can be simplified by assuming that

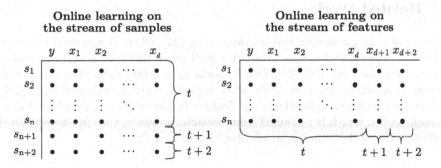

**Fig. 1.** Difference between learning from a stream of samples (left) and a stream of features (right). In both cases, we have $n$ samples and $d$ features at time $t$. However, at time $t+1$, we either have one more sample (left) or one more feature (right).

© Springer Nature Switzerland AG 2022
L. Iliadis et al. (Eds.): EANN 2022, CCIS 1600, pp. 223–234, 2022.
https://doi.org/10.1007/978-3-031-08223-8_19

new samples will be available over time. However, this article is concerned with the orthogonal problem—the fast updating of models with the arrival of new features (see Fig. 1).

Interestingly, the authors of this article did not find any publicly available implementation of a classifier, which would satisfy following requirements:

1. it is faster to update the model with a new feature than to train the model from scratch,
2. is more accurate than naive Bayes, which can be straightforwardly updated to learning on a stream of features,
3. and is faster to train than logistic regression, random forest, and gradient boosted trees.

The proposed update of the quadratic discriminant analysis (QDA) to learning on a stream of features satisfies all these requirements.

### 1.1 Quadratic Discriminant Analysis

The authors extend QDA because it is a simple (but nontrivial) model that can be solved analytically. Furthermore, QDA is capable of modeling interactions between features without explicitly defining them in the data preprocessing step. This property differentiates QDA from linear discriminant analysis (LDA). Nevertheless, it is easy to reduce QDA into LDA by using the same covariance matrix estimate for each class. LDA is known to have a good tradeoff between accuracy and runtime [19], is more efficient than logistic regression [6], and can be used for semi-supervised learning (e.g., by shrinking the class conditional covariance matrix estimates toward the shared covariance matrix).

The paper is structured as follows. First, the related literature is discussed in Sect. 2. Then online QDA is proposed in Sect. 3. Empirical comparisons of the obtained accuracy and speed up are in Sect. 4. The paper closes with a discussion of the applications of the online QDA in Sect. 5 and the conclusion in Sect. 6.

## 2     Related Work

Feature stream processing was introduced by [24], where it was used for feature selection. The current state-of-the-art algorithm in this field is online streaming feature selection (OSFS) [20]. OSFS works as a feature-selection filter, which evaluates incoming features. Only when a new feature is evaluated by OSFS to be relevant and non-redundant, the feature is passed to a conventional downstream model, which is retrained from scratch. However, the time to retrain the downstream model remains an unsolved bottleneck [22].

Examples of other feature selection methods that work on a stream of features are a scalable and accurate online approach for feature selection (SAOLA) [23], online stream feature selection method based on mutual information (OSFSMI) [16], online stream feature selection method with self-adaptive sliding window (OSFSASW) [21], geometric online adaption (GOA) [18], and streaming feature selection considering feature interaction (SFS-FI) [25].

Our approach is a departure from the feature selection mindset; it focuses on *updating an offline classifier into an online classifier.*

This update approach was already successfully applied on least squares support vector machine by [15], on a one-layer artificial neural network by [2], and on Bayes classifier by [13].

## 2.1   Unrelated Work

The proposed implementation of QDA can be described as an *incremental algorithm.* However, this term can have several meanings, and we feel the need to explicitly state what our implementation is not, to avoid confusion.

A considerable amount of literature is associated with updating LDA when new samples arrive (see references in [5, Table 1]). However, this article deals with an orthogonal problem when new features arrive. In addition, the proposed QDA does not return an approximate solution (e.g., by iteratively approximating the first few eigenvectors [3]) but returns an *exact solution.*

## 3   QDA Algorithm

In the following text, matrices are denoted by capital letters, e.g., $Z \in \mathbb{R}^{n \times d}$, vectors by boldface characters, e.g., $\mathbf{z} \in \mathbb{R}^d$, and scalars by lowercase characters, e.g., $z \in \mathbb{R}$. $n$ denotes the count of rows and $d$ denotes the count of columns. Unless stated otherwise, vectors are column-vectors, i.e., $\mathbf{z}^\mathsf{T}\mathbf{z}$ is a scalar. Vectors and matrices are indexed with square brackets, e.g., $Z[i,j]$ for $i^{\text{th}}$ row and $j^{\text{th}}$ column, to unite the notion in mathematical equations and pseudocode. For brevity, broadcasting along the vertical is permitted, e.g., $Z - \mathbf{z} = Z - 1_n\mathbf{z}^\mathsf{T}$, where $1_n$ is a vector of ones.

A single data instance $s$ can be scored with QDA using the following equation:

$$Z_k(s) = -\frac{1}{2}(s - \mu_k)^\mathsf{T}\Sigma_k^{-1}(s - \mu_k) - \frac{1}{2}\ln|\Sigma_k| + \ln p_k. \tag{1}$$

where $\mu_k$ is the estimated mean value of instances in class $k$, $\Sigma_k^{-1}$ is the inverse of the covariance matrix for the class $k$, $|\Sigma_k|$ is the determinant of the covariance matrix $\Sigma_k$, and $p_k$ is the prior probability of the class $k$. Instance $s$ is then classified into the class with the highest $Z$ value.

## 3.1 Covariance

The class-conditional sample covariance matrix $\Sigma_{t,k}$ at time $t$ is estimated from the class-conditional data matrix $X_{t,k}$ with

$$\Sigma_{t,k} = \frac{1}{n_k - 1}(X_{t,k} - \mu_{t,k})(X_{t,k} - \mu_{t,k})^\mathsf{T}, \tag{2}$$

where $\mu_{t,k}$ is a class-conditional vector of the feature means, and $n_k$ is the class-conditional sample count. When a new feature $x_{t+1}$ is appended into the data matrix, $X_t$ becomes $X_{t+1}$. The readily available $\Sigma_{t,k}$ is then updated to $\Sigma_{t+1,k}$ with:

$$
\begin{aligned}
x_{t+1,k}^* &= x_{t+1,k} - \bar{x}_{t+1,k}, \\
X_{t+1,k}^* &= [X_{t,k}^*, x_k^*], \\
\Sigma_{t+1,k} &= \left[\Sigma_{t,k}, \tfrac{1}{n_k-1}(X_{t+1,k}^* \cdot x_{t+1,k}^*)\right],
\end{aligned}
\tag{3}
$$

where the covariance matrices is stored in a packed (triangular) format because covariance matrices are always symmetric. For convenience, the $*$ superscript marks the centered matrices through the text. $\bar{x}_{t+1,k}$ is the estimated mean value (a scalar) of vector $x_{t+1,k}$.

## 3.2 Inverse

Inverse of a matrix, as given in Eq. (1), should generally never be explicitly calculated because faster and more numerically stable methods exist [4]. Suppose that we want to solve $x = A^{-1}y$, where $x$ is the unknown vector. Whenever matrix $A$ is symmetric and positive definite, $x$ can be efficiently obtained via the Cholesky decomposition chol [8, Section 4.2.3] followed by backward substitution backward [8, Section 3.1.6]:

$$
\begin{aligned}
R &= \texttt{chol}(A), \\
x &= \texttt{backward}(R, y).
\end{aligned}
\tag{4}
$$

The Cholesky factorization decomposes matrix $A$ into an upper triangular matrix R such that the product of $R$ and its transpose $R^\mathsf{T}$ yields $A$:

$$A = RR^\mathsf{T}. \tag{5}$$

Backward substitution then solves the problem from bottom to top (hence, the name):

$$
\begin{aligned}
x[d] &= y[d]/R[d,d], \\
x[i] &= \left(y[i] - \sum_{j=i+1}^{d} R[i,j]x[j]\right) / R[i,i], \quad i \in [1, d-1].
\end{aligned}
\tag{6}
$$

Herein, an important factor is that both the Cholesky decomposition and backward substitution can be efficiently updated when a new column is added to matrix $A$. The Cholesky decomposition can be updated with `cholinsert`, which is a built-in function in Octave or Julia. Rank-one update of backward substitution is visually represented in Fig. 2. Since the sample covariance matrices are always symmetric and positive definite when the features are linearly independent, we can use the Cholesky decomposition in QDA. Further discussions regarding the steps to be taken if this assumption is violated are detailed in Sect. 3.6.

## 3.3 Determinant

The determinant of matrix $A$ can be obtained as the product of the squared diagonal elements of `chol(A)`:

$$|A| = \prod_{i=1}^{d} R[i,i]^2, \tag{7}$$

where $d$ is the size of $R$.

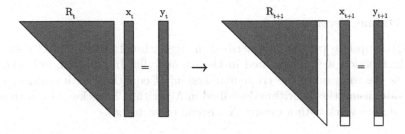

**Fig. 2.** Updating the system of equations by appending a single column into triangular matrix $R$

Whenever the logarithm of the determinant is needed, as in Eq. (1), it is possible to avoid unnecessary overflows by summing the logarithms of the diagonal elements of `chol(A)`:

$$\ln|A| = \ln \prod_{i=1}^{d} R[i,i]^2 = 2 \cdot \sum_{i=1}^{d} \ln(R[i,i]). \tag{8}$$

Because `cholinsert` does not change the values of the old Cholesky decomposition $R_t$ (it simply appends a new column), it is possible to update the logarithm of the determinant in real time:

$$\ln|A_{t+1}| = \ln|A_t| + 2 \cdot \ln(R_{t+1}[t+1,t+1]), \tag{9}$$

where $R_{t+1}[t+1,t+1]$ is the bottom right number in triangular matrix $R_{t+1}$.

## 3.4   Vectorization

Equation (1) is given only for a single sample. To score all new samples at once, first note that:

$$b^\mathsf{T} A^{-1} b = b^\mathsf{T}(RR^\mathsf{T})^{-1} b \tag{10}$$

$$= b^\mathsf{T}(R^{-1})^\mathsf{T} R^{-1} b \tag{11}$$

$$= (R^{-1}b)^\mathsf{T}(R^{-1}b), \tag{12}$$

where $b$ is a vector, $R$ is the Cholesky decomposition of $A$. From this, we obtain a scoring function for matrix $X$:

$$Z_k(x) = -\frac{1}{2}\sum_d \left(R_k^{-1}(X - \mu_k)\right) \circ \left(R_k^{-1}(X - \mu_k)\right) - \frac{1}{2}\ln|\Sigma_k| + \ln p_k. \tag{13}$$

where $\circ$ is element-wise multiplication, $\mu_k$ is the class-conditional mean of the training data, $R_k$ is the Cholesky decomposition of the $\Sigma_k$ covariance matrix, and $R_k^{-1}X$ is solved with backward substitution.

## 3.5   Online Version

The QDA update process is described in Algorithm 1, where `cholinsert` is a built-in function as implemented in Octave or Julia. In addition, `solveinsert` updates the solution of the triangular system of equations with multiple right-hand sides using the algorithm described in Algorithm 2 (backward substitution, but scaled to work with a matrix $X$ instead of vector $x$).

---

**Algorithm 1:** Updating QDA when a new feature is inserted.

---

**Input**: new feature, $x_{t+1}$; label conditional sample count, $m$; label conditional logarithm of prior probability, $lp$; label conditional feature means, $\mu_t$; label conditional centered features, $X_t^*$; label conditional Cholesky decomposition, $R_t$; and label conditional logarithm of determinant, $ld_t$; $t$ is the count of features, $k$ is the class

**Output**: $\mu_{t+1}, X_{t+1}^*, R_{t+1}, ld_{t+1}, Z_{t+1}$

1  **foreach** $k \in K$ **do**

2  $\quad \mu_{t+1,k} = [\mu_{t+1,k}, \bar{x}_{t+1,k}]$                               /* Mean vector */

3  $\quad X_{t+1,k}^* = [X_{t,k}^*, x_{t+1,k}^* - \bar{x}_{t+1}]$                    /* Centered matrix */

4  $\quad \sigma_k = \frac{1}{m_k - 1} \cdot x_{t+1,k}^* \cdot X_{t+1,k}^*$           /* Covariance vector */

5  $\quad R_{t+1,k} = \text{cholinsert}(R_{t,k}, \sigma_k)$                          /* Cholesky decomposition */

6  $\quad ld_{t+1,k} = ld_{t,k} + 2 \cdot \ln(R_{t+1,k}[t+1, t+1])$                  /* Log determinant */

7  $\quad A_{t+1,k} = \text{solveinsert}(A_{t,k}, R_{t+1,k}, X_{t+1}^*)$            /* Solve equations */

8  $\quad Z_{t+1,k} = lp_k - \frac{1}{2}\sum(A_{t+1,k} \circ A_{t+1,k}) + ld_{t+1,k}$ /* Discrimination score */

9  **end**

---

---

**Algorithm 2:** Function `solveinsert` updates the solution of a triangular system of equations with multiple right-hand side for $A \cdot R = X$.

---

**Input:** $A_t, R_{t+1}, X_{t+1}$, where $t$ is the count of features

**Output:** $A_{t+1}$

1  $A_{t+1} = [A_t, (X_{t+1}[:, t+1] - A_t[:, 1:t] \cdot R_{t+1}[1:t, t+1])/R_{t+1}[t+1, t+1]]$

---

### 3.6 Regularization

One of the key problems of QDA is how to reliably estimate the covariance matrices. Equation (2) presents an empirical estimate of the sample covariance matrices. However, these sample covariance matrices suffer from a high variance of the parameter estimates as the count of the parameters to estimate grows quadratically with the number of features $d$ and linearly with the number of the classes $k$.

When the count of the samples is small relative to $d$ and $k$, it is frequently beneficial to assume that the covariance matrices are identical and use a single shared covariance matrix $\Sigma_t$ in place of $\Sigma_{t,k}$:

$$\Sigma_t = \frac{(n_1 - 1)\Sigma_{t,1} + (n_2 - 1)\Sigma_{t,2} + \ldots + (n_k - 1)\Sigma_{t,k}}{(n_1 - 1) + (n_2 - 1) + \ldots + (n_k - 1)}, \tag{14}$$

where $n$ with the index is the number of samples in the class. This variant of QDA is known as linear discriminant analysis (LDA).

Another common issue with QDA is the invertibility of the sample covariance matrices [11]. This can be remedied with shrinking toward the identity matrix [12]:

$$\Sigma_{t,k} = (1 - \lambda)\Sigma_{t,k} + \lambda I, \tag{15}$$

where $I$ is the identity matrix and $\lambda$ is a shrinkage coefficient, $\lambda \in (0, 1)$.

For an improved predictive accuracy, regularized discriminant analysis (RDA) [7] can be used, where the covariance matrix is a linear combination of the shared covariance matrix, the class conditional covariance matrix, and the identity matrix:

$$\Sigma_{t,k} = (1 - \alpha - \lambda)\Sigma_t + \alpha\Sigma_{t,k} + \lambda I, \tag{16}$$

where $\alpha$ is a tunable weight, $\alpha \in (0, 1 - \lambda)$.

# 4    Experiments

## 4.1    Speed

The proposed implementation of QDA is evaluated on the OpenML-CC18 bench-marking suite [1]. This suite includes 72 datasets, from which datasets that include nominal features or missing values were excluded, as the implementation does not directly support them.

Two algorithms were compared: QDA learning from scratch with scikit-learn 0.24.0 QDA as the reference versus the proposed QDA update by feature insert. For each of these two scenarios, the training and scoring times were recorded on each of the datasets. Brier scores (a calibration measure for classification) were also measured to validate that the quality of the predictions is equivalent. Since the Brier scores were indeed identical between the implementations, we do not report them.

Because some datasets have collinear features, as indicated by the high correlation coefficients in the last column in Table 1, regularized covariance matrices: $(1 - \lambda) \sum_k + \lambda I$ were used, where $\lambda = 0.02$. A constant regularization was used, as the aim of the experiment was not to find the best possible regularization coefficients but to compare runtimes.

Median runtimes from 15 iterations are provided in Table 1. The proposed updatable QDA was always faster than scikit-learn QDA. Notably, there was a 1000-fold increase in speed in five cases. Based on the code profiling, SVD decomposition is the bottleneck in scikit-learn implementation. For the description of how to use SVD for discriminant analysis, see for example [11]. The code for the result replication is available at github.com/janmotl/qda.

## 4.2    Accuracy

Since we are generally interested not only in runtime but also accuracy of the classifiers, QDA was compared to naive Bayes, k-nearest neighbours, logistic regression, random forest, and gradient boosted trees. Because of the page limit, the design of the experiment and the obtained results are available at github.com/janmotl/qda.

**Table 1.** Training and scoring times in seconds for scikit-learn QDA and the proposed updatable QDA, when the last feature is inserted. Dataset metadata: count of samples, features, classes, and the maximal absolute Person's correlation coefficient between two different features in the dataset. Predictions from scikit-learn and the proposed QDA are identical. The datasets are ordered by the obtained speed up.

| Dataset | scikit-learn | Proposed | Speed up | Samples | Features | Classes | Corr |
|---|---|---|---|---|---|---|---|
| mfeat-morphological | 0.015 | 0.014 | 1.10 | 2000 | 6 | 10 | 0.97 |
| balance-scale | 0.004 | 0.004 | 1.15 | 625 | 4 | 3 | 0.00 |
| wilt | 0.006 | 0.004 | 1.38 | 4839 | 5 | 2 | 0.96 |
| diabetes | 0.004 | 0.003 | 1.71 | 768 | 8 | 2 | 0.54 |
| vehicle | 0.010 | 0.005 | 1.77 | 846 | 18 | 4 | 1.00 |
| blood-transfusion | 0.005 | 0.003 | 1.79 | 748 | 4 | 2 | 1.00 |
| segment | 0.022 | 0.010 | 2.21 | 2310 | 19 | 7 | 1.00 |
| banknote-authentication | 0.007 | 0.003 | 2.44 | 1372 | 4 | 2 | 0.79 |
| climate-model | 0.006 | 0.003 | 2.45 | 540 | 20 | 2 | 0.11 |
| phoneme | 0.010 | 0.004 | 2.45 | 5404 | 5 | 2 | 0.32 |
| kc2 | 0.008 | 0.003 | 2.94 | 522 | 21 | 2 | 1.00 |
| wdbc | 0.009 | 0.003 | 3.50 | 569 | 30 | 2 | 1.00 |
| steel-plates-fault | 0.042 | 0.012 | 3.61 | 1941 | 27 | 7 | 1.00 |
| letter | 0.334 | 0.090 | 3.71 | 20000 | 16 | 26 | 0.85 |
| jungle_chess_2pcs | 0.081 | 0.021 | 3.92 | 44819 | 6 | 3 | 0.02 |
| pendigits | 0.097 | 0.023 | 4.18 | 10992 | 16 | 10 | 0.86 |
| pc1 | 0.013 | 0.003 | 5.00 | 1109 | 21 | 2 | 1.00 |
| kc1 | 0.019 | 0.003 | 6.30 | 2109 | 21 | 2 | 1.00 |
| qsar-biodeg | 0.019 | 0.003 | 7.06 | 1055 | 41 | 2 | 0.92 |
| mfeat-zernike | 0.090 | 0.013 | 7.08 | 2000 | 47 | 10 | 1.00 |
| wall-robot-navigation | 0.049 | 0.007 | 7.31 | 5456 | 24 | 4 | 0.63 |
| pc3 | 0.025 | 0.003 | 8.02 | 1563 | 37 | 2 | 1.00 |
| texture | 0.153 | 0.019 | 8.07 | 5500 | 40 | 11 | 1.00 |
| satimage | 0.105 | 0.011 | 9.40 | 6430 | 36 | 6 | 0.96 |
| pc4 | 0.026 | 0.003 | 9.64 | 1458 | 37 | 2 | 1.00 |
| mfeat-karhunen | 0.127 | 0.013 | 9.82 | 2000 | 64 | 10 | 0.57 |
| analcatdata_authorship | 0.052 | 0.005 | 10.38 | 841 | 70 | 4 | 0.71 |
| GesturePhaseSegmentation | 0.136 | 0.012 | 11.17 | 9873 | 32 | 5 | 0.94 |
| mfeat-fourier | 0.172 | 0.013 | 13.17 | 2000 | 76 | 10 | 0.68 |
| optdigits | 0.243 | 0.017 | 14.42 | 5620 | 64 | 10 | 0.93 |
| first-order-theorem-proving | 0.184 | 0.011 | 17.11 | 6118 | 51 | 6 | 1.00 |
| numerai28.6 | 0.765 | 0.033 | 23.32 | 96320 | 21 | 2 | 0.86 |
| spambase | 0.091 | 0.004 | 23.62 | 4601 | 57 | 2 | 1.00 |
| ozone-level-8hr | 0.085 | 0.003 | 29.33 | 2534 | 72 | 2 | 1.00 |
| semeion | 0.624 | 0.012 | 50.07 | 1593 | 256 | 10 | 0.81 |
| mfeat-factors | 0.686 | 0.014 | 50.67 | 2000 | 216 | 10 | 1.00 |
| mfeat-pixel | 0.796 | 0.010 | 83.44 | 2000 | 240 | 10 | 0.94 |
| cnae-9 | 0.986 | 0.011 | 88.31 | 1080 | 856 | 9 | 1.00 |

(*continued*)

**Table 2.** (*continued*)

| Dataset | scikit-learn | Proposed | Speed up | Samples | Features | Classes | Corr |
|---|---|---|---|---|---|---|---|
| isolet | 11.465 | 0.051 | 224.41 | 7797 | 617 | 26 | 1.00 |
| madelon | 1.893 | 0.004 | 515.26 | 2600 | 500 | 2 | 0.99 |
| har | 9.689 | 0.014 | 670.19 | 10299 | 561 | 6 | 1.00 |
| Fashion-MNIST | 101.438 | 0.086 | 1177.68 | 70000 | 784 | 10 | 0.96 |
| Devnagari-Script | 731.853 | 0.484 | 1511.97 | 92000 | 1024 | 46 | 0.97 |
| mnist_784 | 145.914 | 0.091 | 1600.96 | 70000 | 784 | 10 | 1.00 |
| Bioresponse | 40.582 | 0.004 | 9068.45 | 3751 | 1776 | 2 | 0.98 |
| CIFAR_10 | 2130.479 | 0.084 | 25385.96 | 60000 | 3072 | 10 | 0.98 |

# 5   Discussion

## 5.1   Feature Selection

The ability to quickly insert new features can be used, for example, to speed up forward variable selection with LDA, as implemented in greedy.wilks() [17].

## 5.2   Limitations

The online version of QDA inherits all the disadvantages of offline QDA, namely high sensitivity to outliers and difficulties with the accurate estimation of the covariance matrices, which can be addressed with robust statistical estimates [10] and covariance shrinking [12], respectively. Missing values in the estimate of the covariance matrix can be handled as described by [14]. And a mixture of numerical and nominal features can be handled with one of the methods described by [9].

# 6   Conclusion

The key to learning on a stream of features with QDA is to use the Cholesky decomposition and cholinsert function in place of the matrix inverse. This method, together with an efficient update of the covariance matrices, reduced the computational complexity of the QDA update when a new feature was added, from $\mathcal{O}(nd^2+d^3)$ to $\mathcal{O}(nd+d^2)$. This is equivalent to the reduction by $d$ (the number of features). The proposed QDA returns identical predictions to scikit-learn QDA while being 1000 times faster. In the accuracy comparison, the need to regularize the estimated covariance matrices was identified. The proposed regularized discriminant analysis on a stream of features is statistically significantly more accurate than naive Bayes (at $p = 0.01$) and comparable to regularized logistic regression, k-nearest neighbors, and gradient boosted trees while in runtime it is much closer to naive Bayes.

**Acknowledgments.** We are grateful to Karel Klouda, Oliver Schulte, and anonymous reviewers for constructive comments on earlier drafts of this article. This research was supported by Grant Agency of the Czech Technical University in Prague (SGS17/210/OHK3/3T/18) and Czech Science Foundation (GAČR 18-18080S).

# References

1. Bischl, B., et al.: OpenML Benchmarking Suites, pp. 1–6. arXiv (2017)
2. Bolon-Canedo, V., Fernández-Francos, D., Peteiro-Barral, D., Alonso-Betanzos, A., Guijarro-Berdiñas, B., Sánchez-Maroño, N.: A unified pipeline for online feature selection and classification. Expert Syst. Appl. **55**, 532–545 (2016). https://doi.org/10.1016/j.eswa.2016.02.035
3. Dagher, I.: Incremental PCA-LDA algorithm. CIMSA **4**, 97–101 (2010). https://doi.org/10.1109/CIMSA.2010.5611752
4. Davis, T.A.: Algorithm 9xx: FACTORIZE: an object-oriented linear system solver for MATLAB. ACM Trans. Math. Softw. **39**(4), 1–18 (2013). https://doi.org/10.1145/2491491.2491498
5. Dhamecha, T.I., Singh, R., Vatsa, M.: On incremental semi-supervised discriminant analysis. Pattern Recogn. **52**, 135–147 (2016). https://doi.org/10.1016/j.patcog.2015.09.030
6. Efron, B.: The efficiency of logistic regression compared to normal discriminant analysis. J. Am. Stat. Assoc. **70**(352), 892–898 (1975). https://doi.org/10.1080/01621459.1975.10480319
7. Friedman, J.H.: Regularized discriminant analysis. J. Am. Stat. Assoc. **84**(405), 165–175 (1989). https://doi.org/10.1080/01621459.1989.10478752
8. Golub, G.H., Loan, C.F.V.: Matrix Computations, 4th edn. Johns Hopkins, Baltimore (2013)
9. Huberty, C.J., Wisenbaker, J.M., Smith, J.D., Smith, J.C.: Using categorical variables in discriminant analysis. Multivariate Behav. Res. **21**(4), 479–496 (1986). https://doi.org/10.1207/s15327906mbr2104_7
10. Jiang, J.H., Chen, Z.P., Xu, C.J., Yu, R.G.: Robust linear discriminant analysis for chemical pattern recognition. J. Chemom. **13**, 3–13 (1999). https://doi.org/10.1002/(SICI)1099-128X(199901/02)13:1⟨3::AID-CEM524⟩3.0.CO;2-R
11. Kalina, J., Valenta, Z., Tebbens, J.D.: Computation of regularized linear discriminant analysis. In: Computing Statistics International Conference, pp. 128–133 (2015)
12. Ledoit, O., Wolf, M.: Improved estimation of the covariance matrix of stock returns with an application to portfolio selection. J. Empir. Financ. **10**(5), 603–621 (2003). https://doi.org/10.1016/S0927-5398(03)00007-0
13. Liyanage, Y.W., Zois, D.S., Chelmis, C.: On-the-Fly Joint Feature Selection and Classification, pp. 1–12. arXiv (2020)
14. Lounici, K.: High-dimensional covariance matrix estimation with missing observations. Bernoulli **20**(3), 1029–1058 (2014). https://doi.org/10.3150/12-BEJ487
15. Ojeda, F., Suykens, J.A., De Moor, B.: Variable selection by rank one updates for least squares support vector machines. In: 2007 International Joint Conference Neural Networks, pp. 2283–2288. IEEE, August 2007. https://doi.org/10.1109/IJCNN.2007.4371314
16. Rahmaninia, M., Moradi, P.: OSFSMI: online stream feature selection method based on mutual information. Appl. Soft Comput. J. **68**, 733–746 (2018). https://doi.org/10.1016/j.asoc.2017.08.034

234     J. Motl and P. Kordík

17. Roever, C., et al.: The klaR package (2006)
18. Sekeh, S.Y., Ganesh, M.R., Banerjee, S., Corso, J.J., Hero, A.O.: A Geometric Approach to Online Streaming Feature Selection. arXiv (2019)
19. Tjen-Sien, L., Wei-Yin, L., Shih, Y.S.: A comparison of prediction accuracy, complexity, and training time of thirty-three old and new classification algorithms. Mach. Learn. **229**, 203–229 (1992). https://doi.org/10.1023/A:1007608224229
20. Wu, X., Yu, K., Wang, H., Ding, W.: Online streaming feature selection. In: International Conference Machine Learning, pp. 1159–1166 (2010)
21. You, D., et al.: Online feature selection for streaming features using self-adaption sliding-window sampling. IEEE Access **7**, 16088–16100 (2019). https://doi.org/10.1109/ACCESS.2019.2894121
22. Yu, K., Ding, W., Simovici, D.A., Wu, X.: Mining emerging patterns by streaming feature selection. KDD, pp. 60–68 (2012). https://doi.org/10.1145/2339530.2339544
23. Yu, K., Wu, X., Ding, W., Pei, J.: Towards scalable and accurate online feature selection for big data. In: Proceedings - IEEE International Conference Data Mining, ICDM 2015, pp. 660–669 (2015). https://doi.org/10.1109/ICDM.2014.63
24. Zhou, J., Foster, D., Stine, R., Ungar, L.: Streaming feature selection using alpha-investing. In: KDD, pp. 384–393 (2005). https://doi.org/10.1145/1081870.1081914
25. Zhou, P., Li, P., Zhao, S., Wu, X.: Feature interaction for streaming feature selection. IEEE Trans. Neural Networks Learn. Syst. **32**(10), 1–12 (2020). https://doi.org/10.1109/TNNLS.2020.3025922

# Learning Image Captioning
# as a Structured Transduction Task

Davide Bacciu[✉] and Davide Serramazza[✉]

Dipartimento di Informatica, Università di Pisa, L.Go B. Pontecorvo 3, Pisa, Italy
davide.bacciu@unipi.it, davide.serramazza@fileli.unipi.it

**Abstract.** Image captioning is a task typically approached by deep
encoder-decoder architectures, where the encoder component works on
a flat representation of the image while the decoder considers a sequential representation of natural language sentences. As such, these encoder-
decoder architectures implement a simple and very specific form of structured transduction, that is a generalization of a predictive problem where
the input data and output predictions might have substantially different structures and topologies. In this paper, we explore a generalization
of such an approach by addressing the problem as a general structured
transduction problem. In particular, we provide a framework that allows
considering input and output information with a tree-structured representation. This allows taking into account the hierarchical nature underlying both images and sentences. To this end, we introduce an approach
to generate tree-structured representations from images along with an
autoencoder working with this kind of data. We empirically assess our
approach on both synthetic and realistic tasks.

**Keywords:** Structured transductions · Image captioning · Learning
for structured data

## 1 Introduction

Image captioning is a long-standing problem for the machine vision community
with clear practical implications for automating a widespread and time-intensive
task usually performed by humans. From a computational perspective, this is
a significantly hard task involving both computer vision and natural language
processing (NLP) challenges. The former is necessary to capture image content
while the latter one is necessary to generate a syntactically and semantically
well-formed natural language sentence.

The performance of image captioning systems have been far from allowing
practical applications for years, until the community has started exploring deep
learning architectures mixing different neural models for visual and language
components. Such heterogeneous neural models are integrated together following an encoder-decoder architecture, popularized by the sequence-to-sequence
models for machine translation [4,8]. The typical scheme is to have as encoder

© Springer Nature Switzerland AG 2022
L. Iliadis et al. (Eds.): EANN 2022, CCIS 1600, pp. 235–246, 2022.
https://doi.org/10.1007/978-3-031-08223-8_20

a convolutional neural network (CNN) which encode the image in the latent representation, and as recurrent or transformer-based decoder transforming this representation in a sentence. The pioneering model, introducing this kind of architecture is the *Neural Image Caption Generator* [17], often shortened as *NIC*. This model employed as encoder the state-of-the-art CNN at the time [9], which is a modified version of Inception network [14], while the decoder was made up of an Embedding Layer and a standard LSTM. Several works have been developed starting from this initial intuition, such as [19], where the NIC model has been enriched with an attention mechanism.

The perspective that we would like to bring with this work is that the learning task solved by popular image captioning approaches in literature is a simple and restricted form of structured transduction.

In this paper, we specifically explore a novel tree-structured representation for both images and sentences within an image captioning application. In literature works, in fact, both input images and target captions are processed from the encoder and decoder without taking into account the dependencies they have: CNN process fixed image sub-windows while the decoder generates the words not considering the sentence structure.

We put forward the following contributions: (i) we introduce an algorithm to label a tree describing the hierarchy in the image components, with convolutional information; (ii) we introduce a deep encoder-decoder model for learning tree structured transduction between images and sentences; (iii) we develop code to build a synthetic image captioning dataset composed of images of nested geometric shapes. Finally we perform a comparison among our structured data/model and a standard one taking as baseline our implementation of the NIC model both on synthetic and realistic datasets.

## 2   Background on Learning for Structured Data

Learning approaches dealing with tree-structured data typically follow a *recursive* approach [6] which operate through a straight generalization of the RNN concept of state update. In a RNN we compute a vectorial encoding $h_t = f(h_{t-1})$ for the $t$-th element of the sequence by considering the state of its predecessor $h_{t-1}$. In a recursive model, we compute the vectorial encoding of the $n-th$ node by considering information from some of its neighboring nodes: which are these considered neighbors usually depends by the parsing direction.

The most popular choice, especially in classification tasks, is bottom-up, where the tree is visited from leaves to root. This defines a straightforward node neighborhood, which is the set of node children, leading to the general recursive state update $h_n = f(x_n, h_{\mathcal{CH}(n)})$, where $h_{\mathcal{CH}(n)}$ denotes the concatenation of the states for all children $\mathcal{CH}(n)$ of node $n$ and $f$ can be interpreted as a generic non-linear transformation implemented by a neural layer.

The actual instantiation of the recursive state encoding depends on the nature of the learning model and its stationarity assumptions. In [2,3], this is modelled as a state transition distribution whose computation is made feasible through a mixture-based factorization. Recursive bottom-up neural approaches have been proposed since [6], while [16] more recently introduced an LSTM-based recursive network with two alternative children aggregation approaches. The *Child-Sum Tree-LSTM* encodes trees without considering the position of nodes (ordering) with respect to their siblings, combining the children states before multiplying them to a single parameter matrix $W^r$. The *N-ary Tree-LSTMs* discriminates children by their position with respect to the siblings, each with a position-specialized weight $W_l^r$.

The top-down approach visits the tree from root to leaves, while the neighborhood of a node for state update purposes simply becomes its parent. This defines models that do not depart much from a standard recurrent model for sequences (given that there is in both cases a single predecessor). Top-down tree models have found wider application in tree generation [5], rather than tree encoding.

# 3 Image Captioning as Structured Transduction

The problem of learning tree transductions is to infer a transformation of an input structure $\mathbf{x}$ into an output $\mathbf{y}$ which can have (and in our application certainly have) radically different topologies. This transduction is learnt from pairs of input-output trees $(\mathbf{x}, \mathbf{y})$ just like in any standard supervised learning task. The problem of learning general tree transductions is still an open one: see [1] for a survey.

Before delving into the proposed model, we introduce the notation used in the paper. We consider labeled rooted trees where $n_i \in \mathcal{U}$ denotes the $i$-th tree node whose direct ancestor, called *parent*, is referred to as $pa(n_i)$. A node $n$ can have a variable number of direct descendants called *children*, such that the $l$-th child of node $n$ is denoted as $ch_l(n)$, while $\mathcal{CH}(n) = n_1, \ldots, n_c$ denotes the set of $c$ node children, where $c$ is the node degree/arity. The pair $(n, m) \in \mathcal{E}$ is used to denote an edge between the node $n$ and its children $m$; two nodes $j$ and $m$ having the same parent $n$ are called siblings. Finally we use $E_v$ to refer to the embedding of a node/set of node $v$ (e.g. $E_{\mathcal{CH}}(n)$ is the embedding of node $n$ children).

## 3.1  Generating Tree-Structured Image Representations

In this work, we use two different representations of images as tree data: one that is general and that we used with realistic datasets; the second specific to the synthetic dataset. In both cases, the tree represents a hierarchy among the image regions, where nodes are labeled with region appearance information extracted by a CNN. We release the code for image to tree transformations here[1].

---

[1] https://github.com/davide-serramazza/image_captionig_tree2tree_input-target_processing.

The first approach builds the tree leveraging a hierarchical segmentation. Tree topology is obtained by processing the structure returned by the GLIA segmentation algorithm [13]. This creates a *Merge tree* in which each node represents an image region. The tree is built starting from the leaves, which are regions found by an over-segmentation of the images. At each iteration two neighborhood regions are connected together following a saliency function, which decides the merge priority of nodes until a full tree is built. After this step, an optimal segmentation is found by identifying an optimal subset of *Merge tree* nodes. A factor graph is built in which the node set is the same as in the merge tree. Each merge of a node and its children in the *Merge tree*, is considered as a clique $p_i$ in the factor graph. Each node of the graph is assigned to a $\{+1, -1\}$ label, indicating whether its children merge or not, solving a constrained optimization problem based on the merging probabilities computed from a boundary classifier. The final tree describing the segmentation is made up of all the nodes whose labels are $+1$ and the parent label is $-1$.

The result of this first step is a tree representing the hierarchical segmentation of an image but this does not convey information about the content of regions represented in tree nodes. To achieve this, we label each node by leveraging information from a CNN. In this first tree representation, the information comes from an Inception-V3 [15] pre-trained network to be as close as possible to the NIC baseline.

We use different labelling strategies for the different node types there are in the tree: leaves, which are the only nodes representing single images segments, are labelled using the activation of the last layer before the inception module which results in a tensor of shape $W \times H \times 192$ with $W$ and $H$ varying with the sizes of the original images. From the segmentation map, we can then tell which of these vectors are influenced by the pixels belonging to the image region associated to the leaf and compute their average: this vector (of size 192) is the final leaf label.

The internal nodes are labeled with the max-pooling of their children labels and the root is labeled with the activation of the dense layer before the logits in the CNN, that is a 2048 dimensional vector.

The image trees for the specific synthetic dataset can be straightforwardly built from the generative grammar used to create the images. This involves a hierarchy of possibly nested geometric forms, and the tree encodes this nesting relationship in its layers. For node labelling, we rely again on a pretrained CNN (a *resNet152* [7] in this case). The same labelling strategy is used for both internal nodes and leaves since in this case they both represent single image segments: we gather local information from the second to last *residual module* of the network resulting in a $W \times H \times 1024$ tensor, while for the root we again use the activation of the neurons before the logits (a 2048 dimensional vector). The resulting trees mix global information in the root with local information about the different shapes in all the other nodes.

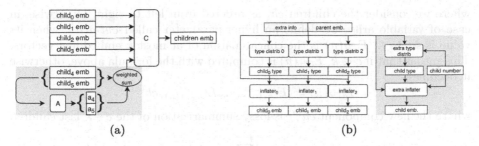

**Fig. 1.** Tree encoder-decoder architecture for structured captioning. In (a) is shown the encoder architecture of the *child embedder* with *cutarity* set to 5: the first 4 children embeddings are processed independently by the network, while the other ones are aggregated into a single embedding using an attention network and fed as 5-th input. In (b) the *Node Inflater* decoder architecture with *cutarity* set to 4: for the first 3 children, distribution types and embedding are computed by dedicated copies of the same networks, while all the remaining children, differentiated using their number, are handled by two other networks.

## 3.2 Deep Model for Tree-Structured Captioning

Our deep model for tree transduction can handle different tree topologies and different node types. We use the term node type to refer to the kind of labels a node can have (e.g. dense/categorical/mixture) and its dimension. The key idea in processing trees nodes is to have a common embedding space E in which each node type $t_i$ of the input tree, coming from the space $\mathbf{V}_{in_i}$, is projected to. Symmetrically each node type $t_j$ of the output tree (lying in the space $\mathbf{V}_{out_j}$) are generated from E. This can be achieved by combining different feed-forward sub-networks with *tanh* activation.

Figure 1 provides a view of the encoder-decoder structure of our model. The encoder processes the input tree in a bottom-up fashion, using two kinds of sub-networks: for each node type of input tree, the encoder instantiates a *Leaves embedder* and a *Children embedder*.

The first one projects each leaf in the embedding space E. Each node type $t_i$ has its own network implementing a function $V_{in_i} \rightarrow$ E. The actual network is a single dense layer with the suitable shape, namely the input shape is the same as $V_{in_i}$ and the output one is the same of the embedding space E.

The *Children embedder* sub-network, instead, is used for internal nodes: its task is to embed the current node label along with its children embedding to get a new one describing all subtrees rooted in the current node. For an internal nodes of type $t_i$, having $c$ children, it implements a function $E^c \times \mathbf{V}_{in_i} \rightarrow$ E. Its concrete application is a feed-forward network computing a function

$$e_n = f(x_n, E_{\mathcal{CH}}(n))$$

The actual value of $E_{\mathcal{CH}}(n)$ is decided by its arity: if the current node has a fixed arity then:

$$E_{\mathcal{CH}}(n) = [E_{ch_1(n)}, \ldots, E_{ch_c(n)}]$$

where we consider the children $ch_i$ as ordered from left to right. Otherwise, in case of variable arity, we define an hyper-parameter called *cut-arity*: when its value is set to $k$, $E_{CH}(n)$ is the concatenation of at most $k$ embedding vectors. This means that if $c < k$, $E_{CH}(n)$ is computed with the formula above, otherwise it becomes:

$$E_{CH}(n) = [E_{ch_1(n)}, \ldots, E_{ch_{k-1}(n)}, ch^{(a)}]$$

where the new component $ch^{(a)}$ is lossy summarization of the $c - k$ last children

$$ch^{(a)} = \sum_{i=k}^{i=c} E_{ch_i} * a_i.$$

The architecture of this last component is shown in Fig. 1a. By iterating this process on tree nodes, we eventually obtain a root embedding which is also the latent representation of the whole input tree.

The decoder is almost symmetric to the encoder with the additional task to generate the tree structures which are unknown at generation time. These tasks are realized by two components: The *Value Inflater* generates a label for a specific node starting from its embedding. It is a single-layer feed-forward network which, for each node type $j$, implements a function $E \rightarrow V_{out_j}$.

The other component, *Node Inflater* is the most complex module in the whole autoencoder. It aims to expand the tree frontier by generating children for a node: two kinds of different sub-networks are involved in a sequential flow. The first one generates a distribution over types for each child of a node. This is done by a feed-forward network, implementing the function

$$D = [d_1, \ldots, d_c] = f(e_n, e_r, x_n) \tag{1}$$

where $D$ is the probability distribution among all the possible children types, $e_n$ and $e_r$ are the current node $n$ and root embedding, respectively. Moreover, a special *nochild* type is used to stop children generation.

The second sub-network generates an embedding for each child: it is a feed-forward network implementing a function

$$E = [e_1, \ldots, e_c] = f(e_n, e_r, x_n, D) \tag{2}$$

which has the same arguments of the function 1 with the addition to the previously computed distribution $D$, so that its embeddings are generated conditioned on the previously chosen node types.

In case of variable arity, we rely another time to the *cutarity* hyper-parameter, as shown in Fig. 1b. If its value is set to $k$, the first $k - 1$ children are generated in parallel using $2(k-1)$ copies of the two networks described above. Please note that these $k - 1$ children can also be assigned to the *nochild* value.

The remaining children (from the $k$-th onwards) are generated sequentially using two other networks (referred as *extra node distrib* and *extra inflater* in Fig. 1b), until a child with *nochild* type is generated. For the $i$-th children the Eq. 1, computed from the first sub-network becomes

$$D = f(e_n, e_r, x_n, \text{one-hot}(i))$$

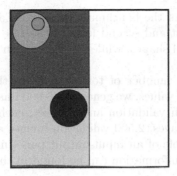 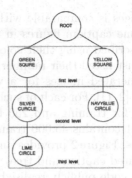

**Fig. 2.** Sample image and its tree (for which the three levels are highlighted) generated by our code. The only associated caption is "A green square and a yellow square: the first one containing a silver circle in turn containing 1 other shape; the second one containing a navy Blue circle" (Color figure online)

and the function 2 computed from the second sub-network turns into

$$E = f(e_n, e_r, x_n, D, \text{one-hot}(i)).$$

Using the sub-networks described above the decoder is able, starting from the root, to generate children, their embedding and associated labels, for each node being processed. For further details on the model, the reader is referred to the code available here[2].

## 4  Empirical Analysis

### 4.1  Dataset Preparation and Experimental Setup

Our experimental analysis is based on two realistic benchmark datasets for image captioning, Flickr30K [20], msCoco [12], and a novel synthetic dataset used to assess the capabilities of learning structured transductions in a controlled setting. Flickr30K contains a total of 31.783 images split in 29.783 for training, 1.000 for validation and 1.000 for testing. msCoco has a bigger average image size, compared to Flickr30k: the 2014 version used in this paper contains 82.783 training images and 40.504 validation images, each labelled with at least 5 captions. Roughly other 41.000 images have been released as blind test set for the different competitions based on this dataset. In order to cover the lack of a labelled test set, many early works, as for instance NIC and Treetalk [11], have extracted 4.000 random images from the validation set and used them as test set. We also follow this split for comparison purposes.

The images of our synthetic dataset represent nested geometric shapes (squares and circles) of 15 different colours, arranged in at most 3 nesting levels. Each shape can contain a variable number $n \in [1, 4]$ of other shapes and the size

---

[2] https://github.com/davide-serramazza/image_captionig_tree2tree.

of the images is comparable with that of the benchmark datasets. Each image has only one caption: figures in the first and second level of the tree are completely described using their colours and shapes, while for the ones in the third level are just listed their number.

We generated images for a varying number of total shapes in the figure, ranging in [2, 11]. For each of such range values, we generated 5.000 images, split into 4.500 for training and 250 for both validation and test set, each. Overall our dataset contains 45.000 training images, 2.500 validation images and 2.500 test images. Figure 2 provides an example of an input-output pair (image with the associated caption and tree). More information can be found in the dataset generation code publicly realised here[3].

The experimental analysis compares the NIC baseline with structured models. For fairness of comparison, the baseline with the benchmark datasets uses an Inception v3 CNN, while a resNet is employed in the synthetic one. In our implementation of NIC, images have been pre-processed according to what is required from the used CNN, while in target sentences we assign a token to each word having a sufficient number of occurrences. Lastly, we add after the beginning and before the ending of each sentence, respectively, the special tokens $< start >$ and $< end >$.

Regarding data for our model, input trees are generated as described in Sect. 3.1 while target ones are obtained by running the Stanford parser [10] on the related captions. This kind of tree has two different node types, internal POS tag nodes and word leaves: for both of them we assign a class for each different possible value we find in the dataset. Finally we assess also the performances of a third model (only with the two benchmark datasets) that is a hybrid one: it has a standard flat encoder and the structured decoder of our model.

We also extended our decoder in Sect. 3.2 to first generate tree topology, POS tag locations and labels along with word node locations. After that, the word nodes are decoded from the corresponding vocabulary word labels using a sequential decoder, similar to NIC, but with known decoded sequence topology (i.e. the generated tree leaves), therefore not needing $< start >$ and $< end >$ tokens.

For our experiments, we follow the setup of the original NIC paper, differing only on 3 points: we do not use ensemble models, we assign a $< unk >$ tokens to words having less than 10 occurrences rather than 5 (since we found slightly better results) and we do not make fine-tuning of the CNN weights for the NIC baseline. Finally for the beam size, in the experiments with the realistic datasets we use the size reported in [17] that is 20, while for the synthetic one we use the value reported in the updated version [18], namely 3.

We conclude this section by describing the model selection setup. For each experiment, we use hold out search to select the best model and then train the selected configuration on the union of training and validation samples. The metrics used in evaluating the obtained captions are *Bleu*-1 up to 4, *Rouge* and *CIDEr* and *Meteor*. In evaluating captioning performances of our model,

---

[3] https://github.com/davide-serramazza/Geometry-dataset.

**Table 1.** Different captioning performance scores for models trained using Flickr 30k and MSCOCO 2014

| Model | Dataset used | Bleu-1 | Bleu-2 | Bleu-3 | Bleu-4 | Rouge | CIDEr | Meteor |
|---|---|---|---|---|---|---|---|---|
| NIC baseline | Flickr | 0.638 | 0.417 | 0.273 | 0.175 | 0.401 | 0.415 | 0.189 |
| seq2tree | Flickr | 0.604 | 0.403 | 0.267 | 0.148 | 0.338 | 0.358 | 0.184 |
| tree2tree | Flickr | 0.585 | 0.387 | 0.256 | 0.169 | 0.33.8 | 0.361 | 0.181 |
| NIC baseline | mscoco | 0.634 | 0.453 | 0.321 | 0.231 | 0.408 | 0.654 | 0.241 |
| seq2tree | mscoco | 0.622 | 0.445 | 0.316 | 0.228 | 0.398 | 0.612 | 0.231 |
| tree2tree | mscoco | 0.618 | 0.435 | 0.299 | 0.215 | 0.389 | 0.567 | 0.220 |
| NIC baseline | synthetic | 0.851 | 0.792 | 0.723 | 0.647 | 0.743 | 4.566 | 0.450 |
| tree2tree | synthetic | 0.979 | 0.933 | 0.918 | 0.903 | 0.949 | 7.064 | 0.723 |

**Table 2.** Precision and recall for both baseline and our model using the synthetic dataset

| | First level | | Second level | | Third level | |
|---|---|---|---|---|---|---|
| Model | Precision | Recall | Precision | Recall | Precision | Recall |
| NIC baseline | 0.587 | 0.639 | 0.121 | 0.102 | 0.235 | 0.294 |
| Our model | 0.986 | 0.985 | 0.437 | 0.432 | 0.638 | 0.634 |

the words are extracted from tree leaves left to right composing the predicted sentence.

## 4.2 Results

**Captions Evaluation.** Table 1 reports the test caption scores for the three datasets.

We first analyze the synthetic dataset, for which in Table 2 it is possible to analyse also precision and recall of geometric shapes. We consider a positive match only if in the generated caption both colour and shape are correctly identified. With this dataset, our autoencoder (*tree2tree*) is the best in each score with a large margin over the baseline. With a so high value of all scores, we can state that our model have learnt images and parse trees structures. Moreover in the major part of the case also the shapes are descripted correctly. It is important to notice that the worst scores are for the second level rather than the third since as shown in Fig. 2, shapes in the last layer are not fully described.

Using the realistic dataset we have another scenario: with Flickr 30k, the NIC baseline is the best model with a neat margin over the other two. The first of our models is the flat encoder/structured decoder (*seq2tree*). It is close to the baseline for some metrics such as Bleu-2, Bleu-3 and Meteor, for which the average difference was 2.89%, while it is really far in other metrics as CIDEr, Rouge and Bleu-4 for which the average difference is 14.83%. The other model, is slightly worse in Bleu-1, Bleu-2 and Bleu-3 score but consistent in all the other

**Table 3.** Comparison of statistics of the 6 more frequent nodes in the generated trees and related nodes in the ground truth (test set). The term gts stands for ground truth trees, which are the trees obtained from Stanford parser. To be notice that the 11 top frequent pos tags are the same for both trees set

| POS node type | Average height | | Occurrences % | | Average children | |
|---|---|---|---|---|---|---|
| | gts | Our model | gts | Our model | gts | Our model |
| NP | 3.742 | 3.732 | 26.21 | 26.29 | 2.948 | 2.953 |
| NN | 4.981 | 4.952 | 17.20 | 17.11 | 1.0 | 1.0005 |
| DT | 4.864 | 4.854 | 15.24 | 15.27 | 1.0 | 1.0002 |
| JJ | 5.054 | 5.030 | 14.80 | 15.3 | 1.0 | 1.0002 |
| CC | 4.115 | 4.131 | 6.83 | 6.864 | 1.0 | 1.0004 |
| VBG | 4.508 | 4.435 | 4.29 | 4.248 | 1.0 | 1.0 |

metrics if compared to our other model. Indeed from *tree2tree*, we got a slightly better performance using CIDEr score and moreover in the Bleu-4 score it have an advantage of more than 2 points over *seq2tree*, being close to the baseline.

The results achieved on msCoco show a thinner margin for the baseline. The average score difference with *seq2tree* shrinks from 8.32%, to 2.83%. The only metric that has a really relevant difference is CIDEr having a gap of 6.92%.

Finally, even though using msCoco as dataset, the gap from *tree2tree* and the baseline model is reduced as well, it is not as competitive as the mixed one: even in some metrics the gap is reduced, some others still show a consistent gap.

**Trees Evaluation.** Along with the caption, we want also to assess the quality of the generated parse trees. Since directly comparing trees can be cumbersome, we focused our evaluation on verifying if some relevant proprieties of parse trees are preserved in the generated ones. We report statistics just for the synthetic dataset since they are very close to the ones.

In a parse tree, each POS node either has other POS children or a single word child. We empirically verify that only 0.014% of generated POS tag nodes have two children of different kinds and no POS tag nodes have more than one-word children. These values suggest that the structure of the parse trees is well-understood and well-replicated by our model.

We also report some statistics from generated and ground truth trees to verify how close they are. In the ground truth ones, the average POS nodes number per tree is 46.80 while the average word nodes are 30.14, In the generated trees we have respective values of 46.60 and 30.02. Moreover, also the proportion $\frac{|POS\ nodes|}{|word\ nodes|}$ is almost the same, having a value of 1.552 for both trees.

Finally, we collect the 6 top frequent types of POS nodes and we compute their average height, average children number and percentage of their occurrences over the total number of nodes. From Table 3, in which these values are reported along with the related ground truth ones we can notice that they are very close. Among the others, we want to stress the values for the average children number. Each of them, except *NP*, describe just a single word indeed in the ground truth trees they have an average children number of exactly 1.0. In the generated trees they either have an exact value of 1.0 or a value a little bit higher suggesting that they have more than one child just in a few cases.

## 5   Conclusions

We have presented a novel perspective over image captioning, leveraging an encoder-decoder architecture but with a data representation that explicitly models the hierarchy in the data for both images and sentences. To this end, we introduced a novel model to learn non-isomorphic tree transductions, capable of learning a mapping between input and target trees, enriched with the addition of a linguistic module in the decoder: the original parts are used to generate tree topology, POS tag and word nodes location and POS tag node values. Only word nodes values are in charge of the linguistic module.

Thanks to the encoder-decoder architecture it is also possible to have a mixed model using structured (hierarchical) representation for the input and the other opposite for the output.

We compared the captioning performances against the NIC baseline both on realistic benchmark datasets and on a synthetic one: in the first case our models, especially *seq2tree* have reached interesting results while in the second one our *tree2tree* model is the best by a large margin.

We also verified the quality of the generated trees, comparing them with the target ones produced from the Stanford parser. From this comparison, we can conclude that generated tree structures and POS tag nodes are closely matching the ground truth ones.

As a future work, we plan to explore the effect of introducing higher quality semantic labelling in the image tree and consider larger scale tasks, to determine if the subobptimal performance of the tree-based captioning models is due to quality and size of the data sample.

**Acknowledgments.** This work has been supported by the Italian Ministry of Education, University, and Research (MIUR) under project SIR 2014 LIST-IT (grant n. RBSI14STDE).

## References

1. Bacciu, D., Bruno, A.: Deep tree transductions - a short survey. In: Oneto, L., Navarin, N., Sperduti, A., Anguita, D. (eds.) INNSBDDL 2019. PINNS, vol. 1, pp. 236–245. Springer, Cham (2020). https://doi.org/10.1007/978-3-030-16841-4_25
2. Bacciu, D., Micheli, A., Sperduti, A.: Compositional generative mapping for tree-structured data-part I: bottom-up probabilistic modeling of trees. IEEE Trans. Neural Netw. Learn. Syst. **23**(12), 1987–2002 (2012). https://doi.org/10.1109/TNNLS.2012.2222044

3. Bacciu, D., Micheli, A., Sperduti, A.: An input-output hidden Markov model for tree transductions. Neurocomputing **112**, 34–46 (2013)
4. Cho, K., et al: Learning phrase representations using RNN encoder-decoder for statistical machine translation. arXiv preprint arXiv:1406.1078 (2014)
5. Dong, L., Lapata, M.: Language to logical form with neural attention. arXiv preprint arXiv:1601.01280 (2016)
6. Frasconi, P., Gori, M., Sperduti, A.: A general framework for adaptive processing of data structures. IEEE Trans. Neural Netw. **9**(5), 768–786 (1998). https://doi.org/10.1109/72.712151
7. He, K., Zhang, X., Ren, S., Sun, J.: Deep residual learning for image recognition. arxiv 2015. arXiv preprint arXiv:1512.03385 (2015)
8. Hochreiter, S., Schmidhuber, J.: Long short-term memory. Neural Comput. **9**(8), 1735–1780 (1997)
9. Ioffe, S., Szegedy, C.: Batch normalization: accelerating deep network training by reducing internal covariate shift. In: International Conference on Machine Learning, pp. 448–456. PMLR (2015)
10. Klein, D., Manning, C.D.: Accurate unlexicalized parsing. In: Proceedings of the 41st Annual Meeting of the Association for Computational Linguistics, pp. 423–430 (2003)
11. Kuznetsova, P., Ordonez, V., Berg, T.L., Choi, Y.: TreeTalk: composition and compression of trees for image descriptions. Trans. Assoc. Comput. Linguist. **2**, 351–362 (2014)
12. Lin, T.-Y., et al.: Microsoft COCO: common objects in context. In: Fleet, D., Pajdla, T., Schiele, B., Tuytelaars, T. (eds.) ECCV 2014. LNCS, vol. 8693, pp. 740–755. Springer, Cham (2014). https://doi.org/10.1007/978-3-319-10602-1_48
13. Liu, T., Seyedhosseini, M., Tasdizen, T.: Image segmentation using hierarchical merge tree. IEEE Trans. Image Process. **25**(10), 4596–4607 (2016)
14. Szegedy, C., et al.: Going deeper with convolutions. In: Proceedings of the IEEE Conference on Computer Vision and Pattern Recognition, pp. 1–9 (2015)
15. Szegedy, C., Vanhoucke, V., Ioffe, S., Shlens, J., Wojna, Z.: Rethinking the inception architecture for computer vision. arxiv 2015. arXiv preprint arXiv:1512.00567 1512 (2015)
16. Tai, K.S., Socher, R., Manning, C.D.: Improved semantic representations from tree-structured long short-term memory networks. arXiv preprint arXiv:1503.00075 (2015)
17. Vinyals, O., Toshev, A., Bengio, S., Erhan, D.: Show and tell: a neural image caption generator. corr abs/1411.4555 (2014). arXiv preprint arXiv:1411.4555 (2014)
18. Vinyals, O., Toshev, A., Bengio, S., Erhan, D.: Show and tell: lessons learned from the 2015 MSCOCO image captioning challenge. IEEE Trans. Pattern Anal. Mach. Intell. **39**(4), 652–663 (2016)
19. Xu, K., et al.: Show, attend and tell: neural image caption generation with visual attention. In: International Conference on Machine Learning, pp. 2048–2057. PMLR (2015)
20. Young, P., Lai, A., Hodosh, M., Hockenmaier, J.: From image descriptions to visual denotations: new similarity metrics for semantic inference over event descriptions. TACL **2**, 67–78 (2014)

# Reconstructing Electricity Profiles in Submetering Systems Using a GRU-AE Network

Serafín Alonso[✉] [iD], Antonio Morán[iD], Daniel Pérez[iD], Miguel A. Prada[iD], Juan J. Fuertes[iD], and Manuel Domínguez[iD]

Grupo de Investigación en Supervisión, Control y Automatización de Procesos Industriales (SUPPRESS), Escuela de Ing. Industrial, Informática y Aeroespacial, Universidad de León, Campus de Vegazana s/n, 24007 León, Spain
{saloc,a.moran,dperl,ma.prada,jjfuem,manuel.dominguez}@unileon.es
http://suppress.unileon.es

**Abstract.** Data are key for providing added value in the Industry 4.0 paradigm, benefiting differentiation and innovation. However, high quality data, i.e., reliable and accurate data from sensors, are required. Nowadays, energy meters are being installed in many industries to achieve holistic submetering systems. In these systems, data can be lost due to meter faults, maintenance, power failure or communication drops, affecting negatively the data quality crucial for monitoring and decision making. Therefore, missing data should be filled. In this paper, we propose a method (GRU-AE) based on a denoising autoencoder (AE) with gated recurrent unit (GRU) layers in order to reconstruct electricity profiles that contain missing samples in submetering systems. GRU-AE is able to capture temporal and meter relations, filling gaps in the electricity profiles. Two implementations are presented: multi-head GRU-AE and multi-feature GRU-AE. The proposed method has proved to be more effective reconstructing electricity profiles in submetering systems than a similar approach that models each meter independently. GRU-AE could be useful even when more than one meter provide incomplete or no data at the same time. Both GRU-AE implementations provide similar reconstruction errors. However, a multi-feature GRU-AE could be more efficient in large submetering systems.

**Keywords:** Signal reconstruction · Electricity profiles · Submetering systems · GRU neural networks · Autoencoders

## 1 Introduction

Data play an important role in the Industry 4.0 era. Nowadays, industrial systems generate large volumes of data, at a high rate and from heterogeneous

Grant PID2020-117890RB-I00 funded by MCIN/AEI/10.13039/501100011033.

© Springer Nature Switzerland AG 2022
L. Iliadis et al. (Eds.): EANN 2022, CCIS 1600, pp. 247–259, 2022.
https://doi.org/10.1007/978-3-031-08223-8_21

sources, due to the increasing number of sensors in the industry [23]. Data storage, processing and monitoring are main topics in the Industry 4.0 framework, since data contain intrinsic information of the industrial systems operation that can be exploited. Therefore, data are key for providing added value in the industry, benefiting differentiation and innovation [15]. Furthermore, the increasing cost of energy is nowadays a great challenge for all sectors, but specially for industry. With the aim of optimizing energy consumption, smart energy meters are being installed in many industries, achieving holistic submetering systems [11].

Handling data in industry requires high quality data, i.e., reliable and accurate data from sensors. However, there are possible sources of errors in the measurement process such as their installation method, principle of measurement, sensor precision, ambient conditions or electrostatic and electromagnetic interferences, which lead to unreliable data. Errors are not only introduced by the sensor, but also by control and acquisition (SCADA) systems or communication networks due to power failures, communication drops or maintenance. As a result, different types of errors are found in sensor data, including outliers, missing data, bias, drift, noise, constant value, uncertainties and stuck-at-zero [20]. Missing data or gaps are one of the most common problems in industrial applications, leading to a smaller size of trusted data that degrades their quality and biases the results and conclusions [20]. Therefore, a preprocessing step is required to handle missing values or gaps (and other potential errors) before further processing. The treatment of missing data from sensors aims to reconstruct data by filling existing gaps, i.e. empty observations from sensors (see Fig. 1).

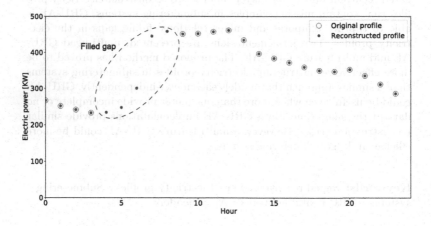

**Fig. 1.** Reconstructing electricity profile with gaps.

Energy meters are able to measure, storage and communicate data [19] and are located in the energy supply and distribution systems, covering upstream as well as downstream strategic points. Thus, there are relations among meters since, for instance, the sum of energy measured by downstream meters should be the energy measured by an upstream meter. In this paper, we propose an autoencoder with recurrent layers in order to reconstruct electricity profiles containing missing samples in submetering systems. The proposed method considers all meters within a submetering system jointly, instead of contemplating each meter independently, in order to capture relations and interactions among meters. This method also extracts temporal patterns, with the final aim of filling potential gaps in the electricity profiles.

The structure of this paper is as follows: the state of the art is reviewed in Sect. 2. The proposed method is presented in Sect. 3. Section 4 describes the experiments, presents the results and discusses them. Finally, in Sect. 5, conclusions are exposed.

## 2    Related Work

Current smart meters enable the massive collection of consumption data whose analysis provides useful information about industrial systems or customers' habits. Several methods have been investigated, obtaining insights to improve services, management and profits related to energy management [4,22]. Examples of these methods are clustering approaches that have been studied for electrical load pattern grouping [6] and load classification in smart grids environments [24]. Similar techniques based on the $k$-means algorithm were implemented to load and state estimation of domestic [3] and medium voltage smart meters [2] with missing data. Moreover, techniques for analyzing and preventing non-technical losses in power distribution systems were reviewed in detail in [1].

In addition, the progression of smart meters has brought complex scenarios related to diverse technology, data analysis algorithms and frameworks that still have open challenges [4]. The creation of submetering networks makes it possible measuring data not only from the main supply but also from intermediate points in the energy distribution network [18]. A method based on support vector machines was deployed to predict the hourly electricity load of buildings with submetering devices [9]. Electricity submetering data were also used for developing an hourly cooling load prediction model, "RC-S" method, improving the accuracy of previous ones [13].

A common approach is the use of energy disaggregation techniques such as non-intrusive load monitoring (NILM) [12,26] which provide estimations of individual consumption in relation to the total energy measurement. These algorithms include methods ranging from hidden Markov models to deep neural networks [14,27]. A function is computed for obtaining that relation so that corresponding individual estimations can be used for filling the gaps of failed measurements [10]. The main problem occurs when there are gaps affecting the total consumption, which hampers the correct computation of individual estimations.

On the other hand, machine learning methods have been developed for energy consumption forecasting, also combining them in hybrid models [7]. In this sense, deep recurrent neural networks have been evaluated for short-term building energy predictions [8] and multi-step ahead time series prediction [5] showing an enhancement with respect to previously proposed methods. To address the problem of missing data, three different architectures of autoencoders –convolutional, long short-term memory (LSTM) and feed-forward– have been developed for short-term time series reconstruction, which could also be used for predicting indoor environment [16]. Then, these architectures have been also applied to the signal reconstruction of room temperature measurements with applicability in different domains [17].

This work aims to advance the study of recurrent autoencoders in order to explore its performance in reconstructing time series data. This addresses the problem of missing values in submetering systems. The proposed method is able to model temporal information accurately including long-term dependencies and, at the same time, to acquire the information about the submetering system. As main drawback, this method requires a vast amount of data from multiple meters and so, long time for training. The proposed method could be applied not only to reconstruct electricity profiles previously to detect anomalies or characterize consumers but also in other engineering areas, for instance, in structural and mechanical processes, as well as, in environment and climate and medical fields.

## 3  The Proposed Method

The proposed method should be able to learn to reconstruct each meter data in a submetering system, i.e. the output data (reconstructed) should match the input data. However, potential missing samples should be considered in the input data. Moreover, the proposed method should consider temporal information, since electricity profiles from meters possess certain periodicity (daily, weekly, monthly, etc.). Finally, the proposed method should learn the relations among meters within a submetering system, since it could useful to estimate missing samples in data from one of the meters based on trusted data from other meters.

For that purpose, the proposed method is based on a denoising autoencoder with recurrent layers. The autoencoder (AE) architecture is in charge of recreating input data whereas the recurrent network is used for capturing temporal patterns in electricity profiles. If input data only contain trusted data, it must be corrupted by randomly turning some of the input values in the training data set to zero in order to generate missing values [21]. Gated Recurrent Units (GRU) are chosen instead of other recurrent neural networks, such as Long Short-Term Memory (LSTM) since they are simpler, train faster and perform better with fewer training data [25]. The proposed method (GRU-AE) can be implemented following two different deep structures: a multi-head structure (**Multi-head GRU-AE**), in which an independent GRU is used to process each meter data, and a multi-feature structure (**Multi-feature GRU-AE**), in which only one GRU with several features (as many features as meters) is used to process together each meter data. Figure 2 shows the two implementations of the proposed method: A multi-head GRU-AE implementation is depicted in Fig. 2a and a multi-feature GRU-AE is shown in Fig. 2b.

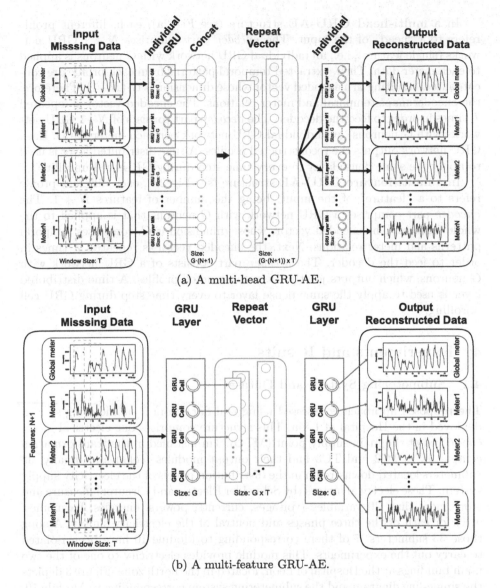

(a) A multi-head GRU-AE.

(b) A multi-feature GRU-AE.

**Fig. 2.** The proposed method (GRU-AE).

Let us define a submetering system containing one global meter together with $N$ downstream submeters. These meters provide data and the profiles are generated by windowing meter data with size $T$. For example, if daily electricity profiles are used (very common), the window size $T$ will be one day. Therefore, the input to the proposed method is the electricity profiles with missing samples (corrupted values) and the output of the method is the complete electricity profiles.

In a **multi-head GRU-AE** structure (see Fig. 2a), each different profile refers to a "head" of the input. The *encoder* part comprises $N + 1$ GRU networks (single feature), i.e., an individual GRU network with $G$ neurons is applied to each meter data. Then, extracted temporal patterns from each profile are concatenated, resulting in a encoded vector whose dimension is $G \cdot (N+1)$. Therefore, the encoder maps temporal and meter relations. The encoded vector is repeated $T$ times in order to feed the decoder. The *decoder* part consists of $N+1$ GRU networks with $G$ neurons (an individual GRU network per each meter data). Each GRU network outputs the reconstructed profiles. A time distributed layer is used to apply the same dense layer to every time step during GRUs cell unrolling.

In a **multi-feature GRU-AE** structure (see Fig. 2b), each different profile refers to a "feature" of the input, being the number of features $N + 1$. The *encoder* part comprises a GRU network with $G$ neurons that is applied to the whole features. The encoded vector, whose dimension is $G$, comprises temporal patterns and meter relations. Next, the encoded vector is repeated $T$ times in order to feed the decoder. The *decoder* part consists of a GRU network with $G$ neurons, which outputs jointly the reconstructed profiles. A time distributed layer is used to apply the same dense layer to every time step during GRU cell unrolling.

## 4    Experiments and Results

### 4.1    Submetering System and Dataset

The proposed approach is assessed using real data from a submetering system deployed in the Hospital of León. This structure comprises one electrical meter connected at the main supply point (MTC), 3 m installed in the transformation centers TC1, TC2 and TC3 and their output modules (cells) and, finally, 33 submeters located downstream in the distribution panels of the electricity supply system. These electrical meters (by Schneider Electric and Circutor) measure and store more than 30 variables (voltages, currents, powers, energies, harmonics, etc.) for each of the three phases and neutral of the electricity supply. Among those 33 submeters, 7 of them corresponding to Module 10 have been isolated to carry out the experiments. This module provides electricity to one of the two main buildings at the Hospital of León, located in the north zone. Figure 3 depicts the single-line diagram and the submetering system corresponding to Module 10. Electricity is supplied to Module 10 from TC1. For that purpose, downstream, a transformer 13.2 KV/400 V is used to reduce the voltage. A meter installed in the output cell measures overall electricity supply to the north building. In turn, module 10 supplies electricity to 6 zones in the north building. An individual meter is connected to each zone. Table 1 lists the mentioned meters corresponding to Module 10.

Data were collected from this submetering system using a sampling period of 1 min, but then data were resampled each 1 h in order to build daily electricity profiles. Only trusted data were selected, so that electricity profiles for 504 days

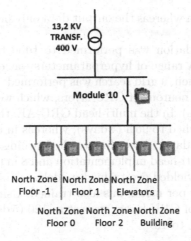

**Fig. 3.** Electrical submetering scheme of the module 10 at the Hospital of León.

**Table 1.** Electrical meters located in the north building at the Hospital of León (Module 10).

| Meter no. | Zone |
|-----------|------|
| #0 | Module 10 |
| #1 | North Zone Floor -1 |
| #2 | North Zone Floor 0 |
| #3 | North Zone Floor 1 |
| #4 | North Zone Floor 2 |
| #5 | North Zone Elevators |
| #6 | North Zone Building |

with no errors were used. As a result, the dataset comprises 504 daily electricity profiles with 24 samples for 7 m (a global meter and 6 submeters).

## 4.2 Experiments

Before proceeding with the experiments, the dataset described above was standardized between $[-1, 1]$ and split into training and validation dataset (70% of data) and test dataset (30%). Since the original dataset only contains trusted data, gaps were generated for each meter. Random gaps with different positions and lengths were introduced in all meters, being the percentage of missing samples over 27% of total samples. All potential combinations were considered, i.e., faults could appear in one meter, two meters or even in all meters at the same time. The dataset was augmented to include trusted and vacant data, so the overall size was 64512 (504 × 128) electricity profiles. Note that input data has trusted and unfilled data whereas the output data only possesses the corresponding trusted data.

A 10-fold cross-validation was performed to tune the hyperparameters of the proposed method. A range of hyperparameters was established after several preliminary runs and, then, a grid search was performed. The main parameter to tune was the number of neurons of GRU layers, which were chosen between 24 h (1 day) and 168 h (7 days). In the multi-head GRU-AE, the number of neurons of GRU layers was established to 96 h (4 days), whereas in the multi-feature GRU-AE, it was set to 144 (6 days). According to the learning curves, training epochs were set to 10 in the multi-head implementation and 8 in the multi-feature one. A high number of epochs yielded overtrained models, so this choice was dismissed. An individual GRU-AE per meter was also trained. Using the same procedure, the number of neurons of GRU layers was set to 120 (5 days) for each meter and training epochs were set to 10.

## 4.3   Results and Discussion

Reconstruction errors are computed only with respect the missing samples. MAPE (Mean Absolute Percentage Error) and RMSE (Root Mean Square Error) have been chosen as evaluation metrics.

Table 2 presents reconstruction errors using validation dataset. This table contains mean and standard deviation values of MAPE and RMSE errors, which were computed for each fold and each meter (global meter #0 and submeters #1, #2, ... ,#6). Moreover, average (Avg.) errors were computed as global errors for overall submetering system. Multi-head GRU-AE yields average errors (both MAPE and RMSE) slightly lower than 5, while multi-feature GRU-AE provides average errors slightly higher than 5, so both implementations of the proposed method give similar results. On the contrary, average errors provided by an individual GRU-AE per meter are considerably higher (MAPE is over 8 and RMSE is over 9). The errors are analogous for all methods with regard to the number of GRU neurons. It can be pointed out that multi-head GRU-AE with 96 neurons (4 days), multi-feature GRU-AE with 144 neurons (6 days), and individual GRU-AE per meter with 120 neurons (5 days) provide the lowest average errors. Multi-feature GRU-AE and individual GRU-AE per meter are able to capture the periodicity (5–7 days) of the electricity profiles better since working days have a high consumption while weekends possess a moderate consumption. There are clear differences in both errors among meters. For example, meters with a high range (#0, #1 and #6 with, respectively, 600, 90 and 145 kW) possess low MAPE errors but high RMSE errors. On the contrary, MAPE and RMSE errors for the remaining meters with lower ranges (#2, #3, #4 and #5) are homogeneous. Meter #1 requires special attention since it has errors above the average values. It could be due to the nature of the consumption in this building zone where several loads are turned on-off and therefore, the electricity profiles in this zone are very shifting. In general, all standard deviations are very low, indicating minimal variability of the results with each fold.

**Table 2.** Reconstruction errors using validation dataset.

| Method | Neur. (GRU) | #0 | #1 | #2 | #3 | #4 | #5 | #6 | Avg. |
|---|---|---|---|---|---|---|---|---|---|
| | | MAPE (mean ± std) | | | | | | | |
| GRU-AE (Multi-head) | 24 | 2.92 ± 0.14 | 9.82 ± 0.32 | 3.72 ± 0.19 | 6.38 ± 0.52 | 5.37 ± 0.29 | 3.44 ± 0.09 | 3.75 ± 0.21 | 5.06 ± 0.25 |
| | 48 | 2.75 ± 0.13 | 9.42 ± 0.30 | 3.63 ± 0.14 | 6.02 ± 0.41 | 5.12 ± 0.27 | 3.32 ± 0.11 | 3.48 ± 0.20 | 4.82 ± 0.22 |
| | 72 | 2.67 ± 0.19 | 9.07 ± 0.25 | 3.67 ± 0.15 | 6.00 ± 0.34 | 5.08 ± 0.22 | 3.37 ± 0.15 | 3.45 ± 0.15 | 4.76 ± 0.21 |
| | 96 | 2.66 ± 0.16 | 9.06 ± 0.22 | 3.66 ± 0.12 | 5.88 ± 0.39 | 5.09 ± 0.28 | 3.31 ± 0.15 | 3.38 ± 0.25 | **4.72 ± 0.22** |
| | 120 | 2.72 ± 0.18 | 8.98 ± 0.41 | 3.69 ± 0.15 | 5.93 ± 0.33 | 5.06 ± 0.29 | 3.28 ± 0.11 | 3.48 ± 0.17 | 4.73 ± 0.23 |
| | 144 | 2.77 ± 0.20 | 9.06 ± 0.28 | 3.72 ± 0.15 | 6.03 ± 0.46 | 5.17 ± 0.31 | 3.26 ± 0.06 | 3.46 ± 0.24 | 4.78 ± 0.24 |
| | 168 | 2.67 ± 0.19 | 9.10 ± 0.34 | 3.70 ± 0.18 | 5.96 ± 0.38 | 5.03 ± 0.30 | 3.35 ± 0.14 | 3.48 ± 0.24 | 4.75 ± 0.25 |
| GRU-AE (Multi-feature) | 24 | 3.30 ± 0.16 | 10.20 ± 0.42 | 3.85 ± 0.17 | 6.70 ± 0.37 | 5.84 ± 0.31 | 3.69 ± 0.17 | 4.16 ± 0.21 | 5.39 ± 0.26 |
| | 48 | 3.26 ± 0.18 | 10.02 ± 0.30 | 3.79 ± 0.17 | 6.67 ± 0.37 | 5.88 ± 0.36 | 3.60 ± 0.18 | 4.08 ± 0.20 | 5.33 ± 0.25 |
| | 72 | 3.04 ± 0.15 | 9.75 ± 0.36 | 3.77 ± 0.20 | 6.52 ± 0.33 | 5.75 ± 0.29 | 3.58 ± 0.18 | 4.10 ± 0.20 | 5.22 ± 0.24 |
| | 96 | 3.04 ± 0.15 | 9.61 ± 0.33 | 3.78 ± 0.19 | 6.53 ± 0.31 | 5.69 ± 0.30 | 3.62 ± 0.21 | 4.10 ± 0.18 | 5.20 ± 0.24 |
| | 120 | 3.00 ± 0.13 | 9.56 ± 0.30 | 3.82 ± 0.21 | 6.49 ± 0.41 | 5.68 ± 0.36 | 3.65 ± 0.18 | 4.10 ± 0.23 | 5.19 ± 0.26 |
| | 144 | 2.97 ± 0.14 | 9.60 ± 0.39 | 3.78 ± 0.19 | 6.50 ± 0.36 | 5.66 ± 0.35 | 3.63 ± 0.15 | 4.08 ± 0.20 | **5.17 ± 0.25** |
| | 168 | 3.03 ± 0.17 | 9.54 ± 0.44 | 3.74 ± 0.17 | 6.53 ± 0.41 | 5.71 ± 0.33 | 3.62 ± 0.15 | 4.08 ± 0.22 | 5.18 ± 0.27 |
| GRU-AE (Per meter) | 24 | 5.77 ± 0.34 | 12.04 ± 0.49 | 4.54 ± 0.14 | 13.47 ± 0.96 | 8.89 ± 0.39 | 6.22 ± 0.21 | 6.97 ± 0.46 | 8.27 ± 0.43 |
| | 48 | 5.75 ± 0.38 | 11.99 ± 0.49 | 4.54 ± 0.12 | 13.17 ± 0.85 | 8.94 ± 0.52 | 6.30 ± 0.48 | 7.03 ± 0.52 | 8.24 ± 0.48 |
| | 72 | 5.73 ± 0.25 | 11.90 ± 0.47 | 4.54 ± 0.12 | 13.50 ± 1.04 | 8.90 ± 0.51 | 6.17 ± 0.29 | 7.02 ± 0.54 | 8.25 ± 0.46 |
| | 96 | 5.80 ± 0.35 | 11.97 ± 0.48 | 4.52 ± 0.13 | 13.55 ± 1.09 | 8.96 ± 0.45 | 6.24 ± 0.25 | 6.91 ± 0.43 | 8.28 ± 0.45 |
| | 120 | 5.81 ± 0.34 | 11.88 ± 0.41 | 4.55 ± 0.09 | 13.14 ± 1.06 | 8.90 ± 0.43 | 6.23 ± 0.33 | 6.93 ± 0.56 | **8.20 ± 0.46** |
| | 144 | 5.80 ± 0.34 | 11.87 ± 0.50 | 4.54 ± 0.10 | 13.54 ± 0.92 | 8.91 ± 0.38 | 6.31 ± 0.48 | 6.84 ± 0.52 | 8.26 ± 0.46 |
| | 168 | 5.85 ± 0.36 | 12.02 ± 0.50 | 4.53 ± 0.13 | 13.35 ± 0.98 | 8.82 ± 0.53 | 6.18 ± 0.37 | 6.75 ± 0.46 | 8.21 ± 0.48 |
| | | RMSE (mean ± std) | | | | | | | |
| GRU-AE (Multi-head) | 24 | 14.47 ± 0.96 | 6.85 ± 0.14 | 1.63 ± 0.09 | 1.97 ± 0.21 | 3.06 ± 0.14 | 1.59 ± 0.06 | 4.41 ± 0.21 | 4.85 ± 0.26 |
| | 48 | 13.82 ± 0.98 | 6.67 ± 0.22 | 1.61 ± 0.07 | 1.90 ± 0.22 | 2.94 ± 0.13 | 1.55 ± 0.06 | 4.12 ± 0.22 | 4.66 ± 0.27 |
| | 72 | 13.40 ± 1.28 | 6.58 ± 0.22 | 1.62 ± 0.06 | 1.93 ± 0.17 | 2.95 ± 0.17 | 1.57 ± 0.09 | 4.10 ± 0.22 | 4.59 ± 0.32 |
| | 96 | 13.38 ± 1.38 | 6.63 ± 0.22 | 1.63 ± 0.06 | 1.85 ± 0.19 | 2.94 ± 0.18 | 1.55 ± 0.11 | 4.07 ± 0.33 | **4.58 ± 0.35** |
| | 120 | 13.83 ± 1.23 | 6.65 ± 0.20 | 1.64 ± 0.06 | 1.90 ± 0.21 | 2.95 ± 0.18 | 1.53 ± 0.07 | 4.23 ± 0.31 | 4.68 ± 0.32 |
| | 144 | 14.12 ± 1.67 | 6.77 ± 0.14 | 1.65 ± 0.06 | 1.95 ± 0.28 | 3.02 ± 0.16 | 1.54 ± 0.08 | 4.34 ± 0.48 | 4.77 ± 0.41 |
| | 168 | 13.45 ± 1.41 | 6.81 ± 0.19 | 1.65 ± 0.07 | 1.90 ± 0.20 | 2.91 ± 0.18 | 1.57 ± 0.10 | 4.19 ± 0.28 | 4.64 ± 0.35 |
| GRU-AE (Multi-feature) | 24 | 16.57 ± 0.82 | 6.93 ± 0.19 | 1.68 ± 0.07 | 2.14 ± 0.14 | 3.32 ± 0.15 | 1.73 ± 0.05 | 4.77 ± 0.21 | 5.31 ± 0.23 |
| | 48 | 16.22 ± 1.08 | 6.84 ± 0.19 | 1.67 ± 0.08 | 2.13 ± 0.17 | 3.33 ± 0.16 | 1.68 ± 0.06 | 4.65 ± 0.24 | 5.22 ± 0.28 |
| | 72 | 15.35 ± 1.11 | 6.75 ± 0.20 | 1.66 ± 0.08 | 2.09 ± 0.16 | 3.27 ± 0.12 | 1.67 ± 0.06 | 4.66 ± 0.16 | 5.06 ± 0.27 |
| | 96 | 15.23 ± 0.92 | 6.66 ± 0.16 | 1.66 ± 0.08 | 2.05 ± 0.14 | 3.21 ± 0.12 | 1.67 ± 0.07 | 4.67 ± 0.21 | 5.02 ± 0.24 |
| | 120 | 14.94 ± 0.90 | 6.60 ± 0.23 | 1.67 ± 0.08 | 2.01 ± 0.13 | 3.20 ± 0.14 | 1.67 ± 0.04 | 4.61 ± 0.22 | 4.96 ± 0.25 |
| | 144 | 14.87 ± 0.83 | 6.60 ± 0.23 | 1.66 ± 0.08 | 2.01 ± 0.16 | 3.18 ± 0.15 | 1.66 ± 0.04 | 4.61 ± 0.22 | **4.94 ± 0.24** |
| | 168 | 15.19 ± 1.15 | 6.62 ± 0.28 | 1.65 ± 0.08 | 2.05 ± 0.15 | 3.22 ± 0.15 | 1.66 ± 0.04 | 4.62 ± 0.24 | 5.00 ± 0.30 |
| GRU-AE (Per meter) | 24 | 33.83 ± 1.65 | 8.51 ± 0.26 | 2.02 ± 0.06 | 5.20 ± 0.28 | 5.73 ± 0.20 | 3.63 ± 0.13 | 9.89 ± 0.59 | 9.83 ± 0.45 |
| | 48 | 33.83 ± 1.98 | 8.46 ± 0.23 | 2.02 ± 0.06 | 5.14 ± 0.31 | 5.76 ± 0.25 | 3.68 ± 0.23 | 9.97 ± 0.67 | 9.84 ± 0.53 |
| | 72 | 33.51 ± 1.25 | 8.41 ± 0.25 | 2.02 ± 0.05 | 5.23 ± 0.23 | 5.77 ± 0.26 | 3.61 ± 0.18 | 10.05 ± 0.73 | 9.80 ± 0.42 |
| | 96 | 33.77 ± 1.69 | 8.43 ± 0.27 | 2.02 ± 0.06 | 5.15 ± 0.33 | 5.78 ± 0.20 | 3.68 ± 0.12 | 9.92 ± 0.52 | 9.82 ± 0.46 |
| | 120 | 33.74 ± 1.49 | 8.36 ± 0.24 | 2.03 ± 0.05 | 5.15 ± 0.32 | 5.76 ± 0.27 | 3.66 ± 0.17 | 9.83 ± 0.71 | **9.79 ± 0.46** |
| | 144 | 33.88 ± 1.57 | 8.38 ± 0.21 | 2.02 ± 0.05 | 5.22 ± 0.23 | 5.77 ± 0.15 | 3.67 ± 0.23 | 9.74 ± 0.72 | 9.81 ± 0.45 |
| | 168 | 34.34 ± 1.79 | 8.40 ± 0.25 | 2.02 ± 0.06 | 5.21 ± 0.26 | 5.71 ± 0.28 | 3.63 ± 0.16 | 9.67 ± 0.68 | 9.85 ± 0.50 |

Table 3 presents reconstruction errors using test dataset for each meter (global meter #0 and submeters #1, #2, ... ,#6). Moreover, average (Avg.) errors were computed as global errors for overall submetering system. Test experiments were performed using the hyperparameters that gave the best results in the validation step, i.e., a multi-head GRU-AE with 96 neurons, a multi-head GRU-AE with 144 neurons and an individual GRU-AE per meter with 120 neurons. As expected, test errors (MAPE and RMSE) are slightly higher than validation errors. Both implementations (multi-head and mul-feature GRU-AE) yield similar errors (around 5), whereas an individual GRU-AE per meter provides errors which are almost double (MAPE is over 9 and RMSE over 11). Global meter (#0) has the highest RMSE errors, but the lowest MAPE errors.

It presents smooth profiles with maximum power values. Again, electricity profiles from meter #1 are more difficult to reconstruct due to their irregular nature.

**Table 3.** Reconstruction errors using test dataset.

| Method | Neur. (GRU) | Meters | | | | | | | |
|---|---|---|---|---|---|---|---|---|---|
| | | #0 | #1 | #2 | #3 | #4 | #5 | #6 | Avg. |
| | | MAPE | | | | | | | |
| GRU-AE (Multi-head) | 96 | 3.28 | 8.50 | 4.31 | 6.15 | 6.91 | 3.96 | 4.25 | 5.34 |
| GRU-AE (Multi-feature) | 144 | 3.58 | 8.24 | 4.26 | 5.81 | 6.50 | 4.41 | 4.32 | 5.30 |
| GRU-AE (Per meter) | 120 | 6.31 | 11.35 | 4.98 | 12.12 | 10.50 | 7.27 | 11.95 | 9.21 |
| | | RMSE | | | | | | | |
| GRU-AE (Multi-head) | 96 | 17.05 | 6.56 | 1.88 | 2.03 | 3.60 | 1.77 | 5.05 | 5.42 |
| GRU-AE (Multi-feature) | 144 | 18.08 | 6.36 | 1.85 | 1.94 | 3.36 | 1.91 | 5.08 | 5.51 |
| GRU-AE (Per meter) | 120 | 37.34 | 9.16 | 2.18 | 4.99 | 6.80 | 4.32 | 18.64 | 11.92 |

Summarizing the results, the proposed method based on a denoising autoencoder with GRU layers (GRU-AE) is promising for reconstructing electricity
profiles in the industry, although it could also be applied to reconstruct signals
in other domains. GRU-AE method is able to take advantage of the temporal information, as well as of the relations among meters (or other sensors) in
submetering systems. Therefore, GRU-AE method is more efficient filling gaps
when the whole submetering system is considered, instead of reconstructing each
meter data independently. Using the proposed method, electricity profiles with
over 27% of missing samples can be reconstructed with an error around 5% if the
whole submetering system is addressed. Furthermore, this method would be useful even when more than one meter provide incomplete or no data at the same
time. Regarding to which implementation (multi-head or multi-feature GRU-
AE) should be selected, it can be stated that both implementations yield comparable results, but multi-feature GRU-AE would be preferred in large submetering systems with many meters. In this case, both training and inference times
required by a multi-head GRU-AE could be much longer due to the high number of patterns resulting in the concatenation layer. In contrast, multi-feature
GRU-AE would have more bounded times.

# 5    Conclusions

In this paper, we propose a method (GRU-AE) based on a denoising autoencoder (AE) with GRU recurrent layers in order to reconstruct electricity profiles containing missing samples in submetering systems. GRU-AE is able to capture temporal and meter relations, filling potential gaps in the electricity profiles. Two GRU-AE implementations are presented: a multi-head GRU-AE in which an independent GRU (one feature) is used to process each meter data and a multi-feature GRU-AE in which only one GRU with several features (as many features as meters) is used.

The proposed method has proved to be more effective reconstructing electricity profiles in submetering systems than using a similar approach for each meter independently. The reconstruction errors are considerably lower. GRU-AE is able to fill gaps even when more than one meter provide incomplete or no data at the same time. Both GRU-AE implementations provide similar reconstruction errors. However, a multi-feature GRU-AE could be more efficient with a high number of meters in the submetering system.

As future work, other recurrent networks such as LSTM and BiLSTM could be assessed, despite of the fact that the training would be more costly and difficult. Furthermore, 1-dimensional CNNs could bring significant improvements, especially separable CNNs that fit the structure of submetering data. Furthermore, additional stacked layers and nonlinear activation functions could help to capture more relations among meters and an attention layer based on meters could also improve the results. Additionally, results and discussion could be extended by considering longer gaps or even by predicting non-existent profiles due to persistent faults in the time. Reconstruction errors should be assessed in several scenarios.

# References

1. Ahmad, T.: Non-technical loss analysis and prevention using smart meters. Renew. Sustain. Energy Rev. **72**, 573–589 (2017)
2. Al-Wakeel, A., Wu, J., Jenkins, N.: State estimation of medium voltage distribution networks using smart meter measurements. Appl. Energy **184**, 207–218 (2016)
3. Al-Wakeel, A., Wu, J., Jenkins, N.: K-means based load estimation of domestic smart meter measurements. Appl. Energy **194**, 333–342 (2017)
4. Alahakoon, D., Yu, X.: Smart electricity meter data intelligence for future energy systems: a survey. IEEE Trans. Industr. Inf. **12**(1), 425–436 (2016). https://doi.org/10.1109/TII.2015.2414355
5. Chandra, R., Goyal, S., Gupta, R.: Evaluation of deep learning models for multi-step ahead time series prediction. IEEE Access **9**, 83105–83123 (2021). https://doi.org/10.1109/ACCESS.2021.3085085
6. Chicco, G.: Overview and performance assessment of the clustering methods for electrical load pattern grouping. Energy **42**(1), 68–80 (2012)
7. Deb, C., Zhang, F., Yang, J., Lee, S.E., Shah, K.W.: A review on time series forecasting techniques for building energy consumption. Renew. Sustain. Energy Rev. **74**, 902–924 (2017)

8. Fan, C., Wang, J., Gang, W., Li, S.: Assessment of deep recurrent neural network-based strategies for short-term building energy predictions. Appl. Energy **236**, 700–710 (2019). https://doi.org/10.1016/j.apenergy.2018.12.004

9. Fu, Y., Li, Z., Zhang, H., Xu, P.: Using support vector machine to predict next day electricity load of public buildings with sub-metering devices. Procedia Eng. **121**, 1016–1022 (2015). https://doi.org/10.1016/j.proeng.2015.09.097

10. García-Pérez, D., Pérez-López, D., Díaz-Blanco, I., González-Muñiz, A., Domínguez-González, M., Cuadrado Vega, A.A.: Fully-convolutional denoising auto-encoders for NILM in large non-residential buildings. IEEE Trans. Smart Grid **12**(3), 2722–2731 (2021). https://doi.org/10.1109/TSG.2020.3047712

11. Halstenberg, F.A., Lindow, K., Stark, R.: Implementation of an energy metering system for smart production. In: Hu, A.H., Matsumoto, M., Kuo, T.C., Smith, S. (eds.) Technologies and Eco-innovation towards Sustainability II, pp. 127–137. Springer, Singapore (2019). https://doi.org/10.1007/978-981-13-1196-3_11

12. Hart, G.W.: Nonintrusive appliance load monitoring. Proc. IEEE **80**(12), 1870–1891 (1992)

13. Ji, Y., Xu, P., Duan, P., Lu, X.: Estimating hourly cooling load in commercial buildings using a thermal network model and electricity submetering data. Appl. Energy **169**, 309–323 (2016). https://doi.org/10.1016/j.apenergy.2016.02.036

14. Kelly, J., Knottenbelt, W.: Neural NILM: deep neural networks applied to energy disaggregation. In: Proceedings of the 2nd ACM International Conference on Embedded Systems for Energy-Efficient Built Environments, pp. 55–64 (2015)

15. Klingenberg, C.O., Borges, M.A.V., Antunes Jr, J.A.V.: Industry 4.0 as a data-driven paradigm: a systematic literature review on technologies. J. Manuf. Technol. Manag. **32**(3), 570–592 (2021). https://doi.org/10.1108/JMTM-09-2018-0325

16. Liguori, A., Markovic, R., Dam, T.T.H., Frisch, J., van Treeck, C., Causone, F.: Indoor environment data time-series reconstruction using autoencoder neural networks. Build. Environ. **191**, 107623 (2021). https://doi.org/10.1016/j.buildenv.2021.107623

17. Liguori, A., Markovic, R., Frisch, J., Wagner, A., Causone, F., Treeck, C.: A gap-filling method for room temperature data based on autoencoder neural networks. In: Proceedings of IBPSA Building Simulation Conference, September 2021

18. Morán, A., Alonso, S., Pérez, D., Prada, M.A., Fuertes, J.J., Domínguez, M.: Feature extraction from building submetering networks using deep learning. Sensors **20**(13) (2020). https://doi.org/10.3390/s20133665

19. Sun, Q., et al.: A comprehensive review of smart energy meters in intelligent energy networks. IEEE Internet Things J. **3**(4), 464–479 (2016). https://doi.org/10.1109/JIOT.2015.2512325

20. Teh, H.Y., Kempa-Liehr, A.W., Wang, K.I.-K.: Sensor data quality: a systematic review. J. Big Data **7**(1), 1–49 (2020). https://doi.org/10.1186/s40537-020-0285-1

21. Vincent, P., Larochelle, H., Lajoie, I., Bengio, Y., Manzagol, P.A.: Stacked denoising autoencoders: learning useful representations in a deep network with a local denoising criterion. J. Mach. Learn. Res. **11**, 3371–3408 (2010)

22. Wang, Y., Chen, Q., Hong, T., Kang, C.: Review of smart meter data analytics: applications, methodologies, and challenges. IEEE Trans. Smart Grid **10**(3), 3125–3148 (2018)

23. Yan, J., Meng, Y., Lu, L., Li, L.: Industrial big data in an industry 4.0 environment: challenges, schemes, and applications for predictive maintenance. IEEE Access **5**, 23484–23491 (2017). https://doi.org/10.1109/ACCESS.2017.2765544

24. Yang, S.l., Shen, C., et al.: A review of electric load classification in smart grid environment. Renewable Sustain. Energy Rev. **24**, 103–110 (2013)

25. Yang, S., Yu, X., Zhou, Y.: LSTM and GRU neural network performance comparison study: taking yelp review dataset as an example. In: 2020 International Workshop on Electronic Communication and Artificial Intelligence (IWECAI), pp. 98–101 (2020). https://doi.org/10.1109/IWECAI50956.2020.00027
26. Zeifman, M., Roth, K.: Nonintrusive appliance load monitoring: review and outlook. IEEE Trans. Consum. Electron. **57**(1), 76–84 (2011)
27. Zoha, A., Gluhak, A., Imran, M.A., Rajasegarar, S.: Non-intrusive load monitoring approaches for disaggregating energy sensing: a survey. Sensors **12**(12), 16838–16866 (2012)

# Trend and Seasonality Elimination from Relational Data

Jan Motl[✉][iD] and Pavel Kordík[iD]

Czech Technical University Prague, Prague, Czech Republic
jan.motl@fit.cvut.cz

**Abstract.** Detrending and deseasoning is a common preprocessing step in time-series analysis. We argue that the same preprocessing step should be considered on relational data whenever the observations are time-dependent. We applied Hierarchical Generalized Additive Models (HGAMs) to detrend and deseason (D&D) 18 real-world relational datasets. The observed positive effect of D&D on the predictive accuracy is statistically significant. The proposed method of D&D might be used to improve the predictive accuracy of churn, default, or propensity models, among others.

**Keywords:** Time series · Relational learning · Propositionalization

## 1 Introduction

This article is concerned with feature extraction from relational data for supervised learning, like classification or regression. The studied problem is not new and is called propositionalization [14]. But one aspect of propositionalization was frequently ignored in the early propositionalization literature: the data are frequently not just relational, but also temporal. The ignorance of the temporal parts in relational data is quite understandable—neither processing of relational or temporal data is trivial when we want to do it right. This article attempts to narrow the gap between these two worlds by introducing one basic concept from time-series modeling to the realm of propositionalization: *the trend and season removal from relational data*. A simple example of relational data is in Fig. 1.

target table

| target id | target timestamp | target |
|---|---|---|
| 1 | 2021-02-01 00:00:00 | A |
| 2 | 2021-02-01 00:00:00 | B |
| 3 | 2021-02-01 00:00:00 | B |
| 4 | 2021-02-01 00:00:00 | A |

1:n

non-target table

| target id | timestamp | numerical attribute |
|---|---|---|
| 1 | 2021-01-01 07:10:04 | 1999 |
| 1 | 2021-01-22 09:45:05 | 3200 |
| 2 | 2021-01-07 11:30:52 | 43 |
| 4 | 2021-01-05 14:02:32 | 199 |
| 4 | 2021-01-05 14:02:32 | 210 |
| 4 | 2021-01-27 13:41:41 | 250 |

**Fig. 1.** Example relational data: We wish to predict `target` based on timestamped `numerical attribute`.

L. Iliadis et al. (Eds.): EANN 2022, CCIS 1600, pp. 260–268, 2022.
https://doi.org/10.1007/978-3-031-08223-8_22

To illustrate the importance of detrending, consider a predictive model built on financial data. If the model was built on raw data, the accuracy of the model would likely degrade faster than if we build the model on inflation-adjusted ("deflated") data.

To illustrate the importance of deseasoning, consider observing a person for a month. If the person went swimming in a river once during that month, we might want to make different conclusions about the person when that month is June than if the month was January.

To describe the proposed temporal normalization, we have to introduce the basics of propositionalization in Sect. 2 and the relevant parts from time-series analysis in Sect. 3. We then follow with the description of the proposed temporal decomposition on relational data in Sect. 4, performed empirical evaluation in Sect. 5, and the results in Sect. 6. The results are discussed in Sect. 7 and concluded in Sect. 8.

## 2    Propositionalization

Propositionalization is a process of conversion of relational data into the attribute-value format, which conventional machine-learning algorithms can understand (see [14]).

There are many propositionalization methods. In this article we use PredictorFactory[1]. But there are many others, which differ in the direction of data propagation (in [15], the target, which we wish to predict, is propagated to the data, while in [14] the data are propagated toward the target) or the count of the used models (in [15] and [14], only one model is used, while Guo [8] uses as many models, as there are tables in the database).

In this article, when we are talking about propositionalization, we assume that the `target`, which we wish to predict, resides in `target table` (observe Fig. 1). The moment when we wish to make the prediction is defined by `target timestamp`. And the entity for which we wish to make the prediction is defined by `target id`.

To predict the target from other tables than the `target table`, we have to link the tables together. This is done with joins over foreign key constraints [15]. The end state of this *target propagation* is that each table in the database contains the `target column`, `timestamp`, and `id` from the `target table`.

The relationship between the target table and other tables does not always have to be 1:1. When the relationship is 1:n, the content of the tables is *aggregated* to the level of the data in the `target table`. Examples of common aggregate functions for numerical attributes include `min`, `max`, `avg`, `count`, and `stddev`.

The final step of propositionalization then consists of *joining* all the features from the propagated and potentially aggregated tables into a single table in attribute-value format.

---

[1] www.predictorfactory.com.

## 3    Detrending and Deseasoning

The trend and seasonality can be removed with classical methods from time-series analysis like Seasonal and Trend decomposition using Loess (STL) [5], Holt-Winter's seasonal method [10] or Seasonal Autoregressive Integrated Moving Average (SARIMA) [2].

However, these methods are not directly applicable to our data because common implementations of these methods cannot directly deal with:

1. non-uniformly spaced samples [6] (e.g., `non-target table` in Fig. 1 is not sampled at periodic intervals),
2. multiple values per sample period [11,21] (e.g., the $4^{nth}$ and the $5^{nth}$ records in the `non-target table` have the same `timestamp`),
3. hierarchical dependencies between the data [12,13,16] (e.g., `target id 1` in the `non-target table` has, on average, higher `numerical attribute` than `target id 2`).

The listed deficiencies can be handled by Hierarchical Generalized Additive Models (HGAMs) [19]. HGAMs are a combination of Generalized Additive Models (GAMs) [9] and Hierarchical Generalized Linear Models (HGLMs) [4]. GAM part takes care of modeling seasonality with cyclic cubic regression splines, while HGLM part takes care of modeling trends and non-independence in the data that arises from hierarchical structures. Note that HGAMs, just like GAMs or HGLMs, can handle non-uniformly spaced samples and multiple values per sample period.

## 4    Method

Assuming additive decomposition, a time-series $y$ at time $t$ can be written as $y_t = S_t + T_t + R_t$, where $S_t$ is the seasonal component, $T_t$ is the trend component, and $R_t$ is the remainder component.

However, in this article, we assume that the data have a two-level hierarchical structure. The first level of data clustering is defined by `target id`. The second level is the whole population. This hierarchical structure is used because it allows us to model both 1:1 and 1:$n$ relationships between `target id` and data in a relational dataset.

A two-level hierarchical time-series can be written as $y_{t,i} = S_t + T_t + T_{t,i} + B_i + R_{t,i}$, where $i$ is a specific `target id`, $S_t$ is the population seasonal component, $T_t$ is the population trend component, $T_{t,i}$ is the trend of $i$ (random slope in HGLM literature), $B_i$ is the bias of $i$ (random intercept in HGLM literature), and $R_{t,i}$ is the remainder component.

Furthermore, we want to support exogenous variables in the decomposition because the data in the tables do not have to be always commensurable. For example, `transaction` table in Financial dataset [1] contains all possible types of transactions, differentiated by columns `type` and `operation` (the used datasets

are discussed in Sect. 5). To block the effect of the exogenous variables, we write
the decomposition as:

$$y_{t,i} = \beta X_{t,i} + S_t + T_t + T_{t,i} + B_i + R_{t,i}, \tag{1}$$

where $X_{t,i}$ is a vector of exogenous variables (fixed effects in HGLM literature)
and $\beta$ is a vector of regression coefficients. An example decomposition is in Fig. 2.

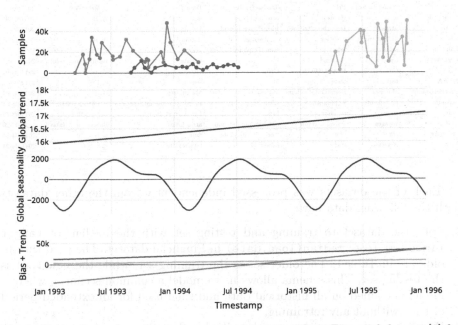

**Fig. 2.** Example decomposition of `transaction.value` from Financial dataset [1] for
incoming transactions.

## 5  Experiments

In the introduction, we argued that the trend and seasonality of data are important. However, does it really impact the quality of the prediction? And if yes,
how much?

To answer these questions, we empirically compare accuracies of models build
on raw data vs. temporarily normalized data on 18 real (non-artificial) temporal
datasets from relational repository [17] (see the list in Table 1). These datasets
were selected, because they follow the data structure depicted in Fig. 1.

**Table 1.** List of the used relational datasets from relational repository [17]. Regression and polynomial classification problems were converted to binary problems with the logic described in Classes column. Threshold column defines the split to training and testing set.

| Dataset | Target table | Target column | Target id | Target timestamp | Classes | Threshold |
|---|---|---|---|---|---|---|
| Accidents | nesreca | klas_nesreca | id_nesreca | cas_nesreca | B, not B | 2001-06-30 |
| Airline | On_Time | ArrDel15 | rownum | FlightDate | 0, 1 | 2016-01-16 |
| BasketballMen | teams | rank | tmID, year | year | ≤ 4, >4 | 1974 |
| BasketballWomen | teams | playoff | tmID, year | year | N, Y | 2003 |
| CCS | transactions_1k | Price | TransactionID | Date | ≤ 500, >500 | 2012-08-24 |
| Financial | loan | status | account_id | date | A, B | 1997-02-05 |
| FNHK | pripady | Delka_hospitalizace | Identifikace_pripadu | Datum_prijeti | ≤ 7, >7 | 2014-06-16 |
| Geneea | hl_hlasovani | vysledek | id_hlasovani | datum | A, R | 2014-12-02 |
| Lahman | salaries | salary | teamID, playerID, lgID | yearID | ≤ 500000, >500000 | 1998 |
| LegalActs | legalacts | ActKind | id | update | Solution, not Solution | 2012-07-24 |
| NBA | Game | ResultOfTeam1 | GameId | Date | -1, 1 | 2014-04-02 |
| NCAA | target | team_id1_wins | id | season | 0, 1 | 2012 |
| PremierLeague | Matches | ResultOfTeamHome | MatchID | MatchDate | -1, 1 | 2014-01-01 |
| Seznam | probehnuto | kc_proklikano | client_id, sluzba | month_year_datum_transakce | ≤ 1000, >1000 | 2014-08-01 |
| Stats | users | Reputation | Id | LastAccessDate | ≤ 10, >10 | 2014-03-29 |
| VOC | voyages | arrival_harbour | number, number_sup | arrival_date | Batavia, not Batavia | 1723-07-20 |
| Walmart | train | units | store_nbr, item_nbr | date | ≤ 10, >10 | 2013-04-15 |
| Yelp | Reviews | stars | review_id | review_date | ≤ 3, >3 | 2011-04-25 |

Each of the datasets was processed independently from the other datasets with the following data flow:

1. Split the dataset to training and testing set with the median of `target timestamp` (e.g.: `median(loan.date)` in Financial dataset. The used thresholds are in Table 1. The older set is the training set, while the newer set is the testing set. This schema allows us to model a common scenario, where a model is trained on all historical data and then used for an extended period of time without any retraining.
2. Perform target propagation, as described in Sect. 2.
3. Fork the flow into the challenger and the baseline group. In the challenger group, we perform temporal normalization. In the baseline group, we keep data as they are. Temporal normalization consists of:
   (a) HGAM training on the training data (we use `mgcv` package in R as illustrated in Listing 1).

```
library(mgcv,lubridate)
fit = gamm(numerical_attribute ~ 1 + exogeneous_attribute + timestamp +
    s(wday(timestamp), bs="cp", k=7), data=df, method="REML",
    random=list(timestamp_as_num=~target_id, target_id=~1))
```

**Listing 1.** Example R code for trend and seasonality fitting. The input data frame `df` is a join of the 2 tables from Fig. 1.

   (b) Global trend $T_t$ and global seasonality $S_t$ removal from both training and testing data.

To see whether it is actually beneficial to perform both detrending and deseasoning, we also evaluate flows, where we only perform detrending, respectively deseasoning.

4. Aggregate numerical attributes with the following aggregate functions: min, max, avg, count, sum, and stddev as described in Sect. 2. We also test adding of local trend $T_{t,i}$ from Equation (1) to the set of aggregates in separate flows.
5. Join the aggregated attributes into a single table.
6. Train Random Forest [3] on the propositionalized training data. We could have chosen any other classifier, but we chose Random Forest, because it can handle dirty data (missing values, outliers, mixture of categorical and numerical attributes, collinearity, etc.) and delivers good results even without meta-parameter tuning [7].
7. Evaluate area under receiver operating characteristics curve (AUC-ROC) on the testing set. We could have chosen any other measure. However, we chose AUC-ROC because ranking measures are generally more sensitive to changes in the prediction than thresholding measures, like classification accuracy (ranking measures detect changes at all possible thresholds while thresholding measures detect changes only at one threshold).

## 6   Results

Empirical results in Table 2 suggest that detrending, deseasoning, and inclusion of trend among the set of the utilized aggregates is better than the baseline, which works on raw data and does not use trend aggregate.

A one-tailed Wilcoxon signed-rank test indicated that AUC-ROC of propositionalization on detrended and deseasoned data with trend as an additional feature generative function was statistically significantly higher than AUC-ROC of baseline propositionalization with $p < 0.00048$.

## 7   Discussion

The empirical results suggest that all the tested enhancements: detrending, deseasoning, and trend feature generative function are overall improving the accuracy of the classification models. This improvement is statistically significant, although when averaged over all the tested datasets, the improvement is modest (1 percent point). In the following paragraphs, we explain the observation and list the limitations of the performed study and the implemented method.

**Table 2.** The effect of global temporal normalization and inclusion of local trend as a feature on testing AUC-ROC. D&D stands for detrended and deseasoned. Bold font indicates the best result for a dataset.

| Dataset | Baseline | Detrended | Deseasoned | D&D | D&D with trend |
|---|---|---|---|---|---|
| Accidents | 0.73 | 0.73 | **0.74** | **0.74** | **0.74** |
| Airline | 0.80 | 0.81 | **0.85** | **0.85** | **0.85** |
| BasketballMen | 0.65 | 0.64 | 0.65 | 0.65 | **0.66** |
| BasketballWomen | 0.63 | 0.63 | 0.63 | 0.63 | **0.64** |
| CCS | 0.69 | **0.70** | **0.70** | **0.70** | **0.70** |
| Financial | 0.87 | 0.89 | 0.89 | **0.90** | **0.90** |
| FNHK | 0.70 | 0.72 | **0.74** | 0.73 | 0.73 |
| Geneea | 0.77 | 0.77 | **0.78** | **0.78** | **0.78** |
| Lahman | **0.58** | **0.58** | **0.58** | **0.58** | **0.58** |
| LegalActs | 0.93 | 0.93 | **0.94** | 0.93 | 0.93 |
| NBA | 0.60 | **0.62** | 0.60 | **0.62** | **0.62** |
| NCAA | **0.70** | **0.70** | 0.69 | **0.70** | **0.70** |
| PremierLeague | **0.67** | **0.67** | **0.67** | **0.67** | **0.67** |
| Seznam | 0.85 | **0.87** | **0.87** | **0.87** | **0.87** |
| Stats | 0.75 | 0.75 | 0.75 | 0.75 | **0.76** |
| VOC | 0.93 | 0.93 | 0.93 | 0.93 | **0.94** |
| Walmart | 0.56 | **0.59** | 0.57 | **0.59** | **0.59** |
| Yelp | 0.84 | **0.85** | 0.84 | **0.85** | **0.85** |
| Average ↑ | 0.74 | 0.74 | 0.75 | 0.75 | 0.75 |
| Wins and ties ↑ | 3 | 8 | 9 | 12 | 16 |

## 7.1 When the Method Works

A good candidate dataset for temporal normalization has the following properties:

1. The dataset is affected by a linear trend and the dataset contains data for long enough to observe the effect of the trend.
2. Each `target id` contains at least 10 observations, from which the `trend` could be estimated.
3. The training set captures at least 2 full seasonal cycles, from which the seasonal pattern could be estimated.

## 7.2 When the Method Fails

While sport is affected by the seasons (e.g., Winter sports are generally more popular during the cold seasons than during the hot seasons), the tasks associated with the sports datasets in the relational repository (BasketballMen, BasketballWomen, Lahman, NBA, NCAA, PremierLeague) is the prediction of which of the teams wins the match. And we did not observe strong seasonality associated with this task.

### 7.3   Limitations of the Study

We have only evaluated the impact of detrending and deseasoning on numerical attributes while ignoring categorical attributes. But in principle, a categorical attribute can always be converted to a set of numerical attributes with the existential quantifier or count aggregates [20].

When multiple seasonal effects with different periods are present, we can incorporate multiple seasonal effects as described in [18, Equation 8]. Similarly, interactions between the seasonal effects can be modeled as in [18, Equation 9]. However, the effect of these "complications" was not evaluated.

Another limitation is that we do not model a mixture of seasonal patterns. E.g., in Financial dataset, we can identify two groups of clients based on their income: clients that are getting the 13. and the 14. paycheck (they have almost twice as high incomes in June and December than in any other month) and clients that are not getting the 13. and the 14. paycheck (they have the same paycheck each month). The model in Eq. (1) treats these two groups as a single group because the information about the number of paychecks is not explicitly present among the exogenous variables $X$ but is a latent information. Hence, when we deseason the data, the transactions of clients with the 13. and the 14. paycheck get currently undercorrected, while the transactions in the second group of the clients get overcorrected. In principle, the two groups can be identified with clustering based on dynamic time warping distance. And each cluster can then have its seasonal pattern. But fixing these deficiencies is future work.

## 8   Conclusion

We proposed a method for trend and seasonality from relational data, which works on non-uniformly spaced samples, multiple values recorded at the same time, and which respects dependencies in hierarchical data. The method is based on Hierarchical Generalized Additive Models and it improves the testing ROC-AUC of the downstream classifier on average by 1 percent point.

**Acknowledgments.** We would like to thank the anonymous reviewers; their comments helped to improve this paper. The reported research has been supported by the Grant Agency of the Czech Technical University in Prague (SGS20/213/OHK3/3T/18) and the Czech Science Foundation (GAČR 18-18080S).

## References

1. Berka, P.: Workshop notes on Discovery Challenge PKDD'99. Technical report, University of Economics, Prague (1999)
2. Box, G.E.P., Jenkins, G.M., Reinsel, G.C., Ljung, G.M.: Time Series Analysis: Forecasting and Control. Wiley, Hoboken (2015)
3. Breiman, L.: Random forest. Mach. Learn. **45**(5), 1–35 (1999)
4. Breslow, N.E., Clayton, D.G.: Approximate inference in generalized linear mixed models. J. Am. Stat. Assoc. **88**(421), 9 (1993)

5. Cleveland, R.B., Cleveland, W.S., McRae, J.E., Terpenning, I.: STL: a seasonal-trend decomposition. J. Off. Stat. **6**(1), 3–73 (1990)
6. Eckner, A.: A note on trend and seasonality estimation for unevenly-spaced time series. Eckner. Com R (2011), 1–8 (2012)
7. Fernández-Delgado, M., Cernadas, E., Barro, S., Amorim, D.: Do we need hundreds of classifiers to solve real world classification problems? J. Mach. Learn. Res. **15**, 3133–3181 (2014)
8. Guo, H., Viktor, H.L.: Multirelational classification: a multiple view approach. Knowl. Inf. Syst. **17**(3), 287–312 (2008)
9. Hastie, T., Tibshirani, R.: Generalized additive models. Stat. Sci. **1**(3), 297–310 (1986)
10. Holt, C.C.: Forecasting seasonals and trends by exponentially weighted moving averages. Int. J. Forecast. **20**(1), 5–10 (2004)
11. Hsiao, C.: Panel data analysis-advantages and challenges. TEST **16**(1), 1–22 (2007)
12. Hyndman, R.J., Athanasopoulos, G., Shang, H.L.: HTS: an R package for forecasting hierarchical or grouped time series. Stat. Softw. (2014)
13. Karmy, J.P., Maldonado, S.: Hierarchical time series forecasting via support vector regression in the European travel retail industry. Expert Syst. Appl. **137**, 59–73 (2019)
14. Knobbe, A.J., de Haas, M., Siebes, A.: Propositionalisation and aggregates. In: De Raedt, L., Siebes, A. (eds.) PKDD 2001. LNCS (LNAI), vol. 2168, pp. 277–288. Springer, Heidelberg (2001). https://doi.org/10.1007/3-540-44794-6_23
15. Krogel, M.-A., Wrobel, S.: Transformation-based learning using multirelational aggregation. In: Rouveirol, C., Sebag, M. (eds.) ILP 2001. LNCS (LNAI), vol. 2157, pp. 142–155. Springer, Heidelberg (2001). https://doi.org/10.1007/3-540-44797-0_12
16. Liu, Z., Yan, Y., Hauskrecht, M.: A flexible forecasting framework for hierarchical time series with seasonal patterns: a case study of web traffic. In: 41st International ACM SIGIR Conference on Research & Development in Information Retrieval, SIGIR 2018, pp. 889–892 (2018)
17. Motl, J., Schulte, O.: The CTU Prague Relational Learning Repository. arXiv (2015)
18. Ollech, D.: Seasonal adjustment of daily time series. J. Time Ser. Econom. **13**(2), 235–264 (2021)
19. Pedersen, E.J., Miller, D.L., Simpson, G.L., Ross, N.: Hierarchical generalized additive models in ecology: an introduction with MGCV. PeerJ **5**, 2019 (2019)
20. Perovšek, M., Vavpetič, A., Kranjc, J., Cestnik, B., Lavrač, N.: Wordification: propositionalization by unfolding relational data into bags of words. Expert Syst. Appl. **42**(17–18), 6442–6456 (2015)
21. Verma, V., Gagliardi, F., Ferretti, C.: On pooling of data and measures On pooling of data and measures. Technical Report November, Università di Siena (2009)

# Deep Learning/Blockchain

# A Blockchained Secure and Integrity-Preserved Architecture for Military Logistics Operations

Konstantinos Demertzis[1,2](✉), Panagiotis Kikiras[3], and Lazaros Iliadis[4]

[1] Department of Forestry and Management of the Environment and Natural Resources,
Democritus University of Thrace, Orestiada, Greece
kdemertz@fmenr.duth.gr

[2] School of Science and Technology, Informatics Studies, Hellenic Open University,
Patras, Greece

[3] Department of Computer Science, University of Thessaly, 35100 Lamia, PC, Greece
kikirasp@uth.gr

[4] School of Civil Engineering, Democritus University of Thrace, Kimmeria, Xanthi, Greece
liliadis@civil.duth.gr

**Abstract.** The employment of 5G Internet of Things (5G-IoT), smart automation, and AI analytics can provide improved military logistics, by enhancing inventory control, reordering, accuracy, flexibility mobility, and real-time monitoring, from the factory and warehouses to the battlefield. On the other hand, there are inherent risks that include cybersecurity issues, such as authentication, integrity, privacy, and confidentiality of the communicated data. Moreover, there are concerns relevant to prioritization, scalability, resilience, and continuous availability of the military supply chain operations. This paper introduces the development of a holistic blockchain integrity-focused scalable architecture, based on two main principles: the data is not stored in a central point and therefore make it vulnerable to attack and sensitive data is not transmitted through open communication channels. Fully homomorphic encryption is used to perform calculations and analysis. Remote independent observers who are eligible to have information access or to search for specific content with visual output, cannot determine the source of the information. The proposed architecture is based on the *Hyperledger Fabric* Project which provides the foundation for developing modular applications or solutions, allowing plug-and-play components, such as consensus and membership services. Its modular and versatile design satisfies a broad range of military operations. Besides, it offers a unique consensus approach that enables scalable performance, while preserving integrity and security. The significance of the proposed architecture is highlighted, by demonstrating its employment in the ammunition supply chain (from production to remote mobile ammunition consumers). Finally, the paper discusses the utilization of the architecture to other domains of military operations, beyond logistics such as C2 systems.

**Keywords:** Hyperledger Fabric · Integrity-preserving · Security · Scalability · Authentication · Prioritization · Blockchain · Logistics · Military operations

© Springer Nature Switzerland AG 2022
L. Iliadis et al. (Eds.): EANN 2022, CCIS 1600, pp. 271–283, 2022.
https://doi.org/10.1007/978-3-031-08223-8_23

# 1 Introduction

The introduction of 5G, IoT and Industrial Internet of Things (IIoT) technologies, smart automation, Artificial Intelligence (AI), and Big Data analytics, has simplified and enhanced the communication between humans and machines [1–3]. Furthermore, these technologies have improved the extraction, processing, and analyzing logistics' and supply chain management information [4, 5]. In particular, military logistics, include a much wider range of functions than commercial ones [6, 7]. Thus, expandability of timely Information Technology innovations, can enhance security, trust, transparency, and efficiency, at operational, strategic, and tactical levels of military operations [8]. In essence, military logistics are not limited to supply chain management, but they are also extended to the provision of all those operations required by a modern army [9, 10]. From a strategic point of view, they can be expanded even further to the Production Industry (industrial logistics) and to the Defense Industry (defense logistics). It is a fact that during military operations, logistics and their respective supportive processes, can play a crucial role in the successful outcome of a military operation. The inability to properly or timely supply or support a military unit is maybe, the most important factor that can lead to failure in the battlefield.

Attempting a detailed mapping of the military logistics, we could say that it is the science of planning and conducting the mobility and maintenance of the armed forces. More specifically, the respective responsibilities include the following: design, development, acquisition, storage, movement, distribution, maintenance, disposal or evacuation army material, transports, acquisition, construction, maintenance and disposal of facilities, providing medical support and military health services. Military logistics include both the development of stocks-warehouses and the maintenance of weapons and forces [7, 9]. Thus, they can be ranked in three different levels, as follows:

1. Production Logistics or Acquisition Logistics. This level of military logistics is related to the research procedures, design, development, manufacture and acceptance of material. They comprise of the following: standardization and interoperability, contracts, quality assurance, spare parts supply, defense reliability and analysis, safety standards for equipment, production specifications and processes, testing and inspections (including providing necessary installations) coding, equipment documentation, configuration control, and modifications.
2. Consumer Logistics or Operational Logistics. This level is related to the receipt of the raw product, to the storage and transportation, including repairing and maintaining or disposing, and the provision of necessary services. The most important processes are the following: inventory control, supply or construction of facilities (excluding any hardware and facilities required to support production logistics) motion control, reliability and fault reporting, safety standards for storage, transportation, and handling, as well as related training.
3. In-Service Logistics. It is the part that bridges production with consumer logistics. It includes functions related to the supply, receipt, storage, distribution, and disposal of material, at the military internal level operations. This internal support is related to activities required to ensure that army systems/equipment/services are available on a 24/7 readiness.

In conclusion, the effective organization and management of all levels of military logistics are directly related to high operational readiness, at a tactical, operational, and strategic level. Respectively, their real-time management helps to improve situation awareness, risk analysis, optimal decision support making for peacekeeping or war operations [11–13].

In recent years, blockchain technology has attracted everyone's attention, as it has managed to redefine the financial industry, offering advanced services and applications that until recently were unthinkable to implement. But the real revolution is related to supply chain management and logistics [14–16]. A blockchain is essentially a series of data entries, where each new group of entries - a block - is uniquely linked via an algorithmic relation. This creates a unique digital signature. Every change in a block, affects the whole chain and therefore it is extremely difficult to impossible to alter the data, without being finally traced [17].

In this context, blockchain can revolutionize the supply chain as it can eliminate the need for physical data managers, while rationalizing the associated costs and enhancing the security and efficiency of military logistics' operations. In addition, it is possible throughout the information life cycle, to enter new data and correct potential errors. However, each action remains visible forever to all participants, without the possibility of deletion. This approach facilitates the secure and transparent exchange of data, providing consent and traceability [16, 18, 19].

## 2    Proposed Architecture

It is necessary to overcome the problems identified in the ways of handling military logistics' facilities. It is also necessary to safely provide general data related to military supply [1–3]. This paper proposes the development of a holistic blockchain, secure and integrity-preserved scalable architecture for military logistics operations [4]. The proposed architecture has two main characteristics: No sensitive data is transmitted through communication channels, even if these channels can provide encryption and they are characterized by a high level of physical and logical security, and there is no single universal data storage point. This means that there is no central point of attack from which data leaks can occur. In this way, the proposed architecture ensures data integrity in military logistics', while providing consent in the ways of their use and inherent traceability potentials.

The features of the proposed system's architecture, allow the optimal management of complex situations related to data management, in military logistics operations. Thus, it implements an optimal hybrid system with the most technologically advanced methods. The design of the system is based on a multi-layered, modular architecture. Its distributed design allows its potential interconnection with existing systems. The separate architectural levels incorporated by the proposed architecture are presented in detail below.

### 2.1    The Blockchain Architecture

The blockchain architecture works as a distributed database or global registry, which maintains logs of all network's transactions. A transaction is a time-stamped record that specifies each operation, its identity its type and the participants. Transactions are combined into blocks, which are sorted based on a cryptographic hash [5, 6].

An open public-private key pair is formed for each user, which is linked to the corresponding account. It is used to sign a transaction and to clearly identify ownership of a function. A hash function with all transaction information is computed, to form a block in the blockchain. The hash value is used to calculate the hash of the block. Thus, the transaction information becomes unchanged and ensures the security, authenticity, and durability of the data storage in the blockchain. If there are conflicting transactions in the network, only one of them is selected to be part of the block [7].

The blocks are added to the blockchain at regular intervals, in order to form a linear sequence where each block states the hash of the previous block, thus forming a chain of blocks. This chain is maintained by the network's nodes. Each node is able to execute and record all the running transactions. This means that each blockchain user has access to the entire transaction log and can check the hash of each new block, in order to determine the correctness of the transaction. Thus, it is possible to reach a common consensus when performing the functions [8, 9].

The proposed architecture is based on Hyperledger Fabric [10], which is a foundation for developing applications or solutions with a modular architecture. It allows the creation of separate security levels and licenses, only for certified users [11]. The architecture of

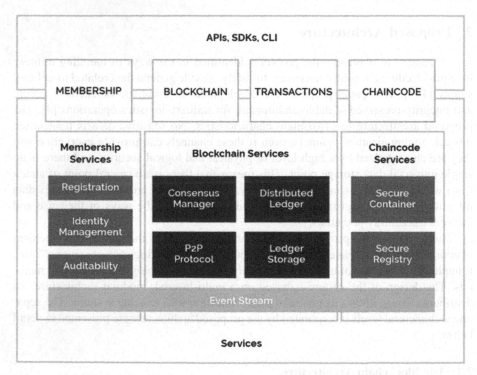

**Fig. 1.** Architecture of the Hyperledger Fabric

the Hyperledger Fabric and the general services it integrates are shown in the following diagram [15].

It is ideal for managing military assets' interests as it achieves transaction confidentiality and selective access between authorized participants. Also, an important feature that enhances Hyperledger Fabric-based implementation, is that the framework is based on the Byzantine Fault Tolerant (BFT) consent algorithm (a mechanism that enables a decentralized, trustless network to function even in the presence of malfunctioning or malicious nodes). Thus, the Hyperledger order service is jointly controlled by network's members, a process which guarantees coverage or the ability to reach consensus, even if there are rival nodes (malicious) or if the nodes are offline [12].

According to the Hyperledger Fabric, each component/actor has an identity and policies which constitute the mechanism for infrastructure management, as they define access control and governance. There are several types of Policies, namely: Channel, Channel Modification, Access Control Lists, Chain Code Lifecycle, and Chain Code Endorsement. Peers are a fundamental element of the network, because they host ledgers and smart contracts. Moreover, peers have an identity of their own and they are managed by the administrator of an organization. Hyperledger Fabric, supports secure communication between nodes, using Transport Layer Security (TLS). They apply both one-way (server only) and two-way (server and client) authentication. In addition, the cryptographic operations performed by nodes, can be delegated to a Hardware Security Module (HSM) that protects the private keys and handles cryptographic operations. Thus, it allows the peers to endorse transactions and ordered nodes, in order to sign blocks without exposing their private keys [10, 13, 14]. The proposed blockchain secure and integrity-preserved scalable architecture depicted in the following Fig. 2.

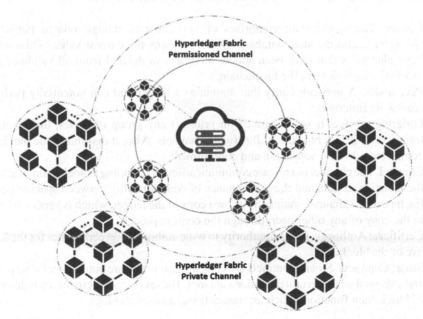

**Fig. 2.** The proposed blockchain secure and integrity-preserved scalable architecture

The architecture of the proposed framework has the capacity to employ different types of Blockchain, which can be characterized by various ways of using and providing the military logistics' data. Specifically [11, 12, 15]:

1. Private Blockchains: They are under the control of an entity, which exclusively ensures the control of the participation-validation of the data-interfaces that it holds. The entity has the right to override, edit or delete the necessary blockchain entries. Entities are organizations with their own equipment, laboratories, collection or distribution centers, collaborating bodies, and units.
2. Permissioned Blockchains: They have rules that define who can participate in the validation process or who can make transactions. They may have full or limited access (depending on the case). They can also provide special rights to each participant, with the ability to perform specific functions such as reading, accessing, and writing information.

Practically, in the proposed modular scheme, *Private* and *Permissioned* Blockchains coexist. Thus, they are making different license levels for different categories of participants, absolutely necessary [16]. Each involved entity may require partial access to the available information. A graph of the proposed scalable architecture is shown in the following Fig. 1, where any node can be expanded in a new blockchain network.

The development of the new blockchains is related to the ways of using and disposing the data – applications of the military logistics operations. They are applying the necessary distinct license levels, for the different categories of participants and for the different types of information access [17].

The following components are used to implement each blockchain [15]:

1. Ledger. The world state comprises of two separate though related parts, the blockchain, and the state database, which contains the current value of the set of key-value pairs that have been added, modified, or deleted from all validated and blocked transactions in the blockchain.
2. Peer nodes. A network entity that maintains a ledger and can potentially perform read/write functions.
3. Ordering service. It serves (based on priority) any group of nodes, that requests transactions in one block, for all network channels. Also, it distributes the blocks to connected peers for validation and commitment.
4. Channel. The channel is a private communication, overlapping a blockchain. It allows the isolation of data and the maintenance of confidentiality between specific peers. Each peer in a channel, maintains its own copy of the ledger, which is kept consistent to the copy of any other peer, through the consent process.
5. Certificate Authority. It is the authority to issue authorization certificates for the legal use of the blockchain.
6. Smart Contracts. Smart Contracts are code programs that are automatically activated and executed when certain conditions are met. These contracts activate a whole range of blockchain functions, such as: transactions, queries and logs.

Respectively, and based on the above components, the proposed architecture consists of specific layers. A general description of these layers is presented below:

1. Consensus Layer. It is responsible for establishing an agreement on the order and on the confirmation of the correctness of all transactions on blockchain.
2. Communication Layer. It is responsible for the transfer of messages between the peer nodes.
3. Authentication Layer. It is responsible for the authentication of users', for the control of their rights, and for the consolidation of trust in the blockchain.
4. API Layer. It is the application programming interface [18] that allows external applications or users to interact with the blockchain.
5. Smart Contracts Layer. It enables the provision of controlled access to the directory, and it is responsible for supporting the consistent information update.
6. Overlay layer. This is an additional level, used to map the communication network between the participating devices – nodes. It is responsible for providing the available services and applications, to the network. This level forms an overlapping network over the existing physical one. Its nodes can be considered as connected by virtual or logical links, each of which corresponds to a path in the underlying network.

The specific levels ensure the uninterrupted operation of the system and the fully interoperable reliability of the participating infrastructures in a simple and safe mode.

## 2.2 Encryption Architecture

The transition to distributed architectures is imperative, due to the necessity for strong encryption mechanisms, capable to ensure that calculations are performed on encrypted data [19]. Based on this principle, the data can remain confidential during processing, while allowing the performance of useful calculations, even if they are stored in unreliable distributed resources or heterogeneous networking environments. This process is achieved using fully *homomorphic encryption* [20, 21], which is an advanced technique allowing calculations on encrypted data. The idea behind homomorphic encryption is based on the use of an algebraic system that allows authorized third parties to perform a variety of calculations on encrypted data [22, 23]. Flow encryption is performed in order to create an advanced control mechanism, capable to control potential leakage of confidential data. It is based on the use of polynomial rings. The cryptographies of the polynomials are calculated by applying noisy linear transformations that include the public key to each polynomial. Numerical operations are then performed on the encrypted flow data. As long as the accumulated noise in the calculations does not exceed a certain limit, the computational output can be decrypted with a linear transformation that includes the private key [24–26].

A fully homomorphic cryptosystem is typically a set of four efficient algorithms (KeyGen; Encrypt; Decrypt; Eval). The first three are used for Key Generation, Encryption and Decryption. The Eval algorithm is associated with a family of functions $F$. Each function $f \in F$ accepts a cipher $\{c_i\}_{i=1}^n$ as input and calculates the cipher $c$ that is decrypted according to the input $f(m_1, \cdots, m_n)$ [20, 23, 24].

$$\text{Eval}\big(f, \text{Encrypt}_K(m_1), \cdots, \text{Encrypt}_K(m_n)\big) = \text{Encrypt}_K(f(m_1, \cdots, m_n)) \quad (1)$$

In general, the encryption process involves adding noise to the original message. This noise is controllable and can be corrected by a decryption (by the corresponding key holder), in a manner analogous to an error correction code. If the noise grows, then no one can proceed with the decryption.

Implementation includes the original CS cryptosystem which has a security parameter $\lambda$ and consists of the following algorithms [20, 21, 25]:

1. KeyGen $\left(1^{\lambda}\right) = p$, a random integer $\lambda^2$ bit.
2. Encrypt $(p, m) = m' + pq$, where $m'$ a random integer $\lambda$ bit with $m' = m$ mod 2 *and* $q$ a random integer $\lambda^5$ bit.
3. Decrypt$(p, c) = (c \bmod p) \bmod 2$ or equal.
4. Decrypt$(p, c) = (c \bmod 2) \oplus (c \div p \bmod 2)$

In addition to the basic encryption, the proposed architecture includes methods providing optimal parameters used for the initial encryption setting and for the calculations that reflect the occurring noise. Thus, the architecture fully ensures security between the trading parties.

## 3   Secure and Private Transaction to Transfer Ammunition

The capabilities of the *Hyperledger Fabric* can be combined to enable powerful chaincode based applications. For example, an ammunition transfer scenario, could be implemented using secure and private military data information, as follows [15]:

1. A specific batch of ammunition may be tracked by a Unique Identifier (UUID) that is a key label comprising of 128-bits. In the public chaincode state of the blockchain, only the ammunition UUID is recorded.
2. The chaincode requires that any transfer request must originate from the owning military unit, and the key is bound by a military regulator who must endorse any transfer requests.
3. The private data of the military unit that contains the details about the batch of ammunition are locked by a hash of the UUID. Other organizations in the blockchain service, can only see the hash of the ammunition.
4. The military regulator is a member of each collection and therefore it has access to the private data of each transaction request.

Based on the above assumptions, a blockchain transaction to transfer ammunition would unfold as follows [15]:

1. The logistic department of a military unit, has struck a deal after successful bidding, a transport service office to transfer ammunition for a certain price.
2. The military office passes the military secrecy details about the ammunition transfer on their private blockchain node.
3. The secret data are encrypted by using homomorphic encryption and the hash is published to the open blockchain channel.

4.  The transport service office verifies the hash of the private details matches the on-chain public hash.

5.  The transport service office invokes chaincode to record their transport deal details in their own private data collection. The chaincode is invoked on the military unit office peer, and on the military's regulator peer that is required by the security transaction policy.

6.  The military unit invokes chaincode to transfer ammunition, passing in the hash of the private details and transport deal details information. This is performed, in order to meet the endorsement security policy of the public key, as well as the policies and private data regulations from the military regulators.

7.  The chaincode is used by the military regulator in order to verify that the submitting military unit is the owner, the private details on the hash in the blockchain collection, and the transport deal details information of the transport service office. The chaincode then writes the proposed updates for the public key and the private details to the transport service office. Prior to final endorsement, the endorsing military regulator ensures that the data is secure and private, and it is not disseminated to any other unauthorized or authorized peers.

8.  The transport service office submits the block transaction with the public deal data and private data hashes for transaction ordering, and it is distributed to all channel peers in the blockchain.

9.  Each peer's block validation logic will consistently verify the endorsement security and privacy policy was met. Moreover, it verifies that the public and private state that was read in the chaincode has not been modified by any other transaction since chaincode execution.

10. All peers commit the transaction as valid, since it passed validation checks.

11. With the transaction completed, other channel members interested in the asset may query the history of the public key to understand its provenance. However, they will not have access to any private details unless a military regulator shares it encrypted in the private blockchain channel.

The following Fig. 3 presents the secure and private transactions, related to the ammunition transfer as imposed by the proposed blockchain architecture.

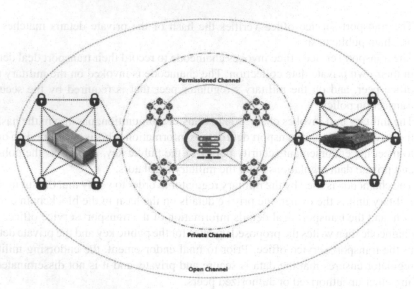

**Fig. 3.** Secure and private proposed architecture

The basic ammunition transfer scenario could be extended for other considerations. For example, the transfer chaincode could verify that a payment record is available to satisfy payment delivery requirements, or to verify that a bank has submitted a letter of credit, prior to the execution of the transfer chaincode. Instead of transactors directly hosting peers, they could transact through custodian organizations who are running peers [13, 27, 28].

## 4 Conclusion

The paper at hand has introduced the idea of prototyping the proposed architecture, as a universal method capable to meet all requirements of military logistics. This approach combines the most up-to-date methods, and it is running under an adaptable, flexible, and easy-to-use operating environment, aiming to complete specialized processes for the military logistics applications of the modern armed forces.

The features of the proposed architecture, allow the monitoring, analysis, and management of complex situations related to military logistics. It optimally combines and implements a hybrid system with the most technologically advanced IT methods that enhance the security and privacy of military operations.

It should be emphasized that the proposed architecture can be applied to a number of C2 applications. The following Fig. 4, presents an extensive architectural standardization of the introduced model, which clearly demonstrates that it is possible to extend the scope of the system to a number of novel C2 applications.

Specifically, an extension of this architecture can integrate the edge network. Any edge device (sensors, readers, gateways) can transfer local data to cloud systems, by using any available communication system for real-time analysis. For example, Unmanned Aerial Vehicles (Drones, UAVs) are one of the most important information gathering

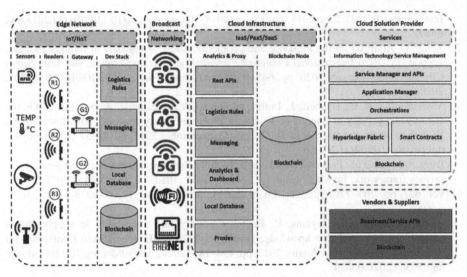

**Fig. 4.** An extension of the proposed blockchained scalable architecture

systems. However, if they are not incorporating smart applications, their use can be considered as rather passive, as these are unable to utilize the data in real-time [10, 29, 30].

To the above issue, the proposed architecture can enrich unmanned flying vehicles with real-time machine vision and machine hearing techniques. These services can be provided by using Cloud Robotics' applications, which allow machines with sensors to use cloud resources in real-time. In this way any video data stream, can pass through real-time identification of target objects (e.g., small boats). This process will enable real time perception of a situation (e.g., identifying shooting sounds). Moreover, it can offer marking of specific spatial locations (e.g., coordinates of target). Overall, this approach can successfully perform decision-making in order to impose proper actions (e.g., activation of rapid reaction units).

Based on this architecture, the data can be converted to decision-support information, which can be available whenever required, without the need for physical access. Similar applications are also directly related to high operational readiness on a tactical, operational, and strategic level. They can help to improve situational awareness, risk analysis, optimal decision making, timely response to a given event, and planning support for conducting control operations related to it.

## References

1. Yang, X., Gong, Y., Chang, L.I.: Analysis model of bottleneck sections in military logistics network. In: 2010 International Conference on Logistics Systems and Intelligent Management (ICLSIM), January 2010, vol. 3, pp. 1957–1960. https://doi.org/10.1109/ICLSIM.2010.546 1267
2. Zhai, C., Jiang, X., Zhang, Y., Liu, N.: Research on the optimization of military supplies under big data background. In: 2018 International Conference on Big Data and Artificial

Intelligence (BDAI), June 2018, pp. 18–23 (2018). https://doi.org/10.1109/BDAI.2018.854 6629

3. Zeng, Y.: Analysis on the influence and countermeasures of big data in military logistics support. In: 2020 International Conference on Intelligent Transportation, Big Data Smart City (ICITBS), January 2020, pp. 648–651 (2020). https://doi.org/10.1109/ICITBS49701. 2020.00142

4. Vasilomanolakis, E., Daubert, J., Luthra, M., Gazis, V., Wiesmaier, A., Kikiras, P.: On the security and privacy of Internet of Things architectures and systems. In: 2015 International Workshop on Secure Internet of Things (SIoT), September 2015, pp. 49–57 (2015). https:// doi.org/10.1109/SIOT.2015.9

5. Demertzis, K., et al.: Federated blockchained supply chain management: a cybersecurity and privacy framework. In: Maglogiannis, I., Macintyre, J., Iliadis, L. (eds.) AIAI 2021. IAICT, vol. 627, pp. 769–779. Springer, Cham (2021). https://doi.org/10.1007/978-3-030-79150-6_60

6. Sahai, S., Singh, N., Dayama, P.: Enabling privacy and traceability in supply chains using blockchain and zero knowledge proofs. In: 2020 IEEE International Conference on Blockchain (Blockchain), August 2020, pp. 134–143 (2020). https://doi.org/10.1109/Blockc hain50366.2020.00024

7. Jiang, C., Ru, C.: Application of blockchain technology in supply chain finance. In: 2020 5th International Conference on Mechanical, Control and Computer Engineering (ICMCCE), September 2020, pp. 1342–1345 (2020). https://doi.org/10.1109/ICMCCE51767.2020.00294

8. Yousuf, S., Svetinovic, D.: Blockchain technology in supply chain management: preliminary study. In: 2019 Sixth International Conference on Internet of Things: Systems, Management and Security (IOTSMS), July 2019, pp. 537–538 (2019). https://doi.org/10.1109/IOTSMS 48152.2019.8939222

9. Yue, Y., Fu, X.: Research on medical equipment supply chain management method based on blockchain technology. In: 2020 International Conference on Service Science (ICSS), December 2020, pp. 143–148 (2020). https://doi.org/10.1109/ICSS50103.2020.00030

10. Ahmed, M., Reno, S., Akter, N., Haque, F.: Securing medical forensic system using hyper-ledger based private blockchain. In: 2020 23rd International Conference on Computer and Information Technology (ICCIT), September 2020, pp. 1–6 (2020). https://doi.org/10.1109/ ICCIT51783.2020.9392686

11. Aleksieva, V., Valchanov, H., Huliyan, A.: Implementation of smart-contract, based on hyper-ledger fabric blockchain. In: 2020 21st International Symposium on Electrical Apparatus Technologies (SIELA), June 2020, pp. 1–4 (2020). https://doi.org/10.1109/SIELA49118. 2020.9167043

12. Alshalali, T., M'Bale, K., Josyula, D.: Security and privacy of electronic health records sharing using hyperledger fabric. In: 2018 International Conference on Computational Science and Computational Intelligence (CSCI), September 2018, pp. 760–763 (2018). https://doi.org/10. 1109/CSCI46756.2018.00152

13. Mohite, A., Acharya, A.: Blockchain for government fund tracking using Hyperledger. In: 2018 International Conference on Computational Techniques, Electronics and Mechanical Systems (CTEMS), September 2018, pp. 231–234 (2018). https://doi.org/10.1109/CTEMS. 2018.8769200

14. Park, W.-S., Hwang, D.-Y., Kim, K.-H.: A TOTP-based two factor authentication scheme for hyperledger fabric blockchain. In: 2018 Tenth International Conference on Ubiquitous and Future Networks (ICUFN), July 2018, pp. 817–819 (2018). https://doi.org/10.1109/ICUFN. 2018.8436784

15. Hyperledger – Open Source Blockchain Technologies. https://www.hyperledger.org/. Accessed 15 Jan 2022

16. D'Acquisto, G., Domingo-Ferrer, J., Kikiras, P., Torra, V., de Montjoye, Y.-A., Bourka, A.: Privacy by design in big data: an overview of privacy enhancing technologies in the era of big data analytics. arXiv151206000 Cs (2015). https://doi.org/10.2824/641480

17. Demertzis, K., Iliadis, L., Tziritas, N., Kikiras, P.: Anomaly detection via blockchained deep learning smart contracts in industry 4.0. Neural Comput. Appl. **32**(23), 17361–17378 (2020). https://doi.org/10.1007/s00521-020-05189-8

18. Demertzis, K., Iliadis, L.: SAME: an intelligent anti-malware extension for Android ART virtual machine. In: Núñez, M., Nguyen, N.T., Camacho, D., Trawiński, B. (eds.) ICCCI 2015. LNCS (LNAI), vol. 9330, pp. 235–245. Springer, Cham (2015). https://doi.org/10. 1007/978-3-319-24306-1_23

19. Bringer, J., Chabanne, H., Patey, A.: Privacy-preserving biometric identification using secure multiparty computation: an overview and recent trends. IEEE Signal Process. Mag. **30**(2), 42–52 (2013). https://doi.org/10.1109/MSP.2012.2230218

20. Kogos, K.G., Filippova, K.S., Epishkina, A.V.: Fully homomorphic encryption schemes: the state of the art. In: 2017 IEEE Conference of Russian Young Researchers in Electrical and Electronic Engineering (EIConRus), October 2017, pp. 463–466 (2017). https://doi.org/10. 1109/EIConRus.2017.7910591

21. Mohan, M., Devi, M.K.K., Prakash, V.J.: Homomorphic encryption-state of the art. In: 2017 International Conference on Intelligent Computing and Control (I2C2), June 2017, pp. 1–6 (2017). https://doi.org/10.1109/I2C2.2017.8321774

22. Shen, T., Wang, F., Chen, K., Wang, K., Li, B.: Efficient leveled (multi) identity-based fully homomorphic encryption schemes. IEEE Access **7**, 79299–79310 (2019). https://doi.org/10. 1109/ACCESS.2019.2922685

23. Sendhil, R., Amuthan, A.: A descriptive study on homomorphic encryption schemes for enhancing security in fog computing. In: 2020 International Conference on Smart Electronics and Communication (ICOSEC), September 2020, pp. 738–743 (2020). https://doi.org/10. 1109/ICOSEC49089.2020.9215422

24. Ogiela, M.R., Oczko, M.: Comparison of selected homomorphic encryption techniques. In: 2018 IEEE 32nd International Conference on Advanced Information Networking and Applications (AINA), February 2018, pp. 1110–1114 (2018). https://doi.org/10.1109/AINA.2018. 00159

25. Kim, J., Yun, A.: Secure fully homomorphic authenticated encryption. IEEE Access **9**, 107279–107297 (2021). https://doi.org/10.1109/ACCESS.2021.3100852

26. Behera, S., Prathuri, J.R.: Application of homomorphic encryption in machine learning. In: 2020 2nd PhD Colloquium on Ethically Driven Innovation and Technology for Society (PhD EDITS), August 2020, pp. 1–2 (2020). https://doi.org/10.1109/PhDEDITS51180.2020.931 5305

27. Kim, Y., Kim, K.-H., Kim, J.-H.: Power trading blockchain using hyperledger fabric. In: 2020 International Conference on Information Networking (ICOIN), January 2020, pp. 821–824 (2020). https://doi.org/10.1109/ICOIN48656.2020.9016428

28. Wutthikarn, R., Hui, Y.G.: Prototype of blockchain in dental care service application based on hyperledger composer in hyperledger fabric framework. In: 2018 22nd International Computer Science and Engineering Conference (ICSEC), August 2018, pp. 1–4 (2018). https://doi.org/ 10.1109/ICSEC.2018.8712639

29. Banerjee, B.P., Raval, S., Cullen, P.J.: UAV-hyperspectral imaging of spectrally complex environments. Int. J. Remote Sens. **41**(11), 4136–4159 (2020). https://doi.org/10.1080/014 31161.2020.1714771

30. Booysen, R., et al.: Detection of REEs with lightweight UAV-based hyperspectral imaging. Sci. Rep. **10**(1), 17450 (2020). https://doi.org/10.1038/s41598-020-74422-0

# An IoT Authentication Framework for Urban Infrastructure Security Using Blockchain and Deep Learning

Anastasios Panagiotis Psathas$^{(\boxtimes)}$ ⓘ, Lazaros Iliadis ⓘ, Antonios Papaleonidas ⓘ, and Dimitris Bountas ⓘ

Department of Civil Engineering-Lab of Mathematics and Informatics (ISCE), Democritus University of Thrace, 67100 Xanthi, Greece
{anpsatha,liliadis,papaleon,dibounta}@civil.duth.gr

**Abstract.** Internet of Things (IoT) enables increased connectivity between devices. However, this benefit also intrinsically increases cybersecurity risks as cyber attackers are provided with expanded network access and additional digital targets. To address this issue, this paper presents a holistic digital and physical cybersecurity user authentication framework, based on Blockchain and Deep Learning (BLDE) algorithms. The introduced user authentication framework, provides an additional layer of resilience against Cybersecurity attacks that may arise through the IoT. Moreover, it controls digital access through the seven OSI layers and via the physical user's identity, such as finger prints or self-images, before the user is accepted in the IoT network. Finally, it offers many layers of security through its decentralized and distributed nature, in order to reduce the system's vulnerability from cyber threats.

**Keywords:** IoT · CNN · MLP · Blockchain · Cybersecurity · Deep Learning · Distributed · Decentralized

## 1 Introduction

The evolution of technology continues its rapid course. The vast number of applications used by individuals or groups, for either personal or commercial use, keeps increasing. The acceptance of Internet-of-Thing (IoT) was determinant for the growth of these applications in the daily life [1].

The term IoT was introduced in the literature by Kevin Ashton in 1999 [2] to describe a system in which its objects could connect to the Internet via sensors using RFID (Radio Frequency Identification) technologies. Nowadays, IoT is defined as a network of physical objects, (e.g., appliances, vehicles, buildings) which contain embedded electronic systems, software, sensors, which allow real time monitoring and control of devices through web connectivity. It allows these objects to be controlled remotely, through a network's infrastructure, creating interaction opportunities among the physical world and the computer systems [3]. Furthermore, IoT relies on technology that includes sensors and actuators which are part of everyday smart systems, like smart homes and smart

© Springer Nature Switzerland AG 2022
L. Iliadis et al. (Eds.): EANN 2022, CCIS 1600, pp. 284–296, 2022.
https://doi.org/10.1007/978-3-031-08223-8_24

vehicles. Each object is identified separately from a built-in computer system and it can operate both autonomously, as well as in collaboration with the rest of the internet infrastructure [4]. However, the increasing use of computer networks, interconnected systems and IoT devices, paved the way for the exploitation of new cyber threats and risks. Cyber attackers are provided with expanded network access and additional digital targets [5]. Despite the tremendous development in network security, the existing solutions are not able to completely defend network and IoT systems, against potential malicious threats [6]. Thus, the deployment of new approaches and methodologies is imperative.

The traditional security techniques such as hardware and software firewalls, user authentication and data encryption, is one way to defend IoT [7]. *Intrusion Detection Systems* (IDS), a rapidly growing field of study, were also suggested in order to facilitate system's security. Using patterns of benign traffic and normal behavior or specific rules that describe a specific attack, IDSs can distinguish between normal and malicious actions [8]. Thus, several *Machine Learning* (ML) and *Deep Learning* (DL) techniques tried to integrate for Cyber Intrusion Detection (CID) [9]. However, in 2008, Nakamoto, presented the *Blockchain* into a peer-to-peer (P2P) electronic cash system. Transactions were verified and linked each other in an open distributed ledge, making almost impossible for someone to tamper the information of any block [10]. This approach, offered the IoT and computer system defenders, an additional asset towards the enhancement of cybersecurity.

Blockchain architecture, enables the digitalization of contracts as it provides both authentication between parties and information encryption, that gradually increments while it is processed in a decentralized network such as the IoT [11]. Due to these features, Blockchain (BLCH) has been already applied in Cryptocurrency, Smart Contracts, Intelligent Transport Systems and Smart Cities [12].

To address the increased cybersecurity risk and threats of the IoT, this paper introduces the *Urban Infrastructure Security* framework (UINSE). UINSE is a hybrid holistic digital and physical authentication framework, based on BLCH technology and DL techniques.

The rest of the paper is organized as follows. Section 2 performs a literature review of IoT Cyber Security and the contribution of Blockchain Technology on it. Section 3 describes Blockchain, the DL Techniques and provides the architecture of the proposed model and its description. Section 4, pinpoints the most significant issues of the model and proposes solutions. Section 5 concludes the manuscript.

## 2  Literature Review

Yu et al. [13], have developed a Support Vector Machine model (SVM) to detect *traffic flooding* attacks. In the attack experiment, the system gathered *Simple Network Management Protocol* (SNMP) information from the victim using SNMP query messages, achieving an attack detection rate over 99.40%, whereas the classification accuracy was 99.53%. Kulkarmi and Venayagamoorthy (2009) [14], proposed a MLP to estimate the *suspicion factor* that indicates whether an IoT device is the victim of a Denial of Service (DoS) attack. If the output of the MLP exceeds a threshold, the IoT device under test, shuts down both the *Media Access Control* (MAC) and the *Physical* (PHY) layer functions to save energy and to extend the network's life. Branch et al. (2013) [15], applied the k-Nearest Neighbor (K-NN) algorithm to address the problem of unsupervised outlier detection in a *Wireless Sensor Network* (WSN). This is a flexible approach, capable to define outliers with reduced energy consumption. In 2017, Shi et al. [16], developed a Deep Learning approach to perform user authentication. The *Channel State Information* (CSI) features of the Wi-Fi signals were initially extracted and the DNN algorithms were applied to detect spoofing attackers. In the testing phase, they achieved high spoofing detection rates and successful user identification. Bostani & Sheikhan [17], introduced a real-time hybrid intrusion detection framework, using the *Optimum-Path Forest* Clustering algorithm, achieving high performance indices' values for the cases of the *sinkhole* and *selective-forwarding* attacks in a real-world application.

Pointcheval [18] presented a linear scheme based on an N-P Perceptron problem suited for smart cards applications. Kinzel et al. [19], trained two multilayer neural networks (NNs) on their mutual output bits with discrete weights, in order to achieve a synchronization that can be applied to secret key exchange over a public channel. Klimov et al. [20] applied the above NN on three *Cryptanalytic* attacks (*Genetic, Geometric and Probabilistic*). Volna et al. [21] employed feed forward NNs to perform encryption and decryption with a continuously changing key. Yayık et al. [22] presented a two-stage cryptography NN. The first stage generates neural network-based pseudo random numbers. In the second phase, a NN encrypts information based on the non-linearity of the model.

After Nakamoto's revolutionary application of Blockchain (BCH) Technology on Bitcoin transactions [10], BCH has attracted the interest of many researchers as it is almost impossible for a third party to tamper it, due to the vast processing power required. In 2017, Xu et al. [23] proposed a punishment scheme, based on the action record of the blockchain, to suppress the attack motivation of edge servers and mobile devices in the edge network. Cha et al. [24] utilized a blockchain network as the underlying communication architecture to construct an ISO/IEC 15408-2 compliant security auditing system. Gai et al. [25] developed a conceptual model for fusing blockchain and cloud computing technologies over three deployment modes: Cloud over Blockchain, BCH over Cloud and a mixed case. In 2018, Gupta et al. [26] announced a Blockchain consensus model for implementing IoT security. Agrawal et al. [27] used Blockchain to continuously evaluate legitimate presence of a user in a valid IoT-Zone, without any kind of user's intervention. In 2019, Serrano, proposed a BCH Random Neural Network model (BRNN), which was applied on an IoT AAA server, covering both the digital 7 layers of the OSI Model and the physical user's credentials (e.g. passport or biometrics). BRNN had 1 hidden layer using as many neurons as the input. The signal of a mobile device was used as input and the output was the credentials, i.e., the private key and the biometric characteristics. The weights are stored (without specifying the actual location). After each iteration, the previous Hidden Layer was added to the input layer and the number of hidden layer neurons increased to equal the number of input neurons. Then the previous weights are recalled, the neurons are re-trained and the new weights are re-stored elsewhere [28]. Moreover, Giannoutakis et al., introduced a BCH approach to support the cybersecurity mechanisms of smart homes installations, focusing on the immutability of users and devices that constitute such environments [29]. Finally, Demertzis et al. [30], suggested a Blockchain Security architecture, that aims to ensure network communication between traded Industrial IoT devices, following the Industry 4.0 standard, based on Deep Learning *Smart Contracts*.

## 3 Architecture of the Urban Infrastructure Security Framework (UINSE)

The introduced UINSE framework employs a Deep Learning scheme following a Convolutional architecture. Its security is ensured by employing a Blockchain network. More specifically, UINSE employs a *Convolutional Neural Network* (CNN) for self-image or fingerprint recognition, a *Multi-Layer Perceptron* (MLP) to control the digital access through the seven *Open System Interconnection* (OSI) layers, and a *Blockchain* architecture for the storage and validation of all "transactions" between the user and the IoT devices.

Apart from the innovative combination of the aforementioned subsystems, another contribution of this research is that the weights used by the CNN and the MLP, are stored distributed in a computer network outside the IoT system and they are gathered only to be used in the authentication process. Last but not least, the whole BLCH process is applied, using a decentralized network of nodes (*miners*) that perform storage and validation of the Blockchain.

### 3.1 The Blockchain and Deep Learning Subsystems

Blockchain is an append-only decentralized digital ledger that is supported by cryptography [31]. It provides a platform to process trusted transactions (TXs) without third-party involvement. Each request has a record in the form of a chain of blocks with a digital signature for verification. Since the ledger is generated and maintained by all participants equally within the system [32] and there is no central server to manage the activity, blockchain holds tamper-proof and immutable information in a secure and encrypted manner. BCH uses a *Peer-to-Peer* (P2P) network, in which every node corresponds to an existing network-user or to a new user who is allowed to join in a secure manner.

Whenever a new node joins the network, it gets the full copy of the blockchain. When a new request is generated, a block is created and it is sent to every other node in the network. Once verified by all nodes to make sure it is not tampered with, it is added to the chain. All nodes follow a consensus to verify the validity of the block. Each time a node gets a blockchain for verification, all others match it with its BCH whereas the blocks that are tampered with, are rejected. The developed Consensus is called *Proof-of-Work* (PoW) [31]. It is an algorithm, used to confirm TXs and to produce new blocks to the chain. The PoW uses random calculations to solve the complex cryptographic puzzle (sufficient number of leading zeros in hash combinations) which requires adequate computing power [33].

A MLP is a feed forward NN, which comprises of $n$ layers [34, 35]. It should be clarified that $W_M$ a matrix comprising of the weights located between the M-$1st$ and the M$th$ layer. The vector $b_M$ is the bias vector of the M$th$ layer [36]. A CNN is defined as a Deep NN that extracts features at a higher resolution, and converts them into more complex features at a coarser resolution, as presented in Fig. 1. CNN comprises of

*Convolutional, Pooling* and *Fully-Connected* layers [37]. The feature value at location $(x, y)$ in the $k^{\text{th}}$ feature map of the $M^{\text{th}}$ layer, is calculated as follows:

$$feature_{x,y,k}^{M} = W_k^{M^T} X_{x,y}^{M} + b_k^{M} \tag{1}$$

where $X_{x,y}^{M}$ is the input patch centered at location $(x, y)$, $W_k^{M}$ is the weight vector of the $k$th filter, and $b_k^{M}$ is bias term of the $M^{\text{th}}$ layer. The activation value $activate_{x,y,k}^{M}$ and the pooling value $pool_{x,y,k}^{M}$ of the Convolution feature $feature_{x,y,k}^{M}$ can be calculated as follows:

$$activate_{x,y,k}^{M} = activation(feature_{x,y,k}^{M}) \tag{2}$$

$$pool_{x,y,k}^{M} = pooling(feature_{a,c,k}^{M}), \ \forall \ (a, c) \in N_{x,y} \tag{3}$$

where $N_{x,y}$ is a local neighborhood around location $(x, y)$. The nonlinear activation functions are the ReLU, the *Sigmoid*, and the Tangent Hyperbolic (*Tan*H). Either Average or MaxPooling operators can be applied.

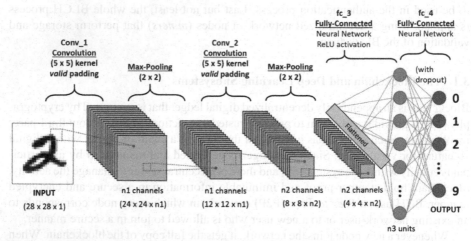

**Fig. 1.** Architecture of the digit recognition CNN which comprises of two Convolution, two Maxpooling, and two Fully Connected Layers.

The following Fig. 2, presents the architecture of the *Authentication* subsystem.

The offline part of the scheme, comprises of a computer where the following are stored:

- **Database:** The database contains the credentials of each user who is credible and authorized to access the Home's IoT system. More specifically, the image(s)/ fingerprint(s) of each credible user is stored in the database as well as the following authentication credentials that cover the 7 layers of the OSI model (Fig. 3) namely: the MAC address of the user's device, the IP (if it is static) the protocol used in the Port layer (UDP, TCP) and the ID of the device to which each credible user can have access.

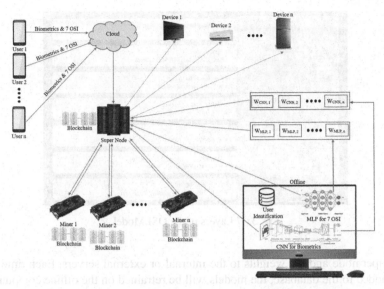

**Fig. 2.** Architecture of the authentication subsystem of the UINSE

- **MLP:** The architecture of the MLP can be tailored during the installation of the system by experienced stuff who will be allowed to choose the number of the hidden layers (not more than three). However, an MLP with two hidden layers will be used as the default one. The Input Layer vectors comprise of the users' credentials related to the 7 layer of OSI Model (Fig. 3), as well as the IDs of the devices for which access is permitted. The output is either 1 or 0 corresponding to permit or decline access authorization (Binary Classification). The model will be trained during installation by the experienced stuff. Its final architecture, without the values of node weights, will be stored in the super node. The nodes' weights will be stored on different secure servers, either inside the house or elsewhere. In Fig. 2, the external weights' servers are denoted as $W_{MLP,1}$, $W_{MLP,2}$, ..., $W_{MLP,n}$ where $W_{MLP,1}$ contains the weights of the first hidden layer of the MLP, $W_{MLP,2}$ contains the weights of the second hidden layer and so on.
- **CNN:** The CNN will have a default architecture, however the user will be able to choose any of certain specific proposed architectures that are well-known in the literature like AlexNet [40], BGG-16 [41] and ReseNet-50 [42]. The CNN will accept user's image (s)/fingerprint (s). The output will be authorization acceptance or rejection (Binary Classification). The CNN model will be trained and its architecture will be stored in the super node, while the weights for the layers will be stored on different secure servers, either inside the house or elsewhere. In Fig. 2, the external weights servers are denoted by $W_{CNN,1}$, $W_{CNN,2}$, ..., $W_{CNN,n}$ where $W_{CNN,1}$ contains the weights of the first Convolution Layer of the CNN, $W_{CNN,2}$ contains the weights of the second Convolution layer and so on.

The computer that will be trained and will contain the database with the credentials of the users, will be permanently offline, except when it will send the networks' details

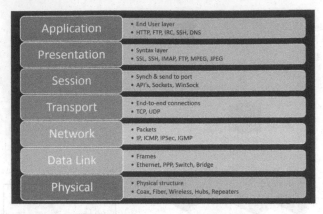

**Fig. 3.** 7 Layers of the OSI Model.

to the super node and the weights to the internal or external servers. Each time a new user is added to the database, the models will be retrained on the offline computer, and the weights will be redistributed to the servers.

The IoT devices will be connected to the *Super Node*, which will be either a computer with features related to the house appliances, or to a supercomputer in a different space, maybe rented from a company. The user can access the IoT devices only after the whole validation process will be successfully performed by the *super-node* and the *miners*. The authorization process will consist of two basic stages, the validation of the users' credentials and the creation and integration of the blocks in the blockchain.

Starting from the process of validating the user's credentials, when a user wants to connect or wants to give a command to a device connected to the IoT of the house, he/she will send the respective biometrics, the credentials related to the seven layers of the OSI model and the device to be connected. This will be done through the Internet in the Super Node. Super Node does the following:

1. Calls the weights of the MLP and the CNN from external Servers.
2. Places the user's credentials on the appropriate network. The images and fingerprints on the CNN and everything else on the MLP and finally it applies the algorithms.
3. Checks if the NNs' results authorize the user to use the corresponding device.
4. At the same time it checks if there is a block of the blockchain in which the specific credentials of the user on the specific device have been rejected.
5. Deletes the weights of the NNs
6. Creates a new block transaction.
7. Broadcasts the new transaction to the Miners
8. After the verification or the rejection of the new block by the miners the Super Node forwards the user's action on the appropriate device or completely prevents the user from authorizing the device.

The architecture of the proposed Blockchain model, related to steps 4, 6, 7 are described in the following Fig. 4.

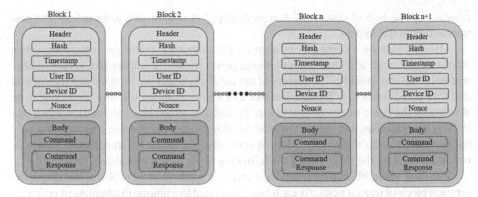

**Fig. 4.** The architecture of the proposed blockchain subsystem

Apart from the Hash of the block, the attributes that have been incorporated in block header for the designed system are as follows:

- **Hash of the previous block**: The block always keeps the hash of the previous block to make the blockchain tamper-proof.
- **Timestamp**: A timestamp has been added in the block to record the event start and finish time in the device/computer and is stored as a log or metadata as temporal information.
- **Nonce**: A nonce is a randomly generated number that is required for the miners as a target value of mathematical calculation to perform Proof of Work (PoW).
- **UserID**: This attribute keeps the credentials of source device from where the command is coming (including and the features that are not used in NN).
- **DeviceID**: This attribute keeps the address of the destination device to which the command has been targeted.

The attributes that have been incorporated in the block body for the designed system are as follows:

- **Command**: The command of the user (**UserID**) to the corresponding device (**DeviceID**)
- **Command Response**: Verified or Reject, depending on whether the user is authorized to perform the specific command in the specific device.

After the description of the Blockchain subsystem's architecture (Fig. 4), step 4 of the Super Node has been clarified. Super Node checks if the combination of the following properties *User ID, Device ID, Command* has been rejected before. If this is the case, it is rejected again. Thus, in step 5, the super node checks the results of the NNs and the existing Blockchain and creates a transaction of the aforementioned features, with the **Hash of the previous block,** the **timestamp** of the requested **Command** the **UserID** the **DeviceID**, and the **Command Response**. This transaction can be either verified or rejected by the hybrid system. If accepted, step 7 is responsible to broadcast the new transaction to the miners.

Miners could be a computer or a group of computers, inside or outside the urban infrastructure, with adequate computational power to solve complex blockchain mathematical problems quickly. The miners of the network, select the broadcasted transaction and they transform it to a 'block'. The block of transactions should wait for a PoW to be verified by the other miner nodes, before its addition to the blockchain. It is a fact that PoW is a mechanism that slows down the development of the blocks. This makes it very hard to tamper with the blocks. More specifically, if a block is tampered, the offensor needs to calculate the PoW for all the following blocks, which is almost impossible.

The PoW is established by resolving a complex mathematical problem that is specific for each block of transactions. As each block is related to a unique mathematical problem, every miner has to strive on a distinct unique case, which is a tedious task requiring adequate computational power [38].

PoW is a powerful method that has proved to achieve the highest level of security in blockchain systems. When the Super Node (SN) receives the command from the authorized user to perform an activity, it finds the blockchain ledger in its database. If the previous ledger is found, the SN generates a block transaction and updates the previous ledger; otherwise, it generates a new blockchain ledger and creates a block transaction. Then, it broadcasts a new block to all miners through a P2P server. The SN automatically detects the miners based on which miner has strong connectivity and availability. The miners validate the new block against the blockchain, or against the last n blocks in the blockchain. After this process of validation, the miners perform mining by finding a hash output for the data in its block for verification. The fulfilment of the block verification process, leads all miners to check the target referenced device in the incoming request. The targeted miner accepts the activity and waits for the acknowledgment of the other miners to perform the requested action.

After Miners validate the new block, and decide to reject it or to append it to the blockchain, they make the blockchain public to the Super Node who already has acces to the previous block. Thus, if the new blockchain broadcasted by the miners, has the new block, the SN offers access to the user of the IoT device, else authorization is denied (step 8).

## 4   Discussion

The introduced framework follows a complex process, which combines state-of-the art technologies, such as Blockchain and Machine Learning algorithms. It shows high levels of tolerance against cyber threats, as it contains many levels of security. The combination of Blockchain, MLP and CNN makes the process tamper proof. Both the credentials of the user and the process itself are validated.

However, due to the complexity of the security process, some issues may arise. The proposed framework ensures that only authorized users can have access to the IoT network and its corresponding devices. If a potential user wants to turn on a device (e.g., the air condition, or the water heater) he/she does not consider the response time important (wether it is 1 min or half a minute). Nevertheless, there are some other actions that may require faster response, depending on the type of the infrastructure. This type of potential problem, can be resolved to negligible levels with a plethora of actions. First of all, the keeper of the infrastructure, could choose a small number of hidden, Convolutional or Maxpooling layers in order to simplify the used networks. Second, the PoW could be applied only on a part of the blockchain (e.g., on the last 10 blocks). This could significantly reduce complexity and running time. Furthermore, fast access (if not default) can be offered for some commands of low risk (e.g. turn on and off the lights) which will required only the credentials of the users (or only Biometrics, for even less complexity). This strategy could skip the mining process in order for these actions to be performed instantly.

The complexity of the proposed framework is an issue that requires further attention in a future research effort. To achieve the aforementioned architecture, it is understood that the Super Node must be a computer or a network of computers with high standard features. Furthermore, there is a need for internal or external storing space (servers or other computers) in which the weights of the NNs will be stored. Last but not least, the miners' infrastructure that requires significant processing power, is quite expensive. Expensive Graphic Processing Units are required for the implementation of this framework [39].

However, there could be two potential solutions to address this issue, which could lead to a lighter version of such a system. The first is to limit the architecture of the proposed approach, to an offline computer (not necessarily of a high standard). This solution can have one computer with high computational power to be used for the SN, and one to be used as external or internal server (for the storage of all the weights). Moreover, it will comprise of two miners, one to solve the complex mathematical problem for the case of the new block, and one to be used for the validation of the blockchain after the new block is added. Although this architectural reduction reduces security levels, it still offers a high level of protection, as the basic idea behind the methodology still exists.

The second solution presupposes the establishment of a company that will offer the above services. The basic concept behind the company's establishment will be to serve not one homeowner, but many at the same time, using the same resources. The company will supply all miners, all servers needed for the weights, and all super nodes required to control the security process.

Thus, a user will give a monthly subscription to rent a company's super node. The super node of the company will be established inside the infrastructure, or it will be used remotely from the physical space of the company. The total number of miners will be used for the validity of the blockchain of several distinct infrastructures. Finally, the storing servers are easy to implement for all of the weights of all costumers. The company's costs related to energy consumption or maintenance of existing buildings, or the purchase of new super nodes for the users, will be covered by the fund created by the monthly subscriptions.

To make the scenario realistic, a large number of subscribers are needed, as for each new subscriber, there are already storing servers and miners, and only the super node will be needed. That is, as the number of users increases linearly, the company's revenue will increase linearly. Sticking to the second solution, a different approach for the Miners could be applied. Instead of purchasing equipment from the company, existing miners on the market could be used. For example, a miner mining bitcoin could apply validation for a company subscriber and could be paid with the companies' token. This token can then be used by the miner to be paid for the received services from the company. This way the company will only need to purchase the storing servers and the super nodes.

## 5 Conclusion and Future Work

In this manuscript, the authors introduce a holistic theoretical approach, for the authorization of a user to access a device via the IoT of a civil infrastructure. The architecture of this approach comprises of the state-of-the art technologies, like Blockchain Technology and DL techniques (MLP, CNN). The methodology offers many layers of security, making the whole process tamper proof. It uses Biometrics and other credentials derived from the 7 layers of OSI model, in order to validate the user identity, as well as, Blockchain Technology for storing and validating the whole process. A significant part of the process is decentralized and distributed, making the whole process even less prone to cyber threats. As all approaches to cyber security have weaknesses, this one also addresses some important issues which were discussed in detail in Sect. 5. In the same section, solutions were proposed to address the problems and difficulties that arise, mainly due to the complexity of methodology.

This specific holistic approach is not case depended and it can be properly tailored for any type of urban-civil infrastrucrue. For example, it could be used on a rising bridge, so that it can be opened to allow ships to pass safely, without the risk of someone not being authorized to affect the state of the bridge. However, this paper describes only the foundations of such a framework. Future research will focus in the application of a respective framework in a real residence after receiving funding from a research project. This could serve as a pilot for further introduction of these technologies in real life.

## References

1. Alqahtani, H., Sarker, I.H., Kalim, A., Minhaz Hossain, S., Ikhlaq, S., Hossain, S.: Cyber intrusion detection using machine learning classification techniques. In: Chaubey, N., Parikh, S., Amin, K. (eds.) COMS2 2020. CCIS, vol. 1235, pp. 121–131. Springer, Singapore (2020). https://doi.org/10.1007/978-981-15-6648-6_10
2. Ashton, K.: That 'Internet of Things' thing. RFID J. **22**(7), 97–114 (2009)
3. Wortmann, F., Flüchter, K.: Internet of things. Bus. Inf. Syst. Eng. **57**(3), 221–224 (2015)
4. Stojkoska, B.L.R., Trivodaliev, K.V.: A review of Internet of Things for smart home: challenges and solutions. J. Clean. Prod. **140**, 1454–1464 (2017)
5. Andrea, I., Chrysostomou, C., Hadjichristofi, G.: Internet of Things: security vulnerabilities and challenges. In: IEEE Symposium on Computers and Communication, pp. 180–187 (2015)
6. Mohammadi, S., Mirvaziri, H., Ghazizadeh-Ahsaee, M., Karimipour, H.: Cyber intrusion detection by combined feature selection algorithm. J. Inf. Secur. Appl. **44**, 80–88 (2019)
7. Tavallaee, M., Stakhanova, N., Ghorbani, A.A.: Toward credible evaluation of anomaly-based intrusion-detection methods. IEEE Trans. Syst. Man Cybern. Part C (Appl. Rev.) **40**(5), 516–524 (2010)
8. Buczak, A.L., Guven, E.: A survey of data mining and machine learning methods for cyber security intrusion detection. IEEE Commun. Surv. Tutor. **18**(2), 1153–1176 (2015)

9. Psathas, A.P., Iliadis, L., Papaleonidas, A., Bountas, D.: A hybrid deep learning ensemble for cyber intrusion detection. In: Iliadis, L., Macintyre, J., Jayne, C., Pimenidis, E. (eds.) EANN 2021. PINNS, vol. 3, pp. 27–41. Springer, Cham (2021). https://doi.org/10.1007/978-3-030-80568-5_3

10. Nakamoto, S.: Bitcoin: a peer-to-peer electronic cash system. Decentralized Bus. Rev. 21260 (2008)

11. Huh, S., Cho, S., Kim, S.: Managing IoT devices using Blockchain platform. In: International Conference on Advanced Communication Technology, pp. 464–467 (2017)

12. Li, X., Jiang, P., Chen, T., Luo, X., Wen, Q.: A survey on the security of blockchain systems. Futur. Gener. Comput. Syst. **107**, 841–853 (2020)

13. Yu, J., Lee, H., Kim, M.S., Park, D.: Traffic flooding attack detection with SNMP MIB using SVM. Comput. Commun. 31(17), 4212–4219 (2008)

14. Kulkarni, R.V., Venayagamoorthy, G.K.: Neural network based secure media access control protocol for wireless sensor networks. In: Proceedings of the International Joint Conference on Neural Networks, pp. 3437–3444, June 2009

15. Branch, J.W., Giannella, C., Szymanski, B., Wolff, R., Kargupta, H.: In-network outlier detection in wireless sensor networks. Knowl. Inform. Syst. **34**(1), 23–54 (2013)

16. Shi, C., Liu, J., Liu, H., Chen, Y.: Smart user authentication through actuation of daily activities leveraging WiFi-enabled IoT. In: Proceedings of the ACM International Symposium on Mobile AdHoc Networking and Computing, pp. 1–10, July 2017

17. Bostani, H., Sheikhan, M.: Hybrid of anomaly-based and specification-based IDS for Internet of Things using unsupervised OPF based on MapReduce approach. Comput. Commun. **98**, 52–71 (2017)

18. Pointcheval, D.: Neural Networks and their Cryptographic Applications. Livre des resumes Eurocode Institute for Research in Computer Science and Automation, 1–7 (1994)

19. Kinzel, W., Kanter, I.: Interacting neural networks and cryptography secure exchange of information by synchronization of neural networks. In: Kramer, B. (eds.) Advances in Solid State Physics. ASSP, vol. 42, 383–391. Springer, Heidelberg (2002). https://doi.org/10.1007/3-540-45618-X_30

20. Klimov, A., Mityagin, A., Shamir, A.: Analysis of neural cryptography. In: Zheng, Y. (ed.) ASIACRYPT 2002. LNCS, vol. 2501, pp. 288–298. Springer, Heidelberg (2002). https://doi.org/10.1007/3-540-36178-2_18

21. Volna, E., Kotyrba, M., Kocian, V., Janosek, M.: Cryptography based on the neural network. In: European Conference on Modelling and Simulation, pp. 1–6 (2012)

22. Yayık, A., Kutlu, Y.: Neural network based cryptography. Int. J. Neural Mass - Parallel Comput. Inf. Syst. **24**(2), 177–192 (2014)

23. Xu, D., Xiao, L., Sun, L., Lei, M.: Game theoretic study on blockchain based secure edge networks. In: IEEE International Conference on Communications in China, pp. 1–5 (2017)

24. Cha, S.-C., Yeh, K.-H.: An ISO/IEC 15408-2 compliant security auditing system with blockchain technology. In: IEEE Conference on Communications and Network Security, pp. 1–2 (2018)

25. Gai, K., Raymond, K.-K., Zhu, L.: Blockchain-enabled reengineering of cloud datacenters. IEEE Cloud Comput. **5**(6), 21–25 (2018)

26. Gupta, Y., Shorey, R., Kulkarni, D., Tew, J.: The applicability of blockchain in the Internet of Things. In: IEEE International Conference on Communication Systems & Networks, pp. 561–564 (2018)

27. Agrawal, R., et al.: Continuous security in IoT using blockchain. In: IEEE International Conference on Acoustics, Speech and Signal Processing, pp. 6423–6427 (2018)

28. Serrano, W.: The blockchain random neural network in cybersecurity and the Internet of Things. In: MacIntyre, J., Maglogiannis, I., Iliadis, L., Pimenidis, E. (eds.) AIAI 2019. IAICT, vol. 559, pp. 50–63. Springer, Cham (2019). https://doi.org/10.1007/978-3-030-19823-7_4

29. Giannoutakis, K.M., et al.: A blockchain solution for enhancing cybersecurity defence of IoT. In: 2020 IEEE International Conference on Blockchain (Blockchain), pp. 490–495. IEEE, November 2020

30. Demertzis, K., Iliadis, L., Tziritas, N., Kikiras, P.: Anomaly detection via blockchained deep learning smart contracts in industry 4.0. Neural Comput. Appl. 32(23), 17361–17378 (2020)

31. Yaga, D.J., Mell, P.M., Roby, N., Scarfone, K.: Blockchain technology overview. Nat. Inst. Standards Technol., Gaithersburg, MD, USA, Technical report 8202 (2018)

32. Yu, Y., Li, Y., Tian, J., Liu, J.: Blockchain-based solutions to security and privacy issues in the Internet of Things. IEEE Wirel. Commun. 25(6), 12–18 (2018)

33. Arif, S., Khan, M.A., Rehman, S.U., Kabir, M.A., Imran, M.: Investigating smart home security: is blockchain the answer? IEEE Access 8, 117802–117816 (2020)

34. Yeung, D.S., Li, J.C., Ng, W.W., Chan, P.P.: MLPNN training via a multiobjective optimization of training error and stochastic sensitivity. IEEE Trans. Neural Netw. Learn. Syst. 27(5), 978–992 (2015)

35. Baek, J., Choi, Y.: Deep neural network for predicting ore production by truck-haulage systems in open-pit mines. Appl. Sci. 10(5), 1657 (2020)

36. Liu, W., Wang, Z., Liu, X., Zeng, N., Liu, Y., Alsaadi, F.E.: A survey of deep neural network architectures and their applications. Neurocomputing 234, 11–26 (2017)

37. O'Shea, K., Nash, R.: An introduction to convolutional neural networks. arXiv preprint arXiv: 1511.08458(2015)

38. Lin, I.-C., Liao, T.-C.: A survey of blockchain security issues and challenges. Int. J. Netw. Secur. 19, 653–659 (2017)

39. Wilson, L.: GPU prices and cryptocurrency returns. Appl. Financ. Lett. 11(1), 2–8 (2022)

40. Krizhevsky, A., Sutskever, I., Hinton, G.E.: ImageNet classification with deep convolutional neural networks. Adv. Neural Inf. Process. Syst. 25, 1097–1105 (2012). https://dl.acm.org/doi/10.5555/2999134.2999257

41. Simonyan, K., Zisserman, A.: Very deep convolutional networks for large-scale image recognition. arXiv preprint arXiv:1409.1556(2014)

42. He, K., Zhang, X., Ren, S., Sun, J.: Deep residual learning for image recognition. In: Proceedings of the IEEE Conference on Computer Vision and Pattern Recognition, pp. 770–778 (2016)

# Human Activity Recognition Under Partial Occlusion

Ioannis-Aris Kostis[1], Eirini Mathe[2], Evaggelos Spyrou[1,3]($\boxtimes$),
and Phivos Mylonas[2]

[1] Department of Computer Science and Telecommunications,
University of Thessaly, Lamia, Greece
espyrou@uth.gr
[2] Department of Informatics, Ionian University, Corfu, Greece
{c17math,fmylonas}@ionio.gr
[3] Institute of Informatics and Telecommunications, National Center for Scientific
Research – "Demokritos", Athens, Greece

**Abstract.** One of the major challenges in Human Activity Recognition
(HAR) using cameras, is occlusion of one or more body parts. However,
this problem is often underestimated in contemporary research works,
wherein training and evaluation is based on datasets shot under laboratory conditions, i.e., without some kind of occlusion. In this work we propose an approach for HAR in the presence of partial occlusion, i.e., in case
of up to two occluded body parts. We solve this problem using regression, performed by a deep neural network. That is, given an occluded
sample, we attempt to reconstruct the missing information regarding
the motion of the occluded part(s). We evaluate our approach using a
publicly available human motion dataset. Our experimental results indicate a significant increase of performance, when compared to a baseline
approach, wherein a network that has been trained using non-occluded
samples is evaluated using occluded samples. To the best of our knowledge, this is the first research work that tackles the problem of HAR
under occlusion as a regression problem.

**Keywords:** Human activity recognition · Deep learning · Regression

## 1 Introduction

Human activity recognition (HAR) still remains one of the most challenging
computer vision-related problems. It may be defined as the recognition of some
human behaviour within an image or a video sequence. An activity (or "action")
may be defined as a type of motion performed by a single human, taking place
within a relatively short time period (however, not instant) and involving multiple body parts [23]. This informal definition differentiates activities from gestures; the latter are typically instant and involve at most a couple of body parts.
Similarly, interactions may involve either a human and an object or two humans
and group activities involve more than one humans. Typical HAR applications

© Springer Nature Switzerland AG 2022
L. Iliadis et al. (Eds.): EANN 2022, CCIS 1600, pp. 297–309, 2022.
https://doi.org/10.1007/978-3-031-08223-8_25

include, yet are not limited to video surveillance, human-computer/robot interaction, augmented reality (AR), ambient assisted environments, health monitoring, intelligent driving, gaming and immersion, animation, etc. [3,20,23].

There exist several HAR approaches that are based on either wearable sensors or sensors installed within the subject's environment. In the former case, the most popular ones include smartwatches, hand/body worn sensors, smartphones, etc. Moreover, in the latter case, typical sensors include video/thermal cameras microphones, infrared, pressure, magnetic, RFID sensors [5] etc. However, it has been shown that wearable sensors are not preferred by the users, while their usability is below average [12,18]. Moreover, overloading the users' environment with a plethora of sensors may be an expensive task, requiring in some cases many interventions in home furniture and/or appliances, e.g., in case of a home environment. Therefore, several low-cost solutions tend to be based solely on cameras, detecting activities using the subjects' motion. Although such approaches are low-cost and demonstrate more than satisfactory performance in laboratory conditions, in real-life situations they suffer from viewpoint and illumination changes and occlusion.

In previous work [19] we dealt with the problem of viewpoint invariance and demonstrated that the decrease of accuracy due to viewpoint changes may be limited when using more than one cameras. Also, recent advances in technology have allowed for camera sensors that also capture depth information and perform significantly better in low-light conditions. Therefore, from the three aforementioned problems, occlusion is the one that introduces most limitations. Also in previous work [7] we assessed how partial occlusion of the subject affects the accuracy of recognition. We simulated occlusion by removing parts of captured visual data and showed that partial occlusion of the subject, in certain cases significantly affected the accuracy of recognition. To tackle this limitation, in this work we aim to reconstruct occluded data, upon formulating this problem as a regression task. We use a deep neural network approach, whose input is a human skeleton, with one or more body parts removed, so as to simulate occlusion. The network is trained to output the skeleton upon estimating the missing parts. We demonstrate that this approach is able to significantly increase accuracy.

The rest of this paper is organized as follows: In Sect. 2 we present research works that aim to assess or even tackle the effect of occlusion in HAR-related scenarios. Then, in Sect. 3 we present the proposed regression methodology. Experimental results of are presented in Sect. 4. Finally, conclusions are drawn in Sect. 5, wherein plans for future work are also presented.

## 2    Related Work

During the last few years, a plethora of research works focusing on HAR, based on 2D representations of skeletal data have been presented [6,9,11,14,15,21,22]. Moreover, a may be found in [23]. However, although it is widely accepted that occlusion consists one of the most important factors that compromise the performance of HAR approaches [10], resulting to poor or even unusable results, few are those works that focus either on studied its effects on the performance of recognition or even attempt to overcome them.

To begin with, in the work of Iosifidis et al. [10], a multi-camera setup, surrounding the subject was used for HAR. In order to simulate occlusion, they first trained their algorithm using data from all available cameras and then evaluate using a randomly chosen subset. More specifically, they made the assumption that due to occlusion, not all cameras were simultaneously able to capture the subject's motion. However, we should note that in all cases more than one cameras were able to capture the whole body of the subjects. Also, recognition of a given activity took place upon combining results only from those cameras that are not affected at any means by occlusion. In the work of Gu et al. [8], randomly generated occlusion masks were used in both training and evaluation. Note that each mask caused the occlusion of more than one 2D skeletal joints. Then, and in order to reconstruct the skeleton, they used a regression network. Liu et al. [17] studied two augmentation strategies for modelling the effect of occlusion. The first discarded independent keypoints, while the second discarded structured sets of keypoints, i.e., those composing main body parts. Note that in this work occluded samples were included in the training process. Moreover, the authors herein made the assumption that the torso and the hips were always visible. Their recognition approach was based on learning view-invariant, occlusion-robust probabilistic embeddings. Similarly, Angelini et al. [2] also included artificially occluded samples within the training process. In that case, samples were created by randomly removing body landmarks according to a binary Bernoulli distribution. Their recognition approach was based on pose libraries which included several pose prototypes. When dealing with missing body parts, they exploited the aforementioned libraries either by matching occluded sequences to pre-defined prototypes, based on high-level features, or by filling missing parts upon searching through the pose libraries. In case of short-time occlusions, they used an interpolation approach.

Finally, in previous work [7] we performed a study, wherein our main goal was to assess the effect of occlusion of body parts, within a HAR approach. We created artificial occluded activity samples, by manually removing one or two body parts (i.e., upon removing subsets of skeleton joints). We made the following assumption: occlusion was continuous during the whole duration of activity and concerned the same part(s). For HAR, we used a deep neural network, that had been trained using only non-occluded samples, i.e., contrary to [2,8,17]. Also, in our study the whole skeleton was never "visible" as it was in the work presented in [10]. Finally, Gu et al. [8] proposed a regression-based approach which was limited to pose estimation.

# 3  Methodology

## 3.1  Occlusion of Skeletal Data

As in previous work [7,19], the proposed approach uses as input 3D trajectories of human skeletons. In 3D HAR problems, subjects perform actions in space and over time. We consider skeleton representations as sets of 3D joints. We use skeleton data that have been captured using the Microsoft Kinect v2 RGB/depth camera.[1] A human skeleton comprises of 25 joints, organized as a graph; each node corresponds to a body part such as arms, legs, head, neck etc., while edges follow the body structure, appropriately connecting pairs of joints. In Fig. 1 we illustrate a skeleton extracted using Kinect. Note that joints are shown as being grouped; each group corresponds to a body part, i.e., an arm, a leg or the torso. In the context of this work, an activity is considered to be a temporal sequence of 3D skeleton representations. For the sake of explanation, a visual example of an activity is illustrated in Fig. 2.

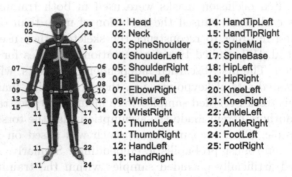

| | |
|---|---|
| 01: Head | 14: HandTipLeft |
| 02: Neck | 15: HandTipRight |
| 03: SpineShoulder | 16: SpineMid |
| 04: ShoulderLeft | 17: SpineBase |
| 05: ShoulderRight | 18: HipLeft |
| 06: ElbowLeft | 19: HipRight |
| 07: ElbowRight | 20: KneeLeft |
| 08: WristLeft | 21: KneeRight |
| 09: WristRight | 22: AnkleLeft |
| 10: ThumbLeft | 23: AnkleRight |
| 11: ThumbRight | 24: FootLeft |
| 12: HandLeft | 25: FootRight |
| 13: HandRight | |

**Fig. 1.** The 25 skeletal joints extracted by Microsoft Kinect, divided into five main body parts – blue: torso, red: left hand, green: right hand, magenta: left leg, orange: right leg. (Color figure online)

As it has already been mentioned in Sect. 1, occlusion may compromise the performance of HAR, in real-life scenarios. Within the context of several applications such as ambient assisted environments, AR environments etc., occlusion typically occurs due to e.g., activities taking place behind furniture, or e.g., due to the presence of more than one people in the same room. Of course, it should be obvious that occlusion of e.g., the legs when the subject performs the action "kicking" results to a significant loss of visual information, which in turn may result to failure of recognition. Although the aforementioned example is quite extreme, it is common sense that partial occlusion may hinder the effectiveness of HAR approaches. We should herein note that most large-scale public motion-based datasets such as the PKU-MMD dataset [16] have been created under ideal laboratory conditions, thus occlusion is prevented. Thus, since the creation of a large scale dataset is a time consuming task, we decided to follow an approach such as the one of Gu et al. [8]. More specifically, we manually discard subsets of joints that correspond to body parts, assuming that the these parts remain occluded during the whole action. For the sake of explanation, a visual example of an activity upon occlusion is illustrated in Fig. 2.

---

[1] https://developer.microsoft.com/en-us/windows/kinect.

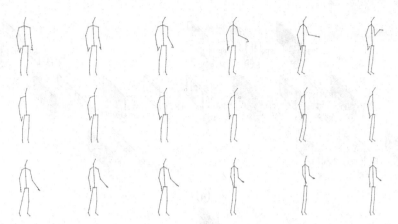

**Fig. 2.** Example skeleton sequences of the activity *handshaking*. First row: skeletons include all 25 joints; Second row: joints corresponding to left arm have been discarded; Third row: joints corresponding left arm have been reconstructed.

## 3.2   Regression of Skeletal Data

The input of our approach consists of temporal sequences of 3D skeleton data, i.e., as described in Subsect. 3.1. Upon imposing a linear interpolation step between consecutive timeframes so as to address temporal variability of activities, we set the length of all activity examples equal to $T_m$, i.e., to the size of the longest one in duration. Note that if the desired length is not reached upon one interpolation step, the process is repeated until the desired length is reached. As we will mention in Sect. 4, we use a dataset that has been captured using 3 cameras. Therefore, as we wish to exploit all possible information, we use the corresponding 3 skeleton sequences as input. We also assume that in every case of occlusion, the same missing body part(s) is (are) occluded in all 3 sequences.

The core philosophy of our approach is that since occlusion practically causes missing values (i.e., in our case some of joints of the skeleton are removed), we may formulate the problem of "reconstructing" those missing values as a regression task. More specifically, let $\mathbf{X}$ denote the original skeleton sequence and $\mathbf{X_o}$ the sequence resulting upon occlusion. The goal of regression is ideally to estimate a function $f$, so that $\mathbf{X}_r = f(\mathbf{X_o}) + \epsilon$, where $\mathbf{X}_r$ denotes the reconstructed skeleton sequence and $\epsilon$ is some error value, to be minimized.

To this goal, we use a Convolutional Recurrent Neural Network (CRNN) model, whose aim is to estimate the missing (occluded) data (joints). Its architecture is illustrated in Fig. 3a and is described in short as follows: The input of the network constitutes of sequential data from 3 cameras. Each camera provides a skeletal sequence under a different viewpoint. Given that in every sequence up to 2 skeletons are included (i.e., in case of interactions between 2 subjects), and each skeleton comprises 25 3-D joints, and the duration of the sequence is $T_m$, input layer size is $T_m \times 150$. Those three input branches are each filtered by a stack of 2 2-D convolutional layer, followed by a max-pooling layer that performs

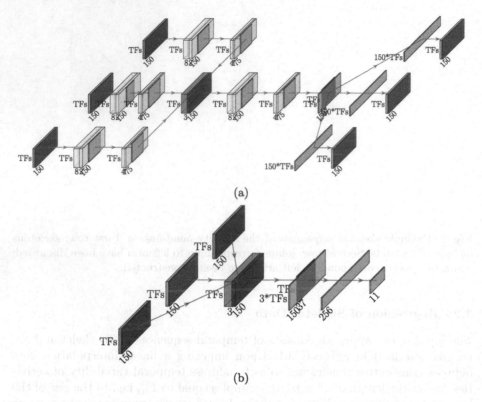

**Fig. 3.** (a) The CRNN that has been used for regression of skeletal joint sequences; (b) The RNN that has been used for classification. Layers have been colored as follows: Gray: input/output, concatenated, Light Orange: 2D convolutional, orange: max pooling, Light Blue: (input layer of) LSTM, Purple: fully connected (dense). Figure best viewed in color. (Color figure online)

$1 \times 2$ sub-sampling. This process repeats after the three branches are concatenated into a single tensor. This single tensor is again filtered by a stack of 2 2-D convolutional layer, followed by a max-pooling layer that performs $1 \times 2$ sub-sampling. The output of this layer constitutes the input to an LSTM layer, whose goal is to harness temporal information of skeletal data. Then, 3 parallel dense layers of size $T_m \times 150$ follow. They are ultimately reshaped to three $T_m \times 150$ output layers. For loss computation, the Mean Square Error (MSE) has been used.

At this point we would like to note that the reason for the use of an asymmetrical kernel (i.e., $1 \times 2$) is that while being sub-sampled this way, information is compressed only along the spatial coordinates' axes, leaving temporal information intact. We experimentally verified that this kernel choice led to a significant improvement of the performance of the network.

The occluded data $\mathbf{X}_o$ are given as input in both training and testing phases of the network. Also, the targets of the network are the non-occluded data $\mathbf{X}$; these data are to be estimated by the network, i.e., its output are reconstructed data $\mathbf{X}_r$. Thus, the network is train to learn $f$, while minimizing $\epsilon$. As we mentioned in Subsect. 3.1, each skeleton joint has its own id. Therefore, in a real-life application, we could easily identify missing (occluded) joints. Bearing this in mind, we opted to train one network per occlusion case, ending up with 8 different networks. Therefore, given an input skeletal sequence, it is fed to the appropriate network, upon identifying missing joints.

At this point, the trained network serves as a mean to reconstruct missing skeletal data of a given skeletal sequence. For the sake of explanation, a visual example of an activity upon reconstruction is illustrated in Fig. 2. Thus, we are able to proceed with its classification into one of the pre-defined classes. This is performed using a second network, whose architecture is based on an LSTM layer and is illustrated in Fig. 3b. As expected, data collected from three cameras constitute again the input of this network. The three branches are concatenated into a single tensor, serving as input to the LSTM layer. The latter is followed by another dense layer of size 11, i.e., equal to the number of classes and constitutes the output layer of the network. During training, the non-occluded data $\mathbf{X}$ serve as input data to the network, thus no occlusion information is used. During testing, its input is a reconstructed skeletal sequence $\mathbf{X}_r$.

# 4   Experiments and Results

## 4.1   Dataset

Since to the best of our knowledge such a large scale dataset consisting of 3D skeletal data does not exist, we used part of the PKU-MMD dataset [16]. Note that this dataset consists of activities that have been recorded using Microsoft Kinect v2 sensor. In order to produce results comparable to the ones of our previous work [7], we have selected the same 11 classes, i.e.: *eat meal snack* (10), *falling* (11), *handshaking* (14), *hugging other person* (16), *make a phone call answer phone* (20), *playing with phone tablet* (23), *reading* (30), *sitting down* (33), *standing up* (34), *typing on a keyboard* (46) and *wearing a jacket* (48). Numbers in parentheses denote the corresponding class ids and will be used at the remaining of this paper. A total number of 1000 samples has been used for training, 100 for validation, while 400 samples have been used for testing.

## 4.2  Experimental Setup and Network Training

Experiments were performed on a personal workstation with an Intel$^{TM}$i7 4770 4-core processor on 3.40 GHz and 16GB RAM, using NVIDIA$^{TM}$Geforce GTX 1050Ti GPU with 4 GB VRAM and Ubuntu 20.04 (64 bit). The deep architecture has been implemented in Python, using Keras 2.4.3 [4] with the Tensorflow 2.5 [1] backend. All data pre-processing and processing steps have been implemented in Python 3.9 using NumPy and SciPy. For the training of the estimator, we used the LeakyReLU activation function, except from the LSTM layer wherein the tanh function was used, and the last dense layer wherein linear activation function was used. For the training of the classifier, the LeakyReLU and tanh activation functions were used respectively, except from the last layer, wherein the softmax activation function was used. Furthermore, we set the batch size to 5 and 10 for the training of the classifier and the estimator respectively. The final values of the aforementioned parameters were decided upon a trial and error process. The Adam optimizer was utilized in both cases, the dropout was set to 0.3, set the learning rate to 0.001 and trained for 50 epochs, using the loss of the validation set calculated via MSE as an early stopping method, in order to avert overfitting. Moreover, since the duration of each activity was set to 150 frames, upon interpolation, the size of the input data was 3 × 150 × 150. Finally, the kernel size of the Conv2D layers was set to 3 × 3 and the stride was set to 1, due to the layers' filter dimensions that left no margin for further tuning.

## 4.3  Results

For the experimental evaluation of the proposed methodology, we considered eight cases of body part removal, so as to simulate occlusion. More specifically, we removed one arm/leg, both arms/legs, one arm and one leg from the same side. For comparison, we also performed experiments without any body part removal. In every case we evaluated classification upon removal and upon reconstruction. Experimental results are depicted in Table 1, wherein as "baseline," we denote the methodology of [7], while using the herein presented network architecture. The weighted accuracy (WA) was 0.92 without any body part removal. Moreover, it ranged between 0.21–0.90 in case of some body part removal, while it ranged between 0.70–0.91 upon reconstruction. In 7 out of 8 cases, significant improvement was observed, in terms of WA, while performance was almost equal in case of removal of Left Leg. Intuitively, one should observe that the majority of the activities we used to evaluate our approach mainly consists of upper body motion (i.e., left and/or right arm). Upon careful observation of the samples of the datasets, this assumption has been verified. This is also reflected to the results of Table 1, wherein it may observed that in cases of occluded arms the improvement is significantly large, with most notable example the case of both arms, wherein WA improves from 0.21 to 0.70.

Upon careful observation of the confusion matrices depicted in Fig. 4, for each occlusion case we should notice the following, when comparing with the case where all joints had been used: a) in case of any occluded arm, class *make a phone call/answer phone* is often confused with *playing with phone/tablet* and class *eat meal/snack* is often confused with *reading*; b) in case of occluded left leg, class *wear jacket* is often confused with *reading* or *standing up*; and c) finally, in case of both arms occluded, 7 classes show adequate performance.

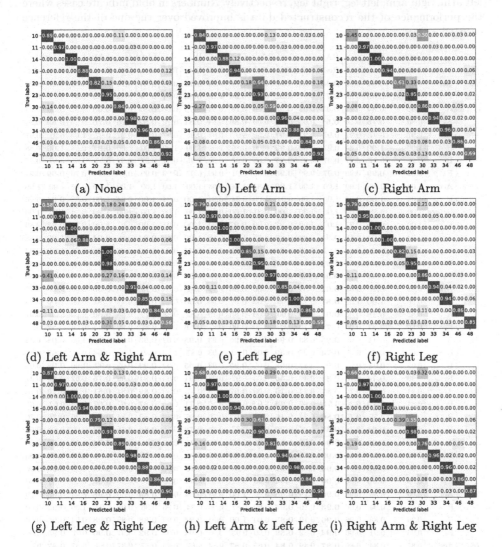

(a) None          (b) Left Arm          (c) Right Arm

(d) Left Arm & Right Arm     (e) Left Leg          (f) Right Leg

(g) Left Leg & Right Leg   (h) Left Arm & Left Leg   (i) Right Arm & Right Leg

**Fig. 4.** Normalized confusion matrices using min-max normalization, for classification (a) without removing any body part, (b)–(i) upon removing the body part(s) denoted in the caption of the corresponding subfigure.

**Table 1.** Experimental results of the proposed approach. "Rec." and "Ref." denote reconstructed and reference case (see Sect. 3). Acc, P, R, $F_1$, WA denote Accuracy, Precision, Recall, $F_1$ score and Weighted Accuracy, respectively. By "None" we denote the case wherein all body parts are included. LA, RA, LL, RL denote the occlusion of left arm, right arm, left leg, right leg, respectively. Numbers in bold indicate cases where the performance of the reconstructed data is improved over the one of the reference case.

| | | None | LA | | RA | | LA&RA | | LL | | RL | | LL&RL | | LA&LL | | RA&RL | |
|---|---|---|---|---|---|---|---|---|---|---|---|---|---|---|---|---|---|---|
| Class | Metric | Baseline | Rec. | Ref. | Rec. | Ref. | Rec. | Ref. | Rec. | Ref. | Rec. | Ref. | Rec. | Ref. | Rec. | Ref. | Rec. | Ref. |
| 10 | Acc | 0.90 | **0.84** | 0.11 | **0.45** | 0.03 | **0.58** | 0.00 | 0.79 | 0.92 | **0.79** | 0.66 | **0.87** | 0.74 | **0.68** | 0.21 | **0.66** | 0.24 |
| | P | 0.83 | **0.68** | 0.29 | **0.77** | 0.17 | **0.52** | 0.00 | **0.94** | 0.78 | **0.83** | 0.81 | 0.79 | 0.82 | **0.72** | 0.31 | 0.74 | 0.75 |
| | R | 0.89 | **0.84** | 0.11 | **0.45** | 0.03 | **0.58** | 0.00 | 0.79 | 0.92 | **0.79** | 0.66 | **0.87** | 0.74 | **0.68** | 0.21 | **0.66** | 0.24 |
| | $F_1$ | 0.86 | **0.75** | 0.15 | **0.57** | 0.05 | **0.55** | 0.00 | **0.86** | 0.84 | **0.81** | 0.72 | **0.82** | 0.78 | **0.70** | 0.25 | **0.69** | 0.36 |
| 11 | Acc | 0.97 | 0.97 | 0.97 | 0.97 | 0.97 | **0.97** | 0.00 | 0.97 | 0.97 | 0.95 | 0.97 | 0.97 | 0.97 | 0.97 | 1.00 | 0.97 | 0.97 |
| | P | 1.00 | **1.00** | 0.84 | 0.97 | 1.00 | **0.92** | 0.00 | 0.86 | 1.00 | 1.00 | 1.00 | 1.00 | 1.00 | **0.97** | 0.54 | **1.00** | 0.88 |
| | R | 0.97 | 0.97 | 0.97 | 0.97 | 0.97 | **0.97** | 0.00 | 0.97 | 0.97 | 0.95 | 0.97 | 0.97 | 0.97 | 0.97 | 1.00 | 0.97 | 0.97 |
| | $F_1$ | 0.99 | **0.99** | 0.90 | 0.97 | 0.99 | **0.95** | 0.00 | 0.91 | 0.99 | 0.97 | 0.99 | 0.99 | 0.99 | **0.97** | 0.70 | **0.99** | 0.92 |
| 14 | Acc | 1.00 | 0.88 | 1.00 | 1.00 | 1.00 | **1.00** | 0.81 | **1.00** | 0.94 | 1.00 | 1.00 | 1.00 | 1.00 | **1.00** | 0.94 | 1.00 | 1.00 |
| | P | 1.00 | **1.00** | 0.94 | 1.00 | 1.00 | 0.94 | 1.00 | 0.94 | 0.94 | **1.00** | 0.84 | **1.00** | 0.84 | **1.00** | 0.88 | **0.94** | 0.76 |
| | R | 1.00 | 0.88 | 1.00 | 1.00 | 1.00 | **1.00** | 0.81 | **1.00** | 0.94 | 1.00 | 1.00 | 1.00 | 1.00 | **1.00** | 0.94 | 1.00 | 1.00 |
| | $F_1$ | 1.00 | 0.93 | 0.97 | 1.00 | 1.00 | **0.97** | 0.90 | **0.97** | 0.94 | **1.00** | 0.91 | **1.00** | 0.91 | **1.00** | 0.91 | **0.97** | 0.86 |
| 16 | Acc | 0.88 | **0.94** | 0.88 | **0.94** | 0.88 | **0.88** | 0.69 | **1.00** | 0.88 | **1.00** | 0.88 | **0.94** | 0.88 | **0.94** | 0.81 | **1.00** | 0.88 |
| | P | 1.00 | 0.88 | 0.93 | 0.94 | 1.00 | **0.93** | 0.85 | 0.94 | 1.00 | **0.94** | 0.93 | **1.00** | 0.93 | **1.00** | 0.76 | **1.00** | 0.82 |
| | R | 0.88 | **0.94** | 0.88 | **0.94** | 0.88 | **0.88** | 0.69 | **1.00** | 0.88 | **1.00** | 0.88 | **0.94** | 0.88 | **0.94** | 0.81 | **1.00** | 0.88 |
| | $F_1$ | 0.93 | **0.91** | 0.90 | **0.94** | 0.93 | **0.90** | 0.76 | **0.97** | 0.93 | **0.97** | 0.90 | **0.97** | 0.90 | **0.97** | 0.79 | **1.00** | 0.85 |
| 20 | Acc | 0.82 | **0.18** | 0.03 | **0.61** | 0.39 | 0.00 | 0.00 | **0.85** | 0.79 | 0.82 | 0.88 | 0.79 | 0.88 | **0.30** | 0.00 | 0.39 | 0.97 |
| | P | 0.96 | **1.00** | 1.00 | **0.87** | 0.13 | 0.00 | 0.00 | **0.97** | 0.96 | **0.90** | 0.48 | **0.96** | 0.47 | **0.91** | 0.00 | **1.00** | 0.16 |
| | R | 0.82 | **0.18** | 0.03 | **0.61** | 0.39 | 0.00 | 0.00 | **0.85** | 0.79 | 0.82 | 0.88 | 0.79 | 0.88 | **0.30** | 0.00 | 0.39 | 0.97 |
| | $F_1$ | 0.89 | **0.31** | 0.06 | **0.71** | 0.19 | 0.00 | 0.00 | **0.90** | 0.87 | **0.86** | 0.62 | 0.87 | 0.90 | **0.45** | 0.00 | **0.57** | 0.27 |
| 23 | Acc | 0.95 | 0.93 | 0.98 | **0.95** | 0.83 | **0.98** | 0.05 | **0.95** | 0.93 | **0.95** | 0.02 | **0.93** | 0.05 | 0.91 | 1.00 | **0.98** | 0.05 |
| | P | 0.85 | **0.61** | 0.55 | **0.74** | 0.27 | **0.39** | 0.06 | 0.89 | 0.93 | 0.87 | 1.00 | 0.89 | 1.00 | **0.64** | 0.45 | **0.67** | 0.17 |
| | R | 0.95 | 0.93 | 0.98 | **0.95** | 0.83 | **0.98** | 0.05 | **0.95** | 0.93 | **0.95** | 0.02 | **0.93** | 0.05 | 0.90 | 1.00 | **0.98** | 0.05 |
| | $F_1$ | 0.90 | **0.74** | 0.70 | **0.83** | 0.40 | **0.56** | 0.05 | 0.92 | 0.93 | **0.91** | 0.05 | **0.91** | 0.09 | **0.75** | 0.62 | **0.80** | 0.07 |
| 30 | Acc | 0.84 | 0.60 | 0.70 | **0.87** | 0.24 | **0.16** | 0.00 | **0.97** | 0.76 | 0.87 | 0.89 | **0.89** | 0.84 | **0.81** | 0.30 | **0.76** | 0.70 |
| | P | 0.84 | **0.79** | 0.36 | 0.54 | 0.69 | **0.33** | 0.00 | 0.64 | 0.80 | **0.71** | 0.65 | **0.87** | 0.67 | **0.67** | 0.24 | 0.62 | 0.65 |
| | R | 0.84 | 0.59 | 0.70 | **0.86** | 0.24 | **0.16** | 0.00 | **0.97** | 0.76 | 0.86 | 0.89 | **0.89** | 0.84 | **0.81** | 0.30 | **0.76** | 0.70 |
| | $F_1$ | 0.84 | **0.68** | 0.48 | **0.67** | 0.36 | **0.22** | 0.00 | 0.77 | 0.78 | **0.78** | 0.75 | **0.88** | 0.75 | **0.73** | 0.27 | 0.68 | 0.68 |
| 33 | Acc | 0.98 | **0.96** | 0.74 | **0.94** | 0.06 | **0.91** | 0.00 | 0.85 | 0.98 | 0.94 | 0.98 | 0.98 | 0.98 | **0.94** | 0.11 | **0.96** | 0.00 |
| | P | 0.98 | 0.96 | 0.97 | **0.98** | 0.75 | **0.98** | 0.00 | **0.98** | 0.98 | 0.96 | 0.98 | 0.98 | 0.98 | 0.98 | 1.00 | **0.98** | 0.00 |
| | R | 0.98 | **0.96** | 0.74 | **0.94** | 0.06 | **0.91** | 0.00 | 0.85 | 0.98 | 0.94 | 0.98 | 0.98 | 0.98 | **0.94** | 0.11 | **0.96** | 0.00 |
| | $F_1$ | 0.98 | **0.96** | 0.84 | **0.96** | 0.11 | **0.94** | 0.00 | 0.91 | 0.98 | 0.95 | 0.98 | 0.98 | 0.98 | **0.96** | 0.20 | **0.97** | 0.00 |
| 34 | Acc | 0.96 | 0.89 | 0.96 | **0.96** | 0.19 | **0.46** | 0.00 | **1.00** | 0.94 | **0.94** | 0.90 | **0.89** | 0.85 | **0.98** | 0.54 | **0.96** | 0.00 |
| | P | 0.96 | 0.94 | 0.96 | **0.93** | 0.10 | **0.94** | 0.00 | 0.87 | 0.96 | 0.94 | 0.96 | 0.96 | 0.98 | 0.94 | 1.00 | **0.94** | 0.00 |
| | R | 0.96 | 0.88 | 0.96 | **0.96** | 0.19 | **0.85** | 0.00 | **1.00** | 0.94 | **0.94** | 0.90 | **0.88** | 0.85 | **0.98** | 0.54 | **0.96** | 0.00 |
| | $F_1$ | 0.96 | 0.91 | 0.96 | **0.94** | 0.32 | **0.89** | 0.00 | 0.93 | 0.95 | **0.94** | 0.93 | **0.92** | 0.91 | **0.96** | 0.70 | **0.95** | 0.00 |
| 46 | Acc | 0.87 | 0.84 | 0.89 | **0.87** | 0.49 | **0.84** | 0.65 | **0.87** | 0.84 | 0.87 | 0.87 | 0.87 | 0.87 | 0.84 | 0.87 | **0.87** | 0.65 |
| | P | 0.97 | **0.94** | 0.56 | **0.89** | 0.31 | **0.97** | 0.08 | **0.97** | 0.97 | 0.94 | 1.00 | 0.97 | 0.97 | **0.91** | 0.33 | **0.91** | 0.49 |
| | R | 0.86 | 0.84 | 0.89 | **0.86** | 0.49 | **0.84** | 0.65 | **0.86** | 0.84 | 0.86 | 0.86 | 0.86 | 0.86 | 0.84 | 0.86 | **0.86** | 0.65 |
| | $F_1$ | 0.91 | **0.89** | 0.69 | **0.88** | 0.38 | **0.90** | 0.14 | **0.91** | 0.90 | 0.90 | 0.93 | 0.91 | 0.91 | **0.87** | 0.48 | **0.89** | 0.56 |
| 48 | Acc | 0.92 | **0.92** | 0.28 | **0.69** | 0.13 | **0.56** | 0.00 | 0.59 | 0.85 | 0.85 | 0.85 | 0.90 | 0.90 | **0.90** | 0.05 | **0.87** | 0.13 |
| | P | 0.84 | 0.68 | 0.82 | **0.84** | 0.71 | **0.59** | 0.00 | **1.00** | 0.89 | **0.89** | 0.62 | **0.73** | 0.64 | **0.83** | 0.67 | 0.89 | 1.00 |
| | R | 0.92 | **0.92** | 0.28 | **0.69** | 0.13 | **0.56** | 0.00 | 0.59 | 0.85 | 0.85 | 0.85 | 0.90 | 0.90 | **0.90** | 0.05 | **0.87** | 0.13 |
| | $F_1$ | 0.88 | **0.78** | 0.43 | **0.76** | 0.22 | **0.58** | 0.00 | 0.74 | 0.87 | **0.87** | 0.72 | **0.80** | 0.74 | **0.86** | 0.10 | **0.88** | 0.23 |
| all | WA | 0.92 | **0.82** | 0.68 | **0.84** | 0.40 | **0.70** | 0.21 | 0.89 | 0.90 | **0.90** | 0.80 | **0.91** | 0.80 | **0.84** | 0.48 | **0.86** | 0.41 |

# 5   Conclusions and Future Work

In this paper we presented an approach for human activity recognition under occlusion, which was based on a convolutional recurrent neural network model and used as input 3D skeleton joint sequences. We simulated occlusion by removing one or two body parts (i.e., sets of joints corresponding to arms and/or legs). By using the aforementioned model, we managed to reconstruct missing joints using regression. We showed that this way, we could achieve a significant boost of performance in a classification task of 11 activities. This could be of great utilization e.g., in AR environments and applications, where such performance plays a significant and important role for the overall user experience and also may act as a means of assessing user engagement, e.g., when a visitor of a museum makes a phone call while interacting with an AR application, this should be an indicator of low engagement, while when she/he is reading in front of an AR screen, this should be an indicator of high engagement. Moreover, another important field of application would be an ambient assisted environment, where the goal is to detect activities of daily living (ADLs) [13].

Future research work may focus on several aspects of the problem of occlusion. Firstly, we would like to investigate cases such as temporally partial occlusion. Then we would like to investigate the use of other deep neural network architectures, such as generative adversarial networks (GANs). Moreover, we would like to perform experiments using full PKU-MMD and possibly other datasets. We would like to perform comparisons of the given approach to one that uses occluded samples for training the neural network that we have herein used for classification, without a regression step. Finally, we plan to perform real-life experiments within the AR environment of the Mon Repo project[2].

**Acknowledgements.** This research was co-financed by the European Union and Greek national funds through the Competitiveness, Entrepreneurship and Innovation Operational Programme, under the Call «Special Actions "Aquaculture" - "Industrial materials" - "Open innovation in culture"»; project title: "Strengthening User Experience & Cultural Innovation through Experiential Knowledge Enhancement with Enhanced Reality Technologies - MON REPO"; project code: $T6YB\Pi$ - 00303; MIS code: 5066856

# References

1. Abadi, M., et al.: TensorFlow: a system for large-scale machine learning. In 12th USENIX Symposium on Operating Systems Design and Implementation (OSDI 2016) (2016)
2. Angelini, F., Fu, Z., Long, Y., Shao, L., Naqvi, S.M.: 2D pose-based real-time human action recognition with occlusion-handling. IEEE Trans. Multimed. **22**(6), 1433–1446 (2019)

---

[2] https://monrepo.online/.

3. Antoshchuk, S., Kovalenko, M., Sieck, J.: Gesture recognition-based human–computer interaction interface for multimedia applications. In: Jat, D.S., Sieck, J., Muyingi, H.N.S.-N., Winschiers-Theophilus, H., Peters, A., Nggada, S. (eds.) Digitisation of Culture: Namibian and International Perspectives, pp. 269–286. Springer, Singapore (2018). https://doi.org/10.1007/978-981-10-7697-8_16
4. Chollet, F., et al.: Keras (2015). https://github.com/fchollet/keras
5. Debes, C., Merentitis, A., Sukhanov, S., Niessen, M., Frangiadakis, N., Bauer, A.: Monitoring activities of daily living in smart homes: understanding human behavior. IEEE Sign. Process. Mag. **33**(2), 81–94 (2016)
6. Du, Y., Fu, Y., Wang, L.: Skeleton based action recognition with convolutional neural network. In: 2015 3rd IAPR Asian Conference on Pattern Recognition (ACPR), pp. 579–583. IEEE (2015)
7. Giannakos, I., Mathe, E., Spyrou, E., Mylonas, P.: A study on the effect of occlusion in human activity recognition. In: The 14th PErvasive Technologies Related to Assistive Environments Conference, pp. 473–482 (2021)
8. Gu, R., Wang, G., Hwang, J.N.: Exploring severe occlusion: multi-person 3D pose estimation with gated convolution. In: 2020 25th International Conference on Pattern Recognition (ICPR), pp. 8243–8250. IEEE (2021)
9. Hou, Y., Li, Z., Wang, P., Li, W.: Skeleton optical spectra-based action recognition using convolutional neural networks. IEEE Trans. Circ. Syst. Video Technol. **28**(3), 807–811 (2016)
10. Iosifidis, A., Tefas, A., Pitas, I.: Multi-view human action recognition under occlusion based on fuzzy distances and neural networks. In: Proceedings of the 20th European Signal Processing Conference (EUSIPCO). IEEE (2012)
11. Ke, Q., An, S., Bennamoun, M., Sohel, F., Boussaid, F.: SkeletonNet: mining deep part features for 3-D action recognition. IEEE Sign. Process. Lett. **24**(6), 731–735 (2017)
12. Keogh, A., Dorn, J.F., Walsh, L., Calvo, F., Caulfield, B.: Comparing the usability and acceptability of wearable sensors among older Irish adults in a real-world context: observational study. JMIR Mhealth Uhealth **8**(4), e15704 (2020)
13. Lawton, M.P., Brody, E.M.: Assessment of older people: self-maintaining and instrumental activities of daily living. Gerontol. **9**(3 Part 1), 179–186 (1969)
14. Li, C., Hou, Y., Wang, P., Li, W.: Joint distance maps based action recognition with convolutional neural networks. IEEE Sign. Process. Lett. **24**(5), 624–628 (2017)
15. Liu, M., Liu, H., Chen, C.: Enhanced skeleton visualization for view invariant human action recognition. Pattern Recogn. **68**, 346–362 (2017)
16. Liu, C., Hu, Y., Li, Y., Song, S., Liu, J.: PKU-MMD: a large scale benchmark for continuous multi-modal human action understanding. arXiv preprint arXiv:1703.07475 (2017)
17. Liu, T., et al.: View-invariant, occlusion-robust probabilistic embedding for human pose. Int. J. Comput. Vis. **130**(1), 111–135 (2022)
18. Majumder, S., Mondal, T., Deen, M.J.: Wearable sensors for remote health monitoring. Sensors **17**(1), 130 (2017)
19. Papadakis, A., Mathe, E., Spyrou, E., Mylonas, P.: A geometric approach for cross-view human action recognition using deep learning. In: 11th International Symposium on Image and Signal Processing and Analysis (ISPA). IEEE (2019)
20. Ranasinghe, S., Al Machot, F., Mayr, H.C.: A review on applications of activity recognition systems with regard to performance and evaluation. Int. J. Distrib. Sens. Netw. **12**(8), 1550147716665520 (2016)

21. Vernikos, I., Mathe, E., Papadakis, A., Spyrou, E., Mylonas, P.: An image representation of skeletal data for action recognition using convolutional neural networks. In: Proceedings of the 12th ACM International Conference on PErvasive Technologies Related to Assistive Environments, pp. 325–326, June 2019
22. Wang, P., Li, W., Li, C., Hou, Y.: Action recognition based on joint trajectory maps with convolutional neural networks. Knowl.-Based Syst. **158**, 43–53 (2018)
23. Wang, P., Li, W., Ogunbona, P., Wan, J., Escalera, S.: RGB-D-based human motion recognition with deep learning: a survey. Comput. Vis. Image Underst. **171**, 118–139 (2018)

# Using a Deep Neural Network in a Relative Risk Model to Estimate Vaccination Protection for COVID-19

Gabriela Suchopárová[1,2,4] , Petra Vidnerová[1,4] , Roman Neruda[1,4(✉)] ,
and Martin Šmíd[3,4]

[1] Institute of Computer Science, Czech Academy of Sciences, Prague, Czech Republic
{suchoparova,petra,roman}@cs.cas.cz
[2] Faculty of Mathematics and Physics, Charles University, Prague, Czech Republic
[3] Institute of Information Theory and Automation, Czech Academy of Sciences,
Prague, Czech Republic
smid@utia.cas.cz
[4] Centre for Modelling of Biological and Social Processes, Prague, Czech Republic

**Abstract.** The proportional hazard Cox model is traditionally used in survival analysis to estimate the effect of several variables on the hazard rate of an event. Recently, neural networks were proposed to improve the flexibility of the Cox model. In this work, we focus on an extension of the Cox model, namely on a non-proportional relative risk model, where the neural network approximates a non-linear time-dependent risk function. We address the issue of the lack of time-varying variables in this model, and to this end, we design a deep neural network model capable of time-varying regression.

The target application of our model is the waning of post-vaccination and post-infection immunity in COVID-19. This task setting is challenging due to the presence of multiple time-varying variables and different epidemic intensities at infection times. The advantage of our model is that it enables a fine-grained analysis of risks depending on the time since vaccination and/or infection, all approximated using a single non-linear function. A case study on a data set containing all COVID-19 cases in the Czech Republic until the end of 2021 has been performed. The vaccine effectiveness for different age groups, vaccine types, and the number of doses received was estimated using our model as a function of time. The results are in accordance with previous findings while allowing greater flexibility in the analysis due to a continuous representation of the waning function.

**Keywords:** Deep learning · Risk model · Immunity waning

## 1 Introduction

Survival analysis models have been extensively studied as a statistical and computational tool to tackle the time-to-event estimation. Applications of time-

© Springer Nature Switzerland AG 2022
L. Iliadis et al. (Eds.): EANN 2022, CCIS 1600, pp. 310–320, 2022.
https://doi.org/10.1007/978-3-031-08223-8_26

to-event predictions are important in various fields from medicine (patient survival prediction) to finances (credit scoring) or engineering (failure of machines). Recently, these tools have been applied in the epidemiological context to study the effect of vaccination or post-infection immunity to the risk of contracting the disease. Several studies make use of collected COVID-19 infection data to build survival models for specific geographical regions and events, such as infection, hospitalization or death [1, 14, 16].

Cox proportional hazards model [3] represents a classical statistical tool to assess the relation between baseline characteristics (covariates) of item studied (e.g. a person in a population) and the risk of its event (e.g. the COVID-19 infection). This approach often yields to reliable and robust models under rather strong constrains – linearity of the model, proportionality of the hazards, and a lack of time-dependent covariates. Several neural network extensions of Cox model have been proposed to alleviate those limitations, such as [8], which we use as a foundation of this work, and extend it further.

The main contributions of this paper are the following. We present a deep network model for relative risk prediction which is non-linear, non-proportional and can deal with time-varying covariates. This model can be seen as an extension of the pycox library capable of handling time dependencies of data. The model is then used in a case study of waning of post-vaccination or post-infection immunity in COVID-19 in the Czech Republic.

## 2  Related Work

Early works on application of neural networks for survival analysis were considering relatively simple feedforward networks used as estimators of proportional hazards. Liestøl and Anderson [10] implemented a neural network classifier (either linear or with one hidden layer) which estimated conditional probabilities of event in discrete time intervals corresponding to network outputs based on input covariates.

The direct risk predicting models were proposed by Faraggi and Simon [4]. They replaced the Cox linear predictor by a neural network, which was a one hidden layer perceptron in their case. Biganzoli [2] proposed the first time-encoded model by adding the time interval as an input variable along covariates to a feed-forward network with entropy error function. Practical results of these early attempts demonstrated modest results with none or moderate improvements over simpler linear model.

Besides neural networks, other machine learning techniques have been used to estimate non-proportional hazards. Namely, the random survival forest [6] model has been used as a benchmark baseline in many studies. The model is an ensemble of decision trees using the log-rank test for splitting criterion, computing the cumulative hazards of the leaves, and averaging them within the ensemble. Authors of [5] use a semi-parametric Bayesian models based on Gaussian processes to estimate the risk based on individual patient's covariates.

In recent years, the application of neural networks have been revisited by making use of learning techniques with encouraging results. Authors of the Deep-Surv model [7] improved the performance of risk predicting models by utilizing state-of-the-art deep networks for estimating non-linear relation of Cox proportional hazards on covariates. Yousefi and colleagues [20] developed a similar framework for neural regressor fitting proportional Cox model with Bayesian hyperparameter search. Changhee and colleagues, in their DeepHit model [9], relax the original Cox constrains by proposing a model that uses a deep neural network to learn the distribution of survival times directly from covariates.

Zhu and colleagues [22] extended the DeepSurv model to use medical images as covariates. They replaced the multi-layer perceptron network by a convolutional network realizing the regression. A recent work [15] describes another convolutional network for survival prediction using images. Their architecture is also able to utilize transfer learning to accommodate for different data.

Several works, such as [11,12,17], revisited and extended the idea of discrete time intervals, and presented various models to compute discrete outputs for survival predictions for several discretized durations. The area of risk predictions in organ transplantation is a common application niche for this approach, with recent paper [13] comparing several machine learning methods, including deep networks, on kidney graft survival prediction.

Finally, authors of [8] extended the approach of risk predicting by deep neural models to more general, non-proportional Cox models, and they also developed a seminal software library pycox[1].

## 3    Preliminaries

Let us consider a non-negative random variable $T$ representing the time-to-event of an item (such as time to death of an individual, or time to failure of a machine). The goal is to model the event distribution as a function of time. We denote $f(t)$ and $F(t)$ the probability density function, and the cumulative distribution function of event time T, respectively, and consider the probability:

$$P(T \leq t) = F(t) = \int_0^t f(s)ds.$$

A *survival function* $S(t)$ is defined in terms of probability of a complement event as: $S(t) = P(T > t) = 1 - F(t)$.

The hazard rate $h(t)$ is defined as a ratio of density and survival functions in a given time: $h(t) = \frac{f(t)}{S(t)}$. The cumulative hazard $H(t)$ is naturally defined as:

$$H(t) = \int_0^t h(s)ds,$$

and it can be used to define values of the survival function:

$$S(t) = e^{-H(t)}$$

---

[1] https://github.com/havakv/pycox.

For the survival data, sometimes the true event time $T$ is not observed because of pre-specified study time limit, or because of an occurrence of a competing event (such as death by other cause). This is called right censoring of data.

Cox proportional hazards model [3] considers a semi-parametric hazard rate form based on covariate variables:

$$h(t|\mathbf{x}) = h_0(t)e^{g(\mathbf{x})}; \quad g(\mathbf{x}) = \beta^T\mathbf{x},$$

where $\mathbf{x}$ is a covariate vector, $\beta$ is a parameter vector, $h_0(t)$ is a (non-parametric) baseline hazard, and the term $e^{g(\mathbf{x})}$ represents a relative risk function, called partial hazard. The predictor $g(\mathbf{x}) = \beta^T\mathbf{x}$ is a linear function of covariate variables. The proportionality assumption states that the hazard functions for any two subjects stay proportional at any point in time, thus the hazard ratio does not vary with time.

The neural extensions to Cox model consider the predictor as a non-linear function $g(\mathbf{x})$ realized by a feedforward neural network. Moreover, the proportionality constraint is often relaxed by defining both the relative risk function, and $g$ as parameterized by time:

$$h(t|\mathbf{x}) = h_0(t)e^{g(t,\mathbf{x})}.$$

Such a model is called relative risk model [8].

# 4   Deep Network Model for Vaccination Waning

Our extensions of the above described model were motivated by the infection protection application described below. The general setup of the model is the same as described above, we consider a relative risk model where the function $g(t, x)$ is realized by deep neural network. Moreover, we consider the covariates $x$ to be time-dependent, and we make a distinction between calendar time $T$ for the environment, and relative time $t$ for covariates. Thus, the desired function has a form of $g(T, x(t))$. We now elaborate on these extensions in a more detail.

We consider a vaccination treatment as one of the important subject covariates. For vaccinated subjects, the time since vaccination represents a highly time-dependent variable that changes every day. The same applies for post-infection immunity and time since previous infection. This was the motivation to extend the model for true time-dependent covariates. On the other hand, the non-vaccinated subjects without previous infection have a constant partial hazard (i.e., independent of time). These subjects have to be considered differently from vaccinated ones in the implementation of the model, which is our second extension of the previous work. The third extension addresses the dependence of the overall hazard function on the actual conditions of pandemics, including non-pharmaceutical interventions or virus variants. Thus, a real (calendar) time is necessary to compute the hazard ratios, while the time-varying covariates depend on relative time. As a consequence, at one real-time point (measuring the objective conditions and influencing the hazard ratios), the subjects can have different time since event (measuring their individual covariates, such as relative time from previous vaccination). In the rest of this section, these three extensions will be described in more detail.

Covariates have remained the one important component of the model that is considered constant in time. There are approaches that deal with changes of covariates in time, such as the partly conditional modeling [21], which for every change in covariate censors the item and create a new one with new covariate value. This approach is not practical for large amount of data with frequent covariate changes.

The deep neural network can naturally handle covariate values changing in time, but it is necessary to extend the computation of the loss function of the model. The loss, called the negative log-likelihood loss, is defined as:

$$Loss = \frac{1}{n} \sum_{i:C_i=1} \log \left( \sum_{j \in R_i} e^{[g(T_i, \mathbf{x_j}) - g(T_i, \mathbf{x_i})]} \right),$$

where for individual $i$ we denote the $T_i$ the event time, and $R_i$ the set of all individuals at risk at time $T_i$. The occurrence of the event is formally expressed as $C_i = 1$. In practice, the set $R_i$ is sub-sampled, and only a subset $R_i'$ of $R_i$ is considered to decrease the computation time. The sub-sampling is done by standard random sampling without replacement choosing only a certain percentage of the data.

Now, we consider that some (or all) covariates are time dependent, i.e. $\mathbf{x_j} = \mathbf{x_j}(t)$, i.e., the new loss is:

$$Loss = \frac{1}{n} \sum_{i:C_i=1} \log \left( \sum_{j \in R_i(T)} e^{[g(T_i, \mathbf{x_j}(t)) - g(T_i, \mathbf{x_i}(t))]} \right).$$

The introduction of relative time $t$ into the previous equation has to be addressed by relating the $t$ to calendar, or real time $T$, which is done in the following way.

For each covariate $\mathbf{x}(t)$ we need to compute $t$ by means of the calendar time $T$ and the event related to the covariate. (E.g., time from vaccination relates to the vaccination event in the past calendar time $T_{EVENT}$. Thus, the value in calendar time $T_R$ is $\mathbf{x}(T_R) = T_R - \mathbf{x}(T_{EVENT})$.

In order to compute the even time $T_i$ in the formula above, we again need to consider the most recent event time with respect to calendar time $T_R$: thus $T_i = T_R - T_i^0$, where the $T_i^0$ is the most recent time of the event (i.e., vaccination or infection).

The value of $\mathbf{g}(T_i, \mathbf{x}(t))$ is then either expressed via the calendar time $T$ as $\mathbf{g}(T, \mathbf{x}(t))$, for vaccinated, or as $\mathbf{g}(0, \mathbf{x}(t))$ for non-vaccinated individuals.

Finally, the real calendar time $T_R$ is used to determine the set $R_i(T_R)$, which is necessary to take into account the individuals to be at risk at given changing conditions in the real time.

Note, that we still use the partly conditional modeling for covariates that do not change much in time, e.g. whether the subject received the second dose of vaccine (not to be confused with the covariate "time since the last dose").

## 5   Experiments

### 5.1   Data and Model

The data set used for this experimental study includes all reported cases of infections, vaccinations, and Covid-related hospital admissions and deaths in the Czech Republic for the period between December 26, 2020 (one day before the vaccination started) and November 30, 2021 (roughly before the Omicron outbreak). Out of these data we have used the period of December 26, 2020 – November 15, 2021 for training, and the last two weeks for validation. The train set was used both for training and the demonstration of results. The split for training and validation was used only to determine the quality of the fit and prevent the overfitting by the choice of stopping criterion. This is a standard policy in risk estimation where we are not primarily concerned with predictions but the focus is on the soundness of the model, expressing the dependence of risk on particular covariates.

The data were preprocessed to form events for our model, which resulted in three data sets containing 27.5 million training patterns with 1.26 million event cases for infection data, 22.4 million with 78.19 thousands event cases for hospitalizations, and 24.1 million with 19.25 thousands event cases for deaths.

The input features to our model include age and sex information of the subject together with information about vaccination status for Pfizer vaccine (non-vaccinated, one or two doses) and times of vaccinations, as well as previous infection flag and time, respectively. We have trained three separate models for infection, hospitalization and death events with the same neural network architecture. We have used a fully connected network with 32–32–64 neurons in hidden layers, trained with Adam optimizer with weight decay, learning rate of 0.001 and batch size 2048. The size of sub-sampling sets for risk evaluation was 100. The number of epochs was determined by decrease in training and validation losses, according to the elbow rule-of-thumb, and the final values are 60 for infections, 600 for deaths and 1500 for hospitalizations. The results we report are mean and 95% confidence intervals of 10 runs with different random seeds.

### 5.2   Results

The results of the three models are presented by means of standard metrics describing the fit of the model in Table 1 and Fig. 1. We report the values of the Brier score, which represents a mean square error of predicted probabilities from real events. The values of Brier score are also plotted with respect to time. The concordance represents covariance-based similarity measure of the predictions with real events. Finally, the negative binary log-likelihood (NBLL) corresponds to a loss used to train the models.

All three standard measures indicate that the models were able to train very well, the hospitalization and death models in particular perform a great fit. More details about the performance of the models can be seen on graphical representation of the waning curves presented on Figs. 2, 3, 4 and 5. The results of all three models correspond to general findings about the vaccine efficiency. The protection against death is the highest (in the order of 90%) and does not wane much in the period of 6 months. The protection against hospitalizations is also strong, starting around 85–90% and decreases to 75–80% within 6 months. The infection protection is lower, starting at the same levels but waning to 50–60% in 6 months. Figure 3 demonstrates that the infection protection is sensitive to age groups as a result of testing and vaccination policies in the course of the pandemics. The decrease of protection against hospitalizations and deaths in young age groups seen on Figs. 5 and 4 is caused by lack of data for these covariates.

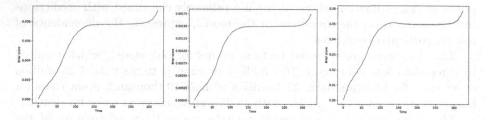

**Fig. 1.** Brier score for hospitalization (left), death (middle), and infection (right) protection with respect to time.

**Table 1.** Evaluation of our models performance with respect to traditional metrics – concordance, Brier score and negative binary log-likelihood (NBLL). The values in table represent mean and standard deviation for 10 runs.

|  | Concordance | | Brier score | | NBLL | |
|---|---|---|---|---|---|---|
|  | Mean | Std | Mean | Std | Mean | Std |
| Infections | 0.6750 | 0.0216 | 0.0426 | 0.0003 | 0.1581 | 0.0021 |
| Hospital | 0.7255 | 0.0019 | $6.354 \times 10^{-3}$ | $5.930 \times 10^{-6}$ | $3.3854 \times 10^{-2}$ | $3.1325 \times 10^{-4}$ |
| Deaths | 0.7776 | 0.0111 | $1.231 \times 10^{-3}$ | $1.213 \times 10^{-6}$ | $8.4879 \times 10^{-3}$ | $3.3529 \times 10^{-4}$ |

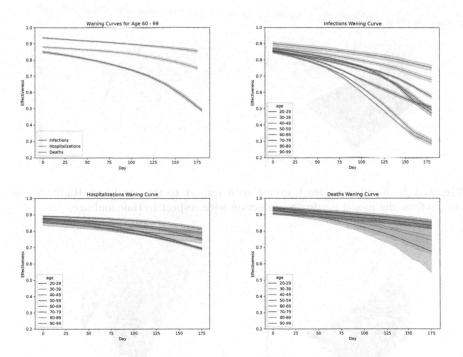

**Fig. 2.** Top left: Waning curves for protection against infection, hospitalization, and death risk for age group 60–69. Top right: Waning curves for infection protection for 10 year interval age groups. Bottom left: Waning curves for hospitalization protection for 10 year interval age groups. Bottom right: Waning curves for death protection for 10 year interval age groups. Dark line represents mean from 10 runs, the shaded area is a 95% confidence interval.

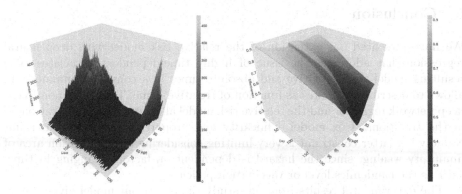

**Fig. 3.** Left: Number of infection events with respect to time and age. Right: Waning curves from the model for infection protection with respect to time and age.

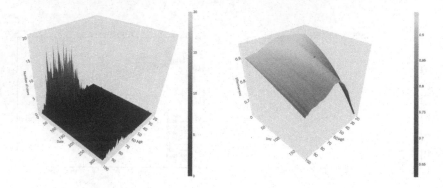

**Fig. 4.** Left: Number of death events with respect to time and age. Right: Waning curves from the model for death protection with respect to time and age.

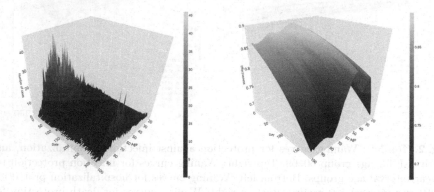

**Fig. 5.** Left: Number of hospitalization events with respect to time and age. Right: Waning curves from the model for hospitalization protection with respect to time and age.

# 6   Conclusion

We have presented our extension of the relative risk model with deep neural regression that addresses the issue of highly time-dependent covariates. The resulting model treats relative and absolute times in a consistent manner and allows to describe covariates as function of (relative) time. The use of non-linear deep network regressor and the relative risk model alleviates two main drawbacks of the traditional Cox model – linearity and proportional hazard constraint. Namely the latter constraint is very limiting considering the application area of immunity waning, since the hazard is dependent on factors changing in time, such as the pandemics level or vaccination policies.

The experimental results from our study show that our model gives results comparable to existing works [1,16,19]. Majority of previous research considers either short time interval of the study (1–2 months), or divides the population into very coarse compartments (both with respect to age or vaccination intervals), and then creates separate models for these. Our approach naturally represents the covariates as continuous, thus we are able to obtain finer results. This can actually bring some drawbacks that we have also demonstrated. Clearly, some data categories are underrepresented, such as young people in hospital and death data sets, which results in poor estimation of their risk values. Also, the data are very unbalanced due to vaccination and testing policies, so the numbers of both infected and vaccinated people vary in time and between age groups substantially.

In the future work we plan to address the problem of unbalanced data in order to achieve smoother estimates of relative risks. Also, from the application point of view, we plan to focus on recent data to estimate the waning curves for the case of omicron virus mutation. Other interesting questions are relative comparisons of vaccine types, or the dependence of combinations or order of vaccination and previous infection events to the waning curve.

**Acknowledgments.** Roman Neruda, Petra Vidnerová and Gabriela Suchopárová acknowledge the institutional support of the Institute of Computer Science, Czech Academy of Sciences RVO 67985807. This research was partially supported by the SVV project number 260 575. Gabriela Suchopárová was supported by Charles University Grant Agency project no. 246322.

# References

1. Berec, L., et al.: Real-life protection provided by vaccination, booster doses and previous infection against Covid-19 infection, hospitalisation or death over time in the Czech Republic: a whole country retrospective view. medRxiv (2021). https://doi.org/10.1101/2021.12.10.21267590, https://www.medrxiv.org/content/early/2021/12/12/2021.12.10.21267590
2. Biganzoli, E., Boracchi, P., Mariani, L., Marubini, E.: Feed forward neural networks for the analysis of censored survival data: a partial logistic regression approach. Stat. Med. **17**(10), 1169–1186 (1998). https://doi.org/10.1002/(SICI)1097-0258(19980530)17:10⟨1169::AID-SIM796⟩3.0.CO;2-D
3. Cox, D.R.: Regression models and life-tables. J. Royal Stat. Soc. Series B (Methodol.) **34**(2), 187–220 (1972). http://www.jstor.org/stable/2985181
4. Faraggi, D., Simon, R.: A neural network model for survival data. Stat. Med. **1**, 73–82 (1995). https://doi.org/10.1002/sim.4780140108
5. Fernandez, T., Rivera, N., Teh, Y.W.: Gaussian processes for survival analysis. In: Lee, D., Sugiyama, M., Luxburg, U., Guyon, I., Garnett, R. (eds.) Advances in Neural Information Processing Systems, vol. 29. Curran Associates, Inc. (2016). https://proceedings.neurips.cc/paper/2016/file/ef1e491a766ce3127556063d49bc2f98-Paper.pdf
6. Ishwaran, H., Kogalur, U., Blackstone, E., Lauer, M.: Random survival forests. Ann. Appl. Stat. **2** (2008). https://doi.org/10.1214/08-AOAS169
7. Katzman, J.L., Shaham, U., Cloninger, A., Bates, J., Jiang, T., Kluger, Y.: DeepSurv: personalized treatment recommender system using a cox proportional hazards deep neural network. BMC Med. Res. Methodol. **18**, 1471–2288 (2018)
8. Kvamme, H., Borgan, Ø., Scheel, I.: Time-to-event prediction with neural networks and cox regression. J. Mach. Learn. Res. **20**(129), 1–30 (2019). http://jmlr.org/papers/v20/18-424.html

9. Lee, C., Zame, W., Yoon, J., van der Schaar, M.: DeepHit: a deep learning approach to survival analysis with competing risks. In: Proceedings of the AAAI Conference on Artificial Intelligence, vol. 32(1), April 2018. https://ojs.aaai.org/index.php/AAAI/article/view/11842

10. Liestøl, K., Andersen, P.K., Andersen, U.: Survival analysis and neural nets. Stat. Med. **13**(12), 1189–1200 (1994). https://doi.org/10.1002/sim.4780131202, https://onlinelibrary.wiley.com/doi/abs/10.1002/sim.4780131202

11. Lin, R.S., Horn, S.D., Hurdle, J.F., Goldfarb-Rumyantzev, A.S.: Single and multiple time-point prediction models in kidney transplant outcomes. J. Biomed. Inform. **41**(6), 944–952 (2008). https://doi.org/10.1016/j.jbi.2008.03.005, https://www.sciencedirect.com/science/article/pii/S1532046408000439

12. Luck, M., Sylvain, T., Cardinal, H., Lodi, A., Bengio, Y.: Deep learning for patient-specific kidney graft survival analysis. CoRR abs/1705.10245 (2017). http://arxiv.org/abs/1705.10245

13. Naqvi, S.A.A., Tennankore, K., Vinson, A., Roy, P.C., Abidi, S.S.R.: Predicting kidney graft survival using machine learning methods: prediction model development and feature significance analysis study. J. Med. Internet Res. **23**(8), e26843 (2021). https://doi.org/10.2196/26843, https://www.jmir.org/2021/8/e26843

14. Tang, P., et al.: BNT162b2 and mRNA-1273 COVID-19 vaccine effectiveness against the SARS-CoV-2 Delta variant in Qatar. Nat. Med. **27**(12), 2136–2143 (2021)

15. Tarkhan, A., Simon, N., Bengtsson, T., Nguyen, K., Dai, J.: Survival prediction using deep learning. In: Greiner, R., Kumar, N., Gerds, T.A., van der Schaar, M. (eds.) Proceedings of AAAI Spring Symposium on Survival Prediction - Algorithms, Challenges, and Applications 2021. Proceedings of Machine Learning Research, vol. 146, pp. 207–214. PMLR, 22–24 March 2021. https://proceedings.mlr.press/v146/tarkhan21a.html

16. Tartof, S., et al.: Effectiveness of mRNA BNT162b2 COVID-19 vaccine up to 6 months in a large integrated health system in the USA: a retrospective cohort study. Lancet **398**, 1407–1416 (2021)

17. Topuz, K., Zengul, F.D., Dag, A., Almehmi, A., Yildirim, M.B.: Predicting graft survival among kidney transplant recipients: a Bayesian decision support model. Dec. Supp. Syste. **106**, 97–109 (2018). https://doi.org/10.1016/j.dss.2017.12.004, https://www.sciencedirect.com/science/article/pii/S0167923617302233

18. Townsend, J., Hassler, H., Wang, Z., Miura, S., Singh, J., Kumar, S., et al.: The durability of immunity against reinfection by SARS-CoV-2: a comparative evolutionary study. Lancet Microbe **2**(12), 1407–1416 (2021)

19. Voysey, M., Clemens, S.C., Madhi, S., Weckx, L., Folegatti, P., Aley, P., et al.: Safety and efficacy of the ChAdOx1 nCoV-19 vaccine (AZD1222) against SARS-CoV-2: an interim analysis of four randomised controlled trials in Brazil, South Africa, and the UK. Lancet **397**, 99–111 (2021)

20. Yousefi, S., et al.: Predicting clinical outcomes from large scale cancer genomic profiles with deep survival models. Sci. Rep. **7**(1), 11707 (2017). https://doi.org/10.1038/s41598-017-11817-6

21. Zheng, Y., Heagerty, P.J.: Partly conditional survival models for longitudinal data. Biometrics **61**(2), 379–391 (2005). https://doi.org/10.1111/j.1541-0420.2005.00323.x, https://onlinelibrary.wiley.com/doi/abs/10.1111/j.1541-0420.2005.00323.x

22. Zhu, X., Yao, J., Huang, J.: Deep convolutional neural network for survival analysis with pathological images. In: 2016 IEEE International Conference on Bioinformatics and Biomedicine (BIBM), pp. 544–547 (2016)

# Machine Learning for Medical Images/Genome Classification

# A Gene Ontology-Driven Wide and Deep Learning Architecture for Cell-Type Classification from Single-Cell RNA-seq Data

Gianmarco Coppola[1], Antonino Fiannaca[2]([✉]) [iD], Massimo La Rosa[2] [iD],
Laura La Paglia[2] [iD], Alfonso Urso[2] [iD], and Salvatore Gaglio[1,2] [iD]

[1] Dipartimento di Ingegneria, Università degli studi di Palermo, Viale Delle Scienze,
ed. 6, Palermo, Italy
[2] ICAR-CNR, National Research Council of Italy, Via Ugo La Malfa 153,
Palermo, Italy
antonino.fiannaca@icar.cnr.it

**Abstract.** Recent advances in single-cell RNA-sequencing in order to study cells in biology, and the increasing amount of data available, led to the development of algorithms for analyzing single cells from gene expression data. In this work, we propose an artificial intelligence architecture that classifies cell types of human tissue. This architecture combines a deep learning model based on the convolutional neural network (CNN) with a wide model. The classification model integrates the concept of functional genes neighbourhood, based on Gene Ontology, in the CNN model (deep part) and the information on biologically relevant marker genes for each cell type in the underlying human tissue (wide part). This approach leads to a gene ontology-driven wide and deep learning model. We tested the proposed architecture with seven human tissue datasets and compared achieved results against three reference literature algorithms. Although the cell-type classification problem is heavily data-dependent, our model performed equal or better than the other models within each tissue.

**Keywords:** Single-cell RNA-sequencing · Cell-type classification ·
Wide and deep learning · Gene ontology

## 1 Introduction

Single-cell RNA sequencing (scRNA-seq) technology refers to sequencing a single-cell genome or transcriptome. It gives information on the quantity and type-composition of the RNA population in a single cell of a specific tissue [9]. The main advantage of this technique is the characterization of highly specific cell types of different cells populations within different tissues and in different biological conditions. The strength of scRNA-seq methods lies in their ability in

© Springer Nature Switzerland AG 2022
L. Iliadis et al. (Eds.): EANN 2022, CCIS 1600, pp. 323–335, 2022.
https://doi.org/10.1007/978-3-031-08223-8_27

individually cells separation, allowing the extraction of cell-by-cell gene expression values from a tissue. Thus, cell-type classification can be applied at different depths, also discriminating between cell subtypes belonging to the same main cell type, based on the level of detail required by research target. Moreover, it avoids data noise caused by the influence of other cells and it allows more accurate measurement of gene expression for each cell within a tissue. In biology, "cell typing" means classifying different cells that share similar morphological or phenotypic features. Cells can have the same genotype, but they can belong, morphologically, to different cell classes due to their differential gene expression. avoiding data noise caused by the influence of other cells and allowing more accurate measurement of gene expression for each cell within a tissue, In this context, automatic classification task through artificial intelligence and machine learning techniques [23,24] has proven a valid instrument [1]. Correct cell types identification is necessary to study tissue and organs development, especially for functional cells production for cell therapies and disease modelling. A fundamental contribution of cell-type classification also lies in oncology. Indeed, single-cell typing in cancer research has contributed to give information related to the landscape of tumour cells and immune cells surrounding them, the behaviour of tumour microenvironment and cell heterogeneity. Moreover, cell type classification would contribute to understanding the tumour biology better and assist in the identification of novel markers, rare subgroups of patients and evolution patterns of cancer phenotypes [13].

This work proposes a computational architecture that exploits two main concepts: the functional relationships among genes and the use of biologically relevant marker genes. Specifically, for the classification task, we first try to integrate the concept of genes neighbourhood within a cell into a deep learning algorithm, giving relevance to the closest genes within a cell from a semantic and functional point of view. Secondly, we combine this information with biologically relevant marker genes extraction for each cell type.

## 2    Related Works

There are several methods to analyse cell types based on scRNA-seq data, like clustering, classification and lineage tracing. In particular, exponential growth in cells and samples number led to the adaptation and development of supervised classification methods for automatic cell identification or classification [1,31]. Cell-type classification can be performed by mapping differentially expressed genes with prior knowledge of cell markers like SCSA [7] and scCATCH [19] algorithms. These methods require updated, relevant genes databases since this information is fundamental to recognise each cell type. To support this, the amount of scRNA-seq data is increasing, thus expanding database marker genes, which will become increasingly populated and available in research. Another cell-type classification strategy compares similarities between a single cell and a bulk or single-cell RNA-seq profile reference database to find potential cellular identities. Several methods including SingleR [4], CHETAH [15], scmap [16], scID [5], scPred [3], ACTINN [18], singleCellNet [22], SciBet [17], CellAssign [28], SCINA [29] belong to this category. These approaches based on reference databases have the advantage to automatically and rapidly classify cell types on a large variety of test sets. Still, they also severely limit cell types extraction dependent on the reference database. Fortunately, recent advances in deep learning have enabled significant progress in the ability of artificial intelligence techniques to integrate big data, including existing knowledge, and learn arbitrarily complex relationships. For this reason, recently, there are also deep learning architectures in literature; one of them is scDeepSort [20], a method that exploits genes relationships in a graph neural network (GNN), or sigGCN [25], based on two parallel networks, a convolutional graph network (GCN) and a neural network (NN).

Two models inspired the architecture proposed in this work: 1) an ontology-driven convolutional neural network (ODCNN) for cancer detection [6] and 2) a "wide and deep learning" model for automatic single-cell typing (scWDL) [26]. The former exploits the concept of functionally and semantically close genes in a convolutional neural network through a 1D convolution operation for cancer detection in human tissue. The latter extends the "wide and deep learning" architecture (WDL) proposed by Google for recommendation systems [10] to the cell-type identification in scRNA-seq data and integrates biologically relevant genes provided by literature into the wide part of a WDL architecture. Our approach combines those two methods by integrating the ontology-based ODCNN model on the deep part of the scWDL approach to exploit the contribution of both functional genes relationships and biologically relevant marker genes.

## 3    Materials and Methods

In this section we introduce the datasets and the proposed architecture for cell-type classification. First of all we describe main features of human tissues scRNA-seq data; then we focus on data pre-processing; finally we present our gene ontology-driven WDL (GOWDL) architecture for cell-type classification from single-cell RNA-seq data. All the phases we discuss below were performed in Python programming language (except for dataset normalization, performed in R programming language).

### 3.1    Datasets

We selected datasets containing scRNA-seq data from different human tissues. All chosen datasets are already normalized (log2) or have been normalized if containing raw counts. Normalization was performed with Seurat package [12] of R programming language, a tool designed for quality control, analysis and exploration of scRNA-seq data, with the $normalization.method = "LogNormalize"$ method. Table 1 summarizes information about all the datasets considered in our study. We chose different tissue datasets, to show proposed architecture's ability to identify cell types in different conditions and with different classes. Furthermore, datasets have a fairly high number of samples per cell type. Datasets include blood, breast, kidney, lung, pancreas and melanoma tissues. Bio-marker genes, that is signature genes that characterize specific cell types, were obtained from CellMatch [19].

**Table 1.** Overview of chosen single-cell RNA-sequencing human tissue dataset.

| Dataset | Tissue type | Source | Starting dimensions (cells x genes) | Normalization | Cell-type number after filtering | Mean number of marker genes per cell-type |
|---|---|---|---|---|---|---|
| Blood | Normal | [14] from Immune Cell Atlas | (13 316 x 21 814) | No | 7 | 5 |
| Breast | Normal | [27] from Stromal cell diversity in negative breast cancer | (24 271 x 28 118) | No | 16 | 13 |
| Kidney | Normal | [21] from Kidney Cell Atlas ("mature human kidneys" dataset) | (7 803 x 33 694) | No | 7 | 129 |
| Lung | Normal | [20] from Human Cell Landscape | (24 051 x 20 021) | No | 11 | 14 |
| Pancreas | Normal | [11] from GEO: GSE81547 | (2 544 x 19 644) | Yes | 6 | 10 |
| Melanoma 1 | Tumor | [26] from GEO: GSE123813 | (53 030 x 22 961) | Yes | 4 | 61 |
| Melanoma 2 | Tumor | [26] from GEO: GSE72056 | (4 645 x 23 686) | No | 6 | 55 |

## 3.2   Data Pre-processing

As mentioned before, raw counts dataset were normalized. After normalization (if necessary), we performed a data pre-processing pipeline composed of different phases.

**Cells Filtering.** In this step, because CellMatch database does not contain gene markers of each cell type, we removed cells without relevant genes. In addition, we replaced cell sub-types with their main cell types using the data provided in [19] (e.g. we considered a basal epithelial cell as an epithelial cell). The last part of this step is the removal of the poorly represented classes: we maintained only the cells belonging to classes with at least 0.05% of total samples, as done in [20].

**Genes Filtering.** Next step of pre-processing is gene filtering, consisting into the following two sub-phases.

- **Filtering based on GO terms**. Because our computational model is based on Gene Ontology [8] (see next Section), we discarded all genes that do not appear as GO nodes (GO terms) in the Gene Ontology graph.
- **Biologically relevant genes extraction**. For each cell, we extracted and removed from the original datasets the gene expression values of the genes representing bio-markers of any cell types, according to CellMatch. Those genes were assembled into a novel dataset of so called biologically relevant genes.

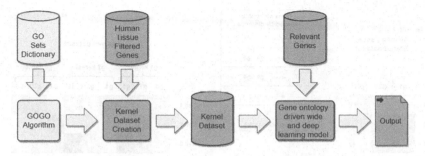

**Fig. 1.** Cell-type classification pipeline: green color represents the main line, while grey color describes a sub-phase. Kernel dataset creation processes input data to generate a kernel-organized dataset depending on the genes distance matrix (obtained from GOGO algorithm). Gene ontology-driven wide and deep learning model (GOWDL) is trained to predict cell types from the kernel dataset and gives an output with the classification results. (Color figure online)

### 3.3  Proposed Architecture

Our computational architecture is shown in Fig. 1. It is composed of two main processing steps. The former, namely Kernel dataset creation, organizes input datasets in a way they can be analysed in the latter, called Gene ontology-driven wide and deep learning model. That phase involves the training of a model that takes into account functional similarity among genes and a supervised learning procedure based on a customized deep learning architecture.

**Kernel Dataset Creation.** Our goal in this phase is to compute a functional distance among genes and then organize input dataset for learning the model in the next processing step. For this reason, we referred to Gene Ontology (GO) [8]. GO is, in fact, the world's largest knowledge base of information about genes functionality. It represents a direct acyclic graph (DAG), where each node is called GO term and each edge is a relationship between them. A GO term is a textual description of some gene function. We relied on GOGO algorithm [30] to compute genes distance, based on the number of GO terms associated with each gene. GOGO algorithm defines a measure of similarity between GO terms, based on their information content and on the number of children that each GO term has within the Gene Ontology. GO uses three DAGs to define the functions of a gene product: molecular function ontology (MFO), biological process ontology (BPO), and cellular component ontology (CCO). In particular, GOGO computes a matrix of genes similarity values for each of those ontologies, where each entry is a similarity value from a gene to another one, based on chosen ontology.

We have processed similarity matrices obtained as output of GOGO algorithm and transformed them into distance matrices. Given a similarity value $S_{g_1 g_2}$ corresponding to the similarity between gene $g_1$ and gene $g_2$, correspond-

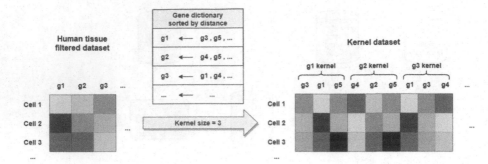

**Fig. 2.** Schematic representation of the kernel dataset organization process. The hue of green color within the cells of the matrix indicates the level of gene expression in a given cell (a darker green means that the gene has a high expression value within that cell, while a green more clear indicates a lower expression value). (Color figure online)

ing distance value $D_{g_1 g_2}$ between the two genes is given by:

$$D_{g_1 g_2} = 1 - S_{g_1 g_2} \tag{1}$$

We performed this computation for each of the BPO, CCO and MFO ontologies, with a total of three output distance matrices. From these three distance matrices we computed a further matrix, where each element is the average between the elements in the corresponding position of the three matrices. Given the GOGO distance matrix, we designed an algorithm that generates a so-called kernel dataset, starting from the dataset filtered by genes and by cells. Assuming to choose $n$ as kernel size, the kernel dataset is computed by taking the $n - 1$ genes closest to each of the genes in the dataset. For each cell, $C$, every gene, $g$, in the dataset is replaced by a mask (kernel) of $n$ elements, , where the expression value of $g$ is in the center of the mask, and the remaining $n - 1$ surrounding elements of the mask are the expression values of the $n - 1$ genes closest to $g$, in descending order (Fig. 2). Therefore the kernel dataset is a dataset with the same row number as the input dataset, but with a number of columns given by:

$$N_{ColumnsKernelDataset} = N_{ColumnsInputDataset} \cdot Size_{Kernel} \tag{2}$$

A dataset with a similar structure will be the input for the convolutional neural network (CNN) part of the proposed deep learning architecture.

**Gene Ontology-Driven Wide and Deep Learning Model.** Final step of the architecture is cell-type classification performed by the Gene ontology-driven wide and deep learning (GOWDL) model, as shown in Fig. 1 (b). As previously explained, the model is inspired by the wide and deep learning model (WDL) [10, 26] and by an ontology-driven convolutional neural network [6] based on gene functional distance. GOWDL is composed of two main components, as depicted in Fig. 3:

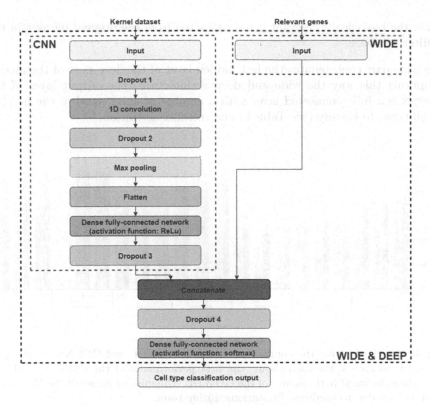

**Fig. 3.** Schematic representation of GOWDL network layers.

- **Deep part**. Deep component of a network generalizes data patterns, that in a classification task allows the network to recognize, starting from a limited set of labelled input samples, new examples never seen before and assign them to a membership class. In the model proposed in this work, the deep part consists of a CNN with a 1D convolution layer which strides along the kernel dataset rows (Fig. 1). Kernel stride is equal to size of the kernel chosen in the kernel dataset creation step, so that all and only the closest genes to the gene in the center of the mask are considered for convolution operation, and then the convolutional kernel strides to next genes set. The deep part has also a max pooling layer, three dropout layers, to avoid overfitting, a flatten layer and, at the end, a fully connected layer with ReLU activation.
- **Wide part**. The wide component of the network is a generalized linear model based on a small set of raw input features. The characteristic of a wide network is the memorization of data patterns starting from a reduced set of features, giving relevance to them, so that they can be considered relevant by the architecture. The wide part works better when dealing with very sparse input data, since in these cases only the deep part suffers from generalization difficulties [10]. In our model the wide part emphasizes the relevant features,

i.e. the biologically relevant genes extracted from the original dataset in the filtering phase.

The wide part concatenates the last hidden layer of the deep part of the model, composing this way the wide and deep architecture. The output layer of the network is a fully connected layer with a number of units equal to the number of cell types to classify (see Table 1) and softmax activation.

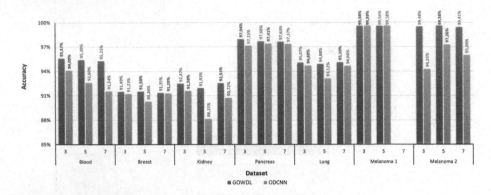

**Fig. 4.** Bar chart shows the comparison between GOWDL and ODCNN accuracy at varying kernel sizes. For each tissue, the best performance of the ODCNN is always lower than the worst performance of the GOWDL. The missing values of the Melanoma 1 dataset are due to hardware limitations during tests.

## 4    Results

In this section we present the design phase of the classifier, focusing on the parameters fine-tuning, the training and test procedure, and the results comparisons of our classification model with other cell-type classification models.

### 4.1    Classifier Design

To design the GOWDL model and find optimal parameters for the classification, we ran, using a ten-fold cross validation procedure, a comprehensive series of experiments leading to the final parameters of the architecture shown in Fig. 3. A large part of experiments involves kernel size (and stride) for the CNN 1D convolution step (stride is always equal to the kernel size). The graph in Fig. 4 shows the comparison between accuracy values versus kernel size of the GOWDL model and the ODCNN model. For a fair comparison, the input of ODCNN is the same as the deep part of the GOWDL but also includes the set of relevant genes (representing the input of the wide part of the GOWDL model). Results show that the GOWDL model always performs better than ODCNN, except in Melanoma 1 dataset, where we could not complete the experiment due to

**Table 2.** GOWDL model performance.

| Dataset | Precision | Recall | F1-score | Accuracy |
|---|---|---|---|---|
| Blood | 95.72% | 95.57% | 95.60% | 95.57% |
| Breast | 91.67% | 91.50% | 91.49% | 91.50% |
| Kidney | 92.77% | 92.53% | 92.55% | 92.53% |
| Pancreas | 98.00% | 97.94% | 97.91% | 97.94% |
| Lung | 94.89% | 95.10% | 94.80% | 95.10% |
| Melanoma 1 | 99.60% | 99.58% | 99.58% | 99.58% |
| Melanoma 2 | 99.58% | 99.58% | 99.55% | 99.58% |

hardware limits. There is no correct and stable value for kernel size in all datasets, the results vary according to the dataset and the marker gene set. Typically, increasing kernel size, a maximum accuracy value is reached, after which the performance of the model decreases.

Another set of experiments involved the value of the dropout layers, which, according to [2], can imply a considerable variation in performances. We choose to tune the parameters of the four dropout layers of the model (see Fig. 3) with the smallest dataset, i.e. the Pancreas dataset, and then we applied the obtained results to all the other datasets. The tested dropout values were in the [0, 0.75] range. We also perform different 10-fold validation runs, varying the initial random seed. The model shows robustness to random seed applied in splitting input data: at varying seed, model performance is more or less constant. The variance is quite low (about $10^{-3}$) depending on seed variation, demonstrating that the model is not influenced by data initialization.

Also, we performed further experiments leading to a good parameters configuration for all the selected datasets. The model parameters are as follows: four dropout layer values are respectively, 0.5, 0.75, 0.25 and 0.25. The convolutional layer has 64 filters, with the stride equal to kernel size and a ReLU activation function. The fully-connected layer has 128 units. We used the categorical cross-entropy loss function and the accuracy metric during the training. Finally, we ran 100 epochs and adopted a batch size of 128.

### 4.2   Training and Testing Procedure

To train and evaluate the proposed model, we chose a k-fold cross validation, with $k = 10$. Specifically, we applied a stratified k-fold cross validation, a variant of k-fold cross validation that splits data into $k$ fold, where each fold contains approximately the same percentage of samples of each target class of the entire dataset, preserving original data distribution in splitting operation. In this way the model is trained and tested on folds, where data are distributed as in the original data, without differences due to the splitting step, which could lead to missing classes (with a few examples in the complete dataset) in some folds.

332     G. Coppola et al.

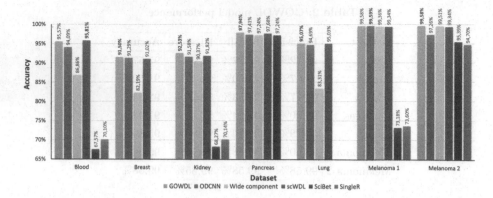

**Fig. 5.** Bar chart shows the comparison between GOWDL, ODCNN, Wide component, scWDL, SciBet and SingleR. For some tissues, the bad performances (or the missing values) of SciBet and SingleR are due to their training set, which does not contain the specific human tissue dataset.

Stratified 10-fold cross validation is a valid technique with scRNA-seq datasets, since they are very sparse and have highly unbalanced classes (cell-types).

To evaluate goodness of our model classification, we computed precision, recall, F1-score and accuracy for each tissue datasets. Table 2 shows the performance of the model for each dataset.

We compared our model to its two components: ODCNN (deep part only) and the wide part only (a model with a single input layer and an output layer with only relevant features in input). We also compared GOWDL to scWDL model to which it is inspired, SciBet and SingleR (two architecture in the literature), these comparisons are showed in Fig. 5. The figure clearly shows how GOWDL outperforms two pre-trained reference cell-type classification models, i.e. SciBet and SingleR. The proposed method provides higher accuracy (except for the "Blood" dataset) with respect to the scWDL model. Furthermore, it performs better than the ODCNN component (except for the "Melanoma 1" dataset), which includes no information about functional distances between genes. In the same way, the "Wide" component, which uses only biologically relevant genes, cannot reach the same accuracy as GOWDL. This result demonstrates how combining the two components overcame single ones.

## 5   Conclusions and Future Works

The proposed gene-ontology driven wide and deep learning model for scRNA-seq cell-type classification was applied to different tissue types, both normal and tumour. Results show it performs well (reaching equal or better results) concerning the other literature classification models. Even though this classification problem is highly data-dependent (e.g., according to NGS sequencing technology, data sparsity, availability of known marker genes and tissue type), the proposed algorithm shows overall good performances for all the tested datasets.

This model can provide a valuable contribution in precision medicine, where the proper identification of the cell-type composition in the tumour tissue of a patient could provide critical information for diagnosis and personalized treatment. As future work, we plan to use an adaptive kernel size that can provide better results for each tissue, according to a threshold value on the GO dictionary that can suggest how many neighbours genes should be considered. Also, we want to push our architecture to a deeper level of classification: we believe that the proposed hybrid learning approach could classify well at cell sub-types level. In the near future, in fact, the availability of scRNA-seq data and marker genes will increase over time so that it will be possible to classify even more cell sub-types belonging to a cell-type family.

# References

1. Abdelaal, T., et al.: A comparison of automatic cell identification methods for single-cell RNA sequencing data. Genome Biol. **20**(1), 194 (2019). https://doi.org/10.1186/s13059-019-1795-z
2. Ahmed, O., Brifcani, A.: Gene expression classification based on deep learning, pp. 145–149 (2019). https://doi.org/10.1109/SICN47020.2019.9019357
3. Alquicira-Hernandez, J., Sathe, A., Ji, H.P., et al.: scPred: accurate supervised method for cell-type classification from single-cell RNA-seq data. Genome Biol. **20**(1), 264 (2019). https://doi.org/10.1186/s13059-019-1862-5
4. Aran, D., Looney, A.P., Liu, L., et al.: Reference-based analysis of lung single-cell sequencing reveals a transitional profibrotic macrophage. Nat. Immunol. **20**(2), 163–172 (2019). https://doi.org/10.1038/s41590-018-0276-y
5. Boufea, K., Seth, S., Batada, N.N.: scID uses discriminant analysis to identify transcriptionally equivalent cell types across single-cell RNA-seq data with batch effect. iScience **23**(3), 100914 (2020). https://doi.org/10.1016/j.isci.2020.100914
6. Canakoglu, A., Nanni, L., Sokolovsky, A.: Designing and Evaluating Deep Learning Models for Cancer Detection on Gene Expression Data, pp. 249–261 (2020). https://doi.org/10.1007/978-3-030-34585-3_22
7. Cao, Y., Wang, X., Peng, G.: SCSA: a cell type annotation tool for single-cell RNA-seq data. Front. Genet. **11**, 490–490 (2020). https://doi.org/10.3389/fgene.2020.00490
8. Carbon, S., Douglass, E., et al.: The gene ontology resource: enriching a GOld mine. Nucleic Acids Res. **49**(D1), D325–D334 (2021). https://doi.org/10.1093/nar/gkaa1113
9. Chen, G., Ning, B., Shi, T.: Single-cell RNA-seq technologies and related computational data analysis. Front. Genet. **10**, 317 (2019)
10. Cheng, H.T., Engineer, S.S., Research, G.: Wide & deep learning: Better together with tensorflow, https://ai.googleblog.com/2016/06/wide-deep-learning-better-together-with.html
11. Enge, M., et al.: Single-cell analysis of human pancreas reveals transcriptional signatures of aging and somatic mutation patterns. Cell **171**(2), 321–330.e14 (2017). https://doi.org/10.1016/j.cell.2017.09.004
12. Hao, Y., et al.: Integrated analysis of multimodal single-cell data. Cell (2021). https://doi.org/10.1016/j.cell.2021.04.048

13. Idikio, H.A.: Human cancer classification: a systems biology- based model integrating morphology, cancer stem cells, proteomics, and genomics. J. Cancer **2**, 107–115 (2011)

14. Institute, B.: Study: ICA: blood mononuclear cells (2 donors, 2 sites). https://singlecell.broadinstitute.org/single_cell/study/SCP345/ica-blood-mononuclear-cells-2-donors-2-sites

15. de Kanter, J.K., Lijnzaad, P., Candelli, T., et al.: CHETAH: a selective, hierarchical cell type identification method for single-cell RNA sequencing. Nucleic Acids Res. **47**(16), e95–e95 (2019). https://doi.org/10.1093/nar/gkz543

16. Kiselev, V.Y., Yiu, A., Hemberg, M.: scmap: projection of single-cell RNA-seq data across data sets. Nat. Meth. **15**(5), 359–362 (2018). https://doi.org/10.1038/nmeth.4644

17. Li, C., Liu, B., Kang, B., et al.: SciBet as a portable and fast single cell type identifier. Nat. Commun. **11**(1), 1818 (2020). https://doi.org/10.1038/s41467-020-15523-2

18. Ma, F., Pellegrini, M.: ACTINN: automated identification of cell types in single cell RNA sequencing. Bioinformatics **36**(2), 533–538 (2019). https://doi.org/10.1093/bioinformatics/btz592

19. Shao, X., Liao, J., Lu, X., et al.: scCATCH: automatic annotation on cell types of clusters from single-cell RNA sequencing data. iScience **23**(3), 100882 (2020). https://doi.org/10.1016/j.isci.2020.100882

20. Shao, X., Yang, H., Zhuang, X., et al.: scDeepSort: a pre-trained cell-type annotation method for single-cell transcriptomics using deep learning with a weighted graph neural network. Nucleic Acids Res. **49**(21), e122–e122 (2021). https://doi.org/10.1093/nar/gkab775

21. Stewart, B.J., Ferdinand, J.R., Young, M.D., et al.: Spatiotemporal immune zonation of the human kidney. Science **365**(6460), 1461–1466 (2019). https://doi.org/10.1126/science.aat5031

22. Tan, Y., Cahan, P.: SingleCellNet: a computational tool to classify single cell RNA-seq data across platforms and across species. Cell Syst. **9**(2), 207-213.e2 (2019). https://doi.org/10.1016/j.cels.2019.06.004

23. Urso, A., Fiannaca, A., La Rosa, M., Ravì, V., Rizzo, R.: Data mining: classification and prediction. In: Encyclopedia of Bioinformatics and Computational Biology, pp. 384–402. Elsevier (2019). https://doi.org/10.1016/B978-0-12-809633-8.20461-5

24. Urso, A., Fiannaca, A., La Rosa, M., Ravì, V., Rizzo, R.: Data mining: prediction methods. In: Encyclopedia of Bioinformatics and Computational Biology, pp. 413–430. Elsevier (2019). https://doi.org/10.1016/B978-0-12-809633-8.20462-7

25. Wang, T., Bai, J., Nabavi, S.: Single-cell classification using graph convolutional networks. BMC Bioinform. **22**(1), 364–364 (2021). https://doi.org/10.1186/s12859-021-04278-2

26. Wilson, C.M., Fridley, B.L., Conejo-Garcia, J.R., et al.: Wide and deep learning for automatic cell type identification. Comput. Struct. Biotechnol. J. **19**, 1052–1062 (2021). https://doi.org/10.1016/j.csbj.2021.01.027

27. Wu, S.Z., Roden, D.L., Wang, C., et al.: Stromal cell diversity associated with immune evasion in human triple-negative breast cancer. EMBO J. **39**(19), e104063–e104063 (2020)

28. Zhang, A.W., O'Flanagan, C., Chavez, E.A., et al.: Probabilistic cell-type assignment of single-cell RNA-seq for tumor microenvironment profiling. Nat. Meth. **16**(10), 1007–1015 (2019). https://doi.org/10.1038/s41592-019-0529-1

29. Zhang, Z., Luo, D., Zhong, X., et al.: SCINA: a semi-supervised subtyping algorithm of single cells and bulk samples. Genes **10**(7), 531 (2019). https://doi.org/10.3390/genes10070531

30. Zhao, C., Wang, Z.: GOGO: an improved algorithm to measure the semantic similarity between gene ontology terms. Sci. Rep. **8** (2018). https://doi.org/10.1038/s41598-018-33219-y

31. Zhao, X., Wu, S., Fang, N., Sun, X., Fan, J.: Evaluation of single-cell classifiers for single-cell RNA sequencing data sets. Brief. Bioinform. **21**(5), 1581–1595 (2020). https://doi.org/10.1093/bib/bbz096

# Brain Tumour Segmentation on 3D MRI Using Attention V-Net

Charul Giri[✉], Jivitesh Sharma, and Morten Goodwin

Center for Artificial Intelligence Research (CAIR), University of Agder,
Kristiansand, Norway
{charul.giri,jivitesh.sharma,morten.goodwin}@uia.no

**Abstract.** Brain tumour segmentation on 3D MRI imaging is one of the most critical deep learning applications. In this paper, for the segmentation of tumour sub-regions in brain MRI images, we study some popular architecture for medical imaging segmentation. We further, inspired by them, proposed an architecture that is an end-to-end trainable, fully convolutional neural network that uses attention block to learn localization of different features of the multiple sub-regions of a tumour. We also experiment with a combination of the weighted cross-entropy loss function and dice loss function on the model's performance and the quality of the output segmented labels. The results of the evaluation of our model are received through BraTS'19 dataset challenge. The model can achieve a dice score of 0.80 for the whole tumour segmentation and dice scores of 0.639 and 0.536 for the other two sub-regions within the tumour on the validation dataset.

**Keywords:** Brain tumour segmentation · MRI · 3D segmentation · Medical imaging · Deep learning · Attention · V-Net

## 1 Introduction

A brain tumour is an abnormal growth of a mass of cells in parts of brain. A tumour can be benign or cancerous. Among various kinds of brain tumours gliomas are the most common one. In the segmentation part, the focus is on gliomas. Common symptoms of gliomas include headaches, memory loss, confusion and decline in brain functioning. The task of brain tumour segmentation is to separate healthy tissues from tumour regions such as advancing tumour, necrotic core and surrounding edema.

The utilization of imaging technology has increased drastically with all the improvement in the science and technology in the last couple of decades, as a result of which today a number of different imaging modalities are available suiting the need of the diagnostic measure, example Alzheimer's detection [5]. Various types of imaging techniques used in medical radiation are MRI (Magnetic Resonance Imaging), PET (positron emission tomography) Scan, Ultrasounds, CT (Computer Tomography) Scans, X-Rays etc. All these imaging techniques work slightly differently from each other.

L. Iliadis et al. (Eds.): EANN 2022, CCIS 1600, pp. 336–348, 2022.
https://doi.org/10.1007/978-3-031-08223-8_28

In this study we have used MRI images for the segmentation task as the data was readily available in this format. To create MRI image, strong and uniform magnetic fields are required. The strength is measured in Tesla('T'). A MRI sequence is a particular set of setting of pulse sequences and pulsed field gradients to create MRI images with specific properties. Gliomas are the most common type of brain tumours and can be further divided into High Grade Gliomas (HGG) and Low Grade Gliomas (LGG) based on the growth rate.

As pointed out precisely by [8] that manual segmentation of tumours could be bias based on the relevant experience of the person and their subjective decision making since there are yet no standard protocols to be followed. This gives the rise to the need of having automatic segmentation systems. This task becomes even more complex for medical image segmentation as it consists of 3D images and highly unbalanced class distribution. The irregular shapes, size, location, heterogeneous appearance of the tumours adds up the challenges to the task. Brain tumour segmentation models are computationally and architecturally complex, but obtain high performance. We aim to further boost performance of a state-of-the-art 3D segmentation model called V-net. To do this, we propose a novel additive attention module with a modified V-net architecture. This module encourages the model to focus on relevant sub-regions of the 3D brain scans.

The rest of the paper is divided into the following sections: Sect. 2 briefly describes some of the relevant research work conducted on medical image segmentation, Sect. 3 proposes our attention 3D V-Net model, Dataset and training details are given in Sect. 4, while the experiments and results are shown in Sect. 5 and finally, Sect. 6 concludes the paper with future research direction.

## 2   Related Work

The need of automation of biomedical imaging analysis has been there for long. In early times low-level pixel processing and mathematical model based systems were used to solve a set tasks. Gradually the focus shifted to more modern approaches which includes utilizing the potential of rapid-growing filed of Artificial Intelligence. The related work revolves around medical image segmentation for brain tumours. In this section we will study some of the work that has been done for the segmentation of medical imaging using deep learning for Brain tumour.

[14] proposed an Enhanced Convolutional Neural Networks where they divided the segmentation task into two parts, first preprocessing with image enhancement and second is to calculate the segmented mask using Hybrid Convolutional Neural Networks. They also introduced a novel loss optimization function called Novel BAT optimization algorithm (NOBA) which uses the concept of echolocation mechanism to calculate the difference between an optimal and non-optimal error.

[13] proposed a 2D architecture called U-Net. It is a key architecture in medical image segmentation. The model has great ability to localize the features and inspired a lot more models. For example [4] proposed a memory efficient

version of U-Net regularized using auto-encoders to segment brain tumours. A combination of mean-squared error and Kullback-Leibler loss was used to as a loss function for the encoder, while SoftDice loss was used to train the U-Net inspired network.

While most of the studies focused on medical image segmentation using patches or 2D slices, authors in [9] proposed an architecture capable of performing volumetric segmentation of medical imaging called V-Net. The applied their model to the segmentation task on the Promise 2012 dataset. The introduction of residual blocks in their network ensured the convergence of the model much faster compared to other studies. [1] in their work made use of two cascaded CNNs inspired from V-Net architecture and modified residual connections for brain tumour segmentation problem. Their first network segments the overall tumour and the second network then delineation of the different tumour regions using the output of first network as input. Their study contributed toward BraTS'17 challenge. Inspired from U-Net, [2] propose a 3D version of it, called 3D U-Net, which became another one of the key architectures for biomedical imaging segmentation. [17] also heavily used U-Net architecture in their study for segmentation of brain tumours in BraTS'18 challenge. They exploit a 3D U-Net based model to first locate the tumours in the brain and an another but more complex and smaller 3D U-Net to further segment the localized tumour into its sub-regions. [15] also create a 2 staged 3D U-Net framework, where they utilized the potential of image super-resolution CNN (SRCNN) to process the MRI images at full resolution. They first detected the ROI from the full volumes and predicted the segmented masks from these ROIs.

Since 3D CNNs have large memory consumption, and 2D CNNs while having low memory requirement ignore the 3D context in the data, [16] proposed a novel framework to use 2.5D CNN, that is a trade-off between memory consumption, model complexity and receptive field. They evaluated their model on BraTS'17 data and ranked second in the challenge. They propose a test-time augmentation technique claiming to improve segmentation accuracy.

DeepMedic [7] is a multi-scale deep 3D CNN for lesion segmentation. The architecture consists of two parallel convolutional pathways. The pathways process images at different resolutions giving it a better receptive field for the final classification. Inspired from DeepMedic, [7] proposed their architecture as extended DeepMedic with residual connections. They tested their results on BraTS'15. The residual connections gave a modest but consistent improvement.

Many researches revolved around the idea of using encoder-decoders to segment lesions in brain. [10] proposed encoder-decoder based architecture to segment tumours in 3D MRI images. They also used a variational-autoencoder joined to the main architecture, to reconstruct the input image and regularize the shared decoder. The architecture ranked $1^{st}$ place in the BraTS 2018 challenge.

In this paper, we augment the 3D V-Net architecture with an attention module. This results in an improvement in performance for brain tumour segmentation on 3D MRI images.

# 3  Proposed Architecture: Attention V-Net

In this section we propose the attention V-Net architecture for brain tumour segmentation. V-Net [9] was first proposed in 2016. It gained popularity because of it's efficiency and accuracy in "PROMISE 2012" [3] dataset challenge for volumetric binary segmentation of prostate gland. V-Net also uses volumetric convolutions as opposed to 2D slices or patches used by other deep learning models for medical imaging. Our model is very much inspired from the V-Net architecture, leveraging the potential of end-to-end trained fully convolutional neural networks to process MRI images. All the models explained above focused on binary segmentation but in this study our focus is on segmenting multiple classes of tumour sub-regions. We take the full advantage of skip connections, residual connections and have added novel attention blocks in our model to tackle the complexity of this task. The proposed model uses volumetric convolutions to process MRI images.

The model comprises of an analysis path (contraction) and a synthesis path (expansion). In the analysis path there are 4 down-transition stages (including one input transition stage) where at each stage downsampling and convolutions happen on the input. In the synthesis path there are 5 up-transition stages.

At each stage in the analysis path, there are 3D convolutional layers sequentially increasing from one to four. The input is passed to these convolution layers, followed by ReLU6 non-linearity and then a batch normalization layer. Each convolution layer uses 3D kernels with size $3 \times 3 \times 3$. A residual function is learnt by adding the input of each stage with output of the last convolution layer of that stage. At the end of each analysis stage a downsampling operation is performed by convolution with $2 \times 2 \times 2$ voxels wide kernels applied with stride 2 to reduce the resolution of the feature maps. Downsampling helps to increase the receptive field. Each stage outputs double the number of feature maps with half of the input resolution. For downsampling use of convolution layers with strides, over pooling layers is inspired from [9]. As suggested in [9] switching pooling layers to convolution layers also results in a smaller memory footprint.

The right part of the model called synthesis path decompresses the signal until the original size is reached. At each stage in the synthesis path, the number of 3D convolution layers decrease from five to one sequentially, making it a mirror image of the analysis path. At each stage the input is upsampled using de-convolution layers to increase the size of the feature maps. Inspired from [13] and [2] we have implemented horizontal skip connections in our model as well. The output of the respective skip connection and the output of the last stage are used to create an attention block which is explained in more details below. The output of this attention block is then concatenated with the output of the last stage again. This is treated as the input for the current stage in the synthesis path. This input is then processed by the convolution layers present in the block followed by ReLU6 layer again. The convolution layers use 3D kernels of size $3 \times 3 \times 3$. The number of kernels in each convolution layer at a stage is half the number of kernels in the convolution layers present in the last stage. The learnt residual is added to this output similar to the analysis block. This process is repeated at each stage. In the final output stage, the last convolution layer computes the four feature maps, one for the background and the rest three for the sub-regions of the tumour. In this way the synthesis path gathers the necessary information and assembles it produce the final output of four channel volumetric segmentation of the tumours. Figure 1 presents our proposed model.

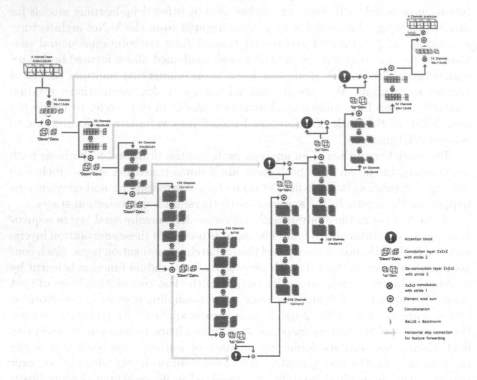

**Fig. 1.** Proposed attention VNet

1. **Horizontal Skip Connections and Residual Connections**: Skip connections as the name suggests skip some part of the network and feeds or adds the output of one layer to the output of another layer beyond the next layer. In our model, we have used two kinds of skip connection, a) a horizontal skip connection and b) a short residual connection.

   In our model the horizontal skip connection helps in the forwarding the extracted features from the analysis path to the synthesis path as shown in Fig. 2. The output from each stage to analysis goes to the next stage, but along with that it also goes to the attention block in the corresponding synthesis stage. In this way it helps our attention block to focus on the localization of the features. In each stage of both analysis and synthesis path, a residual connection [6] is also present. A residual connection is a kind of skip connection which allows smooth information flow from one layer to another

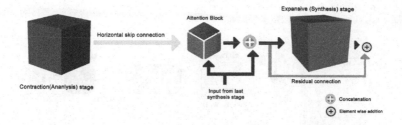

**Fig. 2.** Horizontal skip connection

by bypassing some layers in deep neural networks. A tradition deep learning model learns a mapping M, from an input x to output y.

$$M(x) = y \tag{1}$$

A residual connection tries to learn the difference between a mapping applied to x and the original input x, given by

$$R(x) = M(x) - x \tag{2}$$

Transforming Eq. 2, we get the mapping from a residual connection as

$$M(x) = R(x) + x \tag{3}$$

Since our model is a deep 3D CNN, it is prone to suffer from vanishing gradient problem during backpropagation. Residual connections helps in avoiding this problem because of skipping trait as mentioned earlier.

2. **Attention Blocks**: The attention block in our model is used to highlight the salient features transferred through the horizontal skip connection and remove the irrelevant and noisy responses. Figure 5 gives an outline of the attention blocks we have used in our model.

   The attention block in our model takes two inputs: 1) from the horizontal skip connection coming from the corresponding analysis block of the contraction path as mentioned above and 2) from the upsampled output of the previous synthesis block in the expansive path. In the attention block, individual convolutions of $1 \times 1 \times 1$ are applied on both the inputs. We have then applied addition operation on these two vectors following the norm of additive attention, and then passed it through ReLU6 layer to add non-linearity. Then one more $1 \times 1 \times 1$ convolution operation is performed on the resultant with sigmoid activation applied, creating a voxel-wise mask. We then multiply this result with the $2^{nd}$ input of this attention block. This is the final output of this attention block which is then concatenated with the output of the current stage in the synthesis block, and is passed to the next stage as input and as well as a residual connection. This motivation of this attention block is taken from [11] with some minor changes. Mathematically the attention block is given as:

$$A_{att} = \psi^T(\sigma_1(W_x^T x_i + W_g^T g_i + b_x)) + b_\psi \tag{4}$$

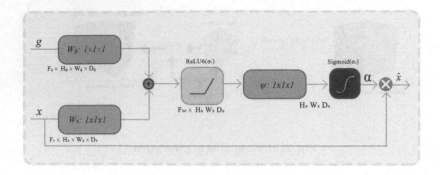

**Fig. 3.** Attention block

$$\alpha_i = \sigma_2(A_{att}(x_i, g_i; \theta_{att})), \tag{5}$$

where $\sigma_1$ is the *ReLU6* non-linearity in our block, $g_i$ and $x_i$ are the two inputs to the attention blocks, and $W_g$ and $W_x$ are the corresponding convolution layers as explained above. $\psi$ is the last $1 \times 1 \times 1$ convolution transformation followed by the sigmoid activation function ($\sigma_2$). $\alpha_i$ is called the activation coefficient. $\theta_{att}$ is the set of parameters containing, $W_x$, $W_g$, $\psi$ and bias terms $b_x$, $b_\psi$.

## 4 Dataset and Training

**Dataset.** The Brain tumour Segmentation (BraTS) challenge focuses on the evaluation of the methods for brain tumour segmentation in multi-parametric magnetic resonance imaging (mpMRI) scans. In this study we have used the latest dataset available at the time from BraTS called BraTS'19. The dataset consists of mpMRI scans of 335 subjects in training set and 125 subjects in validation set.

The standard preprocessing done by BraTS on the MRI images in the dataset includes co-registering the MRI images to a common anatomical template from [12], skull stripping and resampling to a uniform isotropic resolution of 1 $mm^3$. The further preprocessing done on the dataset is the intensity normalization, N4 bias correction and downsampling of the MRI images.

**Training.** The model was trained with 335 MRI images collected from BraTS'19, resized to $96 \times 112 \times 96$ and spatial resolution of $1 \times 1 \times 1$ mm$^3$ in axial view. The input to the model consists of the four MRIs stacked upon each other (T1, T1Gd, T2 and T2-FLAIR), resulting in a input of shape $4 \times 96 \times 112 \times 96$. The model takes a batch size of 12. Like most of the medical segmentation task, we also faced the problem of highly unbalanced classification of the labels in our dataset. To get around this problem we experimented with weighted cross-entropy and dice loss functions. In the final experiments we have used the compound loss which a combination of weighted cross-entropy and dice loss. Cross-entropy is a distribution-based loss and dice loss is a region based loss, so combining these two losses we can improve both classification and localization of the labels in our dataset. Weighted cross-entropy is defined as

$$WCE\ loss(x, class) = w[class] \left( -x[class] + log \left( \sum_j exp(x[j]) \right) \right) \qquad (6)$$

and Dice loss tries to optimize dice coefficient is given as:

$$D = 1 - \frac{2\sum_i^N p_i g_i}{\sum_i^N p_i^2 + \sum_i^N g_i^2} \qquad (7)$$

So, the resultant loss we are trying to optimize is an addition of the two losses. We have initialized our segmentation model with He initialization too. We have trained our model for 10,000 epochs with an initial learning rate of 0.01 with a scheduled drop of factor 0.1 after every 2000 epochs. To optimize the loss we have used Adam optimizer. A dropout of factor 0.2 is used with all the convolution layers. Nearest interpolation is used to resample the segmented labels to the original size. We compare the difference in using the CE loss alone versus the combination of CE and Dice loss as shown in Fig. 4.

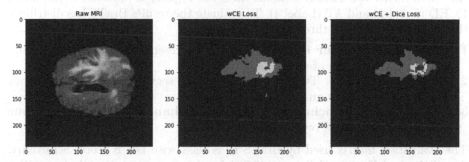

Along with experimenting with our model, we also performed some experiments with 3D U-Net and V-Net to compare our model performance. We trained all three model with the same parameter settings. We limited the number the training epochs to 1000 only. This was done due to time and memory constraints. We calculated the dice score for each of the label. The comparison results are presented in the next section.

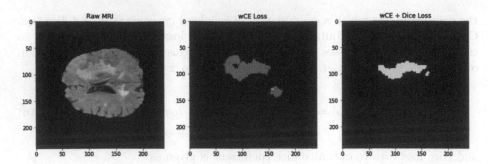

**Fig. 4.** Performance of CE vs CE+Dice

## 5   Experiments and Results

To evaluate the performance of our segmentation model, we have used the validation set of 125 MRIs from BraTS. The ground truths of the validation set are not made available by BraTS. The segmented labels have to uploaded on the challenge website to get the segmented results.

### 5.1   The Evaluation Criteria

As stated earlier the dataset contains three sub-regions of tumours: NCR (Label 1), ED (Label 2) and AT (Label 4). To evaluate the results BraTS has distribute the segmented labels in three classes as follows:

1. **WT: Whole tumour Extent.** WT class represents the whole tumour and is given by the union of all labels.
2. **TC: tumour Core.** TC class represents the segmentation of the tumour core outline. It is the union of label 1 and 4
3. **ET: Active/enhancing and the non-enhancing/necrotic tumour regions.** This class is represented by label 4.

The evaluation matrix used by BraTS'19 is class wise DICE score, Sensitivity, Specificity and Hausdorff distance (95%) for the classes mentioned above. Dice score measures the area of overlap between the ground truth and the predicted label. It is similar to F1 score and using the definition of true positive (TP), false positive (FP), and false negative (FN), it can be written as:

$$DSC = \frac{2TP}{2TP + FP + FN} \tag{8}$$

Hausdorff distance is a surface distance measure. It measure the distance between two boundaries, in our case boundary of prediction and ground truth segment. A bidirectional Hausdorff distance between two sets X and Y is given as:

$$HD(X,Y) = max(hd(X,Y), hd(Y,X)) \tag{9}$$

where,

$$hd(X,Y) = \max_{x \in X} \min_{y \in Y} \|x - y\|_2 \tag{10}$$

## 5.2   Evaluation

We have presented some examples to visualize the performance of our model in Figs. 5 and 6. In Fig. 5 some examples from training dataset are given showing a raw fMRI image, the corresponding ground truth provided by BraTS and the labels segmented by our model. The official results of the evaluation matrix for our segmented labels received from BraTS are mentioned in Table ??

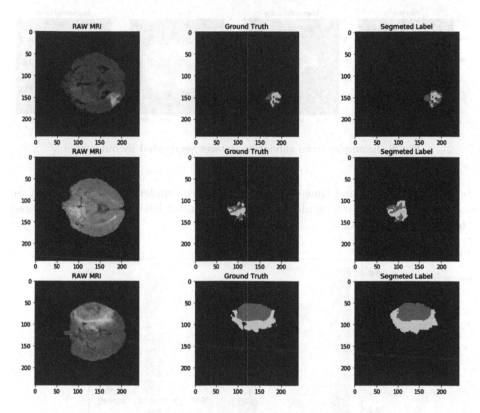

**Fig. 5.** Examples from training dataset segmented by our model

Figure 6 presents some samples of the segmented labels from validation dataset segmented by our model. As can be seen from both training and validation sample segmented results, the model is able to detect the tumour sub-regions very well especially the whole tumour area. The model pays deep attention on both the shape and location of the tumour regions. We did a thorough analysis of the segmented labels for the localization of the whole tumour from the training dataset (since ground truths aren't available for validation data) and found that the model can effectively localize the tumour. In the Fig. 7 below, we have compared our model with V-Net and 3D U-Net when run with the same setting for 1000 epochs. We had to limit this comparison experiment to 1000 epochs

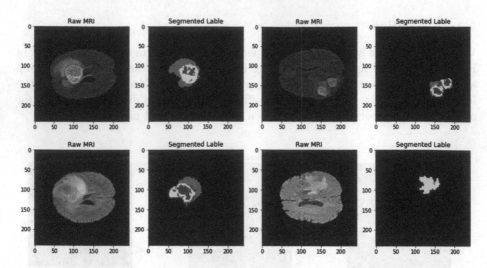

**Fig. 6.** Examples from validation dataset segmented by our model

because of memory and time constrains. When run under same environment we can see clearly that our model converges to a much better accuracy compared to the other two models.

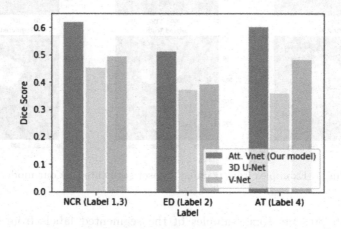

**Fig. 7.** Performance comparison on training data for different labels when trained for 1000 epochs

Since the ground truth were not available, segmented labels for the validation set were uploaded on the BraTS website, and were evaluated on their server using the matrices defined above. The official results of our segmented labels received from BraTS are mention in Table 1. From these two tables we observed that the model obtains good performance for the segmentation of the whole tumour area but is overfitting for the other two classes, especially ET. This is because of the highly unbalanced number of the classes.

**Table 1.** Evaluation Metrices for validation data

|            | WT    | TC    | ET    |
|------------|-------|-------|-------|
| Dice       | 0.800 | 0.639 | 0.536 |
| Hausdorff95 | 15.04 | 20.06 | 16.23 |
| Sensitivity | 0.854 | 0.621 | 0.586 |
| Specificity | 0.985 | 0.996 | 0.996 |

# 6   Conclusion and Future Work

In this paper, we proposed a novel 3D CNN architecture for the segmentation of brain tumours. We modify the V-Net by introducing an attention module and skip connections. The model can predict the segmentation mask with good accuracy for the whole tumour. But we saw it overfitting for the other two sub-regions of a tumour, named enhancing tumour (ET) and tumour core (CT). This is because of highly unbalanced label classes as these classes contain only 22% and 18% of the whole, tumour. The model segmented labels for these classes with high accuracy in the training dataset show the models' ability to learn these small patterns but lacks generalization. The future work involves improving the model's generalization ability with better data augmentation techniques to increase the size of the training data, hence increasing the times an under-represented class label appears during training.

# References

1. Casamitjana, A., Catà, M., Sánchez, I., Combalia, M., Vilaplana, V.: Cascaded V-Net using ROI masks for brain tumor segmentation. In: Crimi, A., Bakas, S., Kuijf, H., Menze, B., Reyes, M. (eds.) BrainLes 2017. LNCS, vol. 10670, pp. 381–391. Springer, Cham (2018). https://doi.org/10.1007/978-3-319-75238-9_33
2. Çiçek, Ö., Abdulkadir, A., Lienkamp, S.S., Brox, T., Ronneberger, O.: 3D U-Net: learning dense volumetric segmentation from sparse annotation. In: Ourselin, S., Joskowicz, L., Sabuncu, M.R., Unal, G., Wells, W. (eds.) MICCAI 2016. LNCS, vol. 9901, pp. 424–432. Springer, Cham (2016). https://doi.org/10.1007/978-3-319-46723-8_49
3. Litjens, G., et al.: Evaluation of prostate segmentation algorithms for MRI: the PROMISE12 challenge. Med. Image Anal. 18(2), 359–373 (2014)
4. Frey, M., Nau, M.: Memory efficient brain tumor segmentation using an autoencoder-regularized U-Net. In: Crimi, A., Bakas, S. (eds.) BrainLes 2019. LNCS, vol. 11992, pp. 388–396. Springer, Cham (2020). https://doi.org/10.1007/978-3-030-46640-4_37

5. Giri, C., Goodwin, M., Oppedal, K.: Deep 3D convolution neural network for Alzheimer's detection. In: Nicosia, G., et al. (eds.) LOD 2020. LNCS, vol. 12565, pp. 347–358. Springer, Cham (2020). https://doi.org/10.1007/978-3-030-64583-0_32

6. He, K., Zhang, X., Ren, S., Sun, J.: Deep residual learning for image recognition (2015)

7. Kamnitsas, K., et al.: DeepMedic for brain tumor segmentation. In: Crimi, A., Menze, B., Maier, O., Reyes, M., Winzeck, S., Handels, H. (eds.) Brainlesion: Glioma, Multiple Sclerosis, Stroke and Traumatic Brain Injuries. BrainLes 2016. LNCS, vol. 10154, pp. 138–149. Springer, Cham (2016). https://doi.org/10.1007/978-3-319-55524-9_14

8. Malathi, M., Sinthia, P.: Brain tumour segmentation using convolutional neural network with tensor flow. Asian Pac. J. Cancer Prev. **20**(7), 2095–2101 (2019)

9. Milletari, F., Navab, N., Ahmadi, S.-A.: V-Net: fully convolutional neural networks for volumetric medical image segmentation (2016)

10. Myronenko, A.: 3D MRI brain tumor segmentation using autoencoder regularization. In: Crimi, A., Bakas, S., Kuijf, H., Keyvan, F., Reyes, M., van Walsum, T. (eds.) BrainLes 2018. LNCS, vol. 11384, pp. 311–320. Springer, Cham (2019). https://doi.org/10.1007/978-3-030-11726-9_28

11. Oktay, O., et al.: Attention U-Net: Learning where to look for the pancreas (2018)

12. Rohlfing, T., Zahr, N., Sullivan, E., Pfefferbaum, A.: The SRI24 multichannel atlas of normal adult human brain structure. Hum. Brain Map. **31**, 798–819 (2009)

13. Ronneberger, O., Fischer, P., Brox, T.: U-Net: convolutional networks for biomedical image segmentation. In: Navab, N., Hornegger, J., Wells, W.M., Frangi, A.F. (eds.) MICCAI 2015. LNCS, vol. 9351, pp. 234–241. Springer, Cham (2015). https://doi.org/10.1007/978-3-319-24574-4_28

14. Thaha, M., Pradeep Kumar, K., Murugan, B., Dhanasekeran, S., Vijayakarthick, P., Selvi, A.: Brain tumor segmentation using convolutional neural networks in MRI images. J. Med. Syst. **43**, 294 (2019). https://doi.org/10.1007/s10916-019-1416-0

15. Wang, C., MacGillivray, T., Macnaught, G., Yang, G., Newby, D.E.: A two-stage 3D Unet framework for multi-class segmentation on full resolution image. arXiv abs/1804.04341 (2018)

16. Wang, G., Li, W., Ourselin, S., Vercauteren, T.: Automatic brain tumor segmentation based on cascaded convolutional neural networks with uncertainty estimation. Front. Comput. Neurosci. **13**, 08 (2019)

17. Weninger, L., Rippel, O., Koppers, S., Merhof, D.: Segmentation of brain tumors and patient survival prediction: methods for the BraTS 2018 challenge. In: Crimi, A., Bakas, S., Kuijf, H., Keyvan, F., Reyes, M., van Walsum, T. (eds.) BrainLes 2018. LNCS, vol. 11384, pp. 3–12. Springer, Cham (2019). https://doi.org/10.1007/978-3-030-11726-9_1

# Development of an Algorithmic Model to Reduce Memory and Learning Deficits on Trisomic Mice

Eleni Gerasimidi$^{(\boxtimes)}$ and Lazaros Iliadis

Department of Civil Engineering, Democritus University of Thrace, 67100 Xanthi, Greece
elgerasimidi@gmail.com, liliadis@civil.duth.gr

**Abstract.** For many decades, scientists have been interested in finding cures for diseases due to the human genome. Down Syndrome is the most common genetic disorder and one of the most common causes of learning and memory deficits. It is a condition that has long preoccupied the scientific community, with the finding of treatments being limited to the individual conditions caused by the Syndrome. It is easy to see that finding a cure for Down Syndrome requires systematic and long-term research. Scientists will need to use whatever means at their disposal, with technological aids being the ones of most interest. Artificial Intelligence has managed to offer much to humanity, despite the short time that has elapsed since its appearance on the scientific firmament. Its discoveries in every scientific field have paved the way for the solution of problems that have occupied scientists for years, while her entry into our daily lives has managed to facilitate her to a great extent. This research aims to introduce Machine Learning (ML) models capable to improve the memory and to reduce the learning deficits of mice with Down Syndrome, that were used as experimental animals. The experimental datasets were developed by Higuera et al., 2015 and Ahmed et al., 2015, and they are related to the levels of proteins present in the brainstem of mice. They are publicly available, by the UCI (University of California Irvine) Open Database. The emerged ML models are very promising and they deserve further attention by the scientific community.

**Keywords:** Reducing memory and learning deficits · Machine learning · Trisomic mice · Memantine · k-Fold cross validation · SMOTE · Random Forest · J48 · Naïve Bayes · Multilayer perceptron

## 1 Introduction

Down Syndrome or Trisomy 21 or Trisomy G is a genetic disorder caused by the presence of an extra copy (or part of an extra copy) of chromosome 21[11]. That condition results on having three instead of the normal two chromosomes 21 in the human's genome. This anomaly is reproduced in every cell of the human body as the fetus develops. Most do not consider it a disease, as people with Down Syndrome do not suffer from it [16]. It is estimated that internationally the incidence in infants is about 1: 800 births per year, while in Greece research indicates that the birth rate of children with Down Syndrome is 1 in 770 births per year [9]. A key factor influencing this ratio is the age of the mother

© Springer Nature Switzerland AG 2022
L. Iliadis et al. (Eds.): EANN 2022, CCIS 1600, pp. 349–360, 2022.
https://doi.org/10.1007/978-3-031-08223-8_29

[10]. It has been estimated that the incidence of Down Syndrome births in a 20-year-old mother is 1:2000, while in a 40-year-old mother, the incidence is 1:100 or less [10].

Regarding the types of Down Syndrome, three categories seem to have been distinguished depending on the characteristics of the individuals in each of them. These categories are Typical Trisomy 21, Mosaic Type, and Displacement [16]. Typical Trisomy 21 is the most common form of Down Syndrome. It occurs in about 90–95% of cases [13]. This form is due to the appearance of an extra chromosome in the 21st pair of human chromosomes. The Mosaic Type is a rarer form of Down Syndrome. This type occurs in about 2–5% of the population with the reported Syndrome [16]. In the Mosaic, the initial fertilization is normal, with the zygote (first cell) having a normal number of chromosomes. Incomplete division appears to occur at some point, early in the course of cell division. Thus, people with Mosaic have two types of cells, those with a normal number of chromosomes and those with the above chromosome 21 [17]. The ratio of normal and trisomic cells determines the percentage of Mosaic. Displacement is an even rarer form of Down Syndrome that occurs in only 2% of people with Down Syndrome [16]. This form is hereditary. During the Displacement, a portion of chromosome 21 breaks down and attaches to another chromosome. Due to that, we have a normal number of copies of chromosome 21, but we also have extra material on it, which is on another chromosome. The detached portion of chromosome 21 is usually found on chromosome 14, and less frequently on chromosome 22 or another chromosome [2].

The fact that Down Syndrome is due to a genetic defect, which means that the genetic material is affected, creates complications in many systems of the human body. This does not mean that the symptoms will be the same in every appearance of the Syndrome [4]. In terms of brain function, the mental retardation of people with Down Syndrome ranges from varying levels, from severe to mild [5]. Usually, we still see influences on short-term memory and the ability to think and hear. These, it is possible to distinguish them from an early age. No cure has been found yet for Down Syndrome. There are only treatments for some of the individual problems that occur due to the Syndrome.

Studies have shown that human chromosome 21 bears a striking resemblance to the corresponding chromosome 16 present in mice [12]. Thus, a trisomy on chromosome 16 (Ts16) of mice could be an ideal organism model for the study of Down Syndrome [11]. Nevertheless, mice with trisomy 16, on chromosome 16, rarely survive after birth, deeming them unsuitable for the study of behavior and their postnatal development [14]. This is attributed to the presence of more genes on chromosome 16 of mice than on human chromosome 21, thus making it necessary to find one more specialized model mouse with trisomy. The Ts65Dn trisomic mouse model first appeared in 1993 [3]. It is a model more similar to human trisomy 21 than the Ts16 trisomic mouse. Ts65Dn cells have an additional copy of a gene fragment of chromosome 16 as well as an additional copy of a gene fragment of chromosome 17 [14]. On this model there are great similarities in terms of behavioral abnormalities and cognitive skills [14]. In this research, the experimental data to be used are derived exclusively from Ts65Dn trisomic mice.

This is an innovative research effort. To the best of our knowledge, it is the first time that such a comprehensive in-depth research has been conducted on this specific subject, using Artificial Intelligence algorithms and Data Pre-Processing Methods. So far, it has been adopted Deep Neural Networks using multiple Hidden Layers for proper feature selection [1]. However, this is the first time that an in-depth AI trisomic mice behavior modeling research effort using a wide spectrum of Machine Learning algorithms is published in the literature.

## 2  Experiments Description

Human chromosome 21 has been shown to encode more than 500 genes but the number of those associated with learning disabilities is unknown [6]. Due to the increased number of genes being encoded, their overexpression disrupts many biological processes, such as those related to its normal development and the function of the brain. Thus, for the development of a drug, we ought to first look for disorders in paths critical to learning and memory and then attempt to correct the discovered disorders. To investigate the normal responses to learning, the scientists measured the levels of approximately 80 proteins in subcellular fractions in areas of the wild type mice's brain exposed to an environment of fear. In them, about half of the proteins responded to learning in at least one area of the brain. Moreover, they studied the effect of memantine on protein expression, whether we are in a fear environment or not. Similarly, we analyzed protein expressions in a trisomic mouse model, Ts65Dn. These mice fail to learn in a fear environment, but only if they were first exposed memantine was their learning "rescued". Comparing protein expressions in trisomic mice that fail to learn in a fear environment, in trisomic mice whose learning has been rescued and in normal mice exposed to the same environment can draw a lot of data on protein levels expressed in successful, failed and rescued learning, differences in protein levels during memantine therapy but also differences in protein expression levels between a normal mouse and a trisomic.

   The use of Machine Learning methods is important for the processing of such data. Both supervised and unsupervised learning are particularly useful for the analysis of biological data. In the reported study Higuera et al., 2015 [6] was deemed more appropriate to use the unsupervised learning algorithm SOM (Self Organizing Maps), which has proven in the past to be a popular and useful bioinformatics tool. In said research, SOM was applied to expression data 77 proteins obtained from the nuclear-enriched fraction of normal and trisomic mice. While using SOM, they have managed to separate the mice that differ in genotype, treatment and learning success, thanks to the differences in the produced proteins' levels.

### 2.1  Experimental Data and Methodology

All protein data in the experiment, came from male mice's brains, up to 3 months old, both Ts65Dn trisomic mice and normal control/wild-type control mice [6]. In order to transfer the mice to a fear environment, we used the method of CFC (Context Fear Conditioning) [6]. According to this methodology the mice were divided into two groups, that of Context-Shock (CS) and that of Shock-Context (SC). The mice of the first group were initially transferred to a cage. There, after they were released to explore for a few minutes, they received a brief electric shock. Normal mice, after this process seem to learn and consequently freeze (immobilize) when exposed to the same cage again. On the contrary, the mice of the second group are left to explore inside the cage after they have initially received an electric shock. Thus, normal mice do not freeze (do not immobilize) when are placed back in the cage, which proves to us that they do not learn to relate the cage with the electric shock. Unlike normal mice, Ts65Dn do not appear to learn in a CS environment. This lack of learning is observed to be corrected by a memantine injection before the procedure. In order to check the results of the injection, a saline mixture was injected, without the introduction of any drug, for both groups. From the above methodology it appears that we had to create four groups of mice for Ts65Dn: CS-memantine, CS-saline, SC-memantine and SC-saline. Respectively, the same categories were also created for control mice, finally offering us eight categories of mice [6]. The following observations emerged from the eight classes of mice:

- In control mice in CS environment with memantine injection (c-CS-m) normal learning was observed (10 mice).
- In control mice in CS environment with saline injection (c-CS-s) normal learning was observed (9 mice).
- In control mice in SC environment with memantine injection (c-SC-m) failed learning was observed (10 mice).
- In control mice in SC environment with saline injection (c-SC-s) failed learning was observed (9 mice).
- In Ts65Dn mice (trisomic mice) in CS environment with memantine injection (t-CS-m) rescued learning was observed (9 mice).
- In Ts65Dn mice (trisomic mice) in CS environment with saline injection (t-CS-s) failed learning was observed (7 mice).
- In Ts65Dn mice (trisomic mice) in SC environment with memantine injection (t-SC-m) failed learning was observed (9 mice).
- In Ts65Dn mice (trisomic mice) in SC environment with saline injection (t-SC-s) failed learning was observed (9 mice) [6] (Fig. 1).

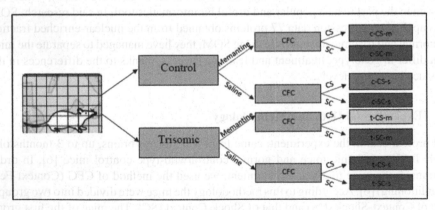

**Fig. 1.** The eight classes of mice

The data used are the expression levels of 77 proteins or modifications of protein that produced detectable signals in the nuclear cortex of the mice's brains. 38 control and

34 trisomic mice were used, therefore a total of 72 mice. 7–10 mice were distributed in each of the 8 groups/classes. For the experiment, 15 measurements of each protein were taken per mouse. So, in total there were 38 × 15 or 570 measurements per protein for control mice and 34 × 15 or 510 measurements per protein for trisomic mice [6]. Each of the above measurements can be calculated as a separate sample/mouse. Because measurement mechanisms are very sensitive, they can create technical problems that require the deletion of data from individual points. Therefore, in the final data set there were missing values, so for some proteins we had less than 15 measurements.

## 3 Data Preprocessing

To create the ML model, data from the UCI Machine Learning Repository [15] have been used. Typically, the first step was data pre-processing (DAP) in order to determine the existence of extreme values, as well as gaps, or symbols that will not allow the model to convergence. The DAP was done in Microsoft Excel, considering the proteins, the genotypes, the treatments and the behaviors as independent features and the class of the mice as the target one. Moreover, two files were developed as follows: The first comprises of the proteins and the respective classes and the second comprises of the proteins, the genotypes and the classes. In the second file, the control mice were assigned the value 1 and the Ts65Dn trisomic mice the value 0 (Fig. 2).

| | A | B | C | D | E | F | G | H | I | J | K |
|---|---|---|---|---|---|---|---|---|---|---|---|
| 1 | MouseID | DYRK1A_N | ITSN1_N | BDNF_N | NR1_N | NR2A_N | pAKT_N | pBRAF_N | pCAMKII_N | pCREB_N | pELK_N |
| 2 | 309_1 | 0,503644 | 0,747193 | 0,430175 | 2,816329 | 5,990152 | 0,21883 | 0,177565 | 2,373744 | 0,232224 | 1,750936 |
| 3 | 309_2 | 0,514617 | 0,689064 | 0,41177 | 2,789514 | 5,685038 | 0,211636 | 0,172817 | 2,29215 | 0,226972 | 1,596377 |
| 4 | 309_3 | 0,509183 | 0,730247 | 0,418309 | 2,687201 | 5,622059 | 0,209011 | 0,175722 | 2,283337 | 0,230247 | 1,561316 |
| 5 | 309_4 | 0,442107 | 0,617076 | 0,358626 | 2,466947 | 4,979503 | 0,222886 | 0,176463 | 2,152301 | 0,207004 | 1,595086 |
| 6 | 309_5 | 0,43494 | 0,61743 | 0,358802 | 2,365785 | 4,718679 | 0,213106 | 0,173627 | 2,134014 | 0,192158 | 1,50423 |
| 7 | 309_6 | 0,447506 | 0,628176 | 0,367388 | 2,385939 | 4,807635 | 0,218578 | 0,176233 | 2,141282 | 0,195188 | 1,442398 |
| 8 | 309_7 | 0,428033 | 0,573696 | 0,342709 | 2,334224 | 4,47313 | 0,225173 | 0,184004 | 2,012414 | 0,195789 | 1,612036 |
| 9 | 309_8 | 0,416923 | 0,564036 | 0,327703 | 2,260135 | 4,268735 | 0,214834 | 0,179668 | 2,007985 | 0,189803 | 1,424601 |
| 10 | 309_9 | 0,386311 | 0,538428 | 0,31772 | 2,125725 | 4,06395 | 0,207222 | 0,167778 | 1,861514 | 0,180684 | 1,261891 |

**Fig. 2.** A partial view of the available data attributes

The open-source WEKA software was employed to develop the ML models. WEKA (Waikato Environment for Knowledge Analysis) is a software environment for Machine Learning and Data Mining [18]. It not only provides a huge variety of classification, regression, clustering and correlation algorithms, but it also provides the user the ability to pre-process data and to visualize the results [7]. Using the WEKA software, as mentioned above, the following software algorithms were employed to extract the most robust classifier namely: The Random Forest, J48, Naive Bayes and Multilayer Perceptron. The Random Forest and J48 algorithms belong to the category of Tree Classifiers, the Naive Bayes algorithm belongs to the family of Bayesian Classifiers, while the Multilayer Perceptron algorithm is a typical Neural Network approach.

### 3.1 k-Folds Cross Validation

According to the method of Cross-validation, the dataset is randomly divided into k subsets (folds), with a specific number of vectors (According to the existing literature, the most used are the 3-fold, 5-fold and 10-fold). Then the training process is repeated k times (k-cycles). Each time, the k-1 folds are used for training the algorithm, whereas the remaining fold is used for testing. This process is repeated k times with the subset that is singled out for testing, changing each time. As performance indicators are taken, the average of the corresponding errors is used to determine the level of model's convergence. The choice of the number of folds depends on the size of the available dataset. Thus, a large number of folds might offer higher accuracy, higher error range, and high execution time while a smaller the number of folds might result in smaller accuracy and smaller execution time [8]. In the upcoming research, the 10-fold approach has been employed.

## 4    Development of Machine Learning Models

### 4.1    Models Using Proteins as Independent Variables

The first ML model was developed in WEKA, by considering all proteins as independent parameters and the classes of mice as depended. Overall, 78 attributes were used, from which 77 were the input ones, related to various types of proteins.

During pretreatment, we detected and subtracted an extreme value, which was found in one of the mouse measurements with ID 365_14, in the RRP1_N protein and in the c-SC-m class, with a negative value, which is not consistent with all other positives. It also needed to be done delete the measurements in mice that showed gaps, resulting in working with the remaining 552 cases-measurements (instances) of the 1080 measurements.

After determining the final datasets, the multi-class classification effort was initiated by employing the four algorithms mentioned in the previous section. Several algorithms were used, among the plethora of algorithms and approaches contained in the Classify tab of Weka. The purpose of this process is the classification of mice, given only the values of their proteins.

#### 4.1.1    ML Model Specifically Based on Proteins

The dataset can be considered as "imbalanced". It is a fact, that most machine learning techniques will have low performance indices for the minority class which is usually the most important. To address this problem the SMOTE (Synthetic Minority Oversampling Technique) method was applied. This method composes new examples (data records) from the minority class [8]. This is an effective way of data enhancement and it can be very effective. Specifically, a random record A from the minority class is selected and also k records from its nearest neighbors (usually k = 5). A neighbor B is selected at random and a synthetic example is created at a randomly selected point between the two selected attributes A and B [8]. As the target is the highest possible accuracy, the SMOTE Oversampling technique was applied on the data records of the minority class (c-CS-m) via the WEKA platform. The classes records for each class were: 45 records for the c-CS-m class (minority class), 75 records for the c-CS-s class, 60 records for the c-SC-m class, 75 records for the c-SC-s class, 90 records for the t-CS-m class, 75 records for the t-CS-s class, 60 records for the t-SC-m class and 72 records for the t-SC-s class. It has been shown that the imaging of proteins shows infinitesimal differences. After this process, the developed model has been significantly improved.

### 4.1.2 ML Model Based on Proteins and Genotypes

At this point, in addition to proteins, the genotype (whether a mouse is trisomic or not) was also considered as independent variable, in an effort to achieve higher classification accuracy. As a result, both the number of attributes and the input data vectors have increased. Overall, we have 79 input attributes (78 proteins and 1 genotype) plus 1 output. Moreover, 552 data records emerged comprising of experimental measurements from the instances. The target was the development of the most suitable model, that could bring the scientists closer to the cure of memory loss and learning deficits in mice. Thus, in this effort the proteins and the genotype were the independent variables, whereas the 8 classes of mice were the depended. The developed model successfully classifies the mice in the proper class, based on their proteins and on their status (trisomic or control). Several experiments were performed by employing several Machine Learning algorithms following a k-fold cross validation (k-fCV) approach. The Synthetic Minority Oversampling Technique was also employed on the (c-CS-m) minority class.

## 5  Attributes Selection

In order to develop the most suitable model, we worked by reducing the parameters and by using only those that could give us a more powerful model. For this purpose, the WEKA's tab, Select Attributes was chosen and the attribute evaluator, CfsSubsetEval (Correlation-based Feature Selection) that uses the GreedyStepwise search method, was employed.

The CfsSubsetEval is a simple filter algorithm that sorts features' subsets according to a searching, correlation-based, evaluation function. According to it, irrelevant attributes should be ignored, because they will have a low correlation with the class. In addition, the unnecessary functions should be deleted, as they will be highly correlated with one or more of the other features. The acceptance of a possibility will de-pend on the extent to which it provides classes in areas of the presence space that they have not already been provided by other functions.

Using the CfsSubsetEval on the file with only the proteins as independent variables, we get a subset of only 24 of the 77 proteins. These proteins emerged as a subset of proteins that are highly correlated with the classes. The subset we chose to consider, contains proteins that are more than 50% correlated to each other. This means that there are other subsets with less correlation between them. We chose this specific subset because it offered (when applied) the best accuracy results compared to the rest. After this procedure, we run the same four algorithms, this time using only the subset of proteins as inputs (Table 1).

**Table 1.** Attributes subset of 24 proteins

| DYRKIA_N | SOD1_N | AcetylH3K9_N | SNCA_N |
|---|---|---|---|
| pCAMKII_N | P38_N | RRP1_N | Ubiquitin_N |
| pERK_N | DSCR1_N | ARC_N | pGSK38_Tyr216_N |
| pPKCAB_N | pP70S6_N | Tau_N | pCFOS_N |
| AKT_N | pPKCG_N | GluR3_N | H3MeK4_N |
| BRAF_N | S6_N | pCASP9_N | CaNA_N |

In the second case, where we have as independent variables the proteins and the genotype, the use of the CfsSubsetEval offers a subset of 20 attributes, 19 of the 77 proteins and the genotype. As mentioned above, this subset emerged as a subset of attributes that are highly correlated with classification according to the filter. Likewise, the subset we chose to take contains proteins that are more than 50% correlated with each other. As before, we run again the same four algorithms and compare the results (Table 2).

**Table 2.** Subset of the attributes of 20 proteins

| pCAMKII_N | DSCR1_N | ADARB1_N | GluR3_N | pCFOS_N |
|---|---|---|---|---|
| BRAF_N | pNUMB_N | AcetylH3K9_N | pCASP9_N | H3MeK4_N |
| SOD1_N | pPKCG_N | RRP1_N | SNCA_N | CaNA_N |
| P38_N | S6_N | ARC_N | pGSK38_Tyr216_N | Genotype |

## 6  Comparative Analysis

The developed ML models were compared in terms of their precision and speed. The necessary accuracy information can be obtained from the respective confusion matrices and the precision tables, produced by Weka. The confusion matrix clearly presents exactly how many mice-instances should be in each specific class and they were actually correctly classified. Moreover, it shows how many of them were missclassified. On the other hand, the Weka precision table clearly presents the values of the accuracy indices. More specifically, in the accuracy table we can see the TP Rate (True Positive Rate – Sensitivity), the FP Rate (False Positive Rate), the Precision, the Recall, the F1-Score, the MCC (Matthews Correlation Coefficient), the ROC Area (Receiver Operating Characteristics) and the PRC Area (Precision-Recall Curves) accuracy indices. Last but not least, we can find the time taken for this model to build. Below there are presented the accuracy table and the confusion matrix of the two best algorithms of all combinations, either with SMOTE or without (Fig. 3, Tables 3, 4 and 5).

```
=== Detailed Accuracy By Class ===

            TP Rate  FP Rate  Precision  Recall  F-Measure  MCC    ROC Area  PRC Area  Class
            1,000    0,000    1,000      1,000   1,000      1,000  1,000     1,000     c-CS-m
            1,000    0,002    0,987      1,000   0,993      0,992  1,000     1,000     c-CS-s
            0,983    0,000    1,000      0,983   0,992      0,991  1,000     0,998     c-SC-m
            1,000    0,000    1,000      1,000   1,000      1,000  1,000     1,000     c-SC-s
            0,989    0,000    1,000      0,989   0,994      0,993  1,000     0,999     t-CS-m
            1,000    0,000    1,000      1,000   1,000      1,000  1,000     1,000     t-CS-s
            1,000    0,002    0,984      1,000   0,992      0,991  1,000     1,000     t-SC-m
            1,000    0,000    1,000      1,000   1,000      1,000  1,000     1,000     t-SC-s
Weighted Avg. 0,996  0,001    0,996      0,996   0,996      0,996  1,000     1,000
```

**Fig. 3.** Accuracy table for each class using Random Forest without SMOTE

**Table 3.** Confusion matrix of the multilayer perceptron with SMOTE

| Confusion Matrix | | | | | | | | |
|---|---|---|---|---|---|---|---|---|
| a | b | c | d | e | f | g | h | <-- classified as |
| 90 | 0 | 0 | 0 | 0 | 0 | 0 | 0 | a=c-CS-m |
| 0 | 75 | 0 | 0 | 0 | 0 | 0 | 0 | b=c-CS-s |
| 0 | 0 | 60 | 0 | 0 | 0 | 0 | 0 | c=c-SC-m |
| 0 | 0 | 0 | 75 | 0 | 0 | 0 | 0 | d=c-SC-s |
| 0 | 0 | 0 | 0 | 90 | 0 | 0 | 0 | e=t-CS-m |
| 0 | 0 | 0 | 0 | 0 | 75 | 0 | 0 | f=t-CS-s |
| 0 | 0 | 0 | 0 | 0 | 0 | 60 | 0 | g=t-SC-m |
| 0 | 0 | 0 | 0 | 0 | 0 | 0 | 72 | h=t-SC-s |

**Table 4.** Performance of Proteins' model in testing without using SMOTE

| ALGORITHM | TP | FP | Precision | Recall | F-Measure | MCC | ROC Area | PRC Area |
|---|---|---|---|---|---|---|---|---|
| Random Forest | 0.996 | 0.001 | 0.996 | 0.996 | 0.996 | 0.996 | 1.000 | 1.000 |
| J48 | 0.889 | 0.016 | 0.890 | 0.889 | 0.890 | 0.874 | 0.946 | 0.838 |
| Naïve Bayes | 0.882 | 0.016 | 0.893 | 0.882 | 0.883 | 0.869 | 0.993 | 0.963 |
| Multi Layer Perceptron | 1.000 | 0.000 | 1.000 | 1.000 | 1.000 | 1.000 | 1.000 | 1.000 |

**Table 5.** Performance of Proteins' model with SMOTE

| ALGORITHM | TP | FP | Precision | Recall | F-Measure | MCC | ROC Area | PRC Area |
|---|---|---|---|---|---|---|---|---|
| Random Forest | 1.000 | 0.000 | 1.000 | 1.000 | 1.000 | 1.000 | 1.000 | 1.000 |
| J48 | 0.935 | 0.010 | 0.935 | 0.935 | 0.935 | 0.925 | 0.967 | 0.905 |
| Naïve Bayes | 0.899 | 0.014 | 0.910 | 0.899 | 0.901 | 0.889 | 0.993 | 0.963 |
| Multi Layer Perceptron | 1.000 | 0.000 | 1.000 | 1.000 | 1.000 | 1.000 | 1.000 | 1.000 |

It should be clarified that all indices refer to the testing process. Concerning the file, where the only independent variables were the proteins, it is clearly shown that the Multilayer Perceptron algorithm seems to have the best fit. Its precision is as high as 1. Moreover, Random Forest is second with precision up to 0.99. The precision of J48 and Naïve Bayes reach the value 0.89. Moreover, the above performance indices improve when the SMOTE oversampling is employed for the above aforementioned algorithms, though the differences are not very significant. It should be mentioned that the differences of the performance indices between the Random Forest and the Multilayer Perceptron are minor. However, the SMOTE technique, seems to increase the accuracy of the J48 and the Naïve Bayes algorithms. The only difference between the two best algorithms is in the construction time of the models. We have 1.2 s for the Random Forest (RF) and 23.07 s for the MLP (without SMOTE). On the other hand, the RF needs 0.56 s and the MLP 24.64 s when SMOTE is applied. From these results we consider that the RF is the most successful, with the use of SMOTE (Tables 6 and 7).

**Table 6.** Performance of proteins and genotypes model without SMOTE

| ALGORITHM | TP | FP | Precision | Recall | F-Measure | MCC | ROC Area | PRC Area |
|---|---|---|---|---|---|---|---|---|
| Random Forest | 1.000 | 0.000 | 1.000 | 1.000 | 1.000 | 1.000 | 1.000 | 1.000 |
| J48 | 0.947 | 0.007 | 0.948 | 0.947 | 0.947 | 0.940 | 0.975 | 0.915 |
| Naïve Bayes | 0.913 | 0.012 | 0.921 | 0.913 | 0.914 | 0.904 | 0.997 | 0.982 |
| Multi Layer Perceptron | 1.000 | 0.000 | 1.000 | 1.000 | 1.000 | 1.000 | 1.000 | 1.000 |

**Table 7.** Performance of proteins and genotypes model with SMOTE

| ALGORITHM | TP | FP | Precision | Recall | F-Measure | MCC | ROC Area | PRC Area |
|---|---|---|---|---|---|---|---|---|
| Random Forest | 1.000 | 0.000 | 1.000 | 1.000 | 1.000 | 1.000 | 1.000 | 1.000 |
| J48 | 0.973 | 0.004 | 0.973 | 0.973 | 0.973 | 0.969 | 0.985 | 0.946 |
| Naïve Bayes | 0.920 | 0.012 | 0.928 | 0.920 | 0.920 | 0.911 | 0.997 | 0.983 |
| Multi Layer Perceptron | 1.000 | 0.000 | 1.000 | 1.000 | 1.000 | 1.000 | 1.000 | 1.000 |

Regarding the case, where the proteins and the genotype were the independent variables, we notice a slight improvement for all of the algorithms, with the precision of the Random Forest and the Multilayer Perceptron being up to 1, while the precision of the J48 is equal to 0.94 and the Naïve Bayes 0.92. By using the SMOTE method, the two most precise algorithms show no difference, while the precision of J48 improves to 0.97 and the one of Naïve Bayes' remains stable to the value 0.92. The only thing we could consider as a difference of the two best models, is again the construction time. We have 1.2 s for the RF and 23.07 s for the MLP (without SMOTE). Also, we need 0.56 s for the RF and 24.64 s for the MLP (with SMOTE). From these results we consider that the RF model to be the most robust, with the use of SMOTE (Tables 8 and 9).

**Table 8.** Results with Cfs with proteins as independent variables

| ALGORITHM | TP | FP | Precision | Recall | F-Measure | MCC | ROC Area | PRC Area |
|---|---|---|---|---|---|---|---|---|
| Random Forest | 0.998 | 0.000 | 0.998 | 0.998 | 0.998 | 0.998 | 1.000 | 1.000 |
| J48 | 0.900 | 0.014 | 0.900 | 0.900 | 0.900 | 0.886 | 0.949 | 0.841 |
| Naïve Bayes | 0.918 | 0.012 | 0.921 | 0.918 | 0.918 | 0.907 | 0.993 | 0.966 |
| Multi Layer Perceptron | 1.000 | 0.000 | 1.000 | 1.000 | 1.000 | 1.000 | 1.000 | 1.000 |

**Table 9.** Results with Cfs with proteins and genotype as independent variables

| ALGORITHM | TP | FP | Precision | Recall | F-Measure | MCC | ROC Area | PRC Area |
|---|---|---|---|---|---|---|---|---|
| Random Forest | 0.998 | 0.000 | 0.998 | 0.998 | 0.998 | 0.998 | 1.000 | 1.000 |
| J48 | 0.951 | 0.007 | 0.951 | 0.951 | 0.951 | 0.944 | 0.979 | 0.929 |
| Naïve Bayes | 0.958 | 0.006 | 0.960 | 0.958 | 0.958 | 0.953 | 0.999 | 0.991 |
| Multi Layer Perceptron | 1.000 | 0.000 | 1.000 | 1.000 | 1.000 | 1.000 | 1.000 | 1.000 |

# 7  Conclusion and Discussion

The experiment, on which we relied for our research, focuses on the efficiency of a drug, memantine, in solving learning and memory problems on trisomic mice. The mice we used belonged to two categories, that of control and that of trisomic (Ts65Dn) mice. Specific conditions were selected under which the data received. Based on these data we implemented our own approach, with the use of Machine Learning, in linking numerical data with its reliability drug in each condition.

In the creation of our model four algorithms were selected, Random Forrest, J48, Naïve Bayes, Multilayer Perceptron, the results of which were analyzed and compared extensively. At the same time, we separated our data into two categories, one with only the proteins as independent variables and one with the proteins and the genotype as independent variables. J48 and NB gave us good results but not good enough to make them the most accurate. In contrast, RF and MLP seemed to dominate with their accuracy reaching 100%. Using the SMOTE method, in order to improve any imperfection in the set of all four algorithms was not achieved some notable change. Nevertheless, for the set of data we considered the RF model with SMOTE to be the most complete, due to its accuracy and speed.

The first results concern an algorithmic model that processes the whole set of proteins for the purpose of classifying mice into classes, so if we know where they belong, we can choose which procedure will have an effect on their treatment in learning and memory deficits. In addition, we tried to design a model using only a subset of proteins. We used the Cfs technique for each one of the two categories, mentioned above, testing various subsets, which correlated with each other and we came up with equally good results for a specific set of proteins. In this case, we chose as the most complete model, between

RF and MLP, this of MLP, which, although at a slightly slower speed, reaches 100% accuracy.

Summarizing our work, we conclude that our goal has been achieved, the development of a model that will design the experiment and categorize the data helping to diagnose the effectiveness of a treatment for learning and memory deficits, based on the category to which the mice belong, simply from the data.

In conclusion, we hope our study will be the trigger for utilizing the model for treatment with minimizing, or even eliminating, experiments on animal model organisms and possibly future expansion of the application directly to human data, in a bigger number of treatments.

# References

1. Abdeldayem, S.S., Elhefnawi, M.M.: Deep feature selection for identification of essential proteins of learning and memory in mouse model of down syndrome. arXiv (bioRxiv preprint https://doi.org/10.1101/333849). https://www.biorxiv.org/content/biorxiv/early/2018/05/29/333849.full.pdf. Accessed 20 Apr 22
2. Cummings, M.: Human Heredity: Principles and Issues, 10 edn. Cengage Learning (2013)
3. Davisson, T., et al.: Segmental trisomy as a mouse model for Down syndrome. Faculty Research 1990–1999, 01 January 1993
4. Domino, F.J.: The 5-Minute Clinical Consult 2007, 2007th edn. Lippincott Williams & Wilkins, Philadelphia (2007)
5. Haenlein, M., Kaplan, A.: A brief history of artificial intelligence: on the past, present, and future of artificial intelligence. Calif. Manag. Rev. (2019)
6. Higuera, C., Gardiner, K.J., Cios, K.J.: Self-organizing feature maps identify proteins critical to learning in a mouse model of down syndrome. PLOS ONE (2015)
7. Holmes, G., Donkin, A., Witten, I.H.: «Like: a machine learning workbench» (PDF). In: Proceedings of Second Australia and New Zealand Conference on Intelligent Information Systems, Brisbane, Australia (1994)
8. Iliadis, L., Papaleonidas, A.: Computational Intelligence & Intelligent Agents. Giola Publications (2017)
9. Iliopoulos, D., Kouri, G., Peristeri, V., Rekleiti, A., Andreou, A., Vogiatzis, N.: In the magazine "Cellular"
10. Mohri, M., Rostamizadeh, A., Talwalkar, A.: Foundations of Machine Learning. The MIT Press, Cambridge (2012)
11. Patterson, D., Costa, A.C.: Down syndrome and genetics - a case of linked histories. Nat. Rev. Genet. (2005)
12. Reeves, R.H., et al.: A mouse model for down syndrome exhibits learning and behavioral deficits. Nat. Genet. (1995)
13. Reisner, H.: Essentials of Rubin's Pathology. Lippincott Williams & Wilkins (2013)
14. Rueda, N., Flórez, J., Martínez-Cué, C.: Mouse models of down syndrome as a tool to unravel the causes of mental disabilities. Neural Plast. (2012)
15. https://archive.ics.uci.edu/ml/datasets/Mice+Protein+Expression. Accessed 20 Feb 2022
16. https://www.noesi.gr/book/syndrome/down. Accessed 20 Feb 2022
17. https://www.down.gr/sites/default/files/ti_einai_to_mosaiko.pdf. Accessed 20 Feb 2022
18. https://www.cs.waikato.ac.nz/ml/weka/index.html. Accessed 20 Feb 2022

# Semantic Segmentation of Diabetic Retinopathy Lesions, Using a UNET with Pretrained Encoder

Dimitrios Theodoropoulos[1]([✉])[iD], Georgios C. Manikis[2], Kostantinos Marias[1,2], and Giorgos Papadourakis[1]

[1] Department of Electrical and Computer Engineering, Hellenic Mediterranean University, GR71004 Heraklion, Crete, Greece
dimitheo@ics.forth.gr
[2] FORTH-ICS, Computational Biomedicine Laboratory, Heraklion, Greece

**Abstract.** There are several novel applications of Deep Learning in Medical Imaging and especially in Ophthalmology in order to provide solutions to unmet clinical needs. The research presented in this paper concerns semantic segmentation of lesions regarding Diabetic Retinopathy. Most of the state-of-the-art papers nowadays use Convolutional Neural Networks, Fully Convolutional Networks, and UNETs, a modified version of Convolutional Neural Networks for segmentation tasks. The robustness of UNETs, in conjunction with transfer learning, has been the main strategy to tackle the limitations of the available public datasets. In this paper, the encoder of a UNET has been substituted by MobileNetV2, which constitutes a novel approach for segmenting Diabetic Retinopathy lesions. Results show that the proposed model, in hemorrhages and soft exudates lesions surpasses other similar attempts. In the proposed model, sensitivity reached 0.89 in hemorrhages and 0.97 in soft exudates. Another novelty of the paper is that the results are further analyzed at the lesion level, in contrast to the common pixel-level analysis met in the literature, something that favors a more intuitive evaluation of the model.

**Keywords:** Diabetic retinopathy · Deep learning · Transfer learning · UNET

## 1 Introduction

Diabetic retinopathy (DR) is the most common eye disease related to diabetes mellitus and it's the leading cause of blindness among working age adults [20]. Early detection and treatment are crucial factors in preventing extensive retina damage and even vision loss. In today's practice, DR is diagnosed based on the examination of retina's fundus images by experienced medical practitioners based on the presence of three lesion types (i.e. Exudates, Hemorrhages and Microaneurysms) [21]. However, this is a difficult and time-consuming task which suffers from intra- and inter-observer variability. In addition, the lack of expert

© Springer Nature Switzerland AG 2022
L. Iliadis et al. (Eds.): EANN 2022, CCIS 1600, pp. 361–371, 2022.
https://doi.org/10.1007/978-3-031-08223-8_30

ophthalmologists in many hospitals especially in underdeveloped countries and remote areas is a limiting factor for early detection and staging. In this study, we propose a model based on the UNet architecture with a pretrained encoder to segment each lesion of DR on fundus images.

The advancement of AI technology has enabled the development of deep learning models for fundus analysis in the context of DR. Eftekhari et al. [4] created patches and trained a CNN to extract probability maps. Furtado [6] tested three state-of-the-art models to segment all lesions. He experimented with the famous DeepLabV3 model [2], with FCNs [12], and with a UNET [17]. Khojasteh et al. [11] executed an experiment with 3 cohorts to segment exudates: they trained a CNN, Discriminative Restricted Boltzmann Machines (DRBM) and used a pre-trained residual network and used 3 different classifiers.

Towards more precise segmentation, novel designs are continuously proposed such as dilated convolutions [23] and attention mechanisms [23]. The state-of-art DeeplabV3+ [5,6] uses both dilated convolutions and spatial pyramid pooling in its contracting path and is one of the most promising models in semantic segmentation nowadays.

In this paper, a model for semantic segmentation of DR lesions based on Deep Learning (DL) is proposed. We propose a substitution of the encoding part of UNET, by taking advantage of the robustness of transfer learning. The rationale for this choice is to allow better performance on small and unbalanced datasets. In parallel, the proposed methodology performs the performance analysis based on metrics at lesion level extending pixel-level reporting facilitating a more intuitive evaluation of the model.

This paper is organized as follows: After the introduction, in Sect. 2 the DR and its lesions from the medical perspective are examined. Section 3 presented the modelling approach and architectures used, specifically UNETs and MobiNetV2. Sections 4 and 5 present the experimental results and Sect. 6 a discussion about final results.

## 2    Diabetic Retinopathy Lesions

Diabetic Retinopathy (DR) is a retinal vascular disease that affects the central vision and its main cause is Diabetes Mellitus [1]. DR patients are expected to reach 191 million by 2030 [10]. If the disease evolves without treatment, patients are in danger of becoming blind. Unfortunately, people with DR in the early stages have no warning signs concerning their vision. Only when the disease worsens do patients become aware of the problem. However, fundus images can provide with early signs concerning the onset of the disease that can save many patients from blindness. Fundus images carry important diagnostic information about the eye and enable experts to detect lesions. By examining evolving lesions experts can determine the disease's grade. Consequently, it is important to identify not only the type of the lesions but also their magnitude. There are 3 main types of lesions: Microaneurysms (MAs), hemorrhages (HMs), and Exudates (EXs) [21].

Generally, MAs are the first signs that can be detected from fundus images, indicating DR evolution. MAs are dilation of microvasculature, as a result of disruption of the internal elastic lamina. Their size is normally less than 125 μm and they look like red spots with distinguishable borders, as shown in Fig. 1. When the capillaries collapse, leaking blood forms HMs. They look like MAs but they are bigger in size and have random shapes, as shown in Fig. 1. Splinter hemorrhage occurs in the superficial surface layer and causes more superficial bleeding-shaped flames. EXs are formed when capillaries collapse and leak much more blood. In contrast with former lesions, they are yellowish and have random shapes, as shown in Fig. 1. EXs comprise two types: Hard Exudates (HEs) and Soft Exudates (SEs).

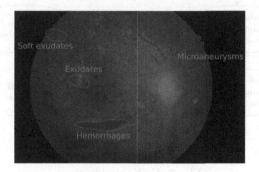

**Fig. 1.** An image exhibiting DR lesions

## 3   DL Architecture Strategy for Semantic Segmentation

Semantic segmentation refers to classifying and subsequently grouping similar structures within the image on the pixel level. Each individual class contains pixels with the same characteristics such as color, intensity, or texture.

Binary segmentation is the simplest category of semantic segmentations. In this case, the pixels may belong either to a positive class (lesion) or to a negative class (healthy). The algorithm presented in this paper creates binary segmentation and is executed as many times as the number of lesions.

After reviewing the available literature, we decided to develop our model based on the UNET architecture. UNETs [17] are a modification of CNNs which were initially targeted at image segmentation of biomedical images. The architecture of a typical UNET, as illustrated in Fig. 2, consists of two paths: the first path is the encoder and is responsible for the feature extraction and compression. The encoder of a UNET is the same as a common CNN, without the fully connected layers. The other path is the decoder and is responsible for synthesis. It consists of upsampling convolutional layers, in addition to residual concatenation connections from the encoder layers. The decoder allows the network to access the spatial information lost at the encoding stage. The resulting output is passed to a convolution layer to construct the segmented image. The architecture of the network is practically symmetric, resembling the "U" letter.

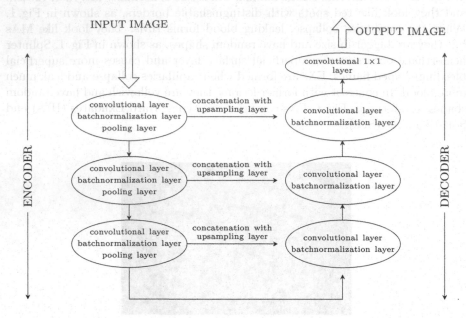

**Fig. 2.** UNET architecture

MobileNetV2 is a modified CNN and its architecture is based upon a series of depthwise and pointwise convolution layers as illustrated in Fig. 3. In the last part, there is a global average pooling layer and a fully connected layer. Due to the structure that requires less computing, it has higher precision and makes it suitable for mobile phones.

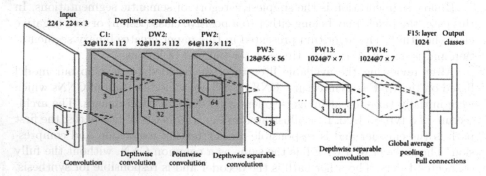

**Fig. 3.** MobileNetV2 architecture [22]

MobileNetV2 uses two global hyperparameters based on depthwise separable convolutions to maintain a balance between efficiency and accuracy. The fundamental principle in MobileNetV2 is the separation of convolution kernels.

By applying depthwise separable convolution, the standard convolution can be divided into a depthwise convolution and a pointwise convolution with a convo- lution kernel.

Our proposed model includes a substitution of the encoder of a UNET with MobilnetV2. The fully connected layer of MobileNetV2, seen in Fig. 3, is excluded and the output of the remaining part is connected with the decoder of the UNET. Additionally, MobileNetV2 is pre-trained on ImageNet [8].

The architecture of the proposed model is shown in Fig. 4. The concatenations begin from 4 inner layers of MobileNetV2 and meet the upsampling layers of the decoder. Each upsampling layer is followed by 2 blocks of convolutional layers, activated with RELU function, and batch normalization layers. A $1 \times 1$ convolutional layer, activated with the sigmoid, function is necessary to restore the dimensions of the output to the dimensions of the input image.

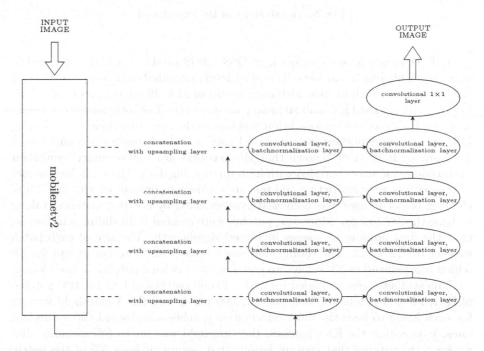

**Fig. 4.** Proposed model's architecture

## 4   Experiments

In order to evaluate the proposed model, various experiments were conducted using as inputs the IDRiD dataset [7]. This specific dataset was chosen among others to train the proposed model because it contains high quality fundus images and precise annotations of DR lesions.

The strategy for the experiments is illustrated in Fig. 5. The process begins with data preprocessing. This is an important and time consuming phase resulting in the data generation of 66,664 patches. Next, the training phase takes place. After the training of the proposed model, the learned model performs the predictions regarding new data, as shown in Fig. 5. The evaluation of the model is discussed in Sect. 5.

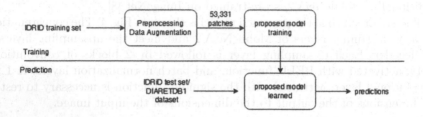

**Fig. 5.** The strategy of the experiment

IDRID images have a resolution of $4288 \times 2848$ pixels, very high compared to other available public datasets. The pixel-level annotated data comprise 81 color fundus images which include 81 binary masks of MA, 40 binary masks of SE, 81 binary masks of hard EX, and 80 binary masks of HE. The total number of masks was 282. It should be mentioned that nowhere in the literature review, concerning DR lesion's segmentation, was reported such a limited number of images used for training. It is widely known that DL networks are "data-hungry" and their performance increases once fed with high-quality, big data. The available number of images was very restrictive and not appropriate to prevent overfitting. Thus, the number of images was increased synthetically, by creating patches, taking as base the 282 images. Moreover, patches were created from sliding windows so that the final number of images increased significantly. The size of each patch was set to $512 \times 512$. The sliding step was 64 pixels in all images except for SE which was reduced to 32 to have an equal number of final patches in each lesion.

The synthetic genesis ended up with 140,000 patches of EX, 140,000 patches of HM, 140,000 patches of MA, and 142,000 patches of SE. A threshold was set for each lesion to keep the most informative patches and discard the redundant ones. Concerning the EXs patches, the threshold was set to 5% meaning that we keep the patches that contain lesions that occupy at least 5% of the patch. The final number of informative EX patches was dropped to 17,016. Similarly, for HMs the threshold was set to 5% and the final number of informative HM patches was reduced to 19,536. Concerning MAs, the threshold was set to 1% and the final number of informative MA patches was decreased to 17,168. Finally, for SEs the threshold was set to 1%, and the final number of informative SE patches was dropped to 12,944. The total number of patches reached 66,664.

Moreover, to prevent overfitting, the size of the dataset was further increased with the augmentation technique, which was applied via ImageDataGenerator [18]. No special image processing technique was applied except for data scaling, reducing the dynamic range of pixel values from 0–1. The absence of special image processing techniques was due to the fact that IDRiD is a qualitative dataset compared to the other publicly available datasets both at the image as well as the annotation level.

In order to train the deep learning network the IDRID dataset was used and it was split into 80% training and 20% testing patches. The training patches were 53,331 and the testing patches 13,333. The learning rate was set to 0.0001 for all the experiments. For the optimization of the loss function, Adam optimizer [9] was implemented with the default settings: $\beta 1 = 0.9$ and $\beta 2 = 0.999$. The batch size was set to 8 for all experiments. The epochs for training differed for each experiment. Specifically, in EX the epochs were 70, in HM 50, in MA 100, and in SE 50 after experimental observations. "Binary cross-entropy" was used as loss function.

The model was trained on a server with an AMD EPYC 7251 8-core 2.9 GHz CPU, RTX 2080Ti 11 GB GPU, and 64 GB RAM, and it was implemented on Tensorflow 2.1.

## 5  Results

One of the novelties introduced in the proposed methodology is that it analyses the results both at pixel and lesion level. The pixel-level analysis takes into account each individual pixel and classifies it into a class, lesion or not. In lesion analysis, a threshold of 50% was set, under which a lesion is not being counted. This analysis is more holistic, leading to a better intuition about the performance of the model.

Table 1 shows the metric's results at pixel-level analysis. Dice coefficient [19] was chosen as a metric of similarity and SEs had the best performance. Specificity is a metric indicating how well the model predicted the negative class, which in our case is the healthy tissue. It is expected to have such a big accuracy because of the high imbalance of the dataset. Most of the pixels in fundus images belong to non-lesion pixels. Sensitivity, on the other hand, is a metric showing how many of the true lesions were correctly predicted. As seen from the results, SEs were predicted with sensitivity 0.97 followed by HMs, EXs, MAs with 0.89, 0.86, and 0.84 sensitivity respectively.

In lesions level analysis Mean IoU [19] was chosen as a metric and SEs had the best performance as indicated in Table 2. Another interesting observation arising from the Sensitivity results is that the area of the lesion seems to be correlated to sensitivity. Generally, it seems that lesions of smaller areas (MAs, EXs) are predicted with higher accuracy compared to lesions of larger areas (HMs, SEs). Specifically, sensitivity in MAS, EXs was 0.97 and 0.93 respectively. In contrast in HMs, SEs sensitivity was 0.60 and 0.84 respectively.

**Table 1.** The metric's results at pixel level for each experiment

| Metric | Exudates | Emorrhages | Microaneurysms | Soft exudates |
|---|---|---|---|---|
| Dice coefficient | 0.83 | 0.85 | 0.85 | 0.95 |
| Recall | 0.85 | 0.89 | 0.84 | 0.97 |
| Precision | 0.90 | 0.91 | 0.95 | 0.96 |
| Sensitivity | 0.86 | 0.89 | 0.84 | 0.97 |
| Specificity | 0.99 | 0.99 | 1.00 | 0.99 |

**Table 2.** The metric's results at lesion level for each experiment.

| Metrics | Exudates | Hemorrhages | Microaneurysms | Soft exudates |
|---|---|---|---|---|
| Sensitivity | 0.93 | 0.60 | 0.97 | 0.84 |
| Precision | 0.73 | 0.72 | 0.95 | 0.96 |
| Mean IoU | 0.75 | 0.78 | 0.75 | 0.93 |

Figure 6 shows an example of how the algorithm predicts whole images of the IDRiD testing dataset as well as the unknown DIARETDB1. The left column displays the original fundus images, the middle column the predictions and the right column the ground truth. Comparing the ground truth of DIARETDB1 with the ground truth of IDRiD dataset, it can be observed that in DIARETDB1 there are no exact borders of the lesion but instead, approximate areas that surround the lesions.

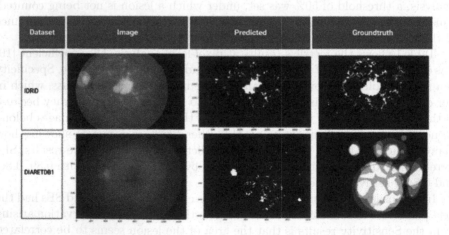

**Fig. 6.** Predictions of the proposed model

Finally, Table 3 summarizes the results of the proposed methodology compared to other techniques. The red color indicates the highest sensitivity in each lesion. The comparison is at pixel level since analysis at lesion level is introduced only in the proposed methodology. Table 3 shows that the Sensitivities of HMs and SEs of the proposed model surpass the existing state of art techniques. More specifically, Sensitivity in HMs reached 0.89 while SEs reached 0.97. In contrast, Sensitivity in EXs 0.86 could not reach 0.99 of [13] and Sensitivity in MAs 0.84 could not surpass 0.87 of [14].

**Table 3.** Metrics in the state-of-art techniques.

| Author | Year | Exudates sensitivity | Hemorrhages sensitivity | Microaneurysms sensitivity | Soft exudates sensitivity | Architecture |
|--------|------|----------|------------|---------------|--------------|--------------|
| OURS | 2021 | 0.86 | 0.89 | 0.844 | 0.97 | UNET WITH PRETRAINED ENCODER |
| [6] | 2021 | 0.94 | 0.87 | 0.48 | 0.87 | DEEPLABV3, FCN, UNET |
| [24] | 2018 | 0.94 | – | – | – | UNET + cGAN |
| [15] | 2018 | 0.92 | – | – | – | UNETs |
| [13] | 2017 | 0.99 | – | – | – | CNN(Le-Net) |
| [10] | 2018 | 0.96 | 0.84 | 0.85 | – | CNN |
| [3] | 2018 | 0.84 | – | – | – | UNET |
| [16] | 2019 | 0.89 | – | – | – | FCN |
| [14] | 2018 | 0.88 | 0.72 | 0.87 | 0.77 | UNET |

# 6 Conclusions

The objective of this paper was to exploit state of art techniques in order to provide a robust DR lesions segmentation method. The presented method, can also be implemented as a mobile phone application which can be the basis of a remote screening diagnostic aid tool for people living in remote areas.

The major problem in many DL tasks is the lack of large and properly curated available datasets. IDRiD dataset was the basis of our training, which is a public dataset. This dataset has qualitative images and annotations but it is highly imbalanced. The preprocessing of IDRiD dataset was based on the most informative patches and an augmentation technique was used to ensure plethora of images to prevent overfitting. Transfer learning was utilized along with the MobileNetV2 architecture, which was pre-trained on ImageNet and constituted the encoder of the proposed UNET. This substitution of the encoder in DR segmentation task was a novel effort and provided encouraging results.

The results of the experiment were very promising and there was no overfitting. This was achieved due to proper preprocessing. The dice coefficient was over 0.83 in all lesions and in soft exudates was 0.95. As far as sensitivity is concerned, all lesions were over 0.84 and the best score was achieved in soft exudates (0.97). Compared to the other state of art techniques, segmentation performance regarding two lesions (SE, HM) surpassed the state of the art.

# References

1. Centers for Disease Control and Prevention (CDC): What is diabetes? May 2021. https://www.cdc.gov/diabetes/basics/diabetes.html. Accessed 28 Nov 2021
2. Chen, L.C., Papandreou, G., Schroff, F., Adam, H.: Rethinking atrous convolution for semantic image segmentation (2017)
3. Chudzik, P., Majumdar, S., Calivá, F., Al-Diri, B., Hunter, A.: Exudate segmentation using fully convolutional neural networks and inception modules. In: Angelini, E.D., Landman, B.A. (eds.) Medical Imaging 2018: Image Processing. SPIE, March 2018. https://doi.org/10.1117/12.2293549
4. Eftekhari, N., Pourreza, H.R., Masoudi, M., Ghiasi-Shirazi, K., Saeedi, E.: Microaneurysm detection in fundus images using a two-step convolutional neural network. BioMedical Eng. On Line 18(67) (2019). https://doi.org/10.1186/s12938-019-0675-9
5. Furtado, P.: Segmentation of diabetic retinopathy lesions by deep learning: achievements and limitations. In: 7th International Conference on Bioimaging, pp. 95–101. SCITEPRESS - Science and Technology Publications, January 2020. https://doi.org/10.5220/0008881100950101
6. Furtado, P.: Using segmentation networks on diabetic retinopathy lesions: metrics, results and challenges. In: Proceedings of the 14th International Joint Conference on Biomedical Engineering Systems and Technologies (BIOSTEC 2021). BIOIMAGING, vol. 2, pp. 128–135. SCITEPRESS - Science and Technology Publications (2021). https://doi.org/10.5220/0010208501280135
7. (IDRiD), I.D.R.I.D., October 2017. https://idrid.grand-challenge.org. Accessed 20 Aug 2021
8. ImageNet: March 2021. https://www.image-net.org/index.php. Accessed 29 Aug 2021
9. keras.io: adam. (2018). https://keras.io/api/optimizers/adam/. Accessed 27 Nov 2021
10. Khojasteh, P., Aliahmad, B., Kumar, D.K.: Fundus images analysis using deep features for detection of exudates, hemorrhages and microaneurysms. BMC Ophthalmol. 18(1) (2018). https://doi.org/10.1186/s12886-018-0954-4
11. Khojasteh, P., et al.: Exudate detection in fundus images using deeply-learnable features. Comput. Biol. Med. 104, 62–69 (2019). https://doi.org/10.1016/j.compbiomed.2018.10.031
12. Long, J., Shelhamer, E., Darrell, T.: Fully convolutional networks for semantic segmentation (2015)
13. Perdomo, O., Arevalo, J., González, F.A.: Convolutional network to detect exudates in eye fundus images of diabetic subjects. In: Romero, E., Lepore, N., Brieva, J., Larrabide, I. (eds.) 12th International Symposium on Medical Information Processing and Analysis. SPIE, January 2017. https://doi.org/10.1117/12.2256939
14. Popli, A., Jindal, G., Pillai, G., Khan, H.R., Agarwal, M., Yadav, V.: Automated hard exudates segmentation in retinal images using patch based UNet, July 2018. https://github.com/apopli/diabetic-retinopathy/blob/master/segmentation-hard-exudates.pdf
15. Appan K., P., Sivaswamy, J.: Retinal image synthesis for CAD development. In: Campilho, A., Karray, F., ter Haar Romeny, B. (eds.) ICIAR 2018. LNCS, vol. 10882, pp. 613–621. Springer, Cham (2018). https://doi.org/10.1007/978-3-319-93000-8_70

16. Si, Z., Fu, D., Liu, Y., Huang, Z.: Hard exudate segmentation in retinal image with attention mechanism. IET Image Process. **15**(3), 587–597 (2020). https://doi.org/10.1049/ipr2.12007

17. Siddique, N., Paheding, S., Elkin, C.P., Devabhaktuni, V.: U-net and its variants for medical image segmentation: a review of theory and applications. IEEE Access **9**, 82031–82057 (2021). https://doi.org/10.1109/access.2021.3086020

18. tensorflow.org: tf.keras.preprocessing.image.ImageDataGenerator, November 2021. https://www.tensorflow.org/api_docs/python/tf/keras/preprocessing/image/ImageDataGenerator. Accessed 20 Nov 2021

19. Tiu, E.: Metrics to evaluate your semantic segmentation model, August 2019. https://towardsdatascience.com/metrics-to-evaluate-your-semantic-segmentation-model-6bcb99639aa2. Accessed 15 Nov 2021

20. Tsiknakis, N., et al.: Deep learning for diabetic retinopathy detection and classification based on fundus images: a review. Comput. Biol. Med. **135**, 104599 (2021). https://doi.org/10.1016/j.compbiomed.2021.104599, https://www.sciencedirect.com/science/article/pii/S0010482521003930

21. Usman Akram, M., Khalid, S., Tariq, A., Khan, S.A., Azam, F.: Detection and classification of retinal lesions for grading of diabetic retinopathy. Comput. Biol. Med. **45**, 161–171 (2014). https://doi.org/10.1016/j.compbiomed.2013.11.014, https://www.sciencedirect.com/science/article/pii/S0010482513003430

22. Wang, W., Hu, Y., Zou, T., Liu, H., Wang, J., Wang, X.: A new image classification approach via improved MobileNet models with local receptive field expansion in shallow layers. Comput. Intell. Neurosci. **2020**, 1–10 (2020). https://doi.org/10.1155/2020/8817849

23. Yu, F., Koltun, V.: Multi-scale context aggregation by dilated convolutions, April 2016, version 3

24. Zheng, R., et al.: Detection of exudates in fundus photographs with imbalanced learning using conditional generative adversarial network. Biomed. Opt. Exp. **9**(10), 4863–4878 (2018). https://doi.org/10.1364/boe.9.004863

16. Si, Z., Liu, D., Liu, Y., Huang, Z.: Hard example segmentation in retinal image with iterative mechanism. IET Image Process. 13(3), 587–597 (2020). https://doi.org/10.1049/ipr2.12030

17. Sandhya, N., Franklin, S., Elliott, C.P., Deyabalan, V., Lee and its variants for weaklabeling segmentations: a review of theory and applications. IEEE Access 9, 82031–82057 (2021). https://doi.org/10.1109/access.2021.3086030

18. Tensorflow.org: TF Keras Preprocessing image dataset Data Generator. November 2021. https://keras.io/api/preprocessing/image/data_generation/ image_dataset_from_directory. Accessed 30 Nov 2021.

19. Tan, H.H., Alom, Z.: Instance aware semantic segmentation model. August 2019. https://towardsdatascience.com/instance-to-evaluate-semantic-segmentation-b0ad9bbefb. Published. Accessed 15 Nov 2021.

20. Rakhlin, A., et al.: Deep learning for diabetic retinopathy detection and classification based on fundus images of retinas. Comput. Biol. Med. 135, 104599 (2021). https://doi.org/10.1016/j.compbiomed.2021.104599. https://www.sciencedirect.com/science/article/pii/S0010482521004790

21. Zhang, Al-Hayani, Alshehabi, S., Tang, A., Khan, S.A., Azam, F.: Detection and classification of retinal lesions for grading of diabetic retinopathy. Comput. Biol. Med. 45, 161–171 (2014). https://doi.org/10.1016/j.compbiomed.2013.11.014. https://www.sciencedirect.com/science/article/pii/S0010482513003150

22. Wang, W., Hu, Y., Zou, T., Liu, H., Wang, J., Wang, X.: A new image classification approach via improved MobileNet models with local receptive field expansion in shallow layers. Comput. Intell. Neurosci. 2020, 1–10 (2020). https://doi.org/10.1155/2020/8817849.

23. Yu, F., Koltun, V.: Multi-scale context aggregation by dilated convolutions. April 2016, version 3.

24. Zhang, M., et al.: Detection of regions of hard exudate in retina photographs with unbalanced learning using conditional generative adversarial network. Biomed. Opt. Exp. 9(10), 1982–4995 (2018). https://doi.org/10.1364/boe.9.001982

# Reinforcement/Adversarial/Echo State Neural Networks

# Echo State Networks in Data Marketplaces for Digital Content Creation

Will Serrano[(✉)]

The Bartlett, University College London, London, UK
`w.serrano@ucl.ac.uk`

**Abstract.** Data marketplaces are the digital platform for data buyers and data sellers to trade information as valuable products or items. The expectation taken for granted from the users of a data marketplace is the truth of the exchanged information. However, the trade of factual data also means the marketable product is no longer unique but a series of replicas. If every user within the data marketplace owns the same information, this data eventually becomes valueless. There are specific instances where the traded products are sought to be always unique, such as predictions or digital art. This paper presents Echo State Networks (ESNs) in data marketplaces that map tradeable data into higher dimensional spaces via the dynamics of a fixed and non-linear reservoir. The reservoir generates unique tradeable data products that can not be replicated, therefore ensuring its exclusivity and commercial value. The validation results show that ESNs can also be applied to generate random tradeable products on different dimensional spaces. Specifically, the reservoir with its associated neural perturbation emulates a digital artist that generates unique and exclusive content based on 2D functions and 3D images.

**Keywords:** Data marketplace · Echo state networks · Reservoir computing · Digital artist · Digital content creation

## 1 Introduction

Reservoir Computing (RC) applies recurrent neural networks to map input data into higher, equal, or lower dimensional computational spaces through the dynamics of a fixed, non-linear system called a reservoir [1]. Echo State Networks (ESNs) are part of reservoir computing composed of a Recurrent Neural Network (RNN) with a sparsely connected hidden layer that generates a complex recursive dynamic system [2]. The key property of ESNs is that although their behaviour is non-linear, the network can create or reproduce specific temporal patterns [3]. This property is due to the only weights modified during the training stage are the neural synapses that connect the hidden neurons to output neurons. Thus, the connectivity and weights of the input hidden neurons are fixed and randomly assigned. The primary process of ESNs is firstly the operation of a random, extensive, fixed, recurring neural network with an input signal to induce a non-linear perturbation signal in each neuron within the reservoir network. Secondly, the desired output signal is connected by a trainable linear combination of

L. Iliadis et al. (Eds.): EANN 2022, CCIS 1600, pp. 375–385, 2022.
https://doi.org/10.1007/978-3-031-08223-8_31

these response signals [4]. Finally, the spatio-temporal patterns of the reservoir after excitation by known inputs are calculated by utilising a training method such as linear or Ridge regression. Therefore, the non-linear dynamical systems serve as a reservoir that enables the computational power of naturally available systems: classical and quantum mechanical [5].

Information is stored in the reservoirs by connecting neurons in recurrent loops where the previous data input affects the following reservoir response recursively. These non-linear dynamics are applied to generate random and unique data transformations that also include alterations within the dimensional space. These properties make ESNs and reservoir computing ideal to create unique data tradeable products in a marketplace as they merge the factual information with random properties by applying the non-linearity properties of the reservoir.

Data marketplaces exchange information between data providers and data consumers. The traditional key roles of the data marketplace are: 1) the collection of a fee from the data buyer via a licensing model, 2) the incentivisation of the data provider via rewards, and 3) the data governance based on structure, security and quality. The additional and innovative task presented by this paper is the generation of unique tradeable content as a value-added service. Data sellers offer atomic data, and data buyers are given a distictinve and random item created from these data atoms by the data marketplace. This exclusive tradeable data content can take the form of images, video or even digital files that create physical items such as drawings or renders.

## 1.1 Research Proposal

This paper presents Echo State Networks (ESNs) in data marketplaces that map tradeable data into higher dimensional spaces via the dynamics of a fixed and non-linear reservoir as a value-added service. The reservoir generates unique tradeable data products that can not be replicated therefore ensuring its exclusivity, uniqueness while guaranteeing its commercial value as a content generation method.

## 1.2 Research Structure

The proposed ESNs model of data marketplaces has been applied to an actual application where tradeable data is based on functions and images. Section 2 provides relevant research background of the Echo Estate Networks, whereasSect. 3 confirms the mathematical model of the ESNs and their application to the data marketplace. Following Sect. 4 presents the experimental and validation results. Finally, conclusions are shared in Sect. 5.

## 2   Research Background

There is extensive research literature within the Echo State Networks (ESNs). The aim of this paper is a practical application of their functionality based on their properties; therefore, only selected research background is described. The external approximation is the development of a Reservoir Computing (RC) that approximates any given filter by finding reservoir and readout maps close to those of the given one. ESNs are universal uniform approximants in the context of discrete-time fading memory filters with uniformly bounded inputs defined on negative infinite times [6]. This approximation is valid for infinite time intervals and guarantees that any fading memory input/output system in discrete time can be realised as a simple finite-dimensional neural network-type state-space model with a static linear readout map. A universal family of ESNs can be generated from elements generated from the echo state and the fading memory properties [7]. Standard ESNs can reach high accuracy when modelling Multiple Superimposed Oscillators (MSOs) with the correct choice of the network parameters. A dual effect within the output feedback strength drives the dynamic reservoir, although this interaction can also block suitable reservoir dynamics on the multiple superimposed oscillators benchmark [8].

Plasticity modifies the strength of the synapses within the reservoir from perturbing activities stimulated by the input based on two rules. The Oja rule alters the strength of the neuron connection or learns over time following the Hebbian rule. If two connected neurons are activated synchronously, the strength of the synaptic weight will increase; however, if they are activated at different times, the synaptic weight will decrease. The Bienenstock-Copper-Munro (BCN) rule also follows the Hebbian rule with a sliding threshold as a stabiliser function. The influence of neural plasticity applied to the randomly assigned weights inside the reservoir on the learning performance of the ESN is analysed based on the prediction and classification performance when offline or online supervised learning algorithms [9]. Local plasticity rules allow different neurons to use different types of plasticity rules (Hebbian and anti-Hebbian) and different parameters. Evolving neural plasticity results in synergistic learning of different neural strength rules, which is essential in improving learning performance [10]. Local plasticity rules can effectively alleviate synaptic interferences within the reservoir structure.

Memory Capacity (MC) in a reservoir measures its ability to store and recall previous in and out signals fed into the network and retrieve past information using the linear combinations of reservoir unit activations. There are optimal spectral radius and norm values for which the memory capacity is maximal. In addition, the reservoir size increases sublinearly the MC [11]. Very sparse reservoirs preserve the maximum MC, whereas the orthogonalisation of properly initialised reservoirs increases the MC significantly. Finally, the MC increases with a decreasing input matrix parameter.

Sparsity, the input and reservoir connections, has a significant role in developing internal temporal representations that possess a more extended short-term memory of previous inputs and a higher dimension. The number of non-zero connections impacts the determination of the richness of the developed representations [12]. While a modest number of recurrent connections is already sufficient for a good performance, maximally sparse input to reservoir connections lead to the best results both in terms of short-term memory and the effective dimension of the state manifold. The concept of consistency as an extension to generalised synchronisation quantifies the degree of functional dependency of a non-linear driven system to its input. Complete consistency is always desirable for reservoir design. The consistency levels based on the principal-component analysis of the high-dimensional response to a memory task is measured to analyse the echo-state property [13]. Inconsistency is not as destructive to fading memory where inconsistent reservoirs perform comparably, and even outperform consistent reservoirs, due to the distribution of signal and noise.

ESNs have a superior capability in modelling non-linear dynamic systems. The relationship between the spectral radius of the internal weights and the capability and performance can be resolved using complex network theory [14]. These models have better prediction capabilities and a wider spectral radius; however, they retain almost the same short-term memory capacity as compared to the conventional ESN model. The smaller the ratio of the scale-free topology over the small-world topology, the better the memory capacity. A graph ESN model is an efficient approach to Recursive Neural Networks modelling extended to deal with cyclic and acyclic, directed and undirected, labelled graphs [15]. The model exploits the fixed contractive state dynamics typical of ESN models where the convergence of the encoding is ensured for a large class of structured data.

Evolutionary computation provides a possible solution for unsupervised learning tasks where no input-output example is available. The concept of evolutionary learning for ESNs is the replacement of the gradient descent used to optimise the outgoing weights by an evolutionary algorithm [16]. The flexibility of evolutionary optimisation enables the optimisation of the outgoing weights and other ESN parameters. Critical phenomena refer to the many interactions that appear in second-order phase transitions and percolation processes. These interactions may occur in the transition region that separates stages such as symmetry properties, macroscopic parameters or structure. Critical ESNs apply the criticality of this phase transition due to their sharp phase transition that depends on the connectivity properties within the reservoir. The recurrent connection structure of ESNs strongly influences the critical phenomenon. A particular small subset of ESNs is much better than ordinary ESNs provided that the topology of the recurrent feedback connections satisfies certain conditions [17]. These conditions are based on the permutation and orthogonal matrices of the network reservoir.

## 3    Echo State Networks in Data Marketplaces

This section presents the mathematical model of Echo State Networks (ESNs) in data marketplaces that map tradeable data into higher dimensional spaces via the dynamics of a fixed and non-linear reservoir. The reservoir generates unique tradeable data products that can not be replicated, ensuring its exclusivity and commercial value. For the ESNs to operate, the reservoir must have the echo state property based on the asymptotic properties of the excited reservoir dynamics to the input signal. The echo state property is guaranteed for any normalised input if the spectral radius is smaller than unity [1].

### 3.1    System Equations

ESNs are composed of an input layer, x(n), of K dimensions that excites the reservoir's neurons that represent the original tradeable data. A recurrent neural network, r(n), is formed of N reservoir units that create the non-linear response signal; r(n) represents the unique tradeable data products generated from the reservoir dynamics. A readout layer, y(n) of L neurons, combines the internal state of the reservoir or the unique tradeable data products into the desired output signal. For this specific Data market application, the desired output signal is the same as the original tradeable data. This approach provides the same boundaries to the reservoir that enhances its non-linear properties. In addition, the reservoir is affected by a random noise signal, v(n). This noise enhances the exclusivity and commercial value of the generated data products (Fig. 1).

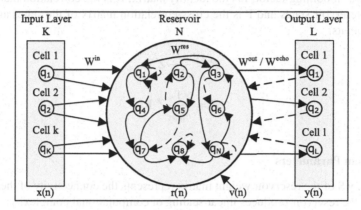

**Fig. 1.** Echo state networks

The equations of ESNs are defined as:

$$r(n+1) = \alpha \cdot r(n) + (1-\alpha) \cdot f\left(W^{res}r(n) + W^{in}x(n+1) + W^{echo}y(n)\right) + v(n) \tag{1}$$

where $W^{in}$ is the N x K data input weight matrix, $W^{res}$ is the N x N reservoir weight matrix of the data marketplace, and $W^{echo}$ is the N × L output feedback or echo matrix; f is a sigmoid function (logistic sigmoid or tanh function) and $\alpha$ is the reservoir leakage rate. The output of the reservoir includes the extended system state, $z(n) = [r(n); x(n)]$ and is defined as:

$$y(n) = g\left(W^{out}z(n)\right) \tag{2}$$

where $W^{out}$ is the L x K + N output weight matrix, and g is the output activation function (identity or sigmoid).

## 3.2 System Learning

ESNs and learning only focus on the output weight matrix, $W^{out}$, as the other ESN weights: W, $W^{in}$ and $W^{fb}$ are fixed. $W^{out}$ is calculated as the linear regression of the training signal y(n) on the extended system state z(n). Two main methods provide this calculation. The first method is the Pseudoinverse denoted as †:

$$W^{out} = (Z^{\dagger}Y)' \tag{3}$$

where Z corresponds to the extended system state matrix z(n) and Y is the desired output vector y(n). The second method is the Ridge regression:

$$W^{out} = \frac{1}{(R + \beta^2 I)} P \tag{4}$$

where β is a smoothing factor, I is the identity matrix, R is the correlation matrix of the extended reservoir states and P is the cross-correlation matrix of the states against the desired outputs:

$$R = \frac{1}{n_{max}} Z' Z \tag{5}$$

$$P = \frac{1}{n_{max}} Z' Y \tag{6}$$

### 3.3  System Parameters

The sparsity S of the reservoir weight matrix represents the connectivity of the response signals in the reservoir produces linear scaling of computational complexity:

$$S = \frac{Non\ zero\ connections}{Reservoir\ size} \tag{7}$$

Memory capacity MC represents the dynamical short-term memory from the RNNs in feedforward configuration where the reservoir states r(n) reflect traces of the past input signals. This short-term memory's capacity MC is defined as:

$$MC = \sum_{i=1}^{i_{max}} MC_k = \sum_{i=1}^{i_{max}} \frac{cov^2(u(t-k), y_k(t))}{var(u(t)) \cdot var(y_k(t))} \tag{8}$$

The spectral radius ρ of the reservoir weight matrix W determines the effective time constant of the echo state network with respect to the decay of impulse response and the range of non-linear interaction of input components through time. ρ(W) < 1 guarantees echo state property in most situations:

$$\rho(W) = \max\ eigenvalue(W) \tag{9}$$

The Input Scaling (IS) defines the level of non-linearity of the reservoir dynamics between a linear medium, to the saturation of the sigmoid and a binary switching dynamics results:

$$IS = range[-IS; IS]\ of\ W^{in} \tag{10}$$

The Output Feedback Scaling (OFS) describes the autonomous pattern generation component from purely input driven to an oscillatory frequency generator:

$$OFS = range[-OFS; OFS]\ of\ W^{out} \tag{11}$$

## 4 Experimental Results

This section presents the experimental results for the proposed echo state networks in data marketplaces. Precisely, a reservoir based on non-linear dynamics and neural perturbations emulates a digital artist to create unique and exclusive content that can not be replicated. This digital artist generates digital content based on 2D functions and 3D images with different dimensional spaces. The application is based on JAVA-Eclipse. The error between the original data product in the input layer and its replica in the output layer is calculated for both algorithms: Pseudoinverse and Ridge regression. The error metric is the current value is calculated following the Root Mean Square Error (RMSE):

$$RMSE = \sqrt{\frac{\sum_{i=1}^{N}(x_i - y_i)^2}{N}} \tag{12}$$

where $x_i$ corresponds to the neurons of the input layer that codify the original tradable data product, $y_i$ represents the desired output with the same as the input for this data marketplace and N the total number of neurons in the output layer.

### 4.1 2D Function Validation

The neurons of the reservoir are excited with three different independent signals: sinusoid, sigmoid and exponential, where each signal dimension of the time series is decoded with its respective input neuron of the ESN. The input layer of the ESN, the reservoir and the output layer are composed of 100 neurons each. Table 1 shows the number of neurons of the reservoir, the algorithm time and the RMSE errors between the input, x(n), and output signals, y(n) and the reservoir, r(n) against the input neural, x(n) layer respectively.

**Table 1.** Data market place – function validation

| Function | Variable | Pseudoinverse | Ridge regression |
|---|---|---|---|
| Reservoir | Neurons | 100 | 100 |
| Sinusoid | Time (s) | 0.126 | 0.125 |
| | r(n) RMSE Error | 3.93E−02 | 2.04E−02 |
| | y(n) RMSE Error | 6.08E−16 | 6.50E−08 |
| Sigmoid | Time (s) | 0.128 | 0.138 |
| | r(n) RMSE Error | 2.90E−02 | 3.84E−02 |
| | y(n) RMSE Error | 6.24E−16 | 8.16E−08 |
| Exponential | Time (s) | 0.118 | 0.128 |
| | r(n) RMSE Error | 1.57E−02 | 1.84E−02 |
| | y(n) RMSE Error | 4.24E−16 | 3.83E−08 |

382    W. Serrano

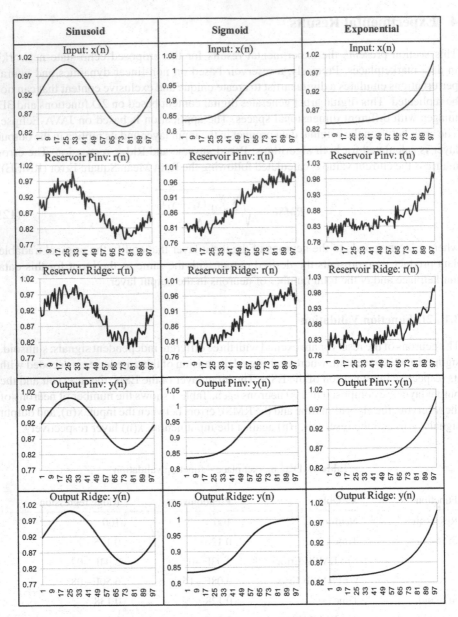

**Fig. 2.** Data market place – function validation

Both algorithms require approximately the same time to calculate the echo state output network weights, $W^{out}$; however, the Pseudoinverse algorithm presents a much lower RSME figure than the Ridge regression. The dynamics of the reservoir, r(n) have a similar representation based on their RSME against the perturbation from the input layer (Table 1). Although the Pseudoinverse algorithm performs better than the Ridge regression when codifying the output data replica, y(n) from the input genuine data product, x(n), the visual representation makes them appear the same. The non-linear dynamics and neural perturbations of the reservoir, r(n) create unique 2D content where the differences can be easily perceived (Fig. 2).

## 4.2  3D Image Validation

The neurons of the reservor are excited with three different independent $25 \times 40$ pixel images: Christmas tree, Rainbow flag and random values where each signal dimension of the time series is decoded with its respective input neuron of the ESn. Each pixel is codified into four neurons that represent the transparency, red, green and blue, respectively. The input layer of the ESN, the reservoir and the output layer are composed of 4,000 neurons each. Table 2 shows the number of neurons of the reservoir, the algorithm time and the RMSE errors between the input, x(n), and output signals, y(n) and the reservoir, r(n) against the input neural, x(n) layer respectively.

**Table 2.** Data market place – image validation

| Function | Variable | Pseudoinverse | Ridge regression |
|---|---|---|---|
| Reservoir | Neurons | 4000 | 4000 |
| Christmas tree | Time (s) | 0.591 | 92.471 |
|  | r(n) RMSE Error | 5.63E−01 | 5.21E−01 |
|  | y(n) RMSE Error | 4.27E−15 | 1.45E−05 |
| Rainbow flag | Time (s) | 0.607 | 117.49 |
|  | r(n) RMSE Error | 1.40E+00 | 1.45E+00 |
|  | y(n) RMSE Error | 2.65E−14 | 1.97E−04 |
| Random values | Time (s) | 0.603 | 138.05 |
|  | r(n) RMSE Error | 2.02E+00 | 2.10E+00 |
|  | y(n) RMSE Error | 1.83E−14 | 7.01E−04 |

The Pseudoinverse algorithm performs better than the Ridge regression in the 3D Image validation in terms of computational time and RMSE error when the number of neurons increases. This difference of error is not visually perceived in the output signal y(n). Similar to the previous validation, the dynamics of the reservoir, r(n), have a similar representation based on their RSME against the perturbation from the input layer (Table 2). The visual representation of the reservoir, r(n), generates random replicas and support echo state networks as a digital artist for content generation (Fig. 3).

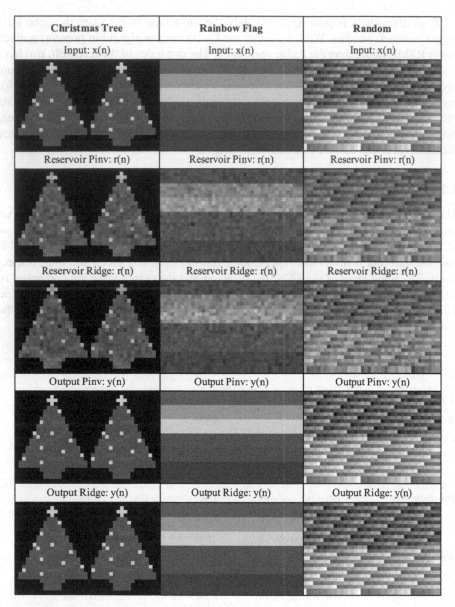

**Fig. 3.** Data market place – image validation

## 5 Conclusions

This paper has presented Echo State Networks (ESNs) in data marketplaces that map tradeable data into higher dimensional spaces via the dynamics of a fixed and non-linear reservoir as a value-added service. The reservoir generates unique tradeable data products that can not be replicated therefore ensuring its exclusivity, uniqueness while guaranteeing its commercial value as a content generation method. The Pesoudoinverse algorithm performs better than the Ridge regression in terms of computational time and RMSE codification error. Future work will analyse the effects of the different reservoir parameters such as sparsity S, Memory capacity MC and spectral radius $\rho$.

# References

1. Jaeger, H.: The "echo state" approach to analysing and training recurrent neural networks. German National Research Institute for Computer Science, pp. 1–43 (2001)
2. Jaeger, H.: Short term memory in echo state networks. Report. German National Research Institute for Computer Science, pp. 1–60 (2002)
3. Maass, W., Natschlager, T., Markram, H.: Real-time computing without stable states: a new framework for neural computation based on perturbations. Neural Comput. **14**(11), 2531–2560 (2002)
4. Jaeger, H.: Discovering multiscale dynamical features with hierarchical echo state networks. Report. School of Engineering and Science, Jacobs University, pp. 1–30 (2007)
5. Schiller, U., Steil, J.: Analysing the weight dynamics of recurrent learning algorithms. Neurocomputing **63**, 5–23 (2005)
6. Grigoryeva, L., Ortega, J.: Echo state networks are universal. Neural Netw. **108**, 495–508 (2018)
7. Gonon, L., Ortega, J.: Fading memory echo state networks are universal. Neural Netw. **138**, 10–13 (2021)
8. Koryakin, D., Lohmann, J., Butz, M.: Balanced echo state networks. Neural Netw. **36**, 35–45 (2012)
9. Yusoff, M., Chrol, J., Jin, Y.: Modelling neural plasticity in echo state networks for classification and regression. Inf. Sci. **364–365**, 184–196 (2016)
10. Wang, X., Jin, Y., Hao, K.: Evolving local plasticity rules for synergistic learning in echo state networks. IEEE Trans. Neural Netw. Learn. Syst. **31**(4), 1363–1374 (2020)
11. Farkas, I., Bosak, R., Gergel, P.: Computational analysis of memory capacity in echo state networks. Neural Netw. **83**, 109–120 (2016)
12. Gallicchio, C.: Sparsity in reservoir computing neural networks. In: International Conference on Innovations in Intelligent Systems and Applications, pp. 1–7 (2020)
13. Lymburn, T., Khor, A., Stemler, T., Corrêa, D., Small, M., Jüngling, T.: Consistency in echo-state networks. Chaos **29**(023118), 1–9 (2019)
14. Cui, H., Liu, X., Li, L.: The architecture of dynamic reservoir in the echo state network. Chaos **22**(033127), 1–12 (2012)
15. Gallicchio, C., Micheli, A.: Graph echo state networks. In: International Joint Conference on Neural Networks (IJCNN), pp. 1–8 (2010)
16. Jiang, F., Berry, H., Schoenauer, M.: Supervised and evolutionary learning of echo state networks. In: International Conference on Parallel Problem Solving from Nature, pp. 215–224 (2008)
17. Hajnal, M., Lorincz, A.: Critical echo state networks. In: International Conference on Artificial Neural Networks, pp. 658–667 (2006)

# Efficient Approaches for Data Augmentation by Using Generative Adversarial Networks

Pretom Kumar Saha[✉] and Doina Logofatu[✉]

Frankfurt University of Applied Sciences, Nibelungenplatz 1,
60318 Frankfurt am Main, Germany
saha@stud.fra-uas.de, logofatu@fb2.fra-uas.de

**Abstract.** In the present and future, data is the most valuable thing in the world. Therefore, it is now a challenge for everyone in every sector to work with data. Collecting data to predict or collecting data to analyze is a very valuable task. Moreover every new research, new machine learning method, and algorithms testing depends on a massive amount of different data. Furthermore, it is also a security issue for many fields to share actual data. It is always hard to find the perfect data set. It is not just about figuring out huge amounts of data. Many other data analysis processes need to be performed on that dataset to make it worthwhile. To overcome this problem, data augmentation is one of the suitable solutions. The idea behind data augmentation is to create a new dataset that depends on some existing dataset features. Generative Adversarial Networks (GANs) are a class of machine learning frameworks introduced by Ian Goodfellow in 2014. They are a game-like way to learn and generate new datasets. GANs have two parts, one is the generator, and the second is the discriminator. They play against each other to win the game. We will use our data set on the GAN model using some specific hyperparameter value and optimizer, which we will find out through our experiment. Finally, we will produce a CSV file with model-generated synthesis data and visualize the performance statistic of our model in the graph. This article will explain the different facts related to Data Augmentation, and GANs.

**Keywords:** Data augmentation · Generative Adversarial Networks · Tabular data

## 1 Introduction

In the world of data aggregate, a large number of different fields of data are required for implementing and testing applications. To evaluate the application and perform in specific scenarios using accurate input is essential for applications. In every area of data sciences, it is tough to collect a significant amount of pertinent information. Gathering valuable facts will be highly cost-consuming in

© Springer Nature Switzerland AG 2022
L. Iliadis et al. (Eds.): EANN 2022, CCIS 1600, pp. 386–399, 2022.
https://doi.org/10.1007/978-3-031-08223-8_32

terms of money, time, staffing, and applications [1]. Feather more, many other related methodologies are connected for data analysis, data cleaning, and so on. It is essential to arrange proper study, guidelines, and training to fulfill all these above factors. To overcome all this complexity and cost, an artificial set of new facts that will contain all the features and properties like actual is the best solution [1]. The data science research literature frequently assumes that the input features for various data analytics procedures is already clean and accurate for consumption [15]. However, cleaning issues in its values or structure consumes a significant portion of professionals time and effort. According to recent polls, data cleansing takes up to 60% of data scientists work [15].

Naturally, most of the information in the business is private and secret. While some databases are freely accessible, new datasets are difficult to come by. Even if owners are ready to provide anonymized datasets, the time and effort required to compile the data and through bureaucracy may deter them [1]. If owners can quickly generate "fake" or synthesized features comparable to actual, friction in data disclosure will be reduced.

Other papers on the scientific approach of Big data development and deployment employ three key levels from a scientific standpoint [11]. Almost every article regarding Big data implementation focuses on Storage, Process, and Analysis in some way. It is a fact that the corporate sector now has a greater need to store and handle data than in the past due to the significant rise in structured and unstructured data (Chen, Mao, and Liu, 2014). Furthermore, large storage systems require adequate and trustworthy interfaces to provide real-time facts for real-time applications (Kambatla, Kollias, Kumar, and Grama, 2014). After information is gathered and stored from numerous sources that create diverse the types (Bolón-Canedo et al., 2015), it is categorized, integrated, and noise and redundancy are removed to reduce redundant storage space and accommodate important information (Chen et al., 2014). We need business software and information systems to analyze (Wang and Hajli, 2017). After, they should explore to make the best use of the information [11]. The input then should be interpreted to make the best use of it. Data analysts and scientists who possess the abilities of a database designer, software programmer, and statistician should be prepared for this purpose by information technology instructors [11]. By Introduce an automated synthesized data generation can resolve all this manual process of research.

In machine learning, a generative model is a subset of unsupervised learning methods. Machine learning is to create models and algorithms that evaluate and comprehend real-world data [19]. In contrast to conventional classification problems, generative models are one of the most promising methods to accomplish this objective [19]. GAN, a novel framework for estimating generative models through an adversarial process, has shown tremendous promise in producing actual data. This article explains GAN and the varients of GAN. The variants of GAN are more relevant to this study.

Some basic problems we faced are summarised as follow:

1. Generate synthesized tabular form given Dataset. The selection of a suitable GAN model is one of the biggest challenges in the thesis.
2. Train a GAN model with generator and discriminator neuron. Find out suitable hyper-parameter values for the GAN model.
3. Select a more appreciated optimizer for the GAN model.
4. Visualized and analyzed the performance of the model.

## 2   Data Augmentation

The term "Data Augmentation" (DA) refers to techniques for expanding the variety of training data without gathering any extra data in the traditional sense. When training ML models, most approaches either add slightly changed copies of existing data or produce synthetic data to have the augmented data work as a regularizer and prevent overfitting [4]. Many computer vision methods, including cropping, flipping, and color jittering, involve DA as an essential part of the training process. A less obvious way to construct augmented instances that capture desirable invariances when the input space is discrete is in natural language processing (NLP) [4]. Supervised, semi-supervised, and unsupervised data augmentation are all types of data augmentation methods [8]. Figure 1 shows the data augmentation categorization. There are two types of Supervised data augmentation: single sample and multi-sample [8]. Supervised data enhancement is based on current data, and it uses pre-set data transformation algorithms to make the changes. It is possible to enrich unsupervised data in two different ways. Data distribution may be learned by models that randomly generate pictures that are consistent with the distribution of the training data set [8]. This approach is known as GAN [6]. Another option is to use the model to learn a data improvement strategy appropriate for the present job. AutoAugment is an example of a symbolic approach.

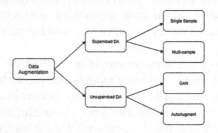

**Fig. 1.** The classification of data augmentation

## 2.1   Existing Methods of Data Generation

It is also feasible to create synthetic tabular data using comparable high-quality models: the implicit joint distribution of columns may be learned from actual data, and synthetic rows can be sampled from that distribution. A few models (MedGAN [2], TableGAN [10], PATE-GAN [7]) have been presented that work by applying fully connected networks or convolutional neural networks directly to tabular data without taking into account the unique situation of modeling tabular data. Although these models perform well on datasets, they have not been thoroughly compared against other statistical models [18].

**Image Data Augmentation:** Computer vision tasks, including picture classification, object recognition, and segmentation, have been particularly influential among popular deep learning applications [13]. In these situations, data augmentation may be a valuable tool for training DL models. Geometric transformations such as Flipping, Rotation, Translation, Cropping, and Scaling, as well as color space transformations such as Color Casting, Varying Brightness, and Noise Injection, may all be applied to a picture with ease [13].

**Speech Data Augmentation:** SpecAugment was developed by Park et al. to improve speech recognition by augmenting input data [9]. Time warping, frequency masking, and time masking are the three most used methods of enhancing data. LibriSpeech basic (LB), LibriSpeech double (LD), Switchboard moderate (SM), and Switchboard strong are the four possible combinations that they introduce in their experiment (SS) [9].

**Text Data Augmentation:** Due to the significant level of linguistic complexity, enhancing text in the NLP discipline is difficult [12]. Not every word can be replaced with a, an, or the like. There aren't synonyms for every term, either. Context is everything and altering a single word changes everything. However, creating an enhanced picture in the computer vision field is much simpler [12]. Even if someone adds noise to the picture or clip off a piece of it, the model will still identify what it is. Symbolic augmentation, Rule based augmentation, Graph structured augmentation, MixUp augmentation, Generative data augmentation, and so on are very popular Text Data Augmentation techniques.

**Tabular Data Augmentation:** Tabular Data Augmentation (TDA) is a new moniker for a technique of modular feature engineering and observation engineering for tabular data that emphasizes the sequence of augmentation to get the best-projected result for a given information set [14]. It solves the issue of how to best represent data to a learning model for the highest prediction accuracy. An augmentation method is any process that alters the underlying data and results in an increase in the amount or quality of the data [14]. Some usable techniques are like Transformation, Mapping, Extraction, Statistical model, and GANs.

## 3　Methodology

An adversarial game is set up using the GAN framework, with a generator and a discriminator as the two participants. The discriminator's job is to tell apart samples from the model from samples from the training data, whereas the generator's job is to confuse the discriminator as much as possible [5]. Using a minimax value function, we may express the goal.

$$\underset{G}{\min}\,\underset{D}{\max}\,f_v(G,D) = \mathbb{E}\left[logD(data)\right] + \mathbb{E}\left[log(1 - D(G(k)))\right] \tag{1}$$

It won't be long until the random variables and distributions needed to understand Eq. 1 are defined. The following is a simple explanation of the two terms in the equation in prose for the time being:

- Train the discriminator to maximize the training data's probability.
- Train the discriminator to reduce the likelihood of the generator's data being sampled. The generator should also focus on an opposing goal: to maximize the discriminator's probability to its samples [5].

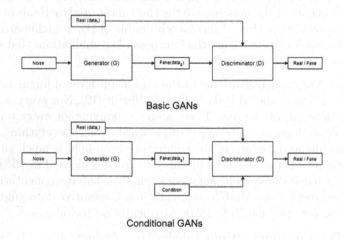

Basic GANs

Conditional GANs

**Fig. 2.** The Architecture of GANs

SGD may be used to train the two players in alternation when they are represented as MLPs by a mathematical model [5].

This paper's contribution is to provide the framework of a conditioning capability. As long as the generator's output and the discriminator's anticipated input are both constrained, we can set up any arbitrary condition $y$ on generation [5] as shown in Fig. 2. In other words, we might say that this condition $y$ engages both the generator and the discriminator in a process of generation or prediction.

## 3.1    Generator

There are many deconvolutional layers in the generator $G$, which makes it a neural network as well. The discriminator's procedure is reversed when $G$ is involved, as illustrated in Fig. 3 [10]. It takes as input a uniformly sampled latent vector $k$ from the unit hypercube space [10]. The input $k$ is transformed into a 2-dimensional matrix, corresponding to a synthetic table row, using several de-convolutional layers.

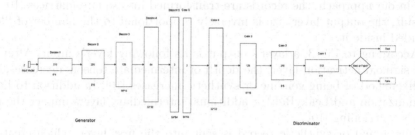

**Fig. 3.** Architecture of the generator and discriminator with 5 layers

The generation of numerical data takes place in two stages. We begin by creating the value scalar $s_i$, and then the cluster vector $c_i$ follows suit. We produce a probability distribution over all potential labels to represent a category characteristic in a single step [17].

We create an attention weight vector $w_t \in \mathbb{R}^t$ and use it to calculate context as

$$w_t = \sum_{i=1}^{t} \frac{expw_t, i}{\sum_j expw_t, j} L_i \qquad (2)$$

Set $w_0$ to be equal to 0. Its output is $L_t$, which we project to a hidden vector $f_t = tanh(lP_L L_t)$, where $lP_L$ is an input parameter that the network has learned over time. $f_t$ has a radius of $n_f$. The concealed vector is then turned into an output variable.

- $b_i = tanh(lP_t f_t)$ is the formula for calculating the value portion of a continuous variable. $f_t$ is the value of the hidden vector at time $t + 1$.
- The result is computed as $a_i = softmax(lP_t f_t)$ if a continuous variable cluster component. $f_t$ is the feature vector for $t+1$.
- The output is a discrete variable if it is $d_i = softmax(lP_t f_t)$. $f_t' = E_i [arg_i \, max \, d_i]$ represents the discrete variable $D_i$ as an embedding matrix $E \in \mathbb{R}^{|D_i| * n_f}$ for time step $t+1$.
- $f_0$ is a particular vector that we learn throughout training.

The discriminator's prediction results may be used to train the generator. That's the idea behind it: the several options for training the generator in our table-GAN [10]. It is possible to use back-propagation to execute this training procedure efficiently.

## 3.2 Discriminator

Using Discriminator, it will be possible to tell if data is legitimate or malicious. More hostile instances will be generated by $G$ based on the detection result, just as it would with regular data [19].

The network that can distinguish one thing from another, $D$ is a neural network taught to differentiate between synthetic records and genuine ones in a table [10]. $D$ is a convolutional neural network (CNN) with many layers. In each layer, the whole input matrix is subjected to a set of trainable filters. Remember that in our approach, the records are transformed into square matrices [10]. As a result, the output layer size is inversely proportional to the number of filters included inside it.

According to Fig. 3, a layer's output is its following layer's input. After the final sigmoid activation layer, the depth of intermediate tensors decreases, and the likelihood of being genuine or synthetic increases [10]. In addition to batch normalization and LeakyReLU , additional intermediary layers impact the network's functioning [10].

One actual or synthetic record is sent into the first layer, which creates a $x * x$ matrices input. By training it on real data, the Discriminator can predict 1 for actual data while predicting 0 for fake data [10].

# 4    Training GANs

First, to train GANs, identify the discriminator parameters that optimize classification accuracy and then identify the generator parameters that confuse the discriminator the most. Figure 5 depicts the training procedure.

$f(G, D)$ is used to assess the training costs since it is dependent on both the generator and the discriminator to work. It is necessary to solve

$$\underset{D}{max}\underset{G}{min} \ f(G, D),$$

where

$$f(G, D) = \mathbb{E}_{p_{data}(data)} log D(data) + \mathbb{E}_{p_g(data)} log(1 - D(data)).$$

One model's parameters are updated while the second model's parameters remain constant throughout training. A static generator is shown to have unique $D^*(data) = p_{data}(data)/(p_{data}(data) + p_g(data))$. For $p_g(data) = p_{data}(data), G$ is equal to the optimum discriminator predicating 0.5 for all samples taken from $data$, as shown by the researchers. The generator is at its best when the discriminator $D$ is completely confused and unable to distinguish between actual samples and false ones.

To get the best results, train the discriminator until it is as good as possible with the current source, and then update the original again [3]. When training the discriminator for a limited number of trials, the discriminator may only be taught for a few iterations before being used with a newer generation. For the generator, this means that instead of using $min_G log(1 - D(G(k)))$, an alternative nonsaturating training criteria is employed, such as $max_G log D(G(z))$.

No matter how many unique solutions exist in theory, GAN training is difficult and unstable for various reasons [3]. Assessing empirical "symptoms" that may be encountered during training may help improve GAN training. Among the signs are:

- problems with model convergence
- As various inputs are used, the generative model "collapses" to produce extremely similar examples
- The discriminator loss rapidly reduces to zero, leaving no route for the generator's gradient to be updated reliably.

As a result, several writers proposed heuristic methods to deal with the problems [3].

To begin, researchers Goodfellow and Salimans et al. hypothesized that GAN training is unstable since the answer to the optimization issue it poses is a saddle point, which is why gradient descent techniques are usually employed to update both the generator's and discriminator's parameters. The example is given by Salimans et al. demonstrates this [3]. However, stochastic gradient descent is often used to update neural networks, and well-developed machine-learning programming environments make it simple to build and update networks using stochastic gradient descent.

Despite an early theoretical approach showing that the generator is optimum when $p_g(data)$ are equal to $p_{data}(data)$, a very tidy conclusion with a strong intuition behind it, actual data samples are found on a manifold in high-dimensional space representations [3]. Consider a data table sample with the values range [0, $\mathbb{R}+$] of size $N * N$, which has a dimensionality of $N^2$. Each dimension accepts values between zero and the highest detectable intensity of the cell value. This is referred to as the $\mathbb{X}$ space. When using $p_{data}$, the data samples provide assistance for a specific issue. Still, they usually only take up the tiniest fraction of the total available space, $\mathbb{X}$. Likewise, the generator's samples should only take up a tiny part of $\mathbb{X}$.

In addition, Goodfellow et al. demonstrated that training $G$ to minimize the Jensen- Shannon (JS) divergence between $p_g(data)$ and $p_{data}(data)$ is equal to reducing $D$, when $D$ is optimum. The update may be less accurate or less significant if $D$ is not optimum [3]. This theoretical discovery has sparked research into alternative distance-based cost functions.

## 5    Dataset

Finding a good dataset for the experiment is a difficult task. For category and numerical data, we are implementing our model. We begin by using a dataset about the European automobile industry which has 9 features including 46405 sets of data. A sample of the dataset is shown below in Table 1.

Table 1. A dataset about the European automobile industry

|   | Mileage | Make | Model | Fuel | Gear | OfferType | Price | hp | Year |
|---|---------|------|-------|------|------|-----------|-------|-----|------|
| 0 | 23500 | BMW | 316 | Diesel | Manual | Used | 6800 | 116.0 | 2011 |
| 1 | 92800 | Volkswagen | Golf | Gasoline | Manual | Used | 6877 | 122.0 | 2011 |
| 2 | 149300 | SEAT | Exeo | Gasoline | Manual | Used | 6900 | 160.0 | 2011 |
| 3 | 96200 | Renault | Megane | Gasoline | Manual | Used | 6950 | 110.0 | 2011 |
| 4 | 156000 | Peugeot | 308 | Gasoline | Manual | Used | 6950 | 156.0 | 2011 |

Another collection of data that we utilize in the experiment is made up of student test scores contain 8 features and 1000 set of data. A sample of the dataset is shown in the following Table 2.

Table 2. A dataset of student test scores

|   | Gender | Race/ethnicity | Parental level of education | Lunch | Test preparation course | Math score | Reading score | Writing score |
|---|--------|----------------|------------------------------|-------|--------------------------|------------|---------------|---------------|
| 0 | Female | Group B | Bachelor's degree | Standard | None | 72 | 72 | 74 |
| 1 | Female | Group C | Some college | Standard | completed | 69 | 90 | 88 |
| 2 | Female | Group B | Master's degree | Standard | None | 90 | 95 | 93 |
| 3 | Male | Group A | Associate's degree | Free/reduced | None | 47 | 57 | 44 |
| 4 | Male | Group C | Some college | Standard | none | 76 | 78 | 75 |

# 6    Experiment and Result Evaluation

The goal of the implementation is to produce a bunch of new data with the help of the Generative Adversarial Networks. Our motive is to use the same algorithm for numerical and categorical tabular data to data augmentation. Preparing the dataset is one of the essential parts of any implementation.

## 6.1    Data Analysis

Preparing data for using them in the proper algorithm, many processes are needed to fulfill the dataset. Developing the dataset with accurate data and rearranging them in the data frame is part of data analysis. Data cleaning, inspection, transformation, and modeling are the main factors considered in this section. We also integrated all the required processes of data analysis for my proposed algorithm.

## 6.2    TGAN Model Setup

We use the processed data set to test our TGAN model. Furthermore, since we employed both category and numerical data, we tested the performance in three distinct methods. One is for numerical data, another is for categorical data, and the third is for a mixture of categorical and numerical data. In addition, we run the model on two distinct datasets to see how they vary. The initial step in the model setup is to choose specific hyperparameters for the model. We fixed the hyperparameter as follows: latent_dim= 100, n_epochs = 5000, n_batch = 8000, and n_eval = 100. We also experiment with other hyper-parameter values. However, with that parameter value, we eventually receive a satisfactory outcome.

For various sorts of data sets, we utilize the same flow. As shown in the diagram Fig. 2, the initial step in this GAN model is to construct the generator. As we can see from the theoretical discussion, the generator plays a vital role in the generation of new data. The discriminator, which is used to examine and determine the correctness of created data. This discriminator is responsible for the whole performance. The final model, which we designate as GAN, combines the generator and discriminator models. We'll train our model with our supplied data set when we finish building this final model. As we explained in the data analysis section, we prepared our data via a series of steps.

### 6.3 Performance Analysis

We encountered several differences in experience when we incorporated numerical and categorical data for various datasets. It is highly typical for all computations to be performed mathematically, making it simple to use numerical data. Beside that, there's a chance to receive a more accurate result in the output. As a consequence, it seems that GAN model is learning to provide more accurate results. If we take a look on the data that are generated from TGAN in the table, then we understand the values of Table 2 are symmetrical as input data (Table 3).

Table 3. GAN generated synthesized numerical data

|   | Mileage | Price | hp | Year |
|---|---------|-------|-----|------|
| 0 | 5.714193e+10 | 1.990812e+10 | 84972.0 | 22164.0 |
| 1 | 3.290286e+09 | 5.752948e+10 | 183475.0 | 22220.0 |
| 2 | 1.680598e+11 | 2.000913e+09 | 108931.0 | 22121.0 |
| 3 | 1.796668e+11 | 7.170141e+09 | 136219.0 | 22162.0 |
| 4 | 5.176544e+10 | 3.075806e+09 | 79564.0 | 22169.0 |

On the other hand, if we observe for a student's performance dataset, we obtain the Table 4 below as a result the left side is the input data and the right is the synthesized data.

**Table 4.** Actual data and GAN generated synthesized numerical data

|   | Math score | Reading score | Writing score | Math score | Reading score | Writing score |
|---|---|---|---|---|---|---|
| 0 | 72 | 72 | 74 | 79.0 | 74.0 | 76.0 |
| 1 | 69 | 90 | 88 | 78.0 | 78.0 | 85.0 |
| 2 | 90 | 95 | 93 | 64.0 | 75.0 | 73.0 |
| 3 | 47 | 57 | 44 | 86.0 | 87.0 | 88.0 |
| 4 | 76 | 78 | 75 | 51.0 | 60.0 | 57.0 |

The same scenario of both categorical and numerical features are used together for student test score data we get the result in the Fig. 4, which is more suitable then the car information result.

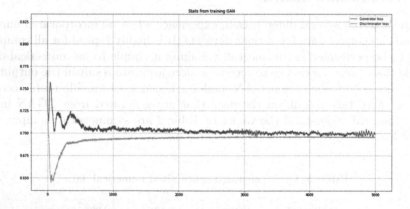

**Fig. 4.** Graphical representation of GAN Model training for student test scores Dataset

So, based on the conversation and the accompanying graph, we can conclude that if the data table has more unique values in categorical features, the GAN model's performance suffers and produce a very distorted result at the end.'

| | gender_female | gender_male | test preparation course_completed | test preparation course_none | math score | reading score | writing score |
|---|---|---|---|---|---|---|---|
| 0 | 1.0 | 0.0 | 0.0 | 1.0 | 64.0 | 67.0 | 74.0 |
| 1 | 1.0 | 0.0 | 1.0 | 0.0 | 84.0 | 96.0 | 98.0 |
| 2 | 0.0 | 1.0 | 0.0 | 1.0 | 82.0 | 63.0 | 65.0 |
| 3 | 0.0 | 1.0 | 0.0 | 1.0 | 78.0 | 79.0 | 69.0 |
| 4 | 0.0 | 1.0 | 0.0 | 1.0 | 62.0 | 60.0 | 48.0 |
| ... | ... | ... | ... | ... | ... | ... | ... |
| 9995 | 1.0 | 0.0 | 1.0 | 0.0 | 93.0 | 98.0 | 99.0 |
| 9996 | 1.0 | 0.0 | 0.0 | 1.0 | 60.0 | 77.0 | 72.0 |
| 9997 | 0.0 | 1.0 | 0.0 | 1.0 | 88.0 | 88.0 | 86.0 |
| 9998 | 1.0 | 0.0 | 1.0 | 0.0 | 75.0 | 83.0 | 84.0 |
| 9999 | 0.0 | 1.0 | 1.0 | 0.0 | 47.0 | 46.0 | 43.0 |

10000 rows × 7 columns

**Fig. 5.** GAN generated synthesized including categorical and numeric data

In the Fig. 5 is represented the final output of the GAN generated synthesized data, containing the categorical and numerical features. As we can see that the categorical features are shown in dummy data format. And we need to apply the process of work to retrieve the actual data from the dummy value. On the other hand, if we look at the numerical value, it seems pretty perfect and similar to the input data.

# 7    Conclusion and Future Work

Transforming data from original records into GAN-recognized input impacts overall performance, demonstrating the importance of representing relational data. A hybrid optimization methodology that co-trains GAN and record representation might lead to some intriguing future work.

We find that GANs are better suited to massive datasets because they can successfully capture correlations between features. That is, we demonstrate that using our approach, we can produce useful synthetic data. The usage of relational databases is widespread, yet modeling them is very challenging. Our architecture is capable of supporting a single table with both numerical and categorical data elements. Eventually, we'll look at utilizing GAN to model sequential data and many tables. Some approaches have difficulty combining tabular data with noise or anomaly. Such instances are inaccessible to the TGAN.

For instance, the model picks up on the basics of data produced from a clean and analyzed data collection. Our method's capabilities may be summed up as follows:

1. Production of high-quality tabular data in real-time, based on specified characteristics.
2. Collection and analysis of any size dataset.
3. The processing time required increases linearly with the quantity of output data.
4. Numeric and categorical data may be processed successfully.

**Future Work.** Machine learning hyper-parameters are parameters that influence how well a system learns. Choosing the proper collection of values while developing a machine learning model, in our instance, the machine learning model is GAN, may be termed Hyperparameter Optimization or Hyperparameter Tuning. Introduce a new Table-GAN which can handle multiple table data input at a time including numerical and categorical value.

# References

1. Calimeri, F., Marzullo, A., Stamile, C., Terracina, G.: Biomedical data augmentation using generative adversarial neural networks. In: Lintas, A., Rovetta, S., Verschure, P.F.M.J., Villa, A.E.P. (eds.) ICANN 2017. LNCS, vol. 10614, pp. 626–634. Springer, Cham (2017). https://doi.org/10.1007/978-3-319-68612-7_71
2. Choi, E., et al.: Generating Multi-Label Discrete Patient Records Using Generative Adversarial Networks. ArXiv:1703.06490 [Cs], January 2018
3. Creswell, A., et al.: Generative Adversarial Networks: An Overview. IEEE Signal Processing Magazine **35**(1), 53–65 (2018)
4. Feng, S.Y., et al.: A Survey of Data Augmentation Approaches for NLP. ArXiv:2105.03075 [Cs], December 2021
5. Gauthier, J.: Conditional Generative Adversarial Nets for Convolutional Face Generation (2015)
6. Goodfellow, I.J., et al.: Generative Adversarial Networks. ArXiv:1406.2661 [Cs, Stat], 1, June 2014
7. Jordon, J., et al.: PATE-GAN: Generating Synthetic Data with Differential Privacy Guarantees (2018)
8. Liu, P., et al.: A survey of text data augmentation. In: 2020 International Conference on Computer Communication and Network Security (CCNS), pp. 191–95 (2020)
9. Park, D.S., et al.: SpecAugment: a simple data augmentation method for automatic speech recognition. Interspeech 2019, pp. 2613–17, September 2019
10. Park, N., et al.: Data synthesis based on generative adversarial networks. In: Proceedings of the VLDB Endowment, vol. 11, no. 10, pp. 1071–83. June 2018
11. Rouhani, S., et al.: What do we know about the big data researches? a systematic review from 2011 to 2017. J. Decision Syst. **26**(4), 368–393 (2017)
12. Shorten, C., et al.: Text data augmentation for deep learning. J. Big Data **8**(1), 101 (2021)
13. Shorten, C., Khoshgoftaar, T.M.: A survey on image data augmentation for deep learning. J. Big Data **6**(1), 60 (2019)
14. Snow, D.: DeltaPy: A Framework for Tabular Data Augmentation in Python. SSRN Scholarly Paper, ID 3582219, Social Science Research Network, 22 April 2020
15. Sukhobok, D., et al.: Tabular data anomaly patterns. In: 2017 International Conference on Big Data Innovations and Applications (Innovate-Data), pp. 25–34 (2017)
16. Umbrich, J., et al.: Quality assessment and evolution of open data portals. In: 2015 3rd International Conference on Future Internet of Things and Cloud, pp. 404–11 (2015)
17. Xu, L.: Synthesizing Tabular Data Using Conditional GAN. Massachusetts Institute of Technology (2020)

18. Xu, L., Veeramachaneni, K.: Synthesizing Tabular Data Using Generative Adversarial Networks. ArXiv:1811.11264 [Cs, Stat], November 2018
19. Yan, Q., et al.: Automatically Synthesizing DoS attack traces using generative adversarial networks. Int. J. Mach. Learn. Cybern. 10(12), 3387–96 (2019)

# Multi-track Transfer Reinforcement Learning for Power Consumption Management of Building Multi-type Air-Conditioners

Yoshifumi Aoki[1]($\boxtimes$), Satoshi Goto[1], Yusuke Takahashi[1], Chuzo Ninagawa[1], and Junji Morikawa[2]

[1] Smart Grid Power Control Engineering Joint Research Laboratory, Gifu University , Gifu, Japan
aoki4423@gifu-u.ac.jp

[2] Mitsubishi Heavy Industries Thermal Systems, Ltd., Tokyo, Japan

**Abstract.** In this paper, we apply reinforcement learning to the power management control of building multi-type air-conditioners. In general, reinforcement learning requires several tens of thousands of training episodes before the control performance reaches a practical level. Therefore, applying it directly to air-conditioning control in 10-min intervals would require unrealistic training days as several years. We attempted to shorten the learning period by learning in advance on a virtual building that emulates the dynamic characteristics of an actual building. Since it is difficult to create exactly the same air-conditioning environment of the actual building, we propose a method to select the closest one from several virtual buildings based on the differences of immediate reward.

**Keywords:** Reinforcement learning · Transfer learning · Building multi-type air-conditioner

## 1 Introduction

In office buildings, the power consumption of air-conditioning accounts for about 40% of the total power consumption [1], and its proper management and control is important from both economic and environmental aspects. In the power management of office buildings, automatic control of building air-conditioning power to achieve energy conservation while minimizing the impact on occupants is essential.

In recent years, there have been many studies on adapting machine learning algorithms to building air conditioning management [2]. However, most of the studies have been conducted on centralized heat source type air-conditioners, and few have been conducted on building multi-type air-conditioners [3].

We have studied a control scheme to adjust the power reduction and room temperature comfort according to the priority for building multi-type air-conditioners [4]. In this previous study, we created a Neural Network: NN which predicts the future power consumption and room temperature and used it to search for the optimal power limitation

L. Iliadis et al. (Eds.): EANN 2022, CCIS 1600, pp. 400–411, 2022.
https://doi.org/10.1007/978-3-031-08223-8_33

command pattern. However, it was necessary to conduct a special operation in the target building for at least one year to collect training data for the NN. This has been a practical problem of the method.

Therefore, in this study, we attempt to use reinforcement learning [5] as a power management control algorithm for building air conditioners to automatically adapt to various air conditioning environments in office buildings. In general, reinforcement learning requires thousands to tens of thousands of trials before the control performance reaches the practical range, and an unrealistically long learning period is required if the learning is performed directly on the actual building.

In order to shorten the learning period in the actual building, we attempted transfer learning approach [6] in which the model is trained using a virtual control target on a computer and then transferred the knowledge to the actual environment.

In this study, a virtual building is developed using an emulator which simulates the dynamic characteristics of the power and room temperature of a building multi-type air-conditioner, and pre-learning is performed on the virtual building to shorten the learning period after the transfer to the actual building. Since there is a difference in the air-conditioning environment (heat load, heat capacity, etc.) between the virtual building and the actual building, we propose a method in which pre-training is performed on multiple virtual buildings in parallel, and the closest virtual building is selected from among them using the difference in immediate reward when training on the actual building.

Experiments on actual buildings are not reproducible and it is difficult to compare with normal operation under the same conditions. Therefore, we confirmed the effectiveness of the proposed method in shortening the learning period by using a virtual building.

## 2 Power Consumption Management System for Building Multi-type Air-Conditioners

Building multi-type air-conditioners, also called VRFs [7], are distributed type air-conditioning system which is widely used in Japan and Asia, especially in small and medium-sized office buildings. In this air-conditioning system, one outdoor unit supplies refrigerant to multiple indoor units, and there are usually several to several dozen outdoor units and several dozen to several hundred indoor units in one office building. Each indoor unit independently controls the refrigerant flow rate, and the refrigerant piping length reaches tens to hundreds of meters, so the pressure and temperature in the refrigerant piping changes in an extremely complicated manner. The refrigerant compressor in outdoor unit accounts for about 90% of the power consumption of the air-conditioning system.

In the power management and control system for building multi-type air-conditioners, it is necessary to manage the power of dozens of outdoor units and room temperature of hundreds of indoor units, which vary in a complicated manner.

In this paper, we assume that the Building Energy Management System (BEMS) determines the hourly power target at the beginning of each day, which is determined by the annual power rate target set by the building manager or the contracted power amount with the power company. Based on this target power amount, the BEMS sends

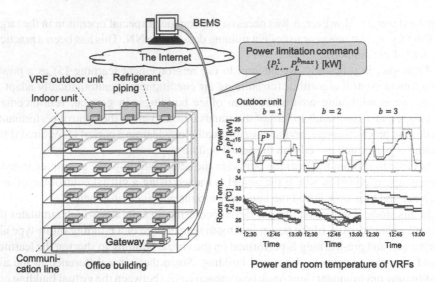

**Fig. 1.** Power consumption management of building multi-type air-conditioners.

power limitation commands $P_L^b$ to each outdoor unit $b$ of the building multi-type air-conditioning system in 10-min intervals to manage and control the power consumption of each outdoor unit, as shown in Fig. 1. At this time, even when there is room for a one-hour target, depending on the location within the building, there may be cases where it is desirable to reduce power consumption even at the slightest sacrifice of room temperature comfort, for example, in entrances and warehouses, and cases where it is desirable to maintain room temperature, for example in server rooms. In other words, the BEMS needs to manage three things: electricity rates in 10-min intervals, room temperature comfort, and the target amount of electricity per hour.

In this research, reinforcement learning algorithm is applied to the power management control for every 10 min and controls the above according to the room temperature priority. However, as we mentioned, reinforcement learning requires several thousand to several tens of thousands of trials and training before the control reaches a practical level, and the training period for the control of every 10 min reaches several years.

Therefore, we created a virtual building that simulates an actual building on a computer in advance to conduct preliminary learning, and then transfer the model to the actual building. In this study, we aim to complete the transfer learning in about 20 days of one summer season.

# 3   Reinforcement Learning for Building Multi-type Air-Conditioners

## 3.1   Q-Learning Control

In this study, Q-learning [8], which is one of the reinforcement learning algorithms, is used for the power management control of building multi-type air-conditioners. We call this control Q-Learning Control (QLC). The state-action value function of QLC is as follows.

$$Q[s(m), a(m)] \leftarrow (1 - \alpha)Q[s(m), a(m)]$$
$$+ \alpha\left\{r(m) + \gamma \min_{a} Q[s(m+1), a(m+1)]\right\} \qquad (1)$$

Here, $Q[s(m), a(m)]$ is the action value function, which represents the value of taking action $a(m)$ in state $s(m)$. $\leftarrow$ denotes the update of the value. The update cycle is $\tau_m = 10$ min, where $m$ is the control frame number which increments every $\tau_m$. $\alpha$ is the learning rate and $\gamma$ is the discount rate. $r(m)$ is the reward and calculated using the evaluation function described in the next section.

In this paper, the state vector $s(m)$ and action value $a(m)$ are as follows.

$$s(m) = \left[T_O(m), T_{SA}^b(m), \hat{W}_{WCAP}^b(m+1)\right]^T \qquad (2)$$

$$a(m) = P_L^b(m+1) \qquad (3)$$

Here, $T_O(m)$ is the outdoor temperature [°C], $T_{SA}^b(m)$ is the average room temperature deviation [°C], and $\hat{W}_{WCAP}^b(m+1)$ is the current residual power [kWh] of one hour. $T_O$ is discretized into three steps, and $T_{SA}^b$ and $\hat{W}_{WCAP}^b$ are discretized into six steps. $P_L^b(m+1)$ represents the power limit command value [kW] for the next control frame, discretized into six steps from 0 to 100% in 20% increments. The $T_{SA}^b(m)$ represent the difference between the set room temperature and the measured room temperature, and it is calculated by the following equation.

$$T_{SA}^b(m) = \frac{\sum_{i=1}^{N_{IU}} C_{Pi}^b\left[T_{Ai}^b(m) - T_{Si}^b(m)\right]}{\sum_{i=1}^{N_{IU}} C_{Pi}^b} \qquad (4)$$

Here, $N_{IU}$ is the number of indoor units, $C_{Pi}^b$ is the rated cooling capacity [kW], $T_{Ai}^b$ is the room temperature [°C], and $T_{Si}^b$ is the set temperature [°C] of indoor unit $i$ connected to outdoor unit $b$.

## 3.2 Definition of Evaluation Function

In this chapter, an evaluation function $J_{QLC}^b$ is defined to calculate the reward of QLC. The evaluation function has three indexes, the electricity price, room temperature comfort, and the excess of the one-hour target power consumption amount.

$$J_{QLC}^b = \alpha^b Y^b(m) + \left(1 - \alpha^b\right)Z^b(m) + \beta^b X^b(m) \qquad (5)$$

where $\alpha^b$ is the balance coefficient between economy and comfort, $\beta^b$ is the excess penalty coefficient for the target electricity quantity, $Y^b(m)$ is the electricity price penalty,

$Z^b(m)$ is the room temperature penalty and $X^b(m)$ is the excess electricity penalty. $Y^b(m)$, $Z^b(m)$ and $X^b(m)$ are calculated by the following euations.

$$Y_{QLC}^b(m) = \frac{1}{R_{max}W_{10max}^b}R(m)W_{10}^b(m) \tag{6}$$

$$Z_{QLC}^b(m) = \left[T_{SA}^b(m)\right]^2 \tag{7}$$

$$X_{QLC}^a(m) = W_{EX}^b(m)^2 \tag{8}$$

Here, $R(m)$ is the unit price of electricity [JPY], $W_{10}^b(m)$ is 10-min power consumption [kWh]. $R_{max}$ and $W_{10max}^b$ are constants for normalization. $W_{EX}^b$ denotes the normalized power excess and is defined by the following equation.

$$if \ W_{10}^b(m) > W_{WCAP}^b(m) \ then \ W_{EX}^b = \frac{W_{10}^b(m) - W_{WCAP}^b(m)}{W_{10max}^b}$$
$$otherwise \ W_{EX}^b = 0 \tag{9}$$

$W_{WCAP}^b$ is the amount of residual power [kWh].

Since $J_{QLC}^b$ is a penalty function (low value means good control), the immediate reward $r^b$ of QLC is calculated by subtracting $J_{QLC}^b$ from the offset value $J_{offset}$.

$$r^b(m) = J_{offsetQLC} - J_{QLC}^b(m) \tag{10}$$

We also define the control score $S_{QLC}$ to evaluate learning progress.

$$S_{QLC} = \frac{r_D - r_{DN}}{r_{DEND} - r_{DN}} \times 10 + 80 \tag{11}$$

where $r_D$ is the total daily reward of $r_{QLC}^b(m)$, $r_{DN}$ is the total daily reward of normal operation, and $r_{DEND}$ is the total daily reward when learning saturated, respectively. 80 points of $S_{QLC}$ means that the control performance of the QLC is equivalent to normal operation, and 90 points means that the control performance reaches equivalent to completion of learning.

# 4    Virtual Building

## 4.1    Dynamic Model of Building Multi-type Air-Conditioner

In this chapter, we define a mathematical model which simulates the power consumption and the room temperature of building multi-type air-conditioner. The power change of outdoor unit is simulated by the following equation.

$$P(t + \Delta t) = P(t) + D(t)\Delta t \tag{12}$$

$$D(t) = S_{OV}^{PL} D_{DWN} + \left(1 - S_{OV}^{PL}\right) \left\{ S_{OV}^{P*} D_{DWN} + \left(1 - S_{OV}^{P*}\right) S_{FR}^{PL} S_{FR}^{P*} D_{UP} \right\} \tag{13}$$

Here, $t$ is a discrete time [s] and $\Delta t$ is the simulation time step [s], where $\Delta t = 10$ [s] in this study. $P(t)$ is an electric power [kW], $D(t)$ is a power change rate [kW/s], $S_{OV}^{PL}$ and $S_{FR}^{PL}$ are the state (0 or 1) of the electric power relative to the power limitation command value $P_L$ [kW], and $S_{OV}^{P*}$ and $S_{FR}^{P*}$ are the status (0 or 1) for the power required for temperature control $P^*(t)$ [kW].

$P^*(t)$ is calculated by a multiple regression equation created by extracting the variables that contribute to the determination of the electric power required for temperature control [9].

The room temperature $T_{Ai}$ [°C] of each indoor unit $i$ is calculated by the following equations.

$$T_{Ai}(t + \Delta t) = T_{Ai}(t) + \Delta T_{Ai}(t)\Delta t \tag{14}$$

$$\Delta T_{Ai}(t) = \frac{1}{C_{Hi}}(Q_{Li}(t) - Q_{ACi}(t)) \tag{15}$$

where $\Delta T_{Ai}(t)$ is the room temperature change rate [°C/s], $C_{Hi}$ is the heat capacity [kW/°C], $Q_{Li}(t)$ is the heat load [kW], and $Q_{ACi}(t)$ is the cooling power of the indoor unit [kW]. The air-conditioning power of the indoor unit, $Q_{ACi}(t)$, is obtained by distributing the air conditioning capacity of the outdoor unit, $Q_{AC}(t)$ [kW], according to the following equations.

$$Q_{ACi}(t) = \frac{S_{THi}C_{Pi}}{\sum_{i=1}^{N_{IU}} S_{THi}C_{Pi}} Q_{AC}(t) \tag{16}$$

$$Q_{AC}(t) = k_{COP}\eta_{COP}P(t) \tag{17}$$

Here, $\eta_{COP}$ is the COP (Coefficient Of Performance) of the outdoor unit, $k_{COP}$ is the COP correction factor based on the outdoor temperature, the total capacity of running indoor unit, and the refrigerant piping length. The $S_{THi}$ is the refrigerant supply state (0 or 1). When the room temperature of the indoor unit reaches the set temperature $T_{Si}$ − 0.5 °C, the electronic expansion valve (EEV) of the relevant indoor unit closes, and the refrigerant supply is stopped ($S_{THi} = 0$). When the room temperature raised up and reached $T_{Si} + 0.5$ °C, the EEV opens ($S_{THi} = 1$).

The heat load $Q_{Li}(t)$ is composed by the following equation.

$$Q_{Li}(t) = Q_{oi}(t) + Q_{Ri}(t) + Q_{Ii}(t) + Q_{Vi}(t) + Q_{Ci}(t) + U_3 \tag{18}$$

Here, $Q_{oi}(t)$ is the heat transfer from exterior walls [kW], $Q_{Ri}(t)$ is the solar radiation load through windows [kW], $Q_{Ii}(t)$ is the internal heat load [kW], $Q_{Vi}(t)$ is the ventilation load [kW], $Q_{Ci}(t)$ is the mutual heat load (cross-effect) with the adjacent indoor unit air-conditioning area, and $U_3$ is the term to simulate the minute-by-minute heat load fluctuation.

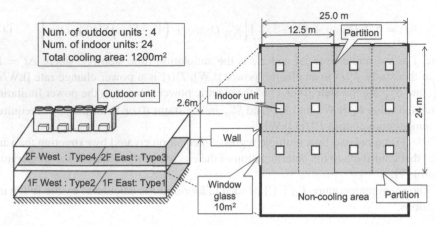

**Fig. 2.** Configuration of the virtual building.

**Table 1.** Specifications of air-conditioners installed in the virtual building.

| Air-con. type | $P_{Rat}$ | $Q_{ACRat}$ | $C_{Pi} \times N_{IU}$ |
|---|---|---|---|
| Type1 | 13.3 kW | 45 kW | 8.0 kW × 6 |
| Type2 | 15.0 kW | 45 kW | 8.0 kW × 5<br>7.1 kW × 1 |
| Type3 | 20.8 kW | 68 kW | 11.2 kW × 6 |
| Type4 | 25.4 kW | 73 kW | 14.0 kW × 5<br>5.6 kW × 1 |

### 4.2 Development of Virtual Building

By using the above mathmatical model, we have created a "virtual building" that assumes a typical office building. The configuration of the virtual building is shown in Fig. 2. The building is a two-story office building with four different types of air-conditioners of Type 1 to Type 4. The specifiacitons of each air-conditioner are shown in Table 1. In the Table 1, $Q_{ACRat}$ is the rated cooling capacity [kW], $P_{Rat}$ is the rated power consumption [kW].

The floors of the virtual building are divided into two by a central partition, and two systems of building multi-type air-conditioners are installed on each floor.

## 5    Multi-track Method

In general, it is difficult to accurately grasp the air-conditioning environment such as heat load or heat capacity of the actual building in advance, and there are some differences between the virtual building and the actual buildings. If these differences are large, the effect of shortening learning period by pre-learning in the virtual building will deteriorate, and it will be difficult to complete the transfer learning in 20 days of summer.

Therefore, as shown in Fig. 3, we prepare multiple derived virtual buildings that assume different air-conditioning environments in advance and complete the pre-learning in each derived virtual building. The learning process in each virtual building is called a "Track". When learning in the actual building, the nearest Track will be selected by comparing difference of immediate rewards of Q-learning, and its state action value will be used for transfer learning. For this selection, we used the reward distance $L_{Rx}$, as the following equation.

$$L_{Rx} = \sqrt{\frac{\sum_{a=1}^{N_a} \sum_{s=1}^{N_s} V_{ACT}(s,a) V_{TRx}(s,a)\{(r_{ACT}(s,a) - r_{TRx}(s,a))\}^2}{\sum_{a}^{N_a} \sum_{s}^{N_s} V_{ACT}(s,a) V_{TRx}(s,a)}} \quad (19)$$

Here, $N_a$ is the number of discretization steps of state $s$ and $N_a$ is the number of discretization steps of action $a$. $V_{TRx}(s,a)$ is the visit experience of the state action pair $(s,a)$ on the pre-training Track $x$ (with visit: 1, without visit: 0), and $V_{ACT}(s,a)$ is the visit experience of the state action pair in the actual building (with visit: 1, without visit: 0). $r_{ACT}(s,a)$ is the average reward in the actual building, $r_{TRx}(s,a)$ is the average reward of the state action pair $(s,a)$ of the Track $x$. We call $r_{ACT}(s,a)$ and $r_{TRx}(s,a)$ "r-Table" and their state action values $Q_{ACT}(s,a)$ and $Q_{TRx}(s,a)$ the "Q-Table".

The reason why r-Table is used for comparison instead of the Q-Table is as follows. If the future state action value is not estimated correctly, the current state action value will also not be estimated correctly, and it will take long time to obtain the correct shape of Q-Table. When the correct state action value is obtained in the actual building, it means that learning has already been completed. The immediate reward can be compared regardless of the learning state of the state action value.

Each day, after the end of the day's control, the Track with the smallest $L_{Rx}$ is selected. Then, the next day, $Q_{TRx}(s,a)$ of the nearest Track is taken over for control.

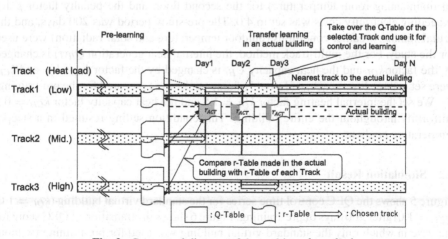

**Fig. 3.** Conceptual diagram of the multi-track method.

As shown in the Fig. 4, immediately after the start of transfer learning on the actual building, $r_{ACT}(s,a)$ has many parts that have not yet been updated, and because the

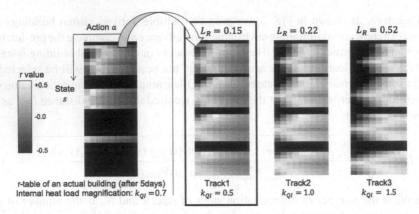

Fig. 4. An example of selection of the nearest track.

values are stored differently from the average reward due to the uncertainty of the air-conditioner, but as the $r_{ACT}(s, a)$ takes shape, a track with heat load characteristics closer to those of the actual building is gradually selected.

# 6 Simulation

## 6.1 Simulation Settings

Since the actual machine test is not reproducible, we conducted a simulation using a virtual building to evaluate the learning progress of the QLC. The evaluation function $\alpha^b$ is set to 0.8 (emphasis on reducing electricity costs) for the first floor and 0.2 (emphasis on maintaining room temperature) for the second floor, and the penalty factor $\beta$ for exceeding electricity costs was set to 4.0. The pre-study period was 200 days, and the actual summer weather conditions (outdoor temperature and solar radiation) were used for the study. For the multi-track method, the internal heat generation $Q_{Ii}(t)$ is changed by the factor $k_{QI}$ and the heat capacity $C_{Hi}$ is changed by the factor $k_{CH}$. $k_{QI}$ and $k_{CH}$ were set to three levels each, and a total of nine tracks were prepared for the pre-training.

We set the internal heating factor $k_{QI} = 1.5$ and the heat capacity factor $k_{CH} = 0.5$ uniformly throughout the entire building. This condition setting resulted in a steeper temperature gradient.

## 6.2 Simulation Result

Figure 5 shows the QLC control time series for the standard virtual building ($k_{QI} = 1.0$, $k_{CH} = 1.0$) after 200 days of pre-training. Figure 6 shows the transition of QLC score for the case in which only the standard virtual building was used for pre-training (without the multitrack method). Figure 7 shows the simulation results for the case in which the multi-track method is used.

As shown in the QLC time series in the Fig. 5, the first floor allowed the room temperature to rise and reduced the power consumption, while the second floor kept the

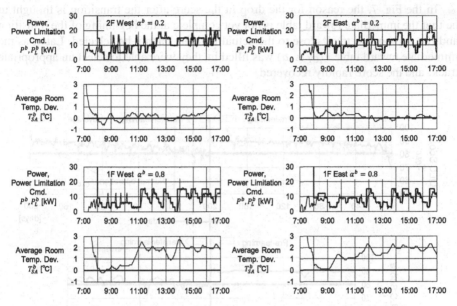

**Fig. 5.** Time series of power and room temperature controlled by the QLC.

average room temperature deviation $T_{SA}^b$ within $+1$ °C, which was the intended control of the evaluation function.

In the case of using only the standard virtual building (without the multitrack method) shown in the Fig. 6, the score does not improve 20 days after the start of transfer learning and remains around 80 points, which is equivalent to normal operation. After that, the score slowly recovers, and it takes almost 8 years (3600 times) to reach the 90-point level. In contrast, with the multi-track method shown in the Fig. 7, the mean score reached the 90-point level within 20 days, and the variance $\pm1\sigma$ was within 80 points.

## 7 Discussion

As shown in the Fig. 6, when there is a large difference between the air-conditioning characteristics of the virtual building and those of the actual building, pre-learning in the virtual building shows little effect in reducing the number of learning days. This is because it takes time to change the shape of the behavioral value function $Q_{ACT}(s, a)$ surface, since the simple Q-learning used in this study updates only one state-action pair per one step of learning.

In the Fig. 7, the reason for the drop in the score after the transition is thought to be that the immediate reward table is not yet complete at the beginning of the transition and the appropriate track close to the actual building cannot be selected. Later, as the immediate reward table $r_{ACT}(s, a)$ was filled in, they were able to select an appropriate track, and the score rapidly recovered.

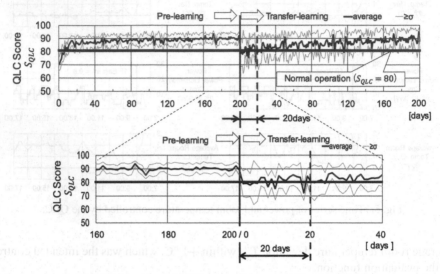

**Fig. 6.** Transition of QLC score without multi-track method.

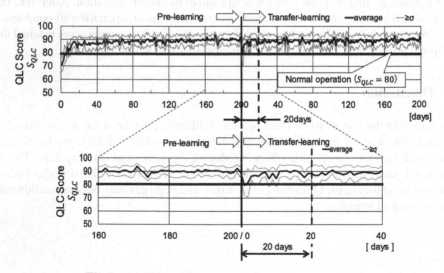

**Fig. 7.** Transition of QLC score with multi-track method.

In this study, we created tracks with only heat capacity and internal heat generation load, but it is also possible to create tracks with other parameters such as ventilation. Since the number of tracks increases exponentially with the number of parameters, it should be noted that the computation time for pre-learning will also increase accordingly. It is necessary to decide which parameters should be selected as tracks by carefully observing how much the parameters affect the control performance.

Even if the number of tracks is increased, the impact on the computation time in the actual building control is expected to be negligible because the multi-track method simply compares r-Tables, $r_{ACT}(s, a)$ with $r_{TRx}(s, a)$.

## 8  Conclusion

In this paper, power management control of building multi-type air-conditioners based on Q-learning algorithm is described. We define a virtual building consisting of dynamic models of electric power and room temperature. In addition to using virtual buildings for pre-training, we proposed the multi-track method of which multiple pre-training sessions are conducted using virtual buildings with different heat load and heat capacity, and verified the effectiveness of the method by simulation.

From the result, we confirmed the multi-track method enabled the power management control to reach the practical level within 20 days.

In the future, we will study more about the parameter combination of the tracks and the algorithm to determine the hourly target power consumption.

## References

1. Council of Australian Governments (COAG) National Strategy on Energy Efficiency: Best Practice Maintenance & Operation of HVAC Systems for Energy Efficiency and Resources, pp. 1–88 (2012)
2. Yu, L., Qin, S., Zhang, M., Shen, C., Jiang, T., Guan, X.: A review of deep reinforcement learning for smart building energy management. IEEE Internet Things J. **8**(15), 12046–12063 (2021)
3. Han, Y., Kim, W.: Development and validation of building control algorithm energy management. Buildings **11**(131), 1–33 (2021)
4. Aoki, Y., Ito, H., Ninagawa, C., Morikawa, J.: Smart grid real-time pricing optimization control with simulated annealing algorithm for office building air-conditioning facilities. In: IEEE International Conference on Industry Technology, Lyon, France, pp. 1309–1313 (2018)
5. Sutton, R.S., Barto, A.G.: Reinforcement Learning: An Introduction. The MIT Press, Cambridge (1998)
6. Pan, J., Yang, Q.: A survey on transfer learning. IEEE Trans. Knowl. Data Eng. **22**(10), 1345–1359 (2010)
7. Goetzler, W.: Variable refrigerant flow systems. ASHRAE J. (2007)
8. Watkins, C.J.C.H., Dayan, P.: Technical note: Q-learning. Mach. Learn. **8**, 279–292 (1992)
9. Matsukawa, S., Ninagawa, C., Morikawa, J., Inaba, T., Kondo, S.: Stable segment method for multiple linear regression on baseline estimation for smart grid fast automated demand response. In: IEEE Innovative Smart Grid Technologies ISGT-Asia, Chengdu, China, pp. 2571–2576 (2019)

# Predicting Seriousness of Injury in a Traffic Accident: A New Imbalanced Dataset and Benchmark

Paschalis Lagias, George D. Magoulas[iD], Ylli Prifti[iD], and Alessandro Provetti[✉][iD]

Birkbeck College, University of London, London, UK
plagia01@dcs.bbk.ac.uk, {g.magoulas,a.provetti}@bbk.ac.uk

**Abstract.** The paper introduces a new dataset to assess the performance of machine learning algorithms in the prediction of the seriousness of injury in a traffic accident. The dataset is created by aggregating publicly available datasets from the UK Department for Transport, which are drastically imbalanced with missing attributes sometimes approaching 50% of the overall data dimensionality. The paper presents the data analysis pipeline starting from the publicly available data of road traffic accidents and ending with predictors of possible injuries and their degree of severity. It addresses the huge incompleteness of public data with a MissForest model. The paper also introduces two baseline approaches to create injury predictors: a supervised artificial neural network and a reinforcement learning model. The dataset can potentially stimulate diverse aspects of machine learning research on imbalanced datasets and the two approaches can be used as baseline references when researchers test more advanced learning algorithms in this area.

**Keywords:** Class imbalance · Data imputation · Feature engineering · Neural networks · Reinforcement learning · Q–learning · Traffic accidents

## 1 Introduction

Nowadays detailed information about traffic accidents is becoming available for independent analysis. Authorities that collect such data may release, along with traditional statistical aggregations, actual data points that are a rich source of information. Apart from time, location, number of vehicles involved and similar factual information, the data record often concerns subjective measures such as the severity of the accident, which is annotated by trained traffic police officers.

In the UK, the Department for Transport (DfT) aggregates and releases a dataset of reference with many details about each accident recorded. While data are available, there is a huge imbalance in the information provided between many minor events, e.g., collisions in parking lots, and the– fortunately less frequent– major events that involve hospitalisation or worse.

© Springer Nature Switzerland AG 2022
L. Iliadis et al. (Eds.): EANN 2022, CCIS 1600, pp. 412–423, 2022.
https://doi.org/10.1007/978-3-031-08223-8_34

Several researchers have examined parts of the UK's DfT traffic accident data in order to answer a variety of research questions. Among them, when it comes to predicting accident severity, [1,2,5] and [6], a central research question is: *"in the scenario of a traffic accident with injuries, how severe is the injury going to be, based on available data on accident conditions, vehicle information etc. ?"* Studies, like the ones cited above, have focused on analysing a specific year or period of traffic data and although they have considered accident severity in general, they did not focus on predicting the seriousness of injuries. This problem comes across as being very challenging because the DfT considers that severity of injury is a *triage*, namely slight, serious, or fatal[1], which leads to a highly-imbalanced distribution of data that impacts the prediction accuracy, especially over minority classes (e.g. fatal accidents), of the methods tested.

Thus the paper considers the prediction of the seriousness of injury as an imbalanced multi–class classification problem. It extends previous work, [1,2, 5] and [6], by applying a systematic data analysis and processing pipeline to combine data from disparate sources of the UK's DfT from years 2005–2018 in order to create a new larger dataset. The pipeline incorporates components for data imputation, based on domain knowledge and the predictive power of variants of Random Forests, and feature importance analysis components, which use categorical feature correlation, mutual feature information and $\chi^2$–tests, with more detailed description of each pipeline component to be presented in a later section.

Lastly, the paper proposes two evaluation approaches to create machine learning predictors using the new dataset. These could be used as baseline references when designing machine learning methods to predict the seriousness of injuries in the scenario of a traffic accident given certain accident conditions, such as involved vehicle information and some personals details (anonymised) of the potentially-injured person and so on.

The rest of the paper is organised as follows. Section 2 presents relevant work, while Sect. 3 describes the data sources that were used. Section 4 describes the components of the pipeline that were used to create the new dataset. The baseline models are presented in Sect. 5, and their evaluation is presented in Sect. 6. The paper ends with conclusions in Sect. 7.

## 2    Relevant Work

UK traffic accident datasets are imbalanced with several missing attributes. Previous studies, [1,2,5,6], attempted to deal with the challenges in these data by limiting the dimensionality of the problem, focusing for example on data from a specific year or period, exploring the potential of specific subsets of attributes that were available across all data points considered, or by transforming the multi–class problem into a binary one. Although overall satisfactory accuracy was produced, all models experienced very low accuracy over minority classes.

---

[1] "Instruction for the completion of accident reports", Dept. for Transport (2005).

More relevant to this paper is the recent effort in [5], where the authors used a variety of tools, such as different statistical methods and Machine Learning (ML) algorithms, in the search for the right "mix" of feature selection and ML algorithm that would provide good predictors for accident severity. The best results were achieved by Random Forests (RFs) running over an input of 14 different features, from, e.g., the age of the driver to the weather conditions. A RF achieved an overall accuracy of 85.08% with 15.12%, 22.03% and 96.58% correct prediction for the fatal, serious and slight class of injuries, respectively. However, the experiments used only c. 136k records from accidents reported in 2016, which is rather limited given the availability of data reported by the DfT[2].

In comparison to that approach, and others cited above, this paper describes a pipeline that includes acquiring, data-cleaning, and inputing long-term accident data (2005–2018) to create a new large dataset for multi–class classification. This can potentially enable ML methods to pick up small fluctuations or relatively rare events (e.g. did not appear in 2015 or 2016), but can determine a non-trivial amount of accident cases, such as ice on the road that does appear only sporadically in the UK but certainly determines a spike in the number and gravity of accidents. Furthermore, the dataset is expanded horizontally by including many new features, in search for non-standard influences.

## 3  Data Sources

The UK's Department for Transport publishes three datasets per year, uploaded in the *Road Safety Data* webpage of the data.gov.uk website:

- **Accidents**, with variables related to accident conditions. Each accident is identified by a unique accident ID, called "Accident Index".
- **Vehicles**, with variables related to vehicle characteristics, driver information and driver action before the accident. Each vehicle is identified with a unique vehicle reference number, "Vehicle Reference", and linked with accidents dataset through an "Accident Index".
- **Casualties**: information about injured individuals, linking an injury with accidents and vehicles through "Accident Index" and "Vehicle Reference".

The paper exploits DfT data from 2005 to 2018, with data from 2019 used for testing. Table 1 shows data distribution in the new aggregated dataset, highlighting the drastic imbalance among the target classes data.

**Table 1.** Distribution of casualty severity in the new aggregated DfT data.

| Slight | 2,539,715 | 87.10% |
|---|---|---|
| Serious | 345,997 | 11.87% |
| Fatal | 30,171 | 1.03% |

[2] https://data.gov.uk/dataset/cb7ae6f0-4be6-4935-9277-47e5ce24a11f/road-safety-data.

# 4    Creating the Dataset

The first phase in creating the new dataset involved accessing and merging data from disparate sources into a single dataset. Next, the work dealt with missing values, running missing value imputation, whenever possible, and assessing the potential importance of each feature for the classification phase.

Imputation was based on domain knowledge and the predictive power of Random Forests. With regards to assessing the potential importance of each feature, which is relevant for machine learning classifiers, various techniques were used. Since most of the variables are nominal, $\chi^2$–tests, Cramer's mutual information, and Theil's U coefficients were used [9]. For correlation of numerical features with nominal ones, the ANOVA test and correlation ratios [9] were computed. Once feature importance analysis and imputation are completed, data can be transformed to an input suitable for classification methods. The details of the data analysis pipeline are presented below.

## 4.1    Dataset Merging

A fragment of the variables for the three datasets (Accidents, Vehicles, Casualties), starting from 2005 and up to 2018, is shown in Table 2, where the target variable, "Casualty Severity", is shown in italics. The datasets were merged by using Accident Index and Vehicle Reference as "foreign keys": using Vehicle Reference, each casualty was matched with a vehicle; pedestrians were matched with vehicles that caused their injury. Next, the output records of the above join were matched with accidents using Accident Index. The final output consists of 2,915,883 data points and 66 variables/features in total (cf. with Table 1).

**Table 2.** Dataset variables

| Accidents | Vehicles | Casualties |
|---|---|---|
| Accident index | Accident index | Accident index |
| Location easting OSGR | Vehicle reference | Vehicle reference |
| Location northing OSGR | Vehicle type | Casualty reference |
| Longitude | Towing and articulation | Casualty class |
| Latitude | Vehicle manoeuvre | Sex of casualty |
| Police force | Vehicle location-restricted lane | Age of casualty |
| Accident severity | Junction location | Age band of casualty |
| Number of vehicles | Skidding and overturning | *Casualty severity* |
| ... | ... | ... |

## 4.2   Dealing with Missing Values

Once merged, the DfT data turned out to be of rather poor quality with only 411,158 data points containing all necessary information, i.e., 86% of the available data points had at least one missing variable value.

Most of the variables in the dataset are categorical with integer encoding, and missing values are represented with $-1$. In addition, some variables include encoding for "unknown" as a separate category, e.g. like the feature Weather Conditions. Initially, the following features were dropped:

- **Accident Index, Vehicle Ref. and Casualty Ref.**: administrative references that are not useful for classification.
- **Age Band of Driver and Age Band of Casualty**: data already include ages for casualties and drivers.
- **Latitude, Longitude and LSOA of Accident Location**: data already include Eastings and Northings.
- **Did Police attend the Scene of the Accident, Accident Severity and Number of Casualties**: post-accident information is not included in the research.
- **Road Maintenance Worker, Journey Purpose of Driver and Engine Capacity**: these variables have an excessive number of either missing, "unknown" or "not applicable" values. Regarding Engine Capacity, many of the available values were found to be inconsistent with the Vehicle Types.

Lastly, for Urban or Rural Area, Sex of Casualty, Sex of Driver, Pedestrian Location, Pedestrian Movement and Light Conditions, all values for "unknown" were re-encoded as missing values with $-1$.

## 4.3   Missing-value Imputations Based on Domain Knowledge

Domain knowledge was derived from available DfT documentation about accident data gathering and relevant guidelines. That was further informed by critical analysis and reasonable assumptions based on the known variables, and used for manual imputation of the missing values as follows:

- Missing values for Car Passenger, which were related to Casualty Type of buses and vans, were replaced with "Not car passenger" value.
- It was assumed that bicycles, motorcycles and mobility scooters have no Towing or Articulation.
- Bicycles, horses, motorcycles and trams cannot be classified as left or right hand drive vehicles. A new category was created for "unknown".
- Many missing values for Junction Location, Junction Detail, Junction Control and 2nd Road Class were corrected, as they referred to accidents that did not occurred near a junction.
- Some missing values for Age of Driver, Age of Casualty, Casualty Home Area Type and Driver Home Area Type were corrected by checking samples where the casualty was the driver.

– All missing values for light conditions were set to "Daylight" after checking Time value of the accident.

Lastly, data points where Eastings, Northings or Time values were missing were dropped from the data. The result of this phase was a record with 53 features and 2,915,387 data points; still 1,471,895 data points, or 50.49% of the total, had one or more missing values.

## 4.4   Time Processing, Feature Correlation and Feature Importance

The next step in the pipeline was to inspect the numerical variables of the produced dataset, assess the importance of features and measure possible correlations and collinearities among variables.

Variables Date and Time were discarded after they were converted into new variables Hour, Month and Year. Next, the following features were treated as numerical: Number of Vehicles, Speed Limit, Age of Casualty, Age of Vehicle, Age of Driver, Location Easting OSGR and Location Northing OSGR. All remaining variables were treated as nominal and represented by discrete values without any form of intrinsic ranking. Casualty Severity, the target variable, is also nominal.

Due to the mixture of nominal and numerical variables in the data, various feature selection and correlation metrics were used (the threshold for considering two features as highly correlated was set to 0.7), depending on the combination of examined features:

– Pearson's correlation was calculated for all pairs of numerical variables.
– A $\chi^2$–squared statistic and mutual information between each categorical variable and Casualty Severity were used to assess the importance of each categorical variables wrt. the target variable.
– the ANOVA F–statistic was calculated to assess the importance of each numerical variable with respect to Casualty Severity.
– Correlation Ratio coefficient for each pair of categorical–numerical variables was employed to check possible correlation in input variables, and confirm the importance of numerical variables wrt. Casualty Severity.
– Cramer's V and Theil's U correlation were calculated for each pair of categorical variables to detect any correlation among input variables. Unlike the rest of correlation coefficients, Theil's U is anti-symmetrical and is based on mutual information (entropy) between two variables.

After assessing features importance, Casualty Type, Vehicle Type and Vehicle Manoeuvre were found to be the most important categorical variables, while Number of Vehicles and Speed Limit were the most important numerical ones. On the opposite end, Carriageway Hazards, Was Vehicle Left Hand Drive and Pedestrian Crossing-Human Control were the least important categorical variables; Eastings and Northings were the least important numerical ones.

Lastly, analysis of feature importance and computation of correlation revealed that:

- Variables Police Force, Local Authority (District), Local Authority (Highway), Eastings and Northings are highly correlated. Only Local Authority (District) was kept as it was found important wrt. Casualty Severity.
- Casualty Type is highly correlated with Casualty Class and Vehicle Type, and it was dropped.
- Variables Casualty Home Area Type and Driver Home Area Type are highly correlated with each other, so the former was dropped.
- Variables 1st Road Number and 2nd Road Number were dropped due to their high cardinality.

### 4.5    Imputation with MissForest

The MissForest algorithm [8] was used to obtain missing–value imputation. MissForest is a type of Random Forest algorithm suitable for handling high–dimensional datasets with mixed data types (categorical and numerical), which is exactly our case. Given the size of the dataset and taking into consideration memory requirements, the procedure was applied iteratively:

1. Speed Limit and Weather Conditions were initially imputed, based on non-missing variables, to increase the number of complete rows.
2. The remaining variables were divided in groups based on topic: Junctions and road classes, Pedestrians, Vehicle–site interaction, Drivers–vehicles, Age of Vehicle and Driver IMD Decile.
3. For each imputed variable, 100 trees were grown.

MissForest imputation produces a new dataset with 2,915,387 data points and 49 features. Note that Casualty Type, Casualty Home Area Type, Police Force and Local Authority (Highway) were excluded from the imputation process. After missing–value imputation was completed, the remaining "unimportant" and highly–correlated features listed in Sect. 4.4 were removed.

## 5    Baseline Models

In this section two approaches are described to create predictors of the seriousness of injury. Creating optimal, or fine–tuned models, is out–of–scope for this article. Instead the aim is to provide a point of reference for researchers to further explore this dataset using machine learning methods. First, supervised learning using a neural network classifier is considered, and then a non–traditional form of learning by reinforcement using Deep–Q Network is explored.

### 5.1    A Supervised Learning Model

A small number of preliminary experiments were conducted to identify an architecture that performs reasonably well, given the imbalanced nature of the dataset, but no serious attempt was made to optimise model or training algorithm hyperparameters. The outcome was a densely–connected artificial neural network (ANN) implemented in Keras with TensorFlow backend:

- **Hidden layers and neurons:** two or three hidden layers were used, with some of the best results presented in the next section.
- **Output layer:** three nodes representing the three classes used by the DfT.
- **Activation functions:** ReLU activations for hidden–layer nodes and Softmax activations for output nones.
- **Optimiser:** the Adam optimiser was used in all experiments.
- **Batch size:** 512 showed better behaviour than 128 or 256.
- **Early stopping:** experimented with 5 and 20 epochs of early stopping.
- **Weight initialisation:** both Glorot and He uniform were tested.
- **Loss function:** the sparse categorical cross entropy was adopted.
- **Class weights:** since the distribution of Casualty Severity is heavily imbalanced, different class weights were tried. The vector of class weights was initially computed as $\frac{|samples|}{|classes|*|frequencies|}$.

## 5.2  A Reinforcement Learning Model

Reinforcement Learning (RL) is not traditionally applied to classification problems, but recent work has shown that it is possible to formulate a classification task as a sequential decision-making problem and solve it with a deep Q–learning network [7]. Moreover, empirical studies demonstrated that this approach can reach strong performance, outperforming other imbalance classification methods, especially when there is high class imbalance [7]. Our RL model followed this approach and was implemented in OpenAI Gym:

1. **Environment:** This was defined as the dataset itself, including the following attributes:
   - **Observation space:** the size of a data sample.
   - **Action space:** taking an action as equivalent of a class prediction, there are three possible actions, one per prediction: slight, serious or fatal.
   - **Step counter:** an integer to track the number of steps the agent has taken in the environment within the same episode.
   - **Weighted action rewards:** a different reward can be earned for correct classification of each class data sample.
   - **Reset function:** it resets the environment at the end of the episode– shuffling data; resetting step counter; retrieving the first training sample.
   - **Step:** a function that makes a Casualty Severity prediction, collects reward and checks if the episode is done. If so, it moves to the next training sample; otherwise, the environment is reset.
2. **Episode:** it starts when the first training sample is read, and it ends when all training samples are classified, or a minority class sample is misclassified.
3. **Reward function:** the recommendations of [7] were followed:

$$
reward = \begin{cases}
1 & if \; label = \; fatal \; and \; prediction \; = \; fatal \\
-1 & if \; label = \; fatal \; and \; prediction \; \neq \; fatal \\
r_1 & if \; label = serious \; and \; prediction = serious \\
-r_1 & if \; label = serious \; and \; prediction \neq serious \\
r_2 & if \; label = \; slight \; and \; prediction \; = \; slight \\
-r_2 & if \; label = \; slight \; and \; prediction \; \neq serious,
\end{cases} \tag{1}
$$

where $r_1$ is the ratio of *Serious injury samples* to *Slight injury samples*, and $r_2$ is the ratio of *Fatal injury samples* to *Slight injury samples*.

4. **Memory:** a facility to save transitions in the environment and sample batches of saved transitions for Q–Network training.
5. **Transition:** it includes the following information:
   - **Current state:** the current training sample.
   - **New state:** the next training sample.
   - **Action taken:** predicted severity.
   - **Reward:** value earned/lost based on prediction and sample actual label.
   - **Episode done flag:** a boolean that indicates episode's completion.
6. **Agent:** an agent has memory, as described above, and holds the following functionality and attributes:
   - **Evaluation and target networks:** it uses one network for training and a second target network, which is updated periodically after a fixed number of steps. This avoids overestimation of Q values and enhances training stability [4].
   - **Action space:** the set of available actions (class predictions).
   - **Hyperparameters:** they relate to training and reward collection, e.g. $\epsilon$ for $\epsilon$–greedy policy, $\gamma$ for reward discount, batch size to sample from Agent's memory, $N$ number of episodes before updating target network and Q–Network optimiser with learning rate.
   - **Save:** a facility to save a transition in Memory and training/target network weights, and the entire memory space.
   - **Load:** a facility to load saved network weights and Memory.
   - **Training:** it updates the training/target network weights.
   - **Action selection:** predicting Casualty Severity for a training sample.

The steps of a full episode within the environment of traffic accidents are:

1. The environment is reset.
2. The agent checks the first training sample and predicts Casualty Severity using the $\epsilon$–greedy policy.
3. A reward, a new training sample and an episode done flag are returned.
4. Agent prediction is compared against actual label and the training network weights are updated by back-propagation with Stochastic Gradient Descent.
5. If a minority sample (serious, fatal) is classified incorrectly, the episode ends and the environment is reset. Otherwise, the agent takes a new step.

Training and target neural networks use the architecture described in Sect. 5.1. However, no Softmax activation is needed, since the RL approach is based on collecting maximum reward from Q values.

# 6    Evaluation

The following experiments could be used as a baseline when optimising similar models or designing more sophisticated approaches. Data and models are available at: https://ale66.github.io/traffic-accident-gravity-predictor/. In this context, different models were trained and tested (cf. with Sect. 5) without hyperparameter optimisation or fine–tuning. In training and validation, 2005–2018 accident data (cf. with Table 1) were used with a 75%–25% split. Different test sets were used, as described below, and the following metrics:

- **Overall classification accuracy:** correctly classified test samples over total number of test samples
- **Class accuracy:** performance in testing on each single class.

## 6.1    Supervised ANN Experiments

Experiments with ANNs were run using different versions of the dataset.

*Experiment 1:* Only full records, c. 411k data points, were used for training and validation in this experiment, i.e. there was no imputation or resampling to treat imbalance. Testing used 2019 data (c. 153k data points). Highest accuracy for fatal injury in testing, 53%, was achieved with an ANN of three hidden layers with 1000 neurons each and class weights 17.5, 2.44 and 0.69 for the fatal, serious and slight classes, respectively. The highest accuracy for the serious–injury class, 66%, was achieved with an ANN of two hidden layers with 2000 and 500 neurons respectively, and class weights of 31.83, 3.04 and 0.38, for the fatal, serious and slight classes, respectively. The highest overall classification accuracy, 77%, and best accuracy per class on average, 56% (44% fatal; 43% serious; 82% slight), were achieved with an ANN of three hidden layers with 1200 neurons each and class weights of 19.5, 3.44 and 0.69 for the fatal, serious and slight classes, respectively.

*Experiment 2:* As above, the full records (c. 411k data points) were used but this time Synthetic Minority Over–sampling Technique (SMOTE), [3], was applied to treat class imbalance. The default value of three neighbours was used for generation of synthetic samples and the output was a new dataset with an equal amount of observations per class. The best test results were achieved with an ANN of three hidden layers with 1200 neurons each: 24% for fatal, 63% for serious, 67% for slight. One of these models also exhibited the best available accuracy for the fatal–injury class (about 25%) with class weights 1.23, 1.07 and 0.89 for the three classes respectively. For the serious–injury class, the best available model achieved an accuracy of 63% with class weights 1, 0.85 and 0.5, for the three classes respectively. Although tests failed to show clear advantage when SMOTE training data are used, fine–tuning deserves some consideration.

*Experiment 3:* This experiment focused on the larger dataset (cf. with Table 1) with imputation, and testing was based on c. 153k data points from 2019. Again, the best results were achieved with an ANN of three hidden layers with 1200 neurons each: 45% for fatal, 57% for serious, and 66% for slight. Best available accuracy for the fatal–injury class was 48% with weights 19.5, 3.44 and 0.69 for the three injury classes respectively. For the serious–injury class, best available accuracy was 64%, with class weights 32.1, 2.81 and 0.38, for the three classes respectively. In comparison, best available results for logistic regression (the stochastic incremental gradient method SAGA and an L2 penalty was used) reached 67% for fatal, 43% for serious, and 63% for slight, indicating that further tuning of the ANN model is needed. Simulations were also run using SMOTE generated data but, as in Experiment 2, test results did not show clear benefits for the minority classes.

## 6.2   Reinforcement Learning Experiments

Q–learning proved to be demanding computationally, although saving and loading memory and network weights may ease some of the burden of training the evaluation and the target networks for thousands of episodes. Different variants of the reward function, Eq. (1), were tried, e.g. different reward ratios, slightly increasing the reward for successful fatal class predictions, reducing even more the reward for predicting correctly light injuries, with no clear benefit. Memory size was set to 1,000,000, $\gamma$ was 0.1, initial $\epsilon$ was 1.0 and final $\epsilon$ was 0.01 after all decrements.

To alleviate computational demands, only the full records, c. 411k data points, were used, keeping 75% for training and 25% for testing, without imputation or resampling. In testing, a Softmax activation was added to the output layer of the target network to generate an injury–class prediction.

As per Sect. 5.2, ANNs with three hidden layers of 1200 neurons each were used. Best available accuracy per class in testing was 29% for fatal, 49% for serious, and 58% for slight, which was achieved after 5800 training episodes. Best available accuracy in testing for the fatal–injury class was 37% after training for 3400 episodes. For the serious–injury class, best available accuracy in testing was 69% by a model trained across 4700 episodes. Increasing the number of training episodes to several thousands has led to overestimation. Clearly that is an issue that deserves further investigation as it has been encountered in RL applications before and various strategies have been proposed, e.g. tuning the rewards, maximising representation diversity or some form of regularisation, which may improve the RL model.

## 7   Conclusions

While several studies have sought to deploy ML to process public traffic accident data, to the best of our knowledge this is the first attempt to create a clean 2005–2018 dataset for predicting the seriousness of personal injuries. There are of course several alternatives that one can explore with respect to improving the data quality and the predictive ability of ML methods. Experiments with the two base models demonstrated that obtaining good accuracy on the minority classes without compromising performance on the majority class is very challenging, and perhaps requires applying more sophisticated approaches.

Although systematic comparison and fine–tuning were out–of–scope for this paper, experiments highlighted the potential of supervised learning. Avenues for further investigation naturally include hyperparameter tuning and model optimisation.

# References

1. Almohimeed, R.: UK traffic accidents - data analysis (10+years) (2019). https://medium.com/@rawanme/
2. Babič, F., Zuskáčová, K.: Descriptive and predictive mining on road accidents data. In: IEEE 14th International Symposium on Applied Machine Intelligence and Informatics (SAMI), pp. 87–92, January 2016. https://doi.org/10.1109/SAMI.2016.7422987
3. Chawla, N.V., Bowyer, K.W., Hall, L.O., Kegelmeyer, W.P.: SMOTE: synthetic minority over-sampling technique. J. Artif. Intell. Res. **16**, 321–357 (2002). https://doi.org/10.1613/jair.953
4. Hasselt, H.v., Guez, A., Silver, D.: Deep reinforcement learning with double q-learning. In: Proceedings of the 30th AAAI Conference on Artificial Intelligence, pp. 2094–2100. AAAI 2016, AAAI Press (2016)
5. Haynes, S., Estin, P.C., Lazarevski, S., Soosay, M., Kor, A.: Data analytics: Factors of traffic accidents in the UK. In: 10th International Conference on Dependable Systems, Services and Technologies, Leeds, United Kingdom, 5–7 June 2019, pp. 120–126. IEEE (2019). https://doi.org/10.1109/DESSERT.2019.8770021
6. Kumeda, B., Zhang, F., Zhou, F., Hussain, S., Almasri, A., Assefa, M.: Classification of road traffic accident data using machine learning algorithms. In: IEEE 11th International Conference on Communication Software and Networks (ICCSN), pp. 682–687 (2019). https://doi.org/10.1109/ICCSN.2019.8905362
7. Lin, E., Chen, Q., Qi, X.: Deep reinforcement learning for imbalanced classification. Appl. Intell. **50**(8), 2488–2502 (2020). https://doi.org/10.1007/s10489-020-01637-z
8. Stekhoven, D.J., Bühlmann, P.: MissForest-non-parametric missing value imputation for mixed-type data. Bioinformatics **28**(1), 112–118 (2011). https://doi.org/10.1093/bioinformatics/btr597
9. Zychlinski, S.: The search for categorical correlation (2018). https://towardsdatascience.com/

# Robotics/Autonomous Vehicles, Photonic Neural Networks

# A Robust, Quantization-Aware Training Method for Photonic Neural Networks

A. Oikonomou[1], M. Kirtas[1]([✉]) [ID], N. Passalis[1] [ID], G. Mourgias-Alexandris[2] [ID], M. Moralis-Pegios[2] [ID], N. Pleros[2] [ID], and A. Tefas[1] [ID]

[1] Computational Intelligence and Deep Learning Group, AIIA Laboratory, Thessaloniki, Greece
{athoikgeo,eakirtas,passalis,tefas}@csd.auth.gr
[2] Wireless and Photonic Systems and Networks Group, Department of Informatics, Aristotle University of Thessaloniki, Thessaloniki, Greece
{mourgias,mmoralis,npleros}@csd.auth.gr

**Abstract.** The computationally demanding nature of Deep Learning (DL) has fueled the research on neuromorphics due to their potential to provide high-speed and low energy hardware accelerators. To this end, neuromorphic photonics are increasingly gain attention since they can operate in very high frequencies with very low energy consumption. However, they also introduce new challenges in DL training and deployment. In this paper, we propose a novel training method that is able to compensate for quantization noise, which profoundly exists in photonic hardware due to analog-to-digital (ADC) and digital-to-analog (DAC) conversions, targeting photonic neural networks (PNNs) which employ easily saturated activation functions. The proposed method takes into account quantization during training, leading to significant performance improvements during the inference phase. We conduct evaluation experiments on both image classification and time-series analysis tasks, employing a wide range of existing photonic neuromorphic architectures. The evaluation experiments demonstrate the effectiveness of the proposed method when low-bit resolution photonic architectures are used, as well as its generalization ability.

**Keywords:** Photonic neural networks · Neuromorphic computing · Neural network quantization

## 1 Introduction

Over the recent years, the applications that are using Deep Learning (DL) are constantly expanding both in industrial and academic communities since they are achieving state-of-the-art performance in complex tasks, such as image classification and time-series forecasting [17]. Despite the fact that DL can effectively tackle such demanding tasks, its application is often restricted because of its high computational cost. High-end hardware accelerators are required to achieve fast

L. Iliadis et al. (Eds.): EANN 2022, CCIS 1600, pp. 427–438, 2022.
https://doi.org/10.1007/978-3-031-08223-8_35

computational operations, such as matrix multiplication that occupies a significant fraction of operations in DL. This demanding nature of DL has fueled the research on low energy and ultra-fast hardware accelerators. Initially, Graphics Processing Units (GPUs) have been used to serve the high computational cost of the training and inference. Nowadays, energy consumption is an increasingly relevant issue [41] and more advanced technologies, such as Tensor Processing Units (TPUs) [13] and novel neuromorphic hardware architectures [11], are applied, achieving even higher frequency rates with lower power consumption.

Neuromorpic photonics is an upcoming and promising technology that has been increasingly gaining more attention in the academic communities since it is able to propagate optical signals in very high frequencies with extremely lower power consumption, employing them to provide the neuron's functionality [1,3,36]. To achieve this, there is a great variety of proposed hardware architectures that use only optical [8,40] and/or conjunctions of electro-optical hardware devices [19]. However, there are limitations that restrict the application of neuromorphic photonics in DL due to their unique nature. Although photonic hardware has great advantages in the development of materials and waveguide technologies [6], managing very fast analog processing and vector-matrix operations with ultra low energy and power consumption [40] in reference to its electronic counterparts, such implementations include analog-to-digital and digital-to-analog conversions significantly degrade bit-resolution [28,39]. Furthermore, most of the photonic architectures currently available face difficulties in deploying traditional activation functions that are typically used in DL, such as ReLU [9]. Instead, PNNs are usually implied on sinusoidal [33] and/or sigmoidal activations [23]. Therefore, training ANNs that are oriented to neuromorphic photonics should consider both the photonic activation function [1,25], and take into account the corruptions that exist due to the use of DACs and ADCs.

Typically, ADCs can be simulated through a quantization process that converts a continuous signal to a discrete one by mapping its continuous set to a finite set of discrete values [34]. This can be achieved by rounding and truncating the values of the input signal. Despite the fact that quantization techniques are widely studied by the DL community [12,16,18], they typically target large convolutional neural networks (CNNs) containing a great amount of surplus parameters with a minor contribution to the overall performance of the model [5,43]. These large architectures are easily compressed, in contrast to smaller networks, such those currently developed for neuromorphic photonics, in which every single parameter has a great contribution on the final output of the model [12]. Furthermore, existing works mainly target dynamic quantization methods, which require extra parameters during inference, or focus on partially quantized models that ignore input and bias [10,12]. These limitations, which are further exaggerated when high-slope photonic activations are used, dictate employing different training paradigms that take into account the actual physical implementation [22].

Indeed, neuromorphic photonics impose new challenges on DL models quantization, requiring the appropriately adaption of the existing methodologies to the unique limitations of photonic substrates, e.g., using smaller models. Furthermore, the quantization scheme applied in neuromorphics is a very simple uniform quantization because it depends on the DAC/ADC modules that quantize the signals equally and symmetrically [28,39]. This differs from the approaches traditionally used in trainable quantization schemes for DL models [31]. Finally, being able to operate on low-precision networks during the deployment can further improve the potential use of analog computing by lowering even more the energy consumption of the developed accelerators [27,38].

This work focuses on training PNNs while taking into account the quantization that occurs during the deployment, employing photonic activation functions. As has been shown, considering actual hardware limitations and corruptions during training can significantly improve the performance of the model during the deployment phase [25,26,32]. To this end, we propose an activation-agnostic, quantization-aware training method oriented for PNNs that enables us to effectively train models in lower precision without significant performance degradation. The proposed quantization-aware training method considers the input and model parameter variances during training and quantizes them accordingly. We evaluate the proposed method on two different photonic architectures used on two traditional image classification tasks applying multi layer perceptron (MLP) and CNNs, respectively, as well as on a challenging time-series forecasting task that involves high frequency financial time series using a state-of-the-art recurrent photonic architecture.

The rest of this paper is structured as follows. Section 2 provides the necessary background on photonic DL, while the proposed method is introduced and described in Sect. 3. Finally, the experimental evaluation is provided in Sect. 4, while the conclusion is drawn in Sect. 5

## 2   Background

Similarly to the software implemented ANNs, photonic ones are based on perceptron with the ultimate goal of approximating a function $f^*$. More precisely, the input signal of the photonic ANN is denoted as $x \in \mathbb{R}^M$, where M represents the number of features. Each sample in the train data set is labeled with a vector $t = 1_n \in \mathbb{R}^N$ where the $n$-th element equals to 1 and the other elements are 0 if it is a classification task ($N$ denotes the number of classes) or a continuous vector $t \in \mathbb{R}^N$ if it is a regression task ($N$ denotes the number of regression targets). MLPs approximate $f^*$ by using more than one layer, i.e., $f_n(...(f_2(f_1(x; \theta_1)\theta_2;)\theta_n) = z_n$ and learn the parameters $\theta_i$ where $0 \leq i \leq n$ with $\theta_i$ consisting of the weights $w_i \in \mathbb{R}^{N_i \times M_i}$ and biases $b_i \in \mathbb{R}^{N_i}$. Subsequently, each layer's output is denoted as $z_i = f_i(y_{i-1}) = w_i y_{i-1} + b_i$. The output of the linear part of a neuron is fed to a non-linear function $g(\cdot)$, named activation function, to form the final output of the layer, $y_i = g(z_i)$

The training of an ANN is achieved by updating its parameters, using the backpropagation algorithm [14], aiming to minimize a loss function $J(y, t)$, where

$t$ represents the training labels and $\mathbf{y}$ the output of the network. Cross-entropy loss is often used in multi-class classification cases $J(\mathbf{y}, \mathbf{t}) = -\sum_{c=1}^{N} t_c \log y_c$.

Except for the feed-forward ANNs, in this paper we also employ a simple-to-apply recurrent neuromorphic photonic architecture. The applied recurrent architecture is benefited from the existing photonic feed-forward implementations [24,37] while using a feedback loop. Following the above notation and the fact that the recurrent architectures accept sequential data as input, let $\mathbf{x}$ be a multidimensional time series, while let $\mathbf{x}_t \in \mathbb{R}^M$ denote $M$ observations fed to the input at the $t$-th time-step. Then, the input signal is weighted by the $i$-th neuron using the input weights $\mathbf{w}_i^{(in)} \in \mathbb{R}^M$. Furthermore, the recurrent feedback signal, denoted by $\mathbf{y}_{t-1}^{(r)} \in \mathbb{R}^{N_r}$, which corresponds to the output of the $N_r$ recurrent neurons at the previous time-step, is also weighted by the recurrent weights $\mathbf{w}_i^{(r)} \in \mathbb{R}^{N_r}$. The final weighted output of the $i$-th recurrent neuron is calculated as $u_{ti}^{(r)} = {\mathbf{w}_i^{(in)}}^T \mathbf{x}_t + {\mathbf{w}_i^{(r)}}^T \mathbf{y}_{t-1}^{(r)}$. Note that we omitted the bias term to simplify the employed notation. Then, this weighted output is fed to the employed photonic non-linearity $f(\cdot)$ to acquire the final activation of the neuron as $y_{ti}^{(r)} = f(u_{ti}^{(r)})$.

In this case of study two photonic activation functions are used. First, the photonic sigmoid activation function is defined as [24]:

$$g(z) = A_2 + \frac{A_1 - A_2}{1 + e^{(z - z_0)/d}} \tag{1}$$

in which the parameters $A_1 = 0.060, A_2 = 1.005, z_0 = 0.154$ and $d = 0.033$ are tuned to fit the experimental observations as implemented on real hardware devices [24].

Also, a photonic sinusoiudal activation function is applied on the experimental evaluations. The photonic layout corresponds to the employing a Mach-Zender Modulator device (MZM) [35] that converts the data into an optical signal along with a photodiode [2]. The formula of this photonic activation function is the following:

$$g(z) = \begin{cases} 0, & \text{if } z < 0. \\ \sin \frac{\pi^2}{2} z, & \text{if } 0 < z < 1. \\ 1, & \text{if } z > 1. \end{cases} \tag{2}$$

It is worth noting that because of the narrow range of the input domain these photonic activations have, training is even more difficult, since the networks tend to be easily saturated, leading to slower convergence or even halting the training.

## 3   Proposed Method

In this work, we propose a quantization-aware training framework that takes into account the quantization error arisen from DACs and ADCs modules in PNNs. In this way, we exploit the intrinsic ability of ANNs to resist to known noise sources when they are first trained to withstand them [25,32]. In this way, the training procedure is adjusted on lower-precision signals, and consequently the quantization error is considered at the loss function and minimized through the optimization process. As a result, the networks trained in a quantization-aware fashion can significantly improve the accuracy during the inference process.

Under the proposed quantization-aware training framework, which is inspired and extends the quantization scheme in [12], every signal that is involved in the response of the $i$-th layer is first quantized in a specific floating range $[p_{min}^{(i)}, \ldots, p_{max}^{(i)}]$. More specifically, it *simulates* the quantization process *during the forward pass*, which means that the input, model's parameters and activation values are stored as floating point numbers enabling us to perform backpropagation as usual. However, during the forward-pass quantization error $\epsilon$ is injected by deploying the rounding of quantization arithmetically in floating point. More precisely, the inputs and the model's parameters are quantized before forward-pass is applied to the layer. In turn, the linear output of the layer is quantized before it is fed to the photonic activation function. As a result, quantization divides the signal by the number of quantization levels in a range depending on the specific bit resolution.

First, every signal involved $p^{(i)}$ is converted to a bit representation by applying the function $Q : \mathbb{R} \rightarrow \mathbb{N}$ formulated as following:

$$p_q^{(i)} = Q(p^{(i)}, s_p^{(i)}, \zeta_p^{(i)}) = clip \left\{ \left\lfloor \frac{p^{(i)}}{s_p^{(i)}} + \zeta_p^{(i)} \right\rceil, q_{min}, q_{max} \right\} \in \mathbb{N}$$

where $p^{(i)} \in \mathbb{R}$, $p_q^{(i)} \in [0 \ldots, 2^B - 1]$ and $B$ denotes the bit resolution of the signal. Variables $s_p^{(i)} \in \mathbb{R}^+$ and $\zeta_p^{(i)} \in \mathbb{N}$ define the quantization parameters of the quantization function $Q$ named *scale* and *zero-point* respectively. The *scale* value is typically represented in the software as a floating-point number and is calculated as follows:

$$s_p^{(i)} = \frac{p_{max}^{(i)} - p_{min}^{(i)}}{q_{max} - q_{min}} \in \mathbb{R}^+ \tag{3}$$

where $q_{min} \in \mathbb{N}^+$ and $q_{max} \in \mathbb{N}^+$ denote the range of an $B$-bit resolution (0 and $2^B - 1$ respectively) while $p_{max}^{(i)} \in \mathbb{R}$ and $p_{min}^{(i)} \in \mathbb{R}$ represents the working range, i.e., maximum and minimum, of a signal. In turn, the zero point is calculated:

$$\zeta_p^{(i)} = clip \left\{ \left\lfloor q_{min} - \frac{p_{min}^{(i)}}{s_p^{(i)}} \right\rceil, q_{min}, q_{max} \right\} \in \mathbb{N} \tag{4}$$

In contrast to [12], we convert $p_q^{(i)} \in [0 \ldots, 2^B - 1]$ to discrete floating arithmetics $p_q^{(i)} \in [p_{min}^{(i)}, \ldots, p_{min}^{(i)}]$ using a dequantization function $D : \mathbb{N} \rightarrow \mathbb{R}$ formulated as following:

$$p_f^{(i)} = D(p_q^{(i)}, s_p^{(i)}, \zeta_p^{(i)}) = s_p^{(i)}(p_q^{(i)} - \zeta_p^{(i)}) \in \mathbb{R} \tag{5}$$

Following the above notation the linear response of $i$-th layer is given by:

$$z_f^{(i)} = Quant(w_f^{(i)} \cdot y_f^{(i-1)} + b_f^{(i)}) \in \mathbb{R}^{N_i} \qquad (6)$$

where $Quant(x)$ denotes process of quantization followed by dequantization of a vector or matrix $x \in \mathbb{R}^{M_i}$, while $w_f^{(i)} \in [w_{min}^{(i)}, \ldots, w_{max}^{(i)}]^{N_i \times M_i}$ and $b_f^{(i)} \in [b_{min}^{(i)}, \ldots, b_{max}^{(i)}]^{N_i}$ denote the quantized weights and biases of $i$-th layer. Note that the $Quant(x)$ function is applied in an element-wise fashion.

Finally, the output $z_f^{(i)}$ passes through the photonic activation function, $g(\cdot)$ of the neuron $y_f^{(i)} = Quant(g(z_f^{(i)}))$. In this way, all signals involved in the layer's output are distributed in a uniform floating range between $p_{min}^{(i)}$ and $p_{max}^{(i)}$ and they can be represented using $B$ bits. Thus, the quantization error is propagated through the network as a noise signal that is taken into account during the training, and the network learns to be aware of it during the deployment. The proposed method is presented for feedforward networks, but without loss of generality it can be applied to RNN architectures as well. Consequently, we can represent the forward pass as a procedure that involves a quantization error that is introduced in the inputs, weights, and activations. We should note that during the training, the quantization effect is simulated while the backpropagation happens as usual, meaning that the original parameters are updated according to the propagated loss.

What significantly affects the amount of quantization error, both in training and inference, is the selected working range, i.e., minimum ($p_{min}$) and maximum ($p_{max}$) values, of a signal on which the scale of uniform buckets depends. To this end, we propose computing the exponential moving average (EMA) for $p_{min}$ and $p_{max}$. We use EMA to eliminate outliers in vectors and matrices and smoothen the process of quantization during the training. In this way, the model becomes more robust to outlier values, especially at the beginning of the training process.

Since the distribution of every signal is transformed during the training, the preferable boundaries of a signal are calculated incrementally at every timestep $t$ as following:

$$\tilde{p}_{max,t}^{(i)} = (\beta/t)p_{max,t}^{(i)} + (1 - (\beta/t))\tilde{p}_{max,t-1}^{(i)} \qquad (7)$$

$$\tilde{p}_{min,t}^{(i)} = (\beta/t)p_{min,t}^{(i)} + (1 - (\beta/t))\tilde{p}_{min,t-1}^{(i)}+ \qquad (8)$$

where $t$ denotes the training iteration, $\beta$ is the weighting parameter of the EMA and the update is applied for $t > \lceil b \rceil$. Note that we calculate the min and max values per vector and/or matrix. Therefore, we use the same min and max for the activations of the same layer, but different ones for different layers.

## 4   Experimental Evaluation

We evaluate the proposed method on two traditional image classification tasks, more specifically on MNIST [4] and CIFAR10 [15], using MLPs and CNNs respectively. Additionally, we employed RNN, to sufficiently cover all possible scenarios, on a challenging forecasting task using high frequency time series limit order book data (FI-2020) [30]. Photonic sigmoid and sinusoidal activation functions are employed in the aforementioned architectures, as given by Eqs. 1 and 2 respectively. We evaluate the performance of the proposed method on different bit resolutions. Also, we compared the proposed method with a post training quantization approach in which the quantization is ignored during the training procedure and is applied during the inference. On the baseline approach, the $p_{min}$ and $p_{max}$ values for each parameter are calculated using the minimum and maximum values of each parameter vector or matrix. This corresponds to the case where the models are deployed directly in photonic hardware, as is currently done in most photonic DL approaches [7,8,21]. In the proposed method, the parameter $\beta$ is set to 2.

## 4.1   Image Classification

We report the average accuracy and the corresponding variance of the evaluation accuracy over 10 training runs in Table 1 and 2 for MNIST and CIFAR10 datasets respectively. More precisely, MNIST [4] dataset consists of handwritten digits, including 60,000 train samples and 10,000 test samples. The digits have been size-normalized, centered in a fixed size, and flattened to one dimension, leading to 784 features per sample. The input flattened images are fed to the first fully connected layer which consists of 10 neurons, then to the second fully connected layer which consists of 20 neurons, and finally to the output layer which consists of 10 neurons. The models are optimized for 100 epochs using the RMSProp optimizer [42] with a learning rate equal to 0.0001. The cross-entropy loss was used as the objective function, while mini-batches of 256 samples were used.

**Table 1.** Evaluating the proposed method on MNIST. Classification accuracy (%) is reported.

| Bits | Photonic Sinusoidal | | Photonic Sigmoid | |
|---|---|---|---|---|
| | Post training | Proposed | Post training | Proposed |
| 8 | $90.12 \pm 1.52$ | $\mathbf{91.21 \pm 0.49}$ | $91.02 \pm 0.81$ | $\mathbf{91.17 \pm 0.33}$ |
| 6 | $86.93 \pm 1.47$ | $\mathbf{91.04 \pm 0.51}$ | $87.01 \pm 0.12$ | $\mathbf{91.02 \pm 0.29}$ |
| 4 | $09.95 \pm 0.00$ | $\mathbf{90.26 \pm 0.77}$ | $09.34 \pm 0.00$ | $\mathbf{90.20 \pm 0.39}$ |
| 2 | $09.97 \pm 0.00$ | $\mathbf{67.63 \pm 2.28}$ | $09.98 \pm 0.00$ | $\mathbf{61.00 \pm 1.95}$ |

As demonstrated in Table 1, the performance of the post training quantization method (columns 2 and 4) is collapsed when the bit resolution is lowered, especially in 2 and 4 bits. The proposed method, which takes into account the quantization during the training phase, can significantly improve the performance in low bit resolutions and resist the corruption occurring in post training quantization. This can be also attributed to the fact that the proposed method is taking into account the bounds of each signal incrementally, since it computes the EMA of the minimum and maximum value of each involved parameter. In this way, it can eliminate outliers that can lead to a wide range of buckets with barely any values. The proposed method (column 3 and 5) exceeds in terms of performance the post training method in all cases irrespective of the model's resolution and/or the applied photonic activation function.

The CIFAR10 dataset includes 50,000 images in the training set and 10,000 in the evaluation set with $32 \times 32$ color image samples containing one of the 10 object classes. The applied CNN consists of four convolutional layers followed by two linear layers. In more detail, the first two convolutional layers consist of $3 \times 3$ kernel size with 32 and 64 filters, followed by a $2 \times 2$ average pooling layer. Then, the other 2 convolutional layers are applied with 128 and 256 filters of size $3 \times 3$ followed by an $2 \times 2$ average pooling. Finally, the features that are extracted are flattened and fed to a linear layer that consists of 512 neurons followed by the final classification layer. The networks are optimized for 250 epochs using RMSProp optimizer [42] using mini-batches of 256 samples with a learning rate equal to 0.0001.

**Table 2.** Evaluating the proposed method on CIFAR10. Classification accuracy (%) is reported.

|  | Photonic Sinusoidal | | Photonic Sigmoid | |
|---|---|---|---|---|
| Bits | Post training | Proposed | Post training | Proposed |
| 8 | $15.22 \pm 1.15$ | $\mathbf{67.64 \pm 1.24}$ | $16.39 \pm 1.15$ | $\mathbf{66.23 \pm 1.23}$ |
| 6 | $15.10 \pm 1.81$ | $\mathbf{66.56 \pm 1.38}$ | $15.76 \pm 0.73$ | $\mathbf{66.50 \pm 1.61}$ |
| 4 | $16.62 \pm 2.44$ | $\mathbf{29.48 \pm 10.43}$ | $16.38 \pm 0.25$ | $\mathbf{65.25 \pm 1.96}$ |

In contrast to the MNIST case, in this experimental evaluation the performance of the baseline approach (columns 2 and 4) collapses even when 8-bit resolution is used. On the other hand, the proposed method (columns 3 and 6), similar to the fully connected case, can significantly resist to such collapse, since it outperforms the baseline approach in all cases. At 4-bit resolution the proposed method cannot fully recover the loss in the accuracy (for the photonic sinusoidal case), yet it can still lead to improvements. Therefore, we can safely draw the conclusion that the proposed can be generalized to CNNs, since it improves the performance of models during the inference for all the experiments conducted.

## 4.2   Forecasting Financial Time Series Analysis

Finally, the dataset that is used to evaluate the photonic recurrent architecture is a high frequency financial time series limit order book dataset (FI-2020) [30] that consists of more than 4,000,000 limit orders which come from 5 Finnish companies. The data processing scheme and evaluation procedure are described extensively in [29]. For the following experiments, splits 1 to 5 were used. The task of the forecast is to predict the movement of the future mid-price after the next 10 time steps which can go down, up or remain stationary.

The DL network that is used for the experiment consists of a recurrent photonic layer with 32 neurons, as described in Sect. 2. The output of the recurrent layer is fed to two fully-connected layers with the first fully connected layer consisting of 512 neurons and the second of 3 neurons. The length of the time series that is fed to the model is 10, which is the current and the past 9 timesteps. The model is optimized for 20 epochs with the RMSprop optimizer, and the learning rate is set to $10^{-4}$.

**Table 3.** Evaluating the proposed method on FI2020. Cohen's $\kappa$ metric is reported.

| | Photonic Sinusoidal | | Photonic Sigmoid | |
|---|---|---|---|---|
| Bits | Post training | Proposed | Post training | Proposed |
| 8 | $0.0502 \pm 0.0218$ | $\mathbf{0.1189 \pm 0.0105}$ | $0.0653 \pm 0.0081$ | $\mathbf{0.1262 \pm 0.0072}$ |
| 6 | $0.0647 \pm 0.0015$ | $\mathbf{0.1170 \pm 0.0115}$ | $0.0656 \pm 0.0061$ | $\mathbf{0.1242 \pm 0.0132}$ |
| 4 | $0.0645 \pm 0.0057$ | $\mathbf{0.1091 \pm 0.0210}$ | $0.0648 \pm 0.0062$ | $\mathbf{0.1232 \pm 0.0517}$ |
| 2 | $0.0370 \pm 0.0069$ | $\mathbf{0.0601 \pm 0.0031}$ | $0.0377 \pm 0.0126$ | $\mathbf{0.0918 \pm 0.0033}$ |

The evaluation results are reported in Table 3. More precisely, we report the mean value of 5 splits using Cohen's $\kappa$ metric [20] to evaluate the performance of the models since the dataset is extremely imbalanced. We observe that the benefits of the proposed method (columns 3 and 6) are crucial for the performance of the models during the inference phase since the post quantization training method (columns 2 and 4) is unable to sustain a reasonable performance. Indeed, the proposed method can significantly improve the inference accuracy irrespective of the photonic activation that is employed, highlighting once again its activation agnostic scope.

## 5   Conclusion

Neuromorphic photonics are an upcoming technology promising to overcome limitations that have become relevant over the recent years providing ultra-high speed and low energy consumption accelerators. At the same time, their application is hindered since it introduces new challenges on the training and deployment of DL, such as easily saturated activation functions and susceptible to different noise source ANNs, e.g., due to quantization. In this paper, we propose a novel activation-agnostic quantization-aware training method that is capable of compensating for quantization noise that arises from ADCs/DACs. As experimentally evaluated, the proposed method is capable of significantly improving the performance of low-bit resolution PNNs by considering quantization during the training. The proposed method builds a robust representation enabling us to decrease memory requirements and computational cost by lowering the bit resolution without significant performance degradation. The proposed method is evaluated on both image classification and time-series analysis tasks, employing a wide range of photonic architectures, outperforming the evaluated baselines.

**Acknowledgements.** The research work was supported by the Hellenic Foundation for Research and Innovation (H.F.R.I.), Greece under the "First Call for H.F.R.I. Research Projects to support Faculty members and Researchers and the procurement of high-cost research equipment grant" (Project Number: 4233)

# References

1. Dabos, G., et al.: End-to-end deep learning with neuromorphic photonics. In: Integrated Optics: Devices, Materials, and Technologies XXV, vol. 11689, p. 116890I. International Society for Optics and Photonics (2021)
2. Danial, L., Wainstein, N., Kraus, S., Kvatinsky, S.: Breaking through the speed-power-accuracy tradeoff in ADCs using a memristive neuromorphic architecture. IEEE Trans. Emerg. Top. Comput. Intell. **2**(5), 396–409 (2018)
3. De Marinis, L., Cococcioni, M., Castoldi, P., Andriolli, N.: Photonic neural networks: a survey. IEEE Access **7**, 175827–175841 (2019)
4. Deng, L.: The MNIST database of handwritten digit images for machine learning research. IEEE Sign. Process. Mag. **29**(6), 141–142 (2012)
5. Esser, S.K., McKinstry, J.L., Bablani, D., Appuswamy, R., Modha, D.S.: Learned step size quantization (2020)
6. Feldmann, J., Youngblood, N., Wright, C., Bhaskaran, H., Pernice, W.: All-optical spiking neurosynaptic networks with self-learning capabilities. Nature **569**(7755), 208–214 (2019)
7. Feldmann, J., et al.: Parallel convolutional processing using an integrated photonic tensor core. Nature **589**(7840), 52–58 (2021)
8. Giamougiannis, G., et al.: Silicon-integrated coherent neurons with 32GMAC/sec/axon compute line-rates using EAM-based input and weighting cells. In: Proceedings of the European Conference on Optical Communication (ECOC), pp. 1–4 (2021)
9. He, K., Zhang, X., Ren, S., Sun, J.: Delving deep into rectifiers: surpassing human-level performance on ImageNet classification. In: Proceedings of the International Conference on Computer Vision, pp. 1026–1034 (2015)
10. Hubara, I., Courbariaux, M., Soudry, D., El-Yaniv, R., Bengio, Y.: Quantized neural networks: training neural networks with low precision weights and activations. J. Mach. Learn. Res. **18**(1), 6869–6898 (2017)
11. Indiveri, G., et al.: Neuromorphic silicon neuron circuits. Front. Neurosci. **5**, 73 (2011)
12. Jacob, B., et al.: Quantization and training of neural networks for efficient integer-arithmetic-only inference. In: Proceedings of the IEEE Computer Society Conference on Computer Vision and Pattern Recognition, pp. 2704–2713 (2018)
13. Jouppi, N.P., et al.: In-datacenter performance analysis of a tensor processing unit. In: Proceedings of the Annual International Symposium on Computer Architecture, pp. 1–12 (2017)
14. Kelley, H.J.: Gradient theory of optimal flight paths. ARS J. **30**(10), 947–954 (1960)

15. Krizhevsky, A., Nair, V., Hinton, G.: CIFAR-10 (Canadian institute for advanced research). http://www.cs.toronto.edu/~kriz/cifar.html
16. Kulkarni, U., Meena, S., Gurlahosur, S.V., Bhogar, G.: Quantization friendly MobileNet (QF-MobileNet) architecture for vision based applications on embedded platforms. Neural Netw. **136**, 28–39 (2021)
17. LeCun, Y., Bengio, Y., Hinton, G.: Deep learning. Nature **521**(7553), 436–444 (2015)
18. Lee, D., Wang, D., Yang, Y., Deng, L., Zhao, G., Li, G.: QTTNet: quantized tensor train neural networks for 3D object and video recognition. Neural Netw. **141**, 420–432 (2021)
19. Lin, X., et al.: All-optical machine learning using diffractive deep neural networks. Science **361**(6406), 1004–1008 (2018)
20. McHugh, M.L.: Interrater reliability: the kappa statistic. Biochemia Medica **22**(3), 276–282 (2012)
21. Miscuglio, M., Sorger, V.J.: Photonic tensor cores for machine learning. Appl. Phys. Rev. 7(3), 31404 (2020)
22. Mourgias-Alexandris, G., et al.: Channel response-aware photonic neural network accelerators for high-speed inference through bandwidth-limited optics. Opt. Express **30**(7), 10664–10671 (2022)
23. Mourgias-Alexandris, G., Tsakyridis, A., Passalis, N., Tefas, A., Vyrsokinos, K., Pleros, N.: An all-optical neuron with sigmoid activation function. Opt. Express **27**(7), 9620–9630 (2019)
24. Mourgias-Alexandris, G., Tsakyridis, A., Passalis, N., Tefas, A., Vyrsokinos, K., Pleros, N.: An all-optical neuron with sigmoid activation function. Opt. Express **27**(7), 9620–9630 (2019)
25. Mourgias-Alexandris, G., et al.: A silicon photonic coherent neuron with 10GMAC/sec processing line-rate. In: Proceedings of the Optical Fiber Communications Conference and Exhibition (OFC), pp. 1–3 (2021)
26. Mourgias-Alexandris, G., et al.: 25GMAC/sec/axon photonic neural networks with 7GHZ bandwidth optics through channel response-aware training. In: Proceedings of the European Conference on Optical Communication (ECOC), pp. 1–4 (2021)
27. Murmann, B.: Mixed-signal computing for deep neural network inference. IEEE Trans. Very Large Scale Integr. (VLSI) Syst. **29**(1), 3–13 (2021)
28. Nahmias, M.A., de Lima, T.F., Tait, A.N., Peng, H.T., Shastri, B.J., Prucnal, P.R.: Photonic multiply-accumulate operations for neural networks. IEEE J. Sel. Top. Quant. Electron. **26**(1), 1–18 (2020)
29. Nousi, P., et al.: Machine learning for forecasting mid-price movements using limit order book data. IEEE Access **7**, 64722–64736 (2019)
30. Ntakaris, A., Magris, M., Kanniainen, J., Gabbouj, M., Iosifidis, A.: Benchmark dataset for mid-price forecasting of limit order book data with machine learning methods. J. Forecast. **37**(8), 852–866 (2018)
31. Park, E., Ahn, J., Yoo, S.: Weighted-entropy-based quantization for deep neural networks. In: Proceedings of the IEEE Conference on Computer Vision and Pattern Recognition (CVPR), pp. 7197–7205 (2017)
32. Passalis, N., Kirtas, M., Mourgias-Alexandris, G., Dabos, G., Pleros, N., Tefas, A.: Training noise-resilient recurrent photonic networks for financial time series analysis. In: Proceedings of the 28th European Signal Processing Conference, pp. 1556–1560 (2021)
33. Passalis, N., Mourgias-Alexandris, G., Tsakyridis, A., Pleros, N., Tefas, A.: Training deep photonic convolutional neural networks with sinusoidal activations. IEEE Trans. Emerg. Top. Comput. Intell. **5**, 384–393 (2019)

34. Pearson, C.: High-speed, analog-to-digital converter basics. Texas Instruments Application Report, SLAA510 (2011)
35. Pitris, S., et al.: O-band energy-efficient broadcast-friendly interconnection scheme with SiPho Mach-Zehnder Modulator (MZM) & Arrayed Waveguide Grating Router (AWGR). In: Proceedings of the Optical Fiber Communication Conference on Optical Society of America (2018)
36. Pleros, N., et al.: Compute with light: architectures, technologies and training models for neuromorphic photonic circuits. In: Proceedings of the European Conference on Optical Communication (ECOC), pp. 1–4 (2021)
37. Rosenbluth, D., Kravtsov, K., Fok, M.P., Prucnal, P.R.: A high performance photonic pulse processing device. Opt. Express **17**(25), 22767–22772 (2009)
38. Sarpeshkar, R.: Analog versus digital: extrapolating from electronics to neurobiology. Neural Comput. **10**(7), 1601–1638 (1998)
39. Shastri, B.J., et al.: Photonics for artificial intelligence and neuromorphic computing. Nat. Photon. **15**(2), 102–114 (2021)
40. Shen, Y., et al.: Deep learning with coherent nanophotonic circuits. Nat. Photon. **11**(7), 441 (2017)
41. Strubell, E., Ganesh, A., McCallum, A.: Energy and policy considerations for deep learning in NLP. arXiv preprint arXiv:1906.02243 (2019)
42. Tieleman, T., Hinton, G.: Lecture 6.5-rmsprop: divide the gradient by a running average of its recent magnitude. COURSERA: Neural Netw. Mach. Learn. **4**(2), 26–31 (2012)
43. Wu, J., Leng, C., Wang, Y., Hu, Q., Cheng, J.: Quantized convolutional neural networks for mobile devices. In: Proceedings of the IEEE Conference on Computer Vision and Pattern Recognition, pp. 4820–4828 (2016)

# Improving Binary Semantic Scene Segmentation for Robotics Applications

Maria Tzelepi[(✉)], Nikolaos Tragkas, and Anastasios Tefas

Aristotle University of Thessaloniki, Thessaloniki, Greece
{mtzelepi,nktragkas,tefas}@csd.auth.gr

**Abstract.** Robotics applications are accompanied by particular computational restrictions, i.e., operation at sufficient speed, on embedded low power GPUs, and also for high-resolution input. Semantic scene segmentation performs an important role in a broad spectrum of robotics applications, e.g., autonomous driving. In this paper, we focus on binary segmentation problems, considering the specific requirements of the robotics applications. To this aim, we utilize the BiseNet model, which achieves significant performance considering the speed-segmentation accuracy trade-off. The target of this work is two-fold. Firstly, we propose a lightweight version of BiseNet model, providing significant speed improvements. Secondly, we explore different losses for enhancing the segmentation accuracy of the proposed lightweight version of BiseNet on binary segmentation problems. The experiments conducted on various high and low power GPUs, utilizing two binary segmentation datasets validated the effectiveness of the proposed method.

**Keywords:** Semantic segmentation · Binary · Bisenet · Robotics · Low power GPUs

## 1 Introduction

Semantic scene segmentation refers to the task of assigning a class label to each pixel of an image, and hence it is also known as pixel-level classification. Semantic scene segmentation is a challenging task involved in numerous robotics applications, such as autonomous driving [1,11,20]. Robotics applications are accompanied by particular computational requirements. That is, the utilized models should be able to effectively operate at sufficient speed, on embedded low power GPUs, while also considering high-resolution input.

Recent advances in Deep Learning (DL), besides other problems [14–16], have provided effective models for addressing the general problem of semantic scene segmentation [7]. The seminal approach introduced fully convolutional neural networks [10]. Subsequently, considerable research has been conducted, focusing on improving the segmentation accuracy [2,9], however, without considering the issue of deployment (inference) speed. That is, most of the existing state-of-the-art DL segmentation models are computationally heavy, and hence ill-suited for robotics applications.

© Springer Nature Switzerland AG 2022
L. Iliadis et al. (Eds.): EANN 2022, CCIS 1600, pp. 439–447, 2022.
https://doi.org/10.1007/978-3-031-08223-8_36

Thus, in the recent literature there have been works that also focus on the deployment speed, providing real-time segmentation models, considering mainly high power GPUs [3,4,6,12,18,19]. A comparative study of current semantic segmentation models considering the inherent computational restrictions in the context of robotics applications is provided in [17]. More specifically, extensive experiments have been conducted on different embedded platforms (e.g., AGX Xavier, NVIDIA TX-2), and also for various input resolutions, ranging from lower to higher ones. From the conducted experiments, it is evident that the Bilateral Segmentation Network (BiseNet) [19] model achieves considerable performance considering the segmentation accuracy-speed trade-off. Towards this end, in this work we employ BiseNet model and we address the problem of binary semantic segmentation considering robotics applications.

The target of this work is to explore ways of improving the performance of BiseNet model both in terms of deployment speed and segmentation accuracy, considering binary segmentation problems. To this aim, we first propose a lightweight version of the model. That is, we propose a lightweight network instead of ResNet-18 [8] that is used in the so-called *context path*. Subsequently, we exploit the available losses. Specifically, apart from the widely used cross entropy (softmax) loss, which is also used in the initial version of BiseNet, we apply hinge loss, since as it is shown in the recent literature, it provides improved accuracy considering binary classification problems [15].

The remainder of the manuscript is structured as follows. Section 2 provides the description of the proposed ways of improving binary segmentation, that is the proposed lightweight version of BiseNet and the investigation on loss functions. Next, Sect. 3 provides the experimental evaluation, and finally conclusions are drawn in Sect. 4.

## 2   Proposed Method

The BiseNet model consists of two paths, that is *Spatial Path* and *Context Path*. The spatial path is used in order to preserve the spatial information and generate high resolution features, and the context path with a fast downsampling strategy is used in order to obtain sufficient receptive field. Furthermore, the model includes two modules, that is a Feature Fusion Module and an Attention Refinement Module, in order to further improve the accuracy with acceptable cost. Finally, apart from the principal cross entropy loss which supervises the output of the BiseNet model, two auxiliary losses are utilized to supervise the output of the context path.

In this work, we propose to replace the ResNet-18 model used in the context path, with a more lightweight model. The proposed model, which is based on the VGG model [13], consists of five pairs of convolutional layers followed by batch normalization and Rectified Linear Unit (ReLU) activation. A max-pooling layer follows each convolutional block. The proposed model architecture is illustrated in Fig. 1. Furthermore, we provide Table 1 which summarizes the design of the proposed model. As it will be presented the modified BiseNet model utilizing the proposed lightweight model in the context path achieves considerable speed improvements.

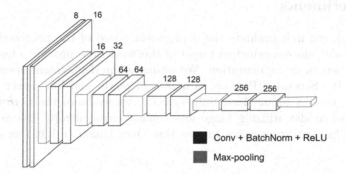

**Fig. 1.** Proposed lightweight model in the context-path: Red boxes represent the max-pooling layers, while the black boxes represent the convolutional layers, followed by batch normalization ReLU activation. The numbers of output channels of each convolutional layer are also depicted. (Color figure online)

**Table 1.** Layers of the proposed fully-convolutional lightweight context-path. *conv3-x* abbreviates a convolutional layer with kernel $3 \times 3$ and $x$ output channels. Batch normalization is applied to each convolutional layer, while ReLU is used as activation function. The maxpool layers downsample by a factor of 2 feature maps.

| Layer | Conv3-8 | Maxpool | Conv3-16 | Maxpool | Conv3-64 | Maxpool | Conv3-128 | Maxpool | Conv3-256 | Maxpool |
|---|---|---|---|---|---|---|---|---|---|---|
| | Conv3-16 | | Conv3-32 | | Conv3-64 | | Conv3-128 | | Conv3-256 | |

Subsequently, since lightweight models usually have inferior performance as compared to their heavyweight counterparts, we explore ways to improve their performance. To achieve this goal, we focus on the loss functions for training the segmentation model. More specifically, even though cross entropy loss is a widely used loss function in DL, in a recent work [15] it has been demonstrated that, considering binary classification problems, hinge loss can achieve improved classification performance. Motivated by the aforementioned observation, in this work, we extend this investigation on binary segmentation problems. Thus, we utilize hinge loss so as to supervise the output of the whole model. Hinge loss per pixel is defined as:

$$\ell_h = \sum_{j=1}^{N_c} max(0, 1 - \zeta\{c = j\}y_j^{last}) \tag{1}$$

where $c \in [1, \cdots, N_c]$ indicates the correct class among the $N_c$ classes, $y_j^{last}$ indicates the score with respect to the $j$-th class, and

$$\zeta\{condition\} = \begin{cases} 1 & \text{, if condition} \\ -1 & \text{, otherwise} \end{cases}$$

In our case, $N_c = 2$, since we deal with binary segmentation problems.

## 3    Experiments

In this work, we first evaluate the deployment speed of the proposed modified BiseNet model, since a principal target of this work is to provide a faster model for binary semantic segmentation. We evaluate the deployment speed in term of Frames Per Second (FPS), on various high power and low power GPUs, as well as for various input sizes. Subsequently, we evaluate the performance of the modified model utilizing hinge loss against cross entropy loss as principal supervised loss, utilizing mean Intersection Over Union (mIOU) as evaluation metric.

### 3.1    Datasets

In this work, we utilize the CityScapes [5] dataset, exploiting only the Human and Vehicle classes, in order to build the two binary segmentation datasets, i.e., *Human Vs Non-Human* and *Vehicle Vs Non-Vehicle*, respectively. The first one consists of 11,900 train images and 2,000 test images, while the second one consists of 2,975 train images and 500 test images.

### 3.2    Implementation Details

All the experiments conducted using the Pytorch framework. Mini-batch gradient descent is used for the networks training, where an update is performed for every mini-batch of 8 samples. Momentum is set to 0.9, while the learning rate policy of the initial work was followed. All the models are trained on an NVIDIA 2080 Ti, and the deployment speed was tested on various low power GPUs.

### 3.3    Experimental Results

In the first set of experiments we evaluate the deployment speed of the proposed modified lightweight BiseNet model against the initial version which uses the ResNet-18 model. We have conducted experiments on a high power NVIDIA 2080 Ti, a high power NVIDIA 2070, a low power NVIDIA Jetson TX-2, and a low power NVIDIA AGX Xavier. Furthermore, we use various input dimensions ranging from $400 \times 400$ to $1024 \times 1024$. The experimental results are illustrated in Tables 2, 3, 4 and 5. Best results are printed in bold. As it is shown, the proposed model runs significantly faster as compared to the initial model, in any considered case. It can also be observed increased discrepancy for lower input sizes.

Moreover, it should be emphasized that the proposed lightweight version of BiseNet accomplishes faster inference speed compared to the original BiseNet model (using ResNet-18), without considerably sacrificing the segmentation accuracy. For example, on the Vehicle dataset, where the proposed lightweight version of BiseNet achieves mIOU 94.82% using the cross entropy loss, the original BiseNet achieves mIOU 95.86%. That is, we sacrifice the segmentation accuracy by roughly 1%, gaining significant speed ups (e.g., on NVIDIA AGX Xavier for input $600 \times 600$, BiseNet runs at 26.78 FPS, while the modified lightweight BiseNet runs at 40.12 FPS).

**Table 2.** Evaluation of speed in terms of FPS utilizing the proposed lightweight model in the context path, against the ResNet-18 on an NVIDIA 2080 Ti.

| Input size | BiseNet–ResNet18 | BiseNet–Proposed |
|---|---|---|
| $1024 \times 1024$ | 66.51 | **75.23** |
| $1280 \times 720$ | 70.69 | **84.06** |
| $800 \times 800$ | 98 | **119.76** |
| $600 \times 600$ | 163.91 | **215.61** |
| $640 \times 360$ | 216.37 | **305.89** |
| $400 \times 400$ | 269.58 | **353.59** |

**Table 3.** Evaluation of speed in terms of FPS utilizing the proposed lightweight model in the context path, against the ResNet-18 on an NVIDIA 2070.

| Input size | BiseNet–ResNet18 | BiseNet–Proposed |
|---|---|---|
| $1024 \times 1024$ | 50.40 | **59.15** |
| $1280 \times 720$ | 56.17 | **66.31** |
| $800 \times 800$ | 77.46 | **93.85** |
| $600 \times 600$ | 125.04 | **166.26** |
| $640 \times 360$ | 184.59 | **251.26** |
| $400 \times 400$ | 237.61 | **315.24** |

Subsequently, the experimental results for evaluating the hinge loss against cross entropy loss, utilizing the proposed lightweight BiseNet model, on the two binary segmentation datasets are presented in Table 6. Best results are printed in bold. As it is demonstrated, hinge loss accomplishes superior performance as compared to the cross entropy loss, considering binary segmentation problems.

444    M. Tzelepi et al.

**Table 4.** Evaluation of speed in terms of FPS utilizing the proposed lightweight model in the context path, against the ResNet-18 on an NVIDIA Jetson TX2.

| Input size | BiseNet–ResNet18 | BiseNet–Proposed |
|---|---|---|
| 1024 × 1024 | 3.98 | **5.02** |
| 1280 × 720 | 4.32 | **5.58** |
| 800 × 800 | 5.71 | **7.69** |
| 600 × 600 | 9.7 | **13.36** |
| 640 × 360 | 14.71 | **21.05** |
| 400 × 400 | 18.82 | **26.42** |

**Table 5.** Evaluation of speed in terms of FPS utilizing the proposed lightweight model in the context path, against the ResNet-18 on an NVIDIA AGX Xavier.

| Input size | BiseNet–ResNet18 | BiseNet–Proposed |
|---|---|---|
| 1024 × 1024 | 11.58 | **15.32** |
| 1280 × 720 | 12.23 | **16.96** |
| 800 × 800 | 16.38 | **23.40** |
| 600 × 600 | 26.78 | **40.12** |
| 640 × 360 | 40.13 | **60.66** |
| 400 × 400 | 52.42 | **77.83** |

**Table 6.** Evaluation on segmentation performance in terms of mIOU (%) utilizing the modified lightweight BiseNet model, for evaluating hinge loss against cross entropy loss.

| Dataset | Cross entropy loss | Hinge loss |
|---|---|---|
| Human Vs Non-Human | 87.82 | **89.23** |
| Vehicle Vs Non-Vehicle | 94.82 | **95.03** |

Furthermore, we note that better segmentation performance is achieved using hinge loss on the original BiseNet model (using ResNet-18), too. For example, on the Vehicle dataset the original BiseNet achieves mIOU 95.86% with cross entropy loss, while hinge loss achieves mIOU 96.40%.

Finally, some qualitative results are presented utilizing the proposed modified model trained for human segmentation and vehicle segmentation in Fig. 2.

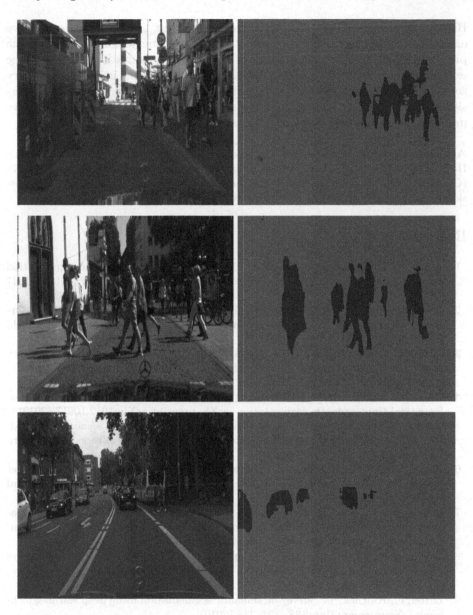

**Fig. 2.** Predictions of the modified lightweight BiSeNet model trained on Human Vs Non-Human and Vehicle Vs Non-Vehicle datasets.

## 4   Conclusions

In this paper, we dealt with binary segmentation problems, utilizing the BiseNet model, which achieves significant performance considering the speed-segmentation accuracy trade-off. First, we proposed a lightweight version of

BiseNet model, in order to improve the deployment speed. Subsequently, we explored different losses in order to enhance the segmentation accuracy of the proposed lightweight version of BiseNet on binary segmentation problems. The experiments conducted on various high and low power GPUs, utilizing two binary segmentation datasets, validated the effectiveness of proposed lightweight version of BiseNet in terms of deployments speed, as well as that hinge loss provides improved performance considering binary segmentation problems.

**Acknowledgment.** This project has received funding from the European Union's Horizon 2020 research and innovation programme under grant agreement No 871449 (OpenDR). This publication reflects the authors' views only. The European Commission is not responsible for any use that may be made of the information it contains.

# References

1. Alonso, I., Riazuelo, L., Murillo, A.C.: Mininet: an efficient semantic segmentation convnet for real-time robotic applications. IEEE Trans. Robot. **36**(4), 1340–1347 (2020)
2. Badrinarayanan, V., Kendall, A., Cipolla, R.: Segnet: a deep convolutional encoder-decoder architecture for image segmentation. IEEE Trans. Pattern Anal. Mach. Intell. **39**(12), 2481–2495 (2017)
3. Chao, P., Kao, C.Y., Ruan, Y.S., Huang, C.H., Lin, Y.L.: Hardnet: a low memory traffic network. In: Proceedings of the IEEE International Conference on Computer Vision, pp. 3552–3561 (2019)
4. Chen, W., Gong, X., Liu, X., Zhang, Q., Li, Y., Wang, Z.: Fasterseg: searching for faster real-time semantic segmentation. arXiv preprint arXiv:1912.10917 (2019)
5. Cordts, M., et al.: The cityscapes dataset for semantic urban scene understanding. In: Proceedings of the IEEE Conference on Computer Vision and Pattern Recognition, pp. 3213–3223 (2016)
6. Emara, T., Abd El Munim, H.E., Abbas, H.M.: Liteseg: a novel lightweight convnet for semantic segmentation. In: 2019 Digital Image Computing: Techniques and Applications (DICTA), pp. 1–7. IEEE (2019)
7. Garcia-Garcia, A., Orts-Escolano, S., Oprea, S., Villena-Martinez, V., Garcia-Rodriguez, J.: A review on deep learning techniques applied to semantic segmentation. arXiv preprint arXiv:1704.06857 (2017)
8. He, K., Zhang, X., Ren, S., Sun, J.: Deep residual learning for image recognition. In: Proceedings of the IEEE Conference on Computer Vision and Pattern Recognition, pp. 770–778 (2016)
9. Lateef, F., Ruichek, Y.: Survey on semantic segmentation using deep learning techniques. Neurocomputing **338**, 321–348 (2019)
10. Long, J., Shelhamer, E., Darrell, T.: Fully convolutional networks for semantic segmentation. In: Proceedings of the IEEE Conference on Computer Vision and Pattern Recognition, pp. 3431–3440 (2015)
11. Milioto, A., Lottes, P., Stachniss, C.: Real-time semantic segmentation of crop and weed for precision agriculture robots leveraging background knowledge in CNNs. In: 2018 IEEE International Conference on Robotics and Automation (ICRA), pp. 2229–2235. IEEE (2018)
12. Poudel, R.P., Liwicki, S., Cipolla, R.: Fast-SCNN: Fast semantic segmentation network. arXiv preprint arXiv:1902.04502 (2019)

13. Simonyan, K., Zisserman, A.: Very deep convolutional networks for large-scale image recognition. arXiv preprint arXiv:1409.1556 (2014)
14. Tzelepi, M., Passalis, N., Tefas, A.: Probabilistic online self-distillation. Neurocomputing (2022)
15. Tzelepi, M., Tefas, A.: Improving the performance of lightweight CNNs for binary classification using quadratic mutual information regularization. Pattern Recogn. 107407 (2020)
16. Tzelepi, M., Tefas, A.: Efficient training of lightweight neural networks using online self-acquired knowledge distillation. In: 2021 IEEE International Conference on Multimedia and Expo (ICME), pp. 1–6. IEEE (2021)
17. Tzelepi, M., Tefas, A.: Semantic scene segmentation for robotics applications (2021)
18. Yu, C., Gao, C., Wang, J., Yu, G., Shen, C., Sang, N.: Bisenet v2: bilateral network with guided aggregation for real-time semantic segmentation. arXiv preprint arXiv:2004.02147 (2020)
19. Yu, C., Wang, J., Peng, C., Gao, C., Yu, G., Sang, N.: Bisenet: bilateral segmentation network for real-time semantic segmentation. In: Proceedings of the European Conference on Computer Vision (ECCV), pp. 325–341 (2018)
20. Zhang, Y., Chen, H., He, Y., Ye, M., Cai, X., Zhang, D.: Road segmentation for all-day outdoor robot navigation. Neurocomputing **314**, 316–325 (2018)

# Online Route Scheduling for a Team of Service Robots with MOEAs and mTSP Model

Raul Alves$^{(\boxtimes)}$ , Clênio E. Silva , and Jefferson R. Souza

Faculty of Computing, Federal University of Uberlandia, Uberlândia, Brazil
{raul,clenio.silva,jrsouza}@ufu.br

**Abstract.** Service robots aim at helping humans in their tasks at home or office. Some tasks can be performed by a team of robots that need to visit target locations in the environment. This problem can be modeled as an instance of the multiple Traveling Salesman Problem (mTSP). The goal of mTSP is to minimize the total distance traveled. However, when the total distance is minimized, some salesmen tend to travel more than others depending on the distribution of the cities. Therefore, balancing individual routes is important to ensure equal battery consumption for the team to complete the task. We proposed a centralized system supported by Multi Objective Evolutionary Algorithms (MOEAs) that generate routes by minimizing the sum of travel distance and standard deviation simultaneously. Experiments were carried out to find MOEAs capable of generation high quality routes in a reasonable amount of time. Moreover, we introduce a novel robot-server architecture that connects robots with our system by means of threads, ROS nodes, and Websocket.

**Keywords:** MOEA · mTSP · Service robots · Online Route Scheduling

## 1 Introduction

Several lines of research into Robotics currently aim at the development of robots for assisting humans in their everyday lives. These robots, also called Service Robots, should perform tasks that are dirty, dull, distant, dangerous, or repetitive to humans.

This paper addresses a problem in which a team of Service Robots has to visit some target locations within an indoor environment to perform any kind of task, such as delivering mail, picking up trash, finding objects, patrolling, etc. In order to perform any of these tasks efficiently, the robots must be able to coordinate their visits.

In this problem, the robots can be anywhere in the environment. Eventually, when they receive a list of target locations, the robots must visit each of them without repetition, and then return to a common spot, such as a charging station.

© Springer Nature Switzerland AG 2022
L. Iliadis et al. (Eds.): EANN 2022, CCIS 1600, pp. 448–460, 2022.
https://doi.org/10.1007/978-3-031-08223-8_37

Thus, to coordinate the visits, a scheduling has to be made to find routes for the robots that cover all locations.

The problem of scheduling visits for a single robot can be seen as an instance of the Traveling Salesman Problem (TSP), which is a combinatorial optimization problem. Combinatorial optimization problems attempt to find an optimal solution from a finite set of solutions. In the TSP, given a set of $n$ cities and the cost of traveling (or distance) between each possible pair, the goal is to find the best possible way of visiting all cities that minimizes the final traveling cost.

While the TSP is restricted to a single salesman, the multiple Traveling Salesman Problem (mTSP) generalizes the problem for multiple salesmen, which is more common in real world applications. Also, each city must be visited exactly once by any salesman, and the total distance of visiting all cities should be minimized.

However, taking into account only the total distance, the distances traveled individually by the salesmen can become imbalanced. For example, when a salesman travels a long distance, the cost of using this salesman to visit all cities in that region is less than the cost of sending another salesman to visit some of them. As a result, some salesmen might travel for long distances, while others stay around the depot. Therefore, for some problems, it is also desired to balance the routes.

This work aims at describing the development of a centralized system to schedule routes for a team of robots using the mTSP model. In this case, cities are target locations to be visited in the environment and salesmen are the robots. The system uses Multi Objective Evolutionary Algorithms (MOEAs) to generate solutions that minimize the total distance traveled by the team and also balance the routes of the robots. In addition, a novel robot-server architecture is proposed to handle the connection between robots and the system using a fast peer-to-peer protocol, called Websocket.

Experiments were carried out on virtual and real environments. For simulation, we ran Robot Operating system (ROS) Gazebo on multiple computers to evaluate time and quality of routes generated by different MOEAs. Moreover, we tested the connectivity of our system to a real robot. Preliminary results show that our system is able to manage the robots visiting in real-time using the proposed algorithms and architecture.

The remainder of the paper is organized as follows. In Sect. 2 lists some related works. The proposed system for solving online multi-robot coordination problem using mTSP model and MOEAS is presented in Sect. 3. Section 4 shows the experiments and their results. Finally, the conclusion and future work are shown in Sect. 5.

## 2   Related Work

Recently, many researches have introduced the concept of mTSP to real multi-robot applications, which we review here.

To understand how to model multi-robot complete coverage path planning problem with mTSP and to solve the task allocation problem, in [10] is proposed a method that use a Genetic Algorithm (GA), which allocates the sub-regions to each robot and gives the robots their visiting orders to the sub-regions.

In order to collaborate with the recent advances in task allocation and planning to service robots, [8] developed a new mTSP methodology to optimize the task-allocation and route-planning for multiple indoor robots with multiple depots.

A GA for solving mTSP while constraining distance between robots is presented in [9]. The algorithm NSGA-II were used as a primary GA, with a secondary GA periodically adding waypoints for greater connectivity.

The problem of assigning a team of autonomous robots to target locations in the context of a disaster management scenario while optimizing several objectives was addressed by [12]. This problem can be cast as a mTSP, where several robots must visit designated locations. Three objectives were considered to be optimized: the total traveled distance, the maximum tour, and the deviation rate.

A bi-objective Ant Colony Optimization was proposed by [1] to solve a multi-robot patrolling problem. It was formulated as a mTSP with single and multiple depot in order to optimize the maximum traveled distance and the total traveled distance simultaneously. Another work with a bio-inspired approach is presented in [13] to resolve cooperative multi-robot task allocation problem. In this case the robots have to minimize the total team cost and, additionally, balance their workloads.

The paper [11], presents an optimization approach that minimizes production time and also the total duration of robot movements in a vehicle production line. The problem was modeled as a generalized mTSP, where was proposed fast algorithm that generates a sequenced near-optimal solution for multi-robotic task sequencing Problem. This algorithm operates on a set of solutions and uses GA mechanisms to converge towards near-optimal solutions.

## 3    Multi-robot Coordination

We proposed a centralized system to generate routes with MOEAs for a team of robots that must visit a set of target locations within an indoor environment. The Figs. 3 and 4 present pictures of the system.

The system's flow is illustrated by Fig. 1. First, the user sets target locations and the return spot on a map of the environment. The robots are displayed in different colors, given their current positions. This hypothetical scenario illustrates the process of Route Scheduling, which works in four steps: set up locations on the map, creation of a complete graph using pre-built paths, tour generation with MOEA.

Then, a complete graph is created with feasible paths, linking target locations, return spot, and all robots. After that, the route scheduling begins by running a MOEA.

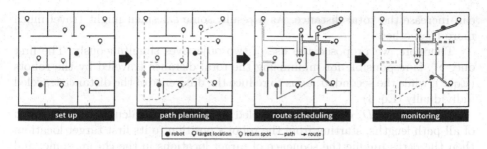

**Fig. 1.** Route scheduling flow. (Color figure online)

Several MOEAs are available on the system, such as: Non-dominated Sorting Genetic Algorithm (NSGA-II) [4], $\epsilon$NSGA-II [6], Reference Vector Guided Evolutionary Algorithm (RVEA) [2], and $\epsilon$MOEA [3].

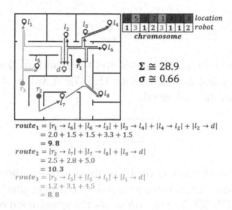

**Fig. 2.** This image depicts the hypothetical route scheduling of Fig. 1.

In order to use the concept of MOEA, some components must be designed regarding the constraints of the problem. For mTSP, we modeled the individual with a single chromosome structured in a 2D-array, as illustrated by Fig. 2. The length of the chromosome is equal to $n$, which is the number of target locations, as they must be visited only once by one of the $m$ robots. Each gene of the chromosome relates a robot to a target location. The sort of the target locations in the chromosome is also important as it shows the sequence in which the robots will perform theirs routes.

The main objective of mTSP is to minimize the total distance traveled by all salesmen. However, it may cause an imbalance in the distance traveled by them. This may occur when a salesman travels far away to visit a city. Since mTSP aims to reduce the total distance, this salesman tends to cover all the cities around, as sending another salesman there, for visiting just a few cities, can increase the total distance. As a result, some salesmen might travel much more than others.

Therefore, we proposed the use of two objectives simultaneously. The first one, $\sum$, is responsible for minimizing the total distance traveled by the robots (Eq. 2), while the second, $\sigma$, aims to reduce the difference of the distance traveled individually (Eq. 3).

The distance $D_i$ of route $R_i$ traveled by robot $r_i$ is calculated by the sum of all path lengths, starting from the robot's position to its first target location, then the paths linking the sequence of target locations in the chromosome, and finally the path from the last target location to the return spot (Eq. 1).

$$D_i = |P_{(r_i, l_1)}| + \sum_{j=1}^{|R_i|} |P_{(j, j+1)}| + |P_{(l_{|R_i|}, d)}| \tag{1}$$

The total distance traveled by the team is given by summing the distance of all routes (Eq. 2)

$$\sum = \sum_{i=1}^{m} D_i \tag{2}$$

To measure how balanced the routes are, the standard deviation is calculated over the distance traveled by each robot (Eq. 3). A value of standard deviation means that the routes are balanced.

$$\sigma = \sqrt{\frac{\sum_{i=1}^{m} (D_i - \overline{D})^2}{m - 1}} \tag{3}$$

The mTSP is a permutation problem as the cities should not be repeated within the chromosome. Therefore, we used a crossover method, called Partially Matched Crossover (PMX) [5], that prevents the generation of invalid individuals as it performs safe permutations between the chromosomes. The PMX makes some changes to avoid repetition, which can generate different genetic structures when compared to the parents.

Once the route scheduling is done, the routes are sent to the robots and the system tracks the execution.

The system, implemented in *Java*, runs on the server-side. It has a Graphical User Interface (GUI) that enables the interaction to the user. This GUI is composed by two panels, one for configuration and another to monitor the execution.

When the user launches the system, the Control Panel appears on the screen. First, the user selects a map file of the desired environment, which is shown on the Execution Panel. At the same time, the system loads a file with several pre-built paths computed off-line with A* that links strategic areas of the map, like rooms and hallways. This paths are used latter to speedup the creation of the complete graph of the map.

Once the system is ready, the robots are able to establish a peer-to-peer connection to the server. To do that, each robot runs a ROS node, built on *Python*, that starts a Websocket connection.

The WebSocket protocol permits a full-duplex communication channels over a single TCP connection with lower overheads, facilitating real-time data transfer from and to the server. This is made possible by providing a standardized way for the server to send content to the client without being first requested by the client, and allowing messages to be passed back and forth while keeping the connection open. In this way, a two-way ongoing conversation can take place between the client and the server.

This is important to our application as the server sends target locations to robots, and the robots send their current positions frequently to the server, without being requested. Websocket also allows to exchange information from heterogeneous technologies, such as *Java* and *Python*.

After the *handshaking* required by the protocol, the system creates a *Thread* for every robot to hold its connection. One of its functions is to update the robot's position. The ROS node of the robot transforms its pose to map coordinate and sends this information to the *Thread*. Then, the *Thread* updates the robot's position on the map of the Execution Panel.

When the robots are properly connected to the system, they appear on the map with different colors along with their IP addresses. After that, the user can easily set the target locations and the return spot by clicking on the map.

Then, the route scheduling can be performed by selecting any MOEA available on the system. Before that, the system computes the complete graph by adapting pre-built static paths with straight lines to link the locations. Thus, the system can estimate the path length from one location to another and calculate the route distance.

At the end, the routes are sent to the *Threads*. Given the sorted list of target locations to be visited, a *Thread* sends the first one to the ROS node which starts the navigation towards it. As the *Thread* tracks the robot's position, when the target location is reached, it is marked as visited and the next one is sent to the robot. When the list becomes empty, the robot navigates to the return spot.

In case a *Thread* loses its connection to the ROS node, due to some failure, it warns the Control Panel that initiates a re-scheduling immediately considering only the remaining target locations and the available robots.

## 4  Experiments and Results

Experiments were carried out to evaluate our Online Route Scheduling System in terms of processing time, quality of routes, and connectivity to robots.

A turtlebot-2 robot [7] was used for these experiments. This robot consists of an Yujin Kobuki base, wheel encoders, wheel drop sensors, an integrated gyroscope, bump sensors, cliff sensors, a 2200 mAh battery pack, a Microsoft Kinect sensor, an Intel NUC i7, a fast charger, a WiFi dongle, and a hardware mounting kit attaching everything together.

The system was tested in two environments. The first one is a simulation environment, called WillowGarage, which is a large area composed by a lot of rooms and hallways. This environment allows us to easily try different scenarios and control several virtual turtlebot-2, running on ROS Gazebo simulator in individual computers. In (Fig. 3), on the right, 3 virtual turtlebot-2 are performing their routes on ROS Gazebo. The image at the bottom shows all 4 computers.

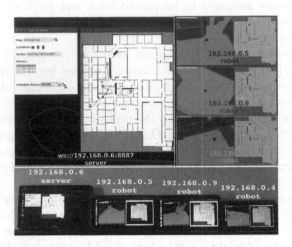

**Fig. 3. Simulation environment.** The system is shown on the left with a map of WillowGarage.

The Fig. 4 shows our second environment, a real house with some rooms and hallways. Its map was acquired by running GMapping algorithm on turtlebot-2. Although we have only one robot for this environment, the system works normally. The main purpose was to test the connectivity of our system to a real robot.

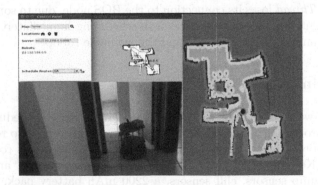

**Fig. 4. Real environment.** The system is shown on top, with a map of the house, during the execution of a route.

For the WillowGarage environment, we set four scenarios with: 1) 2 robots and 10 target locations, 2) 3 robots and 15 target locations, 3) 4 robots and 20 target locations, and 4) 5 robots and 25 target locations.

We ran 10 trials of each MOEA for all scenarios with a maximum Number objective Function Evaluations (NFE) equal to 10,000.

MOEAs return as outputs an approximation of the Pareto Optimal, called Approximation Set, which can be used to measure and compare their quality. They are composed by objective values of non-dominated solutions.

Generational Distance (GD) is the average distance from every solution in the Approximation Set to the nearest solution in a given Reference Set.

The Inverted Generational Distance (IGD) is the inverse of Generational Distance (GD) - it is the average distance from every solution in the Reference Set to the nearest solution in the Approximation Set.

The additive $\epsilon$-indicator, or simply $\epsilon_+$, measures the smallest distance $\epsilon$ that the Approximation Set must be translated by in order to completely dominate the Reference Set. Good proximity and good diversity both result in low values, as the distance that the approximation needs to be translated is reduced. However, if there is a region of the Reference Set that is poorly approximated by the solutions in the Approximation Set, a large is required. Therefore, $\epsilon_+$ indicator can be used to measure the consistency of an Approximation Set.

Spacing indicator measures the uniformity of the spacing between solutions in an Approximation Set. An Approximation Set that is well-spaced will not contain dense clusters of solutions separated by large empty expanses.

The R2-indicator compares the quality of two Approximation Sets based on a set of utility functions. The indicator is weakly monotonic and performs a lower computational overhead than the traditional hypervolume indicator.

The other indicators are presented in Table 1. Considering each indicator, the best values were given by SMS-EMOE, $\epsilon$NSGA-II, NSGA-II, IBEA, and RVEA.

**Table 1. Quality metrics.** 2 robots and 10 target locations.

| Algorithm | GD | IGD | $\epsilon_+$ | Spacing | R2 |
|---|---|---|---|---|---|
| RSO | 360.85 | 645.27 | 613.55 | 461.50 | 5435.55 |
| eNSGAII | 242.21 | **549.52** | 539.25 | 542.26 | 4473.77 |
| NSGAII | 245.31 | **549.52** | 548.83 | 521.50 | 4473.89 |
| SMS-EMOA | **199.39** | 572.37 | **532.44** | 316.08 | 4794.13 |
| NSGAIII | 223.32 | 554.34 | 547.44 | 519.62 | 4478.78 |
| SPEA2 | 212.52 | 571.60 | 547.44 | 480.61 | 4479.48 |
| DBEA | 242.92 | 554.34 | 546.33 | 594.67 | 4858.34 |
| RVEA | 282.61 | 563.36 | 539.25 | 577.35 | **4473.70** |
| PAES | 243.36 | 726.77 | 667.72 | 200.38 | 5877.45 |
| PESA2 | 228.15 | 589.50 | 571.19 | 461.40 | 5092.89 |
| eMOEA | 203.68 | 603.86 | 580.77 | 259.00 | 4879.73 |
| IBEA | 323.61 | 571.60 | 547.72 | **184.46** | 4825.32 |
| Random | 307.11 | 639.71 | 616.05 | 675.77 | 5532.57 |
| VEGA | 370.70 | 668.72 | 651.88 | 251.83 | 5879.97 |

This shows that the MOEAs found more non-dominated solutions in their Approximation Sets for this instance. Although the solutions in each Approximation Sets are non-dominate, they didn't present distant values for $\sigma$ and $\sum$ either, which improved the Spacing indicator for most of the MOEAs.

Random and PAES couldn't find very good solutions in terms of total travel distance and balancing, as their Approximation Sets present.

Therefore, solutions found by them are easily dominated by the other MOEAs, which impacts on indicators such as R2.

Table 2 highlights that $\epsilon$NSGA-II and RVEA are still having the best IGD and R2, respectively. Moreover, $\epsilon$NSGA-II also reached the lowest value for $\epsilon_+$ indicator.

**Table 2.** Quality metrics. 3 robots and 15 target locations.

| Algorithm | GD | IGD | $\epsilon_+$ | Spacing | R2 |
|-----------|--------|---------|---------|--------|---------|
| RSO | 533.51 | 1086.73 | 993.13 | 907.61 | 8826.84 |
| eNSGAII | 269.04 | **763.08** | **738.00** | 183.99 | 6655.05 |
| NSGAII | 207.96 | 852.89 | 747.72 | 113.28 | 6743.25 |
| SMS-EMOA | 244.22 | 886.00 | 817.02 | 199.73 | 7368.30 |
| NSGAIII | 223.04 | 798.54 | 783.83 | 250.61 | 6958.68 |
| SPEA2 | 174.07 | 876.00 | 828.55 | 201.94 | 7470.43 |
| DBEA | 345.58 | 928.17 | 878.13 | 526.10 | 7897.74 |
| RVEA | 198.15 | 808.62 | 743.27 | 107.65 | **6622.55** |
| PAES | 407.09 | 1285.49 | 1054.25 | 61.86 | 9087.91 |
| PESA2 | 178.31 | 953.45 | 904.80 | 60.83 | 8156.49 |
| eMOEA | **129.10** | 941.73 | 847.44 | **54.56** | 7508.85 |
| IBEA | 255.31 | 834.74 | 801.33 | 74.29 | 7225.25 |
| Random | 475.86 | 1087.86 | 1025.08 | 717.74 | 9095.36 |
| VEGA | 465.25 | 1008.40 | 983.27 | 370.25 | 8863.13 |

It was noticed that $\epsilon$MOEA also outperformed other MOEAs in two indicators, GD and Spacing.

Solutions yielded by RSO, PAES, and Random are visibly dominated by the others. On the hand, SPEA-II, NSGA-II, NSGA-III, RVEA are closely to where should be the Pareto Optimal, reflecting on indicators such as GD, IGD, and R2 (Table 3).

**Table 3. Quality metrics.** 4 robots and 20 target locations.

| Algorithm | GD | IGD | $\epsilon_+$ | Spacing | R2 |
|---|---|---|---|---|---|
| RSO | 743.89 | 1503.71 | 1384.80 | 1248.24 | 12231.19 |
| eNSGAII | 222.63 | 1054.42 | 993.27 | 103.29 | 8952.57 |
| NSGAII | **141.54** | 1088.37 | 1007.58 | 67.30 | 9082.32 |
| SMS-EMOA | 193.52 | 1142.27 | 1062.16 | 183.42 | 9573.69 |
| NSGAIII | 206.64 | **1000.47** | 930.63 | 193.48 | 8382.58 |
| SPEA2 | 148.72 | 1088.43 | 1000.22 | 74.73 | 9016.85 |
| DBEA | 491.18 | 1229.05 | 1154.66 | 912.56 | 10406.31 |
| RVEA | 204.99 | 1028.99 | **929.52** | 89.64 | **8380.38** |
| PAES | 279.67 | 1494.64 | 1366.05 | 85.83 | 12308.68 |
| PESA2 | 194.31 | 1262.75 | 1202.86 | 73.51 | 10840.39 |
| eMOEA | 185.18 | 1180.23 | 1109.52 | **46.00** | 9999.19 |
| IBEA | 244.75 | 1039.94 | 1000.63 | 136.04 | 9019.57 |
| Random | 551.20 | 1512.47 | 1366.05 | 573.99 | 12129.32 |
| VEGA | 719.80 | 1330.83 | 1315.77 | 284.79 | 11855.27 |

Table 4 presents the results for our last scenario, with 5 robots and 25 target locations. $\epsilon$NASA-II had the lowest value for 3 of the 5 indicators. $\epsilon$MOEA was the best in GD and PESA-II in Spacing.

**Table 4. Quality metrics.** 5 robots and 25 target locations.

| Algorithm | GD | IGD | $\epsilon_+$ | Spacing | R2 |
|---|---|---|---|---|---|
| RSO | 864.68 | 1961.06 | 1789.38 | 667.30 | 16108.48 |
| eNSGAII | 207.31 | **1299.50** | **1220.63** | 76.35 | **10999.71** |
| NSGAII | 220.30 | 1386.81 | 1311.05 | 100.40 | 11812.91 |
| SMS-EMOA | 287.47 | 1433.22 | 1388.00 | 187.87 | 12071.38 |
| NSGAIII | 217.69 | 1309.24 | 1229.63 | 180.94 | 11070.28 |
| SPEA2 | 211.20 | 1421.90 | 1360.50 | 155.11 | 12258.46 |
| DBEA | 529.72 | 1627.41 | 1556.88 | 385.71 | 14025.94 |
| RVEA | 208.78 | 1312.61 | 1236.88 | 82.52 | 11146.00 |
| PAES | 256.37 | 1920.22 | 1777.86 | 85.18 | 16025.38 |
| PESA2 | 214.23 | 1536.57 | 1478.60 | **56.57** | 13248.54 |
| eMOEA | **202.12** | 1473.49 | 1393.69 | 80.52 | 12557.17 |
| IBEA | 290.28 | 1341.38 | 1306.61 | 82.96 | 11772.88 |
| Random | 783.97 | 1942.69 | 1761.47 | 1056.42 | 15870.78 |
| VEGA | 761.35 | 1598.91 | 1565.77 | 562.95 | 14105.86 |

458     R. Alves et al.

MOEAs from NSGA family have been outperforming their counterparts for a long. In general, regarding the scenarios and indicators used during this experiment, εNSGA-II was the best choice for solving mTSP as it reached the lowest values, or was at least closed to them, in most of the cases.

We compared the elapsed time of εNSGA-II with εMOEA and RVEA, which also provided good results. The Fig. 5 depicts the average time for 10 trials with NFE equal to 10,000. The x-axis of the charts shows the NFE and the values of y-axis are the cumulative time in seconds.

Although εNSGA-II wasn't the fasted MOEA, it can generate high quality solutions in a reasonable time for an online application. For instance, the average time for scheduling routes with 5 robots and 25 target locations was less than 0,2 s.

Our last experiment is regarding the connectivity and response time between the system and robots, which is also important for real-time applications. The results shows that the system can track the robot's position almost instantly.

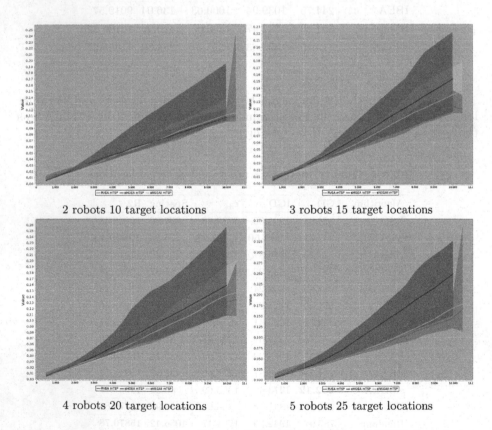

2 robots 10 target locations

3 robots 15 target locations

4 robots 20 target locations

5 robots 25 target locations

**Fig. 5. Elapsed time.** Average time of εNSGA-II, εMOEA, and RVEA in each scenario.

When the ROS node loses the connection and stops sending the localization, due to some robot failure, the system is warned at the same time.

In a multi-robot scenario, when this happens, the system automatically starts a re-scheduling considering the available robots and remaining target locations, and sends new routes to the robots as soon as they are computed.

## 5    Conclusion

This work introduces the problem of scheduling routes for a team of robots in indoor environments. This problem can be seen as an instance of the multiple Traveling Salesmen Problem (mTSP) in which robots are salesmen and cities are target locations to be visited. Since mTSP is classified as NP-hard, approximation and heuristic methods like Evolutionary Algorithms are widely applied as they can find good solutions very quickly.

Although its main objective is to minimize the total route distance traveled by all salesmen, an imbalance in the distance traveled by each of them might occur depending on the distribution of the cities. Therefore, a second objective was taking into account, the minimization of the standard deviation for the route distance.

Given these two objectives, we developed a system to generate routes and track robots positions in real-time using several Multi Objective Evolutionary Algorithms (MOEAs).

Such a system was deployed on a novel Robot-Server Architecture based on ROS and Websocket, which handles the communication between the system and robots. Thanks to this architecture, the system can detects failures on the connection and automatically starts a re-scheduling when some robot goes down.

Experiments were carried out to compare 14 state-of-the-art MOEAs with different performance indicators on real and virtual robot environments.

For future work, we are intended to run experiments with more real robots and compared Websocket to other protocols.

## References

1. Chen, X., Zhang, P., Du, G., Li, F.: Ant colony optimization based memetic algorithm to solve bi-objective multiple traveling salesmen problem for multi-robot systems. IEEE Access 6, 21745–21757 (2018). https://doi.org/10.1109/ACCESS.2018.2828499
2. Cheng, R., Jin, Y., Olhofer, M., Sendhoff, B.: A reference vector guided evolutionary algorithm for many-objective optimization. IEEE Trans. Evol. Comput. 20(5), 773–791 (2016)
3. Deb, K., Mohan, M., Mishra, S.: A fast multi-objective evolutionary algorithm for finding well-spread pareto-optimal solutions. KanGAL Rep. 2003002, 1–18 (2003)
4. Deb, K., Pratap, A., Agarwal, S., Meyarivan, T.: A fast and elitist multiobjective genetic algorithm: Nsga-ii. IEEE Trans. Evol. Comput. 6(2), 182–197 (2002)

5. Goldberg, D.E., Lingle, R., et al.: Alleles, loci, and the traveling salesman problem. In: Proceedings of an International Conference on Genetic Algorithms and their Applications, vol. 154, pp. 154–159. Lawrence Erlbaum Hillsdale, NJ (1985)
6. Kollat, J.B., Reed, P.M.: Comparison of multi-objective evolutionary algorithms for long-term monitoring design. In: Impacts of Global Climate Change, pp. 1–11 (2005)
7. Koubâa, A., et al.: Turtlebot at office: a service-oriented software architecture for personal assistant robots using ROS. In: 2016 International Conference on Autonomous Robot Systems and Competitions (ICARSC), pp. 270–276. IEEE (2016)
8. Mantha, B.R., Jung, M.K., de Soto, B.G., Menassa, C.C., Kamat, V.R.: Generalized task allocation and route planning for robots with multiple depots in indoor building environments. Autom. Constr. **119**, 103359 (2020)
9. Sullivan, N., Grainger, S., Cazzolato, B.: A dual genetic algorithm for multi-robot routing with network connectivity and energy efficiency. In: 2018 15th International Conference on Control, Automation, Robotics and Vision (ICARCV), pp. 1647–1652, November 2018. https://doi.org/10.1109/ICARCV.2018.8581219
10. Sun, R., Tang, C., Zheng, J., Zhou, Y., Yu, S.: Multi-robot path planning for complete coverage with genetic algorithms. In: Yu, H., Liu, J., Liu, L., Ju, Z., Liu, Y., Zhou, D. (eds.) ICIRA 2019. LNCS (LNAI), vol. 11744, pp. 349–361. Springer, Cham (2019). https://doi.org/10.1007/978-3-030-27541-9_29
11. Touzani, H., Hadj-Abdelkader, H., Séguy, N., Bouchafa, S.: Multi-robot task sequencing & automatic path planning for cycle time optimization: application for car production line. IEEE Robot. Autom. Lett. **6**(2), 1335–1342 (2021)
12. Trigui, S., Cheikhrouhou, O., Koubaa, A., Zarrad, A., Youssef, H.: An analytical hierarchy process-based approach to solve the multi-objective multiple traveling salesman problem. Intell. Serv. Robot. **11**(4), 355–369 (2018). https://doi.org/10.1007/s11370-018-0259-8
13. Wei, C., Ji, Z., Cai, B.: Particle swarm optimization for cooperative multi-robot task allocation: a multi-objective approach. IEEE Robot. Autom. Lett. **5**(2), 2530–2537 (2020)

# Towards Using Reinforcement Learning for Autonomous Docking of Unmanned Surface Vehicles

Martin Holen[1]([email]) , Else-Line Malene Ruud[2], Narada Dilp Warakagoda[2,3] ,
Morten Goodwin[1] , Paal Engelstad[3], and Kristian Muri Knausgård[4]

[1] Centre for Artificial Intelligence Research, University of Agder,
Kristiansand, Norway
`martin.holen@uia.no`
[2] Norwegian Defence Research Establishment (FFI), Kjeller, Norway
[3] Institute for Technology Systems, University of Oslo, Oslo, Norway
[4] Top Research Centre Mechatronics, University of Agder, Kristiansand, Norway

**Abstract.** Providing full autonomy to Unmanned Surface Vehicles
(USV) is a challenging goal to achieve. *Autonomous docking* is a sub-
task that is particularly difficult. The vessel has to distinguish between
obstacles and the dock, and the obstacles can be either static or moving.
This paper developed a simulator using Reinforcement Learning (RL) to
approach the problem.

We studied several scenarios for the task of docking a USV in a simulator environment. The scenarios were defined with different sensor
inputs and start-stop procedures but a simple shared reward function.
The results show that the system solved the task when the IMU (Inertial
Measurement Unit) and GNSS (Global Navigation Satellite System) sensors were used to estimate the state, despite the simplicity of the reward
function.

**Keywords:** Simulation · USV · Reinforcement Learning

## 1 Introduction

Autonomous vehicles have attracted significant interest in recent years, in diverse
areas such as drones, self-driving cars, and sea transport [3,21,26,32]. This paper
deals with Unmanned Surface Vessels (USVs), an area that has displayed remark-
able progress in the past few years. There are a few benefits of making the surface
vehicles unmanned, such as removing the cost of the crew, and for shipping, the
possibility of removing crew areas such as cabins and bathrooms [15]; human
factors are also removed [16], such as getting tired, and the ability to see in 360°
around the vessel, continuously.

One of the challenges associated with the development of USVs is that of
docking, as the USV has to navigate through narrow spaces, avoid obstacles,

© Springer Nature Switzerland AG 2022
L. Iliadis et al. (Eds.): EANN 2022, CCIS 1600, pp. 461–474, 2022.
https://doi.org/10.1007/978-3-031-08223-8_38

localize itself and map the environment. Therefore, avoiding collisions while moving in and out of the dock autonomously is a difficult task. It is also important not to crash into other boats, the docks, or other obstacles. Approaching the docks at high speed could damage both the USV and the docks.

In order to solve the task of docking, we applied Reinforcement Learning (RL) which is commonly used in video games and for controlling vehicles and more [7,8,12,17,19,34]. When performing RL, the state is given as the input to the RL algorithm. The output of the RL algorithm is called actions, which are used with the state, the next state, and the reward for improving the reward it receives from the environment. State of the art RL algorithms include Deep-Q Networks (DQN) [19], Deep Deterministic Policy Gradient (DDPG) [17] and Proximal Policy Optimization (PPO) [25]. DQN has shown significant progress for video games [19], though it does not allow for continuous actions. Instead, these algorithms use discretized actions, meaning that the algorithm predicts the action from a finite set of actions, such as keyboard controls for a driving game. Continuous actions allow for a greater degree of control, examples of implementations can be found in [20,28,31,33]. DDPG and PPO can be applied to problems with continuous action spaces [17,25], allowing for more gradual control.

PPO is an algorithm with the benefits of trust region policy optimizations where surrogate objectives do the estimations. The surrogate objectives consist of two components, and it chooses the pessimistic loss, as shown in Eq. 2, which makes sure the policy updates are not too excessive [25]. When using an actor-critic architecture, the overall loss function would consist of the policy loss corresponding to the surrogate objective and the value function loss. This leads to Eq. 3, where the policy loss $L^{CLIP}$ refers to Eq. 2, and value function loss $L^{VF}$ refers to Eq. 1 where the value function loss is the squared error between the predicted value $V_\theta(st)$ and the target value $V_t^{targe}$. The target value is assumed to be the total reward returned by the environment.

In addition to the policy and value function losses, we use an extra loss $S_\pi(...)$ representing the entropy of the policy as shown in 3.

$$L^{VF}(\theta) = (V_\theta(st) - V_t^{targ})^2 \tag{1}$$

$$L^{CLIP}(\theta) = \hat{E}_t[min(r_t(\theta)\hat{A}_t \\ + clip(r_t(\theta), 1 - \epsilon, 1 + \epsilon)\hat{A}_t)] \tag{2}$$

$$L_t^{CLIP+VF+S}(\theta) = \hat{E}_t[L_t^{CLIP}(\theta) - c_1 L_t^{VF}(\theta) \\ + c_2 S[\pi_\theta](st)] \tag{3}$$

There has been significant research on the use of RL for autonomous vehicles, for purposes such as reducing noisy rudder behavior [18], autonomous parking [34] as well as using Deep RL for controlling an Autonomous Underwater Vehicle while being affected by outside disturbances [7]. There is also some work exploring the use of RL algorithms instead of traditional control algorithms [12,27], where it was observed that RL algorithms could predict actions similar to the optimal control algorithms. In addition, they are also able to deal with disturbances observed.

Based on the literature review conducted, there are only a few studies that employ RL for docking of USVs [4,8], though there simulators are to our knowledge, not open-source or freely available. This opens up the need to develop an RL-based simulator that can be used to study an autonomous docking system. The main contribution of our work is the development of a new simulator for docking of USVs. This simulator provides a "standardized" way of creating and testing RL algorithms for docking. It was developed in Unity with the **socketio** module,[1] to control the USV with a programming language such as Python, C# or C++. We have provided the simulator as open-source software.[2]

Our work also demonstrates that it is possible to train an RL algorithm for the task of autonomous docking of USVs using our simulator. The paper proposes a reward function, which is a significant challenge in applying RL for industrial purposes. The solution is developed and validated with the simulator.

This paper is organized as follows: Sect. 2 presents our methods for implementing the simulator and the agents for the environment. Then, the results of our experiments are presented and discussed in Sect. 3, followed by conclusions in Sect. 4.

## 2   Methods

This section will discuss the environment, the agent, and the reward function created for our simulator. First, the environment gives the state to the agent. Then, simultaneously, the agent generates the actions to perform in the environment. Finally, the reward function updates the agent, giving it feedback about its performance.

### 2.1   Environment

The agent's environment is simple, containing land, water, and docks. With the water being the area the USV moves across, the land is the obstacle to avoid, and the docks are the goals. For the agent to learn how to control the USV, it gets a reward from the reward functions. The higher the reward, the more the USV got to or moved towards the docks.

### 2.2   Agent

The agent is the entity that interacts with the environment.[3] It gets information about the environment through the given sensors and generates actions to change

---

[1] https://github.com/udacity/self-driving-car-sim.

[2] https://anonymous.4open.science/r/boatSimulator-3605/.

[3] https://anonymous.4open.science/r/SteeringDockingPaper-98BC/README.md.

the state of the environment. To train this agent, we use the PPO algorithm on a simple Neural Network (NN) [25]. The reason for choosing PPO is that it is among the best algorithms for training in a continuous action space.

**Neural Network.** The Neural Network (NN) used in the study was a simple neural network with three layers, similar to that from ALVINN [23]. It has an input layer, a hidden layer, and an output layer, and all these layers are implemented as fully connected layers. For Scenarios 1,2, and 3, the input layer has 256*256*3 units, the hidden layer has 64 units, and the output layer has three units. The three outputs represent different actions, the first being the force the USV is pushed forward or backwards with, the second being the force to either sides of the USV; lastly a boolean which when it reaches a threshold changes between forward and reverse. Scenario 4 has an input layer with six units, while the hidden layer and output layer have the same number of units as in previous scenarios. The first three scenarios have 12 583 104 weights, while scenario 4 has 576 weights to update. Between each layer, there was a *tanh* activation, suggested by [2]. They are trained until they converge or for 1000 updates of the neural network parameters. Convergence implies that the reward was unchanged for 100 episodes.

## 2.3   Reward Function

One of the challenges with using RL for non-trivial applications is to define an appropriate reward function [4] for the model. It is imperative for the reward function to capture the realistic behavior of the vehicle. The reward function defined in this study is such that it has three main components. Firstly, if the USV completes the episode by going to a dock, the agent receives a reward of +1000. Secondly, the previous distance to the current dock and the new distance are used to calculate how far it traveled, as shown in Eq. 4

$$reward_i = distance_{i-1} - distance_i \qquad (4)$$

Thirdly, a reward of –0.01 is given for each action performed, and this is meant to decrease the amount of stalling done by the vehicle, i.e., sitting in the same location. Using this reward function, we can pick and choose to attempt to find the best fit for each scenario.

## 3   Simulator

We have developed a simulator to study the Reinforcement learning-based approach for docking of USVs. There are several commercially available and open-source software for simulating physics-based environments, like OpenAI Gym [5], Gazebo [14], Unity [13] and Unreal engine [10]. Our simulator was built using the Unity game engine [13] for physics and visualization, SocketIO [24] was used for communication between the environment and the agent, the flow of which can be seen in Fig. 1b. Based on the simulator, a set of scenarios was created where an increasing complexity from one approach to the next.

The USV is controlled by applying forces at the rear of the USV, simulating a physical vehicle. The following sections describe the sensors and control in more detail.

### 3.1 Sensors

For an RL algorithm to understand its environment, it needs sensors, including a camera, an inertial measurement unit (IMU), and a global navigation satellite system (GNSS) sensor. The camera is a built-in sensor in the Unity GameEngine. It captures an RGB image and is an idealized sensor, meaning that it will provide a noise-free picture of the scene. The camera is rotated about the Z-axis, showing a top-down overview of the USV, dock, ocean, and the land, which lies on the x-y plane, simulating a local map made using Lidar/RADAR or a detailed prior map.

Next, we have an IMU sensor, a built-in Unity sensor implemented as a GameObject. A GameObject is an object in the Unity environment that can hold other GameObjects, scripts, and other entities. A given GameObject is associated with a transformation, which includes its position, rotation, and scale [30]. The IMU sensor includes the velocity and angular velocity components along the x, y, and z axes. The GNSS, also a built-in GameObject, is an idealized sensor that gives the exact position in $(x, y, z)$ coordinates and rotation of the USV, the notation of which can be found in Table 1.

**Table 1.** DOF = Degree of freedom, Mot = motion in *axis, Rot = Rotation around the *-axis, FM = Forces and Moments, LAV = Linear and Angular velocities, PEA = Positions and Euler angles

| DOF | | FM | LAV | PEA |
|---|---|---|---|---|
| 1 | Mot xb axis (surge) | X | u | $x^n$ |
| 2 | Mot yb axis (sway) | Y | v | $y^n$ |
| 3 | Mot zb axis (heave) | Z | w | $z^n$ |
| 4 | Rot xb-axis (roll) | K | p | $\phi$ |
| 5 | Rot yb-axis (pitch) | N | q | $\theta$ |
| 6 | Rot zb-axis (yaw) | Z | r | $\psi$ |

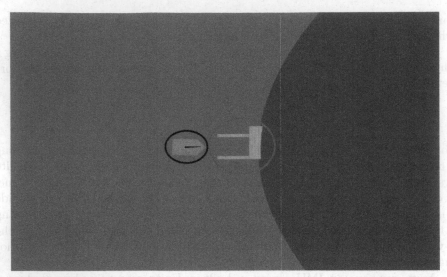

(a) The black circle shows the boat. The red circle showing the dock. While the green is land, and blue is the ocean

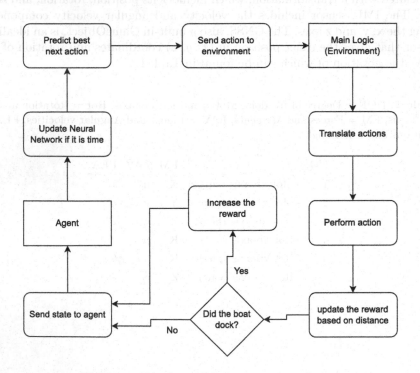

(b) Shows a flow chart of the environment and agent

**Fig. 1.** Shows the environment, as well as a flow chart of how it functions (Color figure online)

## 3.2 Control

Actions from the agent (see Eq. 5) are applied to the USV as shown in Fig. 2. For the actions $(X, Y, r)$ to be applied, they first have to be translated to forces. $X$ is the propulsive force in the body's X direction, $Y$ is the propulsive force in the body's Y direction and $r$ is either –1 or 1 used to change between reverse and moving forwards. As Unity does not consider the bearing of the object, meaning that as the USV turns, the agent will have to take the angle into account when making its prediction. We use the rotation along the $z$ axis of the USV $(\psi)$ to calculate which direction to send the forces. This means that the forces would be added from the rear to the front of the boat when its rotation is 0, but when its rotation is 90, the same force will go from the left (port) to the right (starboard).

The forces to the body are calculated from the three actions (see Eq. 5) to the $F^{body}$ (see Eq. 6). We then use the rotation of USV to calculate the rotational matrix (see Eq. 7) for the Unity coordinate system. $F^{body}$ and $R_\psi$ are then used to calculate the forces $(F^{ENU})$ which are directly applied to the USV (see Eq. 8). The notation of the control equations can be found in Table 1.

$$actions = [X \quad Y \quad r]^T \tag{5}$$

$$F^{body} = [rX \quad Y]^T \tag{6}$$

$$R_\psi = \begin{bmatrix} cos(\psi) & -sin(\psi) \\ sin(\psi) & cos(\psi) \end{bmatrix} \tag{7}$$

$$F^{ENU} = R_\psi^T F^{body} \tag{8}$$

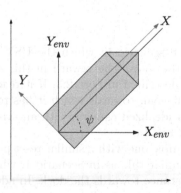

**Fig. 2.** Forces (X, Y) applied on the USV, given the predicted force $(X_{env}, Y_{env})$

# 4   Experiments and Results

This section focuses on the results of each of the four scenarios outlined below. In each scenario, we trained the agent until they converged or for 1000 parameter updates (backpropagations). The number of backpropagations was chosen due to the time constraint.

In order to test our algorithm in the environment, a few different scenarios were defined, each with a differing degree of complexity. We have considered four scenarios, one of which does not include islands (which might hinder the movement of the boat), and the rest include islands. For the latter three scenarios, we use a top-down idealized camera sensor hanging in the air while following the vessel.

These four scenarios differ quite a bit, each with its reward functions and reset system, an overview of which can be found in Table 2. In addition, the last scenario has a different environment setting. In the following, we describe each scenario in more detail.

**Table 2.** Shows the different scenarios implemented. In the table the following X, O actions indicate, X - Yes, O - No. ResetDocked means that the USV is Reset when it is close enough to the dock. ResetOffMap, Resets the USV when it goes off the map. Reset25m means that the USV is Reset when it drives away from its Reset position of 10 m–15 m

| Scenario | Image | Islands | State | ResetDocked | ResetOffMap | Reset25 m |
|---|---|---|---|---|---|---|
| Scenario 1 | X | X | O | O | X | O |
| Scenario 2 | X | X | O | O | X | O |
| Scenario 3 | X | X | O | X | X | X |
| Scenario 4 | O | O | X | X | X | X |

Scenario 1 is a simple scenario in which the USV is reset to its spawning location if it moves off the map. The reward in this scenario is based on the generic reward function described in Sect. 2.3. If it reaches the goal, it is given a new dock as its current goal, towards which it has to navigate again. For its state, it uses a top-down idealized camera, with an arrow pointing towards the current goal as shown in Fig. 1a.

Scenario 2 is also a simple one with a similar reset policy as in Scenario 1. Its reward function has a similar rule as in Scenario 1, where a reward is awarded based on the traveled distance towards the dock. In addition, when attempting to apply an action, this scenario penalizes any actions which are not directing the USV towards the current goal. When an action is bearing towards the goal, with a maximum deviation of 45°, or the predicted force $X$ is lower than 0.5, the forces are applied to the vessel; otherwise, the action is not applied, and the agent receives a penalty. If it reaches the goal, it is given a new dock as its current goal, towards which it has to navigate again. For its state, it uses a top-down idealized camera, with an arrow pointing towards the current goal as shown in Fig. 1a.

Scenario 3 resets the USV for moving off the map, moving further than 25 m away from the goal or reaching its goal. If the USV is reset or is spawning, it is placed within 45° of the current goal and at a distance of 10–15 m. This means that the USV is reset close to the opening of the docks. If it reaches the goal, it is given a new dock as its current goal, which it has to navigate towards it again. The reward function of this scenario is identical to that of Scenario 1. For its state, it uses a top-down idealized camera, with an arrow pointing towards the current goal as shown in Fig. 1a.

Scenario 4 is somewhat more simplistic than the other scenarios as it does not include any islands which might act as obstacles. However, its reset strategy and reward function are identical to Scenario 3. For its state, it uses the IMU and GNSS data, precisely the distance in the x and y-axis, z rotation, z angular velocity, surge, and sway as shown in Fig. 3.

An overview of the scenarios can be found in Table 2.

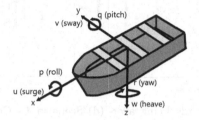

**Fig. 3.** The linear and rotational motion of the boat with respect to the coordinate system of the model, adopted from Fossen [11, 29]

Any reward greater than 700 achieved by the system implies that the USV reached the goal at least once. When the system has reached the goal and has performed more than 2000 actions, the NN parameters are updated; otherwise, the system continues to the next goal. With fewer experiences than the hyper-parameter batch size, the NN cannot sample the memory when updating.

Figure 4d shows that Scenario 4 converged after 100 backpropagations, while Fig. 4c shows that the algorithm did not learn much during this training, but it kept trying new things. Figure 4a and 4b represent scenario 1 and scenario 2, respectively. It is observed that they did not learn much, staying around a reward of –2.9 and deviating only three times around this score.

Table 3 shows the performance between backpropagation 100–200, where scenario 4 had the highest maximum, minimum, and average reward. Table 4 shows that there was little to no performance increase among scenarios 1,2, and 3, though scenario 2 seemed to be most negatively affected.

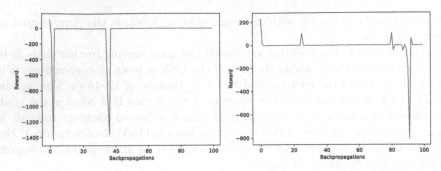

(a) Scenario 1 - Rewards being aver-  (b) Scenario 2 - Rewards being averaged over 10 backpropagations       aged over 10 backpropagations

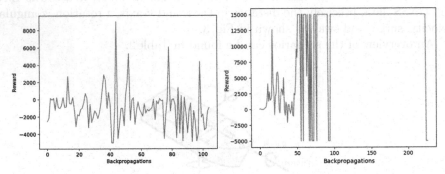

(c) Scenario 3 - Rewards being aver-  (d) Scenario 4 - Converged after only
aged over 10 backpropagations        about 100 episodes

**Fig. 4.** The results of the different scenarios

The Scenarios show that there is a difference in the reward awarded in different scenarios. Scenarios 1 and 2 did very poorly, with essentially no improvement or learning. For Scenario 4, we see a rapid improvement, while Scenario 3 attempted to update the NN but did not converge over the 1000 episodes.

In the different scenarios, the agent has got different types of rewards. In Scenarios 3 and 4, the agents were given positive rewards more often. In Scenarios 1 and 2, the agents have got rewards only occasionally. The results are consistent with these patterns of reward functions showing that Scenario 4 learned more, which can be attributed to the feedback and simplicity of the environment.

Scenario 4 achieved the highest reward consistently after only about 100 backpropagations, with some exploration at the end.

**Table 3.** The nMax is the maximum number of times it reached dock, min is the lowest reward, and AVG is the average reward. These are done for episode 100–200, when scenario 4 converged.

| Scenario | nMax | Min. | AVG. |
|---|---|---|---|
| Scenario 1 | 0.0 | −3.1177 | −2.144 |
| Scenario 2 | 0.0 | −3.0 | −2.4031 |
| Scenario 3 | 15.0 | −5000 | −525.2318 |
| Scenario 4 | 15.0 | 15000 | 15000 |

**Table 4.** The nMax is the maximum number of times it reached dock, min is the lowest reward, and avg is the average reward. These are done for the last 100 episodes of each scenario.

| Scenario | nMax | Min. | AVG. |
|---|---|---|---|
| Scenario 1 | 0.0 | −2.9913 | −2.7341 |
| Scenario 2 | 1.0522 | −1686.1361 | −93.3627 |
| Scenario 3 | 11.74 | −5000 | −525.2318 |
| Scenario 4 | 15.0 | −5000 | 14800 |

Scenario 3 was observed to be varying quite a lot, implying that it was still training, with some substantial variations giving the USV between the maximum and the minimum reward. However, the average reward did not seem to improve much. Given more training time, we assume we could have increased the performance in this scenario. This behavior can be attributed to its higher complexity than that of Scenario 4 due to the camera being its sensor versus IMU and GNSS. Moving from one part of the map to the next is a more complex scenario, so Scenario 1 and Scenario 2 will take significantly longer to train.

Suppose we intend to improve Scenario 1 and 2. In that case, we may perform something similar to the approach in [9], where transfer learning is applied to start from the most straightforward scenario to the most difficult one, i.e., from Scenario 4 through Scenarios 3 and 2 to Scenario 1. Scenario 4 has an important advantage over the other scenarios due to the nature of its state-space where the agent has direct access to distance in $x$ and $y$ along with the angle of rotation to the goal, compared to having to learn this just from the bearings of an arrow pointing towards the goal in other scenarios. In Scenarios 1 and 2, the USV has to move from one dock to the next after it has reached a dock, and they are not spawned in the vicinity of the docks, making them more complex scenarios. However, if given enough time, Scenario 2 should get better feedback than Scenario 1, as Scenario 1 allows for actions that move it away from the next dock, unlike Scenario 2, which penalizes such actions while not performing them.

# 5   Conclusion and Further Work

In this work, we developed a simulator that could be used for RL. The contribution of this work is three-fold. Firstly we present an open-source Unity-based boat simulator for the development of USVs. Secondly, the application of RL to the docking problem was demonstrated in several scenarios; thirdly, a reward function to give feedback to the agents has been defined and studied. Finally, the performance of this simulator was tested in 4 different training scenarios, using IMU and GNSS or a top-down camera as the sensors. Each of these scenarios had a different variant of the reward function and the reset systems.

Our results showed that Scenario 4 converged very quickly while Scenario 1, 2, and 3 took quite long to train. We conclude that Scenario 4 achieved its goal of docking after updating the agent's parameters through only about 100 backpropagations. It was also concluded that scenarios 1 and 2 struggled due to their complexity and may require more feedback or a longer training time.

To improve the training of Scenario 1,2,3, we could use the state data similar to Scenario 4 in addition to the camera. For Scenarios 1 and 2, we could, for example, make checkpoints to provide additional feedback when the USV gets closer to them. It would also be interesting to train these algorithms for a more extended period and observe the changes. Another approach is to transfer the knowledge gathered in a more straightforward scenario to a more complex scenario through transfer learning. As well as developing the simulator further, implementing different propulsion methods, sensors, and developing the reward function. Moreover, lastly, it would be possible to move the simulation to a Gym environment [5] using Gym-unity [1] to train with the standard algorithms from baselines [22] or dopamine [6].

# References

1. ml-agents/gym-unity at main Unity-Technologies/ml-agents. https://github.com/Unity-Technologies/ml-agents/tree/main/gym-unity
2. Andrychowicz, M., et al.: What Matters In On-Policy Reinforcement Learning? A Large-Scale Empirical Study, June 2020. http://arxiv.org/abs/2006.05990
3. Badue, C., et al.: Self-driving cars: a survey. Expert Syst. Appl. **165**, 113816 (2021). https://doi.org/10.1016/J.ESWA.2020.113816
4. Bjering Strand, H.: Autonomous docking control system for the otter USV: a machine learning approach (2020). https://ntnuopen.ntnu.no/ntnu-xmlui/handle/11250/2780950
5. Brockman, G., et al.: OpenAI Gym, June 2016. https://arxiv.org/abs/1606.01540v1
6. Castro, P.S., Moitra, S., Gelada, C., Kumar, S., Bellemare, M.G.: Dopamine: a research framework for deep reinforcement learning, December 2018. https://arxiv.org/abs/1812.06110v1
7. Cui, R., Yang, C., Li, Y., Sharma, S.: Adaptive neural network control of AUVs with control input nonlinearities using reinforcement learning. IEEE Trans. Syst. Man Cybern. Syst. **47**(6), 1019–1029 (2017). https://doi.org/10.1109/TSMC.2016.2645699

8. Cui, Y., Osaki, S., Matsubara, T.: Autonomous boat driving system using sample-efficient model predictive control-based reinforcement learning approach. J. Field Robot. **38**(3), 331–354 (2021). https://doi.org/10.1002/ROB.21990

9. Dosovitskiy, A., Ros, G., Codevilla, F., López, A., Koltun, V.: CARLA: an open urban driving simulator. In: Conference on robot learning, pp. 1–16 (2017)

10. Epic Games, I.: The most powerful real-time 3D creation tool - unreal Engine. https://www.unrealengine.com/en-US/

11. Fossen, T.I.: Handbook of Marine Craft Hydrodynamics and Motion Control, 2nd Edition. 2nd edn. Wiley, Hoboken, April 2021

12. Gaudet, B., Linares, R., Furfaro, R.: Deep reinforcement learning for six degree-of-freedom planetary landing. Adv. Space Res. **65**(7), 1723–1741 (2020). https://doi.org/10.1016/J.ASR.2019.12.030

13. Juliani, A., et al.: Unity: a general platform for intelligent agents, September 2018. https://arxiv.org/abs/1809.02627v2

14. Koenig, N., Howard, A.: Design and use paradigms for Gazebo, an open-source multi-robot simulator. In: 2004 IEEE/RSJ International Conference on Intelligent Robots and Systems (IROS), vol. 3, pp. 2149–2154 (2004). https://doi.org/10.1109/IROS.2004.1389727

15. Kretschmann, L., Burmeister, H.C., Jahn, C.: Analyzing the economic benefit of unmanned autonomous ships: an exploratory cost-comparison between an autonomous and a conventional bulk carrier. Res. Transp. Bus. Manage. **25**, 76–86 (2017). https://doi.org/10.1016/J.RTBM.2017.06.002

16. Kyriakidis, M., et al.: A human factors perspective on automated driving. **20**(3), 223–249 (2017). https://doi.org/10.1080/1463922X.2017.1293187, https://www.tandfonline.com/doi/abs/10.1080/1463922X.2017.1293187

17. Lillicrap, T.P., et al.: Continuous control with deep reinforcement learning. In: 4th International Conference on Learning Representations, ICLR 2016 - Conference Track Proceedings, September 2015. https://arxiv.org/abs/1509.02971v6

18. Martinsen, A.B., Lekkas, A.M.: Straight-Path following for underactuated marine vessels using deep reinforcement learning. IFAC-PapersOnLine **51**(29), 329–334 (2018). https://doi.org/10.1016/J.IFACOL.2018.09.502

19. Mnih, V., et al.: Human-level control through deep reinforcement learning. Nature **518**(7540), 529–533 (2015). https://doi.org/10.1038/nature14236, https://www.nature.com/articles/nature14236

20. Moerland, T.M., Broekens, J., Plaat, A., Jonker, C.M.: A0C: alpha zero in continuous action space, May 2018. https://arxiv.org/abs/1805.09613v1

21. Mousazadeh, H., et al.: Developing a navigation, guidance and obstacle avoidance algorithm for an unmanned surface vehicle (USV) by algorithms fusion. Ocean Eng. **159**, 56–65 (2018). https://doi.org/10.1016/J.OCEANENG.2018.04.018

22. OpenAI: openai/baselines: OpenAI Baselines: high-quality implementations of reinforcement learning algorithms. https://github.com/openai/baselines

23. Pomerleau, D.A.: Alvinn: an autonomous land vehicle in a neural network. Adv. Neural Inf. Process. Syst. (1989). https://proceedings.neurips.cc/paper/1988/file/812b4ba287f5ee0bc9d43bbf5bbe87fb-Paper.pdf

24. Rai, R.: Socket. IO Real-Time Web Application Development - Rohit Rai - Google Books. Packt Publishing Ltd., Birmingham, 1st edn., February 2013. https://books.google.no/books?id=YgdbZbkTDkoC&pg=PT37&dq=socket+io&lr=&source=gbs_selected_pages&cad=2#v=onepage&q=socket%20io&f=false

25. Schulman, J., Wolski, F., Dhariwal, P., Radford, A., Klimov, O.: Proximal policy optimization algorithms, July 2017. https://arxiv.org/abs/1707.06347v2

26. Shao, G., Ma, Y., Malekian, R., Yan, X., Li, Z.: A novel cooperative platform design for coupled USV-UAV systems. IEEE Trans. Ind. Inf. **15**(9), 4913–4922 (2019). https://doi.org/10.1109/TII.2019.2912024

27. Shuai, Y., et al.: An efficient neural-network based approach to automatic ship docking. Ocean Eng. **191**, 106514 (2019). https://doi.org/10.1016/J.OCEANENG. 2019.106514

28. Tang, Y., Agrawal, S.: Discretizing continuous action space for on-policy optimization. In: Proceedings of the AAAI Conference on Artificial Intelligence, vol. 34, no. 04, pp. 5981–5988, April 2020. https://doi.org/10.1609/AAAI.V34I04.6059, https://ojs.aaai.org/index.php/AAAI/article/view/6059

29. Thor I. Fossen: Lecture Notes: TTK 4190 Guidance, Navigation and Control of vehicles. https://www.fossen.biz/wiley/pdf/Ch1.pdf

30. Unity: Unity - Manual: GameObjects. https://docs.unity3d.com/Manual/ GameObjects.html

31. Van Hasselt, H., Wiering, M.A.: Reinforcement learning in continuous action spaces. In: Proceedings of the 2007 IEEE Symposium on Approximate Dynamic Programming and Reinforcement Learning, ADPRL 2007, pp. 272–279 (2007). https://doi.org/10.1109/ADPRL.2007.368199

32. Vásárhelyi, G., Virágh, C., Somorjai, G., Nepusz, T., Eiben, A.E., Vicsek, T.: Optimized flocking of autonomous drones in confined environments. Sci. Robot. **3**(20) (2018). https://doi.org/10.1126/SCIROBOTICS. AAT3536/SUPPL_FILE/AAT3536_SM.PDF, https://www.science.org/doi/abs/ 10.1126/scirobotics.aat3536

33. Veelen, M.v., Spreij, P.: Evolution in games with a continuous action space Matthijs van Veelen · Peter Spreij (2008). https://doi.org/10.1007/s00199-008-0338-8

34. Zhang, P., et al.: Reinforcement learning-based end-to-end parking for automatic parking system. Sensors **19**(18), 3996 (2019). https://doi.org/10.3390/ S19183996, https://www.mdpi.com/1424-8220/19/18/3996/htmwww.mdpi.com/ 1424-8220/19/18/3996

# Text Classification/Natural Language

# An Exploration of Semi-supervised Text Classification

Henrik Lien[2], Daniel Biermann[2], Fabrizio Palumbo[1(✉)],
and Morten Goodwin[1,2]

[1] Artificial Intelligence Lab (AI Lab), Institutt for Informasjonsteknologi,
Oslo Metropolitan University, Oslo, Norway
`fabrizio@oslomet.no`
[2] Centre for Artificial Intelligence Research (CAIR), Department of ICT,
University of Agder, Grimstad, Norway
`{daniel.biermann,morten.goodwin}@uia.no`

**Abstract.** Good performance in supervised text classification is usually obtained with the use of large amounts of labeled training data. However, obtaining labeled data is often expensive and time-consuming. To overcome these limitations, researchers have developed Semi-Supervised learning (SSL) algorithms exploiting the use of unlabeled data, which are generally easy and free to access. With SSL, unlabeled and labeled data are combined to outperform Supervised-Learning algorithms. However, setting up SSL neural networks for text classification is cumbersome and frequently based on a trial and error process.

We show that the hyperparameter configuration significantly impacts SSL performance, and the learning rate is the most influential parameter. Additionally, increasing model size also improves SSL performance, particularly when less pre-processing data are available. Interestingly, as opposed to feed-forward models, recurrent models generally reach a performance threshold as pre-processing data size increases.

This article expands the knowledge on hyperparameters and model size in relation to SSL application in text classification. This work supports the use of SSL work in future NLP projects by optimizing model design and potentially lowering training time, particularly if time-restricted.

**Keywords:** Machine learning · Text classification · Semi-supervised learning

## 1 Introduction

Text classification has many useful application areas, for example, classifying emails, medical texts, or even sentiments. Manual text classification is unfeasible due to significant time and economic costs. Artificial Intelligence (AI) techniques automate text classification tasks, making text classification cheaper and practical. Within AI, neural networks using traditional supervised learning often require a substantial amount of labeled data to achieve good text classification

© Springer Nature Switzerland AG 2022
L. Iliadis et al. (Eds.): EANN 2022, CCIS 1600, pp. 477–488, 2022.
https://doi.org/10.1007/978-3-031-08223-8_39

performance. Unfortunately, obtaining labeled data frequently requires domain-specific expertise. In contrast, getting an extensive volume of unlabeled data is often free and simple. There is a significant amount of research within the exciting area of semi-supervised learning (SSL) for text classification. The SSL technique exploits both unlabeled and labeled data to achieve improved classification performance.

## Semi-supervised Learning
The field of machine learning frequently draws a line between *supervised learning* and *unsupervised learning* [4]. Supervised learning uses a dataset containing data (x-samples) and respective labels/targets (y-samples). In contrast, unsupervised learning uses a dataset containing data (x-samples) but not labels (y-samples). *SSL* uses both supervised and unsupervised learning [6,22]. SSL aims to increase the performance of either the supervised or unsupervised approach. It exploits knowledge from both approaches. In particular, if labeled data is challenging to obtain, using unlabeled data can be significantly useful. For successful use of SSL, three *assumptions* need to be satisfied: the smoothness assumption, the cluster assumption, and the manifold assumption [6, p. 6].

## Pre-training
Unsupervised pre-training utilizes labeled and unlabeled data within two phases. Parameters for unsupervised pre-training are static within feature extraction techniques. They can, however, be modified during the supervised fine-tuning within pre-training techniques. Before supervised learning, unlabeled data moves the decision border towards potentially more relevant areas with pre-training methods. Unsupervised pre-training of a model commonly lowers the required volume of labeled data necessary to achieve good performance. Downstream NLP tasks then became simpler and cheaper to implement. Unsupervised pre-training also makes it possible to fine-tune a model to multiple downstream tasks, reducing training time and regularly improving downstream performance. Pre-training research is therefore valuable within NLP.

## Impact of Parameters on SSL Performance
It is challenging to define precise circumstances where an SSL technique is effective. It is important to highlight that unlabeled data does not always improve results [19]. Previous literature has shown decreased performance as a result of SSL, a phenomenon probably under-reported because of publication bias [22]. Several articles have investigated the use and implementation of SSL [6,13,16,18,22], but it is still unclear how to maximise its performance. This is especially true when good results are reached using purely supervised classifiers, and deploying SSL are more likely to degrade performance. There are multiple parameters that can significantly impact SSL performance within text classification. These include:

## Pre-training Data Size
Raffel [17] et al. and Baevski et al. [2] show that reducing the volume of pre-training data can result in performance degradation since a large network could overfit on a small quantity of pre-training data. Raffel et al. [17] recommend

utilizing a significant amount of pre-training data. Importantly, obtaining additional unlabeled data is inexpensive and straightforward.

**Model Size**
Enlarging network size and/or training time generally improve results [17]. According to a recent paper by Bender et al. [3], the expanding scale of language models, estimated by volume of training data and parameters, has been a significant trend within NLP.

**Hyperparameters**
There is much literature showing that hyperparameters are very relevant for achieving good performance with SSL. Devlin et al. [8] observe that using a significant amount of data and increasing the number of hyperparameters, improves results particularly for GLUE [20]. In the RoBERTa paper [15], Liu et al. show that hyperparameters have a significant impact on SSL performance. You et al. [21] show that with 32k as batch size, BERT training time can be shortened significantly without affecting performance. Dai and Le [7] show that LSTM models can be trained and reach good performance on multiple text classification tasks, with fine adjustment of hyperparameters. It is important to highlight that some hyperparameters have bigger impact on the model performance than others. According to Goodfellow et al. [9], "The learning rate is perhaps the most important hyperparameter". However, there is not a significant volume of research exploring the impact of parameters on SSL performance for text classification.

This article explores the impact of hyperparameters, including pre-training data size and model size, on an SSL algorithm employed in a text classification task. A limited number of epochs and smaller models are used, due to hardware limitations. A program for running experiments is written based on code from an earlier project [14].

## 2    Methods

**Structure of Experiments**
Two experiment types are run for each model: Supervised learning (SL) experiments and Semi Supervised Learning (SSL) experiments. SL experiments train the models with labeled data only, without pre-training. SSL experiments pre-train the models using unlabeled data first. Then, the model is fine-tuned with labeled data.

- **Feed-Forward Model**
  It contains an embedding layer, a dropout layer, two hidden layers, and one or multiple output layers. It uses a single output layer for the text classification task because this requires only a single output. For the pre-training task with predicting two or three masked tokens, it uses two or three output layers. These output layers are sharing hidden layers. Therefore, this model does multi-task pre-training with hard parameter sharing.

- **GRU Model**
  This model contains an embedding layer, a dropout layer, a GRU layer, a dense hidden layer followed by a ReLU activation function, and a single or two/three output layers. The output layers are similar to the output layers in the feed-forward model.
- **Sequence to Sequence (Seq2seq), Classifier**
  It contains an encoder and a decoder. The decoder implements an attention mechanism. The encoder contains an embedding layer, a dropout layer, a bidirectional GRU layer, and the *hidden* layer. The decoder contains an embedding layer, a dropout layer, a GRU layer, an *energy* layer, and an output layer. The implemented *Seq2seq* model with attention mechanism is based on code from GitHub by aladdinpersson [1]. This model does single-task learning during pretext task training. Pretext task training uses the *Seq2seq* model, while supervised text classification training uses the *Classifier* model. Both these models contain an encoder. In contrast to the Seq2seq model, the Classifier model does not have a decoder. The Classifier achieved similar performance as the Seq2seq model during testing in a previous project [14]. Therefore, to improve training time, the Classifier model was used when possible. Additionally, in this work, we reference both the *Seq2seq* and *Classifier* model as *Seq2seq* model.

**Data Handling**
For pre-training, training, validation, and testing datasets are created from the original 20newsgroups [11] dataset. This data contains no headers, footers, or quotes. Unwanted characters are removed from this data. Data is split into sentences containing at the minimum 11 words. For each sentence, a sliding 10-word window iterates over the words. For each 10-word sequence, the words "*sos*" and "*[MASK]*" are inserted before the 10 words themselves. This includes the "*sos*" and "*[MASK]*" tokens in the resulting tokenizer. The eleventh word is also used, mainly because of using the codebase from the previous project [14]. Both supervised and downstream text classification training use data from the original Banking77 dataset [5]. A testing dataset is also obtained from [5] and used in experiments as validation data.

**Experimental Procedure**
After creating the 11-word datasets from the 20newsgroups and Banking77 datasets, both supervised learning and SSL experiments are run for each model. The vocabulary used by the tokenizer is limited to words that appear at least twice in the data. A downstream task experiment initializes model weights with the best model weights obtained during pretext task training. Best model weights achieve the lowest validation loss. If not pre-trained, model weights are randomly initialized. A model trains and validates for a particular number of epochs. The pre-training uses a masking pretext task. The "*[mask]*" token replaces two or three random tokens in the sequence and the objective is to predict the masked tokens. During pre-training or validation, each batch uses dynamic masking. By randomly masking sequences in each batch, the pre-training dataset is enlarged artificially. Sequences in pre-training batches randomly mask during both training and validation. For training, the cross entropy loss is calculated and model parameters are updated using the Adam optimizer.

**Hyperparameters**

This article uses two baseline hyperparameter configurations for experimentation. The *Vanilla configuration*, is meant to represent a typical configuration of hyperparameters used in machine learning. The *SOTA configuration*, is partly based on hyperparameters in two GitHub projects [10,12], based on a paper [7] by Dai and Le. The SOTA configuration masks three tokens in each ten-word sequence. This results in a masking of 30% for each 10-word sequence. Additionally, supervised, pre-training, and downstream training use 200 epochs each during experimentation.

Table 1 summarizes the hyperparameters used in this study. Additional controlled parameters are:

- Dataset size. The number of 10-word sequences created from the 20newsgroups dataset, to generate training, validation, and testing datasets. Used sizes range from 25k to 500k.
- Training, validation and test ratio. Ratios of 80%/10%/10% are used.
- 15 Newsgroups from the 20newsgroups dataset are used.
- Length of word sequences. 10-word sequences are generated from the 20newsgroups dataset.

**Model evaluation**

We evaluate the performance of the models not by an absolute measure but with a relative measure called *SSL performance*. The lowest achieved text classification validation loss using supervised learning, minus the lowest achieved text classification validation loss using SSL. This measure allows us to easily see if a model benefits from using a SSL scheme or not.

$$\text{SSL performance} = L_S - L_{SSL} \tag{1}$$

In Eq. 1, $L_S$ is the text classification loss using purely supervised learning, and $L_{SSL}$ is the text classification loss using SSL.

## 3   Results

**Impact of Hyperparameters Configuration and Model Size on the SSL Performance**

Figure 1 shows the impact of hyperparameter configuration and model size on the SSL performance for each model, represented as the mean and variance of 10 simulations each. For all models with SOTA configuration, SSL performance improves compared to the Vanilla configuration. This improvement supports the hypothesis that the hyperparameters configuration significantly impacts SSL performance. Ten simulations are not a substantial number of simulations for each model, so this figure should not be observed as significantly conclusive. As expected, more extensive models improve SSL performance compared to smaller models.

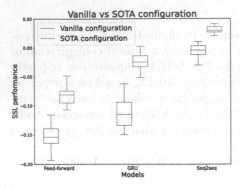

**Fig. 1.** Vanilla configuration versus SOTA configuration, using 25k pre-training data, 200 epochs for each training phase, and ten simulations for each configuration.

**Table 1.** Baseline vanilla configuration and SOTA configuration hyperparameters for experimentation

| Hyperparameter | Vanilla | SOTA |
|---|---|---|
| Embedding size | 512 | 256 |
| Batch size | 512 | 1024 |
| Hidden size | 1024 | 512 |
| Dropout rate | 0.0 | 0.2 |
| Learning rate | 0.0001 | 0.001 |
| Number of masked tokens | 2 | 3 |

## Impact of Increasing Pre-training Dataset Size on the SSL Performance

To test the impact of the pre-processing data size on the SSL performance we run each model configurations, both Vanilla and SOTA, with different pre-training data size. We expect that increasing the size of pre-training data leads to improved performance across all models. Additionally, based on the results observed in Fig. 1 we expect bigger models to outperform smaller ones. The results of SOTA simulations are shown in Fig. 2. For the feed-forward model, increasing the pre-training data amount leads to an increase in SSL performance. However, for both GRU and Seq2seq models, the SSL performance reaches a

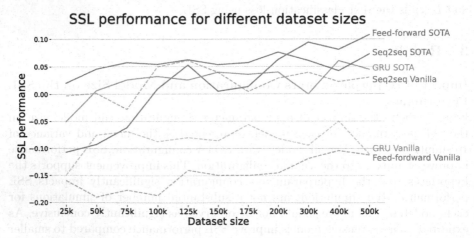

**Fig. 2.** Comparing pre-training data amounts, using SOTA and Vanilla configuration and 200 epochs for each training phase.

plateau when more than 100k sequences are used for pre-training. This experiment shows that a feed-forward model improves SSL performance as long as pre-training data volume increases. Importantly, with a recurrent model, increasing pre-training data size beyond 100k does not improve the SSL performance significantly. This result is unexpected. Next, we investigate the SSL performance across epochs by calculating the loss function for a fix 25K sequences pre-training dataset. This analysis clearly shows that for larger models, the loss graph converges faster (data not shown in this manuscript) and reaches lower values. Both these observations support the idea that more comprehensive models learn more useful features from pre-training data per epoch. These results, taken together with Fig. 2 also show that the more the loss graph converges, the less additional pre-training data improves SSL performance. Increasing pre-training data volume with SOTA configuration results in improved SSL performance for all models with different dynamics, as described in this paragraph. However, when the Vanilla configuration is tested in a similar framework, we observe a small or no impact of pre-training data size on SSL performance. This result is unexpected, particularly for the feed-forward model when compared to the SOTA configuration.

**Impact of Changing Single Hyperparameter on the SSL Performance**
To test the impact of each parameter on the SSL performance of the model and investigate whether the impact depends on other hyperparameters, we modify one parameter at a time while keeping the others constant. Simulations are performed with two different pre-training dataset sizes of 25K and 100K sequences. Only the 100K simulation is presented in Fig. 3. In Fig. 3 the impact of SSL performance is quantified across all models with the SOTA configuration as a starting point. As expected, the learning rate has a crucial impact on the results of the simulation: changing it from 0.001 to 0.0001 significantly lowers the SSL performance across all models. It is of particular interest to investigate the impact of different learning rates on the loss function of the model. In essence, when tested in a Seq2seq model, a higher learning rate (0.001) results in loss graphs converging significantly faster. Thus, indicating that the model has learned more useful knowledge during pre-training leading to improved downstream task performance. Another observation is that changing the dropout rate from 0.2 to 0.0 slightly increases the SSL performance for all models when using 100k dataset size. However, when the 25k dataset size is used (data not presented), changing the dropout rate to 0.0 significantly lowers the SSL performance for all models. This might be due to overfitting during pre-training when using only 25k data samples. This shows that the pre-training dataset size has an impact on the significance of single hyperparameters.

We last simulate the impact of changing single hyperparameters across models using the Vanilla configuration, Fig. 4. Again, the learning rate shows to be an important hyperparameter also for the Vanilla configuration. However, the way the learning rate influences SSL performance in the two configurations is not the same. In the SOTA configuration, decreasing the learning rate leads to lower SSL performance, Fig. 3. Therefore, it might be reasonable to expect

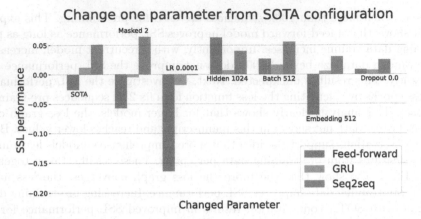

**Fig. 3.** Changing one parameter at a time from SOTA configuration, using 100k pretraining data and 200 epochs for each training phase

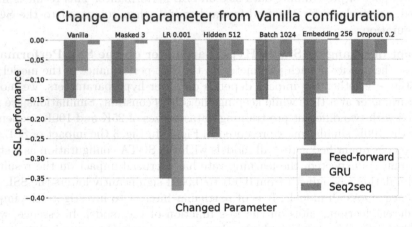

**Fig. 4.** Changing one parameter at a time from Vanilla configuration, using 25k pretraining data and 200 epochs for each training phase

the SSL performance to increase when increasing the learning rate. However, this is not the case. A similar decrease in SSL performance can be seen in the Vanilla configuration when increasing the learning rate from 0.0001 to 0.001, see Fig. 4. This performance indicates that individual hyperparameters can not be tuned independently, and some interplay between hyperparameters exists. Another unexpected result in the Vanilla configuration is that changing the dropout to 0.2 does not change SSL performance as significantly as it did for the SOTA configuration. This result is unexpected.

**Impact of Changing two Hyperparameters on the SSL Performance**
To further understand the relationships between hyperparameters, we continue to modify two hyperparameters at a time, from SOTA configuration, and

quantify the SSL performance. This tests if patterns emerge showing which combination of hyperparameters generally have the strongest impact on SSL performance. Figure 5 shows that both the feed-forward and the Seq2seq model obtain the highest SSL performance when modifying batch size from 256 to 512 and hidden size from 512 to 1024. The GRU model obtains the highest SSL performance when embedding size changes from 256 to 512 and hidden size changes from 512 to 1024. The common factor here is that increasing hidden size from 512 to 1024 makes SSL performance the best for all three models. The differences in SSL performance might not exceed the performance variance. Therefore, if the same experiments are rerun, the results can change. Figure 5 also solidifies that the learning rate is a vital hyperparameter to consider for SSL. When the learning rate changes from 0.001 to 0.0001, performance decreases. Similarly, when dropout is modified from 0.2 to 0.0, SSL performance decrease.

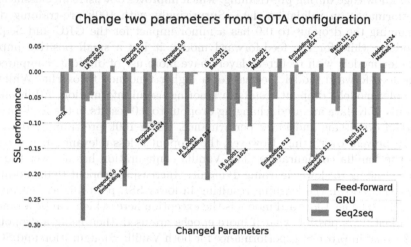

**Fig. 5.** Changing two parameters at a time from SOTA configuration, using 25k pre-training data and 200 epochs for each training phase while keeping everything else fixed.

## 3.1 Discussion

**The Hyperparameters Configuration Has a Significant Impact on the SSL Performance.** Based on the results presented, the hyperparameter configuration significantly impacts SSL performance at least within a fixed number of epochs. The smaller and less sophisticated feed-forward models are frequently more sensitive to hyperparameter modifications. One possible explanation is that less sophisticated models are more dependent on hyperparameters for learning effectively. Potentially, more epochs could allow smaller models to converge more during pre-training and learn more useful knowledge for the downstream classification task. Some hyperparameters have a stronger impact on SSL performance compared to others. Particularly:

- **The learning rate has a significant impact.**
  Increasing the learning rate can lead to a faster model adjustment to the pre-training task. Because the number of epochs is fixed at 200, increasing the learning rate results in more substantial weight modifications per update. This results in faster convergence of the model. A higher learning rate can allow the model to learn more useful features in fewer epochs, resulting in better downstream performance. However, when tested in the Vanilla configuration, a higher learning rate results in a lower SSL performance. A possible explanation can be that the combination of larger embedding size, hidden size, and no dropout may lead to overfitting on pre-training data.
- **The dropout impact on SSL depends on the model.**
  Dropout is known for lowering overfitting and improving generalization in deep neural networks. Adding dropout results in models learning more general knowledge during pre-training, which improves downstream classification performance on validation data. Surprisingly, with 100k pre-training data, changing the dropout to 0.0 has a minor impact for the GRU and Seq2seq models, while for the feed-forward model, it has a small positive impact. Larger models with recurrent layers have more use of dropout, compared to the feed-forward model, because of a higher tendency to overfit. While for simpler models, dropout results in ignoring useful information. Additionally, if only 25K data are used, changing dropout to 0.0 results in the feed-forward model overfitting and lower performance. Using 100k pre-training data will then prevent overfitting. However, the dropout is less relevant when it comes to the Vanilla configuration. The Vanilla configuration has a lower learning rate, leading to slower learning dynamics. Increasing dropout to 0.2 additionally slows down the learning resulting in lower SSL performance within 200 epochs. The feed-forward model is the exception here, which can be a random incident. It is possible that if more epochs are used, then using a dropout of 0.2 would improve SSL performance for both Vanilla configuration and SOTA configuration.

**The Amount of Pre-training Data Improves the SSL Performance**
For hyperparameter configurations tuned for SSL, SSL performance improves for smaller models as pre-training data quantity increases, while larger models reach a performance threshold, at least with a fixed amount of epochs. Therefore, one should experiment with different data volumes and use as little data as possible. This can significantly save training time. One possible explanation for this is that with recurrent layers a model learns faster, and learns a larger number of useful features from pre-training data. This is because of using more parameters. Therefore, more expansive models containing more parameters require less pre-training data to learn the most useful features during pre-training. This is only speculation. It is possible that Fig. 2 looks different with other hyperparameters. Experiments with additional pre-training data are considered future work. For other configurations less suited for SSL, the effect of increasing data quantity is not as significant, particularly for smaller models. This also means that the hyperparameter configuration can be more important than the amount of

pre-training data itself. Using the "wrong" configuration can severely hinder SSL performance even with large amounts of data.

**Larger Models Improve the SSL Performance**
Based on the discussion above, larger models generally show higher SSL performance than smaller models. Our experiments show exceptions to this, but these might occur due to parameter choices. Using additional pre-training data, smaller models can catch up with more extensive models regarding SSL performance. However, throughout this entire study, we do not look at absolute text classification performance. Instead, relative text classification performance is considered. In summary, extensive models show higher SSL performance compared to smaller models - particularly with a smaller volume of pre-training data.

### 3.2  Conclusion

There is a growing interest in SSL research caused by limited labeled data in many domains. However, the setup of SSL neural networks for text classification is cumbersome, frequently based on trial and error, with little knowledge on which setup is beneficial for SSL. Research has shown that SSL does not always improve performance compared to supervised learning. We found that the hyperparameter configuration significantly impacts SSL performance, and the learning rate has the most impact. Hence, experimenting with different hyperparameter configurations can dramatically improve SSL performance. More extensive models often improve SSL performance than smaller models, particularly with a smaller pre-training data quantity. However, as pre-training data size increases, recurrent models generally reach a performance threshold. On the other hand, smaller models can benefit from more pre-training data, especially when hyperparameter configurations are tuned for SSL. Therefore, one should generally experiment using different data volumes for all models. If aiming to achieve the best possible absolute downstream performance, larger and more sophisticated models should be used.

This article explored the impact of hyperparameters, including pre-training data size and model size, on an SSL technique for a text classification task. This exploration improves understanding of which parameters have the most impact on SSL for text classification, making it more manageable to perform SSL work for future NLP projects, particularly if time-restricted. This research also advances the understanding of model size impact on SSL for text classification, enabling a better experience of model selection for SSL designs. With this, we enhance the knowledge of parameter relations, potentially lowering the training time for SSL-based machine learning.

## References

1. aladdinpersson: seq2seq_attention (2021). https://github.com/aladdinpersson/Machine-Learning-Collection/blob/master/ML/Pytorch/more_advanced/Seq2Seq_attention/seq2seq_attention.py. Accessed 3 Jun 2021

2. Baevski, A., Edunov, S., Liu, Y., Zettlemoyer, L., Auli, M.: Cloze-driven pretraining of self-attention networks. arXiv preprint arXiv:1903.07785 (2019)
3. Bender, E.M., Gebru, T., McMillan-Major, A., Shmitchell, S.: On the dangers of stochastic parrots: can language models be too big? In: Proceedings of the 2021 ACM Conference on Fairness, Accountability, and Transparency, pp. 610–623 (2021)
4. Bishop, C.M.: Pattern Recognition and Machine Learning. Springer, New York (2006)
5. Casanueva, I., Temčinas, T., Gerz, D., Henderson, M., Vulić, I.: Efficient intent detection with dual sentence encoders. arXiv preprint arXiv:2003.04807 (2020)
6. Chapelle, O., Schölkopf, B., Zien, A.: Semi-Supervised Learning, September 2006. https://doi.org/10.7551/mitpress/9780262033589.001.0001
7. Dai, A.M., Le, Q.V.: Semi-supervised sequence learning. arXiv preprint arXiv:1511.01432 (2015)
8. Devlin, J., Chang, M.W., Lee, K., Toutanova, K.: Bert: pre-training of deep bidirectional transformers for language understanding. arXiv preprint arXiv:1810.04805 (2018)
9. Goodfellow, I., Bengio, Y., Courville, A., Bengio, Y.: Deep Learning, vol. 1. MIT Press, Cambridge (2016)
10. Chao ji: Semi-supervised-sequence-learning (2021). https://github.com/chao-ji/semi-supervised-sequence-learning. Accessed 3 Jun 2021
11. Lang, K.: Newsweeder: learning to filter netnews. In: Machine Learning Proceedings 1995, pp. 331–339. Elsevier (1995)
12. Lee, D.: Transfer learning for text classification with tensorflow (2018). https://github.com/dongjun-Lee/transfer-learning-text-tf. Accessed 3 Jun 2021
13. Li, Y.F., Zhou, Z.H.: Towards making unlabeled data never hurt. IEEE Trans. Pattern Anal. Mach. Intell. 37(1), 175–188 (2014)
14. Lien, H., Ledaal, B.V.: Semi-supervised learning for text classification (2020). student project in the course IKT442: ICT Seminar 3 at UiA
15. Liu, Y., et al.: Roberta: a robustly optimized bert pretraining approach. arXiv preprint arXiv:1907.11692 (2019)
16. Oliver, A., Odena, A., Raffel, C., Cubuk, E.D., Goodfellow, I.J.: Realistic evaluation of deep semi-supervised learning algorithms. arXiv preprint arXiv:1804.09170 (2018)
17. Raffel, C., et al.: Exploring the limits of transfer learning with a unified text-to-text transformer. arXiv preprint arXiv:1910.10683 (2019)
18. Singh, A., Nowak, R., Zhu, J.: Unlabeled data: now it helps, now it doesn't. Adv. Neural Inf. Process. Syst. 21, 1513–1520 (2008)
19. van Engelen, J.E., Hoos, H.H.: A survey on semi-supervised learning. Mach. Learn. 109(2), 373–440 (2019). https://doi.org/10.1007/s10994-019-05855-6
20. Wang, A., Singh, A., Michael, J., Hill, F., Levy, O., Bowman, S.R.: Glue: a multitask benchmark and analysis platform for natural language understanding. arXiv preprint arXiv:1804.07461 (2018)
21. You, Y., et al.: Large batch optimization for deep learning: training bert in 76 minutes. arXiv preprint arXiv:1904.00962 (2019)
22. Zhu, X.J.: Semi-supervised learning literature survey (2005)

# A Custom State LSTM Cell for Text Classification Tasks

Giannis Haralabopoulos[1]([⊠])[iD] and Ioannis Anagnostopoulos[2]

[1] Henley Business School, University of Reading, Reading, UK
i.haralabopoulos@henley.ac.uk
[2] Department of Computer Science and Biomedical Informatics,
University of Thessaly, Volos, Greece
janag@dib.uth.gr

**Abstract.** Text classification is the task of assigning a class to a document. Machine Learning enables the automation of Text Classification Tasks, amongst others. Recent advances in the Machine Learning field, such as the introduction of Recurrent Neural Networks, Long Short Term Memory and Gated Recurrent Units, have greatly improved classification results. These type of networks include internal memory states that demonstrate dynamic temporal behaviour. In the LSTM cell, this temporal behaviour is supported by two distinct states: current and hidden. We introduce a modification layer within the LSTM cell, where we are able to perform extra state alterations for one or both states. We experiment with 17 single state alterations, 12 for the current state and 5 for the hidden state. We evaluate these alterations in seven datasets that deal with hate speech detection, document classification, human to robot interaction and sentiment analysis. Our results demonstrate an average F1 improvement of 0.5% for the top performing current state alteration and 0.3% for the top performing hidden state alteration.

## 1 Introduction

Machine Learning (ML) enables the automation of a wide range of computer tasks in: Video, Image and Text analysis, Speech recognition and autonomous systems in general. This automation is based in utilising data and training predictive algorithms, such as Support Vector Machines, Decision Trees, Multi-Layer Perceptrons and Neural Networks.

Predictive algorithms have greatly improved in the last decade. Mainly due to the advent of Gated Recurrent Units (GRU), Long Short Term Memory (LSTM) and Deep Learning (DL) networks. These are building upon Neural Network (NN) philosophy, which imitates how a human brain functions, by creating an interconnected network of neurons.

Natural Language Tasks in particular have greatly benefited from the latest NN advancements. In these type of tasks, text is initially analysed and processed through Natural Language Processing (NLP) methods, then, it functions as an input to a NN which provides a prediction to a range of classes. Common

© Springer Nature Switzerland AG 2022
L. Iliadis et al. (Eds.): EANN 2022, CCIS 1600, pp. 489–504, 2022.
https://doi.org/10.1007/978-3-031-08223-8_40

Natural Language Classification tasks are Sentiment analysis [8,19,48], Text Classification [10], Hate speech detection [2] and Spam filter development [1,30]. Recurrent Neural Network (RNN) and its evolutions have played a key role in the performance improvement of these predictive systems.

A RNN is a type of NN that factors in temporal relations. Each RRN neuron has an internal memory state that provides the network with a dynamic temporal behaviour. RNNs were introduced in 1984 by John Hopfield [20] and have since been developed into more complex networks such as LSTMs (1999) [11] and GRUs (2014) [4]. LSTMs are able to access a wider range of contextual information and prevent network decay or exponential growth, when compared to RNNs [14]. LSTMs and GRUs share many similarities, but GRUs lacks one output per cell.

Both networks demonstrate state of the art performance in multiclass and multilabel text classification tasks [17,18]. Multiclass refers to tasks where an item can be classified to more than two classes, while multilabel refers to tasks where each item can be classified to more than one classes at the same time. LSTMs have proved efficient in multiclass and multilabel text classification tasks [17,18]. LSTM network have also been widely used in a variety of NLP tasks. Namely word prediction [43], sentence selection[23], sentence topic prediction [12] and text classification [6,27,28].

Can we improve the performance of an LSTM cell by introducing extra calculations? To answer that, we introduce a modification layer in the LSTM cell architecture. Our goal is to further influence the state outputs, i.e. performing extra state alterations, in each LSTM cell to improve classification performance. We test our approach with 17 different state alterations for the LSTM cell. We evaluate each modification in a state-of-the-art network with two bi-directional LSTM layers in seven diverse text datasets. The evaluation is based in accuracy and three F1 score metrics. Accuracy is important since it's the metric the network is trained upon, while F1 better outlines the classification robustness of our model.

## 2    Related Work

Automated task performance have been greatly improved with the introduction of RNNs and LSTMs in various fields. From the early 2000s s LSTMs have been successfully used in music composition [9], phenom classification [15], speech recognition [13] and face recognition [26]. These are only some of the most prolific applications in the diverse range of fields, where LSTMs have produced improved results upon traditional NNs.

In NLP, LSTMs have been widely used in information retrieval [29], named entity recognition [51], topic modelling [24], machine translation [40], text generation [36], text similarity [49], text summarization [42], sentiment analysis [46] and fake news or hate speech detection [5]. Most of these tasks usually involve a type of classification that predicts the appropriate class for the document at hand. For example, in polarity sentiment analysis these classes are positive and negative sentiment [39], while in emotion sentiment analysis the classes are emotions such as joy, sad etc. [22]. Similarly, for fake news detection a single class is adequate [44], whereas for hate speech detection the classes represent the severity or type of hate observed. The quest for performance in the LSTM cell architecture has been going on for a while, with multiple proposed modifications in diverse fields of applications. Wand et al. [45] integrated batch normalisation in the update function of the LSTM cell. The proposed batch normalisation is applied to all state transitions. The BN-LSTM achieved faster convergence and improved performance upon LSTM. Similarly, Hu et al. [21] introduced an LSTM cell with the capability of trend following of time series data by combining Particle Swarm Optimisation and Gradient Descent selection. The enhanced LSTM cell improved training and testing in three environmental forecasting tasks.

Kalchbrenner, Danihelka and Graves[25] proposed a grid based LSTM network. Although the LSTM cell is untouched in its core, the network layout forces each LSTM cell to interact within a three dimensional structure. Their results suggest that this type of grid improves in parity, addition and memorisation. Chen et al. [3] employed a Tree-LSTM where the input of each cell is based in the input vector and two hidden vectors. They further evaluate a model that uses this enhanced LSTM cells in language inference and conclude that there exists untapped potential in sequential inference. Niu et al. [34] introduced a Hierarchical Multimodal LSTM, which is essentially an extension of the Tree-LSTM with syntax awareness. They evaluate their model in dense visual-semantic embedding and the results suggest that their proposed network can produce well versed phrases. Ye, Li and Chen [50] proposed the M-LSTM where an additional input signal is fed into the LSTM cell. The proposed M-LSTM utilises historical information in the iterative update function. Their network is evaluated in brain dMRI scans with state of the art performance. Qiu et al. [38] altered the LSTM cell by altering the gate mechanisms of the cell. They evaluate their Bidirectional-LTM model in a bearing fault simulation task, where the results suggest a major improvement over Bi-LSTMs. Dai, Li and Li [7] proposed the use of shortcut connections that can bypass the LSTM cell and a spatio-temporal LSTM cell. They test and evaluate their model in dense traffic prediction, where it outperform both M-LSTMs and LSTMs.

Ha, Dai and Le propose a trainable hypernetwork that generated weights for the LSTM network that performs very well in image recognition, language modelling and handwriting generation [16]. Kamil Rocki [41] presented a feedback LSTM that takes into account the difference between prediction and observation. It calculates a prediction error which is used when making new predictions. The performance of feedback LSTMs, in a character prediction task, suggests that their generalisation capability is improved, compared to traditional LSTMs. Wu et al. [47] introduced a Multiplicative Integration LSTM that changes how information flows in the LSTM cell by calculating a Hadamard product. The authors test and evaluate their model in four tasks: Character Level Modelling, Speech Recognition, Skip-through models, Reading and Comprehending. Pulver and Lyu [37] presented the LSTWM with a non-saturating activation function and a combination of multiple inputs. They evaluate their proposed cell and its network in three tasks: text recognition, digit combination and digit recognition. The LSTWM outperforms LSTM, furthermore it achieves that while using fewer parameters in certain occasions. Mittal et al. [32] suggested the use of a reset mechanism within the LSTM cell to reset the internal memory of the cell. Their modified LSTM performed better than LSTM in sign language recognition with a small (¡1000 examples) training dataset.

## 3   Methodology

In this chapter we will present the original LSTM cell structure and our proposed modifications.

### 3.1   The LSTM Cell

The most commonly implemented LSTM cell includes an input gate, an output gate and a forget gate, as illustrated in Fig 1. The cell receives as inputs: an input vector, the hidden state of the previous time step and the cell state of the previous time step. These are then processed through a set of gates and operators to produce the cell state and the hidden state of the current time step, that will be fed to the cell of the next time step.

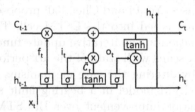

**Fig. 1.** The LSTM Cell

Let us formulate and describe the internal structure in detail. Five different variables interact within the LSTM cell. Initially we have the input vector $x_t$, used alongside the previous hidden state $h_{t-1}$ and biases $b_f$ to produce the forget gate's activation vector, Eq. 1. Where $W$ are the weights of the input and $U$ are the recurrent connections.

$$f_t = \sigma_g(W_f x_t + U_f h_{t-1} + b_f) \qquad (1)$$

Similarly, the activation vector of the input or update gate is calculated based on the input vector $x_t$, the previous hidden state $h_{t-1}$ and biases $b_i$. However, it has its own weights and connections, Eq. 2.

$$i_t = \sigma_g(W_i x_t + U_i h_{t-1} + b_i) \qquad (2)$$

The activation vector of the output gate, Eq. 3, and that of the cell input, Eq. 4, are similarly calculated.

$$o_t = \sigma_g(W_o x_t + U_o h_{t-1} + b_o) \tag{3}$$

$$\tilde{c}_t = \sigma_c(W_c x_t + U_c h_{t-1} + b_c) \tag{4}$$

The calculation of the current cell state is based in all four previous activation vectors, Eq. 5, where $\circ$ symbolises the Hadamard product.

$$c_t = f_t \circ c_{t-1} + i_t \circ \tilde{c}_t \tag{5}$$

The final step is the calculation of the hidden state vector, that factors the latest cell state and the activation vector of the output gate, Eq. 6.

$$h_t = o_t \circ \sigma_h(c_t) \tag{6}$$

where $\sigma_g$ denotes the sigmoid function and $\sigma_{c/t}$ denote the hyperbolic tangent function.

## 3.2  Our Modified LSTM Cell

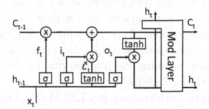

**Fig. 2.** Our modified LSTM Cell

**Fig. 3.** Our stacked LSTM model

**Table 1.** State alterations

| Number | Current | Hidden |
|---|---|---|
| 1 | $c_t = c_t \circ o_t$ | $h_t = c \circ h_t$ |
| 2 | $c_t = c_t \circ h_t$ | $h_t = h_t \circ \sigma_g(c)$ |
| 3 | $c_t = c_t \circ o_t \circ h_t$ | $h_t = c \circ \sigma_g(h_t)$ |
| 4 | $c_t = c_t + c_t \circ h_t$ | $h_t = h_t \circ \sigma_c(c)$ |
| 5 | $c_t = c_t \circ \sigma_g(o_t)$ | $h_t = c \circ \sigma_c(h_t)$ |
| 6 | $c_t = c_t \circ \sigma_g(c_t)$ | |
| 7 | $c_t = c_t \circ \sigma_g(h_t)$ | |
| 8 | $c_t = h_t \circ \sigma_g(c_t)$ | |
| 9 | $c_t = c_t \circ \sigma_c(o_t)$ | |
| 10 | $c_t = c_t \circ \sigma_c(c_t)$ | |
| 11 | $c_t = c_t \circ \sigma_c(h_t)$ | |
| 12 | $c_t = h_t \circ \sigma_c(c_t)$ | |

We introduce a layer before the final current and hidden states are fed to the next LSTM cells. Within this layer we are able to perform any type of modification to the current cell state and/or the hidden state. For our experiment we choose to only alter the current cell state or the hidden state. Although we are able to alter both, we experiment with a single state alteration that will allows for an accurate assessment of the per state alteration and its performance. Furthermore, by only performing a single alteration we minimise the training time increasement, which is bound to happen due to the high dimension of the mathematical objects (Figs. 2 and 3).

Our goal is to improve performance per LSTM cell. Our modified LSTM performs a single extra state process within the current cell that aims to improve cell training and prediction capabilities with no further architectural modifications. We experiment with twelve different current state alterations and five hidden state alterations, Table 1. We mainly focus in a product of the final cell state $c_t$ with the hidden state $h_t$ or vice versa, while in three alterations we experiment with the output gate vector. Each alteration functions as the seventh equation, Table 1, within each LSTM cell.

## 3.3   Model

We evaluate the proposed alterations in a top performing [17,18] Stacked LSTM model. The model utilises a Bag-of-Words embedding layer that replaces each term with a numerical value. A spatial dropout is then applied, before the data is fed into a BI-LSTM. The output of the first BI-LSTM is used as an input of the second BI-LSTM. We then create two information flows, one based on maximum pooling and one on average pooling, which are concatenated before the final fully connected dense layer. This model could be further improved with the addition of other processes, such as pre-trained embeddings or trainable ensembles. The focus, however, is on the LSTM cell performance and further architectural model improvements are out of scope.

### 3.4    Datasets

We evaluate our modification layer in seven diverse text classification datasets.

**Table 2.** Dataset properties

| Dataset | Documents | Classes | MaxLen. | Tokens |
|---------|-----------|---------|---------|--------|
| MLMA | 5647 | 71 | 35 | 14969 |
| SEMEVAL | 6838 | 11 | 33 | 24449 |
| HASOC | 5852 | 4 | 93 | 32168 |
| AG | 120000 | 4 | 122 | 123762 |
| ROBO | 525 | 5 | 29 | 466 |
| CROWD | 40000 | 11 | 34 | 83297 |
| HATE | 1011 | 3 | 611 | 6356 |

The MLMA dataset [35] includes, amongst others, a sentiment label where a tweet is classified as belonging to one or multiple hate-speech categories. The HASOC [31] dataset, which is comprised of social media text instances labelled as: hate-speech, offensive, profane or none. The SEMEVAL dataset [17,33], a collection of Tweets with emotional annotation. A class-balanced hate-speech dataset (HATE) with documents classified in three hate-speech classes: none, hate-speech and severe hate-speech,[1]. A small size multi class dataset of human to robot interaction with specific scenario classes (ROBO) and a crowdsourced emotion dataset, based on annotation received from Crowdflower, (CROWD). The AG News Topic Classification Dataset with topic categories (AG) [52].

The dataset properties prior to pre-processing are displayed in Table 2. Where, 'Items' refers to the numbers of sentences in the dataset, 'Classes' is the number of available classes for any item, 'MaxLen' is the maximum sentence length that directly affects the dimensionality of data in training and 'Tokens' is the number of unique terms in each dataset.

These datasets are pre-processed and cleaned via the exact same process. This process includes a stop word removal, the replacement of contractions based on GloVe, the removal of non alphanumeric characters, lowercase conversion, lemmatisation and infrequent term removal. AGNEWS and TOXIC datasets had to be further reduced via a Term Frequency - Inverse Document Frequency process to improve training time [18].

The pre-processed dataset properties can be seen in Table 3. Our meticulous pre-processing has greatly reduced the number of unique terms in each dataset

---

[1] TEST.

and the maximum sentence length. It marginally reduced the number of available
documents per dataset, with the exception of CROWD were more than two
thirds of the data are removed, due to the short and informal nature of its text
items.

**Table 3.** Dataset properties, post pre-processing

| Dataset | Documents | Classes | MaxLen | Tokens |
|---|---|---|---|---|
| MLMA | 4138 | 48 | 23 | 12018 |
| SEMEVAL | 6495 | 11 | 22 | 14110 |
| HASOC | 1120 | 4 | 42 | 6078 |
| AG | 88431 | 4 | 22 | 4730 |
| ROBO | 254 | 5 | 10 | 149 |
| CROWD | 11377 | 11 | 11 | 1458 |
| HATE | 869 | 3 | 342 | 3235 |

## 4    Evaluation

For each dataset and each state alteration we perform 10 different experimental sessions. Each session has a different random seed and the data is split as
train-validation-test split of 80-10-10 and a 10-fold cross validation. The hyperparameters are exactly the same for each dataset so that we do not introduce
variability in the experiment.

We will present the average percent improvement over these 10 sessions for
each dataset. Due to lack of space we will only present the top-3 performing
current and hidden state alterations on the metrics of: Accuracy, Macro-F1,
Micro-F1 and Weighted F1. Current state alterations are denoted by C-Number,
while hidden state alteration are denoted by H-Number.

### 4.1    Results

Our modified LSTM cell provides accuracy and F1 performance improvement in
six out of seven datasets. HASOC, Table 4, and ROBO, Table 5, results are of
particular interest, since state alterations on HASOC fail to improve micro-F1
score and accuracy, while the same alterations on ROBO greatly improve all
metrics.

**Table 4.** Improvement (%) for HASOC

| Metrics | Accuracy | Macro | Micro | Weighted |
|---|---|---|---|---|
| Baseline | 83.984 | 35.546 | 65.811 | 64.799 |
| C-1 | −0.064 | **1.192** | −0.347 | −0.305 |
| C-4 | −0.101 | 0.202 | −0.460 | −0.527 |
| C-7 | −0.284 | 0.814 | −0.496 | **0.057** |
| H-2 | −0.167 | **−0.152** | −0.266 | −0.086 |
| H-3 | −0.128 | −0.316 | −0.394 | −0.367 |
| H-5 | -0.255 | −0.792 | −0.812 | −0.701 |

**Table 5.** Improvement (%) for ROBO

| Metrics | Accuracy | Macro | Micro | Weighted |
|---|---|---|---|---|
| Baseline | 80.198 | 1.562 | 2.476 | 1.965 |
| C-2 | −0.022 | 42.834 | 22.174 | 21.570 |
| C-5 | 0.087 | 48.085 | 24.028 | 16.320 |
| C-9 | **0.127** | **86.825** | **72.293** | **61.932** |
| H-1 | **0.156** | **96.034** | **68.244** | **57.003** |
| H-2 | −0.003 | 36.926 | 19.060 | 11.098 |
| H-5 | 0.047 | 71.101 | 57.587 | 40.362 |

Regarding HASOC, it is a dataset with small number of documents, small number of classes, high maximum sentence length, relatively high number of tokens and no class balance (74.3% of document belong to a single class). In short, HASOC dataset is a single-class heavy dataset with very few documents and high dimensionality. Our proposed alterations fail to improve training results in HASOC dataset, with the exception of Macro-F1. Unbalanced and small datasets demonstrate an improved classification performance with text augmentation [18].

## 4.2 Results

**Table 6.** Improvement (%) for MLMA

| Metrics | Accuracy | Macro | Micro | Weighted |
|---|---|---|---|---|
| Baseline | 96.642 | 2.123 | 42.642 | 34.077 |
| C-1 | **0.021** | 1.396 | 1.595 | 1.367 |
| C-4 | **0.021** | 1.497 | 1.744 | 1.507 |
| C-6 | 0.018 | **1.595** | **1.891** | **1.585** |
| H-1 | 0.017 | 1.162 | 1.333 | 1.126 |
| H-3 | 0.014 | **1.461** | **1.802** | **1.466** |
| H-4 | **0.018** | 1.084 | 1.235 | 1.058 |

**Table 7.** Improvement (%) for AGNEWS

| Metrics | Accuracy | Macro | Micro | Weighted |
|---|---|---|---|---|
| Baseline | 90.853 | 80.695 | 80.862 | 80.665 |
| C-1 | 0.293 | 1.006 | 0.832 | 1.008 |
| C-3 | 0.241 | 0.869 | 0.700 | 0.870 |
| C-10 | **0.325** | **1.020** | **0.860** | **1.020** |
| H-1 | 0.189 | 0.736 | 0.553 | 0.731 |
| H-3 | 0.262 | **0.908** | **0.731** | **0.900** |
| H-4 | 0.180 | 0.721 | 0.546 | 0.716 |

The most improved classification results are in MLMA and AGNEWS datasets. Current State alterations for MLMA provide up to 1.9% F1 improvement and up to 1% F1 improvement for AGNEWS, Table 6 and 7. With regards to accuracy metrics, it remains relatively unchanged throughout MLMA alterations, while it is improved by up to 0.3% in AGNEWS. Hidden State alterations improve the classification results as well, but perform slightly worse than Current State alterations.

Alterations in CROWD, Table 8, dataset demonstrate a similar performance. Current State alterations improve F1 score, up to 0.65%, while two out of five Hidden State alterations provide some metric-consistent classification improvement. Accuracy metric on Current State alterations is marginally decreased in all 3 top performing Current State alterations, despite the improvements across all F1 metrics.

**Table 8.** Improvement (%) for CROWD

| Metrics | Accuracy | Macro | Micro | Weighted |
|---------|----------|-------|-------|----------|
| Baseline | 89.237 | 13.577 | 26.840 | 24.625 |
| C-5 | −0.045 | **0.770** | 0.249 | 0.398 |
| C-7 | **−0.033** | 0.535 | 0.537 | **0.646** |
| C-11 | −0.041 | 0.668 | **0.608** | 0.591 |
| H-2 | −0.062 | −0.123 | **0.341** | **0.376** |
| H-3 | −0.053 | 0.126 | −0.109 | −0.038 |
| H-5 | −0.034 | **0.414** | 0.217 | 0.354 |

**Table 9.** Improvement (%) for HATE

| Metrics | Accuracy | Macro | Micro | Weighted |
|---------|----------|-------|-------|----------|
| Baseline | 77.397 | 65.710 | 66.101 | 66.714 |
| C-2 | **0.470** | **0.871** | **0.825** | **0.858** |
| C-6 | 0.233 | 0.580 | 0.517 | 0.557 |
| C-8 | 0.193 | 0.585 | 0.487 | 0.506 |
| H-1 | −0.056 | −0.099 | −0.138 | −0.149 |
| H-4 | 0.029 | 0.166 | 0.131 | 0.195 |
| H-5 | **0.248** | **0.641** | **0.544** | **0.589** |

**Table 10.** Improvement (%) for SEMEVAL

| Metrics | Accuracy | Macro | Micro | Weighted |
|---------|----------|-------|-------|----------|
| Baseline | 83.833 | 44.106 | 57.981 | 56.083 |
| C-3 | 0.003 | 0.128 | 0.444 | 0.230 |
| C-6 | **0.099** | 0.199 | **0.448** | **0.246** |
| C-7 | 0.012 | **0.248** | 0.321 | 0.146 |
| H-2 | −0.042 | 0.259 | 0.218 | **0.189** |
| H-3 | **0.026** | 0.167 | **0.277** | 0.098 |
| H-4 | −0.016 | **0.395** | 0.138 | 0.077 |

Hidden state alterations for HATE, Table 9, perform similarly to those of CROWD, where only two out of five provide classification improvements. Improvements from Current State alterations are up to 0.87% with consistent Accuracy improvements as well. SEMEVAL classification demonstrates a slight improvement in both Current and Hidden state alterations, Table 10. The best performing alterations provide 0.45% and 0.28% classification improvement, for current and hidden states respectively.

**Table 11.** Average improvement (%) for current state alterations (excluding ROBO dataset)

| | Accuracy | Macro | Micro | Weighted |
|----|----------|-------|-------|----------|
| 1 | 0.018 | 0.643 | **0.436** | **0.41** |
| 2 | −0.012 | **0.659** | 0.145 | 0.326 |
| 3 | −0.047 | 0.112 | 0.143 | 0.199 |
| 4 | −0.009 | 0.599 | 0.346 | 0.376 |
| 5 | −0.021 | 0.3 | 0.184 | 0.227 |
| 6 | −0.015 | 0.381 | 0.319 | 0.391 |
| 7 | −0.123 | 0.356 | 0.135 | 0.23 |
| 8 | **0.037** | 0.182 | 0.369 | 0.34 |
| 9 | −0.109 | 0.176 | 0.003 | 0.099 |
| 10 | 0.028 | 0.249 | 0.23 | 0.233 |
| 11 | −0.054 | 0.068 | 0.206 | 0.176 |
| 12 | −0.024 | 0.455 | 0.229 | 0.282 |

**Table 12.** Average improvement (%) for hidden state alterations (excluding ROBO dataset)

|   | Accuracy | Macro | Micro | Weighted |
|---|---|---|---|---|
| 1 | −0.05 | −0.301 | −0.027 | −0.055 |
| 2 | −0.047 | 0.24 | **0.305** | **0.317** |
| 3 | −0.065 | **0.312** | 0.276 | 0.242 |
| 4 | −0.13 | −0.038 | −0.145 | 0.026 |
| 5 | **0.008** | 0.2 | 0.085 | 0.165 |

Overall, most Current and Hidden alterations provide meaningful classification improvements. The average alteration improvements presented in Tables 11 and 12 do not include ROBO dataset. Not only ROBO is unique in document and token size, but we also consider the classification improvements in this dataset as outliers.

The best performing Current state alteration ($c_t = c_t \circ o_t$) improves F1 metrics by an average of 0.5%. Even the worst performing ninth Current State alteration ($c_t = c_t \circ \sigma_c(o_t)$) improves F1 metrics by 0.1% on average, Table 11.

Hidden State alterations demonstrated a mixed performance. Three of our proposed alteration improved across all F1 metrics and only one improved across all metrics. The top performing alteration ($h = h \circ \sigma_g(c)$) improved F1 scores by an average of 0.29%, Table 12. However, the worst performing alteration ($h = c \circ h$) not only fails to improve the classification results but reduces them across all metrics.

## 5  Limitations

The modification layer we introduced provides the ability to alter the current and hidden states. Although it is possible to alter both states, in whichever manner, we limit our study in one state alteration per time. Even that single alteration is based on the pre-existing interactions within the LSTM cell. By doing so, we outline the effectiveness of extra single state interactions with minimal resource usage. That doesn't mean that within the modification layer, only pre-existing function can be applied. Not only we are able to include new functions, such as Relu or Softmax, but we can also interact with both Current and Hidden states.

**Table 13.** Epoch training time increase (%) per alteration, MLMA

| Baseline | Alteration | 1 | 2 | 3 | 4 | 5 | 6 | 7 | 8 | 9 | 10 | 11 | 12 |
|---|---|---|---|---|---|---|---|---|---|---|---|---|---|
| 40.6 s | Current | 4.4 | 2.9 | 5.6 | 11.0 | 6.6 | 6.6 | 15.6 | 16.7 | 5.3 | 6.9 | 14.8 | 15.4 |
| | Hidden | 4.5 | 11.8 | 12.0 | 8.8 | 12.6 | | | | | | | |

Furthermore, the modification layer calculates the output of an extra single equation. However, this equation performs a range of calculations amongst tensors, which are mathematical objects of high dimensionality. For example, the number of parameters that is fed to the second LSTM is 1222560 for HATE dataset. On a practical side, any type of extra calculations with similar sized objects will result in increased training time.

As an example, we include the training time increase per state alteration for MLMA dataset, Table 13, to demonstrate the increased resource utilisation on the experiments setup. One initial observation is that the training time increase doesn't necessarily translates to improve classification results. The top performing alterations for MLMA were C-1, C-4 and C-6 for Current State, and H-1, H-3 and H-4 for Hidden. Both states had alterations that required more training time but did not produce better results. We refrain from including a cumulative metric for all datasets, since the increased training time doesn't scale linearly with the dataset size.

**Table 14.** Percentage improvement over baseline for best performing state alterations

| Alteration | Accuracy | Macro | Micro | Weighted |
|---|---|---|---|---|
| $c_t = c_t \circ o_t$ | **0.018** | **0.643** | **0.436** | **0.41** |
| $h = h \circ \sigma_g(c)$ | −0.047 | 0.24 | 0.305 | 0.317 |

# 6    Conclusion

We presented an LSTM modification layer that allows for Current and Hidden state alterations. We experiment with altering one or the other, but the layer provides the ability to alter both at the same time. Our experiments focus on simple product or/and sum equations that aim to perform an extra training step within each LSTM cell. We test 17 different state alterations, 12 for Current state and 5 for Hidden state.

We evaluate the performance of this modified LSTM, and each of the 17 different state alterations, in 7 diverse datasets. These datasets range in document and term size and task. Our datasets are used for Hate-Speech detection, Emotion prediction, News classification and Human to Robot interactions. Our results suggest that both state alterations provide a meaningful classification improvement.

The best performing alterations for each state are presented in Table 14. ROBO dataset exhibits a greater improvement which we consider to be dataset-restricted, thus its improvements are not co-calcualted with the rest of the datasets. Current state alterations provide up to 0.643% Macro-F1 improvement with state alteration number 1: $c_t = c_t \circ o_t$, while Hidden state alterations provide up to $0.317\%$ Weighted-F1 improvement with alteration number 2: $h = h \circ \sigma_g(c)$. Overall, the role of the modification layer is to perform an extra training step within the LSTM cell to improve classification results.

However, these training improvements increase training time. Although the required training time is increased by less than $10\%$, it can be detrimental to the scalability of similar approaches. Ultimately, if the classification task deals with sensitive data, such as health issues or law enforcement, then the increased time requirements can be justified, even when improving classification by $0.5\%$. We only experimented with a single state alteration to better assess the improvement potential of each state. Our results suggest that Current state alterations not only offer better performance but also require, on average, less training time.

We presented an improvement potential inside the LSTM cell. Moving forward, we aim to not only identify the most effective alteration, by collaborating with colleagues from Statistics and Mathematics to optimise our proposed single state alteration, but to experiment with co-occurring alterations for both the Current and the Hidden states or even applying modifications into gated outputs. We believe that the obtained results will spark the interest of fellow scientists to further explore the potential of modifying the LSTM gate or state outputs.

# References

1. Alom, Z., Carminati, B., Ferrari, E.: A deep learning model for twitter spam detection. Online Soc. Netw. Media **18**, 100079 (2020)
2. Aluru, S.S., Mathew, B., Saha, P., Mukherjee, A.: Deep learning models for multilingual hate speech detection. arXiv preprint arXiv:2004.06465 (2020)
3. Chen, Q., Zhu, X., Ling, Z., Wei, S., Jiang, H., Inkpen, D.: Enhanced LSTM for natural language inference. arXiv preprint arXiv:1609.06038 (2016)
4. Cho, K., et al.: Learning phrase representations using RNN encoder-decoder for statistical machine translation. arXiv preprint arXiv:1406.1078 (2014)
5. Chopra, S., Jain, S., Sholar, J.M.: Towards automatic identification of fake news: headline-article stance detection with LSTM attention models. In: Stanford CS224d Deep Learning for NLP Final Project (2017)
6. Dai, J., Chen, C., Li, Y.: A backdoor attack against LSTM-based text classification systems. IEEE Access **7**, 138872–138878 (2019)
7. Dai, S., Li, L., Li, Z.: Modeling vehicle interactions via modified LSTM models for trajectory prediction. IEEE Access **7**, 38287–38296 (2019)
8. Dang, N.C., Moreno-García, M.N., De la Prieta, F.: Sentiment analysis based on deep learning: a comparative study. Electronics **9**(3), 483 (2020)
9. Eck, D., Schmidhuber, J.: A first look at music composition using LSTM recurrent neural networks. Istituto Dalle Molle Di Studi Sull Intelligenza Artificiale **103**, 48 (2002)
10. Fang, W., Luo, H., Xu, S., Love, P.E.D., Lu, Z., Ye, C.: Automated text classification of near-misses from safety reports: an improved deep learning approach. Adv. Eng. Inform. **44**, 101060 (2020)
11. Gers, F.A., Schmidhuber, J., Cummins, F.: Learning to forget: continual prediction with LSTM (1999)

12. Ghosh, S., Vinyals, O., Strope, B., Roy, S., Dean, T., Heck, L.: Contextual LSTM (CLSTM) models for large scale NLP tasks. arXiv preprint arXiv:1602.06291 (2016)

13. Graves, A., Eck, D., Beringer, N., Schmidhuber, J.: Biologically plausible speech recognition with LSTM neural nets. In: Ijspeert, A.J., Murata, M., Wakamiya, N. (eds.) BioADIT 2004. LNCS, vol. 3141, pp. 127–136. Springer, Heidelberg (2004). https://doi.org/10.1007/978-3-540-27835-1_10

14. Graves, A., Liwicki, M., Fernández, S., Bertolami, R., Bunke, H., Schmidhuber, J.: A novel connectionist system for unconstrained handwriting recognition. IEEE Trans. Pattern Anal. Mach. Intell. **31**(5), 855–868 (2008)

15. Graves, A., Schmidhuber, J.: Framewise phoneme classification with bidirectional LSTM and other neural network architectures. Neural Netw. **18**(5–6), 602–610 (2005)

16. Ha, D., Dai, A., Le, Q.V.: Hypernetworks. arXiv preprint arXiv:1609.09106 (2016)

17. Haralabopoulos, G., Anagnostopoulos, I., McAuley, D.: Ensemble deep learning for multilabel binary classification of user-generated content. Algorithms **13**(4), 83 (2020)

18. Haralabopoulos, G., Torres, M.T., Anagnostopoulos, I., McAuley, D.: Text data augmentations: permutation, antonyms and negation. Expert Syst. Appl. 114769 (2021)

19. Haralabopoulos, G., Wagner, C., McAuley, D., Simperl, E.: A multivalued emotion lexicon created and evaluated by the crowd. In: 2018 Fifth International Conference on Social Networks Analysis, Management and Security (SNAMS), pp. 355–362. IEEE (2018)

20. Hopfield, J.J.: Neurons with graded response have collective computational properties like those of two-state neurons. Proc. Natl. Acad. Sci. **81**(10), 3088–3092 (1984)

21. Yao, H., Sun, X., Nie, X., Li, Y., Liu, L.: An enhanced LSTM for trend following of time series. IEEE Access **7**, 34020–34030 (2019)

22. Huang, F., Li, X., Yuan, C., Zhang, S., Zhang, J., Qiao, S.: Attention-emotion-enhanced convolutional LSTM for sentiment analysis. IEEE Trans. Neural Netw. Learn. Syst. (2021)

23. Huang, Y., Wang, W., Wang, L.: Instance-aware image and sentence matching with selective multimodal LSTM. In: Proceedings of the IEEE Conference on Computer Vision and Pattern Recognition, pp. 2310–2318 (2017)

24. Jansson, P., Liu, S.: Topic modelling enriched LSTM models for the detection of novel and emerging named entities from social media. In: 2017 IEEE International Conference on Big Data (Big Data), pp. 4329–4336. IEEE (2017)

25. Kalchbrenner, N., Danihelka, I., Graves, A.: Grid long short-term memory. arXiv preprint arXiv:1507.01526 (2015)

26. Levada, A.L.M., Correa, D.C., Salvadeo, D.H.P., Saito, J.H., Mascarenhas, N.D.A.: Novel approaches for face recognition: template-matching using dynamic time warping and LSTM neural network supervised classification. In: 2008 15th International Conference on Systems, Signals and Image Processing, pp. 241–244. IEEE (2008)

27. Li, C., Zhan, G., Li, Z.: News text classification based on improved BI-LSTM-CNN. In: 2018 9th International Conference on Information Technology in Medicine and Education (ITME), pp. 890–893. IEEE (2018)

28. Liu, G., Guo, J.: Bidirectional LSTM with attention mechanism and convolutional layer for text classification. Neurocomputing **337**, 325–338 (2019)

29. Luukkonen, P., Koskela, M., Floréen, P.: LSTM-based predictions for proactive information retrieval. arXiv preprint arXiv:1606.06137 (2016)
30. Makkar, A., Kumar, N.: An efficient deep learning-based scheme for web spam detection in IoT environment. Futur. Gener. Comput. Syst. **108**, 467–487 (2020)
31. Mandl, T., et al.: Overview of the HASOC track at fire 2019: hate speech and offensive content identification in Indo-European languages. In: Proceedings of the 11th Forum for Information Retrieval Evaluation, pp. 14–17 (2019)
32. Mittal, A., Kumar, P., Roy, P.P., Balasubramanian, R., Chaudhuri, B.B.: A modified LSTM model for continuous sign language recognition using leap motion. IEEE Sens. J. **19**(16), 7056–7063 (2019)
33. Mohammad, S., Bravo-Marquez, F., Salameh, M., Kiritchenko, S.: Semeval-2018 task 1: affect in tweets. In: Proceedings of the 12th International Workshop on Semantic Evaluation, pp. 1–17 (2018)
34. Niu, Z., Zhou, M., Wang, L., Gao, X., Hua, G.: Hierarchical multimodal LSTM for dense visual-semantic embedding. In: Proceedings of the IEEE International Conference on Computer Vision, pp. 1881–1889 (2017)
35. Ousidhoum, N., Lin, Z., Zhang, H., Song, Y., Yeung, D.-Y.: Multilingual and multi-aspect hate speech analysis. In: Proceedings of EMNLP. Association for Computational Linguistics (2019)
36. Pawade, D., Sakhapara, A., Jain, M., Jain, N., Gada, K.: Story scrambler-automatic text generation using word level RNN-LSTM. Int. J. Inf. Technol. Comput. Sci. (IJITCS) **10**(6), 44–53 (2018)
37. Pulver, A., Lyu, S.: LSTM with working memory. In: 2017 International Joint Conference on Neural Networks (IJCNN), pp. 845–851. IEEE (2017)
38. Qiu, D., Liu, Z., Zhou, Y., Shi, J.: Modified bi-directional LSTM neural networks for rolling bearing fault diagnosis. In: ICC 2019–2019 IEEE International Conference on Communications (ICC), pp. 1–6. IEEE (2019)
39. Rao, G., Huang, W., Feng, Z., Cong, Q.: LSTM with sentence representations for document-level sentiment classification. Neurocomputing **308**, 49–57 (2018)
40. Ren, B.: The use of machine translation algorithm based on residual and LSTM neural network in translation teaching. PLoS ONE **15**(11), e0240663 (2020)
41. Rocki, K.M.: Surprisal-driven feedback in recurrent networks. arXiv preprint arXiv:1608.06027 (2016)
42. Song, S., Huang, H., Ruan, T.: Abstractive text summarization using LSTM-CNN based deep learning. Multimedia Tools Appl. **78**(1), 857–875 (2019)
43. Sundermeyer, M., Schlüter, R., Ney, H.: LSTM neural networks for language modeling. In: Thirteenth Annual Conference of the International Speech Communication Association (2012)
44. Umer, M., Imtiaz, Z., Ullah, S., Mehmood, A., Choi, G.S., On, B.-W.: Fake news stance detection using deep learning architecture (CNN-LSTM). IEEE Access **8**, 156695–156706 (2020)
45. Wang, L.-N., Zhong, G., Yan, S., Dong, J., Huang, K.: Enhanced LSTM with batch normalization. In: Gedeon, T., Wong, K.W., Lee, M. (eds.) ICONIP 2019. LNCS, vol. 11953, pp. 746–755. Springer, Cham (2019). https://doi.org/10.1007/978-3-030-36708-4_61
46. Wen, S., et al.: Memristive LSTM network for sentiment analysis. IEEE Trans. Syst. Man Cybern. Syst. (2019)
47. Wu, Y., Zhang, S., Zhang, Y., Bengio, Y., Salakhutdinov, R.R.: On multiplicative integration with recurrent neural networks. Adv. Neural Inf. Process. Syst. **29** (2016)

48. Yadav, A., Vishwakarma, D.K.: Sentiment analysis using deep learning architectures: a review. Artif. Intell. Rev. **53**(6), 4335–4385 (2019). https://doi.org/10.1007/s10462-019-09794-5
49. Yao, L., Pan, Z., Ning, H.: Unlabeled short text similarity with LSTM encoder. IEEE Access **7**, 3430–3437 (2018)
50. Ye, C., Li, X., Chen, J.: A deep network for tissue microstructure estimation using modified LSTM units. Med. Image Anal. **55**, 49–64 (2019)
51. Zeng, D., Sun, C., Lin, L., Liu, B.: LSTM-CRF for drug-named entity recognition. Entropy **19**(6), 283 (2017)
52. Zhang, X., Zhao, J., LeCun, Y.: Character-level convolutional networks for text classification. In: Advances in Neural Information Processing Systems, pp. 649–657 (2015)

# Enhancements on a Pipeline Approach for Abstract Meaning Representation Parsing

Alexandru Frasie[✉], Nicoleta-Teodora Vezan, Georgiana Marian, Florin Macicasan, and Camelia Lemnaru

Romania Department of Computer Science, Technical University of Cluj-Napoca, Cluj-Napoca, Romania
frasie.alexandru@gmail.com

**Abstract.** Abstract Meaning Representation (AMR) parsing attempts to extract a structured representation of a sentence's meaning. This paper enhances an existing processing pipeline for AMR parsing, inspired by state-of-the-art solutions in dependency parsing. It enhances the existing Concept Identification module by using Pointer-Generator Networks. A further considerable improvement of this module is brought by the use of embeddings. An alternative approach is provided through Transformers, an architecture which needs large data-sets to accurately predict concepts. For predicting the relations between concepts, the proposed pipeline combines the two Heads Selection and now trainable Arcs Labelling tasks into a joint Relation Identification module, which enhances the overall performance of edge prediction. The improvements made to this AMR parser have resulted in a completely trainable model that can be improved further with end-to-end training.

**Keywords:** Natural Language Processing · Abstract meaning representation · Concept Identification · LSTM · Pointer-Generator · Transformers · Relation Identification

## 1 Introduction

Abstract Meaning Representation (AMR) has been introduced in [2], aiming to provide a semantically uniform representation for English natural language sentences. The AMR representation of a sentence is achieved by converting it into a Directed Acyclic Graph. The AMR graphs of two different sentences having the same meaning are identical. AMR parsing is the task of generating the AMR graph of a sentence. While there are several recent end-to-end approaches to solving this problem, we address it in a pipelined manner.

The proposed solution is building upon the graph-based parsing pipeline presented in [13]. It splits the task into three steps: Concept Identification (the concepts, representing the labelled nodes in the graph, are extracted from the

© Springer Nature Switzerland AG 2022
L. Iliadis et al. (Eds.): EANN 2022, CCIS 1600, pp. 505–516, 2022.
https://doi.org/10.1007/978-3-031-08223-8_41

sentence, in order), Heads Selection (the arcs of the graph are identified) and Arcs Labelling (the arcs of the graph are labelled). In this paper, we explore two different solutions for Concept Identification: a solution based on LSTMs (Long Short-Term Memories, which are a type of artificial neural networks, based on the RNN architecture and used in the field of deep learning), improving the architecture proposed in [3], and an alternative Transformer-based solution. For the Relation Identification module we propose a solution in which we enhance the previously existent Heads Selection and Arcs Labelling modules. We modeled them to encode concepts, calculate scores based on the DeNSe model, using a single-layer MLP, then treating the two tasks as different types of classification.

The objective of the paper is to present and analyze the enhancements brought to the existing parsing approach by obtaining three configurable, independent, trainable modules that can be further linked in order to perform end-to-end training. The two Concept Identification modules are designed to be interchangeable and the Relation Identification module is configurable so that relation identification and labelling can be performed jointly.

## 2   Related Work

AMR parsing solutions can be categorized into: graph-based, transition-based and sequence-to-sequence. Graph-based models solve this task by predicting the nodes and the arcs present the graph (which is done either together or independently of arc label prediction). Transition-based solutions, introduced in [18], are inspired from dependency parsing, and have been heavily explored in previous years. Sequence-to-sequence models [8] linearize the AMR graph (usually through a DFS traversal) and learn a sequence-to-sequence model to transform the input sentence into the linearized graph.

Graph-based parsing solutions have recently replaced transition-based approaches in the NLP literature for structured learning tasks, as presented by Dozat and Manning in [5]. Consequently, the approach proposed in [13] in the context of AMR relies heavily on them. We build upon that initial pipeline, by tackling individual steps in the pipeline with adaptations of State-of-the-Art solutions, which we review in the following paragraphs.

**Pointer-Generator Networks.** First introduced in [17] for solving the problem of convex hull, Delaunay triangulation, and traveling salesman, the Pointer-Generator Network has been since then used for a variety of Natural Language Processing tasks.

Miao and Blunsom [10] applied the Pointer-Generator on a sentence compression problem, and obtained state-of-the-art results. See proposed in [15] a Pointer-Generator Network that focuses on the abstract summarization problem. The network was designed to reduce repetitiveness and handle out-of-vocabulary words.

**Transformers.** Introduced by Vaswani et al. in [16] for Neural Machine Translation, Transformers provide an alternative to Recurrent Neural Networks. They avoid the use of recurrence (present in the sequence-to-sequence models) by using a Self-attention mechanism, drawing global dependencies between inputs and outputs. To exploit the sequence order, Positional Encodings are added. Transformers introduce the possibility of parallelized training.

The original Transformer architecture [16] consists of a stack of Encoder layers and a stack of Decoder layers. Each stack has a corresponding Embedding, as well as a Positional Encoding layer, which accounts for the word's position in the source sentence. The Decoder output is passed through a final linear layer that generates the output as a word.

As mentioned by Liu in [9], Transformers are effective, yet non-trivial to train. The authors of [4] propose model pre-training for Transformers, by means of transfer learning. Pre-trained models can be used as a starting point, allowing rapid progress when modeling the second task.

**Dependency Parsing Solutions.** In generating the AMR graph, the initial solution [13] is based on the Dependency Neural Selection (DeNSe) model presented by Zhang et al. in [19], which aims to find the head of each word in a sentence. Parsing a sentence and converting it into a graph is discussed by Kolomiyets in [7], while also capturing temporal dependencies between words. For the proposed model, this task has been fully reserved for the Heads Selection module. As inspired from the state-of-the-art solution for capturing relations in NLP proposed by Dozat and Manning in [6], the enhanced Heads Selection module receives a sequence of ordered concepts and uses BiRNNs for learning feature representation of words and also seeks to capture long-term dependencies between them. Using the same approach, the Arcs Labelling module was also constructed on top of Head Selection, transforming them into complimentary modules.

## 3   Approach

The proposed approach consists of two configurable modules: Concept Identification and Relation Identification. The Concept Identification module can be LSTM-based, consisting of an Encoder-Decoder with Attention architecture, or Transformer-based, using Vanilla Transformers. The Relation Identification module combines the previously existent Heads Selection and Arcs Labelling modules and is configurable to predict either solely the edges, or together with their labels.

### 3.1   Concept Identification - LSTM Based

The module is composed of an encoder-decoder LSTM-based architecture, with Bahdanau Attention [1] - to provide contextual information for each word. The model considers additionally three types of specific embeddings (besides the word learned embedding already present in the base model): GloVe embeddings, Character-Level embeddings and Lemma embeddings.

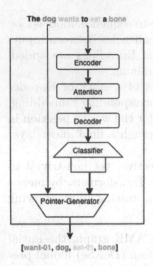

**Fig. 1.** LSTM-based concept identification architecture with pointer generator

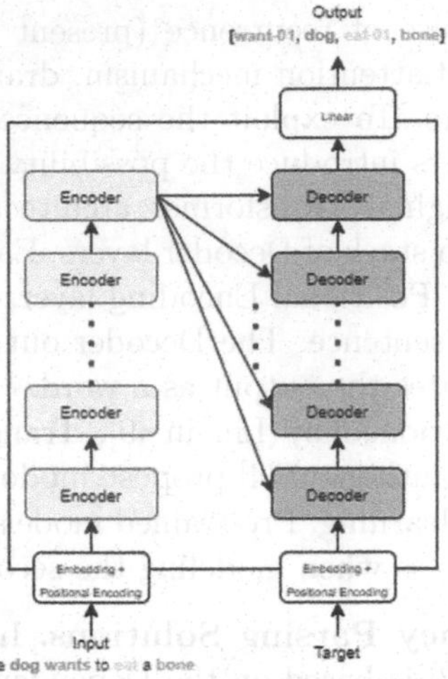

**Fig. 2.** Encoder-Decoder transformer input and output example

**Pointer-Generator.** The Pointer-Generator mechanism adds the ability of the model to copy the words from the original sentence, while maintaining the capacity to generate new words from the vocabulary. In order to switch between functionalities, a generation probability is computed as in (1), similar to the probability presented in [15].

$$pgen = \sigma(\mathbf{w}_h^T \cdot \mathbf{h}_t^* + \mathbf{w}_s^T \cdot \mathbf{s}_t + \mathbf{w}_x^T \cdot \mathbf{x}_t + \mathbf{b}_{ptr}) \tag{1}$$

where the learned parameters are vectors $\mathbf{w}_h^T, \mathbf{w}_s^T, \mathbf{w}_x^T$ and scalar $\mathbf{b}_{ptr}$ and $\sigma$ is the sigmoid function.

After computing the generation probability, the final distribution probability is calculated for the extended vocabulary as in (2). The extended vocabulary is composed of the concepts together with the tokens from the initial sentence.

$$P(w) = pgen * \mathbf{P}_{vocab}(w) + (1 - pgen) \sum_{i:\mathbf{w}_i=w} \mathbf{a}_i^t \tag{2}$$

The loss is further computed with the new extended vocabulary, rather than the concept vocabulary. The main advantage of the pointer generator approach is that if a word is out-of-vocabulary, then the model handles it correctly, due to the $P(w)$. The architecture with the pointer generator added can be seen in Fig. 1.

**Embedding.** The proposed model mainly uses word embeddings, which can be further concatenated with either GloVe, Character-level embeddings and/or Lemma embeddings.

GloVe embeddings are pre-trained, introduced by Pennington et al. in [12]. The model employs the set containing 400.000 words, each having embeddings of 300 dimensions. GloVe embeddings are applied on the input data, in Encoder and then are either fed to the model alone, or concatenated with the word embeddings trained with the model. Similar to [11], Character-level embeddings represent a sub-module that embeds single characters, that are further passed through a Gated Recurrent Unit (GRU). Moreover, Lemma embeddings have the advantage of simplifying the terms and increasing the number of appearances in the input set of specific tokens.

All embedding types are configurable, therefore, they can be concatenated with one another, in order to obtain a better performance.

### 3.2 Concept Identification - Transformer Based

Using Transformers in an AMR context refers to an English-concept translation. Since Neural Machine Translation tasks keep account of the word order in the source and target sentences, the generation of ordered concepts from an English sentence is possible.

The model architecture can be seen in Fig. 2. The input sequence is converted into embeddings, positional encoding is applied and the result is fed to the Encoder stack, producing an encoded representation of the sequence. The target sequence is prepended with a beginning-of-sequence token, converted into embeddings and positionally encoded. The model is auto-regressive, consuming the previously-generated tokens [16].

The Transformer uses different flows during training and inference. On the training flow, teacher forcing is used. The Decoder stack processes the output of the Encoder along with the embedded target sequence to produce an encoded representation of the output. The linear layer converts the Decoder output into word probabilities. The transformer output is compared to the target sequence, back-propagating the loss.

On the inference flow, the target sequence is hidden to the Decoder. The goal of the model is to sequentially produce the output from the input sentence alone, word-by-word, by repeating the decoding process for multiple steps, adding to the output sequence the highest probable token. At each step, the model is fed with the output sequence generated up to the previous time-step.

The Transformer-Based Concept Identification module employs pre-training, by means of transfer learning, a technique that stores knowledge resulted from solving one problem and reuses it to tackle a different problem. The model learns a simple'copy-input' task. The model weights obtained from this task are used to initialize the Encoder weights for the AMR-specific problem.

### 3.3   Relation Identification

The task of relation identification is conceptually separated in two distinct parts. The relations between concepts are established by initially identifying a head for each concept, then assigning a label to that relation (describing its type). In practice, the proposed model jointly predicts the heads and the relations, using the same data structure, but treating the two problems as distinct classifications.

**Heads Selection.** The Heads Selection module aims to find the relations between concepts, more specifically to find a "head" for each concept. The proposed model uses a similar approach to the one introduced in [19], which computes associative scores between concepts in (3) and selects the highest score concept as its head by using the formula in (4).

$$s(\mathbf{a}_i, \mathbf{a}_j) = \mathbf{v}_a^\mathsf{T} \cdot tanh(\mathbf{U}_a \cdot \mathbf{a}_j + \mathbf{W}_a \cdot \mathbf{a}_i) \tag{3}$$

where $\mathbf{a}_i$ and $\mathbf{a}_j$ are vector-based representations of concepts between which the score is computed, $s(\mathbf{a}_i, \mathbf{a}_j)$ is a neural network with a single hidden layer, which computes the associative score between $\mathbf{a}_i$ and $\mathbf{a}_j$; $\mathbf{v}_a \in \mathbb{R}^{2d}$, $\mathbf{U}_a \in \mathbb{R}^{2d \times 2d}$ and $\mathbf{W}_a \in \mathbb{R}^{2d \times 2d}$ are matrices of $\mathbf{s}$.

$$P_{head}(c_j | c_i, S) = \frac{exp(s(\mathbf{c}_j, \mathbf{c}_i))}{\sum_{k=0}^{N} exp(s(\mathbf{c}_k, \mathbf{c}_i))} \tag{4}$$

The current model reuses the same MLP as in [13], but treats it as a binary classification problem instead of multi-class, using a different activation function (sigmoid) and training objective (binary cross entropy). An adjacency matrix is used to store the computed scores between all concepts.

The outcome of the process is a binary adjacency matrix, having entries of value 1, representing the status of EDGE, whereas entries of value 0 are seen as NON-EDGES. For differentiating between EDGES and NON-EDGES, a configurable threshold was established and set by default to 0.5.

**Table 1.** Edge/Non-edge ratio

|       | Positive edges | Negative edges | Total entries | Ratio       |
|-------|----------------|----------------|---------------|-------------|
| Train | 557.824        | 46.342.133     | 46.899.957    | 1.2%/98.9%  |
| Dev   | 27.388         | 3.062.236      | 3.089.624     | 0.8%/99.2%  |

The classes EDGE/NON-EDGE are extremely unbalanced, as it can been seen from Table 1, and nonetheless the preliminary results presented numerous false-positives during prediction, therefore the binary classification suffered some adjustments:

- Creating a mask for sampling negative edges, proportional to the positive edges (*sampling ratio*), representing how many negative edges should be sampled for a positive edge, so a ratio of 1:3 P:N was used.
- Weighting the positive and negative classes differently, so that during score computation the classes would have a specific weight.
- Changing the configurable edge prediction threshold as 0.6, increased from 0.5, in order to predict only edges with higher probability.

**Arcs Labelling.** The Arcs Labelling module was not trainable in [13], so the current approach proposes a model where this is also possible. Arcs Labelling is an addition to Heads Selection, resulting in the Relation Identification module.

Given that in the relation vocabulary there are 158 relation labels, the chosen approach was to treat the task as a multi-class classification. The task is treated similarly to Heads Selection, using the same adjacency matrix. However, for each pair of concepts, a vector of scores of size equal to the number of relation labels in the vocabulary is computed(in our case 158). The result is then passed through a softmax function in order to find the most probable relation label.

The structure of Relation Identification can be seen in Fig. 3, the module being configurable so that it can train solely the Heads Selection module or together with Arcs Labelling.

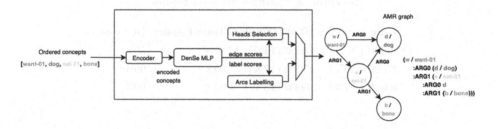

**Fig. 3.** Relation identification architecture

## 4    Experiments and Results

All experiments have been performed on Nvidia DGX, on a single GPU.

### 4.1    Data Analysis

**AMR.** We used the *LDC2016E25-DEFT-Phase-2-AMR-Annotation-R2* dataset to evaluate our approaches. It consists of 39260 English natural language sentences from different domains such as: conversations, web blogs and forums. The examples are split in 3 categories, training examples (36521–93%), validation examples (1368–3.5%), dev examples (1371 - 3.5%).

Upon analysing the examples in the dataset, a series of vocabularies were created, a notable one being the concept vocabulary which consists of 24726 elements, further used for concept identification. A relation vocabulary was established as well, containing a number of 158 different labels which is used in relation identification.

**Synthetic.** Since training Transformer models is a time and memory costly task, a Synthetic dataset has been created for local development. It follows the principle that a sequence-to-sequence model should be able to easily revert any sequence. Therefore, the input is a randomly generated word of fixed length of value 6; the output is the inverted input word.

The vocabulary consists of only 26 tokens (the English alphabet letters), a BOS (Beginning Of Sequence) token and an EOS (End Of Sequence) token. A source-target pair example can be found below:

```
source:   akfgle
target:   elgfka
```

The data split was dataset sizes, splitting the training examples around 85% and the test ones around 15%, as in Table 2.

**Table 2.** Synthetic data-set results

|   | Train examples | Dev examples | Train F-score | Dev F-score |
|---|---|---|---|---|
| 1 | 20000 ( 86%) | 4000 (14%) | 99% | 59% |
| 2 | 30000 ( 88%) | 5000 (12%) | 99% | 99% |
| 3 | 40000 ( 87%) | 6000 (13 %) | 99% | 99% |

**WikiText.** The WikiText Corpus has been used for the task of pre-training the Transformer. The corpus consists of an arrangement of Good and Featured Wikipedia Articles. Wikitext-2, a subset of the corpus, provides 36,718 examples, and is used by the pre-training task for copying the input as output of the model.

### 4.2   Metrics

**F-score.** The Concept Identification module uses F-score to check that the right concepts are predicted, determining the quantitative performance of the module. In the context of Relation Identification, F-Score is also used as a metric on the adjacency matrices. As Heads Selection is treated as a binary classification problem, computing F-Score, Precision and Recall is helpful in order to identity possible problems and improvements, such as over-fitting or predicting numerous false positives.

**Smatch.** The Smatch score is an evaluation metric specifically created to compute the similarity score between two AMRs. It is based on computing the triples present in an AMR graph: relation(variable, value). It computes the maximum match number of triples among all possible variable mappings. In the context of this paper, unlabelled Smatch is used for evaluating the Heads Selection module, and labelled Smatch for the entire Relation Identification module.

### 4.3 Evaluation of Concept Identification - LSTM Model

The LSTM-based Concept Identification module is based on sequence-to-sequence parser with attention mechanism. All the experiments that were performed, with the enhancements mentioned, started from the base-model. The evaluation was made in order to conclude if the added features indeed bring an improvement to the model. The following hyper-parameter tuning has been used for all experiments: word embedding size of 512, hidden size of 1024, character embedding size of 10 and character hidden size of 512.

The best results were obtain for the trained word embeddings concatenated with Character-Level embeddings and GloVe concatenated with Character-Level embeddings. Table 3 presents a comparison of the results obtained from the base model with and without pointer-generator, combined with embeddings.

**Table 3.** Model Results with and without pointer generator

| Approach | Train F-score | Dev F-score |
|---|---|---|
| Base-model without pointer-generator | 86.3% | 57.8% |
| Base-model with pointer-generator | 81% | 60% |
| Trained word embeddings with character-level embeddings | 92% | 63.2% |
| GloVe with character-level embeddings | 88.5% | 63.3% |

### 4.4 Evaluation of Concept Identification - Transformer Model

The Transformer-based Module has been trained on a Synthetic Dataset on a simple task: reverting an input sequence, as well as on the AMR sequence generation problem. The hyper-parameter tuning was made using Popel's suggestions in [14]: 2048 hidden size, 512 embedding dimension, 8 attention heads, 6 encoder/decoder layers, 0.1 dropout and 3e-5 learning rate. Training was performed for 80 epochs.

The purpose of the synthetic task training is to check the correctness of the model, along identifying the needed quantity of data for a proper learning, by looking at the model loss and F-score. Table 2 shows that the results obtained on this task are as expected. As an outcome of these experiments, it was observed that for the largest number of train examples, the model has the least over-fitting.

**Data Sparsity.** A frequent issue in AMR Parsing is that of Data Sparsity: the data-sets consisting of AMR sentence-concept pairs contain thousands of examples compared to NMT data-sets, which have millions. As the number of internal parameters for the Transformer model is enormous, the lack of appropriate examples affects the results of the Transformer in the context of AMR parsing.

A significant effect can be seen on the discrepancy between train and test results. Although the model performs well during training, it has difficulties generalizing to new data.

As Table 4 shows, the test results are influenced by the lack of data. The model has been trained for 200 epochs. For variating teacher forcing, until epoch 80, the F-score increased both on the train and evaluation flow. After that point, only the train F-score increased up to 55%. For fixed teacher forcing, the model reaches 99% F-score after 200 epochs, but learns very little.

**Table 4.** AMR data-set transformer results

| Approach | Train F-score | Dev F-score |
| --- | --- | --- |
| Variate teacher forcing | 16% | 14 % |
| Fixed teacher forcing | 52% | 0.005 % |

### 4.5  Evaluation of Relation Identification

The Relation Identification module is now seen as a conjuncture of Heads Selection and Arcs labelling, but the evaluation was done on the performance of Heads Selection first, and then by adding Arcs Labelling.

A drop-out rate was added to the encoder of the Relation Identification module for obtaining better results. For a better performance, the base model was enhanced with hyper-parameter tuning and usage of embeddings (GloVe and character-level). The results for these experiments can be seen in Table 5.

**Heads Selection.** The experiments were performed using the following hyper-parameter values: embedding size - 150, GloVe embedding size - 50, hidden size - 512, number of layers - 3, DeNSe MLP hidden size - 512, edge threshold - 0.6, sampling ratio - 3, positive class weight - 0.7, negative class weight - 1.0, dropout rate - 0.2. The results were obtained after 40 epochs of training.

**Heads Selection and Arcs Labelling.** When it comes to the Arcs Labelling module, this has been implemented but not yet optimized. However, for the entire module, the official metric of Smatch was used.

**Table 5.** Performance of relation identification

| Flow | F-Score | Precision | Recall | Accuracy | Unlabelled smatch | Smatch |
| --- | --- | --- | --- | --- | --- | --- |
| Train | 81.04% | 75.92% | 88.89% | 96.96% | 86.97% | 61.07% |
| Dev | 53.12% | 43.54% | 70.95% | 93.31% | 71.66% | 36.89% |

# 5   Conclusions

This paper proposes various enhancements to an existing AMR parsing pipeline, adopting state-of-the-art, graph-based solutions from dependency parsing.

For the Concept Identification module, we explored with both a Transformer-based and an LSTM-based approach, for which Pointer-Generator Networks and various embeddings were newly introduced. Pointer-Generator Networks helped the LSTM-based architecture with the over-fitting problem, however the increase in performance was not directly proportional with the complexity of the network. A significant improvement was given by the use of GloVe and Character-level embeddings, which prove to be well-suited for the concept identification problem.

Adapting Transformers led to the discovery that the architecture is sensitive to the quantity of input data with respect to the vocabulary size. The AMR sentence-concept pair data-sets contain a small number of examples compared to machine translation ones, which contain millions of sentences. This issue can be further addressed by augmenting data-sets.

A novel feature for this pipeline is the joint module for Heads Selection and Arcs Labelling, tasks which are based on the same idea taken from NLP dependency parsing approaches for Relation Identification and integrated accordingly. The conjuncture of the two modules resulted in enhancing the accuracy of predicting relations between concepts and offers a more uniform overview of the module, but also makes the final module of the AMR parser to be easier integrable for end-to-end training.

The enhancements brought to this AMR parser result in a fully trainable model which can further be improved by end-to-end training in order to establish how the entire parser performs, on which additional progress can be made.

# References

1. Bahdanau, D., Cho, K., Bengio, Y.: Neural machine translation by jointly learning to align and translate. arXiv preprint arXiv:1409.0473 (2014)
2. Banarescu, L., et al.: Abstract meaning representation for sembanking. In: Proceedings of the 7th Linguistic Annotation Workshop and Interoperability with Discourse, pp. 178–186. Association for Computational Linguistics, Sofia, Bulgaria (2013). https://www.aclweb.org/anthology/W13-2322
3. Batiz, O.B., Helmer, R.P., Pop, R., Macicasan, F., Lemnaru, C.: Concept identification with sequence-to-sequence models in abstract meaning representation parsing. In: 2020 IEEE 16th International Conference on Intelligent Computer Communication and Processing (ICCP), pp. 83–90 (2020)
4. Devlin, J., Chang, M.W., Lee, K., Toutanova, K.: BERT: pre-training of deep bidirectional transformers for language understanding. In: Proceedings of the 2019 Conference of the North American Chapter of the ACL: Human Language Technologies, Volume 1 (Long and Short Papers), pp. 4171–4186. Association for Computational Linguistics, Minneapolis, Minnesota, June 2019
5. Dozat, T., Manning, C.D.: Deep biaffine attention for neural dependency parsing. CoRR abs/1611.01734 (2016). http://arxiv.org/abs/1611.01734

6. Dozat, T., Manning, C.D.: Simpler but more accurate semantic dependency parsing. In: Proceedings of the 56th Annual Meeting of the Association for Computational Linguistics (Volume 2: Short Papers), pp. 484–490. Association for Computational Linguistics, Melbourne, Australia, July 2018
7. Kolomiyets, O., Bethard, S., Moens, M.F.: Extracting narrative timelines as temporal dependency structures. In: Proceedings of the 50th Annual Meeting of the Association for Computational Linguistics (Volume 1: Long Papers), pp. 88–97. Association for Computational Linguistics, Jeju Island, Korea, July 2012
8. Konstas, I., Iyer, S., Yatskar, M., Choi, Y., Zettlemoyer, L.: Neural AMR: sequence-to-sequence models for parsing and generation. In: Proceedings of the 55th Annual Meeting of the ACL (Volume 1: Long Papers), pp. 146–157. Association for Computational Linguistics, Vancouver, Canada, July 2017
9. Liu, L., Liu, X., Gao, J., Chen, W., Han, J.: Understanding the difficulty of training transformers. CoRR abs/2004.08249 (2020). https://arxiv.org/abs/2004.08249
10. Miao, Y., Blunsom, P.: Language as a latent variable: Discrete generative models for sentence compression. Empirical Methods in Natural Language Processings (2016)
11. van Noord, R., Toral, A., Bos, J.: Character-level representations improve DRS-based semantic parsing even in the age of BERT. In: Proceedings of the 2020 Conference on Empirical Methods in Natural Language Processing, pp. 4587–4603, November 2020
12. Pennington, J., Socher, R., Manning, C.D.: Glove: Global vectors for word representation. In: EMNLP, vol. 14, pp. 1532–1543 (2014)
13. Pop, R., Macicasan, F., Lemnaru, C.: A two stage approach for AMR parsing using the concept inference order. In: 2020 IEEE 16th International Conference on Intelligent Computer Communication and Processing (ICCP), pp. 91–98 (2020)
14. Popel, M., Bojar, O.: Training tips for the transformer model. CoRR abs/1804.00247 (2018)
15. See, A., Liu, P.J., Manning, C.D.: Get to the point: summarization with pointer-generator networks. In: Proceedings of the 55th Annual Meeting of the Association for Computational Linguistics, vol. 1, pp. 1073–1083 (2017)
16. Vaswani, A., et al.: Attention is all you need. In: Advances in Neural Information Processing Systems, vol. 30. Curran Associates, Inc. (2017)
17. Vinyals, O., Fortunato, M., Jaitly, N.: Pointer networks. In: Cortes, C., Lawrence, N., Lee, D., Sugiyama, M., Garnett, R. (eds.) Advances in Neural Information Processing Systems, vol. 28. Curran Associates, Inc. (2015)
18. Wang, C., Xue, N., Pradhan, S.: A transition-based algorithm for AMR parsing. In: Proceedings of the 2015 Conference of the North American Chapter of the Association for Computational Linguistics: Human Language Technologies, pp. 366–375. Association for Computational Linguistics, Denver, Colorado, May-Jun 2015
19. Zhang, X., Cheng, J., Lapata, M.: Dependency parsing as head selection. In: Proceedings of the 15th Conference of the European Chapter of the Association for Computational Linguistics: Volume 1, Long Papers, pp. 665–676. Association for Computational Linguistics, Valencia, Spain, Apr 2017

# Text Analysis of COVID-19 Tweets

Panagiotis C. Theocharopoulos[1]($\boxtimes$) (ID), Anastasia Tsoukala[1],
Spiros V. Georgakopoulos[2], Sotiris K. Tasoulis[1], and Vassilis P. Plagianakos[1]

[1] Department of Computer Science and Biomedical Informatics,
University of Thessaly, Lamia, Greece
{ptheochar,antsoukala,stasoulis,vpp}@uth.gr
[2] Department of Mathematics, University of Thessaly, Lamia, Greece
spirosgeorg@uth.gr

**Abstract.** During the COVID-19 pandemic many countries were forced
to implement lockdowns to prevent further spread of the SARS-CoV-2,
prohibiting people from face-to-face social interactions. This unprece-
dented circumstance led to an increase in traffic on social media platforms, one of the most popular of which is Twitter, with a diverse spectrum of users from around the world. This quality, along with the ability
to use its API for research purposes, makes it a valuable resource for
data collection and analysis. In this paper we aim to present the sentiments towards the COVID-19 pandemic and vaccines as it was imprinted
through the users' tweets when the events were actually still in motion.
For our research, we gathered the related data from Twitter and characterized the gathered tweets in two classes, positive and negative; using
the BERT model, with an accuracy of 99%. Finally, we performed various time series analyses based on people's sentiment with reference to
the pandemic period of 2021, the four major vaccine's companies as well
as on the vaccine's technology.

**Keywords:** Text classification · COVID-19 · Vaccines · BERT ·
Sentiment analysis · Twitter

## 1 Introduction

A major pivot in recent human history, specifically in 2020, was boldly highlighted by the COVID-19 global pandemic. Shortly thereafter the year of 2021
is unquestionably marked by the pharmaceutical attempt to shield the masses
against the virus and its variants. The medical scientists seeking out the prevention of the disease were not the only researchers working to prevent a societal
fall. The precariousness of the pandemic set in motion a big part of the research
community to search for patterns of certainty within the data in order to level
the global playing field [22]. Twitter attracted them, as it is a major source for
tagged and specified data aggregation.

At the beginning of the vaccination period citizens were more agreeable to
it, mainly for the purpose of achieving herd immunity against the highly infec-
tious virus as soon as possible, and the realisation of the returning-to-normality

© Springer Nature Switzerland AG 2022
L. Iliadis et al. (Eds.): EANN 2022, CCIS 1600, pp. 517–528, 2022.
https://doi.org/10.1007/978-3-031-08223-8_42

promise [8,15]. However, a significant minority of citizens in many countries expressed a general refusal to vaccination either due to mistrust to the local and global authorities or distrust to the effectiveness, safety and necessity of the COVID-19 vaccines [2].

## 1.1 COVID-19 Vaccines

Leading companies in the pharmaceutical industry attempted to administrate the plans of reconciliation with the help of financial and advertising support of the governments [22]. In some countries, mandates were actually applied with the result of further polarizing the relationships between the governments and the people [6,16]. A geopolitical division based on major vaccine companies also took place, as more vaccines were produced. However, not all of them were globally authorised or approved for emergency administration [3]. The four major vaccine companies that managed to obtain a standing public image, at least in the English speaking world, in the entire Europe and in some African, Oceanian and Asian countries are AstraZeneca, Johnson & Johnson, Moderna and Pfizer. Milken Institute's website about COVID-19 Vaccine Tracker showed on the 18th of December 2020 that 236 vaccines were in development, 38 were then in clinical testing and 7 had reached a regulatory decision [4]. In just a year of clinical trials and regulatory authorization protocols, the four leading vaccines have today managed to get global emergency authorization, with the exception of Cuba, Venezuela and some parts of Africa and Asia. We observe that Twitter and the four leading vaccines share a common factor; the countries that mostly use Twitter are also the ones that have either emergency use or full authorization of these vaccines [3].

## 1.2 Twitter

The Twitter website started as a patchwork infrastructure and organically progressed into an integrating one [14]. Twitter relies on open source tools and a simplistic design to maintain the micro-blogging of its users [14]. The company brought up the innovation of hashtags, when no other social media could filter its content so profoundly. Of course, this asset is its monetization tool for stakeholders and advertisers. In the "Global Impact Report" posted on their website on 2021 Twitter mentions that during the pandemic governments and vaccine companies were amongst various stakeholders contributing to decision-making and the advertising of vaccine campaigns[1]. Among actions taken from 2020 until March 2022 concerning the platform's and its stakeholders' initiative fighting misinformation during the pandemic, Twitter reported about 6,7 thousand account suspensions and 78 thousand content removals[2]

---

[1] https://about.twitter.com/content/dam/about-twitter/en/company/global-impact-2020.pdf.
[2] Twitter COVID-19 Misinformation Report.

## 1.3  Sentiment Analysis

The application of sentiment analysis on data collected from Twitter is considered to be the most commonly applied method among information retrieval work. Sentiment analysis is categorized into mainly two approaches: Machine Learning and Deep Learning. Probabilistic models and simple or complex classification methods based on learning are parts of the first approach, while Neural Networks and transformers constitute the second [23]. Examples of Machine Learning algorithms for stance detection and sentiment analysis are the Support Vector Machine (SVM) and the Naïve Bayes classifier [4]. The most used Deep Learning approaches are the Convolutional Neural Networks and Recurrent Neural Networks with its variant Long short-term memory (LSTM) and transformers such as Open-AI GPT with a unidirectional left-to-right architecture and Bidirectional Encoder Representations from Transformers (BERT) with a bidirectional approach [4].

## 1.4  Paper Outline

The rest of the study has been conducted in five sections. Section 2 represents state of the art related studies. Section 3 states some considerations regarding the Twitter API. Section 4 represents the used data set and describes the proposed methodology. In Sect. 5, the model evaluation and the experimented results have been presented. Finally, Sect. 6 includes the conclusion of the study and future directions.

## 2  Related Work

One of the first published papers regarding vaccine-related tweets applied a comprehensive Latent Dirichlet Allocation (LDA) topic modeling and dynamic sentiment representation. The research examines the subjectivity of the tweets and war-related vocabulary that creates figurative framing [22]. Also [19] calculate sentiment and subjectivity of vaccine tweets, specifically AstraZeneca, Moderna and Pfizer using TextBlob with k-nearest neighbors (k-NN) classification. Sattar et al. used a simplified text processing, TextBlob in combination with VADER to forecast the future vaccine uptake by the end of 2021, leading to mainly neutral and positive sentiments in vaccine related tweets. [18].

Mostly negative sentiments concerning vaccine tweets was the conclusion of this study [17]. In [4] four different methods were presented, namely the Bag of Words (BoW) representation, the Word embedding with machine learning, the Word embedding with Deep Learning and the BERT. By investigating the news against the results, the authors concluded that the occurrence of the tweets follows the trend of the actual events [4]. Again by using BERT model, with the different aim of vaccine misinformation detection in Twitter, this research evaluated it to be the best model of 0.98 precision test in comparison to LSTM and XGBoost [10]

A research approach that probably widens the gap between those who are skeptical against vaccine mandates and those in favor was [11] and it concludes that the anti-vaccine alert-communication aspects on Twitter should be imitated by the pro-vaccine community, by stepping into tactics of opinion manipulation. In the same journal, another interesting paper was published. They applied geographical LDA and word analysis about the US states on COVID-19 vaccines providing with analytical wordclouds and timelines of specific vocabulary used by certain groups [9]. In [12,13], the author identified twelve different communities to related topics from Twitter with uni- and bi-grams by applying graph network analysis. The dataset created from this research was published on the IEEE web portal, which is used in our paper [12,13]. In the [20] study, the authors applied the BERT model to classify the polarity and test the subjectivity of the COVID-19 tweets, with an accuracy of 93.89%.

## 3 Methodology

In this section we present a complete description of the proposed methodology. In particular, for the evaluation of the model, we used a pre-trained model in combination with a labeled dataset. COVID-19 related tweets were gathered via the Twitter API and categorized by a classifier. The classification of the collected data resulted in further analysis through time series. Figure 1 illustrates the overview of the proposed methodology.

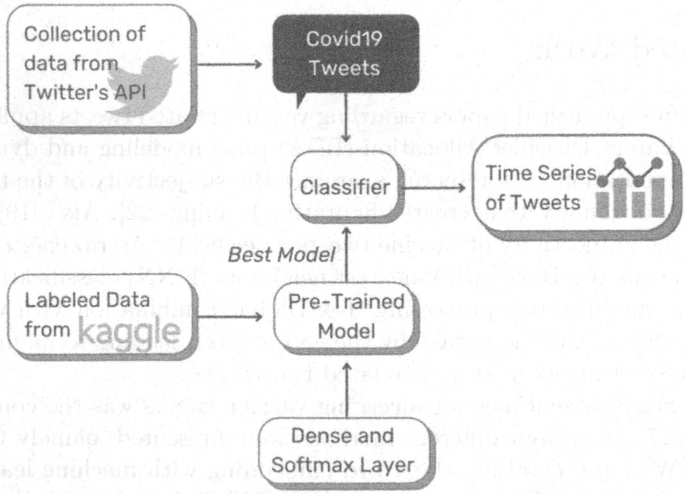


**Fig. 1.** Overview of the proposed methodology

## 3.1    Tweets Hydration

Twitter renewed its privacy policies in March 2020 in relation to the developer's platform and changed the whole tweet parsing procedure. The user profiles were not allowed to be publicly visible, shared or exposing any other sensitive information about the users. However the existence of public databases continued to be available, hence the form of IDs. These IDs can be parsed now through a procedure called hydration, which returns all the embedded information needed [13]. Of course, if the tweet is deleted by the user or filtered out by Twitter it is not hydratable.

## 3.2    Dataset

The first dataset used for this study was a publicly available dataset from a Kaggle competition. Kaggle is a platform for predictive machine learning and analytics competitions [7]. In this work, we used the Sentiment Analysis of Tweets related to the COVID-19 pandemic dataset [1] in order to validate the pre-trained model described in Sect. 3.3. The data from the source was mainly pre-processed and cleaned, but an additional data cleaning procedure has been conducted by removing duplicate entries, stopwords, digits along with hyperlinks, emojis, usernames and punctuation.

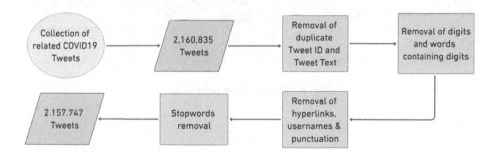

**Fig. 2.** Pre-processing procedure

The second dataset for this study contains tweets related to COVID-19, written in English, during the time period between January 01 2021 and December 31, 2021. Our search was based on a publicly accessible, large-scale COVID-19 tweets dataset [12], at a ratio approximately of 7500 tweets per day. Taking advantage of Twitter's API for hydrating, a process of retrieving a tweet's complete information using its ID. The created dataset attributes are [tweet id],[tweet creation date],[tweet text],[country],[city] and [number of retweets]. Data pre-processing is used for cleaning the collected raw data by extracting duplicate entries, stopwords, digits, as well as hyperlinks, emojis, usernames and punctuation. The pre-processing steps are shown in Fig. 2. After pre-processing, the final number of tweets was 2.157.747. Using a sample of the tweets, we mapped their location

P. C. Theocharopoulos et al.

and presented it in Fig. 3, which can be distinctive for the entire dataset. From the collected tweets, only a significantly small percentage contains location data, due to Twitter's new policy to disable the tweets' location by default. Lastly, the gathered unlabeled tweets were passed on the classifier for polarity labeling.

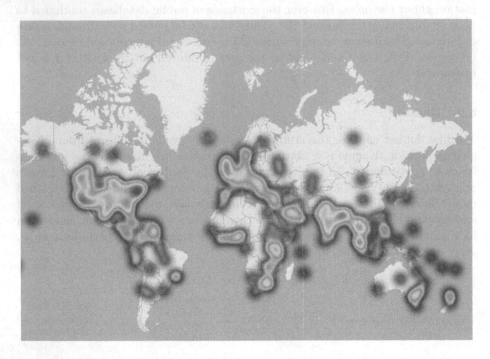

**Fig. 3.** Global tweet heat map

### 3.3 Model

To classify a tweet's polarity into the positive or the negative class, we used the BERT model [5]. The BERT model elevates standard transformers [21] by removing the unidirectionality constraint. Specifically, BERT uses a Masked Language Model (MLM) pre-training objective, which randomly masks a part of a token from the input with the main purpose to predict the original vocabulary id only by its context. The MLM objective can combine the left and the right context, providing us with the ability to pre-train a deep bi-directional transformer dissimilar to a left-to-right model. Additionally, BERT uses the *next sentence prediction* task which gives the ability to pre-train text pairs together. The model has been pre-trained on a plain unlabeled text corpus of the entire English Wikipedia and the BookCorpus. For this study, we train the whole architecture using the train set of tweets from Kaggle. Utilizing the transfer learning technique we start the training from a well known pre-trained model, instead a random weight initialization, updating the weights of the model during the training process. On the pre-trained model we appended a dense and a softmax layer. We used the base model of BERT (Hugging Face) which uses 12 transformer encoders, 12 attention heads and 110 million parameters, instead of the large model that uses 24 transformer encoders, 16 attention heads and 340 million parameters.

## 4    Experimental Results

To investigate the model's performance, we performed 100 independent iterations. In every iteration, the Kaggle's dataset has been shuffled and split into train and test sets, with 70–30 analogy. To prevent overfitting, we performed an early trigger in our model by monitoring the train and validation loss. Once the validation loss reaches its minimum score and starts increasing, we stopped the training and saved the current model. The model showed an average accuracy of 99%, with 0.003 standard deviation, $1.510^{-5}$ variance and an average running time of 42.5 s, running on CUDA. As described, the gathered tweets have been polarized by the classifier, leading to a time series tweet average polarity per day within the year 2021.

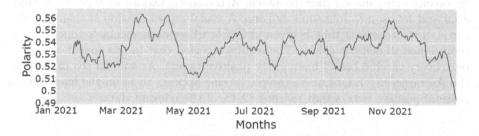

**Fig. 4.** Tweets' polarity over the months

### 4.1    Results and Discussion

After the text classification, we measured the polarity of the average tweet per day. The polarity towards 0 presents negativity and towards 1 presents positivity. The tweets' polarity over time has been visually represented in Fig. 4. In the beginning of 2021, we observe a general neutrality lasting until the middle of March. The period between the middle of March and the end of April is characterized by a large-scale spike of positive tweets. We cross-referenced the media reports from this timespan and found that it coincided with the period with the lowest death rate the UK had seen in six months. Furthermore, at the same time most countries announced the expansion of their vaccination drive to include additional age and professional groups. The polarity decreases rapidly in the first days of May, when, in retrospect, officials from the US authorize the vaccination of children as young as 12 years old. For a long period thereafter the tweets retain a neutral polarity, until November 2021, when a significant flow towards negativity is noticed. This can be explained by the worldwide outbreak of the Omicron variant, in November, and the subsequent take-off in the number of COVID-19 new cases.

**Fig. 5.** Comparison of the COVID-19 vaccines' polarity

In addition, we isolated tweets containing the name of the four major COVID-19 vaccine companies; Pfizer/Biontech, Astrazeneca/Oxford or Vaxzevria, Moderna and Johnson & Johnson's Janssen. A visual representation of their polarity through the course of time is given in Fig. 5, where each vaccine's time series is represented in distinct colors. The results revealed that in the considered timeline, every vaccine brand has mostly positive tweets. As we can see in Table 1, the Astrazeneca/Oxford or Vaxzevria vaccine appears to be in the lead, with a score of positive tweets that reaches 82,4% of the relevant dataset.

**Table 1.** Vaccines' positive rate

| Vaccine brand | Total number of tweets | Positive tweets |
|---|---|---|
| Pfizer/Biontech | 25.447 | 81,8% |
| Astrazeneca/Oxford (Vaxzevria) | 9.474 | 82,4% |
| Moderna | 9.223 | 74,5% |
| Johnson & Johnson's Janssen | 7.297 | 61,2% |

Taking a closer look in Fig. 5, we can see that during the summer and especially within the middle of July and until the middle of August a course towards negativity has been observed. The following events took place over the summer and have been connected with the tweets' polarity concerning the vaccines:

- Israel had already offered a booster shot to its citizens.
- The FDA on July 8th stated that a booster shot was under consideration
- White House announced on August 18, the beginning of booster shots for every adult 8 months after the second dose.

The Moderna vaccine had an immediate course towards the negativity axis, in early November. Around that time the company's CEO made declarations in regard to their product's effectiveness against COVID-19.

Afterwards, we distinguished the vaccines based on their type of technology. The Pfizer/Biontech and Moderna vaccines are classified as mRNA vaccines and the Astrazeneca/Oxford and J&J vaccines as non-mRNA vaccines. Figure 6 shows the overall polarity of each vaccine type. The mRNA vaccines had overall a positive polarity over the non-mRNA vaccines. The non-mRNA vaccines show a negative peak around October 2021, which can be corresponded to the European Medicines Agency (EMA) announcement for a possible new, life-threatening side effect of J&J's vaccine, known as venous thromboembolism (VTE). Both Astrazeneca and J&J vaccines (non-mRNA) have been previously linked with a very rare thrombosis with thrombocytopenia syndrome (TTS).

**Fig. 6.** Comparison of the mRNA and Non mRNA vaccines

We concluded our study, focusing on the polarity of tweets located in the US. Figure 7 shows the average polarity of each state over the year. The states of North Dakota and Alaska have overall more positive tweets. On the other hand, the state of Oregon had tweets with the most negative polarity related to COVID-19.

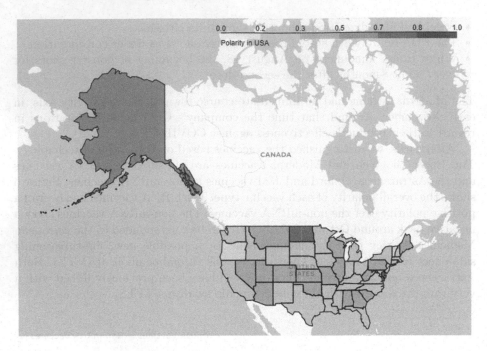

**Fig. 7.** Tweet polarity per US state

# 5    Conclusion

The primary goal of this study is to perform a sentiment analysis with reference of COVID-19 tweets within the year 2021. Taking advantage of an open labeled dataset from a Kaggle competition and a Deep Learning model, BERT, we achieved a validation accuracy as 99%. Then using the unlabeled and preprocessed tweets, we created a sentiment score for each tweet, i.e. 0 for negative and 1 for positive, which lead to an average day polarity time series. The polarity of the tweets reflects exactly the events regarding COVID-19 through the proposed period. Apart from the COVID-19 tweets, we also analyzed the polarity of the COVID-19 vaccines. In general, regardless of the vaccine's technology, the means put into effect in the fight against COVID-19 were well received from Twitter users. The effectiveness of the model brings forth new possibilities for future studies in which we can further develop and improve the performance of other text classification techniques.

**Acknowledgements.** This project has received funding from the Hellenic Foundation for Research and Innovation (HFRI) and the General Secretariat for Research and Technology (GSRT) under grant agreement No. 1901. Also, we gratefully acknowledge the support of NVIDIA Corporation with the donation of the Titan X Pascal GPU used for this research.

# References

1. Sentiment analysis of covid-19 related tweets (2021). https://www.kaggle.com/c/sentiment-analysis-of-covid-19-related-tweets/data

2. Bullock, J., Lane, J.E., Shults, F.L.: What causes covid-19 vaccine hesitancy? ignorance and the lack of bliss in the united kingdom. Humanit. Soc. Sci. Commun. 9(1), 1–7 (2022)

3. contributors, W.: List of covid-19 vaccine authorizations - Wikipedia, the free encyclopedia. https://en.wikipedia.org/w/index.php?title=List_of_COVID-19_vaccine_authorizations&oldid=1081403177 (2022), [Online; accessed 11-April-2022]

4. Cotfas, L.A., Delcea, C., Roxin, I., Ioanăş, C., Gherai, D.S., Tajariol, F.: The longest month: analyzing covid-19 vaccination opinions dynamics from tweets in the month following the first vaccine announcement. IEEE Access 9, 33203–33223 (2021)

5. Devlin, J., Chang, M.W., Lee, K., Google, K., Language, A.: Bert: pre-training of deep bidirectional transformers for language understanding (2019). https://arxiv.org/pdf/1810.04805.pdf

6. Engel-Rebitzer, E., Stokes, D.C., Buttenheim, A., Purtle, J., Meisel, Z.F.: Changes in legislator vaccine-engagement on twitter before and after the arrival of the covid-19 pandemic. Hum. vaccines Immunotherapeutics 17(9), 2868–2872 (2021)

7. Georgakopoulos, S.V., Tasoulis, S.K., Vrahatis, A.G., Plagianakos, V.P.: Convolutional neural networks for toxic comment classification. In: Proceedings of the 10th Hellenic Conference on Artificial Intelligence, pp. 1–6 (2018)

8. Gerretsen, P., et al.: Individual determinants of covid-19 vaccine hesitancy. PLOS ONE 16(11), 1–14 (2021). https://doi.org/10.1371/journal.pone.0258462

9. Guntuku, S.C., Buttenheim, A.M., Sherman, G., Merchant, R.M.: Twitter discourse reveals geographical and temporal variation in concerns about covid-19 vaccines in the united states. Vaccine 39(30), 4034–4038 (2021)

10. Hayawi, K., Shahriar, S., Serhani, M.A., Taleb, I., Mathew, S.S.: Anti-vax: a novel twitter dataset for covid-19 vaccine misinformation detection. Public Health 203, 23–30 (2022)

11. Hoffman, B.L., et al.: # doctorsspeakup: lessons learned from a pro-vaccine twitter event. Vaccine 39(19), 2684–2691 (2021)

12. Lamsal, R.: Coronavirus (covid-19) tweets dataset (2020). https://doi.org/10.21227/781w-ef42

13. Lamsal, R.: Design and analysis of a large-scale covid-19 tweets dataset. Appl. Intell. 51(5), 2790–2804 (2021)

14. Lin, J., Ryaboy, D.: Scaling big data mining infrastructure: the twitter experience. Acm SIGKDD Explor. Newsl. 14(2), 6–19 (2013)

15. Machado, M.D.A.V., Roberts, B., Wong, B.L.H., van Kessel, R., Mossialos, E.: The relationship between the covid-19 pandemic and vaccine hesitancy: a scoping review. Front. Public Health 9, 1370 (2021)

16. Recio-Román, A., Recio-Menéndez, M., Román-González, M.V.: Political populism, institutional distrust and vaccination uptake: a mediation analysis. Int. J. Environ. Res. Public Health 19(6), 3265 (2022)

17. Sarirete, A.: Sentiment analysis tracking of covid-19 vaccine through tweets. J. Ambient Intell. Humanized Comput. 1–9 (2022). https://doi.org/10.1007/s12652-022-03805-0

18. Sattar, N.S., Arifuzzaman, S.: Covid-19 vaccination awareness and aftermath: public sentiment analysis on twitter data and vaccinated population prediction in the usa. Appl. Sci. 11(13), 6128 (2021)

19. Shamrat, F., et al.: Sentiment analysis on twitter tweets about covid-19 vaccines using NLP and supervised KNN classification algorithm. Indones. J. Electr. Eng. Comput. Sci. **23**(1), 463–470 (2021)
20. Singh, M., Jakhar, A.K., Pandey, S.: Sentiment analysis on the impact of coronavirus in social life using the BERT model. Soc. Netw. Anal. Min. **11**(1), 1–11 (2021)
21. Vaswani, A., et al.: Attention is all you need. https://arxiv.org/pdf/1706.03762v5.pdf
22. Wicke, P., Bolognesi, M.M.: Covid-19 discourse on twitter: how the topics, sentiments, subjectivity, and figurative frames changed over time. Front. Commun. **6** (2021). https://doi.org/10.3389/fcomm.2021.651997
23. Zhou, J., Ye, J.M.: Sentiment analysis in education research: a review of journal publications. Interact. Learn. Environ. 1–13 (2020)

# Author Index

Printed in the United States
by Baker & Taylor Publisher Services